THE DIRECTORY
OF AMERICAN
BOOK PUBLISHING

Wall Street About 1825

THE DIRECTORY OF AMERICAN BOOK PUBLISHING

From Founding Fathers
to
Today's Conglomerates

by GEORGE THOMAS KURIAN

SIMON AND SCHUSTER, NEW YORK

Library of Congress Catalog Card Number: 74-16534
Standard Book Number: 671-18745-7

PRINTED IN THE UNITED STATES OF AMERICA

Published by

SIMON AND SCHUSTER
Reference, Technical and Review Book Division
1 West 39th Street
New York, N.Y. 10018

To
my wife
Annie

Photograph Credits

The Publisher wishes to thank the following for their
courteous permission to use pictures from their
respective collections:

Doubleday & Company, Inc.
pp. 105, 107

The Hess Collection, University of Minnesota
page 200

The Grolier Club (photographed by Jay Cantor from Library of Grolier Club)
pp. Frontispiece, 1, 9 (right), 24 (right), 33, 37, 41, 45, 60, 70,
137, 165, 204

The New York Historical Society
page 255

The New York Public Library, Rare Books Collection
pp. 9 (left), 11, 12, 14, 24 (left), 42, 54, 88, 147, 156, 170,
176, 210, 241

Contents

Preface

THE DIRECTORY OF AMERICAN BOOK PUBLISHING has its roots in the fascination I felt as an immigrant for the history and organization of the American book industry. This fascination was sharpened through my own practical involvement in the years that followed with various publishers and soon crystallized into a project that would bring together materials that I had collected on the evolution of book-related institutions in the United States. It seemed to me then that there were two ways to approach this rather formidable task. One was to attempt a broad-brush history of American publishing. However, at that time, there existed two such full-scale histories (Hellmut Lehmann-Haupt's THE BOOK IN AMERICA and Charles Madison's BOOK PUBLISHING IN AMERICA) and a third work, a scholarly three-volume study, by John Tebbel was in the offing.

The other approach — and the one which was finally adopted — was to compile a reference book on the model of J. Kirchner's *Lexikon des Buchwesens,* the celebrated German work for which there still does not exist an American counterpart. Publishing is basically a mosaic and does not lend itself easily to an integrated narrative. On the other hand a somewhat dictionary-type reference book seemed ideally suited to deal with such a fragmented subject. I was confirmed in this belief by Thomas Tanselle's observations in THE HISTORIOGRAPHY OF AMERICAN LITERARY PUBLISHING:

Comprehensive histories of American book production have been attempted...but it seems to me evident that further general histories would, at this stage, be pointless. Before anything approaching a full-scale history of American publishing can be embarked upon, we must have the complete history of the individual publishers that make it up.

Professor Tanselle's words constitute, in part, the *raison d'etre* of this work which is to provide the story of many of the individual American publishing houses in a readily consultable form.

As the work progressed it became possible to enlarge its scope and structure. Several sections of practical value to publishers and editors were added, including a basic bibliography and a glossary of publishing terms and abbreviations. Finally, some illustrations were added. These features will, it is hoped, attract a larger audience than at first envisioned.

Every attempt has been made to include all major publishing houses founded before 1968 and all university presses irrespective of size. But the list is by no means all-inclusive nor is it intended to be. Some editorial prerogative has been exercised in the selection of entries, mostly for reasons of space. All entries have been carefully checked with the help of questionnaires and most of them have been verified by the publishers themselves.

During the course of compiling the book I have incurred an extraordinarily large debt to hundreds of bookmen. To list them would need several pages. I must, in particular, acknowledge my gratitude to all publishers who supplied information and reviewed entries.

Finally, the author will be most grateful for word of omissions and corrections and for suggestions for improvement in succeeding editions.

Pelham,   George Thomas Kurian
New York

I

Founding Fathers
and
Their Enterprises

Aitken, Robert (1734-1802)

Publisher of the first American Bible. Born in Scotland in 1734, Aitken came to the American Colonies in 1769 and entered publishing at Philadelphia, Pennsylvania, a year later. He issued a duodecimo edition of the NEW TESTAMENT in 1777. Encouraged by its success he petitioned the Congress to authorize an American edition of the complete Bible. Congress recommended and sanctioned this work by special resolution. In 1782 the work made its appearance in a 1,400-page single-volume edition of which thirty thousand copies were printed. Unfortunately, the venture was a financial failure because it could not compete with imported Bibles.

Apart from his Bible, Aitken is best known for his publication of THE FABLES OF AESOP AND OTHERS by Samuel Croxall. When Aitken died in 1802 the firm passed to the control of his daughter. She published a four-volume edition of the Bible in 1808.

American Book Company

Organized in 1890 as a New Jersey corporation through the merger of the school departments of the four major publishers of that era: D. Appleton & Company, A.S. Barnes & Company, Ivison, Blakeman, Taylor & Company, and Van Antwerp, Bragg and Company. Each of these four houses agreed to turn over all copyrights, publishing rights, plates, illustrations, etc., on all of their schoolbooks and, in addition, promised not to publish any competing textbooks for at least five years. Harper & Brothers, although not one of the original participants, also sold a large part of its school list to the newly formed corporation.

The first president of the company was Birdseye Blakeman who remained in that position until 1893. He was followed by David B. Ivison (1893-1896); Harry T. Ambrose (1896-1914); Louis M. Dillman (1914-1931); W.T.H. Howe (1931-1939); Frederick H. Blake (1939-1946); Robie D. Marriner (1946-1956); Grant H. Brown (1957-1960); Norvell B. Samuels (1960-1968); Herbert G. Molden (1968); Craig T. Senft (1968-1969); and Charles W. Pepper (1969—).

Capitalized at five million dollars, the company was by far the largest textbook house in the world. It was at once criticized for being a monopoly. This criticism did not stop it from expanding by acquiring other smaller publishing houses such as Werner School Book Company of Chicago, Illinois; Standard School Book Company of St. Louis, Missouri; D.D. Maynard of St. Paul, Minnesota; Cowperthwait and Company of Philadelphia, Pennsylvania; Taintor Brothers and Company of New York City; E.H. Butler and Company, also of Philadelphia; Western School Book Company of Chicago; Sheldon and Company of New York; Williams and Rogers of Rochester, New York; Crane and Company of Topeka, Kansas, and others. In 1908 the company was reorganized as a New York corporation.

As part of its policy of growth the company, until then basically an elementary school publisher, built up a strong high school list and in the early 1930s started a separate college division. In the 1950s Aladdin Books, Inc., was founded as a subsidiary publisher of trade juveniles. In the early 1960s The Learning Center was established with Creative Playthings as a jointly owned company, and a number of joint ventures were launched with Educational Development Laboratory. In 1961 American Book Company acquired McCormick-Mathers Publishing Company (q.v.), and in 1967 it joined Litton Industries as a division of Litton Educational Publishing, Inc.

American Book has been associated with two of the most widely used textbooks ever published: McGUFFEY'S ECLECTIC READERS (q.v.) and Noah Webster's OLD BLUE BACK SPELLER, which has sold over one hundred million copies. The SPELLER was the only textbook ever to be used as a standard article of commerce, like sugar or salt, and sold in general stores across the country. American Book Company also continues to be the sole distributor of Merriam-Webster school dictionaries.

The archives of the company were given to Syracuse University Library in 1967.

American Imprints Inventory

Historical records survey made by the Works Progress Administration in the 1930s under the national editorship of Douglas C. McMurtrie, assisted by state supervisors. The purpose of the catalog was to locate all American imprints prior to 1876, the date of Frederick Leypoldt's AMERICAN CATALOG.

American Sunday School Union

Founded in 1824 at Philadelphia, Pennsylvania, to publish books for children. It first published the new lesson plans drawn up by the New York Association of Sunday School Teachers in 1825. The Union also published nondenominational books and it was one of the earliest organizations to set standards for children's literature. The Union's code of standards included four rules: a book must be moral in content; it must be graded and adapted to children's needs; it must adhere to high standards of style; and it must be American in character. Several series and sets were offered among which were: *A Child's Cabinet Library, Village and Family Library, Sunday School and Family Library,* and *Juvenile Library.*

American Tract Society

Founded in 1825 at New York City through a merger of the New York Religious Tract Society, the New England Tract Society, and about forty smaller groups engaged in the publication and distribution of evangelical literature. Its purpose was "to diffuse a knowledge of . . . Jesus Christ as the Redeemer of Sinners and to promote the interests of vital godliness and sound morality, by the circulation of religious tracts."

The first president of the Society was S.V.S. Wilder, who was both a dedicated evangelizer and an imaginative bookman. Among Wilder's successful promotional methods were a Tract of the Month Program, the use of door-to-door canvassers and field agents divided into sales areas, and the development of special audience categories, such as sailors, children, soldiers, immigrants, travelers, and the blind. Through those means he reached families in the most remote sections of the country and at all levels of society. The tracts were handsomely produced and well illustrated.

Besides religious classics, such as PILGRIM'S PROGRESS, which was published in twenty-five languages, Wilder also published some of the best-known authors of the day: Cotton Mather, Jonathan Edwards, Benjamin Rush, Mason Weems, Timothy Dwight, and Jacob Abbott. The Society became Abbott's general publisher and his book, THE YOUNG CHRISTIAN, was the beginning of a series that included THE CHILD AT HOME and THE MOTHER AT HOME. Thomas H. Gallaudet was another popular author who wrote a series of seven books for Wilder entitled *Scripture Biography.* There was also a *Youth's Biographical Series,* which was later combined with another series, *Youth's Narrative,* to form *Youth's Christian Library* in forty volumes. Other books were published in the Portuguese, Spanish, Swedish and Dutch languages.

During five major wars the Society distributed free evangelical literature to the armed forces. It discontinued book publication in 1948.

Armed Services Editions

Inexpensive, oblong-shaped paperbacks issued to members of the Armed Forces during World War II. Sponsored by the Council on Books in Wartime (1942-46). A total of one hundred and eight million copies of 1324 titles was issued by the Council.

Baker, Voorhis & Company

Founded in 1817 at New York City as Wiley and Halstead, a partnership of Charles Wiley and Oliver Halstead, publishers of law books. When Wiley left in 1820, Halstead continued to publish under his own name until 1830 when he took John Voorhies as a partner. After Halstead's death in 1842 Voorhies continued the firm, publishing many important works on law, including Ogden Hoffman's CHANCERY PRACTICE and John Townsend's CODE OF PROCEDURE.

In 1865, following the death of Voorhies, the firm was acquired by Baker & Godwin along with a partner, William W.L. Voorhis. Baker & Godwin had been founded in 1846 by Peter Carpenter Baker and Daniel Godwin. But William Voorhis was the dominant figure in the partnership and the firm was soon reorganized as Baker, Voorhis & Company. It published many outstanding legal books, such as TOWNSEND ON LIBEL, BLISS ON LIFE INSURANCE, GERARD ON TITLES TO REAL ESTATE, and KERR ON FRAUD AND MISTAKE. The firm was incorporated in 1889. In 1894 it absorbed L.K. Strouse & Company.

In 1940 Baker, Voorhis was acquired by Lawyers Co-operative Publishing Company, and became one of its affiliated imprints. It is no longer an operating company.

Bancroft, Hubert Howe (1832-1918)

Born, Granville, Ohio. Beginning as a bookseller's assistant in Buffalo, New York, he went to California in 1852, and in 1856 established his publishing firm of H.H. Bancroft & Company at San Francisco. His partner was George L. Kenney, a Buffalo colleague. Bancroft started with two religious works: W.A. Scott's THE GIANT JUDGE: OR, THE STORY OF SAMPSON, THE HEBREW HERCULES; and ESTHER, THE HEBREW-PERSIAN QUEEN. As his list grew more titles on California were added: William H. Knight's HAND-BOOK OF THE PACIFIC COAST, Franklin Tuthill's A HISTORY OF CALIFORNIA, and Titus Fey's THE NATURAL WEALTH OF CALIFORNIA.

Bancroft soon branched into law books, publishing, in the course of time, some of the best law books issued in the West including a compilation of the general laws of California in two volumes. He developed a strong educational list, too, with a series called *Pacific Coast School Books*. By 1870 Bancroft was the largest publisher in the West and about half the books published in the region bore his imprint. But his greatest achievement was his thirty-nine volume encyclopedic history of the Pacific Coast area, which he published between 1875 and 1890. Of these volumes twenty-eight are devoted to history proper, five to native races, and six to essays; the entire work bears the impress of Bancroft's organizing capacity. The set, entitled *Bancroft's Works*, was promoted with great energy and enthusiasm and sold by direct mail.

In 1870 the firm name was changed to A.L. Bancroft and Company. In 1886 the establishment was destroyed by fire and was merged with Sumner Whitney Company, law publishers, under the name of Bancroft-Whitney Company. Bancroft-Whitney became noted as the publisher of ANNOTATED REPORTS SYSTEM, which it launched in 1887. In 1919, a year after H.H. Bancroft's death, Bancroft-Whitney was acquired by the Lawyers Co-operative Publishing Company and ceased to exist as an independent imprint.

Banks Law Publishing Company

Founded about 1790 by William Gould as a retail law bookstore in Albany, New York. In 1804 he took his cousin, Anthony Gould, a nephew, William Gould, and his brother-in-law,

David Banks, as partners, whereupon the name became Gould, Banks & Company. A branch was established in New York City with David Banks in charge. In 1857, following the death of Anthony and William Sr., and the retirement of Banks and the junior William Gould, David Banks, Jr., and his brothers, Charles Banks and A. Bleecker Banks, reorganized the firm as Banks & Brothers. In 1895 two new corporations were formed following a second dissolution: Banks & Company in Albany, as successor to Banks, Gould & Company with A. Bleecker Banks as president, and the Banks Law Publishing Company in New York as successor to Banks & Brothers.

In 1910 Banks & Company was acquired by Matthew Bender & Company. In 1926 William E. Baldwin purchased the Banks Law Publishing Company and in 1933 it was merged with the Baldwin Law Publishing Company as the Banks-Baldwin Law Publishing Company of New York and Cleveland (q.v.).

Bay Psalm Book

The first book printed in the United States, in 1640. It was a version of the Psalms translated by a board of divines which included Richard Mather, Thomas Welde and John Eliot.

The book was a crudely printed quarto of 294 pages, unnumbered, bearing neither the printer's nor the compilers' names, nor the place of printing. The title page, however, recorded that it was "imprinted 1640." It is also known as the WHOLE BOOK OF PSALMES.

The BAY PSALM BOOK was printed at the Cambridge Press (q.v.) by Stephen Day, assisted by his son Matthew Day.

Of the first printing of seventeen hundred copies eleven survive.

Irwin P. Beadle & Company

Established in New York City in 1859 by Erastus F. Beadle with Irwin P. Beadle and Robert Adams as partners. The company was to become synonymous with the dime novel, which they invented. The earlier publications of the Beadle brothers were songbooks and cookbooks which they sold for a dime. The Beadle dime novels had orange wrappers, from 100 to 128 pages, and a trim size of 6-5/8 by 4½ inches. They were issued in series at intervals of three to four weeks. In their advertisements they were described as books for the million, which indeed they were.

In 1862 Erastus Beadle and Adams bought out Irwin and in the following year Irwin formed a new partnership with George Munro known as Irwin P. Beadle & Company. Erastus Beadle enjoined the use of the name and thereafter the firm was taken over by Munro. By the end of the Civil War, Beadle & Company was in an established position, publishing not only dime novels but also *American Tales* and the *American Library*.

When Robert Adams died in 1866 his place was taken by his two sons, William and David. David died in 1886 and Erastus Beadle retired in 1889, leaving William Adams as the sole owner of the company. In 1897-98 Beadle & Adams, as the company was known after the Civil War, was purchased by M.J. Ives & Company who continued the Beadle name for a number of years.

Bell, Robert (1732-1784)

Born, Glasgow, Scotland. Came to the American Colonies about 1766 and went into bookselling, printing and publishing in Philadelphia, Pennsylvania. In 1768 he published Sir William Blackstone's COMMENTARIES in five volumes. In 1770 he came to New York City and issued that year, from his shop on Third Street, the first American edition of John Milton's PARADISE LOST. Bell introduced American readers to a wide range of English and European classics, among which were Laurence Sterne's SENTIMENTAL JOURNEY, CHARLES V by William Robertson, and Michel Eyquem de Montaigne's LETTERS. Thomas Paine was a clerk in the Bell establishment for a time and Bell published his former employee's COMMONSENSE. Bell also achieved distinction as a book auctioneer.

A writer of considerable wit, Bell wrote two books: ILLUMINATIONS FOR LEGISLATORS, AND FOR SENTIMENTALISTS and MEMORIAL ON THE FREE SALE OF BOOKS.

Bemis, James D. (1783-1857)

Born Spencer, Massachusetts. In 1804 Bemis established a most remarkable publishing operation in the wilderness town of Canandaigua, New York. It included a newspaper, *The Western Repository,* a bindery, printery, ink-making equipment, type foundry, bookstore, stationery, and a circulating library. Of his ten partnerships, that with John Gould was the first and the most productive. Bemis began publishing in 1805 and the Gould and Bemis imprint appeared first on THE MINUTES OF THE CAYUGA BAPTIST ASSOCIATION, HELD AT PALMYRA, SEPTEMBER 26th AND 27th, 1804. Soon Bemis became "a . . . publisher to the frontier church," with PLAIN AND EASY CATHECISM FOR CHILDREN by Isaac Watts and CALL TO THE UNCONVERTED by Richard Baxter.

Broadening the scope of his titles, he began publishing books dealing with all aspects of frontier life, such as Indian rights, agriculture, Federalism, and the proposed canal from Lake Erie to the Hudson River. Bemis also had a strong textbook list that included John Walker's CRITICAL PRONOUNCING DICTIONARY, Noah Webster's AMERICAN SPELLING BOOK, Lindley Murray's ENGLISH READER, and ELEMENTS OF NUMBERS by Tobias Ostrander. As a Federalist he published Timothy Pickering's THE DANGERS OF THE COUNTRY! . . . EXHIBITING . . . THE IMMINENT DANGER OF AN UNNECESSARY AND RUINOUS WAR and later his POLITICAL ESSAYS, which had the distinction of being the first bound book published in western New York. One perennial title on the Bemis list was James E. Seaver's NARRATIVE OF THE LIFE OF MRS. MARY JEMISON, first published in 1824. Like many other publishers of his time, Bemis published an almanac entitled THE FARMER'S DIARY, OR WESTERN ALMANACK, which throws light on the social life and interests of a frontier settlement.

By 1830 Bemis's health had begun to fail, and although he went to Europe in 1834 for treatment, his malady and infirmity only worsened in the following years. He died in 1857.

The Blakiston Company

Founded in 1843 in Philadelphia, Pennsylvania, by Presley Blakiston and Robert Lindsay under the name of Lindsay and Blakiston. The early list consisted mostly of religious works promoting the Evangelical Lutheran Church. Medical, scientific, and dental titles were gradually added to this list and when these proved more profitable, the partners began to concentrate solely on them. In 1882 the partnership was dissolved when Lindsay retired and it was reorganized as P. Blakiston Son & Company with Blakiston's son, Kenneth M., and Frank W. Robinson as partners. Upon the elder Blakiston's death in 1898 the name was changed to P. Blakiston's Son & Company. In 1939 it was reorganized as The Blakiston Company.

Kenneth Blakiston died in 1937 and the firm was taken over by a group of associates under Horace G. White. It was purchased by Doubleday in 1944 and by McGraw-Hill Book Company in 1954. Currently it operates as a unit of McGraw-Hill Book Company.

Blue and Gold Series

Volumes of collected poems of noted American poets published by Ticknor and Fields. Inclusion in the series, Bliss Perry, the essayist, once remarked, was equivalent to being elected to the French Academy.

Blue Ribbon Books

Organized in 1930 by Dodd, Mead, Harcourt, Brace, Harper, and Little, Brown as a reprint publishing house to compete with Grosset and Dunlap. Eugene Reynal was employed as the first manager. Higher-priced reprints were published under the Halcyon House imprint. In 1933 Reynal bought the firm and four years later he sold it to Doubleday, Doran & Company.

Boni, Albert

Albert Boni started his career with his brother Charles in a Washington Square bookshop in New York City. Together they founded the Little Leather Library, a set of thirty tiny volumes of classics which they sold by mail. When Harry Scherman and Robert Haas took over this venture, Albert Boni joined Horace Liveright in founding Boni and Liveright in 1917. In the same year they launched the *Modern Library*. In 1918 Boni and Liveright separated. A toss of the coin favored Liveright and he bought out the Bonis. Shortly afterwards the Bonis bought the firm of Lieber and Lewis and began to publish on their own, as Albert and Charles Boni.

Among the many Boni projects were the *Cosmos Library,* scientific paperbacks; the *American Library; Studio Books;* and Boni Paper Books, a book club designed to provide its members with twelve new paperbound volumes a year. They had a few successful titles during their brief career: Thornton Wilder's THE CABALA and THE BRIDGE OF SAN LUIS REY; Upton Sinclair's BOSTON; Ford Maddox Ford's A MAN COULD STAND UP; and DOWN THERE: A STUDY OF SATANISM by J.K. Huysmans. The firm succumbed to the Depression in 1930. Later Boni invented the Readex Reading Projector and became president of the Readex Microprint Corporation.

Boston Society for the Diffusion of Knowledge

Founded in Boston, Massachusetts in 1829 for the purpose of issuing "in cheap form a series of works, partly original and partly selected, in all the most important branches of learning."

The Society was established through the initiative of The Society for the Diffusion of Knowledge, a movement for mass literature which began in England in 1827.

The Society's publication program was started in 1831 with the *American Library of Useful Knowledge,* which was the first attempt in the United States to reach the popular market with low-priced books. The first volume declared that the series will contain "works on the most important branches of knowledge as ought to be in the possession of every intelligent family . . . and is to embrace in it only works of permanent value." Further it was noted that "each work shall be written in a style which shall be intelligible to the careful reader although he may have little other previous acquaintance with the particular . . . but the books will not be unworthy of attention of the accomplished author and man of science. . . . It will be no part of their purpose to furnish works of mere entertainment." Each book was priced at 62½ cents.

The venture did not attract enough readers and the Society was short-lived.

Bowker, Richard Rogers (1848-1933)

Born, Salem, Massachusetts. American publisher, author, editor, and bibliographer. Beginning as a contributor to *Publishers Weekly* he later became an associate of Frederick Leypoldt. He went on to become editor of *Publishers Weekly* and head of the parent publishing firm which in 1911 adopted his name.

With Leypoldt and Melvil Dewey he founded the *Library Journal* and helped in the founding of the American Library Association. He was also a tireless champion of the rights of authors and international copyright. Among his books are: COPYRIGHT: ITS LAW AND LITERATURE (1886), and COPYRIGHT: ITS HISTORY AND ITS LAW (1912).

The Bowker Lectures were established in his honor.

Bradford, John (1749-1830)

Set up a press in Lexington, Kentucky, in 1787. The first book to bear his imprint was THE KENTUCKY ALMANACK FOR 1788, which continued in annual publication for twenty years. This was followed by KENTUCKY MISCELLANY, a small volume of poetry. As public printer to Kentucky, Bradford printed the ACTS OF THE KENTUCKY LEGISLATURE and the KENTUCKY SUPREME COURT'S DECISIONS edited by James Hughes.

Bradley, Milton (1836-1911)

Born, Vienna, Maine. In 1869 Bradley published THE PARADISE OF CHILDHOOD, the first kindergarten manual published in America. He also published two magazines for children, the *Kindergarten Review* and *Work and Play.*

Brentano's

Founded in New York City in 1870 as Brentano's Literary Emporium by August Brentano. August Brentano, Jr., became president of the firm in 1882 and Arthur Brentano in 1915.

The firm published books from 1897 to 1933 and became noted as the American publisher of George Bernard Shaw. Lowell Brentano, novelist and playwright, served as editor from 1918 until 1933. The bookstore operation was acquired by Crowell Collier and Macmillan in 1962.

Brewer and Tileston

Founded at Boston, Massachusetts, by John West in 1792. Five years later West took over the publication of the very popular FARMER'S ALMANAC. After a series of reorganizations as Jenks, Hickling, and Swan; Hickling, Swan and Brown; Hickling, Swan and Brewer; and Swan, Brewer and Tileston, toward the 1840s the firm became Brewer and Tileston, a name which it retained as long as it continued to publish — until the end of the century.

Brewer and Tileston is noted as the publisher of Joseph Worcester's dictionary series: A GEOGRAPHICAL DICTIONARY, OR UNIVERSAL GAZETTEER, ANCIENT AND MODERN, in 1817; COMPREHENSIVE PRONOUNCING AND EXPLANATORY ENGLISH DICTIONARY, in 1830; and DICTIONARY OF THE ENGLISH LANGUAGE, in 1860. The publication of the last-named dictionary set off the famous War of the Dictionaries between Worcester and Noah Webster. In addition, Brewer and Tileston published a number of other popular books: Charles A. Goodrich's HISTORY OF THE UNITED STATES, and the NEW ENGLAND HOUSEWIFE'S ANNUAL were two of them. Until a disastrous fire ravaged their premises in 1872 they were regarded as the largest schoolbook publishers in New England.

A.L. Burt Company

Established in 1883 at New York City by Albert L. Burt. He died in 1913 and was succeeded by his son, Harry P. Burt. The latter retired in 1937, selling his business to Blue Ribbon Books. Beginning in 1902 the firm specialized in fiction reprints. Their largest series was *Burt's Home Library,* which included four hundred titles.

Cambridge Press

The first printing establishment set up in the American Colonies. Founded in 1638 in Cambridge, Massachusetts, by Stephen Day(e) and his son, Matthew Day. It was owned by Elizabeth Glover and was located in a house provided by the Harvard Board of Overseers. In 1639 the first publication came off the press: a broadside entitled *Freeman's Oath.* Though no copy of it survives, it is known to have contained only 222 words printed on a half sheet of paper.

Before the end of the year Day brought out his second publication, THE ALMANACK CALCULATED FOR NEW ENGLAND, by Mr. Pierce, Mariner. Not much is known about this pamphlet and less about its author. Day's third product, the famous BAY PSALM BOOK (q.v.)

is regarded as the first book printed in the United States. It was published in 1640 and reprinted in 1647. In the eight years following the original publication of BAY PSALM BOOK the Press produced twelve more books, including almanacs for 1646, 1647 and 1648.

In 1641 Elizabeth Glover married Henry Dunster, president of Harvard College, who then became a partner in the press. Five years later Stephen Day left the press, possibly as a result of differences with Dunster. Matthew Day died in 1649 and from that time until 1692 the press was managed by Samuel Green. During this period 124 books were produced, including Michael Wigglesworth's DAY OF DOOM, the bestseller of the day, John Eliot's INDIAN BIBLE, and books by Richard Mather and Increase Mather.

Before the press finally closed in 1692 it had produced more than two hundred books and pamphlets at the rate of four books a year.

Cape and Smith

Founded in 1929 at New York City as a joint publishing house by Jonathan Cape, British publisher, and Harrison Smith. During the next four publishing seasons they brought out a fine list that included Maxim Gorki's THE BYSTANDER and Robert Graves' GOOD-BYE TO ALL THAT. The firm, however, succumbed to the Depression of 1930 and was dissolved in 1932. Its list was taken over partly by Putnam and partly by Farrar and Rinehart. Smith joined Robert K. Haas in launching Smith and Haas, which was acquired by Random House in 1936.

Carey and Hart

Established in 1828 at Philadelphia, Pennsylvania, by Edward Carey and Abraham Hart. The firm had a promising start with a book that was also their greatest success: A NARRATIVE OF THE LIFE OF DAVID CROCKETT OF THE STATE OF TENNESSEE, written by Davy Crockett himself. Another popular author was

Captain Frederick Marryat. Henry Wadsworth Longfellow edited an anthology for them, POETS AND POETRY OF EUROPE, whose success inspired Rufus Griswold's POETS AND POETRY OF AMERICA, POETS AND POETRY OF ENGLAND, FEMALE POETS OF AMERICA, and PROSE WRITERS OF AMERICA.

Carey died in 1845 and for the next four years Henry Carey Baird was Hart's partner. After Baird left the firm in 1849 Hart carried on alone until 1854, when he decided to retire. The assets of the firm were sold at auction. Hart died in 1884.

Carey, Henry Charles (1793-1879)

Born, Philadelphia, Pennsylvania. Son of Mathew Carey. By 1822 Henry Carey was in control of the firm, M. Carey & Sons of Philadelphia. The same year he acquired a partner, Isaac Lea, his brother-in-law. Eager to expand, Carey opened a branch in New York City under the name of H.C. Carey & Company.

Carey gained national attention with his early successes in publishing: the AMERICAN ATLAS in 1822, a quarto Bible in 1823, Sir Walter Scott's LIFE OF NAPOLEON, Charles Lamb's ESSAYS OF ELIA, and books by Washington Irving and James Fenimore Cooper. In 1833 he published Francis Lieber's ENCYCLOPAEDIA AMERICANA in thirteen volumes, which was a translation of Friedrich Arnold Brockhaus's KONVERSATIONS-LEXIKON. To compete with the magazines of Harper and Scribner, Carey began to publish in 1825 *The Atlantic Souvenir.* Two years later he launched *The American Quarterly Review,* but by 1832 he had sold both magazines.

Carey retired from the firm in 1838 to devote himself to writing. During the next forty years he turned out a number of scholarly books, most of them in the field of political economy. THE PRINCIPLES OF POLITICAL ECONOMY (three volumes), THE PRINCIPLES OF SOCIAL SCIENCE (three volumes), and THE UNITY OF LAW are the most important of his works.

Carey, Mathew (1760-1839)

Born, Dublin, Ireland. Generally regarded as the first book publisher in the United States. He arrived in Philadelphia, Pennsylvania, in 1784, and with $400.00 loaned to him by the Marquis de Lafayette, he launched himself into publishing with the newspaper, *The Pennsylvania Evening Herald.* The following year he began a new periodical, *Columbian Magazine.* Withdrawing from this venture in 1787, he started still another periodical, *American Museum,* which ran until 1792.

He entered book publishing in 1785 and established his reputation by publishing the quarto DOUAY BIBLE in 1789. A Protestant Bible followed a few years later. Bolder and more imaginative than any of his contemporaries, Carey built up a strong list that included works of Sir Walter Scott, ANIMATED NATURE by Oliver Goldsmith, William Guthrie's GEOGRAPHY, CHARLOTTE TEMPLE by Susanna Haswell Rowson, and THE LIFE AND MEMORABLE ACTIONS OF GEORGE WASHINGTON by Parson Mason Locke Weems, the extravagant and colorful salesman whom Carey employed for many years.

Carey's success as a publisher was equalled by his success in bookselling. He developed the exchange system through which large dealers could maintain a full stock by exchanging books with other dealers. In 1801 he was instrumental in establishing the American Company of Booksellers, one of the first trade associations in the field of books. Carey's other pioneering innovations included the employment of full-time proofreaders, the soliciting of advance subscriptions, the use of direct mail and magazine advertising, and the use of traveling salesmen.

In 1825 Carey retired so as to spend all of his time writing. The publishing part of his business he gave to his son Henry and the bookstore to his son, Edward.

A charter member of the Philadelphia Society for the Promotion of National Industry, Mathew Carey wrote books and pamphlets advocating protective tariffs. His chief work, ESSAYS ON POLITICAL ECONOMY, was one of the earliest expositions of the principles of protection. His own AUTOBIOGRAPHY is regarded as good reading for everyone who loves books and bookselling. The Carey-Thomas Award for Creative Publishing honors the pioneering accomplishments of Mathew Carey and Isaiah Thomas (q.v.).

Carleton, George W. (1832-1901)

George Washington Carleton started publishing in New York City in 1857 when he bought a share in the publishing firm of Livermore and Rudd and thereby changed its name to Rudd and Carleton. His first book was a runaway bestseller: NOTHING TO WEAR, a poem by William Allen Butler, followed by NOTHING TO SAY, a poem in similar vein by Mortimer

N. Thompson. Another success was THE LIFE, SPEECHES AND PUBLIC SERVICES OF ABRAHAM LINCOLN, published in 1860, which has been regarded as the first campaign biography of Lincoln. In 1861 Rudd died and Carleton carried on alone under a distinctive colophon which was the Arabic word for books turned upside down.

Carleton's name is associated with the famous humor books of Artemus Ward (Charles F. Browne) and Josh Billings (Henry Wheeler Shaw). ARTEMUS WARD-HIS BOOK was the first of several Ward books that were eventually published collectively in 1898 as THE COMPLETE WORKS OF ARTEMUS WARD. Another satiric collection of military and political humor was THE LIFE AND ADVENTURES . . . OF PRIVATE MILES O'REILLY.

Carleton has also been described as the largest publisher of sensational books by native American authors and in this category could be included TEMPEST AND SUNSHINE and THE ENGLISH ORPHANS by Mary J. Holmes, ST. ELMO by Augusta Evans Wilson, TERRIBLE SECRET, WONDERFUL WOMAN and MAD MARRIAGE by May Agnes Fleming, and books by Miriam Coles Harris, Julie P. Smith and Mary Virginia Terhune (Marion Harland). Carleton also added to his list many translations from the French, including Victor Hugo's LES MISÉRABLES and Jules Michelet's L'AMOUR and LA FEMME.

Carleton published as well a series of information and reference books giving an eager public "much learning in little space" — HANDBOOK OF POPULAR QUOTATIONS, ENCYCLOPAEDIA AND HANDBOOK OF LEGAL INFORMATION, CONDENSED CLASSICAL DICTIONARY, and THE RECORD OF THE YEAR, edited by Frank Moore, which was a digest of important events of the year collected from newspapers and journals.

Another of Carleton's publishing interests was reflected in his courtesy books and "Handbooks of Society," among them being THE ART OF CONVERSATION, THE ARTS OF WRITING, READING AND SPEAKING, THE HABITS OF GOOD SOCIETY, FEMALE BEAUTY AND THE ART OF PLEASING, THE LADIES' AND GENTLEMEN'S ETIQUETTE BOOK, and THE ART OF AMUSING. Though he turned down Mark Twain, Carleton published Bret Harte, Richard Stoddard and Thomas Aldrich. The success of a sketch book called OUR ARTIST IN CUBA led to similar titles: OUR ARTIST IN PERU, OUR ARTIST IN ALGIERS, and OUR ARTIST IN SPAIN, all of which sold widely.

Carleton was aided in his activities by an able associate, George Dillingham. Carleton and Dillingham were deft showmen and some of their techniques anticipated modern publishing. In 1886 Carleton retired from business. Dillingham, who then became head of the firm, continued to offer a wide list of popular books every year until his death in 1895. When Carleton died in 1901 *Publishers Weekly* paid him the ultimate tribute: "There is at least one publisher whom even Lord Byron would not desire to kill, and his name is Carleton."

Robert Carter and Brothers

Founded in New York City in 1834 as a bookshop by Robert Carter, a Scot immigrant, who had come to New York only three years earlier. In 1836 he published his first book, SYMINGTON ON THE ATONEMENT AND INTERCESSION OF JESUS CHRIST, which he described as more "suited to the Covenanters of Scotland two hundred years ago." Nevertheless he sold six thousand copies and was encouraged to go into publishing on a modest scale. His next success was in 1841, Merle d'Aubigné's HISTORY OF THE GREAT REFORMATION in three volumes. By 1848 Carter was so successful that he took in his brothers, Peter and Walter, as partners.

A devout Presbyterian and individualist, Carter issued mostly religious titles, and his *Sunday School Library Series* of over five hundred books has been described as one of the most extensive ever published by a single house. His business did not survive his death in 1889.

The Century Company

Founded in 1881 in New York City by Roswell Smith when he bought Charles Scribner's interest in Scribner and Company, publishers of *Scribner's* magazine and *St. Nicholas* magazine. As a result of this reorganization Scribner and Company was renamed The Century Company and *Scribner's* magazine was retitled *Century*.

The Century Company's first titles drew heavily on the popular articles published in *Century* and *St. Nicholas*. Among these were THE BATTLES AND LEADERS OF THE CIVIL WAR, LINCOLN by John G. Nicolay and John Hay, Joseph Jefferson's AUTOBIOGRAPHY, Frances Eliza Burnett's LITTLE LORD FAUNTLEROY, THE STORY OF THE GOLDEN FLEECE by Andrew Lang, THE HOOSIER SCHOOLMASTER by Edward Eggleston, and Mark Twain's TOM SAWYER ABROAD. Later, Century began publication of a number of original novels. Included among these were: THE RISE OF SILAS LAPHAM by William Dean Howells; Mark Twain's HUCKLEBERRY FINN and PUDD'NHEAD WILSON; Weir Mitchell's HUGH WYNNE; Rudyard Kipling's THE JUNGLE BOOK; and Frank Stockton's THE LADY OR THE TIGER.

A bold and imaginative publisher, Smith engaged William D. Whitney in 1882 to compile THE CENTURY DICTIONARY. When the work was completed in six volumes in 1891 it was hailed as the most monumental lexicographical achievement in the United States up to that time. Two supplementary volumes were issued in 1909. In 1927 the work was compressed into three volumes and published as THE NEW CENTURY DICTIONARY. Two other major reference works undertaken by Smith were the CENTURY CYCLOPAEDIA OF NAMES and the CENTURY ATLAS OF THE WORLD. The former work was reissued in 1954 as the NEW CENTURY CYCLOPEDIA OF NAMES, edited by Clarence L. Barnhart and William D. Halsey.

Smith died in 1890 and was succeeded in the presidency by Frank H. Scott who directed the firm until 1912. Scott was responsible for developing Century's strong college textbook line which included Alexander Smith's chemistry series, the sociology series of E.A. Ross, George L. Burr's history series, Frederick A. Ogg's political science series, C.E. Chadsey's education series, and the Century Readings in English and American Literature.

The firm's fortunes began to decline after 1912 when W.W. Ellsworth became president. W. Morgan Schuster, who followed Ellsworth as president in 1915, failed to revive the company. Enfeebled by the Depression, it was merged with D. Appleton and Company in 1933 to form D. Appleton-Century Company.

Childs, George W. (1829-1894)

Born, Baltimore, Maryland. Childs joined the publishing firm of R.E. Peterson of Philadelphia, Pennsylvania, in 1850 and within two years rose to a partnership. In 1854 the firm was renamed Childs & Peterson. The firm's early list comprised law books, one of which was INSTITUTES OF AMERICAN LAW; a few religious titles; textbooks, such as FAMILIAR SCIENCE and ALGEBRA by Enoch Lewis; reference books like A NEW MEDICAL DICTIONARY; David Wells' YEAR BOOK OF AGRICULTURE; also THE NATIONAL COOK BOOK.

Childs' showmanship soon asserted itself and he promoted one of his titles, ARCTIC EXPLORATIONS by E.K. Kane, with such éclat that it became a national bestseller. But another undertaking, A CRITICAL DICTIONARY OF ENGLISH LITERATURE, AND BRITISH AND AMERICAN AUTHORS by Samuel A. Allibone, proved a loser and brought the firm near to bankruptcy.

Peterson retired in 1860 and Childs, after a brief connection with J.B. Lippincott, established his own imprint. Under his device of the broken sword and quill pen appeared a varied list that included many successful titles: PARSON BROWNLOW'S BOOK, THE MILITARY LAWS OF THE UNITED STATES, LIVES OF THE GENERALS OF THE UNION ARMY, PICTORIAL HISTORY OF THE CIVIL WAR, THE NATIONAL ALMANAC, and FIELDBOOK OF THE AMERICAN REVOLUTION.

In 1863 Childs purchased the *American Publishers' Circular and Literary Gazette* from Charles R. Rode and soon developed it into an "index of the Republic of Letters throughout the World." In 1872 the *Gazette* merged with F. Leypoldt's *Weekly Trade Circular* to become the *Publishers Weekly*. Not long after Childs acquired the *Gazette* he purchased with Anthony J. Drexel the *Public Ledger* of Philadelphia, Pennsylvania. Under his direction the *Ledger* became one of the greatest daily newspapers in the country but it also marked the end of his career as a book publisher. However, he continued to issue occasional books throughout the 1870s.

Robert Clarke & Company

Founded in 1854 when Robert Clarke bought an interest in Lyon and Patterson of Cleveland, Ohio, which then became Patterson & Clarke. Clarke specialized in rare Americana, a field in which he was considered an authority. He became sole owner of the firm in 1857. The next year he took in R.D. Barney and J.W. Dale as partners and bought the lawbook firm of Henry Derby. Reorganized as Robert Clarke & Company, the firm published mainly law books. Reflecting his own interests, Clarke also published many antiquarian books and historical works, of which William H. Venable's BEGINNINGS OF LITERARY CULTURE IN THE OHIO VALLEY was the most important. Clarke's *Ohio Valley Historical Series* is regarded as a mine of historical source material on that region. Another achievement for which Clarke is remembered is the *Bibliotheca Americana,* a systematic catalogue for scholars of American history.

The firm was acquired by W.H. Anderson Company in 1908.

Collier, Peter Fenelon (1849-1909)

Born, County Carlow, Ireland. Collier started his career as a salesman for P.J. Kenedy of New York City, selling Bibles and Catholic books through a deferred-payment plan. Later he began to offer sets of standard authors, including Charles Dickens, Sir Walter Scott and William Shakespeare. In the course of time his sales organization became so efficient that editions of a hundred thousand sets were not uncommon. He divided the United States into departments under able, salaried heads and subdivided those departments into territories under commission agents, so that there was no city or village where his sets were not on sale.

In 1888 Collier launched *Once A Week,* primarily to promote his books. Later renamed *Collier's Weekly,* it developed into one of the important mass market magazines of the first half of the twentieth century. In 1909 Collier announced an ambitious undertaking, *The Harvard Classics,* a fifty-volume collection known as the Five-Foot Shelf, edited by Charles W. Eliot.

Collier was succeeded as head of the firm by his son, R.J. Collier. A year after the death of R.J. Collier in 1918 the firm was acquired by Crowell Publishing Company and the combined business became Crowell-Collier Publishing Company (q.v.).

Comstock, Anthony (1844-1915)

Founder in 1873 in New York City of the New York Society for the Suppression of Vice. He was instrumental in securing the passage of a postal law prohibiting transmission of obscene materials through the mails.

During his busy years as a moral crusader Comstock tracked down many publishers of indecent works, but his puritanical zeal often blurred the distinction between freethinking and pornography. A man single-minded in his own way, he credited himself with having caused fifteen suicides among his victims. He wrote two books: FRAUDS EXPOSED (1880) and TRAPS FOR THE YOUNG (1883).

See: ANTHONY COMSTOCK, ROUNDSMAN OF THE LORD by Heywood Broun and Margaret Leech (1927), and ANTHONY COMSTOCK, FIGHTER by Charles G. Trumbull (1913).

Copeland and Day

Founded in 1893 by Frederick Holland Day and Herbert Copeland in Boston, Massachusetts. They soon built up an impressive list of American authors. Their total output of ninety-six titles included fifty-four books of poems; of the remaining titles, the majority were translations. Included were works by Lionel Johnson, Francis Thompson, Alice Brown, Louise Imogen Guiney, and C.M. Flandrau. Daniel Berkeley Updike has said of these books that they belong among the best printed volumes of the day. The firm did not outlive the century. In 1899 it was acquired by Small, Maynard and Company.

Covici-Friede

A partnership begun in 1928 by Pascal Covici and Donald Friede in New York City. Covici had started a publishing house in Chicago, Illinois, in the early 1920s and Friede was a vice president of Liveright. They began as publishers of bibliophilic books in limited editions and their first major book was Radclyffe Hall's THE WELL OF LONELINESS, which ran afoul of John Sumner who declared it obscene. The ensuing trial aroused great interest in the novel and, when it was cleared by the courts, it became a bestseller.

During their ten years as publishers, the partners issued many books of high quality and their authors included Wyndham Lewis, Albert Einstein, Richard Aldington, Saul Bellow, Arthur Miller, George Gamow, Ludwig Bemelmans, and Gene Fowler. Covici developed close friendships with and was held in high esteem by his authors. He was a lifelong friend of John Steinbeck and felt that his critical judgment was fully rewarded when the latter was awarded the Nobel Prize in 1962. In dedicating EAST OF EDEN to Covici, Steinbeck wrote: "The dedication is to you with all the admiration and affection that have been distilled from our singularly blessed association of many years." Saul Bellow's HERZOG was also dedicated "To Pat Covici, a great editor."

In spite of these successes, the firm became insolvent in 1938. Covici joined Viking as senior editor, taking with him many of his authors, including Steinbeck. Most of the other titles were sold to Nat Wartel's Outlet Book Company which, in time, became Crown Publishers. Some years later Friede joined World Publishing Company.

Crocker & Brewster

Founded in Boston, Massachusetts, by Uriel Crocker and Osmyn Brewster, partners in the publishing firm of S.T. Armstrong, Crocker and Brewster. The firm later was known as Crocker and Brewster when Armstrong retired in 1840. The firm published the *Rollo* books by J.S.C. Abbott. The bookstore of Crocker and Brewster was a favorite gathering place of Boston literati. The partnership lasted for more than seventy-five years. The firm merged with Houghton Mifflin in 1876. *See,* Uriel Crocker's AUTOBIOGRAPHY and MEMORIAL OF URIEL CROCKER.

J.C. Derby & Company

Founded in 1840 in Auburn, New York, by J.C. Derby with H.C. Ivison as partner. Their first book was CONFERENCE HYMNS, WITH TUNES, ADAPTED TO RELIGIOUS MEET-

INGS FOR PRAYERS by the Reverend Josiah Hopkins and Henry Ivison, published in 1844. Norman C. Miller became a partner in 1848 and the company's name was changed to Derby & Miller. By 1853, when Derby left the firm to go to New York, more than one hundred books had been published under this imprint, including LIVES OF MARY AND MARTHA WASHINGTON by Margaret C. Conkling, LIFE OF GEORGE WASHINGTON by Jared Sparks, LIFE OF JOHN QUINCY ADAMS by William H. Seward, and HISTORY OF ALL NATIONS by Charles Augustus Goodrich.

Derby in 1855 set up a new partnership with Edwin Jackson in New York, called Derby and Jackson. This imprint continued until 1861, publishing Oliver Goldsmith, Blaise Pascal, Daniel Defoe, Charles Lamb, Henry Fielding, Tobias George Smollett, and Jane Austen, as well as many American writers. Derby is best known for his book FIFTY YEARS AMONG AUTHORS, BOOKS, AND PUBLISHERS, published by G.W. Carleton in 1884.

Dewey, Melvil (1851-1931)

Born, Adams Center, New York. Inventor of the Dewey Decimal System of book classification. He first published his scheme in 1876 and revised it until 1929. He was a founder of the New York State Library School, the first training school for librarians. He was also one of the founders of the American Library Association and a co-founder of the *Library Journal*.

Dewey was an ardent advocate of simplified spelling, which he used in his own books.

Dick & Fitzgerald

Established in 1851 in New York City by William Brisbane Dick and Lawrence R. Fitzgerald when they took over the firm of Burgess and Garrett. Dick & Fitzgerald specialized in two types of books for which there was an eager public in the latter half of the nineteenth century: self-improvement books and entertainment books. In the first category would fall books with titles as modern as HOW TO BEHAVE IN SOCIETY, THE ART OF DRESSING WELL, THE LADIES' GUIDE TO BEAUTY, THE ART AND ETIQUETTE OF MAKING LOVE and BLUNDERS IN BEHAVIOR CORRECTED. A wide assortment of cookbooks was also offered: THE AMERICAN HOUSEWIFE AND KITCHEN DIRECTORY, HOW TO COOK AND HOW TO CARVE, and HOW TO COOK POTATOES, APPLES, EGGS, AND FISH FOUR HUNDRED DIFFERENT WAYS.

On a higher plane they offered Franz Thimm's FRENCH, GERMAN, SPANISH, and ITALIAN SELF-TAUGHT, and their *Reason Why* series and *Shilling Library of Reference Books*. The *Hand and Pocket Library* offered adventure and detective stories at twenty-five cents each. To meet a different type of need a series of manuals were published on ready reckoning, phonography, taxidermy, horse training, printing, punctuation, health, household pets, needlework, and individual sports.

In the field of entertainment books, the list was even more varied. It included books on popular dances, parlor dramas, palmistry, magic, card games, and song books. These entertainments were brought together in such titles as WHAT SHALL WE DO TONIGHT? OR, SOCIAL AMUSEMENTS FOR EVENING PARTIES; THE SOCIABLE, OR, ONE THOUSAND AND ONE HOME AMUSEMENTS; UNCLE JOSH'S TRUNK-FULL OF FUN; and FIRESIDE GAMES: FOR WINTER EVENING'S AMUSEMENT. For those who wished more specific instruction there were titles such as THE COMPLETE BANJO INSTRUCTOR by Frank Converse, THE AMERICAN HOYLE, THE FIRESIDE MAGICIAN, HYPNOTISM by Lauron W. De Laurence, THE ART OF DANCING by General Edward Ferrero, FANCY COS-

TUMES by Weldon, THE GOLDEN WHEEL DREAM BOOK by Felix Fontaine, and William Brisbane Dick's MYSTERIES OF THE HAND, OR, PALMISTRY MADE EASY.

In the course of time Dick & Fitzgerald became primarily a mail order house. Fitzgerald died in 1881 and William Dick continued the business under the same name until his retirement in 1898, at which time his son, Harris Brisbane Dick, took over the firm and successfully directed it until his death in 1918. Under terms of his will the firm was dissolved but was later reorganized as the Fitzgerald Publishing Corporation, which remained in business until 1940. At that time Rudolph Behrens of Danbury, Connecticut, acquired the Dick and Fitzgerald handbooks and issued them under the name of Behrens Publishing Company.

The imprint has been acquired by Walter H. Baker Company.

Dietz Press

Established in 1890 in Richmond, Virginia, by August Dietz, Sr., as The Dietz Printing Company. In 1939 the company, headed by F. Meredith Dietz and August Dietz, Jr., revived publication of the *Southern Literary Messenger*. The firm was incorporated in 1942 as The Dietz Press, Inc. The press specialized in Virginiana and Southern literature.

Dobson, Thomas

Publisher in 1803 of the first American edition of ENCYCLOPAEDIA BRITANNICA, generally known as DOBSON'S ENCYCLOPAEDIA. He sold the work by subscription. The ENCYCLOPAEDIA was completed in twenty-one volumes with a supplement of three volumes and contained over six hundred copperplates.

M.A. Donohue and Company

Founded in 1861, at Chicago, Illinois, M.A. Donohue and Company was one of the oldest juvenile publishers in the United States. The firm began as Cox and Donohue, bookbinders; by 1880 it became Donohue and Henneberry, printers and publishers. By 1901, when M.A. Donohue bought out Henneberry, the firm was specializing exclusively in children's books and sets.

Hubbard Press has acquired the imprint.

Doran, George H. (1869-1956)

Born, Toronto, Canada. Doran began his career with Fleming H. Revell in Chicago, Illinois. Moving to New York City in 1908 he started his own firm, with the British house of Hodder and Stoughton as a minority shareholder. His first book was Winston S. Churchill's MY AFRICAN JOURNEY. Profits from two early bestsellers, Ralph Connor's THE FOREIGNER and Arnold Bennett's OLD WIVES' TALE enabled him to acquire, in 1910, the firm of A.C. Armstrong and Son. In 1913 he started the *Fifty-cent Fiction Library*. Somerset Maugham and Mary Roberts Rinehart appeared on Doran's 1915 list.

Doran was at the height of his career in the 1920s and with the assistance of his brilliant associates, Eugene Saxton, John Farrar, and Stanley M. Rinehart, he had managed to attract some of the most popular American and British writers of the day. Among them were Aldous Huxley, Arthur Conan Doyle, Hugh Walpole, Marie Corelli, Stephen McKenna, Stephen Vincent Benét, Hervey Allen, Michael Arlen, Ring Lardner, T.E. Lawrence, and DuBose Heyward. He also published James Moffatt's translation of the New Testament.

In 1924 Hodder and Stoughton relinquished their interest in the firm. Three years later Doran accepted a merger offer from the Doubleday organization. The combined firm of Doubleday, Doran and Company became the largest trade publisher in the United States. The partnership came to an end in 1930 when Doran found the new conglomerate uncongenial. In his later years Doran published his memoirs as THE CHRONICLES OF BARABBAS, the title recalling Byron's famous line: *Now Barabbas was a publisher.*

Dornin, Bernard

An Irishman who came to the United States in 1803, Dornin that year set up a bookshop in New York City. By 1805 he was publishing such titles as Oliver Goldsmith's ROMAN HISTORY and James Ferguson's EASY INTRODUCTION TO ASTRONOMY. He began to publish Catholic books in 1806 and moved to Baltimore, Maryland, in 1809. When his firm became bankrupt, he started again in Philadelphia, Pennsylvania, as Bernard Dornin & Company, publishing exclusively Catholic books. He retired in 1824, having published over fifty books and pamphlets.

Paul Elder & Company

Founded in San Francisco, California, by Paul Elder in 1898. In 1899 Morgan Shepard became Elder's partner and Elder and Shepard was formed. In 1903 Shepard retired. The business was then incorporated as Paul Elder and Company. The firm's publications were distinguished by their fine printing.

Elliott, Thomes, and Talbot

Established at Boston, Massachusetts, in 1863 by James R. Elliott, Henry Thomes, and Newton Talbot. In that year they launched the *Ten-Cent Novelettes,* which have been described as the largest and handsomest ten-cent books ever published. These novelettes, issued every month, were bound in pink, and later printed on pink paper, in a format slightly larger than the dime novels. In addition the firm issued the *Brilliant Novelettes,* each priced at twenty cents and containing engravings illustrating a complete story. These two series purveyed adventure, horror, romance, and patriotism. The authors were mostly unknowns, the one exception being Louisa May Alcott.

Elliott left the firm in 1870 to start the *Western World* and the firm was dissolved in the mid-eighties.

Estes & Lauriat

Established at Boston, Massachusetts, in 1872 by Dana Estes and Charles E. Lauriat for the purpose of publishing subscription books in de luxe editions at a moderate price so as to attract a wide audience. A representative title in the firm's early list was F.P.G. Guizot's six-volume POPULAR HISTORY OF FRANCE, which was offered in fifty-five parts at fifty cents each. Similar works were offered at prices ranging from $25 to $60: Charles Knight's eight-volume POPULAR HISTORY OF ENGLAND, Alfred N. Rambaud's three-volume RUSSIA, Victor Duruy's eight-volume ROME, as well as popular travel books, biographies, dictionaries, and encyclopedias. In the field of fiction the firm offered James Osgood's thirty-volume *Library of Novels* and the novels of Alphonse Daudet. Juveniles were particularly successful with the titles CHATTERBOX and CAPTAIN JANUARY by Laura E. Richards heading the list. Hezekiah Butterworth's book of journeys in Europe was the first of seventeen *Zigzag* volumes issued between 1879 and 1895.

In 1898 the partnership was dissolved and Estes took over the publishing division while Lauriat retained the retail bookstore. Estes died in 1909 and his sons managed the business until 1914 when it was sold to L.C. Page and Company. L.C. Page, who was Estes' stepson, continued to promote the Estes titles. The L.C. Page list was sold in 1957 to Farrar & Straus.

Farrar & Rinehart

Founded as a partnership in 1929 in New York City by John Farrar and Stanley M. Rinehart, Jr. Both Farrar and Rinehart had been employees of Doubleday and when they left they arranged to take over some Doubleday titles and contracts. Mary Roberts Rinehart also gave them her books and the firm got off to a good start. Their first list, issued during the Depression, included Mary Rinehart's THE ROMANTICS, DuBose Heyward's THE HALF-PINT FLASK, and Herbert Gorman's THE INCREDIBLE MARQUIS.

The firm's first major success was Hervey Allen's ANTHONY ADVERSE published in 1931. In the same year the firm acquired the books of Cosmopolitan Book Corporation which had published many such popular authors as Faith Baldwin, Louis Golding, and Rex Beach. The accession of these authors resulted in a highly visible trade house and the quality of the list was sustained from year to year. Thus the 1931 list included Philip Wylie and Upton Sinclair, the 1932 list G.K. Chesterton and Evelyn Waugh, the 1933 list Stephen Vincent Benét and Alexander Laing, and the 1934 list Frank Swinnerton and H.S. Canby. Benét proved to be a very loyal author until his death in 1944.

A major undertaking at this period was the *Rivers of America* series, edited by Constance Lindsay Skinner, which received the first Carey-Thomas Award for Creative Publishing. The firm also began to develop a mystery series with the establishment of the Mary Roberts Rinehart Mystery Prize Contest, and a series of volumes on *American Government in Action* proved to be very influential.

The partnership was dissolved in 1945. For further history, *see* Rinehart & Company and Farrar, Straus & Giroux.

Federal Writers' Project

Established in 1934 as a project of the Works Progress Administration with Henry G. Alsberg as director. Also known as Federal One, the Project's most enduring legacy was the fifty-one volume *American Guide Series*. The volumes, some nearly one thousand pages long, are beautifully written narratives mirroring America's landscape and character. The 6,686 writers employed by the project included Nelson Algren, Richard Wright, and Saul Bellow in Chicago, John Cheever and Ralph Ellison in New York, Loren Eiseley in Nebraska, Conrad Aiken in Massachusetts, and Kenneth Rexroth in San Francisco.

Fergus, Robert (1815-1897)

Born, Glasgow, Scotland. In 1840 Fergus joined with William Ellis to form the first publishing house in Chicago, Illinois. Their first book was a slim volume of poetry entitled GLEANINGS OF THOUGHT. In 1843 the partners produced the first regular directory of Chicago entitled GENERAL DIRECTORY AND BUSINESS ADVERTISER OF THE CITY OF CHICAGO, FOR THE YEAR 1844; TOGETHER WITH A HISTORICAL SKETCH AND STATISTICAL ACCOUNT TO THE PRESENT TIME. Another first by Fergus was the first historical work printed in Chicago, MRS. KINZIE'S NARRATIVE OF THE MASSACRE AT CHICAGO, AUGUST 15, 1812. In 1845 appeared THE ROSARIST'S COMPANION: OR, MANUAL OF DEVOUT EXERCISES.

The partnership was dissolved in 1850 and Fergus continued alone until 1871, when the great fire in Chicago destroyed his establishment. Out of this tragic experience came Fergus's greatest project, the *Fergus Historical* series, which eventually numbered thirty volumes. The series was designed to preserve the history of the city that had gone down in flames. In addition Fergus also issued under his imprint the Chicago Historical Society's COLLECTIONS or ADDRESSES. Fergus's interests extended also to genealogies and the Scottish language. A GLOSSARY OF SCOTTISH WORDS is among his later works. He died in 1897.

Fowler and Wells Company

Established in New York City by Orson Squire Fowler and Lorenzo Niles Fowler. They were joined in 1844 by S.R. Wells. As dedicated phrenologists, they used their imprint to promote the science of phrenology. They took over the *American Phrenological Journal and Miscellany* in 1849. Before they closed their business in 1863, they had issued a number of titles on their favorite subject: PHRENOLOGY PROVED, ILLUSTRATED AND APPLIED; HEREDITARY

DESCENT; LOVE AND PARENTAGE; and PHRENOLOGICAL ALMANAC. But their chief claim to fame rests with their publication of the second edition of Walt Whitman's LEAVES OF GRASS, which bore Ralph Waldo Emerson's testimonial.

C.S. Francis & Company

Established in 1826 as a bookstore in New York City by Charles Stephen Francis. Charles Francis was the son of David Francis, a partner in the Boston, Massachusetts, house of Munroe & Francis, publishers of the earliest edition of SHAKESPEARE'S WORKS in America. The Francis store in New York City was a favorite rendezvous for New Englanders and was patronized among others by Aaron Burr, DeWitt Clinton, and James Audubon.

Francis gradually gravitated into publishing. He is best remembered as the publisher of John James Audubon's BIRDS OF AMERICA with four hundred thirty-five plates, in a four-volume elephant folio, priced at $1,000.00. He also brought out MOTHER GOOSE MELODIES and two popular novels: AURORA LEIGH by Elizabeth Browning, and A NEW HOME—WHO'LL FOLLOW? by Caroline Matilda Stansbury Kirkland. The NEW GUIDE TO THE CITIES OF NEW YORK, AND BROOKLYN, AND THE VICINITY, which Francis published in 1853, is regarded as a valuable source book.

Francis retired in 1860 and his business went to James Miller, who had joined the firm as an errand boy in 1835. Miller turned his attention to illustrated gift books and he is generally regarded as the first American to have published these in boxed sets. He also published standard editions of works of Robert Browning, Thomas Gray, Sir Walter Scott, Percy B. Shelley, Thomas B. Macaulay, and Robert Burns, along with popular and practical books such as SCIENCE OF THINGS FAMILIAR and FIVE HUNDRED MISTAKES IN SPEAKING AND READING CORRECTED. His large line of children's titles included ROBIN HOOD and CHILD'S OWN BOOK OF FAIRY TALES. Miller died in 1883.

Franklin, Benjamin (1706-1790)

Born, Boston, Massachusetts. In the summer of 1728 Franklin set up a printing shop called Franklin and Meredith in Philadelphia, Pennsylvania, with Hugh Meredith as his partner. The first work to bear their imprint is generally believed to have been A NEW VERSION OF THE PSALMS OF DAVID by Isaac Watts, published in 1729. Other books bearing Franklin's varying imprints appeared thereafter. Cadwallader Colden's AN EXPLICATION OF THE FIRST CAUSES OF MOTION IN MATTER; THE NEW ENGLAND PSALTER; DISTINGUISHING MARKS OF A WORK OF THE SPIRIT OF GOD by Jonathan Edwards; Daniel Defoe's FAMILY INSTRUCTOR; and DER HOCHERLEUCHTELEN THEOLOGI by Johann Arndt were among Franklin's more important publications during the next three decades. But Franklin is best remembered for POOR RICHARD'S ALMANACK, which he published annually from 1732 to 1757.

As official printer for the States of Pennsylvania, New Jersey and Delaware, Franklin's publications were mostly legislative records, laws, and treaties. The total of his imprints has been estimated at seven hundred and thirty, a hundred fewer than that of Isaiah Thomas. His most productive period was between 1748 and 1776, when David Hall was his partner. The imprint of Franklin & Hall survived through a succession of partnerships well into the twentieth century.

Franklin's contribution to books was not limited to printing and publishing; he founded the first subscription library in Philadelphia, known

18

as the Philadelphia Library, and his bookstores were reputed to be the finest in the American Colonies.

Goodrich, Samuel (1793-1860)

Born, Ridgefield, Connecticut. Goodrich entered publishing in 1812 in partnership with George Sheldon. The firm, based in Hartford, Connecticut, started off with many ambitious ventures among which were Scott's FAMILY BIBLE in five volumes, and an eight-volume edition of Sir Walter Scott's WORKS, also an edition of John Trumbull's POEMS in two volumes. Sheldon died in 1817 and in 1826 Goodrich moved to Boston, Massachusetts.

In 1827 Goodrich issued the first of the *Peter Parley* books for children, one of the most successful series of children's books ever published in the United States. *Peter Parley* has been regarded as one of the best-loved figures in juvenile literature and the total sale of this series has been estimated at over twelve million copies. Most of the books, at an average of ten books a year, were written by Goodrich himself. Goodrich died in 1860.

Gould & Lincoln

Started by Charles D. Gould and Charles S. Kendall when they acquired the bankrupt bookselling business of Joshua Lincoln and William Pierce, of Boston, Massachusetts. The partners began business in 1835 as Gould, Kendall & Lincoln. Kendall withdrew in 1850 and Gould continued, using the name Gould & Lincoln.

Gould's principal aim as a publisher was to bring out books that would, in his own words, "diffuse abroad the pure light of science, learning, and religion." In keeping with this aim he published Arnold Henry Guyot's EARTH AND MAN, ZOOLOGY by Alexander Agassiz and Augustus A. Gould, William Paley's NATURAL THEOLOGY, Francis Wayland's MORAL SCIENCE, and THE PSALMIST, a hymnbook, all of which sold many thousands of copies and made Charles Gould one of the most prosperous publishers of his time.

Gould, Stephen

The first lawbook publisher in the United States. He started his business in New York City in 1790. A relative, William Gould, established a lawbook store in Albany, New York, which continued in business until 1890.

Haldeman-Julius, Emanuel (1889-1951)

Founder of the *Little Blue Books* in 1919. The early *Little Blue Books* were 3½″ by 5″ booklets printed in newspaper column width at Haldeman-Julius's own press in Girard, Kansas. They were priced at twenty-five cents a copy but as the sales increased he reduced the price to five cents. By 1922 the list of 283 titles had sold over twenty-two million copies, mostly by mail order and through newspaper advertising. Later Haldeman-Julius also issued the *Big Blue Books* at fifty cents a copy. Most of the two thousand titles he published during his career dealt with such staple subjects as sex, self-improvement, and amusement. But they included a few works of genuine merit, one of which was Will Durant's THE STORY OF PHILOSOPHY.

By means of flamboyant promotion Haldeman-Julius sold over three hundred million copies of his books, earning the title of "the Henry Ford of publishing." Haldeman-Julius was also an author and among his books are THE COLOR OF LIFE (1920), THE ART OF READING (1922), AN AGNOSTIC LOOKS AT LIFE (1926), MYTHS AND MYTH-MAKERS (1927) and THE BIG AMERICAN PARADE (1929).

After Haldeman-Julius died in 1951 his son, Henry, carried on the business until 1964, when he retired following an obscenity conviction.

Hall, David (1714-1772)

Born, Edinburgh, Scotland. Hall came to America in 1744 and in the same year was hired as a journeyman by Benjamin Franklin's press in Philadelphia, Pennsylvania. He became Franklin's partner in 1748. The firm of Franklin and Hall continued until 1766. After his partnership with

Franklin ended, Hall joined William Sellers, another young English bookseller, to form Hall & Sellers. Hall died in 1772 and was succeeded by his two sons, William and David. The firm appears as Hall and Pierie in 1808 and as Hall and Atkinson in 1815. Through successive changes of partners and names, the house that David Hall founded emerged as the Franklin Printing Company, a name that it retains to this day.

Harris, Benjamin (1673-1716)

Born, London, England. Harris arrived in Boston, Massachusetts, in 1686 and opened a bookshop "by the Town Pump near the Change" and here he published his first book in 1687, JOHN TULLEY'S ALMANACH. Harris also published America's first newspaper, *Publick Occurrences Both Foreign and Domestick,* in 1690. This newspaper unfortunately was suppressed after one issue because Harris had failed to obtain the necessary license to publish. But Harris made an even greater contribution to American publishing when he issued the first edition of THE NEW ENGLAND PRIMER sometime in 1690.

The Norman W. Henley Publishing Company

Established in 1890 in New York City by Norman W. Henley to publish technical and scientific books. The firm purchased Henry Carey Baird & Company of Philadelphia. Henley died in 1945 and the business was carried on by his nephew, Charles E. Henley.

The imprint was acquired by Books, Inc.

B. Herder Book Company

Established in 1873 by Joseph Gummersbach in St. Louis, Missouri, as the American branch of the celebrated German firm of Herder Verlag, which was founded in 1801 by Bartholomäus Herder. The American branch became independent in 1917. Owned by the Gummersbach family, Herder specializes in Catholic publications and textbooks.

Hilliard, William

Hilliard established a printing house in 1800 at Cambridge, Massachusetts. In 1812 he formed a partnership with Jacob Abbott Cummings mainly for the purpose of supplying textbooks to Harvard students. The partnership got off to a good start with an ANCIENT AND MODERN SCHOOL GEOGRAPHY written by Cummings, which became a required text for admission to Harvard College. Another moneymaker was Cummings' QUESTIONS ON THE NEW TESTAMENT. Soon a stream of textbooks issued from the firm, among which were Richard Valpy's GREEK GRAMMAR, Joseph Emerson Worcester's ELEMENTS OF GEOGRAPHY, Levi Hedge's ELEMENTS OF LOGIC, and LECTURES ON RHETORIC AND ORATORY by John Quincy Adams. One textbook, Jacob Bigelow's AMERICAN MEDICAL BOTANY, had the distinction of being the first American book printed with plates in color. In addition to their own publications, Cummings and Hilliard offered imported scholarly works and rare books.

Following the death of Cummings in 1823 the partnership was dissolved, and was reconstituted as Cummings, Hilliard & Company with Timothy Harrington Carter as a new partner. Carter persuaded Hilliard to enter the lawbook field, which in course of time became highly profitable. He was also responsible for introducing Charles C. Little to the firm. Meanwhile Hilliard took in two more partners, John Hubbard Wilkins and Harrison Gray. When Carter left the firm in 1827, it was reorganized as Hilliard, Gray and Company. Little, in charge of the legal division, expanded this department as a major source of income. Hilliard continued to serve as publisher to Harvard College and published many works by its scholars. Two important undertakings at this period were Jared Sparks' LIBRARY OF AMERICAN BIOGRAPHY and SPECIMENS OF FOREIGN STANDARD LITERATURE by George Ripley.

Hilliard's last partner was James Brown, who replaced John Wilkins. A year after Hilliard died in 1836, Little and Brown formed a partnership that, as Little, Brown & Company, was to continue many of the traditions of William Hilliard.

Huebsch, Benjamin W. (1875-1964)

Huebsch began his career as a publisher in New York City about 1905 with the publication of THE CITY THAT WAS: A REQUIEM OF OLD SAN FRANCISCO by Will Irwin. His first list included among other titles Otto Pfleiderer's CHRISTIAN ORIGINS, and C.F.G. Masterman's IN PERIL OF CHANGE. Gelett Burgess's ARE YOU A BROMIDE? was his first popular title but within a few publishing seasons his list included a number of provocative and serious books. Among them were Maxim Gorki's THE SPY, John Spargo's KARL MARX AND SYNDICALISM, Edward Bernstein's EVOLUTIONARY SOCIALISM, William Ellery Leonard's THE POET OF GALILEE, Edwin Markham's THE MARVELLOUS YEAR, Gerhart Hauptmann's THE WEAVERS and ATLANTIS, Auguste Rodin's VENUS, and DISCOVERY OF THE FUTURE by H.G. Wells. He also started *The Art of Life,* a series of fifty-cent books. By 1914 the list of Huebsch books was among the best in the trade.

During the World War I years Huebsch published George Sorel's REFLECTIONS ON VIOLENCE, A TALE OF TWO COUNTRIES by Maxim Gorki, Jules Romains' DEATH OF A NOBODY, Van Wyck Brooks' AMERICA'S COMING-OF-AGE, Ludwig Lewisohn's THE MODERN DRAMA, Percy MacKaye's THE IMMIGRANTS, George Jean Nathan's ANOTHER BOOK ON THE THEATER, Simon Patten's CULTURE AND WAR, Arthur Ransome's RUSSIA IN 1919, and Francis Hackett's IRELAND: A CRITICAL EXAMINATION. Huebsch was the first American publisher of James Joyce and D.H. Lawrence, and he nursed the early efforts of Sherwood Anderson when few others recognized Anderson's talent. He was also an uncompromising foe of censorship and opposed the self-appointed moral guardians of his time even when the Publishers Association maintained discreet neutrality.

In 1919 Huebsch became the publisher of *The Freeman,* a liberal weekly, and with this added burden he began to neglect his book publishing interests. By the end of 1924, when *The Freeman* folded, he found that his book business had dwindled beyond recovery and that most of his authors had left him for other houses. Hence he accepted an offer of a merger from The Viking Press.

The disappearance of the Huebsch imprint from the annals of publishing was deeply regretted by his contemporaries. Huebsch had achieved eminence not by the size of his house but by his keen appreciation of good writing and by his fidelity to ideals. "His seven-branched candlestick," Christopher Morley wrote, "almost always marked a book that had a genuine reason for existence." Huebsch retired from Viking in 1956 but served as a literary adviser until his death. In 1964 he received the first annual Irita Van Doren Literary Award "for more than a half century of tireless devotion to literature." He died later in the same year.

Huebsch was also one of the founders of the American Civil Liberties Union.

Indian Bible

The first Bible printed in the American Colonies, at the Cambridge Press in 1663. It was a translation by John Eliot into the language of the Indians. The occasion moved Cotton Mather to write: "Behold, ye Americans, the greatest honor that ever you were partakers of. The Bible was printed here at our Cambridge, and is the only Bible that ever was printed in all America, from the very foundations of the world . . ." A second edition appeared in 1685. It contained, unlike the first, no English title pages.

Inman, John (1805-1850)

The first house editor in American publishing history. He was hired by J. & J. Harper in 1830 as a reader but he performed editorial functions including styling and proofreading. He later became the editor of the *Commercial Advertiser.*

Ivison, Blakeman, Taylor & Company

Founded in 1828 at New York City by Mark H. Newman. One of his early publications was a graded series of spelling and reading books known as *Porter's Readers*. In 1846 he invited Henry Ivison, a bookseller and publisher in Auburn, New York, to join him as partner. The partnership, known as Mark H. Newman & Company, issued fairly successful textbooks, such as the spellers and readers of Charles W. Sanders.

Newman died in 1851. Five years later Ivison formed a new partnership with H.F. Phinney, changing the partnership name in the process to Ivison & Phinney. Phinney was the father-in-law of James Fenimore Cooper and brought with him to the firm several of the Cooper titles. But the partners began to concentrate on the profitable textbook line and they soon became leading educational publishers.

Ivison was one of the prime movers in setting up the Publishers Board of Trade in 1870 to promote reform in educational publishing. During the Civil War years Ivison & Phinney expanded and prospered with their *Union Readers* as one of their most profitable lines of textbooks.

In 1864 the firm was reorganized. Three new partners were added: Birdseye Blakeman, Augustus C. Taylor, and David B. Ivison, and to reflect this change the firm became Ivison, Phinney, Blakeman & Company. By the time Phinney retired in 1870 the firm had become one of the largest educational publishers in the world with a list of over three hundred schoolbooks including Noah Webster's SCHOOL DICTIONARY, Asa Gray's BOTANY, the Platt Rogers Spencer copybooks, MATHEMATICS by Horatio Nelson Robinson, and William Swinton's OUTLINES OF WORLD HISTORY.

William N. Crane was brought in as a partner to replace Phinney and the firm's name was again changed to Ivison, Blakeman, Taylor & Company. When Henry Ivison retired in 1882 his interest was acquired by his son, David Ivison. Taylor retired five years later and Crane also left the firm about that time.

The imprint was shortened to Ivison, Blakeman & Company in 1887, the remaining partners being Birdseye Blakeman, David Ivison, George R. Cathcart and Louis H. Blakeman. In 1890 the firm merged into the American Book Company (q.v.). Birdseye Blakeman became the first president of American Book Company and David Ivison its second.

James, Joseph A. and Uriah P.

Established in 1832 in Cincinnati, Ohio, by Joseph A. and Uriah P. James as J.A. James & Company. Their first publication was THE EOLIAN SONGSTER, a songbook, which they reissued for many years. Most of their titles in the early years were uncopyrighted classics but a few original works were also published, along with almanacs and children's books. The partnership was dissolved in 1837 but was reorganized ten years later as J.A. and U.P. James.

At the peak of their careers the Jameses were known as the Harpers of the West. In addition to such standard works as books by John Milton, Edward Gibbon, Robert Burns, and Thomas Moore, they published Western Americana, and antiquarian books soon developed into one of the strengths of the firm. Before the Civil War the brothers published two ambitious series called the *Library of American History* and the *Library of General Knowledge*. The partnership was once again dissolved in 1854 but Uriah P. James continued to publish on a modest scale until 1880.

Jewett, John P. (1814-1884)

Born, Lebanon, Maine. Began publishing in Boston, Massachusetts, in 1847. Jewett made his fortune when he published UNCLE TOM'S CABIN by Harriet Beecher Stowe, widely regarded as one of the most influential and popular books of all time. He repeated this success with THE LAMPLIGHTER by Maria Susanna Cummins.

With the profits from his two bestsellers Jewett expanded quickly and his catalogue included theological works, a music encyclopedia, and an edition of Margaret Fuller's WOMAN IN THE NINETEENTH CENTURY. Jewett's firm failed to survive the Panic of 1857.

Johnson and Warner

Founded at Philadelphia, Pennsylvania, by Jacob Johnson and Benjamin Warner in 1808, though Johnson himself was in the book business as early as 1780. Later Warner bought his partner's share and continued to publish a number of children's books. By 1828 the firm was in the hands of McCarty and Davis, a partnership of William McCarty and Thomas Davis. McCarty died in 1831, and, on the death of Davis in 1851, the firm was acquired by Moses Polock, who is best remembered as the friend of Edgar Allan Poe, James Fenimore Cooper, Herman Melville, and Daniel Webster. In 1857 Polock published the first collected edition of Charles Brockden Brown.

The firm disappeared from the publishing annals when Polock died in 1903.

Orange Judd Publishing Company, Inc.

Founded in 1836 in New York City by Charles M. Saxton and Early E. Miles as Miles and Saxton. Miles sold his interest to Saxton and the firm became Charles M. Saxton, Agricultural Book Publishers. When Saxton purchased the *American Agriculturalist,* its editor, Orange Judd, remained as Saxton's associate.

After Saxton's death in 1864, his interest was acquired by Judd and the firm was reorganized as Orange Judd & Company. The firm later went into bankruptcy but was again reorganized in 1883 with David W. Judd, brother of Orange Judd, as president. In 1921 George E. Eiermann purchased the book department. The firm continued to specialize in agricultural, gardening, and pet books.

The imprint was acquired by Howell Book House.

Kennerley, Mitchell (1878-1950)

Kennerley was sent to America in 1896 by John Lane, the British publishers, to open and manage their New York City office. In 1900 he left Lane and became the business manager of *The Smart Set* magazine. The next year he started *Reader's Magazine* which he sold to Bobbs-Merrill in 1904. In 1905 he founded the publishing firm that bore his name.

During the next ten years Kennerley published some critical successes: IMPERIAL PURPLE by Edgar Saltus; Kenneth Brown's SIROCCO; ANACTORIA by Algernon Swinburne; LIFE'S SHOP WINDOW by Victoria Cross; THE MAN SHAKESPEARE AND HIS TRAGIC LIFE STORY by Frank Harris; WINE OF THE PURITANS by Van Wyck Brooks; GREEN CARNATION by Robert Hichens; the poems of Bliss Carman; Joseph Hergesheimer's LAY ANTHONY and MOUNTAIN BLOOD; Edna St. Vincent Millay's RENASCENCE AND OTHER POEMS; Vachel Lindsay's GENERAL WILLIAM BOOTH ENTERS INTO HEAVEN and HANDY GUIDE FOR BEGGARS; Walter Lippmann's PREFACE TO POLITICS and DRIFT AND MASTERY; Ferenc Molnár's THE DEVIL; Frank Swinnerton's GEORGE GISSING; and CHILD OF THE AMAZONS by Max Eastman.

Unorthodox in his tastes, Kennerley encouraged several young and liberal authors who owed to him their first start to fame. In 1913 Kennerley was prosecuted by Anthony Comstock for publishing Daniel C. Goodman's HAGAR REVELLY. He won this case and went on to publish D.H. Lawrence. Kennerley's later list included such authors as Samuel Butler, Lord Dunsany, Leonid N. Andreyev, and Leonard Merrick. Kennerley also published *The Forum,* which served as a vehicle for his nonconformist ideas.

In 1915 Kennerley became the director of the Anderson Auction Company. Thereafter he published only occasional books and gradually disposed of his list. Old and penniless, he ended his own life early in 1950. The type Kennerley, designed by Frederic W. Goudy, was named for him.

Lea, Henry Charles (1825-1909)

Born, Philadelphia, Pennsylvania. Son of Isaac Lea and grandson of Mathew Carey. As head of the firm of Blanchard & Lea and later Henry C. Lea, he was responsible for transforming the firm into a specialized medical book publisher. Lea's achievements as an author are as notable as his contribution to publishing. His works include A HISTORY OF THE INQUISITION OF THE MIDDLE AGES; HISTORY OF WITCHCRAFT, SUPERSTITION AND FORCE; THE MORISCOS OF SPAIN; and HISTORICAL SKETCH OF SACERDOTAL CELIBACY IN THE CHRISTIAN CHURCH.

Ledyard, John

Author of the first copyrighted book in the United States. Ledyard had sailed with Captain James Cook on his third voyage and on his return home had written A JOURNAL OF CAPTAIN COOK'S LAST VOYAGE TO THE PACIFIC OCEAN. In 1790 he appealed to the Connecticut Assembly for exclusive rights to his book. The committee to which his appeal was referred recommended the passage of a general copyright law. The Act for the Encouragement of Literature and Genius which the Assembly thereupon enacted was the basis for the Federal Law of 1790. The Act gave to authors resident in America "the sole liberty of printing, publishing, and vending" any book of their creation, previously unprinted, for a term of fourteen years. Penalties were provided for infringement and methods of registration spelled out. The Act however required the author to set a reasonable price on his book and to furnish the public with a sufficient number of copies.

his time. In 1862 he ventured into book publishing with his first book, PICTORIAL HISTORY OF THE WAR OF 1861. After a series of new novels in 1863 and 1864, a PICTORIAL LIFE OF ABRAHAM LINCOLN followed. Later he issued his HISTORICAL REGISTER OF THE . . . CENTENNIAL EXPOSITION, which was energetically promoted.

Leslie's books were usually arranged in series: *Home Library of Standard Works, Chimney Corner Series, Popular Library Series,* and *Boys Library Series.* His books belonged to the class of railroad literature and were sold by the American News Company at station kiosks and on the trains. However, the crisis of 1877 overtook Leslie and his empire crumbled. He died in 1880 but his widow carried on his business for a time under the legal name of Frank Leslie.

Lewis Historical Publishing Company

Founded in 1877 at Chicago, Illinois, by B.F. Lewis and S.T. Lewis. A New York City branch was founded in 1907 by Marion L. Lewis. The firm specialized in history, biography, genealogy, and state, county, and town histories. The historical works published by the firm include HISTORY OF SOUTH CAROLINA by David D. Wallace, RHODE ISLAND by Charles Carroll, and HISTORY OF NEW YORK STATE edited by James Sullivan.

Leslie, Frank (1821-1880)

Born, Ipswich, England. In 1854 Leslie commenced publication in New York City of *Frank Leslie's Illustrated Newspaper,* which eventually developed into a magazine empire and made its owner one of the most celebrated publishers of

Leypoldt, Frederick (1835-1884)

Born, Stuttgart, Germany. Leypoldt came to America in 1864 and five years later started a bookshop in Philadelphia, Pennsylvania. In 1864 he opened a publishing house in New York City and three years later joined with Henry Holt to found Leypoldt and Holt. The partners began publication of *Literary Bulletin,* a compendium of book trade news. Within a year, however, the partnership was dissolved. Holt kept the trade division and Leypoldt, the *Bulletin.*

Leypoldt now turned his attention to his life-long passion—the publication of bibliographical tools. He founded the *Publishers' and Stationers' Weekly* in 1872, which later merged with the *American Literary Gazette and Publishers' Trade Circular* to become *Publishers Weekly.* He originated the UNIFORM TRADE LIST ANNUAL (now PUBLISHERS' TRADE LIST ANNUAL) and the AMERICAN EDUCATIONAL CATALOG (now TEXTBOOKS IN PRINT). He was one of the founders of the American Library Association and of the *Library Journal.* Another of his ventures was the *Index Medicus.* Five years before his death in 1884 Leypoldt sold his business to his associate, Richard Rogers Bowker.

Liveright, Horace Brisbin (1886-1933)

Born, Osceola Mills, Pennsylvania. Founded the firm of Boni and Liveright in 1917 in New York City with Albert and Charles Boni in order to publish the *Modern Library: the World's Best Books.* The launching of the *Modern Library* was described by Liveright as "the most important event of 1917." In the same year Thomas Seltzer joined the Bonis and Liveright as a partner and became editor for the group. The partners started auspiciously with a list that included UTOPIA OF USURERS by G.K. Chesterton, THE PATH

ON THE RAINBOW by George Cronyn, Theodore Dreiser's FREE and SISTER CARRIE, THE SANITY OF ART by G. B. Shaw, and Henri Barbusse's THE INFERNO. Also included were George Moore's A STORY-TELLER'S HOLIDAY and Joyce Kilmer's POEMS. Soon, however, the flamboyant Liveright and his partners parted company and Liveright bought the firm, although the Boni name was retained in the company's name until 1928.

The change in the structure of the firm did not impair the quality of Liveright's list. In 1919 and 1920 he published such classics as TEN DAYS THAT SHOOK THE WORLD by John Reed, Theodore Dreiser's TWELVE MEN, Upton Sinclair's JIMMIE HIGGINS, TRAVELING COMPANIONS by Henry James, Eugene O'Neill's THE MOON OF THE CARIBBEES, George Moore's AVOWALS, Sigmund Freud's A GENERAL INTRODUCTION TO PSYCHOANALYSIS, Rose Macaulay's POTTERISM, DARK MOTHER by Waldo Frank, and ANCIENT MAN by Hendrik Willem Van Loon.

Liveright's success was due in no small measure to his staff, which at that time included a galaxy of names that became in course of time part of publishing history: Manuel Komroff, Lillian Hellman, Louis Kronenberger, Bennett Cerf, Richard Simon, Edward Weeks, Donald Friede, and Julian Messner. But his greatest asset was T.R. Smith, former managing editor of the *Century* magazine, who helped Liveright to acquire and publish some of the finest works in the decade of the 1920s: T.S. Eliot's THE WASTELAND; Hendrik Willem Van Loon's THE STORY OF MANKIND; Theodore Dreiser's AN AMERICAN TRAGEDY and GENIUS; Ludwig Lewisohn's UPSTREAM; Lewis Mumford's STORY OF UTOPIAS; e.e. cummings' THE ENORMOUS ROOM; GENTLEMEN PREFER BLONDES by Anita Loos; Sherwood Anderson's DARK LAUGHTER; MY LIFE AS AN EXPLORER by Sven Hedin; TRAVELS IN ARABIA DESERTA by C.M. Doughty; SIEGE by Samuel Hopkins Adams; and Edgar Lee Masters' THE NEW SPOON RIVER. *The Black and Gold Library of Classics,* edited by Manuel Komroff, also proved a hugely profitable series.

But Liveright's extravagant habits reduced his earnings and in 1925 he sold the *Modern Library* to Bennett Cerf for $200,000.00. His publishing interests suffered also when he became a theatrical producer in 1924 and spent large sums on the production of such plays as "Firebrand," "Hamlet In Modern Dress," "An American Tragedy," "Dracula," and "The Dagger and the Rose." During his later years he still continued to bring out books as outstanding as THE THIBAULTS by Roger Martin du Gard; Isadora Duncan's MY LIFE; THÉRÈSE by Françoise Mauriac; and Eugene O'Neill's STRANGE INTERLUDE. But Liveright's early fire was gone and the 1929 market crash ended his activities. He died in 1933.

The Liveright imprint was owned since the 1930s by Arthur Pell. In 1969 he sold it to Gilbert A. Harrison of the *New Republic* who revived the firm and built up a strong list. In 1974 the firm was acquired by W.W. Norton but the imprint retains its separate identity.

Longmans, Green & Company

Established in New York City in 1875 as the American branch of the well-known British firm of the same name, founded in 1724 by Thomas Longman. In 1889 the company was converted into a New York partnership with Charles J. Mills as manager. Later he was succeeded by his son, Edward S. Mills. In 1935 the partnership became a New York corporation.

In addition to distribution of British titles the firm had a vigorous program of original publishing in education, religion, and history. Among its notable series have been *Historic Towns, Epochs of American History,* the *American Citizen* series, *Living Thoughts Library,* and *Our Debt to Greece and Rome.* In 1961 its trade titles were sold to David McKay Company; its medical texts went to Little, Brown, and its technical list to Wiley.

Loring, A.K. (1826-1911)

Born, Sterling, Massachusetts. In 1859 Loring started a circulating library in Boston that sold books and stationery. Having thus acquired a knowledge of popular taste he ventured into publishing with a few juveniles. By 1864 he had already established himself in this field with A.D.T. Whitney's FAITH GARTNEY'S GIRLHOOD and had formed an association with Horatio Alger, Jr., whose *Ragged Dick* books were to bring both of them fame and profit. Developing the Horatio Alger formula, Loring brought out many similar series: Virginia F. Townsend's *Breakwater* series, the *Fairy-Folk* series, *Loring's Tales of the Day,* and books for girls by "Laura Caxton" (Elizabeth Parker Comins). Louisa May Alcott was one of Loring's most prolific writers.

In addition to juveniles, Loring published cheap books in series and libraries, some of which were *Books for Young Ladies, Railway Library, Standard English Novels, Select Novels,* and *Popular Books.* Only a step removed were his home manuals, which included such titles as HOW TO FURNISH AND ADORN A HOUSE WITH SMALL MEANS, $5000 A YEAR AND HOW I MADE IT, HOW I MANAGED MY CHILDREN FROM INFANCY TO MARRIAGE, GARDENING FOR MONEY, and DIXIE COOKERY.

Loring was not only a brisk and businesslike publisher, he was also an eccentric man. Toward the late 1870s he began to neglect his book trade and in 1881 he went into bankruptcy.

Lovell, John W. (1851-1932)

Born, Montreal, Canada. In 1876 Lovell established the firm of Lovell, Adam & Company in New York City for the purpose of reprinting cheap editions of British books. His partner was G. Mercer Adam, a fellow Canadian. Shortly thereafter Francis L. Wesson also became a partner and the new imprint of Lovell, Adam, Wesson & Company began to issue the *Lake Champlain Press Series.* In 1877 the partnership was dissolved and Lovell began to publish on his own.

Lovell started as a pirate with the intention of breaking the courtesy of the trade principle of the literary establishment. Inexpensive series soon appeared under his imprint: *The Popular Twelvemos, Standard Histories, Caxton Classics,* and *Editions of the Poets.* In 1881 he reorganized his business, calling it John W. Lovell Company, and the following year he introduced the *Lovell's Library,* a series of paperbacks priced at ten, twenty, or thirty cents. Beginning as a weekly issue, the series grew until, by 1890, it had become a triweekly. Lovell issued his books either in cloth or in paper. Publishing over seven million cheap books a year, he became known as Book-A-Day Lovell.

In 1888 Lovell acquired for a quarter of a million dollars all the plates and stock of the Munro Library. By this time he was publishing over nine series in addition to his *Lovell's Library: American Authors; American Novelists;* the *Occult;* the *Illustrated;* the *Foreign;* the *Rugby;* the *Universal;* the *Franklin;* and the *Red Line.* He also had branches in Boston, Chicago, and London, England.

To further his radical socialist ideas, Lovell launched *Lovell's Political and Scientific Series,* which included among its titles SOCIAL SOLUTIONS by Jean Godin, Albert K. Owen's INTEGRAL CO-OPERATION, Henry George's PROGRESS AND POVERTY, and LABOR AND CAPITAL by Edward Kellogg. His *Occult Series* reflected Lovell's interest in theosophy, and he was also an ardent champion of women's rights.

In 1890 Lovell's publishing activities culminated in the formation of the United States Book Company (q.v.). Within three years, however, this firm went into bankruptcy and by 1900 Lovell had completely disappeared from the annals of publishing. He died in 1932.

McClure, Phillips & Company

Organized by S.S. McClure in New York City in 1899 when Frank N. Doubleday left the earlier firm of Doubleday and McClure to form a new partnership with Walter Hines Page. John Phillips, who had been one of McClure's original partners, managed the new firm.

During the next eight years Phillips built up a successful list that rivaled even that of Doubleday. Among his authors were Willa Cather, Anthony Hope, Ida Tarbell, Frances Hodgson Burnett, Joel Chandler Harris, Booth Tarkington, A. Conan Doyle, H.S. Merriman, Stanley J. Weyman, Joseph Conrad, Arnold Bennett, O. Henry,

William Allen White, Edwin Markham, H. Rider Haggard, Rex Beach, and G. Lowes Dickinson.

Despite these successes the partnership began to break up and in 1907 McClure dropped the name of Phillips from the imprint. Unable to carry on alone, he arranged the sale of his firm to Doubleday, Page and Company.

McGuffey Readers

The most influential and popular book series published in the United States. Its author was William Holmes McGuffey, a Scotsman, professor of Greek and Latin at Miami University.

In 1833 McGuffey was asked by Truman and Smith of Cincinnati, Ohio, to write some school texts. For the modest sum of $1,000 he was to write a primer, four graded readers, and a speller.

The first two readers were published in 1835, the third and the fourth in 1837. A fifth reader and a high school reader were added later. It is estimated that over one hundred and twenty-five million copies of these readers were sold between 1836 and 1920, justifying the claim that no books, except the Bible, have so influenced the American mind.

McLoughlin Brothers

Founded in New York City in 1828 as a printshop by John McLoughlin, a Scot immigrant. He began publishing tracts and "leaflet stories of a semi-religious character" for young readers and these were later collected into one volume as McLOUGHLIN BOOKS FOR CHILDREN. Shortly before 1840 McLoughlin merged his business with that of John Elton. It was then called John Elton & Company. Under this imprint was published ELTON'S COMIC ALMANAC which contained "all the jokes the city would have for a year." McLoughlin's son, John Jr., joined the business in 1841 and when the senior partners retired in 1848 he carried on the firm. When John's brother, Edmund, came into the company in 1850 the firm became McLoughlin Brothers.

The brothers began manufacturing toy books and coloring books, two lines in which they had no domestic competition. Among the titles on their list were MOTHER GOOSE, biographies of heroes such as General Ulysses S. Grant and General William T. Sherman, and the *Happy House Series,* which had illuminated covers.

After the death of John McLoughlin, Jr. in 1907 the firm was managed by his two sons, James G. and Charles. The latter died in 1914 and in 1920 the firm was sold to Milton Bradley Company and reorganized as McLoughlin Brothers, Inc. In 1954 the business was acquired by Grosset and Dunlap.

Maxwell, William (1755-1809)

Pioneer Ohio publisher. He settled in Cincinnati in 1793 and began publication of the first paper in the northwest, *The Sentinel of the North-Western Territory.* Three years later he published the first book printed in Ohio, THE LAWS OF THE TERRITORY OF THE UNITED STATES NORTH WEST OF THE RIVER OHIO, a subscription book of two hundred twenty-five pages more commonly known as MAXWELL'S CODE. *See,* Douglas C. McMurtrie's ANTECEDENT EXPERIENCE IN KENTUCKY OF WILLIAM MAXWELL, OHIO'S FIRST PRINTER.

Maynard, Effingham (1829-1899)

Born, Oxford, Massachusetts. In 1851 Maynard came to New York City to work for the publishing house of Mason Brothers. Later he joined Clark, Austin and Smith, successors to Truman and Smith, publishers of the McGUFFEY READERS. When this firm failed in 1861 Maynard founded the firm of Clark and Maynard with Lucius E. Clark. When Clark retired in 1889 the firm became Effingham Maynard & Company.

In 1893 Maynard joined forces with Edwin C. Merrill to form Maynard, Merrill & Company, of which he remained president until his death in 1899. For some time Maynard was the publisher of John Ruskin's WORKS, including the Brantwood edition.

Melcher, Frederic Gershom (1879-1966)

Born, Malden, Massachusetts. Melcher began his career with Lauriat and Company of Boston, where he served from 1895 until 1913. From 1913 until 1918 he was with W.K. Stewart Company of Indianapolis, Indiana. He became a co-editor of *Publishers Weekly* in 1918 and went on to become its editor and later president of R.R. Bowker Company.

A widely respected bookman, Melcher founded the Children's Book Week in 1919 and established the John Newbery Medal, the Caldecott Medal, and the Carey-Thomas Award for Creative Publishing.

Mentzer, Bush & Company

Established in 1898 in Chicago, Illinois, by John P. Mentzer and Charles F. Atkinson as Atkinson and Mentzer to publish school textbooks. In 1904 the name was changed to Atkinson, Mentzer and Grover and in 1912 back to Atkinson, Mentzer & Company. In 1922 Charles Atkinson left the company; it then became Mentzer, Bush & Company.

The imprint was later acquired by Holt, Rinehart & Winston.

Mosher, Thomas (1852-1923)

Born, Biddeford, Maine. In 1891 Mosher began his career at Portland, Maine, as a literary pirate and publisher with an edition of George Meredith's MODERN LOVE. Obviously following his own tastes, he began a selection of contemporary English poetry, euphemistically called *English Reprint Series,* which included the poems of Dante Gabriel Rossetti, Algernon C. Swinburne, and William Morris. His famous *Bibelot Series* appeared from 1893 to 1897.

Though he never paid any royalty to his authors, Mosher's piracy was redeemed by the beauty and dignity of his little books. "He waylays," said Richard Le Gallienne, "unprotected copyright with such grace that it hardly seems like piracy at all. In fact, I suppose, technically speaking, it is not. Else Mr. Mosher would **not** be permitted to delight us with perhaps the daintiest editions at present being published by any publisher."

After the founder's death in 1923 the press was managed by his widow, Flora Lamb, until 1942, when it was purchased by J.G. Williams of Williams Book Store and relocated in Boston, Massachusetts. Later, under the management of Williams' daughter, the press continued to specialize in literary and scholarly works.

Munro, George P. (1825-1896)

Born, West River, Nova Scotia. Munro began his career with Beadle and Adams in New York City. He left this firm in 1866 and went into partnership with Irwin P. Beadle. Under the latter's name they began the publication of the *New Dime Novels.* Enjoined from using the Beadle name, the firm became George P. Munro.

Munro published Harlan P. Halsey's OLD SLEUTH, THE DETECTIVE, the first of the *Old Sleuth* series of over two hundred titles. Later he brought out the *Old Cap Collier Series, Munro's Ten Cent Novels,* and the *Seaside Series* of reprints. The last series grew to over two thousand titles. He also founded the *Fireside Companion* in 1866.

Munsell, Joel (1808-1880)

Born, Northfield, Massachusetts. Munsell came to Albany, New York, in 1827 and began publishing a newspaper, the *Minerva,* which had only one hundred and fifty subscribers. His first published book was OUTLINE OF THE HISTORY OF PRINTING, in 1839. This was the beginning of a lifelong interest in books, printing, and typography which led him to publish TYPOGRAPHICAL MISCELLANY in 1850, CHRONOLOGY OF PAPER AND PAPER MAKING, and a revised edition of Isaiah Thomas's HISTORY OF PRINTING. Richard de Bury's PHILOBIBLON, the medieval classic on books, was reissued by Munsell in 1861. History was another of his interests, and the ANNALS OF ALBANY, in ten volumes, was one of his most ambitious under-

takings. Munsell was the leader of the Romantic revival of typography and many of his books are considered models of the typographic art.

John Murphy & Company

Established in 1837 by John Murphy, an Irish immigrant, as Murphy and Spaulding, with William Spaulding as his partner. Spaulding later retired and Murphy carried on his business in Baltimore, Maryland, publishing standard Catholic works, one of which was TRANSLATION OF THE DEFINITION OF THE DOGMA OF THE IMMACULATE CONCEPTION. He also published two magazines, *The United States Catholic Magazine* and the *Metropolitan Magazine.* In addition to religious publications, Murphy brought out the MARYLAND CODE in two volumes and the CONSTITUTION OF MARYLAND. In 1872 Murphy published the ST. VINCENT'S MANUAL, a popular Catholic prayer book. By this time he had also branched into schoolbooks and textbooks.

After his death in 1880, Murphy's business was continued by his two sons, Francis K. and Charles Abell. In 1887 the firm was honored by Pope Leo XIII with the title of "Printers and Publishers to the Holy See." A major undertaking of the company at this time was the publication of Cardinal James Gibbons' books.

The imprint was later acquired by P.J. Kenedy.

New England Primer

One of the earliest of children's books published in America and, in terms of its influence on the education of Americans, the most remarkable. It incorporated John Cotton's SPIRITUAL MILK FOR BOSTON BABES IN EITHER ENGLAND DRAWN OUT OF THE BREASTS OF BOTH TESTAMENTS FOR THEIR SOULS NOURISHMENT. Its earliest printing is said to have been between 1686 and 1690. It grew in importance as a teaching tool and the 1727 edition bears the subtitle: *For the More Easy Attaining the True Reading of English.*

It is estimated that during the period from 1680 to 1830 between six and eight million copies of the PRIMER were printed.

No Name Series

A well-known series of prose and poetry by anonymous writers published by Roberts Brothers in Boston, Massachusetts. The first series of fourteen volumes was issued in black and red bindings, 1876-78. The second series was issued in green and gold bindings in twelve volumes, 1879-81. The third series, in brown and gold bindings, was issued in eleven volumes, 1882-87. Thomas Niles was the editor of the series.

Norton, Charles B. (1825-1891)

Born, Hartford, Connecticut. Norton came to New York City in 1850 and set himself up as a bookseller and publisher. Following his interest in scientific bibliography he launched *Norton's Literary Gazette and Publishers' Circular* in 1852. *The Gazette* carried full bibliographical lists and information on the book trade. This was supplemented by annual catalogues. A force in the library and book world, Norton was the prime mover in forming the Book Publishers Association. In 1855 this Association assumed publication of the *Gazette,* converting it into a weekly and retitling it *American Publishers' Circular.*

Norton also published several reference tools for the library world, among which were GUILD'S LIBRARY MANUAL and POOLE'S INDEX TO PERIODICALS.

Ogilvie, John Stuart (1843-1910)

Started his publishing firm as J.S. Ogilvie Company in New York City in 1858. Ogilvie soon became the largest distributor of so-called railroad literature, which consisted of sensational fiction, joke books, and sex books. His business was purchased by the United States Book Company in 1890.

Osgood, James Ripley (1836-1892)

In 1868 Osgood became a partner in Ticknor and Fields at Boston, Massachusetts, which was thereupon renamed Fields, Osgood and Company. In 1867 Osgood went to London, England, to arrange with Charles Dickens for a lecture tour of the United States. In 1871, when Fields retired, Osgood and his associates bought his stock and renamed the firm James R. Osgood & Company.

One of the most energetic and able publishers of his day, Osgood strove to maintain the quality and prestige of the Ticknor and Fields imprint. His books were handsomely produced and the *Publishers Weekly* described his editions of Dante, Homer, and Goethe as "among the greatest triumphs of the publisher's art the world over." Generous and gregarious by nature he attracted some of the best authors of the day: Henry Wadsworth Longfellow, John Greenleaf Whittier, Oliver Wendell Holmes, Bayard Taylor, Bret Harte, Charles Reade, Ralph Waldo Emerson, James Russell Lowell, Nathaniel Hawthorne, and William Dean Howells. But his extravagance became his undoing. As a result of his imprudent financial management he was in chronic need of cash. A devastating fire added to his troubles and he began disposing of a large part of his list to others at the annual trade sales.

He sold his journals, *Atlantic Monthly* and *Every Saturday* to Hurd and Houghton, *Our Young Folks* to Scribner and Company, and *North American Review* to Allen T. Rice. In 1878 he arranged a merger with Henry O. Houghton. The two men were mismatched in every way: Houghton was as thrifty and cautious as Osgood was bold and extravagant. In 1879 they parted company and in 1880 Osgood reestablished his own imprint. In 1881 he launched the *Round Robin Series* of anonymous novels. He was also able to bring back to his house Mark Twain, William Dean Howells, and Henry James.

Misfortune, however, continued to hound Osgood. His edition of Walt Whitman's LEAVES OF GRASS had to be abandoned on account of censorship. His firm went into bankruptcy and was acquired in 1888 by Houghton Mifflin Company. Osgood himself became Harper's representative in London, England. He formed his own firm in London with Clarence W. McIlvaine in 1890. He contracted with Eugene Field and Thomas Hardy to publish their works. Hardy's TESS OF THE D'URBERVILLES appeared under his imprint in 1891. But death cut short his third and last publishing venture in 1892.

The Otterbein Press

Founded in 1833 in Circleville, Ohio, as the publishing arm of the United Brethren in Christ. Its first publication was a hymnal in 1837. In 1853 the press was moved to Dayton, Ohio. The firm specialized in denominational books for the Evangelical United Brethren Church.

Owen, John (1805-1882)

Born, Portland, Maine. Owen went into publishing as a partner of Murray & Nichols, booksellers in Cambridge, Massachusetts, in 1834. He became proprietor of the store in 1836.

Owen published some of the early works of his friend and classmate, Henry Wadsworth Longfellow, including Longfellow's first book of poems, VOICES OF THE NIGHT. Owen also published some of the works of Nathaniel Hawthorne. He gave up his book business in 1848.

Pablos, Juan

The first printer in the Western Hemisphere. He published his first book in Mexico in 1540, a century before Stephen Day's BAY PSALM BOOK.

L.C. Page & Company

Established in 1892 at Boston, Massachusetts, as the Joseph Knight Company, a subsidiary of Estes and Lauriat. The company was reorganized in 1895 with Lewis C. Page as president. The firm name was changed to L.C. Page & Company in 1896. In 1914 it acquired the business of Dana Estes and Company, successor to Estes and Lauriat.

L.C. Page is best remembered as the publisher of Eleanor H. Porter's POLLYANNA, L.M. Montgomery's ANNE OF GREEN GABLES, *The Little Colonel* series by Annie Fellows Johnston, the poems of Bliss Carman, and the fiction of Charles G.D. Roberts and Robert Neilson Stephens.

Lewis C. Page died in 1956 and in 1957 the firm was merged with Farrar and Straus. At the time of the merger its list contained over one thousand titles, most of which were juveniles.

Parks, William (1698-1750)

Born in England in 1698, Parks came to America in 1725 and settled in Annapolis, Maryland, where he became a public printer. Parks is the first known Virginia imprint. In 1730 Parks published his first book, Governor William Gooch's CHARGE TO THE JURY. In the same year he published John Markland's TYPOGRAPHIA, AN ODE TO PRINTING. By 1733, when he published A COLLECTION OF ALL THE ACTS OF ASSEMBLY NOW IN FORCE IN THE COLONY OF VIRGINIA, Parks had established himself as a publisher of major rank. He was active in publishing medical and historical works; in the latter category would fall THE HISTORY OF THE FIRST DISCOVERY AND SETTLEMENT OF VIRGINIA by William Smith, which he brought out in 1747.

Parks has been credited with a number of firsts in American publishing. In 1734 he published the first American book on sports, THE COMPLEAT SYSTEM OF FENCING; OR THE ART OF DEFENCE, IN THE USE OF THE SMALLSWORD by Edward Blackwell. In 1742 he offered the first American cookbook, THE COMPLEAT HOUSEWIFE; OR ACCOMPLISHED GENTLEWOMAN'S COMPANION by an Englishwoman, Mrs. E. Smith. In 1728 he published the earliest known American book of poetry, Edward Holdsworth's MUSCIPULA. Later he encouraged other Southern poets: Richard Lewis,

Ebenezer Cooke, and John Markland. Parks also founded in 1727 the *Maryland Gazette,* which has been generally regarded as one of the best Colonial newspapers.

Perkins, Maxwell Evarts (1884-1947)

Born, New York City. One of the most famous editors in American publishing history. Perkins was a reporter for the *New York Times* from 1907 to 1910. He joined Scribner's in 1914 and rose to be vice president of the company. A painstaking editor, he is credited with making readable the long, sprawling novels of Thomas Wolfe. Other authors whose works passed under his blue pencil were F. Scott Fitzgerald, John Galsworthy, Ring Lardner, and Ernest Hemingway.

Phillips, Sampson & Company

Founded in the early 1840s at Boston, Massachusetts, by Moses Dresser Phillips and Charles Sampson. During its brief but vigorous life the firm achieved recognition as a mass market publisher. By printing large editions and distributing them to as wide a market as possible Phillips, Sampson introduced a new approach to publishing that was later copied by other publishers. They published several editions in various price ranges but the most successful was the Boston Edition that consisted of handsomely produced volumes of the works of Lord Byron, William Shakespeare, Sir Walter Scott, George Moore, Robert Burns, John Milton, and Ben Jonson.

The *Standard Historical Series* sold over one hundred thousand copies every year. Cheaper editions of writings of Thomas B. Macaulay, David Hume, and Edward Gibbon were even more popular. William Hickling Prescott was the most famous author on the Phillips, Sampson list. They published his PHILIP THE SECOND and CHARLES THE FIFTH. Besides Prescott, the firm also published the works of Ralph Waldo Emerson and Henry Ward Beecher. A profitable juvenile department under William Lee published Jacob Abbott's *Rollo* books and other fine se-

ries. A more durable achievement was the founding of the *Atlantic Monthly* in 1857 with James Russell Lowell as first editor. But the end came abruptly in 1859 when both Phillips and Sampson died and the firm fell under the auctioneer's gavel.

The Pilgrim Press

Founded in 1832 in Boston, Massachusetts, as the Congregational Sunday-School and Publishing Society, in association with the Massachusetts Sabbath School Society. It united in 1868 with the Congregational Board of Publication, which had been established in 1829 as the Doctrinal Tract and Book Society. The combined organization became known as The Congregational Sabbath-School and Publishing Society. In 1919 when the Society was incorporated as the Congregational Publishing Society, The Pilgrim Press was adopted as its trade imprint.

The imprint was acquired by United Church Press.

Poor Richard's Almanack

The most popular of early almanacs, published annually by Benjamin Franklin in Philadelphia, Pennsylvania, from 1732 until 1757. The proverbs and homely sayings printed throughout these books have passed into the common speech.

Potter, John E. (1827-1893)

Born, Westerly, Rhode Island. In 1853 Potter set himself up as a publisher in Philadelphia, Pennsylvania, and issued his first book in the same year, Joseph E. Belcher's RELIGIOUS DENOMINATIONS OF THE WORLD. It was an instant moneymaker and sold fifty thousand copies. The profits from this first book enabled Potter to assemble a varied list, but religious titles were his main interest. His Bibles, both Protestant and Catholic, were sold throughout the world. Soon he added textbooks, history, biography, travel, adventure, poetry, fiction, and classics. The greatest Potter successes were David Livingstone's AFRICA, EVERYBODY'S LAWYER, and Timothy S. Arthur's TEN NIGHTS IN A BAR-ROOM.

The firm was enlarged through the admission of four partners: George T. Stuckert, William T. Amies, and Potter's two sons, John E., and Clarence H. In 1874 Potter took over the *American Historical Record* and transformed it into a popular monthly under the title, *Potter's American Monthly of History, Literature, Science and Art.*

Prang, Louis (1824-1909)

Born, Breslau, Silesia. In 1882 he established the Prang Educational Company at Boston, Massachusetts, to promote and publish materials for art instruction in public schools. Prang was the first to apply the term "chromos" to colored reproductions of works of art. The company was sold to a syndicate after the founder's death in 1909. Edwin O. Grover became president of the company in 1912 when its name was changed to The Prang Company.

Frederick Pustet Company, Inc.

Founded in 1865 in New York City as a branch of the German Catholic publishing house established in 1819 in Passau, Germany, by Friedrich I. Pustet. A branch was opened in Cincinnati, Ohio, in 1867.

Incorporated in 1917, the firm published Ratisbon breviaries, missals, and related liturgical publications. Since 1903 the American branch has been managed by members of the Tapke family.

Anson D.F. Randolph & Company

Founded in 1851 in New York City by Anson Davies Fitz Randolph. That year he published his first volume, HINTS TO CHRISTIANS. His

third book, a book of hymns, turned him to the publication of religious poems and hymns. He published many of these; some of them were: CHRIST IN SONG: HYMNS OF IMMANUEL IN ALL AGES, by Philip Schaff; THE CHANGED CROSS AND OTHER RELIGIOUS POEMS; and CHURCH MELODIES by Thomas Hastings.

In time Randolph was publishing sermons, essays and devotional books. In 1896 he became bankrupt, and in 1899 the firm was dissolved.

Randolph was highly regarded by his fellow bookmen and is remembered as the president of the American Book Trade Association.

Redfield, Justus Starr (1810-1888)

Born, Wallingford, Connecticut. Opened a publishing business in New York City in 1841.

Redfield achieved distinction as the publisher of Edgar Allan Poe. He agreed to publish Poe's writings at a time when nearly every publisher had turned Poe down. After Poe's death Redfield acquired the copyrights to all the Poe works from Mrs. Clemm (Poe's mother-in-law) for the sum of $250.00.

Redfield disposed of his business to William J. Widdleton in 1860. Besides Poe, Redfield had published works of William Gilmore Simms, Robert Montgomery Bird, Fitz-Greene Halleck, Alice Cary, and Cornelius Matthews.

Redpath, James (1833-1891)

Born, Berwick-on-Tweed, Scotland. One of the earliest radical publishers in the United States. In 1860 Redpath founded the Haytian Bureau of Emigration to sponsor the immigration of American Negroes to Haiti. To advance his cause he wrote A GUIDE TO HAITI which was published by Thayer and Eldridge. This firm also published other books by Redpath: ECHOES OF HARPER'S FERRY and PUBLIC LIFE OF CAPTAIN JOHN BROWN. When Thayer and Eldridge failed in 1861 Redpath decided to become a publisher. He set up his publishing activities in Boston, Massachusetts.

To Redpath publishing was a crusade for reform and his "Books For The Times" were indeed "cause" books such as THE BLACK MAN by William Wells Brown, Wendell Phillips' SPEECHES, LECTURES, AND LETTERS, Redpath's own PUBLIC LIFE AND AUTOBIOGRAPHY OF JOHN BROWN, John R. Beard's TOUSSAINT L'OUVERTURE, and Louisa May Alcott's HOSPITAL SKETCHES. Reasonably priced and heavily promoted his "Books For The Times" sold well, and the success of this series encouraged him to bring out two more low-priced series, *Books for Camp and Home* and *Books for the Camp Fires*. The latter series consisted of ten-cent books, containing 96 to 124 pages neatly bound with green backs, and were advertised as "the cheapest books of real merit in the market." Along with such classics as editions of Victor Hugo and Honoré de Balzac, adventure and religious titles were offered. The books were sold by all newsdealers, a fact that must have contributed to their popularity.

Redpath continued in publishing until 1864 when he left to join General William T. Sherman's army. He did not return to publishing after the Civil War but engaged in a variety of ventures of which the Lyceum Lecture Bureau was the most famous.

Reynal & Hitchcock

Founded in 1933 in New York City by Eugene Reynal and Curtice Hitchcock. Their aim was to publish a small but distinguished list. They met with early success when they published Lin Yutang's IMPORTANCE OF LIVING and the P.L. Travers' *Mary Poppins* volumes, In 1940, desiring to establish a college division, the partners engaged T.J. Wilson. Before Wilson left, in about a year, he managed to publish a dozen texts covering many fields.

The firm's greatest bestseller was Adolf Hitler's MEIN KAMPF, which they published under an arrangement with Houghton Mifflin. Lillian Smith's STRANGE FRUIT proved to be a controversial novel. During the World War II years the firm published Philip Guedalla's MR. CHURCHILL, Gustav Stolper's THIS AGE OF FABLE, Antoine de Saint-Exupéry's FLIGHT TO ARRAS, THE MAKING OF TOMORROW by Raoul de Roussy de Sales, Rosamond Lehmann's THE BALLAD AND THE SOURCE, Francis Steegmüller's STATES OF GRACE, and Karl Shapiro's poetry.

In 1946 Hitchcock died and shortly afterwards Reynal arranged a merger with Harcourt Brace & Company. In 1956 Eugene Reynal founded his own firm, Reynal and Company, after leaving Harcourt, Brace & Company in 1955.

Richardson, Charles B.

Born, Groton, Connecticut. In 1849 Richardson went to Boston, Massachusetts, where in 1856 he first published a magazine entitled *The Student and Schoolmate*. The next year he launched *Historical Magazine* and *American Notes and Queries,* which was later edited by John Gilmary Shea. Also in 1857 Richardson moved to New York City and took over the business of C.B. Norton. He then issued a series of outstanding books including George Bancroft's HISTORY OF THE UNITED STATES, Benjamin Franklin's LETTERS and AMERICAN HISTORICAL AND LITERARY CURIOSITIES, and the GEORGE WASHINGTON DIARIES.

During the Civil War he began to publish Edward R. Pollard's THE FIRST YEAR OF THE WAR IN 1863, followed by a similar title for the second year and the third year. In 1864 he established the *United States Service Magazine* for Naval and Army personnel. A disastrous fire wiped out his business in 1864. He resumed business within a year with a series of books on the Civil War: SHERMAN AND HIS CAMPAIGNS, GRANT AND HIS CAMPAIGNS, THE LIFE OF STONEWALL JACKSON, and SOUTHERN GENERALS.

Rinehart & Company

When the partnership of John Farrar and Stanley Rinehart was dissolved in 1945 Rinehart took over its assets. He then organized Rinehart & Company in New York City.

Rinehart began with a formidable array of authors and titles: Norman Mailer's THE NAKED AND THE DEAD, Charles Jackson's THE LOST WEEKEND, Frederick Wakeman's THE HUCKSTERS, and Hervey Allen's TOWARD THE MORNING. The firm also owned the *Rivers of American* Series and the Rinehart Editions, a paperback reprint series. But this early impetus was lost during the fifties and the firm merely coasted along on the strength of its backlist. In 1960 the company was merged with Henry Holt and Company to form Holt and Rinehart.

Roberts Brothers

Founded about 1855 in Boston, Massachusetts, by Lewis Augustus Roberts and his two brothers, John and Austin. Hit by the panic of 1857, the business was given up in 1859. Augustus Roberts revived the firm in 1861 as a publisher of photograph albums. In 1864 he hired Thomas Niles as editor and the history of the firm may be said to begin with that appointment. Niles had been a member of the Ticknor and Fields house but had later gone into publishing under the imprint of Whittemore, Niles & Hall. Although by 1857 Niles had built up a varied list of sixty books, unfortunately his firm went down in the panic of that year.

Under the direction of Niles, Roberts Brothers assembled their first list in 1864. It consisted mostly of juveniles. By 1870 Niles was in complete charge of the firm and virtually ran it as

his own. His first great success was LITTLE WOMEN, which he had persuaded Louisa May Alcott to write. Another of his discoveries was Jean Ingelow, whose poems sold widely. In 1870 Niles began to publish George Sand and three years later Helen Hunt Jackson, whose RAMONA sold over three hundred thousand copies. Niles also introduced Philip Gilbert Hamerton, Edwin Arnold, and Robert Louis Stevenson to American readers. In 1876 Niles launched the *No Name Series* of anonymous authors and the *American Tauchnitz Series*.

Anxious to attract American authors, Niles offered them particularly generous terms. His shrewd business sense, combined with sharp critical judgment, made him by 1880 "the boldest publisher in Boston" as *The New York Times* described him. At this time his list of authors included Christina G. Rossetti, Emily Dickinson, Oscar Wilde, Dante Gabriel Rossetti, George Meredith, and William Morris. He had also a perennial bestseller in THE BOSTON COOKING-SCHOOL COOK BOOK by Evelyn Lincoln of the Boston Cooking School.

Niles died in 1894 and Roberts Brothers soon lost its preeminence. In 1896 the firm launched the *Columbian Knowledge Series* and the next year it announced a project first planned by Niles: the Wormsley de luxe edition of Honoré de Balzac's LA COMÉDIE HUMAINE in forty volumes, limited to two hundred and fifty sets. But by this time the firm was only coasting along on the strength of its backlist and lacked the power and discrimination which it had had under Niles. The firm was acquired by Little, Brown in 1898 and thus did not outlive the century.

Roman, Anton (1828-1903)

Born, Bavaria, Germany. Roman opened a bookstore in Shasta, California, in 1853. Discovering that he had more readers than books to supply, he decided to become a publisher. The first book to bear his imprint was AN OUTLINE OF THE HISTORY OF CALIFORNIA, FROM THE DISCOVERY OF THE COUNTRY TO THE YEAR 1849, published in 1860. This was the first of a long line of books which established

Roman as publisher to the frontier state and as an "argonaut of books." Within a few years he issued RESOURCES OF CALIFORNIA by John S. Hittell; A YOUTH'S HISTORY OF CALIFORNIA by Louise Palmer Heaven; LIFE AMONG THE APACHES by John C. Cremony; SCENES OF WONDER AND CURIOSITY IN CALIFORNIA by James Mason Hutchings; SEEKING THE GOLDEN FLEECE: A RECORD OF PIONEER LIFE IN CALIFORNIA by Jacob D.B. Stillman; and SOME OF THE CAUSES WHICH RETARD THE PROGRESS OF CALIFORNIA DEMONSTRATED by John Alexander Ferris.

Roman's interest soon extended farther afield, even to China beyond the Pacific. China intrigued him and he published many books on the subject. Two of these were: CHINESE AND ENGLISH PHRASE BOOK by Benoni Lanctot; CONFUCIUS AND THE CHINESE CLASSICS by A.W. Loomis. He also published schoolbooks, children's literature, and poetry. OUTCROPPINGS: BEING SELECTIONS OF CALIFORNIA VERSE is interesting because it was the first Roman book with which Bret Harte was associated. This association later developed when Roman launched his magazine, *Overland Monthly Devoted to the Development of the Country,* in 1868. Harte contributed six stories to this magazine including THE LUCK OF ROARING CAMP. At about the same time Roman sponsored the *California Medical Gazette.* Three years later he started *The Californian: A Monthly Western Magazine.*

In 1866 Roman established a branch in New York City in association with the firm of William J. Widdleton. But the panic of 1873 hit the firm severely and by 1879 he was forced to go into bankruptcy. He tried to reestablish his business in 1882 but was unsuccessful, and by 1888 Roman had abandoned the book trade permanently. He died in 1903.

The H.M. Rowe Company

Established in 1867 in Baltimore, Maryland, by Warren H. Sadler as the firm of W.H. Sadler in order to publish commercial textbooks. In 1892 H.M. Rowe was admitted as a partner and six years later the business was incorporated as Sadler-Rowe, Inc. In 1907 Rowe acquired Sadler's interest and the firm then became The H.M. Rowe Company. The firm specialized in books in the field of business education.

Row, Peterson & Company

Founded in 1906 at Evanston, Illinois, by R.K. Row and Isaak Peterson. Their first publication was ESSENTIAL STUDIES IN ENGLISH by R.K. Row with Carolyn Robbins. This was the first of a number of phenomenally successful el-hi books that included the FREE AND TREADWELL READER in 1910, the BROWN-ELDRIDGE ARITHMETICS in 1925, and GROWTH OF A NATION by Eugene C. Barker, William Edward Dood and Walter Prescott Webb, in 1928. A drama department, formed in 1929, published many plays for high school use. In 1936 the firm announced the *Alice and Jerry Reading Program,* a new reading system prepared by Mabel O'Donnell. The *Basic Science Uni-Texts* were introduced in 1940. In the 1950s the firm entered the audio-visual field with *Textfilms.*

Peterson died in 1918. Row, who succeeded him as president of the company, died in 1932. The succeeding presidents were William L. Cozzens, Gordon M. Jones, and Maynard B. Hites. Under Hites the firm merged with Harper & Brothers to form Harper & Row.

Roycroft Publishing Shop

Founded in 1895 in East Aurora, New York, by Elbert Green Hubbard. His first book, SONG OF SONGS, was published in 1896. A successful author and publicist, Hubbard promoted his books through an efficient mail order operation. After the death of the founder in 1915 the business was continued by Elbert Hubbard II who sold it to Samuel R. Guard in 1939.

Rudge, William Edwin (1876-1931)

Born, Brooklyn, New York. Rudge began his career as a printer. His press, first located in New York City and then at Mount Vernon, New York, produced many fine books. He was assisted by such book designers as Frederic W. Goudy, Bruce Rogers, Frederic Warde, and W.A. Dwiggins. One of his best-known publications was Mary Vaux Walcott's NORTH AMERICAN WILD FLOWERS in five volumes, published in 1925.

Russell, John (1812-1871)

Born, Charleston, South Carolina. In 1846 Russell established a bookshop in Charleston which soon became a meeting place for the Southern literati. Russell's first publication appeared in the same year, AREYTOS: OR, SONGS OF THE SOUTH by Gilmore Simms. A long list of books followed that were intended to "illustrate Southern history—its traditions and its legends—its scenery and its sentiments." Among them were ANNALS OF TENNESSEE by J.G. Ramsey; REMINISCENCES OF CHARLESTON by Charles Fraser; ICHTHYOLOGY OF SOUTHERN CAROLINA by John Edward Holbrook; and HOUSE AND HOME; OR, THE CAROLINA HOUSEWIFE, by A Lady of Charleston.

In 1857, the year in which *Russell's Magazine* was launched, the firm's name was changed to Russell & Jones, the latter being James C. Jones, Russell's half-brother. For the next three years Russell continued to bring out under the new imprint books of local interest such as HISTORY OF SOUTH CAROLINA by Gilmore Simms, and PLEIOCENE FOSSILS OF SOUTH CAROLINA by Michael Tuomey and Francis S. Holmes.

The firm did not survive the Civil War.

The Saalfield Publishing Company

Established in 1899 by Arthur James Saalfield in Akron, Ohio. He began as a general publisher of trade books, premium books, and subscription books. He acquired the stock of Werner School Book Company and later began to specialize in children's books.

Sabin, Joseph (1821-1881)

Born, Braunston, England. Compiler, BIBLIOTHECA AMERICANA: A DICTIONARY OF BOOKS RELATING TO AMERICA FROM ITS DISCOVERY TO THE PRESENT TIME, twenty-nine volumes, 1868-1936, of which he edited volumes one to fourteen. The remaining volumes were edited by Wilberforce Eames and Robert W.G. Vail. Sabin was also the editor of the *American Bibliopolist*. The book business he established in 1856 was continued by his son, Joseph Sabin (1845-1926).

Benjamin H. Sanborn & Company

Founded in 1898 in Boston, Massachusetts, by Benjamin H. Sanborn when the original firm known as Leach, Shewell, & Sanborn was dissolved. The company's history may be traced back to the famous eighteenth century Boston publishing house of Manning & Loring. Sanborn incorporated his firm in Maine in 1899.

In 1912 W.F. Young acquired control and moved the corporate headquarters to Chicago, Illinois. It expanded its list through the acquisition of Thos. R. Shewell & Company in 1902, Sibley & Company in 1916, and Augsburg Publishing Company in 1940. It was absorbed by the Syracuse, New York, house of L.W. Singer Company in 1956. The latter firm, in turn, was merged with Random House in 1960.

Sheldon & Company

Organized in 1854 in New York City by Smith Sheldon when he bought a controlling interest in Lamport, Blakeman and Law, which thereupon became Sheldon, Lamport and Blakeman. Later Sheldon bought the stock of Lewis Colby and Company, publishers of Baptist books. Two of Sheldon's early successes were C.H. Spurgeon's SERMONS, which sold over three hundred thousand copies, and Hermann Olshausen's COMMENTARIES. Lamport retired in 1856 and Hezekiah Shailer and Melancthon M. Hurd came in as partners. But by 1864 all the partners had withdrawn, leaving Sheldon as sole owner of the company, which was then renamed Sheldon & Company.

Between 1858 and 1867 Sheldon expanded by acquiring the stock of four major publishers: Phillips, Sampson & Company; Pratt, Oakley & Company; Blanchard & Lea; and Mason Brothers. With the help of their lists Sheldon was able to establish himself as an important publisher. Jacob Abbott's *Rollo* books, which he bought from Phillips, Sampson, gave him an established favorite in children's books. The Pratt, Oakley list consisted of several profitable textbooks. Marion Harland's novel, ALONE, which he bought from Derby and Jackson, was a popular bestseller. In addition, Sheldon published Thomas B. Macaulay's ESSAYS, Henry H. Milman's LATIN CHRISTIANITY, and Edward Everett's LIFE OF WASHINGTON. Sheldon died in 1884.

Small, Maynard & Company

Founded in 1897 at Boston, Massachusetts, as a literary house by Laurens Small. In 1899 it took over the Stone and Kimball list. The firm maintained a precarious existence until 1926 when it was absorbed by Dodd, Mead and Company. Among its authors were Bliss Carman, Faith Baldwin, and E.M. Hull. It also issued the short story annuals edited by Edward J. O'Brien and the play anthologies edited by Burns Mantle.

Sower, Christopher (1693-1758)

Born in Germany. The first educational publisher in the United States. Arriving in America in 1724 as a refugee he was able to set up a highly successful press for the settlement of Dunkers in Germantown, Pennsylvania. His first publishing venture in 1733 was a schoolbook, EIN A B C UND BUCHSTABIER BUCH, followed by a German and English grammar in 1747, and the GOLDEN A B C, OR THE SCHOOL OF KNOWLEDGE IN RHYMES, also in German. In 1738 he brought out AN A B C AND SPELLING BOOK TO BE USED BY ALL RELIGIONS WITHOUT REASONABLE OBJECTION. He also published an almanac, THE HIGH GERMAN AMERICAN CALENDAR.

Sower's greatest achievement was his Germantown Bible, the first to be printed in America in a European language. A quarto, bound in beveled boards, it was covered with leather and had strong clasps. A second edition of this Bible was printed in 1763 by Christopher Sower II. The firm continued as publishers of schoolbooks well into the twentieth century under the direction of members of the Sower family.

Steiger, Ernst (1832-1917)

Born, Gastewitz, Germany. Steiger arrived in America in 1855. In 1863 at New York City he purchased a small German news agency which he later converted into a publishing house under his own name.

Steiger's purpose was to publish books for German-Americans, a goal he pursued single-mindedly for fifty years. For them he brought out DEUTSCH-AMERIKANISCHE BIBLIOTHEK, a collection of ten volumes by German-American authors. CALIFORNIEN by Karl Rühl appeared in 1867. Along with German translations of the works of Henry Wadsworth Longfellow, Edgar Allan Poe, John Greenleaf Whittier, and Ralph Waldo Emerson, Steiger published HEIMATHGRÜSSE AUS AMERIKA; DORNROSEN, the first collection of German-American lyrics; as well as the poems of Konrad Krez and Johann Straubenmüller. Steiger's ILLUSTRIRTER VOLKS-KALENDER was designed as an almanac for all classes of Germans in America, and Alexander Schem's DEUTSCH-AMERIKANISCHES CONVERSATIONS-LEXIKON became a cyclopedia of information on German life. The most important of Steiger's publications in this field was GESCHICHTSBLÄTTER, edited by Carl Schurz, in two volumes. This work dealt with the history of German immigration to the United States.

As publisher to The German Society, Steiger issued the PRAKTISCHE RATHSCHLÄGE UND MITTHEILUNGEN FÜR DEUTSCHE EINWANDERER. Only a step removed were his language books and textbooks for German language schools. One of his best works in this area was AHN'S AMERICAN INTERPRETER by Johann Franz Ahn "for Germans to learn English without a Teacher." Ahn was the author of two more German language textbooks, AHN'S NEW PRACTICAL AND EASY METHOD OF LEARNING THE GERMAN LANGUAGE and AHN'S RUDIMENTS OF THE GERMAN LANGUAGE. These works were supplemented by STEIGER'S COLLOQUIAL METHOD OF LEARNING THE GERMAN LANGUAGE and William Grauert's MANUAL OF THE GERMAN LANGUAGE.

Steiger also offered four series of popular German literature: HAUS-BIBLIOTHEK in fifteen volumes; DEUTSCHE BIBLIOTHEK in two hundred volumes; HUMORISTISCHE BIBLIOTHEK in fifty-two volumes; and the JUGEND-BIBLIOTHEK in thirty volumes. To complete the education of the German community, the Steiger catalogue offered a GERMAN-AMERICAN COOKBOOK showing how to cook "in the thrifty German manner . . . with due regard to American market products."

Steiger was largely responsible for introducing and promoting the educational theories of Friedrich Froebel in the United States. To advance Froebel's kindergarten system, Steiger published such books as Adolf Douai's THE KINDERGARTEN: A MANUAL FOR THE INTRODUCTION OF FROEBEL'S SYSTEM and GUIDE TO THE KINDERGARTEN AND INTERMEDIATE CLASS by Elizabeth P. Peabody. Education was one of Steiger's lifelong interests and it found another expression in such ambitious reference books as CYCLOPEDIA OF EDUCATION, DICTIONARY OF EDUCATION, and YEAR-BOOK OF EDUCATION, all by Henry Kiddle and Alexander J. Schem. In 1873 Steiger launched still another enormous project, a catalogue of *The Periodical Literature of the United States of America,* arranged under subject headings.

The First World War dealt a crippling blow to Steiger's operations; he died within months after the United States entered the war. The business continued in existence until 1934, when it was reorganized as The Steiger Company. By 1943, when Ernest Steiger, Jr. committed suicide, the firm had run its course.

Stoddart, Joseph Marshall (1845-1921)

Born, Philadelphia, Pennsylvania, and entered the publishing business in Philadelphia in 1874. His first book was OUT OF THE HURLY BURLY by Charles Heber Clark. From 1875 to 1884 he published the American editions of ENCYCLOPAEDIA BRITANNICA, and from 1883 to 1889 ENCYCLOPEDIA AMERICANA. He also published *Stoddart's Review* from 1880 to 1882. Later Stoddart became well known as the publisher of Gilbert and Sullivan comic operas in America.

Frederick A. Stokes Company

Organized in 1881 as White and Stokes by Frederick A. Stokes and J. Parker White. Two years later when Frank Allen joined as a partner, it became White, Stokes & Allen. In 1887 Stokes bought out his partners and organized the company as Frederick A. Stokes & Brother with his brother, Horace W., as his partner. The firm was incorporated in 1890 as Frederick A. Stokes Company. Among the early associates of Stokes were Maynard Dominick and William Morrow. Dominick was responsible for bringing onto the Stokes list Anthony Hope, W.W. Jacobs, and Marie Corelli.

Stokes encouraged American writers and among the many popular writers whose early works were published under his imprint were Gertrude Atherton, Susan Glaspell, Stephen Crane, Edna Ferber, Louis Bromfield, Robert Barr, and Alfred Henry Lewis. His list also contained a large number of popular juvenile books, including Helen Bannerman's LITTLE BLACK SAMBO and LITTLE BLACK MINGO, Gelett Burgess' GOOPS, Rose O'Neill's KEWPIES, and Hugh Lofting's THE STORY OF DR. DOLITTLE.

By 1900 Stokes was one of the major publishers on the American scene and he stated that his aim was "to supply readers of all ages with good reading, sane and wholesome, yet at the same time vivid, realistic, and entertaining." In keeping with this aim he published books by a number of popular authors. Among them were Robert E. Peary, Robert Hichens, Louis Brandeis, Alfred Noyes, Eden Phillpotts, John Masefield, John A. Spender, Cecil Roberts, and David Graham Phillips. Stokes' interests also touched poetry, art, and music. His list was particularly strong in art with a number of popular series: *Distinguished American Artists, British Artists, Collectors,* and *Masterpieces in Color.* His illustrated art books were generally regarded as the most handsome published up to that time. From 1898 to 1909 Stokes also edited and published *The Pocket Magazine.*

Stokes was highly respected in the publishing community and was for many years the president of the American Publishers Association and later the National Association of Book Publishers. In his role as the elder statesman of publishing Stokes delivered the first Bowker Lecture in 1935. Morrow, his able associate, left to form William Morrow and Company in 1926. After Stokes' death in 1939, declining profits of the company led to its sale, in 1941, to J.B. Lippincott Company.

Founded in 1893 by Herbert Stuart Stone and Ingalls Kimball in Cambridge, Massachusetts. The first book under this imprint was a bibliography of American first editions. Their first list announced their intention to "astound American book-buyers by the mere beauty of manufacture." Within the next three years they published a succession of works that were distinguished for their literary merit as well as by their appearance. Among them were THE HOLY CROSS AND OTHER TALES by Eugene Field; MAIN TRAVELLED ROADS and PRAIRIE FOLKS by Hamlin Garland; HIS BROKEN SWORD by Louise Taylor; A LOVER'S DIARY by Gilbert Parker; LINCOLN'S GRAVE by Maurice Thompson; Edgar Allan Poe's COLLECTED WORKS; John Davidson's PLAYS; POEMS OF THE SYMBOLISTS by Stuart Merrill; George Santayana's SONNETS; THE PLAYS OF MAURICE MAETERLINCK; VISTAS by William Sharp; LAND OF HEART'S DESIRE by William Butler Yeats; Gilbert Parker's PIERRE AND HIS PEOPLE; Paul Verlaine's POEMS. They had only one bestseller in their brief career: THE DAMNATION OF THERON WARE by Harold Frederic. In 1894 they launched *The Chap-Book,* a semimonthly literary magazine devoted to experimental and *avant-garde* literature.

Soon the partners were in financial straits. In 1896 Kimball purchased his partner's share in the business and moved to New York City, where he continued to publish with meager financial resources. He also started a newspaper called *The Daily Tatler,* devoted to cultural interests. His enterprises came to a premature end in 1897.

Meanwhile, Stone resumed publishing in Chicago, Illinois, under the name of Herbert S. Stone & Company. He continued to publish *The Chap-Book* and started *The House Beautiful,* a magazine that continued in publication until 1917. Stone's new books were not so artistically delightful as his earlier publications had been, but they were still impressive. Among them were PROSE FANCIES by Richard Le Gallienne; WHAT MAISIE KNEW by Henry James; George Bernard Shaw's PLAYS PLEASANT AND UNPLEASANT; THREE PLAYS FOR PURITANS by George Moore; FABLES IN SLANG by George Ade; and GRAUSTARK by George Barr McCutcheon. In 1898 he took over the small firm of Way and Williams of Chicago. The firm came to an end in 1906 when Stone sold his book division to Fox, Duffield and Company.

The two hundred and seventy-four books published by Stone and Kimball between 1893 and 1906 are now collectors' items. "Theirs was a list," wrote Frederic G. Melcher, "never to be forgotten by lovers and collectors of books and a record of imaginative creative publishing."

Street and Smith Publications, Inc.

Established in 1855 in New York City by Francis S. Street and Francis S. Smith to publish a weekly family paper entitled *New York Weekly Dispatch* (later *New York Weekly*). When Street died in 1883 his interest was acquired by Francis Smith's son, Ormond Gerald Smith. Under the direction of Ormond Smith and his brother, George Campbell Smith, the firm published numerous dime novel libraries: the *Log Cabin Library,* the *Nugget Library,* the *Nick Carter Detective Library,* the *Diamond Dick Library,* and the *Merriwell Series.* By 1915 the firm discontinued book publication and began to concentrate on special-interest magazines.

Talbot, Christopher

The first Catholic publisher in the United States. In 1784 at Philadelphia, Pennsylvania, he published THE HISTORY OF THE OLD AND NEW TESTAMENTS, INTERSPERSED WITH MORAL AND INSTRUCTIVE REFLECTIONS CHIEFLY TAKEN FROM THE HOLY FATHERS, by J. Reeve. In 1786 Talbot joined Mathew Carey, a fellow Catholic, to establish the *Columbian Magazine.* He died sometime before 1797.

Thomas, Isaiah (1749-1831)

Born, Boston, Massachusetts. Indentured at the age of seven, Thomas became an accomplished printer by the time he was sixteen. In 1770, when only twenty-one, he started at Boston a triweekly tabloid called *The Spy* which soon became the most important paper in the American Colonies. To increase his income, he also published books and pamphlets and a line of almanacs beginning with the MASSACHUSETTS CALENDAR OF 1772, which was retitled THOMAS'S NEW ENGLAND ALMANAC in 1775.

By the end of the Revolutionary War Thomas had established himself as the foremost book publisher in the United States. The timing and selection of his titles showed that he knew how to exploit public taste. For example, during the time of the Shays' Rebellion he published Minot's HISTORY OF THE INSURRECTION IN MASSACHUSETTS, which sold widely. He had a solid backlist of standard legal and medical works including (Sir William) BLACKSTONE'S COMMENTARIES in four volumes. At its peak his company employed one hundred and fifty people, had sixteen presses in constant operation and a chain of eight bookstores, five in Massachusetts, one in Concord, New Hampshire, one in Albany, New York, and one in Baltimore, Maryland.

Between 1784 and 1802 Thomas published over nine hundred books. Textbooks formed the largest part of his list. One of the earliest and the most successful of his textbooks was William Perry's SPELLER which he brought out to compete with Noah Webster's spelling book. Published in 1783, it went through fourteen editions with a total sale of three hundred thousand copies. Another success was William Perry's ROYAL STANDARD ENGLISH DICTIONARY which sold fifty-four thousand copies in four editions. Later Thomas obtained exclusive rights to print Noah Webster's books in New Hampshire, Massachusetts, and Rhode Island. Thomas was also the first American music publisher, with Silas Ballou's NEW HYMNS, ON VARIOUS SUBJECTS, published in 1784, followed in 1786 by LAUS DEO! THE WORCESTER COLLECTION OF SACRED HARMONY.

In addition, Thomas became the first major publisher of children's books in America. His interest in juveniles began when he published several of John Newbery's chapbooks, which had originated in England. The success of these books led him to pirate other British classics for children, including MOTHER GOOSE and ROBINSON CRUSOE. Later he began to publish his own juveniles, in all sixty-six titles in one hundred and nineteen editions. He sold these books in five classes according to size, the smallest priced at four cents and the largest at twenty cents.

Though Thomas is remembered for his juveniles, his greatest achievements were his Bibles. In 1786 he published a children's Bible, followed two years later by A CURIOUS HIEROGLYPHICK BIBLE. Other Bibles followed: a two-volume folio with fifty full-page copperplates, published in 1791, an octavo edition in 1793, and in 1797 a duodecimo standing Bible, generally regarded as one of the most beautiful books published in America up to that time.

Nor did Thomas neglect reference books. His Jeremy Belknap's AMERICAN BIOGRAPHY was the first biographical dictionary to be published in the United States. At the same time he continued to cater to the "mass market" by bringing out Laurence Sterne's SENTIMENTAL JOURNEY, PAMELA by Samuel Richardson, THE VICAR OF WAKEFIELD by Oliver Goldsmith and John Bunyan's PILGRIM'S PROGRESS.

By 1796 Thomas was the most successful publisher in the United States. Thereafter his fortunes declined. In retirement he began his great work on THE HISTORY OF PRINTING IN AMERICA. This was published in 1810 in two volumes. Two years after its completion Thomas sponsored another enterprise for which he is now best remembered: The American Antiquarian Society. The first meeting of the American Society of Antiquaries was held in 1812 when Thomas was elected president, an office that he held until his death in 1831. The Society's charter defined it as an institution for "the collection and preservation of the antiquities of our country, and of curious and valuable productions in art and nature (which) have a tendency to enlarge the sphere of human knowledge, aid in the progress of science, to perpetuate the history of moral and political events, and to improve and instruct posterity." Thomas bequeathed to the Society his library of over three thousand volumes and his large collection of periodicals. The rest of his fortune went to certain other learned societies, organizations of printers, and charitable institutions.

The Carey-Thomas Award for Creative Publishing honors Isaiah Thomas and Mathew Carey as pioneers of the American book industry.

James T. Fields (1817-1881)

Ticknor & Fields

Founded by William D. Ticknor when he took over the retail department of Carter's Old Corner Bookstore in Boston, Massachusetts, in 1832. John Allen was his partner. Allen withdrew from the business in 1834 and Ticknor continued on his own under the name of William D. Ticknor and Company. The firm took on new life when, in 1843, Ticknor made his two clerks, James Thomas Fields and John Reed, his partners and renamed the reorganized firm Ticknor, Reed and Fields. Fields had persuaded Ticknor to publish works of Alfred, Lord Tennyson, and Thomas De Quincey, and the partnership granted to him was in recognition of Fields' wide knowledge of the book trade. In 1854 Reed left to go into banking and the firm then became Ticknor and Fields, the imprint under which it became famous.

Fields' ambition was to specialize in literature as other publishing houses specialized in law or medicine. Fortunately for him, his efforts coincided with the Flowering of New England and nearly all of the great writers gravitated to Ticknor and Fields. Among them were Henry Wadsworth Longfellow, Oliver Wendell Holmes, John Greenleaf Whittier, Nathaniel Hawthorne, Julia Ward Howe, Henry David Thoreau, Robert Browning, Charles Kingsley, Charles Reade, William Makepeace Thackeray, Charles Dickens, Ralph Waldo Emerson, and Harriet Beecher Stowe.

Fields also pioneered in establishing new standards of publisher-author relations. Warren S. Tryon paid Ticknor and Fields the ultimate compliment when he said that the Ticknor and Fields imprint on a book was a sufficient guarantee of its merit. Fields also took care to produce his books handsomely and to promote them vigorously. The *Blue and Gold Editions* of poetry, in particular, were regarded as models of bookmaking.

In 1857 the firm acquired the *Atlantic Monthly* from Phillips, Sampson & Company and Fields took over its editorship in 1861. Ticknor died in 1864. In the reorganization that followed James R. Osgood became a partner in the business and the firm continued to expand. In an effort to diversify, Fields acquired three more magazines: *North American Review, Our Young Folks,* and *Every Saturday.* But by then the pace had slowed and the house entered a period of decline. For a time the firm became Fields Osgood & Company, and later, when Fields retired, James R. Osgood and Company.

For further history, *see* James R. Osgood and Houghton Mifflin Company. *See also,* HAWTHORNE AND HIS PUBLISHER by Caroline Ticknor; MEMOIRS OF JAMES T. FIELDS by Adams Fields.

Trow, John Fowler (1809-1886)

Born, Andover, Massachusetts. Trow went into the printing business in New York City with John T. West as West and Trow. The partnership was dissolved in 1837 and Trow continued alone as John F. Trow & Company. In 1844 he took Jonathan Leavitt as his partner and this partnership lasted until 1849.

Trow did printing, publishing and bookselling. For many years the Trow establishment was the largest printshop in America. He had a large array of Oriental typefaces and he specialized in the printing of original foreign books. As a publisher his greatest success was TROW'S NEW YORK CITY DIRECTORY, which was first issued in 1852.

Trow died in 1886 but the firm remained active until 1918, when it went into bankruptcy.

Truman & Smith

Founded in 1834 in Cincinnati, Ohio. Its early titles included THE CHILD'S BIBLE; SACRED HARP by Lowell Mason and Timothy B. Mason, a collection of church music; INTRODUCTION TO RAY'S ECLECTIC ARITHMETIC by Joseph Ray; and ENGLISH GRAMMAR ON THE PRODUCTIVE SYSTEM by Roswell C. Smith. Beginning in 1836 they published McGUFFEY READERS, an enormously profitable undertaking that established the firm on a sound financial basis.

The partnership was dissolved in 1843. Winthrop B. Smith, the junior partner, formed a new partnership with Edward Sargent and Lowell Mason, Jr. called W.B. Smith and Company. When Smith retired in 1863, the firm was reorganized as Sargent, Wilson & Hinkle, then changed to Wilson, Hinkle & Company in 1868. In 1877 Lewis Van Antwerp took over the firm and renamed it Van Antwerp, Bragg & Company. In 1890 this firm merged into the American Book Company.

The United States Book Company

Organized in 1890 at New York City by John W. Lovell (q.v.) as a gigantic book trust. It bought up cheap reprint libraries such as those of Estes and Lauriat, W.L. Allison and De Wolfe, Fiske, Hurst & Company, Pollard and Moss, Worthington, and many others. In 1890 the company was incorporated in New Jersey with a paid-up capital of three and a quarter million dollars, later increased to five million.

A stream of new series was launched under the imprint: the *Westminster* and the *Columbus,* the *Canterbury* and the *Metropolitan,* the *Leather Clad* and the *Seaside Library,* the *Oxford Edition of Twelvemos* and the *Universal,* the *Political* and *Scientific,* and the *Occult* series. Several satellite companies were established to distribute the books. They included: Lovell, Coryell & Company; Wayside Publishing Company; Seaside Publishing Company; the National Book Company; the International Book Company; Empire Publishing Company; the Lovell Brothers & Company; Prudential Book Company; and Lovell, Gestefeld & Company.

Within three years the bubble burst, bringing to an end the career of the flamboyant Lovell. The firm was succeeded by the American Publishers Corporation, which maintained a precarious existence until 1904.

Usher, Hezekiah (1615-1676)

The first American bookseller. Usher's bookshop in Boston, Massachusetts, established about 1647, was the first in the American Colonies. Following the established custom of English stationers, he had his books printed with the words, "Printed for Hezekiah Usher" on the title page. Usher also did some publishing on his own and John Cotton's SPIRITUAL MILK FOR BOSTON BABES IN EITHER ENGLAND was one of the books which appeared under his imprint. His sons, Hezekiah and John, continued his business after his death.

Walker, James P. (1829-1868)

In 1859 Walker founded the firm of Walker, Wise & Company at Boston, Massachusetts, with Daniel W. Wise as his partner, to print and circulate Unitarian books "for the promulgation of liberal Christianity" in collaboration with the American Unitarian Association. Most of the books which appeared under this imprint reflected the Unitarian credo and the Transcendentalist philosophy that had such strong roots in New England. Among them were: REASON IN RELIGION by Frederic Henry Hedge; Theodore Parker's PRAYERS; William Ellery Channing's WORKS; Andrews Norton's STATEMENT; and STUDIES OF CHRISTIANITY by James Martineau.

Walker's interest in women's rights led to the publication of WOMAN'S RIGHTS UNDER THE LAW by Caroline H. Dall, and EMPLOYMENTS OF WOMEN by Virginia Penny. And as a champion of abolition, Walker published James Kendall Hosmer's COLOR GUARD; THE WHIP, HOE, AND SWORD by George Hughes Hepworth; and SPEECHES, LECTURES, AND LETTERS by Wendell Phillips. Also, a Walker, Wise juvenile division offered a whole catalogue of standard books for the young which included *The Silver Penny Series, Home Story Books, Pioneer Boy Series, All the Children's Library,* the *Union Series,* and A YOUTH'S HISTORY OF THE REBELLION by William Makepeace Thayer. Still another major undertaking of the firm was Henri Martin's HISTORY OF FRANCE, translated into English by Mary L. Booth.

When Daniel Wise left the company in 1865, Walker formed a brief association with Horace B. Fuller. This partnership came to an abrupt end when the American Unitarian Association decided to resume its own publishing. Fuller continued in business for some time longer publishing books and a magazine for children.

The Wartburg Press

Founded originally in 1881 in Columbus, Ohio, as the Lutheran Book Concern by the Evangelical Lutheran Joint Synod of Ohio and other states. As a result of the formation of the American Lutheran Church in 1930 the Lutheran Book Concern was merged with the Wartburg Publishing House. This had been established in 1883 in Waverly, Iowa, by the Evangelical Lutheran Joint Synod of Iowa and other states. The Wartburg Press imprint was adopted in 1944. The imprint was later superseded by that of Augustana Publishing House.

Charles L. Webster & Company

Started by Mark Twain and his nephew, Charles L. Webster, in 1885, at Albany, New York. During a brief life of six years the firm published many successful books including Mark Twain's THE ADVENTURES OF HUCKLEBERRY FINN, General Ulysses Simpson Grant's MEMOIRS, General Philip H. Sheridan's PERSONAL MEMOIRS, General George B. McClellan's MEMOIRS, Henry Ward Beecher's LIFE OF JESUS CHRIST, and the *Library of American Literature,* edited by E.C. Stedman and Ellen M. Hutchinson. Webster died in 1891 and, after a series of unprofitable publishing seasons, the firm went into bankruptcy.

Webster, Noah (1758-1843)

Born, West Hartford, Connecticut. Webster was the first and perhaps the greatest of American lexicographers. He believed that "America must be as independent in literature as she is in politics, as famous for arts as for arms." To help develop a national language he published in 1873 his famous BLUE-BACKED SPELLER which has sold over the years upwards of one hundred million copies. A grammar and a reader followed in succeeding years, the three books forming *A Grammatical Institute of the English Language* (1783-85). In 1806 he edited A COMPENDIOUS DICTIONARY OF THE ENGLISH LANGUAGE and its abridgement, A DICTIONARY . . . FOR THE USE OF THE COMMON SCHOOLS. Both works emphasized American words and simplified spelling. They formed the groundwork for his greatest achievement, AN AMERICAN DICTIONARY OF THE ENGLISH LANGUAGE, published in 1828, the basis of Merriam-Webster unabridged dictionaries.

Webster canvassed actively for the legal protection of the rights of authors and his efforts to secure the passage of the Act of 1790 earned him the title of "father of American copyright." From 1793 to 1798 he was also the editor of New York's first daily newspaper, *The American Minerva.*

Other publications by Webster included DISSERTATIONS ON THE ENGLISH LANGUAGE, A BRIEF HISTORY OF EPIDEMIC AND PESTILENTIAL DISEASES, A HISTORY OF THE UNITED STATES, several textbooks, and a bowdlerized version of the Bible.

The Whole Book of Psalmes
See, Bay Psalm Book.

Wilson, John (1802-1868)

Born, Glasgow, Scotland. He came to Boston, Massachusetts, in 1846 and established a printing business in 1847 under the name of John Wilson & Son. He moved to Cambridge, Massachusetts, in 1865.

The firm printed many books for Harvard University. Wilson also wrote and published three religious works and his TREATISE ON PUNCTUATION AND OTHER PARTS OF COMPOSITION was the most popular printer's manual of his day.

Following Wilson's death in 1868 the business was carried on by his son, John Wilson. In 1879 the younger John Wilson and Charles E. Kentworth bought the Harvard University Press. It was not until 1913 that the Harvard University Press began to publish books under its own imprint.

45

John C. Winston Company

Founded in 1884 in Philadelphia, Pennsylvania, by John C. Winston. His first publication was THE CROWN BOOK OF THE BEAUTIFUL, THE WONDERFUL, AND THE WISE. Winston then arranged with the Publishing Concern of the Methodist-Episcopal Church to take over its International Series of Bibles. This publishing coup enabled him to become, by the turn of the century, the largest manufacturer and publisher of Bibles in the United States.

The firm was incorporated in 1900. Winston was president and Charles F. Kindt was the secretary. Shortly afterwards Winston acquired the Henry T. Coates & Company with its one thousand titles. At the same time the Winston list was broadened to include general publications. The *Griffin Series of Popular Copyright Novels* was begun in 1904. Juveniles were also issued in larger numbers. But the most important undertaking at this time was the NEW UNIVERSAL SELF-PRONOUNCING DICTIONARY OF THE ENGLISH LANGUAGE, which Winston published in various editions.

In the field of trade books under the Winston imprint there were Upton Sinclair's SYLVIA and THE CRY FOR JUSTICE, Stephen McKenna's THE RELUCTANT LOVER, and Helen Cramp's WINSTON COOK BOOK. In 1917 the firm entered the elementary and high school fields with a series of texts in civics, history, grammar, spelling, arithmetic, and language, of which the *Winston Readers* were the most innovative. The series was supplemented by the WINSTON SIMPLIFIED DICTIONARY for schools.

John C. Winston died in 1920 and was succeeded as president of the company by Charles F. Kindt, who had been groomed by Winston to take his place. Kindt launched the twenty-two volume INTERNATIONAL HANDBOOK OF PRACTICAL INFORMATION. In 1923 he brought out the *Clear-Type Classics* which became immensely popular. The trade division published scores of popular titles, such as CROSSWORD PUZZLE BOOK, THE MEMOIRS OF WILLIAMS JENNINGS BRYAN, Macy E. Phillips' EDGAR ALLAN POE, THE EXECUTIVE'S DESK BOOK, Royal Samuel Copeland's HOME MEDICAL BOOK, Herman Hagedorn's

BOOK OF COURAGE, YOUNG FU OF THE UPPER YANGTZE by Elizabeth F. Lewis, and Ely Culbertson's books on bridge. New and improved texts were introduced by the education department, among them, J. Russell Smith's *Human Geography* series, the *New Curriculum Arithmetics,* and *Easy Growth in Reading.*

Charles F. Kindt died in 1938. His son and namesake then became president of the company. Culberton continued to be the firm's most profitable author. LASSIE, COME HOME by Eric Knight was a bestseller during the years of World War II. When the war was over Winston published THE HISTORY OF WORLD WAR II. After 1948 Winston started several new juvenile series, called *Land of the Free, Winston Adventure Books, Winston Science Fiction,* and *Pixie Books.* In 1959 the company launched its *Winston Communication Program,* an elementary text series for the first six grades.

In 1960 the Winston Company was merged with Holt and Rinehart to form Holt, Rinehart & Winston.

Wood, Samuel (1760-1844)

Born, Oyster Bay, New York. One of the earliest juvenile and medical publishers in the United States. His earliest publications were children's primers and spellers. Of these THE YOUNG CHILD'S A B C, OR, FIRST BOOK, illustrated with many copperplate engravings, was the best known. It was written by Wood and published at New York City in 1806. The children's books sold so well that Wood began to specialize in this field. His *New York Readers* were widely adopted and remained in print until the 1880s.

In 1811 Wood admitted into partnership two of his adopted sons, Samuel S. and John. John left later and was replaced by another son, William. William was particularly interested in medicine and when his father retired in 1836 his brother and he began to devote more and more of their attention to building a medical list. The firm was known as Samuel S. and William Wood until Samuel died in 1861. In 1863, William H.S. Wood, William's son, joined the firm as a partner and the name was changed to William Wood &

Company. Publication of general non-medical books was discontinued in 1861 and the backlist was sold to J.H. Vail & Company in 1881.

William H.S. Wood continued to direct the company until his death in 1907, when ownership passed to his three sons, William C., Gilbert C., and Arnold. On the death of the last representative of the Wood family in 1932, the assets of the company were acquired by The Williams and Wilkins Company (q.v.) The Wood list at that time included such medical bestsellers as DISEASES OF THE EYE by C. May, PHYSICAL DIAGNOSIS by F. Dennette Adams, TEXTBOOK OF HISTOLOGY and PHYSICAL SIGNS IN CLINICAL SURGERY by Frederick R. Bailey, Thomas L. Stedman's MEDICAL DICTIONARY, and PRINCIPLES OF BACTERIOLOGY AND IMMUNOLOGY by W.C. Tople/ and Graham S. Wilson. Some of these books are still on The Williams and Wilkins Company list.

Zell, Ellwood

Born, Philadelphia, Pennsylvania. In 1854 Zell bought an interest in Troutman & Hayes and renamed the firm Hayes and Zell. The Civil War disrupted the partnership, Hayes joining the Confederate and Zell the Union Army. When the war ended Zell resumed business as a subscription book publisher. His first book, McKenzie's FIVE THOUSAND RECIPES, was so profitable that he followed it with other titles that soon made him one of the largest subscription book publishers of his time.

ZELL'S ENCYCLOPEDIA, DICTIONARY, AND GAZETTEER was his greatest success. Among his other undertakings were DESCRIPTIVE HAND ATLAS OF THE WORLD, CYCLOPAEDIA OF AMERICAN LITERATURE, ILLUSTRATED BIBLE, and UNITED STATES BUSINESS DIRECTORY.

II

Today's
Publishing Houses

ABC-Clio, Inc.

Founded by Eric H. Boehm in 1953 in Vienna, Austria, with the publication of HISTORICAL ABSTRACTS. In 1960 Boehm established Clio Press in Santa Barbara, California, to continue publication of the ABSTRACTS. Clio Press published its first book titles, GERMAN NATIONAL SOCIALISM and WE SURVIVED, in 1966. In 1969 American Bibliographical Center—Clio Press was incorporated; two years later EBC-Clio was established in Oxford, England.

ABC-Clio is one of the largest bibliographical publishers in the world, focusing on history and related social sciences. Among its major publishing programs are: *Historical Abstracts,* published quarterly in two parts: *Modern History Abstracts* and *Twentieth Century Abstracts; America: History and Life: A Guide to Periodical Literature; ABC POL SCI* (Advance Bibliography of Contents: Political Science and Government); *Artbibliographies* in three parts: *Artbibliographies Modern* (formerly *Literature of Modern Art*); *Artbibliographies Current Titles;* and *Artbibliographies Historical.*

The Clio Book Division currently publishes titles in four series, including: *The Twentieth Century,* edited by Lyman Legters; *Bibliography and Reference,* edited by Eric H. Boehm; *Comparative Government and Politics,* edited by Peter H. Merkl; and *A Bibliography Series on the Study of War and Peace,* sponsored by the Center for the Study of Armament and Disarmament, California State University, Los Angeles, and edited by Richard D. Burns.

AMS Press, Inc.

Organized in 1962 as a reprint publisher. It is the publishing arm of one of New York City's oldest book shops, Abraham's Magazine Service, Inc., which was founded in 1899 and owned by Herman Meyers and Jack A. Abrams. A subsidiary imprint called Paladin Press, devoted to American history, existed for a while.

The major areas of specialization of the press are the humanities and the social sciences. Outstanding reprint projects include JOHNSON'S DICTIONARY, Henry Rowe Schoolcraft's HISTORY OF U.S. INDIAN TRIBES, THE NORTH AMERICAN REVIEW in 175 volumes, TUDOR FACSIMILE TEXTS, and Columbia University's STUDIES IN THE SOCIAL SCIENCES. In 1965 the firm was acquired by Gabriel Hornstein and Maurice Weisbaum.

Abbey Press

Founded in 1889 and currently at St. Meinrad, Indiana, as a publisher of books of general religious interest and dealing with family life. Its books are nonfiction and often issued in paperback.

Abelard-Schuman Ltd.

Established in 1948 in New York City by Lew Schwartz, Canadian-born publisher of trade magazines. In 1953 he acquired Henry Schuman, Inc., which had been started in 1946 by Henry Schuman, a former rare books dealer. The two firms were amalgamated into one organization known as Abelard-Schuman Ltd. with branches in Canada and London, England.

In 1960 Abelard-Schuman acquired Criterion Books and this imprint has been retained for adult and young adult titles. The firm has published such notable authors as Isaac Asimov, Mark Van Doren, Jacques Barzun, Max Frisch, and Charlotte Zolotow.

In 1969 Abelard-Schuman was acquired by Intext, Inc. (q.v.) and operated as a member of the Intext Press Group until 1974 when its author contracts and inventory were purchased by Thomas Y. Crowell.

Abingdon Press

Founded in 1789, Abingdon Press is the oldest religious publisher and the second oldest book publisher in the United States. The evolution of the press follows closely the history of Methodism. In the beginning it was in Philadelphia, Pennsylvania, and was known as The Methodist Book Concern, with John Dickins as the Book

Steward. Its first publication was John Wesley's CHRISTIAN'S PATTERN. In 1804 the headquarters were transferred to New York City. The first branch house was opened in Cincinnati, Ohio, by Martin Ruter in 1820 and chartered in 1839 as the Western Book Concern of the Methodist Episcopal Church.

Then, in 1828, with the beginning of separatism, came various publishing imprints: The Methodist Protestant Church began the Methodist Protestant Book Concern in Baltimore, Maryland, and the Methodist Episcopal Church, South, formed the Methodist Publishing House in Nashville, Tennessee. In 1939, when the three branches of Methodism were joined, the publishing units merged into The Methodist Publishing House. Since the recent Evangelical United Brethren merger with the Methodist Church the publishing firm has been renamed The United Methodist Publishing House.

In 1914 The Methodist Book Concern made Abingdon Press the trade name for its publications. The Methodist Publishing House had established the Cokesbury Press in 1923, while The Methodist Protestant Book Concern had begun using the imprint of Stockton in 1913. Upon unification in 1939 the name of the publishing department became Abingdon-Cokesbury Press, a combination of the names of Thomas Coke and Francis Asbury, Methodism's first bishops, and the location of its first college in Abingdon, Maryland. In 1954 the name Cokesbury was dropped and Abingdon Press was adopted as the over-all title. The retail stores of The United Methodist Publishing House are operated under the name of Cokesbury.

Abingdon has six editorial divisions: religious, general, college, children's special projects, and fine arts, which encompasses Abingdon Audio-Graphics. Abingdon's main strength lies in classics such as THE INTERPRETER'S BIBLE, THE INTERPRETER'S DICTIONARY, the one-volume THE INTERPRETER'S COMMENTARY, and James Strong's EXHAUSTIVE CONCORDANCE OF THE BIBLE. Among more popular titles are RIVERMAN, LETTERS TO KAREN, THE JESUS TRIP: ADVENT OF THE JESUS FREAKS, and BLESS THIS MESS AND OTHER PRAYERS by Jo Carr and Imogene Sorley.

Harry N. Abrams, Inc.

Founded in New York City in 1949 when there was no significant or exclusive art book publisher in America. Since then the firm has established its world-wide reputation as the leading publisher of exceptionally fine artbooks and reproductions.

Harry N. Abrams, the president and chairman of the board of the company, began his innovative, pioneering publishing enterprise with $100,000.00 and a profound commitment to art, scholarship, and fine quality reproduction. His first three titles, VAN GOGH, EL GRECO, and RENOIR, were published in October, 1950, and became the keystone of an important and continuing series, the *Library of Great Painters,* each containing distinguished scholarly texts with fifty large full-color illustrations of an artist's work. Nearly thirty titles in this series have since been published in as many as eight different languages including French, German, Spanish, Italian and Japanese.

Although Europe had been considered the artbook capital of the world, with its fine printing and meticulous craftsmanship, within a few short years Abrams proved that books originating in America could compete successfully in terms of quality and beauty. Absolute fidelity of color reproduction was of utmost importance, and to that was coupled the greatest possible editorial care, under the direction of Milton S. Fox, who was with Abrams since its inception. Three years after its founding, Fritz H. Landshoff joined the company as a vice president, and organized a European office in Amsterdam, thus opening up world-wide marketing possibilities. As a direct consequence, a trend was reversed and Europe began importing artbooks from the United States and selling them successfully. By 1953 four and a half million copies of the thirty-two titles in an early, softcover series, *The Pocket Library,* were sold in this manner alone, at fifty cents each, throughout the continent. Almost overnight the modest Abrams publishing enterprise, centered in New York, had become an important international cultural phenomenon.

Also by 1953, Harry N. Abrams had applied his own merchandising ingenuity to America, adopting for artbooks the distribution techniques of direct mail and book club distribution. In 1952

Abrams arranged with the Book-of-the-Month Club to distribute the ART TREASURES OF THE LOUVRE. Later he created the five-volume HISTORY OF ART for New American Library. Another development was the formation of an art book club, Art Treasures of the World, operated by the Greystone Press. In 1954 Abrams began its Print Division, through which it produced hundreds of large full-color reproductions. Then, in 1959, a subsidiary imprint, Abradale Press, was developed to handle non-artbook titles, including Bibles, a medical encyclopedia, an Italian cookbook and a science series, among others, all produced with the same meticulous care as the Abrams artbooks.

Currently, more than five hundred titles are listed in the Abrams catalogue, including the following series: *The Library of Great Painters, The Library of Great Museums, The Library of Modern Masters,* and *The Library of Art History.* The company is dedicated to the publication of such great American painters as Edward Hopper and Ben Shahn, and it recently had an unprecedented runaway bestseller (at $60.00) in NORMAN ROCKWELL: ARTIST AND ILLUSTRATOR. Commitment to contemporary art is also an original aspect of the company's program, and more than forty titles deal with such recent art movements as Pop Art, Minimalism, Kineticism, and Earthworks, as well as the diverse creative conceptions of the individual artists Johns, Rauschenberg, Gorky, Frankenthaler, Christo, Rivers, and many others. There are, in addition, titles encompassing sculpture, graphic arts, architecture, individual artists, and art history, as well as books of special interest such as the famed SHELL: FIVE HUNDRED MILLION YEARS OF INSPIRED DESIGN, and the recently published THE DOLL, and A TREASURY OF AMERICAN DESIGN.

A large number of Abrams titles are selected by major book clubs each year and a growing number are being used as textbooks in leading universities and high schools throughout the world. The HISTORY OF ART by Professor H.W. Janson of New York University, as an example, has sold since its publication about eight years ago nearly two million copies. It is the standard, authorized survey text on art history through the ages at the college and university level, lively in style, impeccable in scholarship, richly illustrated and beautifully printed and bound. Two other books by Janson were also successful: THE PICTURE HISTORY OF ART and KEY MONUMENTS OF THE HISTORY OF ART.

The Abrams office in Holland, still under the directorship of Fritz H. Landshoff, is responsible for the sale of foreign rights, with many Abrams titles available in as many as ten languages. The Dutch Abrams operation also supervises European production and the acquisition of American rights to European artbooks (such as DALI and the recent WORLD OF M. C. ESCHER). The Abrams office in Tokyo, opened in 1966, now handles the largest part of Abrams book production, as well as the distribution of Abrams titles in Japan.

A part of Abrams specialized activities as publishers, consultants and distributors, are joint ventures with industry, art institutions, and direct mail organizations in America and abroad.

Several prominent bookmen have been associated with Abrams. Harry N. Abrams was a well known figure in the publishing field long before he organized his own company. He had a strong background in the fine arts, having studied fine art with serious artistic ambition at the Art Students League and the National Academy of Design. His interest spread to commercial art and he worked for several years at an advertising agency. In 1936 he became art director of the Book-of-the-Month Club and in 1947 a member of its board of directors. During this period, he designed numerous beautifully illustrated books which the club used as book dividends. He also created and designed the Random House *Illustrated Modern Library* in 1943, and the Grosset & Dunlap *Illustrated Junior Library* in 1945.

Milton S. Fox was vice president and editor-in-chief of the company from its inception until his death in October 1971. He was a professional artist who had been trained at the Cleveland School of Art, the Académie Julian and the École des Beaux Arts in Paris, became art critic for the *Cleveland* (Ohio) *News* in 1930, staff member and supervisor of education at the Cleveland Museum of Art from 1932 to 1944, then until 1950 worked as a screen writer in Hollywood.

Fox wrote extensively on art, was a member of several local and national art education committees and a founder and vice president of the New York Art International.

Fritz H. Landshoff, the executive vice president of Abrams, was born in Berlin, Germany, and received his Ph.D. in literature at the University of Frankfurt. After several years of training in bookstores and publishing houses, he became manager of the Berlin literary publishing house, Gustav Kiepenheuer Verlag. He emigrated to Holland in 1933 and with the Dutch publisher, Querido, founded the Querido Verlag, where he concentrated primarily on publishing exiled German authors such as Thomas Mann, Stefan Zweig, Franz Werfel, among others. After the German occupation of Holland in 1941, he moved to New York and became a partner in the publishing firm of L.B. Fischer. When the war was over, he became co-founder and co-manager of Excerpta Medica, Amsterdam and New York, before joining Harry N. Abrams as an executive and associate.

In April, 1966, Harry N. Abrams, Inc. was acquired by the Times Mirror Company.

Academic Press, Inc.

Founded in 1941 in New York City by Walter J. Johnson and Kurt Jacoby, son and son-in-law respectively of the founder of Akademische Verlag in Leipzig, Germany. Their first publication, in 1942, was the semiannual ARCHIVES OF BIOCHEMISTRY (later, ARCHIVES OF BIOCHEMISTRY AND BIOPHYSICS). This was followed, in 1943, by CHEMISTRY AND METHODS OF ENZYMES by J.B. Sumner and G.F. Somers and VITAMINS AND HORMONES by R.S. Harris and K.V. Thimann.

The firm soon branched out into the publication of journals in the pure and applied sciences. These eventually grew to sixty-five in number. Among them are the *Journal of Colloid Science, Experimental Cell Research, Experimental Parasitology, Virology, Nuclear Science and Engineering, Journal of Molecular Biology, Developmental Biology, Analytical Biochemistry, Journal of Catalysis, Experimental Eye Research,* and *Icarus:*

International Journal of the Solar System. Another program was entitled *Advances* and books in this series dealt with current progress in the discrete scientific fields of protein chemistry and electron physics. The press's treatises, monographs, and symposia include such works as the Harvey Lectures, the six-volume THE CELL: BIOCHEMISTRY, PHYSIOLOGY, MORPHOLOGY, and the five-volume THE BACTERIA: A TREATISE ON STRUCTURE AND FUNCTION. For a while Academic Press distributed the books of Springer-Verlag. In 1961 a college textbook division was established.

In 1969 the firm was acquired, along with its subsidiary, Johnson Reprint Corporation, by Harcourt Brace Jovanovich, Inc.

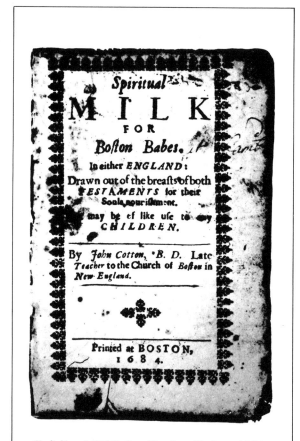

Spiritual Milk for Boston Babes, 1684.
Title Page. One of the first books printed in the American Colonies.

Ace Books

Founded in New York City in 1952. Its first publications were in the form of paperback double-books: two complete novels published back-to-back at the price of one book. Ace continued to release books in this format for about a year until it began to increase its output and to introduce general material. The first important work was JUNKIE by William Burroughs.

Ace Books was the first to publish science fiction in paperback form. The first releases in this field included Leigh Brackett's SWORD OF RHIANNON and CONAN. The Ace backlist now includes 12 Nebula and Hugo Award winners among which are: Frank Herbert's DUNE, Ursula K. LeGuin's LEFT HAND OF DARKNESS, and THE EINSTEIN INTERSECTION and BABEL 17 by Samuel K. Delany.

Ace also offers 30 titles by Edgar Rice Burroughs, 51 by André Norton, and 11 by Robert A. Heinlein, and is active in the Gothic, suspense, occult, and Western fields. Ace Westerns have won two Western Heritage Awards and nine Spur Awards.

Ace Books is now a subsidiary of Charter Communications, Inc.

Acropolis Books Ltd.

Established in 1965. A Washington, D.C.-based publisher of hard and softcover books dealing with social themes.

Addison-Wesley Publishing Company, Inc.

Established in 1942 at Cambridge, Massachusetts, by Lew Addison Cummings and Melbourne Wesley Cummings. Melbourne Cummings (unrelated to Lew Cummings) was sales manager for the Lew A. Cummings Company, a New Hampshire printing firm, when Professor Francis W. Sears of the Massachusetts Institute of Technology (MIT) brought to him the manuscript of a book which he wished to have privately printed. Melbourne Cummings proposed that instead of acting simply as a printer he would like to perform the function of a publisher. Accordingly the firm of Addison-Wesley Press, Inc., was incorporated in New Hampshire, the name being taken from the middle names of its founders.

In 1946 Lew Cummings withdrew from Addison-Wesley and the business continued under the direction of Mel Cummings. In 1947 Addison-Wesley became a Massachusetts corporation and the corporate name was changed in 1952 to Addison-Wesley Publishing Company, Inc.

With ready access to MIT and Harvard scholars the firm obtained a number of them as authors. Its early successes were the three-volume PRINCIPLES OF PHYSICS by F.W. Sears, SPECTROCHEMICAL ANALYSIS by L.H. Ahrens, F.H. Mitchell's FUNDAMENTALS OF ELECTRONICS, and THERMODYNAMICS OF ALLOYS by C. Wagner. Later, Addison-Wesley broadened its list to include chemistry and related sciences. Until 1958 the company specialized in texts at the college level and in that year the international division was established. This division not only sells the parent company's books but also arranges translations and does indigenous publishing. In 1958 the Atomic Energy Commission selected Addison-Wesley as the publisher of its twelve-volume series of papers for the second Atoms-for-Peace Conference in Geneva. Also in 1958 a high school division was established, and in 1961 the company entered the field of elementary school publishing. These two divisions were combined to form a School Division, located in Menlo Park, California. In 1961 a Business and Professional Division was set up.

In the 1960s two of Addison-Wesley's texts were adopted by the nationally televised Continental Classroom Program: PROBABILITY AND STATISTICS by Frederick Mosteller and others, and A STUDY GUIDE TO THE NEW BIOLOGY by Ray Koppelman. In 1968 the company formed a wholly-owned subsidiary, Cummings Publishing Company, Inc., in Menlo Park to specialize in books for the two-year colleges. In 1969 a Juvenile Division was established. This division publishes curriculum-related juveniles under the imprint Addisonian Press and trade juveniles under the imprint Young Scott Books. In 1971 the company acquired W.A. Benjamin, Inc., a publisher of college texts, now based in Menlo Park.

Mel Cummings and his family were sole owners of the company's stock until 1955, when a limited number of shares were made available to employees, authors, and associates. The first public offering of the company's stock was made in 1956. In 1970 Donald W. Jones succeeded Cummings as president of the company.

Aero Publishers, Inc.

Established in 1939 at Fallbrook, California. Publishes books on aviation and space.

Alba House

Founded in 1937 in New York City under the name of St. Paul Publications. In 1961 it was reorganized under the imprint of Alba House, the name standing for the four Gospels, incorporating the initial letters of the four Evangelists: Angelus (angel) for Matthew, Leo (lion) for Mark, Bos (ox) for Luke, and Aquila (eagle) for John. It is owned and operated by the Society of St. Paul, founded in 1914 in Italy, for the purpose of propagating Christian doctrine through the press, radio, television, motion pictures, recordings, and other audio-visual media. The annual output of about twenty-five volumes by Alba House deals mostly with theology, Biblical studies, pastoral work, liturgy, marriage, and family.

Aldine Publishing Company

Established in 1961 by Alexander J. Morin and Daniel E. Levin in Chicago, Illinois. The first book under the new imprint was published in 1962. Its programs are directed entirely toward college, university, and professional audiences and consist of works in the social sciences, including undergraduate and graduate textbooks and professional books. When Atherton Press was ac-

quired in 1971 the name of the firm was changed to Aldine-Atherton, Inc., but upon the disposition of part of the original Atherton list in 1972 the name was changed back to Aldine Publishing Company.

Alec R. Allenson, Inc.

Established in 1924 at Naperville, Illinois, a publisher of religious books.

Allyn and Bacon, Inc.

Founded in 1868 in Boston, Massachusetts, by John Allyn, a publisher specializing in classical textbooks, whose publication rights had been obtained from Harvard University Bookstore. In 1888 George Andrew Bacon joined Allyn as his partner and the name was changed to Allyn and Bacon. Bacon had been the principal of Syracuse High School and publisher of *The Academy,* a journal of secondary education. When Bacon retired in 1923, he left direction of the company with his two sons, Charles Edward and Paul, and they proceeded to build up a sizeable elementary and high school list.

In 1951 the firm was acquired by Prentice-Hall. In the following year a College Division was established. The firm became independent in 1957. Holbrook Press, a wholly-owned subsidiary, was set up in 1966. The Longwood Division, formerly a mail-order operation, was established in 1972.

American Baptist Board of Education and Publication

See, Judson Press.

American Bible Society

Founded in 1816 at New York City "to encourage a wider circulation of the Holy Scriptures

56

without doctrinal note or comment and without profit." Elias Boudinot was the Society's first president. Incorporated in 1841, the Society soon became the largest publisher of Bibles in the world. The Society also publishes a monthly journal, *American Bible Society Record*.

American Chemical Society

Founded in 1876 in New York City. For many years its major activity was to hold monthly meetings at which scientific and technical papers were read. The papers were published in the *Proceedings* which, in 1879, became the *Journal of the American Chemical Society*. In 1920 the Society started the *ACS Monographs Series* which, until 1972, was published by Van Nostrand Reinhold Book Company and its predecessors, Reinhold Publishing Company and Chemical Catalog Company. In 1972 the Society assumed publication of the series.

In 1950 ACS started *Advances in Chemistry,* a series of books devoted to publishing symposia and collections of data. About twelve new titles in this series are published annually. The *Advances* and the *Monographs* are published by the Society's Book Department, which also issues other scientific and reference books and reprint collections. Among the reference books are REAGENT CHEMICALS, which is revised on a five-year cycle, and C. Seidell's SOLUBILITIES OF CHEMICAL COMPOUNDS.

In 1971 the Society entered into an agreement with the Manufacturing Chemists Association to publish the *Chemistry In Action* series of books formerly published by Doubleday. In 1972 the Society commenced publishing *Modern Chemical Technology,* a series of textbooks for the training of chemical technologists. The Society also publishes seventeen research journals and five magazines.

American Education Publications

See, Xerox Education Publications.

American Elsevier Publishing Company, Inc.

Set up in New York City in 1962 as an affiliate of Elsevier Publishing Company of Amsterdam, Holland. The firm specializes in scientific, medical, and technical reference books and textbooks.

American Heritage Publishing Company, Inc.

Established in 1954 in New York City by James Parton with Joseph Thorndike, Jr. and Oliver Jensen as partners. Their purpose was to publish a bimonthly, ad-free, hardcover magazine of American history for a popular audience. The magazine's name, *American Heritage,* was taken from a small quarterly established in 1947 by the American Association for State and Local History. The Association was given the right to elect three members to the company's board of directors and is paid a royalty on sales.

American Heritage soon became the world's largest and best-known history journal. In 1957 the company published the first of a continuing series of illustrated American and world history books, combining well-researched historical pictures with texts by prominent authors. In 1958 the company launched its second hardcover ad-free magazine: *Horizon.* During the sixties American Heritage published a series of more than eighty histories for young readers, el-hi and college textbooks, and several book series for supermarket distribution.

The company's most notable single publication is THE AMERICAN HERITAGE DICTIONARY OF THE ENGLISH LANGUAGE, published in 1969. The dictionary, which took six years and five million dollars to complete, is marketed by Houghton Mifflin Company. Other major publishing achievements include AMERICAN HERITAGE PICTURE HISTORY OF THE CIVIL WAR, which won a special Pulitzer Prize citation; FOUR DAYS, an illustrated historical record of the assassination and burial of President Kennedy; and THE ORIGINAL WATER-COLOR PAINTINGS OF JOHN JAMES AUDUBON FOR THE BIRDS OF AMERICA.

In 1969 the company became a wholly-owned subsidiary of McGraw-Hill, Inc.

American Library Association

Founded at Philadelphia, Pennsylvania, in 1876, the American Library Association is the oldest and largest national library association in the world. In 1909 its headquarters were transferred to Chicago, Illinois. Among its major goals are the promotion of library service of excellent quality, freely available to all; improvement of professional library standards; and the defense of the freedom of the individual to have access to any materials he chooses to read without restriction by censorship.

The Association is governed by an elected council that operates through an administrative body of the council called the Executive Board. ALA activities are carried on through its divisions and their sections: the Association of College and Research Libraries, Public Library Association, Children's Services Division, Young Adult Services Division, Information Science and Automation Division, Library Administration Division, Library Education Division, Resources and Technical Services Division, American Association of School Librarians, Reference and Adult Services Division, Association of Hospital and Institution Libraries, American Library Trustee Association, and Association of State Library Agencies.

In 1886, when the ALA was only ten years old, it founded its own publishing enterprise, calling it simply the Publishing Section. It was formed "to secure the preparation and publication of such catalogs, indexes, and other bibliographical helps as may best be produced by cooperation." Now organized as Publishing Services, this program has as one of its major objectives the creation and publication of professional literature "responsive to the needs, concerns, and goals of the library profession and the American Library Association." More than two dozen periodicals, ranging from newsletters to proceedings, are published by ALA. Among them are *American Libraries,* the official membership publication; *ALA Membership Directory; The Booklist, Choice,* and *RQ,* three review journals; and *Library Technology Reports.*

Perhaps the most important single reference book published by the ALA is GUIDE TO REFERENCE BOOKS. First published in 1902, its compilers have been outstanding authorities on reference books: Alice Bertha Kroeger for the first two editions, Isadore Gilbert Mudge for the next four editions, Constance Mabel Winchell for the seventh and eighth editions, and Eugene Sheehy for the supplements to the eighth edition.

Working tools for librarians, library administrators, and library school students form a major segment of ALA publications program. Among these are: Paul Dunkin's CATALOGING USA; Margaret Mann's INTRODUCTION TO CATALOGING AND THE CLASSIFICATION OF BOOKS, AMERICAN LIBRARY LAWS by Alex Ladenson, ANGLO-AMERICAN CATALOGING RULES by Seymour Lubetzky and C. Sumner Spalding, FUNDAMENTAL REFERENCE SOURCES by Frances N. Cheney, Dorothy Sinclair's ADMINISTRATION OF THE SMALL PUBLIC LIBRARY, and SERIAL PUBLICATIONS by Andrew D. Osborn.

ALA's selection aids and bibliographies provide a firm base for book acquisition. These include BOOKS FOR ELEMENTARY SCHOOL LIBRARIES, BOOKS FOR COLLEGE LIBRARIES, BOOKS FOR JUNIOR COLLEGE LIBRARIES, PERIODICALS FOR SCHOOL LIBRARIES, and AGRICULTURAL EDUCATION IN A TECHNICAL SOCIETY.

American Management Associations

Established in 1923 in New York City through successive mergers of earlier organizations interested in scientific management. The book and periodicals publication program is one of four divisions of AMACOM, the communications arm of AMA. The publications division dates back on a formal basis to 1958.

Judged by the number of titles published annually, AMACOM has been described as the world's largest publisher of management books. Subject areas correspond to AMA's breakdown of the major areas of managerial responsibility: finance, general management, general (office) services, insurance, international management, management systems and sciences, manufacturing, marketing, packaging, personnel, purchasing, transportation and physical distribution, and research and development.

AMACOM publishes the following periodicals: *Management News, Management Review, Personnel, Supervisory Management, Hospital Supervision, Compensation Review,* and *Organizational Dynamics.* It is also the world's leading publisher of programmed instruction materials for management under the trade name Prime[R], and also offers a series of advanced management courses featuring private, self-paced study at home — the Extension Institute of AMA.

American Mathematical Society

Founded in 1888 at Providence, Rhode Island. Publishes technical and scholarly books on mathematics, particularly two major series, *Colloquium Series* and *Math Surveys.*

American Personnel & Guidance Association

Founded in 1952 at Washington, D.C. Publishes books on educational aspects of counseling.

American Philosophical Society

Founded in 1743 in Philadelphia, Pennsylvania; the oldest learned society in the United States. Publishes ten to twelve books annually on the history of science and philosophy.

American Photographic Book Publishing Co., Inc., (Amphoto)

Founded originally in 1888 at New York City, Amphoto publishes exclusively books on photography and also distributes photographic books for both American and foreign publishers. Seymour D. Uslan has been president of the company for many years. It is now a division of Cox Broadcasting Corporation and is located at Garden City, New York.

American Society For Testing And Materials

Founded in 1898 at Philadelphia, Pennsylvania. Publisher of technical and scientific manuals.

American Technical Society

Founded by R.T. Miller, Jr. in 1898 in Chicago, Illinois, in order to publish books and encyclopedia sets on technical subjects. Miller retired in 1940 and the Society was reorganized as a nonprofit foundation under the laws of the State of Illinois.

The Society still publishes textbooks for technical, vocational, occupational and industrial arts classes, and it now offers home study courses in various vocational subjects and study guides in the areas of technical apprenticeship training, adult education, and industrial arts programs.

Amuru Press, Inc.

A firm of Black publishers in New York City that publishes exclusively young Black writers of poetry, short stories, novels, plays, humor and folklore, cartoons, fables, children's stories, and photography.

Anchor Books

The first quality reprint program in soft cover format launched by Doubleday in 1952. It was planned and directed by Jason Epstein.

The W.H. Anderson Company

Founded in 1887 in Cincinnati, Ohio, by William Harvey Anderson "for the sale, purchase, or exchange of new and second-hand law books." His first venture into publishing was WHITTAKER'S OHIO CIVIL CODE, the first edition of which appeared the same year. The company was incorporated in 1902. Six years later Anderson purchased the Robert Clarke Company which had been in business since 1845 and which owned many valuable copyrights including SWAN'S TREATISE and COCHRAN'S LAW LEXICON.

Anderson remained president of the company until his retirement in 1930. Under him the company published such notable works as PAGE'S OHIO GENERAL CODE, BRANNAN'S NEGOTIABLE INSTRUMENTS, THORNTON ON OIL AND GAS, CLARK ON RECEIVERS, PAGE ON THE LAW OF WILLS, and STEARNS ON SURETYSHIP.

Succeeding presidents of the company were Edwin P. Coke (1930-36), Clifford W. Mueller (1936-50), George C. Trautwein (1950-64), and John L. Skirving since 1964. During Trautwein's tenure the company acquired the *Ohio Law Reporter* magazine and began publishing books sponsored by the National Organization on Legal Problems of Education.

Since 1958 (except for the years 1967 and 1968) the Anderson Company has published the transcript of the annual convention of the American Trial Lawyers Association and other official publications of that organization. Also during this period, the Municipal Codes Division was established. Ordinances have been codified for over two hundred cities and villages.

A major area into which the company has expanded is police science and criminal justice. A new series called *Police Texts* was launched with John L. Klotter and Leo Kanowitz's CONSTITUTIONAL LAW FOR POLICE as the first book. A Police Publications Advisory Board has been set up to assist in the selection of authors and titles.

In 1972 the Jefferson Law Book Company, with headquarters in Washington, D.C., was purchased to expand author and customer contacts in the eastern states.

Ann Arbor Science Publishers, Inc.

Established in 1966 as a subsidiary of the Gelman Instrument Company in Ann Arbor, Michigan. Charles Gelman and Edward Lewis were

the founders. In 1971 the company was reorganized and Edward Lewis became the president. The firm specializes in environmental, biomedical, biochemical, chemical, chemical engineering, and mechanical engineering books. A major publishing achievement was THE PARTICLE ATLAS, EDITION TWO in 1973, a four-volume set three times larger than the original. The company is the world's largest publisher of environmental books for professional and university level use.

Anthroposophic Press, Inc.

Established in 1922 at Spring Valley, New York. Publishes exclusively books by Dr. Rudolf Steiner and works of related authors in American, British and European editions.

Daniel Appleton (1785-1849)

Appleton-Century-Crofts

Established in 1825 in New York City as a dry goods store by Daniel Appleton. The store had a book section that was so profitable that Appleton converted his enterprise into a bookstore in 1831. In the same year he published his first book, a tiny volume measuring three inches square entitled CRUMBS FROM THE MASTER'S TABLE: OR, SELECT SENTENCES DOCTRINAL, PRACTICAL, AND EXPERIMENTAL, compiled by W. Mason. Other religious books followed, but Appleton's piety was so strong that he refused to publish fiction. Appleton's son, William H., who had joined his father's firm in 1830, became a partner in 1838 and the imprint was changed to D. Appleton & Company.

In 1839 the company's flourishing business warranted the opening of a branch office in London, England. In the 1840s the firm began to publish textbooks in Spanish and by the end of the Civil War it held a virtual monopoly in educational and scientific books for the South American market. Another new line was a series of travel guides, beginning in 1847 with APPLETON'S RAILROAD AND STEAMBOAT COMPANION. THE UNITED STATES GUIDE BOOK (later ILLUSTRATED HANDBOOK OF AMERICAN TRAVEL) appeared in 1861, followed by HANDBOOK OF SUMMER RESORTS and EUROPEAN GUIDEBOOK, the latter running into twenty-nine editions between 1870 and 1896. Appleton's *Literary Bulletin* was begun in 1842 as a record of new books. The first juvenile title also appeared in this year: THE CROFTON BOYS by Harriet Martineau.

Daniel Appleton retired in 1848 and the business was taken over by his five sons, with William H. in charge. William's fine literary taste was responsible for bringing into the house such classics as ALICE'S ADVENTURES IN WONDERLAND, John Henry Newman's APOLOGIA PRO VITA SUA, William Cullen Bryant's POEMS, Commodore Matthew C. Perry's A NARRATIVE OF THE EXPEDITION . . . TO JAPAN and Thomas Hart Benton's THIRTY YEARS' VIEW; OR, A HISTORY . . . OF THE AMERICAN GOVERNMENT.

From the beginning schoolbooks had constituted a sizeable part of the Appleton list with *Mandeville Readers, Wright Readers, Perkins Arithmetics* and *Cornell Geographies*. Noah Webster's ELEMENTARY SPELLING BOOK was added to this list in 1855; its sale over the next

hundred years has been estimated at seventy million copies. Another landmark was Appleton's entry into medical publishing, in 1852, with John Appleton Swett's A TREATISE ON THE DISEASES OF THE CHEST. Later Appleton was to bring out the celebrated medical classic, Sir William Osler's PRINCIPLES AND PRACTICE OF MEDICINE.

William Appleton's greatest achievement was the NEW AMERICAN CYCLOPEDIA, edited by Charles Anderson Dana and George Ripley, which George H. Derby called "the greatest literary enterprise ever undertaken and accomplished in America." Compiled at a cost of over one million dollars, it sold one and a half million copies. The AMERICAN ANNUAL CYCLOPEDIA was first issued in 1861. Appleton's CYCLOPEDIA OF BIOGRAPHY, the CYCLOPEDIA OF AMERICAN BIOGRAPHY, edited by James Grant Wilson and John Fiske, and THE LIBRARY OF WONDERS were other major reference works that appeared between 1856 and 1890.

One of the distinguished editors at Appleton at this time was Edward L. Youmans, whose great contribution to the field of scientific literature earned him the title of "interpreter of science to the people." At the urging of Youmans, Appleton published Charles Robert Darwin's THE ORIGIN OF SPECIES, Herbert Spencer's FIRST PRINCIPLES and PRINCIPLES OF BIOLOGY, and Thomas Henry Huxley's MAN'S PLACE IN NATURE. Youmans also initiated a new series of scientific textbooks for the classroom: CLASSBOOK OF CHEMISTRY, CHEMICAL ATLAS, and THE HANDBOOK OF HOUSEHOLD SCIENCE. Out of these efforts grew the *International Scientific Series* through which Youmans introduced the great scientists of the day to the American audience. This series eventually grew to seventy volumes. Youmans also started the *Popular Science Monthly* in 1872 and served as the first editor of *Appleton's Journal* founded in 1869. *Appleton's Journal* expired in 1881 but *Popular Science Monthly* went on to become under various owners a very influential scientific periodical.

William H. Appleton's enterprise was manifest in all departments of publishing. A series of illustrated books, PICTURESQUE AMERICA, PICTURESQUE EUROPE, and PICTURES-QUE PALESTINE, was sold by subscription and met with phenomenal success. Appleton also published a number of memoirs and biographies, including William Henry Seward's AUTOBIO-GRAPHY, General William Sherman's MEM-OIRS, and Adam Badeau's THE MILITARY HISTORY OF ULYSSES SIMPSON GRANT. To compete in the low-priced field Appleton introduced the *New Handy-Volume,* a series of novelettes, *Collection of Foreign Authors,* and the *Town and Country Library,* the latter extending eventually to 312 volumes. In the field of history Appleton's outstanding titles included Jefferson Davis's HISTORY OF THE RISE AND FALL OF THE CONFEDERATE GOVERN-MENT, George Bancroft's HISTORY OF THE UNITED STATES, W.E.H. Lecky's HISTORY OF ENGLAND IN THE EIGHTEENTH CEN-TURY, and John Bach McMaster's HISTORY OF THE PEOPLE OF THE UNITED STATES FROM THE REVOLUTION TO THE CIVIL WAR.

The *International Education Series,* edited by William T. Harris in sixty-four volumes, achieved an influence among educators comparable to that of the *International Science Series* in the scientific community. During this period the trade department brought out such bestsellers as DAVID HARUM by Edward N. Westcott, UNCLE REMUS by Joel Chandler Harris, THE MANX-MAN by Hall Caine, THE RED BADGE OF COURAGE by Stephen Crane, and books by Rudyard Kipling, Arthur Conan Doyle, and Joseph Conrad.

In 1897 the firm was incorporated with a capital of $2,000,000. Two years later William H. Appleton died and was succeeded as president by his son, William Worthen Appleton. W.W. Appleton was not the keen businessman his father had been and financial troubles soon overtook the company, forcing it into receivership. Joseph H. Sears was engaged by the directors to reorganize the company and he was elected president. To make the trade department once again profitable Sears brought in several popular authors: George Moore, Edith Wharton, David Graham Phillips, and Robert W. Chambers. He

also published important nonfiction titles: G. Stanley Hall's ADOLESCENCE, Herbert Spencer's AUTOBIOGRAPHY, and the three-volume CYCLOPEDIA OF AMERICAN GOVERN-MENT.

In 1919 Sears was replaced by John W. Hiltman and the new president was also charged with the task of reviving the company's failing fortunes. One of his first ventures was to launch a new series entitled *The Problems of War and Reconstruction.* Another was to acquire Harold Bell Wright, the popular novelist, as an author. The medical department was also greatly strengthened. This division's most profitable titles were Austin Flint's PHYSIOLOGY OF MAN, Luther Emmett Holt's DISEASES OF INFANCY AND CHILDHOOD and THE CARE AND FEED-ING OF CHILDREN, Whitridge Williams' OB-STETRICS, Hans Zinsser's TEXTBOOK OF BACTERIOLOGY, and THERAPEUSIS OF INTERNAL MEDICINE edited by Frederick Forchheimer. *The Dollar Library* was started in 1927 and *Appleton Biographies* in 1932.

In 1930 Hiltman announced the merger of D. Appleton Company with the Century Company (q.v.) as D. Appleton-Century Company. W. Morgan Schuster became the president of the new firm. Both firms had been hard hit by the Depression but combined they had vigorous trade, educational, and reference lists. In another move toward consolidation, in 1947 a merger was arranged with F.S. Crofts & Company. This latter firm had been started in 1924 by F.S. Crofts as a college textbook house.

The combined firm of Appleton-Century-Crofts was absorbed by Meredith Publishing Company (q.v.) in 1960. In late 1973 Meredith sold the Appleton medical-nursing, professional and reference lines and college texts to Prentice-Hall, Inc. The Appleton-Century-Crofts imprint is being continued only on the medical-nursing books.

Arbor House Publishing Co., Inc.

Established in 1969 at New York City by Donald I. Fine to publish general fiction and nonfiction.

Architectural Book Publishing Company, Inc.

Founded in 1890 in New York City by Paul Wenzel and called by the firm name of Paul Wenzel, to publish architectural and industrial art books. In 1913 a Scribner salesman, Maurice Krakow, joined with Wenzel in a venture to publish a series of monographs on the works of American architects. Architectural Book Publishing Company, as this new firm was called, published its first book in 1913: THE WORK OF CHARLES A. PLATT. A distinguished list of monographs on the works of famous American architects followed.

The Architectural Book Publishing Company bought the firm of Paul Wenzel and was incorporated in 1924. One of its major projects was the great series on town planning by Werner Hegemann, THE AMERICAN VITRIVIUS-CIVIC ART, in four volumes. Another series was *American Architecture in the 20th Century* in folio-sized volumes, with drawings and photographs of buildings by leading architects. The firm also published the works of Samuel Chamberlain: TUDOR HOMES OF ENGLAND; SKETCHES OF NORTHERN SPANISH ARCHITECTURE; and DOMESTIC ARCHITECTURE OF RURAL FRANCE.

On Wenzel's death in 1938 the firm was reorganized and in 1952 Walter Frese, vice president of the company since 1931, founder of Hastings House (q.v.) and a grandson of Paul Wenzel, became sole owner. A successful series completed recently is a five-volume one by Verna and Warren Shipway on the architecture and decorations of Mexican houses and interiors.

Arco Publishing Company, Inc.

Started in 1937 in New York City by Milton Gladstone. Arco originated the idea of test preparation study books. Its first title was CUSTOMS INSPECTOR-CIVIL SERVICE. In 1946 the firm was incorporated with Gladstone as its president.

Arco now publishes over two hundred test titles in civil service, academic tests, medical tests, professional tests, teachers' tests, and has a back list of over 2,300 general trade titles.

The firm also specializes in health food and nutrition, aviation, nautical books, horse and pet books, crafts and hobby, and self-help books. Its outstanding titles include PRACTICE FOR ARMED FORCES TESTS, HIGH SCHOOL DIPLOMA TESTS, FEDERAL SERVICE ENTRANCE TESTS, VETERINARY NOTES FOR HORSE-OWNERS, and VITAMIN E: KEY TO A HEALTHY HEART.

Arlington House, Inc.

Founded in 1965 by Neil McCaffrey at New Rochelle, New York, to provide books for the Conservative Book Club which he had established a year earlier. In 1968 the firm merged with Computer Applications, which later sold it to the Starr Broadcasting Group. In 1968 Arlington established the Nostalgia Book Club and nostalgia is a growing part of its current list. Another successful Arlington program has been the *Dollar Growth Library*. This includes financial and stock market titles.

Arno Press, Inc.

Founded in 1964 in New York City as a printing broker specializing in short-run reprints. The firm commenced its own reprinting activities late in 1966. Fifty-one percent ownership was sold to The New York Times Company in 1968 and the balance of forty-nine percent in 1971. The major activity of the firm is the publication of reprint series and collections, and since 1972 it publishes the library publications of *The New York Times*. A Biographical Directories program was launched in 1974.

Jason Aronson, Inc.

Established at New York City in 1965. Publishes professional books in medicine and the behavioral sciences.

Ashley Books, Inc.

Established in 1971 at Port Washington, New York, the firm is a small publisher of hardcover general trade books.

Asia Publishing House, Inc.

The New York branch of Asia Publishing House, Ltd., based in Bombay, India. Publishes textbooks, scholarly and reference books in the social sciences and humanities. Affiliated British publisher is Asia Publishing House, Ltd. of London.

Association Press

Established in 1907 at New York City to make and distribute pamphlets and books sponsored by the National Council of Young Men's Christian Associations, by which it is still owned. In the first year it published twenty-eight titles designed "to contribute to the making of a Christian character and to the building of a virile Christian manhood." By 1912 the Press had begun to take a significant place in the community of publishers with a developing reputation in the fields of religious education, camping, recreation, physical education, and group work. Association books were further distinguished by a scientific approach to such issues as sex education, smoking, and alcohol.

Under the directorship of Frederick Morgan Harris the Association list was strengthened with authors as renowned as Harry Emerson Fosdick and Dale Carnegie. Fosdick's THE MEANING OF PRAYER, first published in 1916, sold more than 135,000 copies in two years. By 1972 the combined sales of three Fosdick titles, THE MEANING OF PRAYER, THE MEANING OF FAITH, and THE MEANING OF SERVICE, had reached a sales figure of eight hundred thousand copies. Dale Carnegie's first book, PUBLIC SPEAKING AND INFLUENCING MEN IN BUSINESS, was published in 1926 and was reprinted more than fifty times before it went out of print in 1963. In 1962 it was revised by his widow, Dorothy, under the title THE QUICK AND EASY WAY TO EFFECTIVE SPEAKING.

Succeeding Harris as directors of the Press were Spurgeon M. Keeny, Lawrence K. Hall, James Rietmulder, Stanley I. Stuber, and the present incumbent, Robert W. Hill, who also serves as editor-in-chief. Under Lawrence K. Hall, more than twenty million pieces of USO literature were prepared and distributed to servicemen throughout the world. He was also responsible for launching the books of Evelyn Millis Duvall, among which were WHEN YOU MARRY, co-authored by Reuben Hill, and LOVE AND THE FACTS OF LIFE. The latter title has sold over two million copies in the present revised edition.

The list now contains such best-selling authors as Carl F. Burke and Clarence Jordan. The Burke books include: GOD IS FOR REAL, MAN; TREAT ME COOL, LORD; GOD IS BEAUTIFUL, MAN; and DON'T TURN ME OFF, LORD. The Jordan books are the *Cotton Patch Version* series, PAUL'S EPISTLES, LUKE AND ACTS, and MATTHEW AND JOHN. The popular styles of these two authors, couched effectively in the street gang and Southern idiom respectively, were in the vanguard of the "God is Dead" school of religious writing.

The current list maintains traditional strengths of the Press in such fields as adult education, social work, psychology, religion, sex education, the visual arts, sports, and recreation. A new departure is the publication in Russian of two important novels: Alexander Solzhenitsyn's AUGUST 1914 and Mikhail Bulgakov's THE HEART OF A DOG. The nature of present Association Press lists is one of general trade books with a strong accent on leisure time activities and the arts, including THE LIVELY YEARS: 1920-1973, by Brooks Atkinson and Albert Hirschfeld.

Astor-Honor, Inc.

Established in 1957 at Stamford, Connecticut. The firm is the successor to Ivan Obolensky, Inc., and McDowell, Obolensky, Inc. Publishes juveniles under the Astor imprint, paperbacks under the Honor imprint, and adult titles under the Obolensky imprint.

Atheneum Publishers

Organized in 1959 by Alfred Knopf, Jr., Simon Michael Bessie and Hiram Haydn, as a small publishing house in New York City. The partners soon managed to attract a number of distinguished authors including Jan de Hartog, Ignazio Silone, R.H.S. Crossman, Loren Eiseley, Lovat Dickson, Wright Morris, Randall Jarrell, André Schwarz-Bart, Rose Macaulay, Daniel Boorstin, A.J.P. Taylor, and C.H. Waddington. Within a decade the firm also had many bestsellers, among which were T.H. White's THE MAKING OF THE PRESIDENT, (1960, 1964, 1968, 1972), Frederick Morton's THE ROTHSCHILDS, and James D. Watson's THE DOUBLE HELIX.

In the late 1960s. T.J. Wilson joined the firm as an editor. Following disagreements with his partners, Haydn left the firm in 1964 and subsequently began publishing under the imprint of Harcourt Brace Jovanovich. A subsidiary imprint, Russell and Russell, publishes scholarly reprints. Atheneum also publishes an important list of books for younger readers and a selection of quality paperbacks.

The Atlantic Monthly Press

A division of the Atlantic Monthly Company which also publishes the *Atlantic Monthly,* located in Boston, Massachusetts. The first book to be published by the Press was HEADQUARTERS NIGHTS by Vernon Kellogg in 1917. The Press was an outgrowth of the recognition by Ellery Sedgwick, the editor and proprietor of the *Atlantic,* that a literary magazine breeds books, and the early Atlantic books carried the distinct flavor of New England *belles letters.* Editorially the Press got off to a vigorous start but it soon showed signs of wilting as a business enterprise. As a result Sedgwick entered into an agreement with Little, Brown and Company under which Atlantic Monthly Press books were manufactured and distributed by Little, Brown.

In 1938 Edward Weeks succeeded Sedgwick as editor of the *Atlantic* and he became the dominant influence on the Press too. In the forties and fifties the Press published some of the finest authors in the country: Walter Lippmann, Catherine Drinker Bowen, Charles Nordhoff and James Norman Hall, Edwin O'Connor, Samuel Eliot Morison, Stanley Kunitz, and James Hilton. In the sixties it added to its list Alfred Kazin, George F. Kennan, Katherine Anne Porter, Pauline Kael, George Ball, Robert Coles, Francis Steegmuller, Shirley Hazzard, James Alan McPherson and Frances FitzGerald. The Press, under Peter Davison and Robert Manning, could boast that its authors included two Nobel Prize winners, twelve Pulitzer Prize winners, four National Book Award winners, and one John Newbery Medal winner.

In 1971 the largest single undertaking in the history of the Press was published: ATLANTIC BRIEF LIVES: A BIOGRAPHICAL COMPANION TO THE ARTS, edited by Louis Kronenberger.

Auerbach Publishers, Inc.

Founded in 1957 in Philadelphia, Pennsylvania, by Isaac L. Auerbach. Auerbach is one of the world's largest publishers of reference services on the subject of data processing. It first entered publishing with *Auerbach Standard EDP Reports* which, since that time, have become the standard monthly updated encyclopedic reference service throughout the world for qualitative and quantitative analyses of commercially available computer systems. Later the company expanded its services to provide special subject guides, a series of tutorial publications on computer equipment and use.

Augsburg Publishing House

Founded in 1891 in Minneapolis, Minnesota, by the United Norwegian Lutheran Church to make available to the church English translations of Norwegian religious works. Its history, like that of its parent body, represents a long series of unions. Its publishing activities go back in one strain to the publication in 1841 of an English translation of Martin Luther's CATECHISM and in another strain to *The Lutheran Standard,* founded in 1842. In 1917 Augsburg absorbed the Lutheran Publishing House and the Hauge Printing and Publishing Society, both of which had been established in 1878. In 1961 it merged with the Wartburg Press. Wartburg Press itself was a merger between the Lutheran Book Concern and the Wartburg Publishing House.

Throughout its history Augsburg has been especially active in publishing material for religious education at all age levels, emphasizing theological and devotional material. As part of its extensive music publishing program, Augsburg has also been a leader in the publication of choral material, hymnals, and other religious aids. Since 1931 it has published CHRISTMAS: AN AMERICAN ANNUAL OF CHRISTMAS LITERATURE AND ART. While a number of its periodicals have come and gone through the years, *The Lutheran Standard* has continued uninterrupted since 1842. The publishing house is a service unit of The American Lutheran Church and is governed by a Board of Publication elected by the convention of the Church.

Augustana Book Concern

Founded in 1854 by a Swedish Lutheran pastor, T.N. Hasselquist, who set up a small print shop on the first floor of his house in Galesburg, Illinois. During the course of the next three years he printed a series of tracts and pamphlets. Hasselquist moved his press to Chicago in 1858. In the same year the Swedish Lutheran Publication Society was formed, with Hasselquist's press as its nucleus. Badly hit by internal dissension, the Civil War, and the depression of the 1870s, the Society was sold to three partners, Jonas Engberg, Charles P. Holmberg, and C.O. Lindell, who, in 1874, formed the Engberg-Holmberg Publishing Company.

In 1877 a new publication society, the Ungdomens Vänner, was started at Augustana College and was later incorporated as the Augustana Tract Society. In 1889 the Lutheran Augustana Book Concern was established at the Convention of the Augustana Synod at Rock Island, Illinois, as the official publication house of the Synod. In 1903 its name was changed to Augustana

Book Concern. In 1917 it took over the Engberg-Holmberg Publishing Company. The imprint was superseded by that of Fortress Press (q.v.) in 1962.

J. J. Augustin, Inc., Publisher

Established in 1936 in Locust Valley, New York, as an affiliate of J.J. Augustin, Glueckstadt and Hamburg, West Germany. The German firm dates back to 1632 and has been in the Augustin family since 1775. Augustin publishes scientific monographs and books. Its fields are Byzantine history, archaeology, art and orientalia.

Aurora Publishers, Inc.

A small general trade house established in 1969 at Nashville, Tennessee.

The Ave Maria Press

Founded in 1865 at Notre Dame, Indiana, by the Congregation of Holy Cross under the direction of Reverend Edward Sorin. The Press published until 1970 a weekly Catholic magazine called *Ave Maria*. This evolved into another publication called *A.D. Correspondence*, a biweekly in a newsletter format. The Press also has an extensive paperback book publishing operation and is engaged in the distribution of audio-visual materials.

Avi Publishing Company

Organized in New York City in 1921 for the purpose of publishing a trade journal entitled *The Fruit Products Journal*. The president of this company was C.L. Kehrer. In addition to the *Journal,* the company published a number of books in the food products field. Several of these were concerned with fruit and vegetable juices, wine, and other alcoholic beverages. In 1936 the field of publication was expanded to include books on food freezing and frozen foods. The first of these was THE FREEZING OF FRUITS, FRUIT

JUICES & VEGETABLES by Donald K. Tressler and Clifford Evers.

In 1948 the publication of *The Fruit Products Journal* was discontinued and eight years later the Avi Publishing Company, owned at that time by Florence K. Dorin and Christine S. Dorin, was sold to Donald K. Tressler and Gerald A. Fitzgerald. The company was then incorporated in Connecticut and moved to Westport, Connecticut. In 1958 Fitzgerald sold his interest to Tressler. The publishing activities of the company were greatly expanded to include all types of books on food science, food processing, nutrition, agriculture, and horticulture.

The present officers of the company are president and general manager, Dr. Donald K. Tressler, vice president and editor-in-chief, John J. O'Neil, 2nd vice president, Dr. C. Olin Ball, secretary, Lucy Long, and treasurer, Ella W. Tressler. With the exception of the last, all of these officers are well-known food processing and food service experts.

Avon Books

Founded in New York City in 1939 by Joseph Meyer, Avon is the second oldest paperback publishing house in the United States. The firm was acquired by the Hearst Corporation in 1959.

Avon now comprises six imprints: Avon, Bard, Camelot, Discus, Equinox, and Flare. Bard Books are fiction; Discus, nonfiction and educational books; Camelot, juveniles; Equinox, large format serious paperbacks; and Flare, large format specialized titles for a popular market. The firm publishes numerous paperback originals and in 1972 began publishing large format titles in a variety of sizes in reprint and original editions.

BFL Communications, Inc.

Founded in New York City in 1962 as Books For Libraries, Inc. It was originally organized in the late 1940s as an antiquarian mail order business for institutional libraries and operated in California from 1958 to 1962. The name was changed in 1972 to BFL Communications, Inc., a publicly held company with the majority stock controlled by Samuel Hauben and Harvey Paul Roth.

Books for Libraries Press was organized in 1965 as a facsimile reprint publisher of scholarly materials. The press has over seven thousand titles in print and publishes in eight major reprint series: *Essay Index Reprints, Granger Index Reprints, Short Story Index Reprints, BCL Select Bibliographies Reprints, The Black Heritage Library Collection, Biography Index Reprints, Play Anthology Reprints, American Fiction Reprints.*

BFL Micropublications was set up in 1972 to publish scholarly materials in microform. In 1971 BFL acquired Nash Publishing Corporation (q.v.). A trade division, The Library Press, was begun in 1969 under Melvin J. Lasky and sold in 1973 to Open Court Publishing Company of LaSalle, Illinois.

BNA Books

See, Bureau of National Affairs, Inc.

The Baker & Taylor Co.

Founded in 1828 in Hartford, Connecticut, as D.F. Robinson and Company, booksellers and publishers. In 1834 Henry Z. Pratt entered the firm and in 1835 it moved to New York City and was known as Robinson, Pratt & Co. From then until 1885 its name changed a number of times, reflecting the changes in partnerships: Pratt, Woodford and Co.; Farmer, Brace & Co.; Pratt, Oakley and Co.; Oakley Mason and Co.; Mason, Baker and Pratt; and The Baker & Taylor Co.

The last-named partnership, between James S. Baker and Nelson Taylor, was formed in 1885. In the same year it started a book publishing division. For the next twenty-nine years a number of fine books were published. Among them were COOPER'S VIRGIL; GREENLEAF'S ENGLISH GRAMMARS; COMSTOCK'S OUTLINES OF CHEMISTRY, PHYSIOLOGY, BOTANY, MINERALOGY, and NATURAL HISTORY OF BIRDS, the first elementary works on these sciences published in this country; also DR. PETER BULLION'S ENGLISH

GRAMMAR, and BULLION'S LATIN and GREEK series of textbooks. Herbert S. Baker became the firm's president in 1912. Two years later he sold his book list to Doubleday and decided to devote the firm's activities to book jobbing.

In 1948 the company moved to Hillside, New Jersey. For many years William A. Hunter was president of the company and was very instrumental in its present growth. Upon his death in 1965, Jack D. Willis was named president, and he holds that position today. The firm is now one of the largest book wholesalers, and is operated as a division of W.R. Grace & Co. In the last ten years, The Baker & Taylor Co. has grown from one location in New Jersey to five plants located strategically throughout the United States: the Eastern Division in Somerville, New Jersey; Midwest Division in Momence, Illinois; Western Division in Reno, Nevada; Southwest Division in Clarksville, Texas; and Southeast Division in Commerce, Georgia. An Inspection Center for Books and Media is also operated in Los Angeles, California.

Baker Book House

Established in 1939 in Grand Rapids, Michigan. A modest program was carried on until 1949 when a full-fledged publication division was established. Baker publishes books promoting evangelical Christianity and a scripture-based life-view. A major part of the firm's list consists of reference works and textbooks for seminaries, Bible schools and colleges and ministers.

Among Baker's publishing achievements are THE TWENTIETH CENTURY ENCYCLOPEDIA OF RELIGIOUS KNOWLEDGE edited by Everett F. Harrison, THE NEW SCHAFF-HERZOG ENCYCLOPEDIA OF RELIGIOUS KNOWLEDGE, BAKER'S BIBLE ATLAS by Charles F. Pfeiffer, BAKER'S DICTIONARY OF THEOLOGY edited by Everett F. Harrison, BAKER STUDIES IN BIBLICAL ARCHAEOLOGY, DAVIS DICTIONARY OF THE BIBLE, Cruden's UNABRIDGED CONCORDANCE, and the recently published BAKER'S DICTIONARY OF CHRISTIAN ETHICS, edited by Carl F.H. Henry.

Walter H. Baker Company (Baker's Plays)

Descended from the Herbert Sweet Company, Boston, Massachusetts, play publishers founded in 1845. In 1851 the Sweet Company was acquired by William H. Spencer, who carried on the business until his death in 1870. Later the firm was merged with Lee and Shepard. The play publishing division was managed until 1885 by George M. Baker and Company. In 1892, Walter H. Baker, brother of George M., formed a partnership with Frank E. Chase as Walter H. Baker Company. In 1920 Chase sold his interest to Theodore Johnson who became sole owner of the company after Baker's death in 1929. Johnson retired in 1951. The firm took over the assets of Fitzgerald Publishing Company.

Now known as Baker's Plays, the firm is directed by M. Abbott Van Mostrand.

Ballantine Books, Inc.

Founded in New York City in 1925 by Ian Ballantine with Bernard Shir-Cliff, Bruno Stefanoni, and Houghton Mifflin Company as partners. The company was sold to Intext in 1969.

Ballantine's growth has been based on two significant publishing concepts: the publication of paperbound originals and the development of books in categories and series: science fiction, war, and Westerns. In 1967 Ballantine successfully introduced the paperbound gift book with Sierra Club's IN WILDERNESS IS THE PRESERVATION OF THE WORLD. The gift book series was expanded to include art books and craft books at $3.95. NORMAL ROCKWELL was the first art book and TIE AND DYE the first of the craft books.

In 1968 Ballantine introduced the illustrated, larger format paperback when it issued the first four books in the *Illustrated History of World War II* series. The books combined picture and text in a fully integrated well-designed book. The success of the four books led to the introduction of the series into regular publication in 1969. The illustrated concept was expanded in 1971 to an auto series and one on World War I. In 1969 a new imprint was launched—Walden Books—

aimed primarily at a college audience. Regional publishing was started in 1969 with two books on the Pacific Northwest. Their success led to the creation of a new imprint, Comstock Editions, which is distributed exclusively in the western United States. In 1970 Beagle Books was launched to gain an entry into the women's market. On January 1, 1973, Ballantine Books was purchased by Random House.

Ballinger Publishing Company

See, J.B. Lippincott Company.

Bancroft-Whitney Company

See, Hubert Howe Bancroft; also, Lawyers Cooperative Publishing Company.

Banks-Baldwin Law Publishing Company

Founded in 1804 in New York City by David Banks as Gould and Banks. The name was later changed to Banks & Company and then to Banks Law Publishing Company. In 1913 William Edward Baldwin established the Baldwin Law Book Company in Louisville, Kentucky. This company published the official statutes of Kentucky. In 1919, while continuing to operate his Kentucky company, Baldwin moved to Cleveland, Ohio, and set up the Baldwin Law Publishing Company of Ohio. The major publication of this new company was its 1921 edition of the OHIO CODE.

In 1924, Baldwin moved to New York City and became the president of Banks Law Publishing Company. Two years later he purchased the Banks Law Publishing Company from the Banks family. In 1933 he consolidated the operations of his three companies under the title of Banks-Baldwin Law Publishing Company, as an Ohio corporation. The company was the official printer for the court reports of many states. Until the late 1920s, when publication was taken over by the Government Printing Office, the Banks Law Publishing Company also published the official edition of the UNITED STATES SUPREME COURT REPORTS. Currently, Banks-Baldwin Law Publishing Company specializes in the publication of local statutes and legal practice services

for the State of Ohio and the Commonwealths of Kentucky and Pennsylvania.

Bantam Books, Inc.

Organized in 1945 in New York City by Ian Ballantine, with Grosset and Dunlap and Curtis Publishing Company as major shareholders. Bantam Books went on sale with twenty-five paperback titles, each priced at twenty-five cents, with the promise of four more titles a month to follow. Ian Ballantine had a flair for promotion, and Bantam (a name suggested by a young Grosset editor, Bernard Geis) placed emphasis from the start on point-of-sale displays, cooperative advertising, blowup posters, and promotion tie-ins.

But by 1950 the paperback industry was in trouble and Bantam's problems were heightened by Ian Ballantine's departure in 1952. To replace him the board of directors in 1954 chose Oscar Dystel, former editor-in-chief of *Coronet.* Under Dystel the company cut its wholesale inventories and fashioned a new publishing and distributing concept. In 1964 Curtis sold its thirty percent holdings to Grosset and Bantam became a wholly-owned subsidiary of Grosset and Dunlap. In 1968 the National General Corporation purchased Grosset and Dunlap, thereby acquiring both Bantam Books and Transworld, Bantam's British subsidiary.

Bantam's boldest venture in original publishing is the *Bantam Extra,* or instant books. The first Extra, THE REPORT OF THE WARREN COMMISSION ON THE ASSASSINATION OF PRESIDENT KENNEDY, sold one and a half million copies. Bantam's dictionary series includes six foreign language dictionaries and an English one. Bantam's first venture in quality paperbacks was the *Pathfinder Editions,* started in 1963 with twenty-five titles. The school and college market is served by over seven hundred and fifty titles, including science, mathematics, literature, language, and drama. In 1970 a new division was formed, Premium Ventures, renamed in 1973 Premium Marketing Division, responsible for premium, mail order, and other special bulk sales.

Early in 1974 Bantam was sold to American Financial Corporation. In November 1974 American Financial sold Bantam outright to IFI International, an Italian holding company.

Barclay House Books

Established in 1968 at Chatsworth, California. A paperback division of American Art Enterprises, Inc. Issues a limited annual list of both fiction and nonfiction.

Alfred Smith Barnes (1817-1888)

A.S. Barnes & Company, Inc.

Founded in 1838 in Hartford, Connecticut, by Alfred Smith Barnes with Charles Davies as a partner. Barnes had learned the book trade as an employee of D.F. Robinson & Company, then one of the largest publishers of schoolbooks in America.

The firm's only initial asset was a series of mathematical texts prepared by Davies. Barnes promoted the series by acting as his own traveler, going directly to schools. In 1840 the concern was moved to Philadelphia, Pennsylvania, and five years later to New York City. Here Barnes began to issue a series of schoolbooks that made the firm well-known in the country. Among them were Richard Green Parker and James M. Wat-

son's READERS, Stephen W. Clark's ENGLISH GRAMMAR, James Monteith's GEOGRAPHY series, Theodore Parker's NATURAL PHILOSPHY, and Fulton and Eastman's BOOKKEEPING. Later he combined his textbooks into a complete series known as *The National Series of Standard School Books.*

In addition to textbooks Barnes ventured into hymn books and books on physical education, history, and pedagogy. The PLYMOUTH COLLECTION OF HYMNS AND TUNES compiled by Henry Ward Beecher and published in 1855 was the first of many hymn books that bore the Barnes imprint. A series of books for teachers, beginning with David Perkins Page's THEORY AND PRACTICE OF TEACHING, grew into the *Library of Professional Pedagogy.*

In 1848 Davies sold his interest in the firm to Edmund Dwight from whom it was acquired by Barnes' brother-in-law, Henry L. Burr.

From 1859 until 1865 the firm was known as Barnes and Burr. The name of A.S. Barnes & Company was adopted in 1865. In the same year Barnes' son, Alfred Cutler Barnes, became a partner. He succeeded his father as head of the firm in 1888. Two years later the Barnes imprint was merged with that of the American Book Company. In 1909 the firm was revived as the A.S. Barnes Company with Henry Burr Barnes as president and with a list of educational titles acquired from E.L. Kellogg and Company. It was again reorganized in 1918 under John Barnes Pratt as president. The following year Pratt took over the firm's most profitable lines—hymn books and books on physical education, sports, folk dance, and allied fields.

The company was incorporated in 1930. Rinehart and Company acquired an interest in it in 1951 but resold its equity four years later. In 1958 the A.S. Barnes Company was purchased by Thomas Yoseloff and it is now managed by Thomas and Julien Yoseloff.

Barnes & Noble Books

Established in 1874 by C.M. Barnes in Wheaton, Illinois, as a jobbing business in second-hand schoolbooks. It moved to Chicago within a year, where it was incorporated in 1894 as the C.M. Barnes Company. The founder retired in 1902 and his son, W.R. Barnes, became president. John W. Wilcox joined the firm in 1898 and ten years later the firm became the Barnes-Wilcox Company.

In 1917 W.R. Barnes sold his interest in the company and came to New York City where he bought a partnership in Noble and Noble, which then became Barnes & Noble. W.R. Barnes was president of the new firm and G. Clifford Noble its secretary-treasurer. In 1929 Noble withdrew, selling his stock to John Wilcox Barnes, grandson of C.M. Barnes, and J.W. Wilcox. John Barnes became president of the company in 1942.

The firm did not enter the publishing field until 1931 when it issued AN OUTLINE OF THE HISTORY OF EUROPE, 1500-1848, by Henry W. Littlefield. This publication led to Barnes & Noble's most famous program, *The College Outline Series*. John W. Barnes died in 1964 and five years later the company was sold to Amtel, Inc. In 1971 Harper & Row acquired the imprint, and reorganized it as Barnes & Noble Books, a wholly-owned subsidiary.

Clarence L. Barnhart, Inc.

Founded at Bronxville, New York, by Clarence Lewis Barnhart, distinguished American editor and lexicographer. Beginning with the AMERICAN COLLEGE DICTIONARY in 1948, Barnhart has planned and edited some of the finest contemporary reference works. They include the NEW CENTURY CYCLOPEDIA OF NAMES, WORLD BOOK ENCYCLOPEDIA DICTIONARY, the Thorndike-Barnhart series of school dictionaries, and THE BARNHART DICTIONARY OF NEW ENGLISH SINCE 1963. Barnhart's son, Robert K., serves as managing editor.

Richard W. Baron Publishing Co., Inc.

A small publishing house in New York City, whose general trade books are distributed by E.P. Dutton.

Barre Publishing Company, Inc.

Started in 1956 at Barre, Massachusetts, as an outgrowth of the *Barre Gazette*, a weekly newspaper that has been published continuously since 1834. The *Gazette* was purchased in the mid-fifties by Alden P. Johnson. The first book, A HISTORY OF THE EARLY AMERICAN CIRCUS, appeared in 1956 bearing the *Barre Gazette* imprint. The present imprint was adopted in 1962. Johnson operated the company as sole proprietor and editor-in-chief until 1969. When Alden Johnson died in 1972, Ronald P. Johnson, who joined the firm in 1964, succeeded him as president.

Beginning as a publisher of local histories, photographic essays, and New Englandiana, Barre has expanded its list over the years and now offers books in the fields of art, history, marine, and travel. In cooperation with the American Antiquarian Society it produces important reference works and bibliographies of the Colonial period.

Barre, along with its subsidiary, The Imprint Society, was purchased in May 1974 by Crown Publishers, Inc., but will continue to operate independently as a wholly-owned subsidiary.

Barron's Educational Series, Inc.

Established in Brooklyn, New York, in 1939 as Barron's Textbook Exchange by Manuel H. Barron and Edward R. Barron. The partnership was dissolved in 1943 and a new partnership was created with Manuel H. Barron and Gloria M. Barron as the principals. Publishing commenced at this time with two series: *Barron's Regents Exams and Answers* and *College Review Books*. The first of the Review Books was the ESSENTIALS OF GREEK AND ROMAN CLASSICS, published in 1946.

In 1945 the company was reorganized as Barron's Educational Series, Inc., with headquarters at Great Neck, New York. The publishing program was expanded to include college guidance, social studies, foreign language, translations from foreign classics, and a series of theater classics for the modern reader. In 1965 the company was again relocated, this time at Woodbury, New York.

Barron's 450 titles in print include series on *Politics of Government, Regents Exams and Answers, Book Notes, Critical Studies, College and High School Reviews, Profiles In-Depth of American Colleges, College Board Achievement Tests, Foreign Language Verbs,* and *Theater Classics.*

Basic Books, Inc., Publishers

Founded in 1951 at New York City by Arthur J. Rosenthal, its president and editor-in-chief for the next twenty years.

During its early years of publishing, Basic Books adopted a method of marketing that made it possible to form a house dedicated to scholarly backlist titles and partially eliminate the pressure of the hunt for the bestseller. This method was to start a specialized book club in each new area of publishing *before* issuing lists in that field. These clubs included Basic Books Service (behavioral sciences), The Library of Science (physical and natural sciences), and The Readers' Subscription (humanities). At the time of their sale in 1960 to Crowell Collier Macmillan, the membership of Basic Books' book clubs totaled over one hundred and fifty thousand members.

Basic Books' first area of specialization was psychiatry and psychoanalysis, and its list of authors soon became a Who's Who in that field. Authors who appeared on Basic Books' list in the 1950s included Sigmund Freud, Jean Piaget, Gardner Murphy, Karl Menninger, and Franz Alexander.

At the end of its first decade of publishing, two brilliant editors joined Basic Books. Leon Swirsky, one of the founders of *Scientific American,* became science editor, and Irving Kristol, co-founder of *Encounter* magazine, became editor for the social sciences.

In the course of the 1960s, largely as a result of the efforts of Irving Kristol, executive vice president, Basic Books began to move solidly into all areas of the social sciences. Sociology, especially, came to feature prominently on the list, but political science, economics, and history also became areas of interest. By 1969, when Basic Books was acquired by Harper & Row, it was a publishing firm covering the full range of the social sciences, with an annual list of some seventy to seventy-five titles.

Arthur Rosenthal resigned in 1972 to accept the directorship of Harvard University Press, and Erwin A. Glikes, formerly a dean at Columbia University and then executive vice president of Basic Books, became president and publisher of the company.

William L. Bauhan, Inc.

Established in 1929 at Peterborough, New Hampshire. Specializes in regional and scholarly books on New Hampshire.

Beacon Press

"In the autumn of 1824, thirty or forty of the leading men of Boston (Massachusetts), members of the Anonymous Association, had met to consider the importance of distribution of Unitarian books . . . The result was the American Unitarian Association, formed by the Berry Street Conference of Ministers on May 25, 1825. It proposed 'to publish and distribute books and tracts inculcating correct views of religion in such a form and at such a price as shall afford all an opportunity of becoming acquainted with Christian Truth.' " (*See:* Jeanette Hopkins, BOOKS THAT WILL NOT BURN, Boston, 1954.)

A number of books were published during those early years by Crosby, Nichols and Company. Then, in 1854, the executive committee of the Association, under S.K. Lothrop, voted to raise $50,000 "to be employed in the printing, distribution, and sale of religious books and pamphlets." That same year the Association issued its first book under its own imprint—Cyrus Augustus Bartol's GRAINS OF GOLD—and plans were made for three special series: *The Biblical Library, The Theological Library,* and *The Devotional Library.*

In 1902 Livingston Stebbins (appointed agent by AUA President Samuel A. Eliot) created a new imprint, Beacon Press, for "publishing books dealing with ethical, sociological, philanthropic, and similar subjects, as well as those of a more strictly religious nature." However, the output of the Press continued to be modest until 1945 when Melvin Arnold was appointed as its director. With him the Press entered an era of growth and strength. He initiated such series as *Studies in Freedom and Power, Studies in Church and State, Ancient Roots of Modern Thought, The Beacon Schweitzer Series, Wit and Wisdom Series, Harvard Studies in Altruism,* and *Studies in Soviet Tyranny.*

In 1956 Thomas Bledsoe replaced Arnold as director but he left two years later in the midst of mounting financial difficulties.

Beacon Press had been incorporated in 1954, but it was not able to publish as a Unitarian house without subsidy, and in 1958 Beacon Press was again set·up as a part of the Unitarian Department of Publications. Edward Darling became the acting director and a three-man committee was empowered to run the Press. With the merger of the Unitarians and the Universalists in 1961, Edward Darling was appointed director of the Publications Department of the Unitarian Universalist Association. In 1962 Gobin Stair was appointed director of Beacon Press and during the following few years the Press grew in size and importance. In 1972 Beacon Press was once again set up as a separate entity, but this time still within the Association, with its own board of directors responsible for the editorial and financial affairs.

Beacon Press has a tradition of bold and responsive publishing which has been asserted with such titles as Paul Blanshard's AMERICAN FREEDOM AND CATHOLIC POWER, George C. Stoddard's KREBIOZEN: THE GREAT CANCER MYSTERY, and THE PENTAGON PAPERS/THE GRAVEL EDITION. The Press has published Herbert Marcuse, Barrington Moore, Jurgen Habermas, Raymond Firth, and others. Its mission is to discover, develop, and make public ideas that further understanding of how our society operates and how values are reflected in patterns of social obligation. Thus the Press provides resources for those attempting either constructive change within the society or personal adjustment to the dilemmas it poses.

The Beacon Press is also a liberal press, willing to present the idea that is controversial or unpopular, or in some cases suppressed. A liberal religious press such as this one must accept the risks of freedom so that it can act as a channel of communication from the individual through to the public of prophetic ideas.

As a religious press, Beacon Press seeks to maintain its independence and to do this it must make its own way. This requires highly skilled distribution and business methods and unusual and innovative editorial decisions.

Books such as CONCERNING DEATH by Earl Grollman, BEYOND GOD THE FATHER by Mary Daly, AGING IN AMERICA by Bert Smith, as well as the standbys in the Beacon backlist of ONE-DIMENSIONAL MAN by Herbert Marcuse and STUDIES ON THE REFORMATION by Roland Bainton, demonstrate the active participation of Beacon Press in current affairs and ideas. Well-written, successful books sell and return a healthy income with which new books are sought, edited, and distributed. The Press is required to be nonprofit by its charter and yet it also must break even, and this it must achieve by the excellence of its books and the support of the readers.

Behavioral Publications, Inc.

Established in 1965 at New York City by Sheldon R. Roen to publish the *Community Mental Health Journal.* In 1969 it became a wholly-owned subsidiary of Human Sciences, Inc. Patrick McLoughlin joined Behavioral Publications as president in late 1969. Describing itself as the human sciences publisher, Behavioral expanded into related fields. Currently it publishes nine journals, children's books, and five tests in the fields of psychology and education. Its books are distributed to the trade through Independent Publishers Group.

Behrman House, Inc.

Established 1920 in New York City as Behrman's Jewish Book House. Specializes in religious books on Jewish themes.

Bellman Publishing Company

Founded in 1934 in Boston, Massachusetts. Specializes in subscription and reference books in the educational and guidance field.

Belmont Tower Books, Inc.

Established in 1960 at New York City with Harry Shorten as publisher and president of the company. The company publishes paperback reprints and originals.

Matthew Bender & Company, Inc.

Founded in Albany, New York, in 1887 by Matthew Bender, a former law book salesman. He was soon joined by two of his three sons, Matthew, Jr., and John T. The firm was incorporated in 1915. About this time it also acquired the stock of Banks & Company and the Fallon Law Book Company. Many leading New York State and national publications were produced, including COLLIER ON BANKRUPTCY, BENDER'S FORMS FOR THE CONSOLIDATED LAWS, and many other volumes of text and forms.

Matthew Bender, Jr. succeeded his father as president of the firm while John T. became the editorial and marketing head. Toward the end of the 1920s the third generation of Benders began to appear on the scene. Matthew Bender III brought along a classmate from Yale, Richard Reiner, and together with John T. Bender, Jr., effected the rapid development of the enterprise in several directions, including initiation of most of the current bestselling publications: MOORE'S FEDERAL PRACTICE, RABKIN AND JOHNSON'S FEDERAL INCOME, GIFT AND ESTATE TAXATION, and CURRENT LEGAL FORMS. Bender's FORMS FOR THE CIVIL PRACTICE and the fourteenth edition of COLLIER ON BANKRUPTCY were the first standard law books to be published in loose-leaf form.

In 1963 the Benders sold their interest to The Times Mirror Company but John T. Bender continued for a time as president of Bender. Later Matthew T. Birmingham, Jr., was appointed to succeed him. Under Birmingham's leadership, within a few years, the company's business, staff and sales force were doubled.

Benefic Press

Founded in 1960 as the publishing arm of the Beckley-Cardy Company of Westchester, Illinois. The Beckley-Cardy Company had entered publishing in 1913 with supplementary reading books for the primary grades and various manuals and guides to help teachers. In 1926 this publishing activity was expanded to include basic textbooks. The first of these was the *Adventures in Storyland,* a series consisting of basic readers for the primary grades. Later series were in the fields of science, health, spelling, and social studies. As the publishing volume grew it was decided to establish a new imprint for the book division. The Benefic Press thus came into being in 1960. Among Benefic's most successful series have been the *Teenie Weenie, Cowboy Sam,* and *Dan Frontier* books.

The Benjamin Company, Inc.

Organized in New York City in 1948 by Roy Benjamin as The Benjamin Agency, a sales promotion company. It became a partnership when his brother, Ted Benjamin, joined in 1953. The Benjamin Agency developed the concept of insert advertising in Pocket Books and other leading paperbound lines. The sale of books in bulk for premium and promotion uses developed into an important part of the company's operations during the late 1950s, and in 1958 the name was changed to The Benjamin Company. In 1964 the partnership was replaced by a corporate structure, under the name of The Benjamin Company, Inc. The publishing ventures of the company date from this period.

The company, best described as a publishing/marketing organization, combines the traditional functions of a publisher with the sales goals of its business and association clients. It provides books and booklets for public relations, sales promotion, advertising, incentive, public service, and promotional programs. It specializes in the creation and production of hardcover and softcover editions which are published for sponsoring firms or in association with national organizations. The published book is used as a promotional tool by the sponsor and is sold to the trade, either as an imprint of The Benjamin Company, or under the aegis of one or more leading distributing publishers, such as Simon & Schuster, Inc., Harper & Row, Prentice-Hall, Scribner's, etc.

Benco Editions, which are either original books or other publishers' titles adapted for premium or promotional use, identify one imprint of The Benjamin Company. Another major imprint is that of "A Benjamin Company/Rutledge Book" for those titles prepared by the Rutledge Books division of Ridge Press, Inc., for publication by The Benjamin Company, Inc.

Among the more important books published recently for commercial or association sponsors are: HISTORICAL TREASURY OF AMERICAN GUNS (Remington Arms), THE FIRST FIFTY YEARS (National Football League), CAVALCADE OF BROADCASTING (National Association of Broadcasters), CONSUMER'S BUYING GUIDE (Better Business Bureau), MAXWELL HOUSE COFFEE COOKBOOK (General Foods), HOW TO MANAGE YOUR MONEY (Marine Midland and Mellon Banks), CAMPING (Ford), BRINGING UP BABY (Gerber), COMPLETE CHEESE COOKBOOK (Kraftco), OLYMPICS (Toyota), PORTABLE ELECTRIC COOKERY (Sunbeam), HOW TO GAIN FINANCIAL INDEPENDENCE (National Association of Mutual Savings Banks) and YOU (National Bank of North America). The creation of a series of books and booklets forming a health and welfare line has been a major Benjamin development of the 1970s.

One of the more innovative functions of the company involves the publication of "adapted"

books, booklets, condensations or excerpts from other publishers' titles. Millions of special edition books have been used by promotion-minded firms. Recent examples include Gillette's use of MY TURN AT BAT (Pocket Books), Mueller's adaptation of PASTA (Pyramid Books), Jacobsen's excerpt of "Make Friends With Your Lawn" from Jerry Baker's PLANTS ARE LIKE PEOPLE (Nash), and Lark Cigarette's giveaway of BARBECUE COOKBOOK (TRP).

W.A. Benjamin, Inc.

Founded in 1962 in New York City by William A. Benjamin. The backers included several outstanding physical scientists including John D. Roberts and David Pines. The company's program was restricted to the physical sciences and mathematics. Sometime later, the company went public through a stock offering. In 1970 Benjamin became a wholly-owned subsidiary of Addison-Wesley Publishing Company and the company headquarters were moved to Menlo Park, California. The company also acquired a new president, David C. Bull.

The company carries on intensive publishing in its four original fields: physics, chemistry, biology, and mathematics. In addition it has added psychology with BASIC PSYCHOLOGY by Howard H. Kendler, and electronics with ELECTRONICS FOR SCIENTISTS by H.V. Malmstadt and C.G. Enke. Outstanding textbooks in chemistry include CHEMICAL PRINCIPLES by R.E. Dickerson, H.B. Gray, and G.P. Haight, Jr., and BASIC PRINCIPLES OF ORGANIC CHEMISTRY by J.D. Roberts and M. Caserio. In the life sciences J.D. Watson's MOLECULAR BIOLOGY OF THE GENE and A.L. Lehninger's BIOENERGETICS have found wide acceptance. Introductory physics texts include PHYSICS I by E. Huggins and INTRODUCTORY PHYSICS by R. Karplus.

In addition to specific subject areas the company is committed to research and publication in the field of innovative methods and materials. One such program is the *Keller Plan for a Personalized System of Instruction.*

Chas. A. Bennett Co., Inc.

Established in 1899 in Peoria, Illinois, by Charles A. Bennett for the publication of the *Manual Training Magazine*. In 1903 the imprint "The Manual Arts Press" was adopted. Two years later it published its first book, Murray's PROBLEMS IN WOODWORKING. The business was incorporated in 1909. The magazine was discontinued in 1939. In the same year, L.L. Simpson succeeded the founder as president of the company.

In 1949, the firm's fiftieth anniversary, the name was changed to Chas. A. Bennett Co., Inc. Upon L.L. Simpson's death in 1952 Richard H. Simpson became president. The firm specializes in school texts for shop, crafts, art, and homemaking.

W.S. Benson & Company

Established in 1919 at Austin, Texas, the company publishes textbooks and supplementary readers in both English and Spanish, principally for the elementary grades.

Robert Bentley, Inc.

Established in 1949 at Cambridge, Massachusetts. Publishes a limited list principally dealing with automobiles and sports cars; also books by and about Montessori.

Benziger Bruce and Glencoe, Inc.

Incorporated in Delaware in 1972 as a wholly-owned subsidiary of Macmillan, Inc. The firm was created by the merger of three imprints: Benziger, Inc., Bruce Publishing, and Glencoe Press, to form a broad-based educational publisher. No books are published under the joint imprint; rather, books are published under each of the imprints.

Benziger was founded in 1853 as an American branch of the Swiss firm which had been established in Einsideln, Switzerland, by Joseph Charles Benziger in 1792. In 1860 J.N. Adelrich Benziger and Louis Benziger began to publish books in America. A Cincinnati branch was opened in 1860, a Chicago branch in 1887, a San Francisco branch in 1929, and a Boston branch in 1937. In 1867 the Holy See conferred on the firm the title of "Printers to the Holy Apostolic See." Besides religious books, travel books, and text books, Benziger published an illustrated Catholic monthly entitled *Benziger's Magazine*. The firm also published the highly successful *New Century Catholic Readers*. Benziger continued under the original family ownership until 1969, when it was acquired by Macmillan, Inc. Benziger publishes a wide range of materials for the entire elementary and high school markets. Major series include: *The Word is Life,* a series for Catholic religious education; *The Benziger Readers,* developed on the linguistic approach to reading; and *The Web of Life,* a series of environmental readers.

Bruce Publishing Company was founded in 1891 in Milwaukee, Wisconsin, by William George Bruce. Bruce was also originally a Catholic publisher but later developed a strong list in vocational and industrial education. Bruce was acquired by Macmillan, Inc. in 1968. Bruce concentrates on vocational and industrial education where its strongest titles include BASIC ELECTRONIC SYSTEMS TECHNOLOGY, COMPREHENSIVE GENERAL SHOP and THE PIPEFITTER'S AND PIPEWELDER'S HANDBOOK.

Glencoe Press was founded as a division of Macmillan Publishing Company, Inc., to publish for the junior college market. It rapidly became a major publisher of books on criminal justice, fire science, and business education. Some of its titles, such as HUMAN NATURE by James F. Downs, MICROBIOLOGY AND HUMAN DISEASE by George A. Wistreich and Max D. Lechtman, and MYTH AND THE AMERICAN EXPERIENCE by Nicholas Cords and Patrick Gerster, are widely used in both two-year and four-year colleges.

Norman S. Berg, Publisher

Established in 1965 at Dunwoody, Georgia, a small personal publishing house issuing general trade books including fiction, biography, history, poetry and juveniles.

Berkley Publishing Corporation

Established in New York City in 1954 by Charles Byrne and Frederick Klein. They began by producing two magazines which were discontinued at the end of ten months. Then, in 1955, they started Berkley Books in paperback which were distributed at first by American News Company and later by Kable News Company. Eventually three imprints were developed: an adult line called Berkley Medallion Books, a juvenile line called Berkley Highland, and a third called Diamond Books, which was short-lived.

In 1965 G.P. Putnam's Sons bought the firm and it has been operating as a division of Putnam's since that time. The president of the corporation is Stephen Conland, who has held the office since 1958.

The major Berkley series are in the areas of mysteries and Japanese novels. A hardbound line has also been launched, with PLAIN SPEAKING: AN ORAL BIOGRAPHY OF HARRY S. TRUMAN by Merle Miller as its most notable title.

Berlitz Publications, Inc.

Founded in 1878 in Providence, Rhode Island, by Maximilian D. Berlitz to publish books for the Berlitz School of Languages. The firm specializes in self-instruction language books, travel phrase books, and phonographic materials for language-learning. The firm was acquired by Crowell Collier & Macmillan in 1965. It is now a division of Macmillan, Inc.

Bethany Fellowship, Inc.

Founded 1946 at Minneapolis, Minnesota. Publishes evangelical, religious books.

The Bethany Press

Founded in 1954 at St. Louis, Missouri, as the Publications Department of Disciples of Christ. Specializes in hymnals and inspirational books.

Better Homes & Gardens Books

Established in 1930 at Des Moines, Iowa, Better Homes and Gardens Books is the consumer book division of Meredith Corporation, publisher of *Better Homes & Gardens* magazine. The division publishes books related to or derived from the magazine and dealing with all phases of home and family services, including cooking, gardening, sewing, decorating. Meredith Corporation also operates the Better Homes & Gardens Family Book Service, a book club, and conducts an active mail order department.

The Bibliographical Society of America

Founded in 1904 at New York City and incorporated in 1927. *The Papers* of the Society are published quarterly. In 1937 the Society completed the publication of Joseph Sabin's DICTIONARY OF BOOKS RELATING TO AMERICA. The Society has also sponsored publication of THE UNION LIST OF NEWSPAPERS (1937); the BIBLIOGRAPHY OF INTERNATIONAL CONGRESSES AND CONFERENCES (1938); INCUNABULA IN AMERICAN LIBRARIES, A SECOND CENSUS (1940); THE COST BOOKS OF TICKNOR AND FIELDS (1949); A BIBLIOGRAPHY OF OLIVER WENDELL HOLMES (1953); SUPPLEMENT TO SEYMOUR DE RICCI'S CENSUS OF MEDIEVAL AND RENAISSANCE MANUSCRIPTS IN THE UNITED STATES AND CANADA (1962);

Frederick Goff's INCUNABULA IN AMERICAN LIBRARIES, A THIRD CENSUS (1964); Margaret Stillwell's THE AWAKENING OF INTEREST IN SCIENCE DURING THE FIRST CENTURY OF PRINTING: 1450-1550 (1970); Donald Eddy's A BIBLIOGRAPHY OF JOHN BROWN (1972); THE BEGINNING OF THE WORLD OF BOOKS, 1450 to 1470 — A CHRONOLOGICAL SURVEY OF THE TEXTS CHOSEN FOR PRINTING (1972); Denis Woodfield's SURREPTITIOUS PRINTING IN ENGLAND, 1550 to 1640; Goff's INCUNABULA IN AMERICAN LIBRARIES — A SUPPLEMENT TO THE THIRD CENSUS; and the ongoing project, BIBLIOGRAPHY OF AMERICAN LITERATURE.

Biblo & Tannen Booksellers & Publishers, Inc.

Founded in 1928 in New York City by Jack Biblo and Jack Tannen as an antiquarian bookshop. In 1957 the firm entered the field of reprint publishing. Among the outstanding reprints published by the firm are Sir Arthur Evans' THE PALACE OF MINOS, the COOK ZEUS in three volumes, and books by Franz Boas and Benedetto Croce. A subsidiary, the Canaveral Press, has reissued the works of Edgar Rice Burroughs.

Binfords & Mort, Publishers

Founded in 1891 by Peter Binford and his brother Maurice in Portland, Oregon, as the Metropolitan Printing Company. In 1930 they published their first book, CATHLAMET ON THE COLUMBIA, a little frontier classic by Thomas Nelson Strong. Peter set the entire book by hand and it is still in print.

In 1938 the name of the firm was changed to Binfords & Mort, Publishers, partly at the suggestion of Thayer Hobson, president of William Morrow, then the firm's distributor in the eastern United States, and partly to include Ralph Mort, a nephew, who had become a partner. The firm's output steadily increased during this period and many of its titles became classics in Northwest literature: BEFORE THE COVERED WAGON by Philip Parrish, GENERAL HISTORY OF OREGON by Charles H. Carey, WILD FLOWERS OF THE PACIFIC COAST by Leslie Haskin, SWIFT FLOWS THE RIVER by Nard Jones, and the Oregon, Washington, and Nevada volumes in the *American Guide Series*.

In the 1930s Peter's son, Thomas, and Maurice's sons, Ormond and Maurice, Jr., entered the firm. Among the major projects initiated by the second generation Binfords are: HISTORY OF WASHINGTON by Cecil Dryden, SCENIC GEOLOGY OF THE PACIFIC NORTHWEST by Leonard Ekman, EAST OF THE CASCADES by Phil F. Brogan, HISTORY OF MONTANA by James M. Hamilton, FISHWHEELS OF THE COLUMBIA by Ivan Donaldson, and ANCIENT TRIBES OF THE KLAMATH COUNTRY by Carrol B. Howe.

In 1973 the publishing firm of Binfords & Mort was purchased by Thomas Binford, who will continue publishing books pertaining to the Pacific Northwest.

Walter J. Black, Inc.

Started in New York City in 1923 by Walter J. Black as the Plymouth Publishing Company. Black originally undertook to publish one-volume editions of the works of William Shakespeare for sale by mail; successful in this venture, he gradually expanded his list of classical authors. In 1941 Black established the Classics Club, offering selections from classical authors in one of the first specialized book clubs. In 1942 he started the Detective Book Club, which offers its members a monthly volume containing three complete mystery and detective novels. In 1950 the complete works of Zane Grey were offered to readers by mail.

After moving the company's headquarters to Roslyn, New York, in 1953, Walter J. Black died in 1958 and the presidency of the company was assumed by his son, Theodore M. Black. Since then three new book clubs have been established: The Erle Stanley Gardner Mystery Library (1964), The Golden Giants DeLuxe Classics

(1968), and the Inner Circle (1971). In 1971 the operations of the firm were extended to Canada.

Black Sparrow Press

Established in 1968 at Los Angeles, California. Issues *avant-garde* poetry and prose.

John F. Blair, Publisher

Set up in 1954 at Winston-Salem, North Carolina, a small privately-held publisher of general trade books.

Bloch Publishing Company

Founded in 1854 by Rabbi Isaac Meyer Wise and his brother-in-law, Edward Bloch, as Bloch and Company, in Cincinnati, Ohio. Bloch is the oldest Jewish publisher in the United States.

Bloch's earliest publications were prayer books, Bibles, and Hebrew-English texts for religious schools. For the increasing number of German-speaking Jewish immigrants Bloch published THE AMERICAN ISRAELITE in English and DIE DEBORAH in German. Other notable publications of the early period were Wise's prayerbook, MINHAG AMERIKA, and THE ESSENCE OF JUDAISM, M. Mielziner's THE JEWISH LAW ON MARRIAGE AND DIVORCE and INTRODUCTION TO THE TALMUD. In 1880 the *Proceedings* of the Rabbinical Literary Association of the Reform Rabbis were issued under the title *The Hebrew Review*. At the same time popular literature—poetry and drama—was not neglected. In 1873 a monthly for children entitled *The Sabbath Visitor* was launched.

Charles E. Bloch entered the business in 1878. Under his management a branch was established in Chicago, Illinois, where, in 1891, he began publishing *The Reform Advocate* under the editorship of Emil G. Hirsch. In 1901 the activities of the Bloch Printing and Publishing Company in Chicago and Bloch and Company in Cincinnati were combined and moved to New York City under the name of Bloch Publishing Company.

Bloch's contribution to Jewish publishing is reflected in the important classics that it has published: THE SUFFERING OF THE JEWS DURING THE MIDDLE AGES by Leopold Zunz, revised and edited by George A. Kohut (1907), Ibn Gabirol's MIBHAR PENINIM by A. Cohen (1925), the popular edition of the PIRKE ABOT with an introduction and notes by I. Gorfinkle (1913), H.G. Enelow's MENORAT-HA-MAOR (1929-32) in four volumes, and Meyer Waxman's A HISTORY OF JEWISH LITERATURE (1930) in four volumes.

In addition to publishing, Bloch acts as a major supplier of Judaica from all publishers as well as distributor for European and Israeli publishers. Under the direction of the fourth generation Bloch, Charles E., the firm steadfastly continues to dignify the publication and sales of books of Jewish as well as general interest from its new location in New York City.

Benjamin Blom, Inc.

Established in 1963 at New York City as a general trade house. Specializes in reprints.

Clark Boardman Company, Ltd.

Established in 1916 at New York City by P. Clark Boardman, Alvin Weisker, and Edward S. Morse, all of whom were former associates of Lawyers Co-operative Publishing Company. The company was for many years a dealer and supplier of law books, with publishing a minor activity. However, around 1967 the emphasis shifted to publishing. The firm is currently active in publishing in most areas of the law. Specialized related series of law books are being published in the following subject areas: intellectual property, New York practice, criminal law, securities regulation, and real property law.

In 1973 the company acquired a wholly-owned subsidiary, Trade Activities, Inc., since 1902 publisher of various books and magazines for the patent and trademark bar. The Trade Activities publications are being continued in their existing format.

Board of Educational Ministries of the American Baptist Churches of the U.S.A.

See, Judson Press.

The Bobbs-Merrill Company, Inc.

Founded in 1838 in Indianapolis, Indiana, by Samuel Merrill and E.H. Hood as a bookstore. In 1839 Merrill acquired Hood's interest. On Merrill's death the business passed to his son, Colonel Samuel Merrill, Jr. After the Civil War the name was changed several times: Merrill, Field & Company; Merrill, Hubbard & Company; and Merrill, Meigs and Company. In 1885 it merged with Bowen, Stuart and Company to become the Bowen-Merrill Company. In 1890 the Colonel retired and his stock was transferred to his son, Charles W. Merrill. In 1895 W.C. Bobbs became president of the company and in 1903 his name replaced Bowen's in the title.

As Merrill, Meigs and Company the firm's first venture into publishing was in 1861 with REPORTS OF THE SUPREME COURT OF INDIANA, edited by Benjamin Harrison. It soon developed a strong legal division which was expanded in 1899 through the acquisition of the legal titles of Houghton Mifflin and the American Publishers Company of Norwalk, Ohio. In addition to DIGESTS and STATUTES for several states, Bobbs-Merrill published THOMPSON'S COMMENTARIES ON THE LAW OF NEGLIGENCE and COMMENTARIES ON THE LAW OF PRIVATE CORPORATIONS, both in six volumes, ELLIOTT'S RAILROADS in five volumes, and CONTRACTS in eight volumes.

The firm's trade list began with the publication of James Whitcomb Riley's THE OLD SWIMMIN' HOLE in 1884. Charles Major's WHEN KNIGHTHOOD WAS IN FLOWER was the first of a series of bestsellers that owed much of their success to spectacular promotion. Bobbs-Merrill was one of the earliest publishers to take full-page advertisements in newspapers to announce forthcoming books. Maurice Thompson's ALICE OF OLD VINCENNES, THE WONDERFUL WIZARD OF OZ by Frank Baum, and THE CIRCULAR STAIRCASE by Mary Roberts Rinehart became phenomenal successes through such advertising.

Bobbs headed the firm until 1926 when he was succeeded as president by J.J. Curtis. Curtis was responsible for reviving the fortunes of the company with a fresh spate of popular books including John Erskine's THE PRIVATE LIFE OF HELEN OF TROY and Bruce Barton's two notable books, THE MAN NOBODY KNOWS and THE BOOK NOBODY KNOWS. In 1929 the firm went public to raise the funds necessary to acquire the equity of Bobbs from his estate.

Curtis died in 1931 and four years later D. Laurance Chambers was appointed president. Chambers initiated such distinguished series as *The American Lake, American Trails, Notable American Trials* and *Makers of American Tradition.* With Hiram Haydn as editor, in the early fifties Bobbs-Merrill brought out many popular fiction and nonfiction titles.

In 1958 Howard W. Sams acquired the company and proceeded to reinvigorate all of its departments. The juvenile department was strengthened through the energetic promotion of the *Childhood of Famous Americans* series, the *Raggedy Ann* books, and the introduction of new projects such as *The Best Children's Literature.* Sams' interest in scientific reference books was reflected in such titles as MODERN SCIENCE DICTIONARY by A. Hechtlinger and THE AUDIO CYCLOPEDIA by H.W. Tremaine. The firm also started publication of the highly profitable THE JOY OF COOKING by Irma Rombauer and Marion Rombauer Becker.

Expanding further in the textbook field, Bobbs-Merrill acquired the Public School Publishing Company, the C.A. Gregory Publishing Company, the Liberal Arts Press, and the elementary list of Charles Scribner's Sons. In 1960 a paperback line, Charter Books, was launched. In 1965 Leo C. Gobin was appointed president of Bobbs-Merrill and a vice president of Howard W. Sams & Company, Inc. The Odyssey Press and Pegasus Division of Western Publishing Company were acquired by Bobbs-Merrill in 1970.

Bobley Publishing

Set up in 1958 in Woodbury, New York, as a division of Illustrated World Encyclopedia, Inc., by Edward Bobley and Harry W. Bobley. In addition to ILLUSTRATED WORLD ENCYCLOPEDIA, the firm publishes a Book-of-the-Year, a Science Annual, ILLUSTRATED LIBRARY OF LITERARY TREASURES, and other educational reference books. The ownership is closely held in the Bobley family.

Bollingen Series

A series of scholarly books on psychology, mythology, and related subjects sponsored by the Mellon Foundation and published by Pantheon Books until 1967 and by Princeton University Press since then.

Book-of-the-Month Club, Inc.

Established in New York City by Harry Scherman and Max Sackheim in 1926. Scherman and Sackheim had been in the advertising business where one of their accounts was the *Little Leather Library*. Scherman's idea was to launch a club whose members would buy books regularly. The principles upon which it was organized were "convenience, reading fulfillment, guidance by experts, and continuity." The partners invited Robert K. Haas to join the new enterprise.

The first panel of judges included H.S. Canby, Dorothy Canfield Fisher, Heywood Broun, Christopher Morley, and William A. White. The first selection in 1926 was sent to 4,750 subscribers, who had agreed to take twelve books a year at the publisher's prices. Later the required minimum number of books was reduced to four and one book was given free for every two books purchased. Premium books were also offered to attract new members. During the early 1930s Haas and Sackheim left and Scherman carried on alone.

In the 1930s another innovation was introduced when the club began to print its own editions, paying royalties to publishers and a fee for the use of their plates. Business increased substantially after World War II and the Book-of-the-Month Club became a major force in the publishing world. Scherman died in 1970 and Axel Rosin, who had been president since 1960, became chief executive. In 1973 Rosin became chairman of the board of directors and Edward Fitzgerald was elected president.

The Book-of-the-Month Club is the most influential book club in the United States, with a membership of over one and a quarter million.

In March 1974 the BOMC undertook to manage and operate for Time Incorporated Book Clubs, Inc. the Sports Illustrated Book Club and the Fortune Book Club.

Books For Libraries, Inc.

See, BFL Communications, Inc.

Boston Technical Publishers

Organized in 1963 at Boston, Massachusetts, to publish scientific and technical books, it distributes the publications of the British Institute of Electrical Engineering.

Thomas Bouregy & Company, Inc.

A New York City publisher of fiction, Gothics and juveniles. Its affiliate, Airmont Publishing Company, is a reprint house.

R.R. Bowker Company

Founded in 1872 in New York City by Frederick Leypoldt as *The Publishers and Stationers' Weekly Trade Circular* (renamed *Publishers Weekly* in 1873). Leypoldt was a bibliographic genius who originated such valuable book tools as PUB-

LISHERS TRADE LIST ANNUAL and AMER-
ICAN EDUCATIONAL CATALOG. In 1879
Leypoldt sold his business to his associate, Richard Rogers Bowker, and in 1911 the firm was
renamed R.R. Bowker Company. When Bowker
died in 1933 Frederick Melcher became president.
In 1968 the firm was acquired by Xerox Corporation and it is now part of Xerox Education
Group.

Apart from *Publishers Weekly* and *Library
Journal,* Bowker publishes magazines and books
for the library and book world. Among them
are: BOOKS IN PRINT; SUBJECT GUIDE TO
BOOKS IN PRINT; *Previews;* LITERARY
MARKET PLACE; AMERICAN BOOK PUB-
LISHING RECORD; CHILDREN'S BOOKS IN
PRINT; EL-HI TEXTBOOKS IN PRINT;
AMERICAN LIBRARY DIRECTORY; PUB-
LISHERS TRADE LIST ANNUAL; THE
READER'S ADVISER; THE BOWKER AN-
NUAL OF LIBRARY AND BOOK TRADE
INFORMATION; AMERICAN BOOK TRADE
DIRECTORY; PAPERBOUND BOOKS IN
PRINT; and AMERICAN MEN & WOMEN
OF SCIENCE.

Bowmar

Established 1966 at Glendale, California, as a
publisher of juvenile books and multi-media materials.

Boyd & Fraser Publishing Company

A small publisher of college texts and supplementary reading materials, established in 1970 at San
Francisco, California.

Bradbury Press, Inc.

Established in 1968 at Scarsdale, New York, as
a small publisher of children's books. They are
distributed by Henry Z. Walck, Inc.

Branden Press, Inc.

Located at Boston, Massachusetts, a publisher
of general trade books.

Brandon Books

Established 1962 at Chatsworth, California, as a
paperback division of American Art Enterprises,
Inc.

Charles T. Branford Company

Established in 1925 at Newton Centre, Massachusetts. The firm took over the Medici Society of
America and Ralph T. Hale & Company, successor to Hale, Cushman & Flint. Specializes in
books on arts and crafts, natural history, gardening, and sports.

George Braziller, Inc.

Founded in New York City in 1954 by George
Braziller as a publishing house specializing in
hardback reprints. Earlier, Braziller had estab-
lished two book clubs, the Book Find Club in
the 1940s and the Seven Arts Society in the 1950s.
By 1955 he began to turn, as had Alfred A.
Knopf before him, to Europe for manuscripts.
Interested in the anti-novel movement, he began
to publish Nathalie Sarraute, Claude Simon,
Claude Mauriac, Yves Berger, and Julien Cracq.
Later he became the American publisher of Jean-
Paul Sartre.

Braziller has developed a number of series in
the fields of literature and the arts among which
are: *The Library of Illuminated Manuscripts,
Arts of Mankind, Great Drawings of the Louvre
Museum, Great Draughtsmen, Great Ages of
World Architecture, Masters of World Architec-
ture, Makers of Contemporary Architecture, New
Directions in Architecture, Planning and Cities,
Great Religions of Modern Man, Patterns of
Myth, Cultures of Mankind, American Epochs,*

American Culture Series, and *Braziller Series of Poetry.* In 1965 Georgy Kepes was engaged to edit a series entitled *Vision and Value,* based on his famous seminars on communication. More recently ecology and environment have dominated the list with such titles as THE ARTS OF THE ENVIRONMENT; FREDERICK LAW OLMSTED AND THE AMERICAN ENVIRONMENTAL TRADITION; THE DOMINATION OF NATURE; and THE FUTURE OF THE OCEANS.

Brigham Young University Press

Established in 1967 at Provo, Utah, with Ernest L. Olson as director. It publishes books under three imprints: the University Press for the scholar, Young House for books in religion, and University Publications for the lay reader. Because Brigham Young University is owned by the Church of Jesus Christ of Latter-Day Saints a number of Press titles are particularly directed to members of the Church. Church histories and doctrinal books form an important segment of the Press list. It also publishes extensively in the scholarly book field.

Broadman Press

Founded in 1934 at Nashville, Tennessee, as the publishing arm of the Sunday School Board of the Southern Baptist Convention. Broadman was coined from the last names of John Albert Broadus and Basil Manly, Jr., secretary and president respectively of the first Sunday School Board. The first books to bear this imprint appeared in 1934, although the general book publishing program of the Sunday School Board goes back to 1898 when it issued its first trade book, THE STORY OF YATES THE MISSIONARY. Only twelve books were published from 1898 to 1913 and only thirty-five new general titles were added in the next eight years. From 1922 to 1930 the number of books published ranged from seventeen to twenty-eight titles per year. Broadman now releases about sixty new titles each year.

Major publishing programs since 1956 include ENCYCLOPEDIA OF SOUTHERN BAPTISTS, a two-volume reference work; THE BIBLE STORY BOOK; Broadman Readers Plan, a book club founded in 1964; the twelve-volume BROADMAN BIBLE COMMENTARY, and the one-volume TEACHER'S BIBLE COMMENTARY. Starbooks and Inner-Circle Books are other series published by Broadman.

Broadman's publications are designed for the general religious market. Specifically denominational books are published under the auspices of the Convention Press, also owned and operated by the Sunday School Board.

Broadside Press

A Detroit, Michigan, publisher specializing in poetry by Black authors. Also publishes books of criticism of Black poets as well as biographies.

Bro-Dart Publishing Company

Publishing division of Bro-Dart, Inc., a general wholesaler of books to the trade. The publishing program includes bibliographic works for schools and libraries. General offices are at Williamsport, Pennsylvania.

The Brookings Institution

Founded in 1927 as an independent organization with headquarters in Washington, D.C. devoted to non-partisan research, education, and publication in economics, government, foreign policy, and the social sciences generally. Its principal purposes are to aid in the development of sound public policies and to promote public understanding of issues of national importance. The Institution was incorporated in 1927 through a merger of the Institute for Government Research, founded in 1916, the Institute of Economics, founded in 1922, and the Robert Brookings Graduate School of Economics and Government, organized in 1924. The consolidated institution was named in honor of Robert Somers Brookings, a St. Louis businessman whose leadership had shaped the earlier organizations.

The publishing activities of the Institution are restricted to manuscripts arising from the Institution's own research and take the form of books, research reports, *Brookings Papers on Economic Activity,* and reprints of selected articles by staff members from professional journals and other publications. Publications arise from the Institution's three research programs (economics, government, and foreign policy). Many appear in series: *Studies in the Regulation of Economic Activity; Studies in Defense Policy; Studies of Government Finance; Studies in Presidential Selection; Studies in Social Economics; Studies of Unionism in Government;* and *Studies in Wage-Price Policy.*

See, Charles B. Saunders, Jr., THE BROOKINGS INSTITUTION: A FIFTY-YEAR HISTORY (Brookings, 1966).

Brooks/Cole Publishing Company

See, Wadsworth Publishing Co., Inc.

Wm. C. Brown Company, Publishers

Established in 1944 by William C. Brown in Dubuque, Iowa. Brown started by purchasing the publishing rights to twenty-six college level texts, including Frank Hill and Roland Searight's A STUDY OUTLINE AND WORKBOOK IN THE ELEMENTS OF MUSIC and the *Jaques Picture-Key Nature Series.* The company expanded during the 1950s and 1960s, keeping pace with the upsurge in the education industry.

In the 1960s the *Brown Physical Education Activities* series was introduced and the company entered such other major growth disciplines as data processing and career education. At the same time traditional lines in art, music, education, biology, English, and speech were strengthened.

Brown has two subsidiary imprints. Kendall/ Hunt Publishing Company provides specialized

publishing service in guide books, manuals, and workbooks, and the Wm. C. Brown Reprint Library specializes in reprinting scholarly works in limited editions for colleges and libraries.

Brown University Press

Founded in 1932 at Providence, Rhode Island. The list of the Press is devoted primarily to scholarly monographs and to books about Rhode Island and New England. Among its major scholarly series are: *Brown Egyptological Studies* and *Brown University Slavic Reprints.* Blake studies, which are a specialty of the Press, include A BLAKE DICTIONARY by S. Foster Damon.

Brunner/Mazel, Inc.

Established in 1945 at New York City. Publishes a limited list of books for professionals in the fields of psychology, psychiatry, neurology, social work and special education.

Bucknell University Press

Organized in 1969 as a branch of the Associated University Presses, Inc., of Cranbury, New Jersey. The scholarly activities of the Press take place at Bucknell University; the production, copyediting, and distribution of books are done in Cranbury. James F. Carens was the first director of the Press; Michael Payne is its current director.

In addition to a general list of scholarly publications, the special publishing programs of the Press are: the series, *Irish Writers,* edited by Professor Carens and consisting of studies of about forty Irish writers of the nineteenth and twentieth centuries; *The Primates,* a series on the naturalistic behavior of non-human primates, edited by Douglas K. Candland; and the *Bucknell Renaissance Texts,* edited by Guido A. Guarino, containing English translations of works by Italian humanists.

Bureau of National Affairs, Inc.

Developed at Washington, D.C., in 1933 as an outgrowth of the *United States Daily,* a national newspaper of record, established in 1926 by David Lawrence. When the *Daily* became the weekly *U.S. News* (later *U.S. News and World Report*) the Bureau of National Affairs, Inc. was spun off as a separate organization charged with the mission of carrying on in-depth reporting of Washington developments in specific fields: patents, trademarks and copyright; labor management relations; and the Supreme Court. The first BNA book was a PRIMER OF LABOR RELATIONS published in 1937.

In 1946 U.S. News Publishing Corporation sold Bureau of National Affairs, Inc., to a group of its employees. Since that time it has been an independent company owned wholly by its employees. In 1947 BNA had one of its proudest moments when THE NEW LABOR LAW, containing an extensive analysis and complete legislative history of the Taft-Hartley Act, was published on the same day the Act was enacted over President Truman's veto.

Many BNA books have gained acceptance as definitive works in the fields of law, labor-management relations, management, accounting, and government regulation. These include HOWELL's COPYRIGHT LAW by Alan Latman; SUPREME COURT PRACTICE by Robert L. Stern and Eugene Gressman; HOW ARBITRATION WORKS by Frank and Edna Asper Elkouri; ROBERTS' DICTIONARY OF INDUSTRIAL RELATIONS by Harold S. Roberts; SILVERBERG'S HOW TO TAKE A CASE BEFORE THE NATIONAL LABOR RELATIONS BOARD by Kenneth C. McGuiness; and MEDIATION AND THE DYNAMICS OF COLLECTIVE BARGAINING by William E. Simkin. For many years BNA Books and the UNESCO have jointly published a compilation of laws and international treaties concerned with copyright protection: COPYRIGHT LAWS AND TREATIES OF THE WORLD. A similar compilation dealing with design laws, DESIGN LAWS AND TREATIES OF THE WORLD, is published jointly by BNA Books and Sansom-Sijthoff, a Dutch publisher.

In 1971 BNA Books launched its first textbook series, *Labor Relations and Social Problems,* prepared by The Labor Law Group.

Burgess Publishing Company

Founded in 1925 in Minneapolis, Minnesota, as a medium-sized publisher. Its organization followed the success of a book for an ecology class at the University of Minnesota which had been published by Burgess-Beckwith, Inc.

At first the firm tended to specialize in laboratory manuals and syllabi and to maintain a somewhat regional approach to its publishing program. But by the 1930s the firm was publishing college textbooks on a national scale. The 1960s saw Burgess enter the field of instructional systems for individualized learning. Audio-Tutorial Systems was set up as a division in 1964. In recent years the firm has begun to publish books in the social sciences and the humanities.

Cadillac Publishing Company, Inc.

Established in 1940 in New York City. The firm took over the titles of Ken Publishing Company, Inc. In 1973 the company launched a successful one-volume encyclopedia. Specializes in reference books for the mail order market.

Cahners Books

Founded in 1968 as a division of Cahners Publishing Company of Boston, Massachusetts, publishers of trade magazines. Although there was no formal book operation before 1968, Cahners magazine divisions had generated more than forty specialized books for the audiences of their magazines. On an informal basis book production and sales grew over the years. The first step toward integrating the various books into a single list was taken in 1968 with the agreement to co-publish with Gower Press of London, England, four general business management books.

Cahners Books specializes in books of interest to managers, technical people, and educators in food service and lodging, manufacturing, transportation and distribution, building and construction, electronics, engineering, marketing, packaging, materials handling, purchasing, plastics, and glass making and ceramics. It also publishes books sponsored by professional and trade associations, such as the Standards Engineers Society and the Society of the Plastics Industry, Inc., and its list includes a large line of annual directories. Cahners books can be roughly divided into two general areas: career development and career education. Many of the titles are used as textbooks in colleges, special high school programs, vocational schools, and for on-the-job training. The company is currently producing new titles at the rate of fifty a year and importing another twenty-five new titles per year.

Cahners also distributes titles published by Herman Publishing Service, Industrial Education Institute, Conover-Mast, Industrial Publications, *Institutions/Volume Feeding Magazine,* Medalist Publishing, Rank-Wharfedale, and the Barnes & Noble Professional Engineering Career Development Series. In addition, it operates special-interest book clubs for business and industry.

Callaghan & Company

Founded in 1864 in Chicago, Illinois, by Bernard Callaghan under the name of Callaghan and Cutler, a legal publishing firm for the Middle West. In 1870 the name was changed to Callaghan & Cockroft, but the business was completely destroyed by the Chicago fire of 1871. Callaghan resumed business as Callaghan and Company in 1873. In 1916 E.I. Cudahy purchased control of the company. In 1951 E.I. Cudahy was succeeded in the presidency by Michael Cudahy. The Cudahy Publishing Company and John Byrne Company are wholly-owned subsidiaries.

Cambridge Book Company

Organized in 1942 at New York City. Now a division of The New York Times Media Corporation, the company publishes textbooks and related materials at the elementary, high school and junior college levels.

Cambridge University Press, American Branch

Established in New York City in 1949. The Cambridge University Press for nearly a century had been represented in the United States by The Macmillan Company. The parent press was established in Cambridge, England, in 1521 when John Siberch, University Printer, issued his first book. A succesor, John Legate, produced in 1591 the first CAMBRIDGE BIBLE, giving Cambridge its claim to be the oldest Bible publisher in the world. The American Branch, of which F. Ronald Mansbridge was the first manager, is one of the two editorial offices of Cambridge University Press, the other being still at Cambridge, England.

The Cambridge University Press imprint is associated with notable books in certain fields, especially mathematics, history, classics, philosophy, and the natural sciences. The alltime bestseller of the Press is THE NEW ENGLISH BIBLE, copublished with Oxford University Press, which has sold over five million copies, but it is best known for its great multi-volume series and its histories: CAMBRIDGE ANCIENT HISTORY; MEDIEVAL; and MODERN — the last now superseded by the CAMBRIDGE NEW MODERN HISTORY. Other multi-volume works include Joseph Needham's SCIENCE AND CIVILIZATION IN CHINA, THE MATHEMATICAL PAPERS OF ISAAC NEWTON, QUILLER-COUCH-DOVER WILSON SHAKESPEARE TEXTS, SHAKESPEARE SURVEY, and BIBLIOGRAPHY OF ENGLISH LITERATURE.

The American Branch maintains a special department for the promotion of Cambridge scholarly journals, the number of which has doubled in a little over twenty years. The list now includes journals edited in the United States, among them being *Comparative Studies in Society and History, International Journal of Middle East Studies,* and *Language in Society.* One of the outstanding authors associated directly with the American Branch was George Gamow, whose MR. TOMP-KINS introduced thousands of students painlessly to the mysteries of atomic physics. A publication which proved even more popular in the United States than in England was C.P. Snow's Rede Lecture, THE TWO CULTURES AND THE SCIENTIFIC REVOLUTION.

In January 1971 Jack Schulman succeeded F. Ronald Mansbridge as director of the American Branch.

The Cardavon Press, Inc.

Established 1929 at Avon, Connecticut. Publishes fine illustrated editions for The Limited Editions Club, The Heritage Club, and others.

Carolrhoda Books, Inc.

Established in 1969 at Minneapolis, Minnesota, a small publisher of juvenile picture story books.

Catholic Press

Currently a division of Consolidated Book Publishers at Chicago, Illinois. Issues Catholic Bibles, missals, prayer books, and religious reference books in English, Spanish, French, Portuguese and Italian languages.

The Catholic University of America Press

Established in 1939 in Washington, D.C. and incorporated in 1941. In 1971 it became affiliated with Consortium Press of the McGrath Publishing Company. The Press publishes only in four

fields: language and letters, society in historical perspective, philosophy, and religion. Several series in philosophy and religion are well established: *The Fathers of the Church,* translations of patristic writings into modern English; *Studies in Christian Antiquity; Studies in Philosophy* and *The History of Philosophy,* edited by John K. Ryan.

The Press also publishes three journals: *The American Ecclesiastical Review, The Catholic Historical Review,* and *Anthropological Quarterly.*

The Caxton Printers, Ltd.

Founded in 1903 and incorporated in 1907 in Caldwell, Idaho, by Albert E. Gipson. The firm was an outgrowth of a small farm paper called *The Gem State Rural* which Gipson had first published in 1895. In the 1920s this paper was sold to the Cowles Publishing Company of Spokane, Washington, and Caxton, then under the direction of J.H. Gipson, son of Albert Gipson, began to produce a small but regular book list—as many as five titles a year.

In 1937 a fire destroyed the entire plant and business. Publishing was soon resumed, however, and by 1952 Caxton had a solid backlist of two hundred seventy-five titles, of which nearly half consisted of books on Western Americana. Caxton was one of the first of the small, independent, regional publishers to bring out a regional title illustrated in full color. The book, STEENS MOUNTAIN by Russell Jackman, Charles Conkling and John Scharrf, won critical acclaim. Another title, SNAKE RIVER COUNTRY by Bill Gulick, was equally successful.

Now a multi-division corporation, the publishing operation is directed by Gordon Gipson.

Century House, Inc.

Established in 1942 at Watkins Glen, New York, Century is a small publisher specializing in Americana, art, music, antique and hobbies books.

Chanticleer Press, Inc.

Set up in 1941 in New York City by Paul Steiner as a subsidiary of the British publishing house of Adprint, Ltd. In 1952 Steiner assumed full ownership of the company.

The Press was a pioneer in the packaging of books, especially illustrated books in the fields of natural history and art. Among such creations are *Living Animals of the World,* in seven volumes; *The Continents We Live On,* in six volumes; *The Worlds of Science,* in seven volumes; and the single-volume, THE BRITANNICA EN-CYCLOPEDIA OF AMERICAN ART.

The firm also sponsors international co-editions, having pioneered in this field and been among the first, possibly the first, to develop the practice of joint printings with text changes.

Charter Communications, Inc.

Located in New York City, the parent conglomerate company whose other divisions and companies include: Ace Books, Inc., Dauntless Books, Inc.; G & D Publications Inc.; Harle Publications, Inc.; U.S. Electronic Publications; Charter School Books.

The Chatham Press, Inc.

Established in 1967 at Chatham, Massachusetts, by John V. Hinshaw for the purpose of publishing regional Cape Cod books. The company moved to Old Greenwich, Connecticut, in 1969 and expanded its list to include regional titles from other areas.

Christopher Harris joined the company in 1970 and in 1971 the firm moved to offices in Riverside, Connecticut. In 1973 George Rinehart became vice president for sales and marketing; Harris was elected president of the company and Hinshaw became the publisher. Chatham Press books are distributed to the trade by E.P. Dutton & Co., Inc.

Chatham publishes approximately eighteen titles a year, ranging from National Park guides to large format, pictorial works.

The first American Geography, 1784

Chelsea House, Publishers

Established in 1966 at New York City. Specializes in multi-volume reference works in history, law and art. Also publishes general trade books in association with various publishers.

Chelsea Publishing Company, Inc.

Established in 1944 in New York City, a small publishing house that issues scientific and mathematical books.

Chemical Publishing Company, Inc.

Started in 1934 when Harry Bennett bought the backlist of the defunct Chemical Publishing Company of Easton, Pennsylvania. Dorothy Fracht purchased the company in 1951. In 1964 Anita Wiener became a partner. The company, now located in New York City, publishes and imports scientific and technical books with emphasis on chemistry.

Childrens Press

Organized in 1945 as a wholly-owned division of Regensteiner Publishing Enterprises, Inc. of Chicago, Illinois. It began as a publisher of coloring books, cut-out books, and picture books in 1946. Early in 1948 it began to publish books for school libraries. Childrens Press was one of the first publishers to offer factual materials for primary grades with its *True Book* and *I Want To Be* series, and was the first trade book publisher to offer a library binding. Other major publishing programs consist of *Young People's Science Encyclopedia, Enchantment Of* series, and the *You* series for junior and senior high schools.

The Press acquired Melmont Publishers in 1959, Elk Grove Press in 1972, and Golden Gate Press in 1973.

The Child Study Press

Publishing division of the Child Study Association which was founded in 1888 at New York City. Issues general and professional books and pamphlets on child development, family life, parent education and counseling, etc.

Chilton Book Company

Established in 1955 as the Book Division of Chilton Company, a publisher of trade journals and magazines, based in Philadelphia, Pennsylvania.

Beginning with several automotive books and a small core of titles purchased from Conover-Mast, the division expanded with the acquisition in 1958 of Greenberg: Publisher. In 1964 the company was divided into the Trade Book Division with Nic. Groenevelt as general manager and the Educational Book Division with Charles Heinle, who had been the Book Division's general manager since 1955, in charge. By 1967 all the titles from the Educational Book Division, other than foreign language textbooks, had been transferred to the Trade Book Division. During that year the Trade Division changed its name from Chilton Books, a Division of Chilton Company, to its present name.

The Educational Book Division was incorporated in 1969 as the Center for Curriculum Development. It then expanded its program of developing printed and audio-visual materials for the teaching of foreign languages in schools and colleges. The Center distributes all publications of Librairie Marcel Didier, Max Hueber Verlag, and several other foreign publishers. Transferred to Rand McNally on a licensing arrangement in 1972, the Center was relocated in Chicago, Illinois.

Nic. Groenevelt continued as general manager and vice president until 1971 when he was succeeded by Bruce Andresen. In 1972 William D. Byrne was appointed to succeed Andresen. In 1973 Jack Kelly became editor-in-chief.

Chilton's major publishing programs include: *Chilton's Creative Crafts Series,* a complete line of consumer and vocationally-oriented automotive repair manuals, and individual repair guides for

American and imported cars, motor cycles and recreational vehicles; an expanding selection of books on modern journalism techniques; and a collection of titles in various technical fields, such as instrumentation.

Christian Publications, Inc.

Founded in 1886 at Harrisburg, Pennsylvania, by A.B. Simpson to publish books on missionary work. Its first publication was Simpson's THE KING'S BUSINESS. In 1912 Simpson relinquished ownership and the firm was incorporated as The Christian Alliance Publishing Company. It was renamed Christian Publications, Inc., in 1932. The firm publishes denominational books for The Christian and Missionary Alliance.

The Christian Science Publishing Society

Founded in its present form by a deed of trust executed in 1898 by Mary Baker Eddy, the discoverer and founder of Christian Science. Its offices are in Boston, Massachusetts. Though a predecessor of the same name formed in 1886 carried out somewhat similar functions, the history of the present Society begins with the deed of trust in 1898. The purpose of the Society was defined as one "of more effectively promoting and extending the religion of Christian Science." The publication of Mary Baker Eddy's own works, including SCIENCE AND HEALTH WITH KEY TO THE SCRIPTURES and the CHURCH MANUAL is a separate function not related to the Society. The Society's own first publication was the CHRISTIAN SCIENCE HYMNAL.

The books and pamphlets published by the Society deal almost exclusively with the history, teachings, organization, and healing outreach of Christian Science. An exception is to be found in the booklet reprints of special series of *Christian Science Monitor* articles which have dealt with such subjects as ecology, diplomacy, narcotics, youth, and the judiciary. These reprints, as well as the INDEX TO THE CHRISTIAN SCIENCE MONITOR, are published by University Microfilms of Ann Arbor, Michigan.

In addition to supplying Christian Science Reading Rooms throughout the world, the Society acts as distributor of Bibles, Bible commentaries, and dictionaries published by other firms. A long-established relationship with Oxford University Press has resulted in the latter's producing Bibles to match all editions of SCIENCE AND HEALTH. A few books originally published by commercial publishers have also been taken over by the Society. These include Erwin D. Canham's COMMITMENT TO FREEDOM, DeWitt John's THE CHRISTIAN SCIENCE OF LIFE, and the three-volume life of Mary Baker Eddy by Robert Peel.

Chronicle Books

Established in 1966 at San Francisco, California, as the book division of The (San Francisco) Chronicle Publishing Company. Publishes a small general nonfiction list annually in both cloth and paper bindings, specializing in Californiana and Western Americana.

Citadel Press, Inc.

Started in New York City in 1939 by Abraham Lieberman and Morris Sorkin as the Remainder Book Company dealing in publishers' overstocks. In 1940 the firm entered publishing under the imprint of Citadel Press with the publication of low-priced cloth reprints. In 1959 the company discontinued its remainder operation and began to devote itself to publishing. In the same year a quality paperback reprint line was launched. In 1966 Allan J. Wilson became a partner in the firm.

Citadel specializes in books about films, the occult, theater, and psychology. Fiction is occasionally published. In 1970 the company was acquired by Lyle Stuart, Inc., and it now operates as a wholly-owned division.

Arthur H. Clark Company

Founded in 1902 in Cleveland, Ohio, by Arthur H. Clark, a naturalized American who, as a member of the board of directors of Burrows Brothers, had been principally responsible for their publication of the monumental JESUIT RELATIONS AND ALLIED DOCUMENTS in seventy-three volumes. Clark specialized in the publication of significant documents and monographs relating to the American past. His first project was THE HISTORIC HIGHWAYS OF AMERICA, OR THE HISTORY OF AMERICA AS PORTRAYED IN ITS HIGHWAYS OF WAR, COMMERCE, AND SOCIAL EXPANSION. Between 1904 and 1907 he published Reuben Gold Thwaites' EARLY WESTERN TRAVELS, 1748-1846, in thirty-two volumes, a project which won immediate acclaim.

Over the next twenty-five years Clark produced a larger selection of significant Western titles than any other publisher in the United States. Notable among these were John James Audubon's WESTERN JOURNAL, 1849-1850 (1905); Emma Helen Blair's INDIAN TRIBES OF THE UPPER MISSISSIPPI VALLEY AND REGION OF THE GREAT LAKES (2 vols., 1911); James A. Robertson's LOUISIANA UNDER THE RULE OF SPAIN, FRANCE, AND THE UNITED STATES (2 vols., 1911); Charles Knowles Bolton's magnificent edition of Father Kino's HISTORICAL MEMOIR OF PIMERÍA ALTA (2 vols., 1919); Granville Stuart's FORTY YEARS ON THE FRONTIER (2 vols. 1925); LeRoy R. Hafen's THE OVERLAND MAIL, 1849-1869 (1926); Clarence A. Vandiveer's THE FUR TRADE AND EARLY WESTERN EXPLORATION (1929); and Earle R. Forrest's MISSIONS AND PUEBLOS OF THE OLD SOUTHWEST (1929).

While Clark built his reputation chiefly with books on western North America, he by no means neglected other areas of historical interest. Over the years he produced such distinguished histories as Arthur W. Calhoun's SOCIAL HISTORY OF THE AMERICAN FAMILY (3 vols., 1917-19); Charles O. Paullin's AMERICAN COLONIAL GOVERNMENT, 1696-1765 (1912); the eleven-volume DOCUMENTARY HISTORY OF AMERICAN INDUSTRIAL SOCIETY, 1649-1880 (1909-1910), edited by John R. Commons and others; PLANTATION AND FRONTIER DOCUMENTS, 1649-1863 (2 vols., 1910) edited by Ulrich B. Phillips; CROWN COLLECTION OF PHOTOGRAPHS OF AMERICAN MAPS by Archer Butler Hulbert (5 vols., 1904-1908); Herbert M. Sylvester's INDIAN WARS OF NEW ENGLAND (3 vols., 1910); and the 55-volume prize-winning PHILIPPINE ISLANDS, 1493-1898, edited by Blair and Robertson. In 1929 Fred A. Shannon's ORGANIZATION AND ADMINISTRATION OF THE UNION ARMY (2 vols., 1928) won the Pulitzer Prize.

In 1930 Clark decided to go west himself and moved to Glendale, California, where he launched the *Southwest Historical* series and the *Pacific Historical Review*. Clark died in 1951 and control of the company passed to his son, Arthur H. Clark, Jr., and Paul Galleher, an associate. Under their direction the bibliographical file on Western Americana has been expanded and facsimile series were launched. The firm also undertook one of its most impressive projects to date: THE FAR WEST AND THE ROCKIES, 1810-1875, a series of fifteen volumes edited by LeRoy R. Hafen and his wife, Ann W. Hafen. Also published by the firm over the past twenty-five years is a ten-volume series, *The Mountain Men and the Fur Trade of the Far West*, and many other multi-volume series including *Western Frontiersmen, Spain in the West, Western Lands and Waters, Northwest Historical, Far West and the Rockies, Early Western Travels,* and *American Waterways*.

Cliff's Notes, Inc.

Established in 1958 in Lincoln, Nebraska, by Clifton K. Hillegass, a long-time associate of Nebraska Book Company. The firm specializes in the publication of paperback literature, study aids, and review books. The first series to be published, *Cliff's Notes,* was initiated with the release of sixteen titles. In 1964 a second series, the *Complete Study Editions,* was launched. In 1969 the company entered the subject matter review book field with *Cliff's Course Outlines.* In 1972 *Cliff's Keynote Reviews* were incorporated into the program with twenty-one initial volumes. This series, acquired from Amtel, was originally published by Barnes & Noble as *Keynotes.*

Collectors Editions Limited

Organized in 1968 at New York City, its publications are distributed by Litton Educational Publishing, Inc. These are original books and reprints in the art reference and social history fields.

College and University Press

Founded in 1958 in New Haven, Connecticut, by I. Frederick Doduck under the title of College and University Press Services, Inc. The company was formed to perform editing, manufacturing, and distributing functions for its own books as well as books of other trade and scholarly publishers. The Press acquired the paperback rights to Twayne's *United States Authors Series* which, when completed, will contain over three hundred and fifty titles. The Press also publishes the *Masterworks of Literature Series* and *Alcohol Studies,* the latter in association with the Rutgers Center of Alcohol Studies. Since 1961 the trade list has been broadened to include behavioral sciences, philosophy, and religion.

William Collins Sons & Company, Ltd.

Founded in 1905 in New York City as the American branch of the British firm which was established in Glasgow, Scotland, in 1819 by William Collins the First. The firm had agents in New York as early as 1881 and in 1890 a New York office had been opened under the name of International Bible Agency. In 1907 the J.C. Winston Company became agents for the Collins Bibles until war conditions in 1917 terminated the agreement. After World War I the Bible line was placed in an agent's hands until a Collins office was reopened in 1923.

The firm also publishes under the imprint Collins Clear-Type Press. In addition to distributing the books of the parent company, the American branch specializes in Bibles, Gem dictionaries, *Collins Classics,* and juveniles. In 1962 Collins, New York, embarked on its first specifically American publishing venture: THE REVISED STANDARD VERSION BIBLE. In 1972, the first title in a new major dictionary program was published — COLLINS ENGLISH-SPANISH: SPANISH-ENGLISH DICTIONARY.

In 1974 Collins merged with World Publishing Company to form Collins-World.

Colorado Associated University Press

In May 1960, the president of the University of Colorado appointed a committee, " . . . to review the university's activities in the field of scholarly publications." The members of this committee elected Ralph E. Ellsworth, director of the libraries, chairman. The following year, in January, the committee issued a report recommending a single university press for all four-year, state-supported institutions of higher education in Colorado because "No one of the eight . . . institutions can afford the staff required to support a university press."

But it was not until 1968 that the Press received its first appropriation from the state legislature. It was a modest sum but enough to employ Roger W. Shugg, then director of the University of New Mexico Press, as a consulting director and his wife, Helen Clapesattle, as a consulting editor. When the legislature provided a larger appropriation in 1969, John T. Schwartz was hired as the first full-time director of the Press.

Since it began, the Press has served the following institutions: Adams State College, Colorado State University, Fort Lewis College, Metropolitan State College, Southern Colorado State College, University of Colorado, University of Northern Colorado, and Western State College. The publishing offices are at Boulder, Colorado.

Notable among the books the Press has published are: Kenneth E. Boulding's COLLECTED PAPERS, Volumes I and II of a projected five volumes; DOS PASSOS' PATH TO U.S.A.: A

Political Biography, 1912-1936, by Melvin Landsberg; U.S. CHINA POLICY AND THE PROBLEM OF TAIWAN; and COSMOLOGY, FUSION AND OTHER MATTERS, a collection of essays in honor of the late George Gamow.

Columbia University Press

Founded in New York City in 1893 by ten trustees of Columbia University with no staff and little money but a firm purpose: "To promote the study of economic, historical, literary, philosophical, scientific, and other subjects; and to promote and encourage the publication of literary works embodying original research in such subjects." To cover its first bill, one for $42.75, nine of the university's trustees reached into their pockets for $5.00 each, giving the Press a credit balance of $2.25. Soon afterwards, in 1894, Seth Low, president of Columbia University and later mayor of New York, contributed a gift of $10,000, and the Press was able to issue its first book, CLASSICAL STUDIES IN HONOR OF HENRY DRISLER.

Firm guidance was provided for many years by Seth Low's successor, Nicholas Murray Butler, who held the title of president of the Press for more than fifty years until 1946, as well as being president of Columbia University from 1902-1945. Butler encouraged the publication of the definitive edition of the works of John Milton, published in eighteen volumes, 1931-38. Also begun under Butler's direction was publication of the impressive series, *Records of Civilization: Sources and Studies;* its first volume was published in 1910 and the most recent, an eighty-seventh, in 1972.

After a somewhat uncertain period, Frederick Coykendall took over the directorship of the Press in 1923 and strengthened its active list as well as its financial base. Following him after World War II was Charles G. Proffitt, who had joined Coykendall as an assistant in 1927 and who retired in 1969 as president and director of the Press. Proffitt was succeeded as president and director by Robert G. Barnes, a former vice president of Doubleday, Inc.

THE COLUMBIA ENCYCLOPEDIA is undoubtedly the best-known publication of the Press. The first edition of this one-volume reference work was published in 1935 under the editorship of Clarke F. Ansley; the second edition was published in 1950; the third in 1963; and a fourth is now in preparation. Other major works published by Columbia include THE COLUMBIA-LIPPINCOTT GAZETTEER edited by Leon E. Seltzer (1952); GRANGER'S INDEX TO POETRY AND RECITATIONS, first published by the Press in 1953 after it was acquired from McClurg; George C.D. O'Dell's monumental ANNALS OF THE NEW YORK STAGE (1927); the four-volume FORMS AND FUNCTIONS OF 20TH CENTURY ARCHITECTURE by Talbot F. Hamlin (1952); and THE PAPERS OF ALEXANDER HAMILTON, a projected twenty-six volume set, of which seventeen volumes have already been published. In 1960 the Press began publishing its *Columbia Paperbacks* series. In 1972 a Columbia book, THE BLUE WHALE by George L. Small, received the National Book Award for science.

Columbia now publishes an average of eighty to one hundred books a year. Of the nearly 4,500 books it has published some 1,300 remain in print. A former subsidiary imprint, King's Crown Press, established in the days when all Columbia University dissertations were required to be published, is no longer active. The Press also distributes the publications of other nonprofit organizations.

F.E. Compton Company

Organized at Chicago, Illinois, in 1907 as F.E. Compton & Company. The company traces its descent from C.B. Beach & Company, which launched the two-volume THE STUDENT'S CYCLOPEDIA in 1893. THE STUDENT'S CYCLOPEDIA was replaced successively by THE STUDENT'S REFERENCE WORK in 1901, and by THE NEW STUDENT'S REFERENCE WORK in 1909. The last edition of THE NEW STUDENT'S REFERENCE WORK, in seven volumes, appeared in 1921. In 1907 Frank E. Compton purchased the sales rights to THE

STUDENT'S REFERENCE WORK from Chandler B. Beach. Compton incorporated his firm in 1912.

In 1918 editorial work began on COMPTON'S PICTURED ENCYCLOPEDIA. The first eight-volume edition of the new encyclopedia appeared in 1922. Under an innovative policy of continuous revision this encyclopedia has been revised at least once a year from that time to the present. It was more heavily illustrated than any of its predecessors or contemporaries; hence the "Pictured" in the title. In 1968 when this innovation had become commonplace the word "Pictured" was dropped from the title.

Other pioneering features of Compton's first edition of the encyclopedia were its Fact-Index and Study Outlines. The Fact-Index combined citations to the body of the encyclopedia with a large number of short entries that would otherwise have cluttered up the text. The Study Outlines (later titled Reference Outlines) methodically organized the major subject classifications covered in the encyclopedia and provided citations to the pages on which each of the topics and subtopics of the outline were treated. In 1924 COMPTON'S was expanded to ten volumes; in 1932 to fifteen; in 1973 to twenty-two.

The first editor-in-chief of the Compton Company was the historian, Guy Stanton Ford, who held the position from 1922 through 1961. In 1953 Charles Alfred Ford became Compton's full-time editorial director, a newly created position which he held until 1961, when he succeeded Guy Stanton Ford as editor-in-chief. Upon his retirement in 1965 Charles Ford was succeeded as editor-in-chief by Donald E. Lawson, who held that position until 1973. A number of able men followed Frank E. Compton as president of the company: Harry C. Johnson, S.J. Gillfillan, and C.E. Snell. It was during Snell's tenure in 1961 that the company was acquired by Encyclopaedia Britannica, Inc., as a wholly-owned subsidiary. Following the acquisition Robert E. Conger was appointed executive director of the company and in 1963 he became chairman of the board of directors. Wilbur S. Edwards then served as president from 1962 to 1965, when the company became a division of Encyclopaedia Britannica, Inc., and when the company was

restablished Edwards served as its president from 1970 to 1973.

As a Britannica subsidiary Compton's achievements include the successful development and marketing of a number of products, such as the sixteen-volume COMPTON'S PRECYCLOPEDIA (1971), the COMPTON YEARBOOK, which has appeared annually since 1959, COMPTON'S ENCYCLOPEDIC DICTIONARY, COMPTON'S ILLUSTRATED SCIENCE DICTIONARY, and COMPTON'S DICTIONARY OF THE NATURAL SCIENCES.

Concordia Publishing House

Founded in 1869 at St. Louis, Missouri, as the publishing arm of The Lutheran Church—Missouri Synod. At first simply called the Synod's printery, the firm received the official name of Concordia Verlag in 1878. By World War I the English equivalent name, Concordia Publishing House, was adopted. The new publishing house was designed to provide hymnals and other books for church use, catechisms, Bible histories, and other texts for use in the Synod's day schools, as well as periodicals for Lutheran homes.

The first publication run off the press was DAS SCHULBLATT, which is still being published under the title of LUTHERAN EDUCATION. A notable achievement spanning the turn of the century was the publication of LUTHERS WERKE, the German language "St. Louis Edition" of Martin Luther's writings, in twenty-five volumes. The modern counterpart to this undertaking is the fifty-six volume American edition of LUTHER'S WORKS, a joint venture with Fortress Press. By arrangement Concordia will produce Luther's exegetical writings, or commentaries (volumes 1-30) while Fortress publishes his Reformation works, the doctrinal and devotional writings. The project is targeted for completion in 1975.

Concordia publishes both scholarly and popular books. A number of European theologians have been translated and published. Concordia's American authors include Martin E. Marty and Jaroslav Pelikan. Books for the general reader, mostly in the devotional field, enjoy wide sales. A favorite among children's books is the *Arch*

Books series. The firm also publishes several dozen periodicals, including *Portals of Prayer,* and curricular materials for its *Mission:Life* educational program.

Concordia has had only five general managers during its long history. The first to head the firm was Martin C. Barthel, who bore the title of book agent. Martin Tirmenstein, his successor, served until 1907, when his place was taken by Edmund P. Seuel. From 1944 to 1971 Otto A. Dorn was the general manager. Ralph L. Reinke took over as president in 1971.

The Conference Board, Inc.

Organized in New York City and publishes periodic studies in business practices, personnel practices, economics and public affairs.

Consolidated Book Publishers

Established in 1913 by John F. Cuneo in Chicago, Illinois. It is presently an independent operating division of a Cuneo-owned group of companies known as Processing & Books, Inc. Consolidated's imprints and subsidiaries include Advance Publishers, Inc., Orlando, Florida, publishers of cookbooks; The Catholic Press, Chicago, publisher of Catholic Bibles and other religious books under its own imprint and that of its Spanish division, La Prensa Catolica; Culinary Arts Institute, Chicago, publisher of cookbooks; John A. Dickson Publishing Company, Chicago, publisher of Protestant Bibles and other religious books; The English Language Institute of America, Inc., Chicago, publisher of home study and self-improvement courses; Harwin Press Limited, England, publisher of cookbooks and religious books; Libros Basicos, S.A., Mexico City, direct-selling organization distributing Bibles, religious books and encyclopedias; Menorah Press, Chicago, publisher of Jewish Bibles.

Previous imprints include the People's Book Club, a joint venture with Simon & Schuster and Sears, Roebuck; Spencer Press, a joint venture with Sears, Roebuck, now owned by Grolier; Columbia Educational books; Timothy Books;

and Panasian Press Limited, Tokyo, Japan, joint venture with a Japanese group that sells encyclopedias and language courses in Japan.

Consolidated's major publishing programs are primarily the development of cookbooks, Bibles, dictionaries, including THE LIVING WEBSTER DICTIONARY OF THE ENGLISH LANGUAGE, and encyclopedias which have, in the past, included THE AMERICAN PEOPLE'S ENCYCLOPEDIA, OUR WONDERFUL WORLD, and the UNIVERSAL WORLD REFERENCE ENCYCLOPEDIA.

In 1969 Kenneth S. Giniger, founder of Hawthorn Books for Prentice-Hall, joined the company and was its president and chief executive officer. He resigned in August, 1974 to devote his time to his own company, The K.S. Giniger Company, Inc. (q.v.).

Cooper Square Publishers, Inc.

Organized in 1961 in New York City as successor to Pageant Books, Inc. Publishes scholarly and reference reprints and original books, including paperbacks.

Corinth Books

A New York City-based publisher of poetry. Books are distributed by Small Publishers Company. Privately held, the editors and owners are Ted and Joan Wilentz.

Cornell Maritime Press, Inc.

Established in 1938 at Cambridge, Maryland. Publishers of maritime, technical, hobby and how-to books.

Cornell University Press

The first university press in America, established in 1865, the year the university itself was founded. It was first accorded official recognition in the university *Register* in 1869. During the first years it printed, and apparently published, in the modern sense, a French reader, some works on American ethnology, and two pamphlets in a scientific series. The Press ceased operating in 1884 during a period of financial difficulties at the university.

The Comstock Publishing Associates was founded in 1893 by two Cornell professors, John H. Comstock and Simon H. Gage, to market their own books, one of which, AN INTRODUCTION TO ENTOMOLOGY, is still in print. It was a successful enterprise, partly because of the publication of Anna Botsford Comstock's HANDBOOK OF NATURE STUDY, now in its twenty-fourth edition. After the death of the Comstocks, the company and its buildings were bequeathed to Cornell University in 1931 and became part of a revitalized Cornell University Press. Comstock Publishing Associates is still used as an imprint by the Press for books published in the fields of nature study and applied biological sciences.

Woodford Patterson was named university publisher (director) in 1931, and Stanley Schaefer became manager of the new enterprise while still a student. Schaefer himself became the publisher in 1940.

When Victor Reynolds became director in 1943, there were one hundred and fifty books in print. During his twenty-year directorship, the annual publishing output grew to between twenty-five and thirty titles, and the backlist grew to four hundred and sixty-five titles. Cornell became, in 1955, the first university press to enter the paperback field.

Roger Howley, the current university publisher, joined the staff in 1963. In the next ten years the staff grew from twenty to forty persons and annual sales more than trebled in volume. The number of manuscripts offered the Press increased from about one hundred in 1963 to more than one thousand in 1972. During the same period the annual publishing program reached a level of eighty-five to ninety books a year, and the number of titles in print grew to nine hundred and fifty.

In addition to increasing its domestic publishing and marketing operations, the Press undertook a major program of copublishing with British firms, and published many works in translation from European languages. In 1969 the Press opened a London office to market books in the British Isles, Europe, Africa, and the Middle East.

The Press now publishes general and specialized nonfiction in nearly all fields of interest, with emphasis on works in history, literary criticism, philosophy, political science, developmental economics, and Russian, Asian, and African studies, as well as selected works of serious fiction, usually in translation.

Cornell Press is financially self-supporting, depending for income on its publishing activities.

Cornerstone Library, Inc.

Founded by Norman Monath in 1960 at New York City. The first eight titles, all of the how-to genre, in softcover and mostly reprints, were issued in January, 1961. This editorial policy has been maintained, with the exception of one hardcover novel published in 1963.

Chief books published by Cornerstone are: THE MODERN FUNDAMENTALS OF GOLF by Ben Hogan; THE MAGIC OF BELIEVING by Claude Bristol; THE MAGIC OF THINKING BIG by David J. Schwartz; PAINTING AS A PASTIME by Winston Churchill; THE ART OF SELFISHNESS by David Seabury; THE PRECISION SYSTEM OF CONTRACT BRIDGE BIDDING by Charles H. Goren; CHESS THE EASY WAY by Reuben Fine; SWIMMING THE SHANE GOULD WAY by Shirley Gould; HOW TO READ A PERSON LIKE A BOOK by Gerard L. Nierenburg; HOW TO HAVE A GREEN THUMB by Ruth Stout.

R.D. Cortina Company, Inc.

Founded in 1882 in New York City by Count Rafael Diez de la Cortina as a language school. Its first title was SPANISH IN 20 LESSONS. The firm was acquired by the Livesey family in 1929. Anthony S. Livesey was president from 1929 to 1970 when he was succeeded by Robert

E. Livesey.

Publishes foreign language texts and recordings for individual study and schools. Maintains branch offices in Europe, Asia, and Central and South America. Institute for Language Study is a subsidiary.

Coward, McCann & Geoghegan, Inc.

Founded in 1927 in New York City by Thomas R. Coward and James A. McCann. Their first book was MacKinlay Kantor's DIVERSEY and their first book for children was MILLIONS OF CATS by Wanda Gag, both published in 1928. Weathering the 1930s Depression, they arranged with Dodd, Mead to handle their sales. In 1933 they bought the Brentano list—with the exception of books by George Bernard Shaw—which contained a number of important authors. In 1936 the company was acquired by G.P. Putnam's Sons and became an autonomous subsidiary.

In the 1930s Coward published a number of distinguished authors, including Thornton Wilder, Alexander Woollcott, Manuel Komroff, and D.B. Wyndham Lewis. A number of European writers were also represented on the list: Siegfried Sassoon, Knut Hamsun, and Christopher La Farge. In addition, the firm published plays by Philip Barry, Elmer Rice, Jean Anouihl, and (Jay Alan) Lerner and (Frederick) Lowe. In the 1940s the firm acquired one of its most popular authors, Elizabeth Goudge.

McCann resigned in 1946 and Coward died in 1957. Walter Minton of Putnam found a new president in John J. Geoghegan. Under Geoghegan's direction the company has emerged as a highly visible trade house, growing rapidly in size and stature. Geoghegan launched the *American Vista Series* in 1960 with such books as LAND OF THE LONG HORIZON by Walter Havighurst and THE ROMANTIC SOUTH by Harnett Kane. In addition to bestsellers such as John Le Carré's THE SPY WHO CAME IN FROM THE COLD, William Golding's LORD OF THE FLIES, and THE CHILD FROM THE SEA by Elizabeth Goudge, the firm also publishes authors as outstanding as Hesketh Pearson, Robert Payne, Monica Dickens, Jack Kerouac, Paul Gallico, Edward Albee, Hans Hellmut Kirst, Ruth

Montgomery, John Braine, and Nicholas Mosley. Geoghegan's role in Coward, McCann's growth was acknowledged in 1971 when the firm was redesignated Coward, McCann & Geoghegan.

In the early 1970s the firm's list has been successfully broadened to include and reflect the emerging social and political issues of the times. Among its titles are: THE REAL MAJORITY by Richard M. Scammon and Ben J. Wattenberg; THE COURT MARTIAL OF LT. CALLEY by Richard Hammer; SOLEDAD BROTHER: THE PRISON LETTERS OF GEORGE JACKSON; THE NEW CHASTITY by Midge Decter; A CHILDHOOD IN PRISON by Pytor Yakir; THE LIVING PRESIDENCY by Emmet John Hughes; UPSTAIRS AT THE WHITE HOUSE by J.B. West and Mary Lynn Kotz; and THE NEW WOMAN'S SURVIVAL CATALOG, edited by Susan Rennie and Kirsten Grimstad.

Crane, Russak & Company, Inc.

Organized in 1972 at New York City by Edward M. Crane, Jr., former president of Van Nostrand, and Ben Russak, former president of American Elsevier. Co-editions with a score of British publishers, including Butterworth's, Edward Arnold, and Heinemann Educational Books, are the main strength of the firm's list. Crane, Russak also publishes an extensive list of books issued by the International Union of Pure and Applied Chemistry.

The company has begun to publish its own primary scientific journals in the fields of the information sciences, optics, and oceanography. It has also started publishing books in cooperation with the Rand Corporation, Stanford Research Institute, and National Strategy Information Center.

Creative Educational Society, Inc.

Started in 1932 by J.C. Mackin and George R. Peterson at Mankato, Minnesota. Their first publishing project was a *Visualized Curriculum Series,* which consisted of 704 photographs printed on card stock, size 8½ x 11, with text material on the reverse side of each picture. A teachers' manual was included with the series. During World War II the company decided to concentrate on educational toys but returned to publishing after the war. In 1956 Creative published a five-volume series entitled *The Community of Living Things* in cooperation with the National Audubon Society. It was an immediate success. A similar project was the *Creative Science Series* produced in co-operation with the American Museum of Natural History.

In 1967 George R. Peterson, Jr., acquired the stock interest of both Mackin and George R. Peterson. One year later Creative formed an affiliated company named Child's World, Inc., which now produces and distributes materials for the early childhood market. In the same year it acquired an audio-visual subsidiary known as Instructional Aids, Inc. Also in 1970 a new imprint was formed: Amecus Street. This imprint publishes photojournalistic books for the educational market.

Crescendo Publishing Company

Organized in 1967 at Boston, Massachusetts, as a publisher of nonfiction trade books and textbooks of music and music personalities.

Thomas Y. Crowell Company

In 1856 Thomas Young Crowell left the sea and took a job with Benjamin Bradley & Co. (established in 1834). He acquired this company in 1870 and set up publishing, parallel with bookbinding, in 1876, in New York City, after acquiring the stock of Warren & Wyman, a religious publisher. His first large success was *Crowell's Red Line Poets*—so-called because there was a red-line border on every page. Encouraged by the success of this project Crowell began to issue *Crowell's Standard Sets:* handsome editions of Robert Browning, William Shakespeare, and other well-known poets.

Religious and inspirational titles also formed a constant and staple element in Crowell's early list. Some of them were vastly successful. Among these were: POOR BOYS WHO BECAME FAMOUS by Sarah K. Bolton, and books by Orison S. Marden and James R. Miller. Like other publishers of his time Crowell issued many profitable series: *The Well Spent Hour Library,* the *Handy Volume Classics,* the *Astor Library,* and the *What Is Worth While* series. The publication of Leo Tolstoy's MY RELIGION led to the publication of a uniform edition of Tolstoy's works. Crowell's *Library of Economics and Politics,* edited by Richard T. Ely, consisted of such scholarly titles as THE LABOR MOVEMENT IN AMERICA. Crowell's traditional interest in reference books began with Peter Mark Roget's THESAURUS, issued in 1886.

In 1900 Crowell moved his Boston bookbindery to New York where he combined it with his publishing operation. The bindery was discontinued in 1920. Thomas Crowell died in 1915 and his son T. Irving Crowell became president of the company. In 1937 Irving Crowell became chairman of the board and his son, Robert L. Crowell, assumed the presidency. The company under Robert Crowell was separated into four divisions: juvenile, trade, reference, and college.

The juvenile list, established in 1886, burgeoned under Elizabeth Riley's management. It published numerous series of children's books, among them *Read-to-Me Storybook* compiled by the Child Study Association of America, *Experiments in Science,* and *Let's-Read-and-Find-Out.* The *Crowell Poets,* a series for high schools, was launched in 1964, and *Crowell Holiday Books* for younger readers appeared in 1965.

Gwen Bristow, the popular novelist, joined Crowell's trade list in 1937 with her bestselling book DEEP SUMMER, soon followed by THE HANDSOME ROAD and THIS SIDE OF GLORY. Her later books, JUBILEE TRAIL, CELIA GARTH, and CALICO PALACE, were even more successful.

The reference division maintained its dominant position with ROGET'S INTERNATIONAL THESAURUS, THE READER'S ENCYCLOPEDIA by William Rose Benét; Harold Wentworth and Stuart Flexner's DICTIONARY OF AMERICAN SLANG; L.V. Berrey and M. Van den Bark's THE AMERICAN THESAURUS OF SLANG; Max J. Herzberg's THE READER'S

ENCYCLOPEDIA OF AMERICAN LITERATURE; THE AMATEUR PHOTOGRAPHER'S HANDBOOK by Aaron Sussman; and Gorton Carruth's ENCYCLOPEDIA OF AMERICAN FACTS AND DATES.

Milestones in the Crowell college textbook list were the famous ECONOMICS: PRINCIPLES AND PROBLEMS, by Lionel D. Edie; Scott's BIOLOGY; Babor's CHEMISTRY; Key's POLITICS, PARTIES AND PRESSURE GROUPS; Baker's PRACTICAL STYLIST; and CULTURE, MAN AND NATURE by Marvin Harris.

The Crowell firm was acquired by Dun and Bradstreet, Inc. in 1968. In 1972 Robert Crowell retired as president and was replaced by Lewis Gillenson, a former vice president of Grosset & Dunlap. Since then, the company has broadened the base of its adult trade list. In 1973 it published one hundred and sixty titles in the fields of fiction, biography, sports, politics, and other nonfiction subjects.

In 1974 Crowell acquired the author contracts and inventory of John Day Company, Abelard-Schuman, Criterion Books, Intext Educational Publishers, and Chandler Publishing Company.

Crowell Collier and Macmillan, Inc.

See, Macmillan, Inc.

Crowell-Collier Publishing Company

Founded in 1877 in Springfield, Ohio, as the Crowell Publishing Company to issue *Farm and Fireside* (renamed *The Country Home* in 1930). Later the firm acquired *Woman's Home Companion* (founded in 1873 as *Ladies' Home Companion*) and the *American Magazine* (founded in 1876 as *Frank Leslie's Popular Monthly*).

In 1919 Crowell Publishing Company took over the assets of P.F. Collier with its profitable subscription book department and the influential periodical, *Collier's Weekly.*

In 1951 the COLLIER'S ENCYCLOPEDIA was published in twenty volumes; it was extended to twenty-four volumes in 1962. An annual supplement, COLLIER'S YEAR BOOK, was also launched in 1951. Other major projects were the *New Junior Classics* and the twelve-volume HISTORY OF THE WORLD, edited by Allan Nevins.

In 1956 the firm decided to suspend all its magazines to concentrate on publishing and education. In 1960 Crowell-Collier acquired a controlling interest in The Macmillan Company and merged with it to form Crowell Collier and Macmillan. In 1973 the firm was renamed Macmillan, Inc. (q.v.).

Crown Publishers, Inc.

Started in New York City in 1933 when Robert Simon and Nat Wartels founded Outlet Book Co. Inc., to deal in publishers' remainders. In 1936 they branched out into original publishing under the name of Crown and later, when the publishing operation was much greater than the remainder operation, the name of the company was changed to Crown Publishers, Inc.

During the ensuing years, besides expanding its list of general trade publishing, which included fiction, nonfiction, and children's books, the company acquired other publishing operations. Among these were Covici-Friede, Lothrop, Lee & Shepard (since sold in 1965 to Scott, Foresman), Howell, Soskin & Co., Long & Smith, Allen, Towne & Heath, Lear Publishers, and Robert M. McBride.

Publishing well over one hundred titles per year, Crown has had many book club selections and bestsellers, including two one million plus copies bestsellers, HOW TO AVOID PROBATE and THE SEARS ROEBUCK CATALOG. A third book, THE JOY OF SEX, is nearing that mark. The majority of Crown's books are published with the expectancy of long-term, steady sales. Crown was the first English language publisher of Sholom Aleichem, and it has an extensive list of collector's books, craft books, art, history, reference and how-to books.

Crown editors have included Edmund Fuller, Hiram Haydn, and Robert Van Gelder, Currently Herbert Michelman is editor-in-chief; Millen Brand and David McDowell head the editorial staff.

Crown's specialized divisions include Bonanza (hardcover reprints); Harmony Books; Lenox Hill (library fiction); Publishers Central Bureau (mail order); Living Language Record and Book courses; Crescent, Avenel, and Gramercy. The firm also acts as distributor for Clarkson N. Potter, Inc., Living Shakespeare, Inc., Sports Car Press, Craft Course Books, and a number of other firms.

Nat Wartels still heads Crown. Robert Simon died in 1966. Alan Mirken is executive vice president. Offices of the company are in New York City, with shipping facilities in Avenel, New Jersey.

In 1974 Crown purchased the Barre Publishing Company, Inc., a trade publisher of nonfiction, and Imprint Society, Inc., publisher of limited editions for subscribers and the institutional markets. Both of these wholly-owned subsidiaries will operate as independent publishers. It also acquired Westover Publishing Company.

Curtis Books, Inc.

Established 1969 at Philadelphia, Pennsylvania, and now a subsidiary of Cadence Industries Corporation. Mainly a direct mail and mail order distributor of nonfiction books.

Da Capo Press, Inc.

See, Plenum Publishing Corporation.

The Stuart L. Daniels Company, Inc.

Founded in 1967 at New York City. Publisher under its own imprint and jointly with other publishers of general nonfiction titles in both hard and softcover, with emphasis on sports, beauty and charm, humor, business, cookbooks, and the theater.

The Dartnell Corporation

Founded in 1917 by John Cameron Aspley at Chicago, Illinois, as the Dartnell Sales Service to produce bulletins for salesmen. Building on this base Dartnell went on to publish books, manuals, newsletters, subscription services, films, and cassettes for business. In addition to subscription services for salesmen, Dartnell has launched several magazines in this field including *Sales Management, Printed Salesmanship, Office Equipment Salesman, The American Salesman, Printing Arts Quarterly* and *American Business*.

Still a closely-held corporation, Dartnell's president after Aspley was B. Gordon Fyfe. In 1965 William Harrison Fetridge became president and still serves in that capacity. Best-known of Dartnell titles are the 1,000-page handbooks offering executives handy desk-reference information in such specific areas as office administration, personnel management, sales management, advertising, marketing, direct mail and mail order operations, sales promotion and public relations.

Other Dartnell publishing activities include the production of business manuals, pamphlets for the guidance of executives, supervisors, foremen, and salesmen, and business record and expense books. Monthly management information services are provided for financial officers, sales/marketing executives, and office administrators. Dartnell also publishes a wide range of business diaries and is today one of the largest producers of management training and sales training films. Its film, "Second Effort" starring Vince Lombardi, is reputed to be the largest-selling industrial film in history. The Dartnell books and films are available in a number of foreign languages.

Dartnell has also acquired the assets of Cambridge Associates, Boston-based publisher of several business newsletters. An educational division of Dartnell serves school administrators, providing both publications and research.

Daughters of St. Paul, Inc.

Founded in 1915 at Boston, Massachusetts. Publishes a wide range of religious and Catholic books, Bibles, biographies, juveniles, and some textbooks.

Daniel Davey & Company, Inc.

Established in 1964 at Hartford, Connecticut. Publishes a small list of scientific and technical books.

F.A. Davis Company

Founded in 1879 in Philadelphia, Pennsylvania, by Frank Allston Davis, a traveler for William Wood and Company. The firm specialized in medical books.

Davis died in 1917 and the company was then operated by his widow, Elizabeth Irene Craven Davis, until 1960, when her nephew, Robert H. Craven, took over. With Clarence W. Taber as editor, Davis became a leading nursing textbook publisher. Taber's own TABER'S CYCLOPEDIC MEDICAL DICTIONARY is one of the best-selling titles on the Davis list.

In 1962 an arrangement was made with Blackwell Scientific Publications of Oxford, England, to publish their books on a cooperative basis in the United States. In the sixties the company expanded into the biological, physical, and the behavioral sciences.

Daw Books, Inc.

Established in 1971 at New York City. Publishes paperbacks, originals and reprints, of science fiction books, which are distributed by New American Library.

John de Graff, Inc.

Established in 1951 at Tuckahoe, New York. Issues small lists of nonfiction titles.

Marcel Dekker, Inc.

Founded in 1963 by Marcel Dekker, son of Maurits Dekker, founder of Dekker and Nordemann, Amsterdam, Holland. Leaving Holland in 1939, Maurits Dekker established American Elsevier and Interscience Publishers in New York City. He served as president of Interscience from 1940 to 1961, at which time he sold the firm to John Wiley. In 1964 Maurits retired as vice president of John Wiley and two years later he joined his son, Marcel Dekker, in the firm of Marcel Dekker, Inc. A subsidiary, Maurits Dekker As-

sociates, acts as an adviser in editorial and marketing programs.

The firm's major publications include monographs, textbooks, journals, and encyclopedias. A multi-volume ENCYCLOPEDIA OF INFORMATION AND LIBRARY SCIENCES is in progress.

Dell Publishing Co., Inc.

Established in New York City in 1921 by George T. Delacorte, Jr. A popular fiction magazine called *I Confess* was the first of over seven hundred magazines which have over the years appeared with the Dell imprint. During the 1940s and 1950s Dell also became synonymous with comic books. In 1942 Dell introduced its first paperback, DEATH IN THE LIBRARY by Philip Ketchum.

Currently Dell publishes a wide range of paperback imprints: *Laurel Editions* at the high school and college levels; *Laurel Leaf Library* for senior and junior high school students; *Yearling Books,* juvenile paperbacks; *Delta Paperbacks,* general adult fiction and nonfiction in more expensive format; and *Dell Purse Books,* 35¢ small paperbacks, covering a wide range of nonfiction, special interest subjects, *e.g.,* calorie counters, horoscopes, puzzles, etc.

The Delacorte Press was established in 1963. In 1968 a second imprint was added: Delacorte Press/Seymour Lawrence. Both publish original fiction and nonfiction in hardcover. In 1964 Dell acquired the Dial Press (q.v.) and Noble and Noble (q.v.) became a wholly-owned subsidiary in 1965.

Dell also publishes cross word puzzle magazines and general interest magazines, etc.

Helen Meyer, who joined Dell in 1923, has served as president of the firm since 1957.

Delmar Publishers

Established in 1945 at Albany, Illinois, by James Dickson, Eugene A. Fink, and Thomas Greenwood. The company published text and work textbooks for both vocational and technical education. These textbooks were distinguished by their unit-lesson format in which short unit-lessons were arranged in order of learning difficulty. Careful attention was paid to presenting the contents at reading levels suited to each student's capabilities and short tests were included to determine students' mastery of the presented information.

The firm experienced steady growth and in 1969 was acquired by Litton Industries, Inc., to be the occupational education arm of Litton Educational Publishing, Inc. Eugene A. Fink continues with the firm as president.

T.S. Denison and Company, Inc.

Established in 1876 in Chicago, Illinois, by T.S. Denison. Eben Norris was the second owner and upon his death the company was acquired by the Brings family and moved to Minneapolis, Minnesota, in 1942. The firm publishes books for the educational market and operates by direct mail without any salesmen in the field.

Denison specializes in series such as *Children's Illustrated Readers, Countries of the World, Men of Achievement, Famous American Heroes and Leaders, Lives of Great Americans,* and *Teaching the Mentally Retarded,* as well as all types of teachers' aids. Its list comprises five thousand titles.

Denlinger's Publishers

Based at Fairfax, Virginia, the firm publishes books on dogs and Americana.

Denoyer-Geppert

Founded in Chicago, Illinois, in 1916 by L. Philip Denoyer and O.E. Geppert. Denoyer was a geography professor and Geppert a mapmaker and this combination of cartography and teaching determined the development of the company. The company produced not only maps and globes but also learning aids, such as charts and biological and anatomical models. In 1968, upon Geppert's retirement, Denoyer-Geppert was acquired by the Times-Mirror Company.

In 1970 Denoyer-Geppert took over the distribution and marketing of the audio-visual division of Popular Science Publishing Company. This division has been renamed Denoyer-Geppert Audio-Visuals. The company is now producing multi-media educational programs in social studies, science, environmental studies, and contemporary problems. Reflecting this emphasis is a new program, *From Subject to Citizen,* a one-year course in American history for secondary students. An environmental geography program has also been developed entitled *Man and Environment: A Changing Relationship. Early Explorations* is a new series of five kits for preschool and kindergarten children designed to teach basic learning skills.

Deseret Book Company

Had its beginnings in 1866 at Salt Lake City, Utah, when George Q. Cannon opened the George Q. Cannon & Sons Book Company. Cannon, who served as a counselor in the First Presidency of the Mormon Church to pioneer colonizer Brigham Young, was also editor of *The Deseret News,* the Church-owned newspaper. Upon his death in 1901 the bookstore was sold to *The Deseret News.* In the meantime, the Sunday Schools of the Church had operated the Deseret Sunday School Union Bookstore. Several years later it was decided to merge the two stores, since they were both operated by organizations of the Church. In October, 1919, the amalgamation took place under the name Deseret Book Company. The firm was later incorporated in 1932 as a tax-paying publishing arm of The Church of Jesus Christ of Latter-day Saints. The first president of the firm was James E. Talmadge, author, and apostle of the Church. His successors have included Melvin J. Ballard, Samuel O. Bennion, George R. Hill, and Marvin J. Ashton, who is now serving. General managers and chief operating officers of the company have been T. Albert Hooper, A. Hamer Reiser, Alva H. Parry, and William James Mortimer, now serving.

In addition to publishing the standard works of the Church, the company publishes about forty general interest hardbound titles yearly. It also operates retail bookstores in Utah and California, and is affiliated nationally with the Association of American Publishers and the American Booksellers Association.

Determined Productions, Inc.

Based in San Francisco, California, publishes popular classic coloring books, datebooks, gourmet cookbooks and travel books.

The Devin-Adair Company

Established in New York City in 1911 by Henry Garrity. The company's first book was a classic travelogue by Garrity entitled MY UNKNOWN CHUM. The company is now owned by the son of the founder, Devin Adair Garrity. In 1970 Devin-Adair moved to Old Greenwich, Connecticut. In the same year the firm started an Ecological Book Club. A second book club, The Veritas Book Club, was begun in 1971.

Devin-Adair publishes primarily four types of books 1) conservative political books, among them being THE ROOSEVELT MYTH by John T. Flynn, THE UNTOLD STORY OF DOUGLAS MacARTHUR by Frazier Hunt, and REFLECTIONS ON THE FAILURE OF SOCIALISM by Max Eastman. 2) modern Irish literary works, which include the poetry of Patrick Kavanagh, Oliver St. John Gogarty and Padraic Colum, the short fiction of Sean O' Faolain, Liam O'Flaherty, and Lord Dunsany, and histories such as THE STORY OF THE IRISH RACE by Seumas MacManus. 3) books on natural history and ecology, and including the following: THE WEB OF LIFE by John H. Storer and *American Naturalists,* a series edited by Farida A. Wiley; also bird books including THE WARBLERS OF AMERICA by Ludlow Griscom and Alexander Sprunt, A GATHERING OF SHORE BIRDS by Henry Marion Hall, and WORLD OF THE GREAT WHITE HERON by Marjory Bartlett Sanger. 4) Americana and biographies dealing with such folk heroes as Butch Cassidy, Roy Bean and Jack Ganzhorn.

Devin-Adair was the first publisher to develop an "organic" list with books by Sir Albert Howard, Eve Balfour, Leonard Wickenden, and J.I. Rodale, whose PAY DIRT (1945) was the first modern American book on organic gardening. Closely allied are a series of popular health books: FEEL LIKE A MILLION by Catharyn Elwood, and GET WELL NATURALLY and STAY YOUNG LONGER by Linda Clark, which have achieved considerable sales records.

The Dial Press

Founded in 1924 in New York City by Lincoln MacVeagh, a former editor at Holt. His partner was Scofield Thayer, publisher of *The Dial* magazine. Elizabeth Bowen's THE HOTEL was the first bestseller on the Dial list. A man of critical judgment, MacVeagh also published among other outstanding books R.H. Mottram's THE SPANISH FARM and W.R. Burnett's LITTLE CAESAR. Later the firm started the *Library of Living Classics,* edited by Manuel Komroff.

When MacVeagh was appointed the American minister to Greece in 1933 he sold the press to Max Salop. Five years later Salop sold it to B.C. Hoffman. Hoffman managed to keep the imprint fairly active, helped by such bestsellers as THE FOXES OF HARROW by Frank Yerby and Gladys Schmitt's DAVID, THE KING. A series of popular anthologies were also brought out entitled *The Permanent Library.* In 1951 the firm was acquired by George Joel. He relinquished ownership to R.W. Baron in 1959.

In 1964 the press was acquired by Dell Publishing Co., Inc., adding another hardcover division to its list of subsidiaries.

Dial published James Baldwin's first book and has continued as his publisher. In addition, Dial is the publisher of Richard Condon, Robert Ludlum and Vance Bourjaily, among many others.

John A. Dickson Publishing Company

Founded in 1901 at Chicago, Illinois. It publishes Protestant Bibles and Bible study books exclusively. Now a subsidiary of Consolidated Book Publishers.

Digest Books

Organized in 1944 by Milton Klein as Gun Digest Publishing Company in Illinois as an adjunct to his Chicago-based chain of Klein's Sporting Goods stores. The first publication was THE GUN DIGEST, an annual reference book and catalog devoted to guns, accessories, and other information for shooters, collectors, hunters and those interested in guns. Klein later sold his stores in order to concentrate on publishing.

Other titles on the Digest list cover various areas of guns and shooting, sports, recreation and the outdoors, nostalgia, dog care and magic. Digest books are distributed to the book trade by Follett Publishing Company. Distribution to all other markets is direct from the publisher.

Dimension Books, Inc.

Established in 1963 at Denville, New Jersey. Publishes Catholic and other religious books.

Dodd, Mead & Company

Founded in 1840 by Moses W. Dodd, a pious Presbyterian who had been trained for the ministry but turned to publishing when he bought John S. Taylor's bookshop in New York City. Dodd's first venture in publishing was the sermons of Reverend Gardiner Spring entitled THE OBLIGATIONS OF THE WORLD TO THE BIBLE. The firm began to prosper after Dodd's son, Frank H., joined the firm in 1859. Under his direction nondenominational books were included in the publishing program. In 1867 Dodd issued his first bestseller—Martha Finley's ELSIE DINSMORE, followed by twenty-eight other ELSIE'S.

When Moses Dodd retired in 1870, Edward S. Mead, Frank's cousin, was invited to join the firm and the partnership became Dodd and Mead. About this time the novels of E.P. Roe, notably his BARRIERS BURNED AWAY, contributed to the prosperity of the firm. Mead himself wrote a good many of the titles, mostly juveniles, under different names. The partners also engaged Hamilton Wright Mabie as literary adviser and scout and Mabie was later to emerge as the high priest of American literary culture.

One steady seller during the early days was Alexander Cruden's CONCORDANCE TO THE BIBLE, and foreign authors formed another major element of the Dodd and Mead list. Frank Dodd's excellent connections with foreign publishers—which he maintained through frequent overseas visits—enabled him to obtain a number of popular authors, including Anthony Trollope, Elizabeth Barrett Browning, Maurice Maeterlinck, Jerome K. Jerome, Marie Corelli, Ian Maclaren, and J. Henri Fabre. In 1895 he began publishing *The Bookman* with Harry Thurston Peck as editor. This magazine flourished until 1933 as the country's leading literary periodical.

Dodd's greatest achievement was the seventeen-volume NEW INTERNATIONAL ENCYCLOPEDIA, under the editorship of Daniel Coit Gilman, Harry Thurston Peck, and Frank Moore Colby. First published between 1902 and 1904, it was revised in 1917 and issued in twenty-four volumes. Meanwhile the trade division brought out such notable books as George Saintsbury's HISTORY OF CRITICISM; THE ORIGINAL JOURNALS OF THE LEWIS AND CLARK EXPEDITION in eight volumes, edited by Reuben Gold Thwaites; Aylmer Maude's two-volume THE LIFE OF TOLSTOY; and books by Gertrude Atherton, Eden Phillpotts, George Barr McCutcheon, and E. Phillips Oppenheim.

Mead died in 1894 and Frank H. Dodd in 1916. Frank H. Dodd's son, Edward H., then became president of the firm and his cousin, Frank C. Dodd, manager of the general book division. In 1917 the company was incorporated. Frank C. Dodd proved to be an enterprising publisher, buying up small firms with potentially valuable lists. By acquiring the American branch of John Lane of London, England, he obtained its single most profitable author, Agatha Christie. Similarly he bought the Moffat, Yard list in 1924 and Small, Maynard and Company in 1926. The latter firm brought to Dodd, Mead Faith Baldwin, Bliss Carman, E.M. Hull, the short story annuals edited by Edward O'Brien, and the play anthologies edited by Burns Mantle. Dodd also joined with three other publishers to establish Blue Ribbon Books in 1930. In the same year the firm launched *American Political Leaders,* a series edited by Allan Nevins. In 1931 Edward H. Dodd yielded the presidency to Frank C. Dodd, and in a move toward consolidation the NEW INTER-NATIONAL ENCYCLOPEDIA was sold to Funk and Wagnalls. When Brentano, George Bernard Shaw's American publisher, discontinued its publishing division during the Depression of the thirties Dodd, Mead arranged with Shaw to issue his works.

In 1934 Dodd took over the lists of two more failing houses: Sears and Company and Duffield and Green, the latter being publishers of H.G. Wells and Edward Lear. At about this time the firm also launched the series, *Great Illustrated Classics,* and introduced two major reference books, INTERNATIONAL CYCLOPEDIA OF MUSIC AND MUSICIANS by Oscar Thompson and B.E. Stevenson's THE HOME BOOK OF QUOTATIONS. The large and active backlist of Dodd, Mead also included works by such established authors as Cornelia Otis Skinner, H.V. Morton, G.K. Chesterton, Max Brand, William Rose Benét, Anatole France, Stephen Leacock, E. Barrington, Rupert Brooke, Maureen Daly, Paul Laurence Dunbar, Walter D. Edmonds, Edwin Way Teale, and Robert Service.

Dodd, Mead's greatest success during the years after World War II was the publication of Winston Churchill's THE HISTORY OF THE ENGLISH-SPEAKING PEOPLES. In 1955 the company acquired the De La Mare Publishing Company's gardening titles. Two years later a college division was established under the direction of William M. Oman.

In 1942 Howard C. Lewis became president of the firm when Frank C. Dodd moved up to the chairmanship. Lewis died in 1952 and was succeeded in the presidency by Edward H. Dodd, Jr. Raymond T. Bond was president from 1957 until 1964, when S. Phelps Platt, Jr., was elected to that post.

Frank Nelson Doubleday (1862-1934)

Doubleday & Company, Inc.

Established in 1897 at New York City by Frank Nelson Doubleday, a descendant of Jonathan Edwards. Doubleday, when a brash young man still in his teens, had started his career as an employee of Scribner's and had risen to become head of the book subscription department and editor of *The Book Buyer.* He remained with Scribner's for eighteen years, working his way up in responsibility, while at the same time gaining additional experience by doing outside jobs for *The New York Times* and other journals. In 1897 he joined forces with S.S. McClure, publisher of *McClure's Magazine,* to set up Doubleday & McClure. Their first book, a collection of stories from *McClure's,* was published in the first year of their operation. Their 1898 list included THE DAY'S WORK by Doubleday's friend Rudyard Kipling, which at once sold over a hundred thousand copies, books by Frank Norris and Henry George, as well as BIRD NEIGHBORS by Doubleday's gifted wife, Neltje Blanchan deGraff, whose pen name was Neltje Blanchan.

In 1900 Doubleday severed his connection with McClure and formed a new partnership with Walter Hines Page. In 1903 this firm was incorporated. Doubleday, Page & Company began as a large-scale publishing house with an extensive list of popular authors, including Rudyard Kipling, Joseph Conrad, Frank Norris, Gene Stratton-Porter, O. Henry and Booth Tarkington.

Doubleday was dubbed "Effendi" by Rudyard Kipling, from his initials F.N.D. In Turkish the word means "Chief." It remained Doubleday's sobriquet, a term of affection and respect. He was very devoted to his authors and the firm's history is marked with many model author-publisher relations.

By 1910 Doubleday, Page had become one of the largest publishing houses in the country, issuing hundreds of books every year, "the wonder of the publishing world." By 1920 two Doubleday authors, Kipling and Selma Lagerlof, had won Nobel Prizes for Literature, and some of the notable books they had published included A GIRL OF THE LIMBERLOST by Gene Stratton Porter, Booth Tarkington's PENROD and THE MAGNIFICENT AMBERSONS, Joseph Conrad's CHANCE and VICTORY, Kipling's JUST SO STORIES, THE JUNGLE by Upton Sinclair, and THE HAUNTED BOOKSHOP by Christopher Morley.

In 1910 Doubleday established its own printing plant, Country Life Press, in Garden City, Long Island, New York, and opened the first Doubleday Book Shop of the future Doubleday chain in Pennsylvania Railroad Station, New York City, to test and develop methods of retail sales and promotion, selling the books of all publishers.

Page was appointed ambassador to Great Britain in 1913 and he left the firm that year. In 1920 Doubleday acquired the well-known British firm of William Heinemann. He moved its offices, as he had his own firm back home, to the countryside away from London. Nelson Doubleday, Effendi's son, joined his father's firm in 1922, and in 1923 he established a new subsidiary, Garden City Publishing Company, to specialize in reprints. This subsidiary introduced such profitable lines as *Lambskin Library, Star Dollar Books,* and the *Sun Dial Library.* The Crime Club, Inc. was launched in 1928 as well as

a special children's department, headed by May Massee, and in 1929 sales operations were started in Canada. During the 1920s Edna Ferber, Margaret Kennedy, Don Marquis, and W. Somerset Maugham joined the Doubleday list; ALICE ADAMS by Tarkington and SO BIG by Edna Ferber became Pulitzer Prize novels, while THE LIFE AND LETTERS OF WALTER HINES PAGE, edited by Burton J. Hendrick, won the 1923 Pulitzer Prize for Biography; and in 1929 JOHN BROWN'S BODY by Stephen Vincent Benét, won the Pulitzer Prize for Poetry. In 1926 Edna Ferber's memorable SHOW BOAT was issued.

In 1927 Doubleday announced the merger of his firm with George H. Doran, to be known as Doubleday, Doran & Company. The combined house became the largest trade publisher in the United States. *Publishers Weekly* considered the merger "the most impressive and dramatic consolidation that has ever been announced in the field of American book publishing." Doran brought with him a formidable list of authors. This included Arnold Bennett, W. Somerset Maugham, Mary Roberts Rinehart, Hugh Walpole, and A. Conan Doyle. But the partnership proved an uneasy one and in 1930 Doran withdrew.

F.N. Doubleday died in 1934, leaving the business to his son, Nelson Doubleday. Nelson had a business acumen and marketing flair that overshadowed even those of his father. He was inexhaustible in his fertile schemes for larger distribution of books to people who never before had bought books. He was quick to see the possibilities in selling books by mail and bought all the outstanding stock of the Literary Guild and made it a wholly-owned subsidiary. He organized the Junior Literary Guild, a book club for young readers, and the Doubleday One Dollar Book Club, as well as the Book League of America, both offering books at bargain prices since they were not new publications. The effectiveness of Nelson's aggressive promotion was evident in the success of two of his new authors. Daphne du Maurier's REBECCA was used by several clubs and was reprinted in numerous inexpensive editions after its first hardcover sale. Kenneth Roberts' books were also spread to their utmost market.

Wastebasket of Frank Nelson Doubleday kept ready for bad manuscripts.

Continuing his expansion in the reprint field, Nelson established Outdoor Books, Heyday House, and Sun Dial Press. He also purchased Windward House and Blue Ribbon Books. In addition, he had five more reprint divisions set up: De Luxe Editions, Halcyon House, Star Dollar Books, Triangle Books, and the New Home Library. At this time, too, the Country Life Press was reorganized into a separate corporation. The World War II years were, as a result of these activities, highly prosperous ones for the publishing company.

Highlight Doubleday publications of the 1930s included: CIMARRON by Edna Ferber; GRAND HOTEL by Vicki Baum; BRAVE NEW WORLD by Aldous Huxley; IT CAN'T HAPPEN HERE by Sinclair Lewis, who became the first American to be awarded the Nobel Prize for Literature; SEVEN PILLARS OF WISDOM by T.E. Lawrence; JAMAICA INN by Daphne du Maurier; NORTHWEST PASSAGE by Kenneth Roberts; and WOODROW WILSON: LIFE AND LETTERS: Vols. VII-VIII, by Ray Stannard Baker, which won in 1939 the Pulitzer Prize for Biography.

Douglas M. Black joined the company as first vice president in 1943 and when, in 1946, the company name was changed to Doubleday & Company, Inc., Black became the president. During that decade both the English and French Doubleday offices were extremely active in scouting for books and authors as well as selling translation and publication rights to Doubleday books. Important books published during the 1940s included IN THIS OUR LIFE by Ellen Glasgow, which won the 1942 Pulitzer Prize for Literature; GEORGE WASHINGTON CARVER by Rackham Holt; THE RAZOR'S EDGE by W. Somerset Maugham; THE BLACK ROSE by Thomas Costain; BASIC HISTORY OF THE UNITED STATES by Charles & Mary Beard; LYDIA BAILEY by Kenneth Roberts; THE GREATEST STORY EVER TOLD by Fulton Oursler, which sold over three million copies in the United States alone. A noteworthy success in 1948 was Dwight D. Eisenhower's CRUSADE IN EUROPE, the first of a half dozen Eisenhower books that Doubleday published.

Nelson Doubleday died in 1949. Called one of the world's leading merchants of books, Doubleday believed that publishing was a business first and a noble calling second.

Under the new president, Douglas M. Black, the transition of the firm to the post-Nelson Doubleday era proved smooth and efficient. In 1951 the company published the THORNDIKE-BARNHART COMPREHENSIVE DESK DICTIONARY, and in 1952 it launched the *Mainstream of America Series,* which in 1956 won the Carey-Thomas Award for Creative Publishing. In 1953 a young Doubleday editor launched *Anchor Books,* the first American paperbound quality reprints and originals, bringing to Doubleday that year's Carey-Thomas Award for Creative Publishing. In 1955 this success was followed with the introduction of *Image Books,* paperbacks of Catholic classics, which received the Thomas More Association Medal for the "most distinguished contribution to Catholic publishing," and Doubleday has since continued active Catholic publishing. In the 1950s some of the notable trade successes were MEMOIRS OF HARRY S. TRUMAN; Amy Vanderbilt's COMPLETE BOOK OF ETIQUETTE, which Doubleday had commissioned; THE SILVER CHALICE by Thomas B. Costain; THE LONELY CROWD by David Riesman; SOMETHING OF VALUE by Robert Ruark; THE ORGANIZATION MAN by William Whyte; EXODUS by Leon Uris; THE DIARY OF ANNE FRANK; and Herman Wouk's THE CAINE MUTINY, a Pulitzer Prize winner. There were five additional Pulitzer Prize winners: THE WAKING by Theodore Roethke; A STILLNESS AT APPOMATTOX by Bruce Catton, which also won the National Book Award; THE TRAVELS OF JAIMIE McPHEETERS by Robert Lewis Taylor; ADVISE AND CONSENT by Allen Drury. The fifth was the special Pulitzer award made for the work of Kenneth Roberts.

Turning toward textbooks, Doubleday issued in 1959 the *Anchor Science Study Series, Made-Simple Books,* and *Tudor-Text Books.*

Early in 1961 John T. Sargent, Nelson Doubleday's son-in-law, became president of the company. Also in 1961 Doubleday acquired Aldus Books, Ltd., an English publishing firm that specialized in international publishing of general knowledge books with text in various languages dubbed in. In 1964 Anchor Books issued the first two volumes of the thirty-eight volume ANCHOR BIBLE, under the general editorship of William F. Albright and David Noel Freedman. A new imprint, Natural History Press, was formed with the American Museum of Natural History to publish books and periodicals sponsored by the museum. In 1965 Doubleday announced *Zenith Books,* a new series dealing with American minority groups. Also in that same year the *Paris Review Editions* were planned in association with George A. Plimpton's *The Paris Review.*

Among Doubleday's bestselling authors during the sixties were Irving Stone, Louis Nizer, Leon Uris, Arthur Hailey, Allen Drury, Norah Lofts, Daphne du Maurier, Victoria Holt, Taylor Caldwell, and Bruce Catton. A major acquisition, also during the sixties, was Feffer and Simons, the American export representatives who handle a sizeable share of book exports. And to expand its share of the rich textbook and reference book markets Doubleday purchased Laidlaw Brothers of River Forest, Illinois, which has become the third largest publisher of textbooks for elementary schools, and the J.G. Ferguson Company of Chicago, Illinois, an independent subscription reference book company. An Educational Systems Division was also established, which put Doubleday into the audio-visual field. This was merged with International Communication Films, Inc., producer of educational films and film-strips, when Doubleday acquired that company in 1967, to become Doubleday Multi-Media. In 1966 Doubleday published its phenomenally successful modern language translation of the Bible, THE JERUSALEM BIBLE, by Father Alexander Jones and a panel of scholars. Six editions have been issued, including one in paperback, and over a million copies of this book have been sold.

As it entered the 1970s Doubleday continued to maintain its position as a giant of the book industry. There are now some twenty Doubleday book clubs catering to all tastes and fashions. There are also Doubleday subscription book clubs in Canada, Australia, New Zealand and Great Britain. In 1970 Samuel S. Vaughan was named publisher of the Doubleday Publishing Division. Doubleday remains still a family, privately-owned company.

Dover Publications, Inc.

Founded in New York City by Hayward Cirker, a former salesman for Crown Publishers, in 1945, to publish scientific reprints on a small scale and to sell them by mail order. Cirker is regarded as one of the early pioneers in inexpensive reprints of classic scientific works. Albert Einstein was one of the earliest Nobel Prize winners on his list, followed by Max Born, Werner Heisenberg, Peter Debye, H.A. Lorentz, Erwin Schrodinger, Romain Rolland, and Max Planck. Anticipating the knowledge explosion in the fifties and sixties, Cirker entered the paperback business at about the same time as Doubleday's Jason Epstein. He was one of the earliest publishers to extend paperbacks into many areas, including mathematics, physics, graphics, design, juveniles, chess, music, crafts, and almost every field of human learning. The Dover company has the unusual ability to reprint scholarly books with a limited market in paperback and at a moderate price. In certain areas such as chess, books on design, music, mathematics and physics, Dover claims that it maintains the world's largest library of inexpensive paperback books.

Despite the vicissitudes of paperback publishing during the past twenty-five years, Dover Publications has maintained its vitality in enlarging its list in many areas and may now be the most important single publisher of quality paperbacks.

The firm is closely held by the Cirker family and, by and large, is still managed and directed by the people who have been with it since its inception.

Drake Publishers, Inc.

Established in 1890 by Frederick J. Drake in Chicago, Illinois, as Frederick J. Drake & Co., Drake was probably the first publisher to produce books in the how-to, craft, and vocational fields. Most of the books were on carpentry, plumbing, blacksmithing, painting, and metalworking, and were written primarily for the layman rather than the professional. After the founder's death in 1912 the firm was managed by L. Brent Vaughan. When Vaughan retired in 1930 he was succeeded by Stafford W. Drake, the founder's son. The business, in turn, passed to Stafford Drake's daughter, Mrs. William Dibble, and her husband. Dibble, who was not a publisher, neglected to update the books or to look for new titles and about 1965 the company slowly drifted into bankruptcy.

In 1967 George Siebel acquired Drake but sold it the next year to Carl Ruderman, then a Henry M. Snyder & Company executive. Ruderman relocated the company in New York City and vitalized it by expanding its automotive workshop and repair manuals, starting the *Dollar Craft Books* for the how-to buff, and establishing two book clubs, Woodworkers Book Club of America and The Sewing Circle Book Club. Drake now publishes only nonfiction and continues the craft and how-to lines.

Drake Books, a subsidiary, handles all mail order and direct sales. Drake is also actively involved in the production of audio-visual cassettes in the how-to and craft fields.

Drama Book Specialists/Publishers

Established in 1967 at New York City as DBS Publications, Inc. Specialize in books on the performing arts.

The Dramatic Publishing Company

Founded in 1885 in Chicago, Illinois, by Charles H. Sergel to publish plays. The company was incorporated in 1887.

Dramatists Play Service, Inc.

Founded in 1936 at New York City. Publishes plays.

Droke House/Hallux, Inc.

Established in 1940 at Anderson, South Carolina, as Droke House Publishers, Inc. Publishes annually a small list of general fiction and nonfiction, specializing in Southern literature.

Duell, Sloan & Pearce

Founded in 1939 by Halliwell Duell, Samuel Sloan, and Charles A. Pearce. The firm began auspiciously with AMERICA WAS PROMISES by Archibald MacLeish. In the course of time they built up a good list of authors that included Benjamin Spock, John O'Hara, Erskine Caldwell, Howard Fast, Carey McWilliams, and Richard Aldington. Erskine Caldwell edited for them a fourteen-volume series on *American Folkways*.

Sloan died in 1945 but the two remaining partners maintained a steady pace of publishing activity until 1961. In that year the firm was acquired by Meredith Publishing Company and was reorganized as a subsidiary.

Dufour Editions, Inc.

Organized in 1946 at Chester Spring, Pennsylvania. Publishes literature and literary criticism, poetry, music, history, and reference books.

Duke University Press

Scholarly publishing at Trinity College, Durham, North Carolina, began in 1897 with the publication of THE PAPERS OF THE TRINITY COLLEGE HISTORICAL SOCIETY. In 1902 the *South Atlantic Quarterly* was launched as a scholarly periodical. But it was not until 1921 that the Press formally took shape under the imprint of Trinity College Press, mainly through the efforts of a number of faculty members. The first book to bear this new imprint was POLITICAL IDEAS OF THE AMERICAN REVOLUTION by Randolph Greenfield Adams (1922).

When Trinity College became one of the undergraduate colleges of the Duke University, Trinity College Press became Duke University Press. The first book published under the Duke imprint was ORIGINS OF THE WHIG PARTY by E. Malcolm Carroll (1925).

From the outset journals have played an important part in the evolution of the Press. In 1926 the Press revived publication of the *Hispanic American Historical Review,* which had been published earlier from 1918 to 1922. In 1929, with the cooperation of the Modern Language Association of America, it began publication of *American Literature.* From 1931 until 1948 the Press published the *Southern Association Quarterly,* official journal of the Southern Association of Secondary Schools and Colleges.

The other journals published by Duke are: *Ecological Monographs,* founded 1931; *Character and Personality* (renamed *Journal of Personality* in 1945), 1932; *Duke Mathematical Journal,* 1935; *Ecology,* 1920, at Duke since 1948; *The History of Political Economy,* 1969; *The Bulletin of the Ecological Society of America,* 1920, at Duke since 1970; and *The Journal of Medieval and Renaissance Studies,* 1971.

Duke has no regional or subject bias and its list does not concentrate on any one discipline or field.

Dunellen Publishing Company, Inc.

Established in 1969 at New York City. Issues the University Press of Cambridge Series in the Social Sciences.

Duquesne University Press

Established in Pittsburgh, Pennsylvania, in 1927. Occasional scholarly publications were issued on an informal basis from 1927 through 1951. In 1951 the Press developed a substantial publishing program under the directorship of Henry J. Koren. As part of this program the famous *Duquesne Studies* were initiated with the publication of the first volume in the *Philosophical Series,* FROM ATOMOS TO ATOM by Andrew G.

van Melsen. In 1965 John J. Foley was appointed director, a position he held until 1969, when John J. Dowds took over.

In 1972 the Press combined its publishing operations with Humanities Press, Inc. Book titles will carry the dual imprint of Duquesne University Press and Humanities Press. From 1951 until 1972 the Press had co-published with Editions Nauwelaerts of Louvain, Belgium.

Duquesne's major area of specialization is phenomenology. It thus concentrates on a region of the intellect rather than on a geographical area, as do a number of other American university presses. The most outstanding title in this program is EXISTENTIAL PHENOMENOLOGY by William Luijpen.

Under the general heading of *Duquesne Studies,* six book series have been published: in 1951, *The Philosophical;* in 1958, *The Spiritan;* in 1960, *The Philological;* in 1963, *The Theological;* in 1965, *The African* and *The Psychological.*

The Press formerly published several journals of which the most important were *The Journal of Ecumenical Studies* and the *Journal of Phenomenological Psychology.*

E.P. Dutton & Company, Inc.

Founded in 1852 in Boston, Massachusetts, by Edward Payson Dutton and Lemuel Ide as Ide and Dutton, distributors of schoolbooks and supplies. They did not venture into publishing until 1855 when they brought out Horace Mann's LECTURES ON EDUCATION. In 1858 Dutton purchased Ide's interest and the firm became E.P. Dutton & Company, publishing mainly denominational books, textbooks and maps. In 1864 Dutton acquired the famous Old Corner Bookstore from Ticknor & Fields. Four years later he took over the business of the General Protestant Episcopal Sunday School Union and the Book Society and established a branch in New York City. In 1869 James R. Osgood and Company of Boston offered its New York business to Dutton on condition that the company make its headquarters in New York and give up its Boston business. This offer was accepted, and the firm moved to New York City.

Dutton, like most of the publishers of his time, published a great many religious books of which three stand out: Dean Farrar's LIFE OF CHRIST; Phillips Brooks' SERMONS; and W.L.M. Jay's SHILOH. Dutton's bookshop at this time has been described as "the largest and handsomest book-store in New York." In 1884 John Macrae joined the firm as an office boy and in 1890 he was sent to England as a representative and buyer. He became a partner in 1900. Macrae went to Europe regularly, crossing the Atlantic one hundred and thirty-four times in all during his lifetime. It was during one of those visits that he arranged with J.M. Dent to publish the *Everyman's Library* in the United States. This series eventually extended to one thousand volumes. Through his English contacts Dutton obtained from Routledge of London their *Universal Library* and the *Muses Library,* as well as the right to publish such authors as George Gissing, W.H. Hudson, Samuel Butler, Max Beerbohm, Hilaire Belloc, G.K. Chesterton, Vincente Blasco-Ibáñez, Arnold Bennett, Leonard Merrick, Mary Webb, H.M. Tomlinson, Henry Williamson, Luigi Pirandello, Evelyn Underhill, and A.A. Milne. Encouraged by the success of *Everyman's Library,* Dutton brought out the series *Library of English Novelists,* the *Temple Shakespeare,* the *Temple Classics,* the *Temple Dramatists,* and many others.

When E.P. Dutton died in 1923, at the age of ninety-two, John Macrae and Henry Clapp Smith became joint trustees of the firm. Five years later the two separated, with Macrae retaining the imprint and Smith the bookstore. In 1929 Macrae made another of his successful discoveries when he published Axel Munthe's THE STORY OF SAN MICHELE. During the 1930s Dutton published such classics as THE FLOWERING OF NEW ENGLAND by Van Wyck Brooks and 1066 AND ALL THAT by Walter C. Sellar and Robert J. Yeatman. And in the early 1940s Dutton made publishing history by issuing John Roy Carlson's UNDER COVER in the face of great opposition. On his death in 1944 Macrae was mourned as the last of the old school of publishers. His son, Elliott Beach Macrae, became president of the company, a position he occupied until he died in 1968.

In 1946 the *Society in America* series was launched with THE PROPER BOSTONIANS by Cleveland Amory as the first title. A new and profitable author was also added to the list when Mickey Spillane's I, THE JURY was published. Macrae's interest in mountaineering led to the publication of several titles on adventure and exploration, especially, ANNAPURNA by Maurice Herzog, John Hunt's THE CONQUEST OF EVEREST, Sir Edmund Hillary's HIGH ADVENTURE, and Heinrich Harrer's SEVEN YEARS IN TIBET.

Dutton's ability to discover and foster new and important authors was again attested when, during the 1950s, it introduced to American readers Lawrence Durrell, Françoise Sagan, Marek Hlasko, Alexander Solzhenitsyn, Jorge Luis Borges, and Yevgeny Yevtushenko. Following the success of Gavin Maxwell's RING OF BRIGHT WATER the firm established the Dutton Animal Book Award, which has been won by such books as Sterling North's RASCAL and Robert Murphy's THE POND. The A.A. Milne books, WINNIE-THE-POOH, THE HOUSE AT POOH CORNER, WHEN WE WERE VERY YOUNG and NOW WE ARE SIX, as well as the Latin WINNIE ILLE PU, have been continuing successes. In 1957 Dutton launched its paperback series known as Dutton Paperbacks.

In 1968, after the death of Elliott Beach Macrae, for a brief period his brother, John Macrae, Jr., was Dutton's fourth president. He relinquished that post to become chairman of the board when his son, John Macrae III, took over the presidency in 1970.

In recent years THE TREE WHERE MAN WAS BORN by Peter Matthiessen and Eliot Porter, and A DIFFERENT WOMAN by Jane Howard, have been notably successful. THE FUNNY LITTLE WOMAN by Arlene Mosel, with illustrations by Blair Lent, was the winner of the coveted Caldecott Award in 1973.

Dutton publishes three annual series: *Best Detective Stories of the Year, Best Sports Stories,* and *Best Science Fiction Stories of the Year.* Dutton is also co-publisher of Windmill Books, Inc., Springfellow Books, Inc., Arthur Fields Books, Inc., Harvard Student Agencies, New Critics Press, Saturday Review Press, and Sunrise Book, Inc. The firm distributes the books of and provides a number of other services for the Richard W. Baron Publishing Company, Inc., Liveright, Nash Publishing, Inc., Garland Publishing, Inc., Transaction Books, Reader's Digest Press, and Chatham Press.

The Economy Company

Founded in 1929 at Oklahoma City, Oklahoma, by David D. Price. The company publishes textbooks and related materials exclusively for the language arts area of the curriculum. Some of those are KEYS TO READING, KEYS TO GOOD LANGUAGE, CONTINUOUS PROGRESS IN SPELLING, and KEYS TO GOOD ENGLISH. Wholly-owned affiliates are Individualized Instruction, Inc., and Educational Guidelines Company.

Edgemoor Publishing Company

Established in 1968 at Houston, Texas. Publishes plays and anthologies for nonprofessional theatre use; also regional books, especially folklore and history.

Educators Publishing Service, Inc.

Based at Cambridge, Massachusetts, a publisher of language arts materials for grades K-12 with special emphasis on remedial reading. Also, other supplementary work-text books.

William B. Eerdmans Publishing Company

Established in 1911 at Grand Rapids, Michigan, as the Eerdmans-Sevensma Company. Its purpose was to publish Biblical and theological works and works in the sciences and the humanities that interact with Christian scholarship and reflect basic Christian concern. By 1915 the company was wholly owned by the founder, William B. Eerdmans, Sr., and since that time it has been known as the William B. Eerdmans Publishing

Company. William B. Eerdmans, Sr., died in 1966 and was succeeded as president by his son, William B. Eerdmans, Jr.

Eerdmans has published both popular books and reference books. In the latter category would fall such major projects as: THE THEOLOGICAL DICTIONARY OF THE NEW TESTAMENT, edited by Gerhard Kittel and Gerhard Friedrich and translated by Geoffrey Bromiley, in nine volumes; STUDIES IN DOGMATICS by G.C. Berkouwer, in twenty volumes; THE NEW INTERNATIONAL COMMENTARY ON THE NEW TESTAMENT, edited by F.F. Bruce, in seventeen volumes; THE NICENE AND POST-NICENE FATHERS, edited by Philip Schaff and Henry Wace, in fifty-two volumes; THE THEOLOGICAL DICTIONARY OF THE OLD TESTAMENT, edited by G. Johannes Botterweck and Helmer Ringgren, in twelve volumes; TYNDALE NEW TESTAMENT COMMENTARY, edited by R.V.G. Tasker, in nineteen volumes; EVANGELICAL THEOLOGY by Helmut Thielicke, in three volumes; FOUNDATIONS OF THEOLOGY by Otto Weber, in two volumes; and CONTEMPORARY WRITERS IN CHRISTIAN PERSPECTIVE, edited by Roderick Jellema, an ongoing series of which by 1973 twenty-eight volumes had been published.

Encyclopaedia Britannica, Inc.

Reorganized in Chicago, Illinois, in 1943 by William Benton under the auspices of the University of Chicago. The ENCYCLOPAEDIA BRITANNICA had been first published in Edinburgh, Scotland, by a "Society of Gentlemen," in three volumes, between 1768 and 1771. The second edition consisted of ten, and the third of eighteen, volumes. In 1812 Archibald Constable acquired the work and issued a vastly improved twenty-volume sixth edition from 1820 to 1823. After Constable's death Encyclopaedia Britannica was bought by Adam Black, another Edinburgh publisher. The famous ninth edition was issued under the imprint of A. & C. Black from 1875 to 1889. It was sold extensively in the United States by Little, Brown and by Scribner.

Toward the turn of the century publication rights were acquired by a group of Americans consisting of James and George Clarke, Horace Hooper, and Walter M. Jackson. They issued a new edition under the sponsorship of *The Times* of London, England. Hooper bought out his partners and began work on the eleventh edition for publication on both sides of the Atlantic, carrying the imprint of the Cambridge University Press. After this edition appeared in 1910-11, and after lengthy litigation, Hooper was confirmed in his purchase of Jackson's interest. A smaller-sized version of the eleventh edition was distributed in the United States by Sears, Roebuck & Company, whose head, Julius Rosenwald, was a friend of Hooper. Rosenwald bought the BRITANNICA in 1920 but resold it two years later to Hooper's widow and her brother, W.J. Cox. Cox launched the fourteenth edition, edited by Franklin Hooper and J.L. Garvin. Beset once again by financial troubles, Cox permitted Rosenwald to reacquire the firm in 1928.

Rosenwald died in 1932 and a year later E.H. Powell, a Sears executive, was appointed to reorganize the ailing Britannica company on modern lines. Powell built up the firm's sales organization, began BRITANNICA JUNIOR encyclopaedia, and introduced such innovations as a library research department and a policy of continuous revision. R.E. Wood, the new chairman of Sears, regarded the encyclopaedia as a liability and offered to donate it to the University of Chicago. The trustees of the university hesitated to accept the gift until William Benton, retired co-founder of the advertising firm of Benton and Bowles and vice president of the university, agreed to provide the working capital and to take over the direction.

Encyclopaedia Britannica, Inc. thus in 1943 came under the control of Benton as chairman and publisher and majority stockholder. Under the arrangement, the University of Chicago was to receive perpetual royalties on the sales of the firm. After a few years the arrangement was changed to give Benton complete ownership and the university a contractual agreement which, by 1974, had returned $46,000,000 to it in royalties and other payments.

Under the guidance of three able presidents, Robert C. Preble, Maurice Mitchell, and Charles Swanson, Encyclopaedia Britannica, Inc. has emerged as one of the largest reference book publishers in the world. The BRITANNICA BOOK OF THE YEAR was launched in 1938 and BRITANNICA WORLD LANGUAGE DICTIONARY in 1954. One landmark publication was THE GREAT BOOKS OF THE WESTERN WORLD (q.v.) developed by Robert M. Hutchins and Mortimer J. Adler and associates in fifty-four volumes, including a two-volume SYNTOPICON, which Adler devised. THE GREAT IDEAS TODAY is issued as an annual supplement to this set. A companion publication, GATEWAY TO THE GREAT BOOKS, a ten-volume set, was published in 1963.

Three important acquisitions of the firm during the sixties were the F.E. Compton Company in 1961, G. & C. Merriam in 1964, and Frederick A. Praeger, Inc., in 1966. For the juvenile market the firm issues BRITANNICA JUNIOR ENCYCLOPAEDIA (first published in 1934 as BRITANNICA JUNIOR), GATEWAY TO THE GREAT BOOKS in ten volumes, and COMPTON'S ENCYCLOPEDIA. The juvenile division also publishes the sixteen-volume YOUNG CHILDREN'S ENCYCLOPAEDIA. An atlas program was begun with BRITANNICA WORLD ATLAS and continues with the BRITANNICA ATLAS. In 1968 a new annual was introduced: BRITANNICA YEARBOOK OF SCIENCE AND THE FUTURE.

Britannica entered the South American market with the Spanish ENCICLOPEDIA BARSA in 1957; a Portuguese edition followed in 1964. Another major international publication began in 1968 with the first volume of the French ENCYCLOPAEDIA UNIVERSALIS being issued in association with the Club Français du Livre (The French Book Club).

Publications sold by Britannica's Home Library Service, which makes books available by mail order, include THE WORLD OF MAN in sixteen volumes, a fourteen-volume ILLUSTRATED FAMILY ENCYCLOPEDIA OF THE LIVING BIBLE, and other books.

Early in 1966 the Encyclopaedia Britannica Educational Corporation was formed to meet changing needs in the development, production and marketing of educational films, other instructional materials and reference books. Nucleus of the firm was a pioneer educational film company purchased in 1943 and named Encyclopaedia Britannica Films, Inc. Publications introduced in 1969 include the three-volume THE NEGRO IN AMERICAN HISTORY and THE ANNALS OF AMERICA, a twenty-volume set including a two-volume CONSPECTUS that traces the life, thought and action of America from 1493 to 1968. A ten-volume MAKERS OF AMERICA appeared in 1971.

Expanding its international operations still further, in 1968 Britannica purchased a substantial minority interest in the Weidenfeld group of companies in London, England. In 1969, Britannica joined Tokyo Broadcasting System, Inc., and Toppan Printing Company to form a joint venture company called TBS-Britannica. This firm began publishing the twenty-eight-volume Japanese-language BRITANNICA INTERNATIONAL ENCYCLOPAEDIA in 1972 and will undertake other educational projects in Japan and the Far East.

In 1970 a subsidiary company, Library Resources, Inc., was set up to engage in micropublishing activities. Its Microbook Libraries include the 19,000-volume LIBRARY OF AMERICAN CIVILIZATION and the LIBRARY OF ENGLISH LITERATURE.

William Benton died in 1973. He had served as chairman and publisher of the company for thirty years, and during this period the volume of Britannica's business had increased more than fifty-fold.

In 1974 the company announced an entirely new edition of the ENCYCLOPAEDIA BRITANNICA incorporating major changes in format and content. In thirty volumes, it would comprise a one-volume topically organized *Propaedia* (or *Outline of Knowledge and Guide to the Britannica*), a main text or *Macropaedia,* in nineteen volumes, and a *Micropaedia* (or *Ready Reference and Index*) in ten volumes, the latter two parts to be alphabetically arranged.

Paul S. Eriksson, Inc.

Organized at New York City in 1960. Publishes a small general trade list annually in both fiction and nonfiction.

M. Evans & Company, Inc.

Organized in 1954 at New York City by Melvin Evans and George C. de Kay as a book packager. Over a nine-year period the firm produced more than one hundred books and series. It published the first list of its own books in 1963. Melvin Evans left the company in 1964; later, Herbert Katz joined the firm as an officer and shareholder.

The Evans list has stressed popular nonfiction and juveniles. Among the first category are such bestsellers as A GIFT OF JOY by Helen Hayes, AEROBICS by Kenneth H. Cooper, ON RE-FLECTION by Helen Hayes, BODY LAN-GUAGE by Julius Fast, OPEN MARRIAGE by Nena and George O'Neill, and ADDITIONAL DIALOGUE by Dalton Trumbo. The Evans juvenile program has included among its authors Ogden Nash, Louis Untermeyer, and Nancy Larrick.

Fairchild Publications, Inc.

Established in New York City in 1890. Issues publications in the fields of fashion, business, home economics, and management.

Fairleigh Dickinson University Press

Founded in 1966 at Rutherford, New Jersey. Though the imprint is controlled by Fairleigh Dickinson University, the Press is managed by Associated Universities Press of Cranbury, New Jersey. The Press publishes scholarly books.

Farnsworth Publishing Company, Inc.

Established in 1963 in Lynbrook, New York, and specializes in business, finance, and insurance.

Farrar, Straus & Giroux, Inc.

Established as a partnership in New York City in 1945 by John Farrar and Roger Straus, Jr.

Later Stanley Young was admitted as a partner and his name was added to the masthead. In the forties and fifties they published a number of successful titles including Carlo Levi's CHRIST STOPPED AT EBOLI, Alberto Moravia's THE WOMAN OF ROME, Martín Buber's AT THE TURNING, and Marguerite Yourcenar's MEM-OIRS OF HADRIAN. In 1951 the firm acquired Creative Age Press and two years later it took over Pellegrini & Cudahy. Following the latter acquisition Sheila Cudahy joined the company as an officer and her name replaced Young's in 1955 in the firm's title. In the same year Robert Giroux joined Farrar, Straus as editor-in-chief.

In the 1950s the trade list included three Nobel Prize winners—T.S. Eliot, François Mauriac, and Juan Ramón Jiménez. The firm also brought out the Vision Books for Catholics, books of Jewish interest such as the fiction of Isaac B. Singer, and *The Great Letters* series. Among the established authors associated with the Farrar, Straus imprint are Bernard Malamud, Anne O'Hare McCormick, Dwight Macdonald, Frank Swinnerton, Colette, Salvador de Madariaga, Isaak Babel, John Berryman, Carlos Fuentes, Mary McCarthy, and Thomas Merton.

In 1957 Farrar, Straus acquired L.C. Page & Company, whose list of over one thousand books included the *Pollyanna Glad Books* and the *Little Colonel series*. Since then the firm has taken over four more houses: McMullen Books, Inc., in 1958. Noonday Press, Inc., in 1960, Octagon Books, Inc., in 1968, and Hill & Wang in 1971.

Sheila Cudahy left the firm in 1955 and Robert Giroux's name was added to the masthead in 1964. The imprints Octagon Books, Noonday Paperbacks, and Sunburst Books are actively used.

Fawcett Publications, Inc.

Established in 1919 when Captain Wilford H. Fawcett began a little bulletin of humorous stories designed to spread cheer among World War I veterans in various hospitals. The bulletin was called *Captain Billy's Whiz Bang* (after the famous World War I artillery shell) and its first printing was only five thousand copies. But soon a national network of magazine distributors was selling over a half million copies a month. Encouraged by the success of *Whiz Bang,* the Fawcett family decided to expand their publishing activities and they moved into the upper floor of a bank building in Robbinsdale, Minnesota. Roscoe Fawcett, Billy's brother, became the publishing editorial director.

Robbinsdale became the birthplace of many magazines bearing the Fawcett imprint: *True Confessions, Mechanix Illustrated,* and the first Fawcett motion picture magazine called *Paris and Hollywood.* Later came *True, Rudder, Woman's Day, Electronics Illustrated,* several detective magazines, and dozens of once-a-year specials. In 1930 the firm moved to Minneapolis, Minnesota, and in 1935 the company's permanent headquarters were moved to Greenwich, Connecticut; shortly afterwards the editorial and advertising offices were set up in New York City. Roscoe Fawcett died in 1936, Captain Billy in 1940, and the task of management then fell upon Billy's four sons.

In the 1950s Fawcett entered book publishing with paperbound Gold Medal Books, joined in 1955 by Crest Books and Premier Books. The Crest titles are paperback reprints and Premier Books are paperbacks geared toward the educational market. Fawcett World Library is the general paperback division of Fawcett Publications. The company is a closely held family-owned corporation.

F.W. Faxon Company, Inc.

Founded in 1881 at Boston, Massachusetts, as Soule and Bugbee, lawbook publisher and bookseller. Bugbee retired in 1884 and the firm was reorganized in 1889 as the Boston Book Company. In the same year Frederick Winthrop Faxon joined the company to work in the newly formed library department and rose to become president in 1913. Faxon bought the company in 1918 and changed its name to F.W. Faxon Company. He continued as proprietor until his death in 1936, when ownership was transferred to Albert H. Davis, a cousin-in-law. The company was in-

corporated in 1951 with Davis as president. Davis retired in 1955 and his son, Albert H. Davis, Jr., was elected president.

The company's publishing programs were determined early by Faxon's enduring interest in libraries and magazines. *The Bulletin of Bibliography,* the company's oldest continuous publication, was established in 1897 as a medium for the publication of articles, bibliographies, reading lists, and other materials helpful to libraries. For a long time Faxon edited the magazine himself and his *Births, Deaths, and Magazine Notes* was a regular feature in it. In 1907 the first volume of the *Useful Reference Series of Books* was published. This series which lists over one hundred publications to date, began as an outgrowth of the *Bulletin of Bibliography.* The MAGAZINE SUBJECT INDEX and the DRAMATIC INDEX, both of which were published annually from 1909 to 1949, also outgrew their original short format in the *Bulletin.* The MAGAZINE SUBJECT INDEX was conceived as a complement to the major indexes of the day, POOLE'S and WILSON'S, and included state historical magazines and other periodicals not listed elsewhere. Other indexes include INDEX TO WOMEN, INDEX TO PROFILE SKETCHES IN THE NEW YORKER MAGAZINE, INDEX TO FAIRY TALES, and CLASSIFIED LIST OF PERIODICALS FOR THE COLLEGE LIBRARY.

Fearon Publishers

Established in 1956 in Belmont, California. Publishes elementary, secondary, and college textbooks. Sponsors the highly innovative *Pacemaker* books on special education. In 1974 the firm was sold to Pitman Publishing Corporation.

Feffer and Simons, Inc.

Organized in New York City in 1956 by Paul E. Feffer and George Calvert Simons as a worldwide export organization. In 1962 it was acquired by Doubleday and Company and it now operates as a wholly-owned subsidiary.

In addition to twelve overseas offices Feffer and Simons owns or controls a number of distribution firms overseas that specialize in the sale of books. These include Feffer and Simons (Nederland) B.V., in the Netherlands, Fleetbooks, S.A., in Switzerland, Transatlantic Book Service in England, Boxerbooks in Switzerland, Distribuidora de Impresos, S.A., in Mexico, and Tudor Distributors, Pty. Ltd. in Australia. It also owns two Spanish language publishing firms, Minerva Books Limited of New York and Compañía General de Ediciones, S.A., in Mexico City. In India the firm of Vakils, Feffer and Simons Pvt. Ltd. specializes in publishing low cost textbooks. The Editorial Services Company, another subsidiary, reprints texts for the college market abroad and purchases overruns of trade books for sale overseas.

Feffer and Simons has served as consultants and advisers to UNESCO, the Asian Productivity Organization, the United States Information Agency, and the Agency for International Development of the United States Department of State.

Frederick Fell Publishers, Inc.

Founded in 1943 in New York City by Frederick Fell. Over the years the firm published under several imprints, including Felco Paperbacks, Frederick Fell, and Lido Paperback Books. A subsidiary, the Arden Book Company, is no longer in existence. Major publishing programs include a *Western Americana* series, *Fell's Business Book Library, Fell's Personal Interest Library,* and *Fell's Self-Help Library.*

Magnet Books, Inc. is now a part of Frederick Fell Publishers, Inc.

J.G. Ferguson Publishing Company

Established in 1956 in Chicago, Illinois. The firm took over the Good Counsel Publishing Company. It was acquired by Doubleday and Company, of which it is now a division. Specializes in subscription and reference books and curriculum materials.

Howard Fertig, Inc., Publisher

Established in 1966, a small privately-owned publisher of scholarly originals and reprints.

The Fideler Company

Established in 1936 at Grand Rapids, Michigan. Publishes elementary and high school textbooks in social studies and language arts.

Fides Publishers, Inc.

Founded in 1944 at Notre Dame, Indiana, by a group of Catholic Actionists headed by Rev. Louis J. Putz, C.S.C. The original purpose of the organization, then known as Apostolate Press and Fides Publishers Association, was to publish materials for the Catholic lay apostolate. As an innovator in the field of religious publishing Fides introduced Cardinal Suhard, Father Henry and many other liberal theologians to the American reading public. During the 1950s and 1960s Fides enjoyed steady growth, expanding into textbooks for Catholic high schools and religious educational materials for all grade levels. In addition to formal textbook programs for use in Catholic high schools, Fides publishes the Dome paperback series on cinema and film education, books for early childhood education, and books of general religious interest.

In 1962 Fides was reorganized as a privately-owned Indiana corporation. One major program is *Teaching Religion Through Literature,* a non-doctrinal approach to teaching religious ideas and values through the use of short stories and poems by famous authors, including Ernest Hemingway, William Faulkner, Anton Chekhov, Robert Frost, and John Steinbeck. Fides has also made available the first American translation of two of Maria Montessori's most famous works, THE SECRET OF CHILDHOOD and THE DISCOVERY OF THE CHILD. In addition, Fides has undertaken the translation into English of the nine-volume GUIDE FOR THE CHRISTIAN ASSEMBLY, a background book of the Mass. Another of their major publishing programs is the forty-eight volume *Theology Today* series. In 1973 Fides published THE LIT BOOK, a guided independent study course in literature which will take the firm into the public school market for the first time.

Field Enterprises Educational Corporation

Established in 1944 by Marshall Field III as Field Enterprises, Inc. in Chicago, Illinois. The firm purchased in 1945 the Quarrie Corporation, publishers of the WORLD BOOK ENCYCLOPEDIA and CHILDCRAFT — THE HOW AND WHY LIBRARY.

The history of WORLD BOOK goes back to 1915 when J.H. Hanson of the Hanson-Bellows Company engaged Michael Vincent O'Shea, famed educator, to revise his NEW PRACTICAL REFERENCE LIBRARY, which he had been publishing for many years as a five-volume set. In 1917 this revised edition appeared under the title, THE WORLD BOOK, ORGANIZED KNOWLEDGE IN STORY AND PICTURES. In 1919 W.F. Quarrie took over the Hanson-Bellows Company and became publisher of the WORLD BOOK. Quarrie and R.G. Lamberson, an able associate, established the company as a going concern, organized an effective field sales force, and undertook the revision of the WORLD BOOK in 1929. The new revision consisted of thirteen volumes, including a reading and study guide with a unit-letter arrangement of volumes. In 1933 the WORLD BOOK was once again revised in a nineteen-volume edition.

In 1934 the company brought out CHILD-CRAFT, a six-volume set that had been prepared on the lines laid down by the first White House Conference on Children and Youth. Described as a complete plan of development for young children's reading, CHILDCRAFT included the best of juvenile literature along with articles on child guidance for parents. The set appeared in two editions, one designed for parents and the other for teachers.

Lamberson became president of the firm in 1940, a post he held until his retirement in 1956. He was responsible for persuading Marshall Field to take over the corporation from the ailing Quarrie in 1945. In 1949 the Quarrie Corporation

became the educational division of Field Enterprises, Inc.; in 1957 it was renamed Field Enterprises Educational Corporation. By 1947, when a new edition of the WORLD BOOK was published under the editorship of J.M. Jones, the company had introduced the principle of continuous revision. An editorial advisory board also adopted the principle that the vocabulary of the articles must be suitable to the students at the grade levels where the subjects are generally studied. In addition, the over-all format and typography were improved with the help of W.A. Dwiggins, the noted typographer.

Bailey K. Howard became president of the corporation in 1957. Under his leadership the revised edition of the WORLD BOOK was published in 1960 in twenty volumes. This included a major innovation: Trans-Vision®, a visual aid composed of several acetate overlays, each showing a discrete element of the illustration. In 1960 Field acquired L.J. Bullard Company, publishers of TEACHERS EXTENSION SET in eight volumes and the HOW AND WHY LIBRARY in seven volumes.

In 1961 the firm introduced the Cyclo-teacher® Learning Aid, a self-instructional teaching machine based on the WORLD BOOK. Several major projects were launched during the 1960s. Among them were THE WORLD BOOK YEAR BOOK (1962), THE WORLD BOOK ENCYCLOPEDIA DICTIONARY, edited by the renowned lexicographer, Clarence L. Barnhart (1963), THE WORLD BOOK ENCYCLOPEDIA SCIENCE SERVICE (1963), THE WORLD BOOK ATLAS (1964), WORLD SCIENCE YEAR (1965), and CHILDCRAFT ANNUAL (1966). CHILDCRAFT and the HOW AND WHY LIBRARY were combined into a fifteen-volume set in 1964. International editions of the WORLD BOOK ENCYCLOPEDIA were also published in Great Britain and Australia. A Braille edition was published in 1961 and a large-type edition in 1964.

Howard V. Phalin succeeded Howard as president of the company in 1964. His successor was Robert R. Barker. William T. Branham became president of the firm in 1971 and chairman of the board of Field Enterprises Educational Corporation in January, 1973. James E. Fletcher became president in January, 1973.

Fleet Press Corporation

Founded in 1955 as the Fleet Publishing Company in New York City. In 1967 the name was changed to Fleet Press Corporation under a new management, with Doris Schiff as president. An associate company known as Fleet Academic Editions was founded in 1969.

Fleet Press publishes books for the young reader. The Fleet Academic Editions publishes books for the college and graduate school reader. A major ongoing project is the publication of the *Nobel Conference Lecture Series* with the assistance of the Advisory Committee of Nobel Laureates.

Fodor's Modern Guides, Inc.

See, David McKay Company, Inc.

Follett Publishing Company

Founded in 1873 in Wheaton, Illinois, by C.M. Barnes as a retail bookstore serving college students. The firm was moved to Chicago in 1875. In 1893 J.W. Wilcox became a partner and in 1894 the company incorporated as C.M. Barnes Company. In 1901 Charles W. Follett entered the firm. Barnes retired in 1902 and his son, W.R. Barnes, assumed the presidency. In 1907 the firm name was changed to C.M. Barnes-Wilcox Company. In 1917 when the Barnes family moved to New York City to eventually found Barnes & Noble, the company became J.W. Wilcox & Follett Company.

By 1923 the company was owned entirely by members of the Follett family. Follett Publishing Company was organized as a publishing division in 1926. Charles Follett was succeeded by Dwight W. Follett as president, and the current president, Robert Follett, is the third generation of the family to lead the company. The company's active imprints include Maxton, Big Table, Follett In-Service Seminars, Educational Opportunity Project, and Follett Educational Corporation.

From its inception Follett has published for both the trade and the educational markets. In the trade area the company has been a major publisher of children's books and adult nonfiction. Foreign language dictionaries and sports books have long been staple items. In the educational area Follett has been primarily involved with providing a broad range of instructional materials for schools. The company has pioneered in the unification of the social sciences, in the use of recordings in music education, in the development of multi-racial textbooks, in the development of programs for early childhood education, in materials for educationally handicapped and slow-learning students, in the beginning-to-read concept, and in basic educational programs for adult illiterates.

Fordham University Press

Established in 1907 by James J. Walsh, Dean of the School of Medicine, Fordham University, Bronx, New York, who served as director of the Press until 1922. From that year until 1936 the Press was managed by five administrators. The first full-time director, Robert E. Holland S.J., served from 1936 to 1946. For the next ten years the titles of the Press were produced and distributed by The Declan X. McMullen Company, Inc.

The Press was reorganized at the beginning of 1957 and Edwin A. Quain, S.J., was appointed director, a post which he held until 1972, when H. George Fletcher succeeded him. Under Father Quain's leadership, the Press developed into a full-time operation, publishing annually some dozen books and journals. The most prestigious of its titles is TRADITIO: STUDIES IN ANCIENT AND MEDIEVAL HISTORY, THOUGHT, AND RELIGION.

Fortress Press

Founded in 1962 at Philadelphia, Pennsylvania, as the trade book division of the Board of Publication of the Lutheran Church in America. It represents a merger of earlier trade names, the Muhlenberg Press, the Augustana Book Concern, and the Finnish Book Concern.

In recent years, Fortress Press has become a major publisher of religious books for lay, clergy, general academic, and scholarly reading audiences. Its annual publishing program includes approximately fifty books. Outstanding titles have recently included DEFINING AMERICA: A CHRISTIAN CRITIQUE OF THE AMERICAN DREAM by Philip Hefner and Robert Benne; the *Hermeneia* series, more than thirty commissioned volumes in "An Historical and Critical Commentary on the Bible" edited by Boards headed by Frank Moore Cross, Jr. and Helmut Koester of Harvard University; the international project of ten volumes on Jewish-Christian relations, COMPENDIA RERUM IUDAICARUM AD MOVUM TESTAMENTUM; a major series of sixteen paperbacks on "Creative Pastoral Counseling and Care" edited by Howard Cline-bell of the Claremont Graduate School of Theology; HOMOSEXUALITY AND COUNSELING by Clinton Jones; PRAYERS FOR LAY MINISTRY by Carl Uehling. Since 1955 Fortress has cooperated with the Concordia Publishing House on the 55-volume edition of LUTHER'S WORKS.

Fortress traces its history for nearly a hundred years. The present director and senior editor is Norman A. Hjelm.

See also Augustana Book Concern and Muhlenberg Press.

The Foundation Press, Inc.

Founded in 1931 at Mineola, New York. Publishes books on law, business, and political science.

Fountainhead Publishers, Inc.

Established in 1960 at New York City. A small privately-owned publisher of hardcover general fiction and nonfiction books.

Franciscan Herald Press

Founded in 1917 at Chicago, Illinois. Publishers of Catholic and religious books, and Franciscan literature.

Burt Franklin

Established in 1943 at New York City. The firm was acquired by Lenox Hill Publishing and Distributing Corporation. Specializes in reprints.

Franklin Book Programs, Inc.

Established in 1952 as a nongovernmental, nonprofit educational corporation whose purpose is to assist international book publishing development with major emphasis on assistance to developing countries. It was funded by the U.S. Government through the efforts of the American Book Publishers Council's Joint International Trade Committee and the American Library Association's International Relations Committee.

Originally established to foster the translation of American books into the languages of Asia and the Middle East, it has evolved into a technical assistance organization, with translations comprising only a small part of its total activity. It is currently supported by grants and contracts with governments, foundations, and corporations. Its board of thirty directors has always included leaders of the American book industry. Board chairmen have been Malcolm Johnson, William E. Spaulding, Henry A. Laughlin, Thomas J. Wilson, W. Bradford Wiley, Edward E. Booher, Raymond C. Harwood, and Martin P. Levin. Presidents have been Datus C. Smith, Jr., Michael Harris, Carroll G. Bowen, and John H. Kyle.

Major assistance programs have been or are being carried out through local offices in Egypt, Iraq, Iran, Afghanistan, Pakistan, Bangladesh, Malaysia, Indonesia, Kenya, Nigeria, Lebanon, Argentina, and Brazil. Individual projects, including surveys, seminars, and special publishing projects, have been carried out in many other countries. All projects conform to Franklin's four basic objectives: (1) To increase local capabilities Franklin assists and trains indigenous organizations in the planning and production of textbooks, classroom magazines, and audio-visual materials for the schools, adult literacy and fundamental education materials, and reference books for the educated citizen. It assists in the development of printing plants, and training of their personnel. (2) To increase the international exchange of books, Franklin sponsors book translations (over three thousand to date); assists publishing organizations in the developing countries to secure translation and reprint rights to American books; sponsors international conferences and seminars to promote the international exchange of books. (3) To strengthen book marketing and distribution Franklin seeks to improve trade practices—advertising and promotion, pricing, discounts, credit, and accounting—and to improve local book trade services it encourages trade publications, national bibliographies, direct-mail lists and services and wholesale operations. It also seeks to alleviate the chronic undercapitalization of publishers in the developing countries. (4) To foster the development of the reading habit, Franklin assists in the development of supplementary reading materials for the schools, sponsors exhibits and related activities to enhance the image of the book in the popular mind, and creates school and village libraries.

The Free Press

Founded in 1947 in Glencoe, Illinois, by Jeremiah Kaplan with the backing of Charles Liebman. Acquired by Crowell, Collier & Macmillan in 1961 and reorganized as a division. Issues college textbooks and professional books, primarily in the social sciences and the humanities.

James E. Freel & Associates

Publisher of college textbooks, located at Cupertino, California. Formerly a subsidiary of John Wiley & Sons, Inc., the company in early 1974 was sold to Page Ficklin Publications of California. Wiley continues to distribute its books.

Miller Freeman Publications, Inc.

Established in 1902 at San Francisco, California. Publishes technical books.

W.H. Freeman and Company

Founded in San Francisco, California, in 1946 by William Hazen Freeman who, for some twenty years, had been a college representative for the Macmillan Company. His purpose was to establish a California-based publishing company, relying on the leading universities of the area for authors, particularly in the natural sciences. The first book, GENERAL CHEMISTRY by Linus Pauling, was an immediate success. Since then Freeman has published over three hundred college textbooks in the sciences, mathematics, and agriculture.

In 1961 the company entered into a joint venture with Scientific American, Inc., wherein the company agreed to publish and promote articles from *Scientific American* magazine as separate publications for classroom use in schools and colleges. In the ensuing decade some thirty-five million of these offprints were sold. More recently topical anthologies and the encyclopedic *Scientific American Resource Library* have been compiled of articles from the magazine. This led in 1964 to the corporate merger of W.H. Freeman and Company and Scientific American, Inc. A further activity of this period was a large and successful project prepared under the auspices of the National Science Foundation: the publication and distribution of the Chemical Education Material Study, which has greatly influenced the teaching of high school chemistry. This project consists of a textbook, lab manual, teacher's guide, achievement exams, etc.

Freeman left the company in 1962 and Stanley Schaefer succeeded him as president. Schaefer is now chairman of the board. He was succeeded as president of the company by Richard W. Warrington in 1973.

Freeman, Cooper & Company

Established in 1964 at San Francisco, California. Publishes college textbooks in science and philosophy.

Samuel French, Inc.

Established in 1850 in New York City by Samuel French as a branch of the English firm which had been started in London in 1830 by the British actor Thomas Hailes Lacy. In 1872 French bought out Lacy.

Among the early French drama series were *French's Standard Drama, French's Minor Drama, French's American Drama,* and *Spencer's Boston Theater.* French also published books on the art of makeup, stage management, and related subjects. In 1871 French's son joined the firm and it was renamed Samuel French & Son.

Samuel French died in 1898. The firm was incorporated in 1899 as Samuel French, Inc. Its specialization is plays and play parts, as well as other books dealing with theatrical arts.

Freshet Press Inc.

Organized in 1969 at Rockville Centre, New York, a small publisher of reprint and original titles dealing with outdoor sports.

Friendship Press

Founded in 1902 at New York City when the Young People's Missionary Movement decided to begin the publication of materials to help people in the churches understand missionary work. This movement merged with Councils of Churches for Home Missions and Councils of Churches for Foreign Missions, becoming in 1911 the Missionary Education Movement of the United States and Canada. This imprint remained active until 1935 when the name Friendship Press was adopted. The parent organization, however, continued to be known as the Missionary Education Movement of the United States and Canada. In 1950 the Movement became a unit of the National Council of Churches of Christ as the Department of Education for Mission.

The Press publishes a series of books, maps, plays, games, etc. on the church in certain areas of the world, such as Africa, India, Southeast Asia, Latin America, and another series on the great issues of the day, *e.g.* affluence and poverty, faith and justice, development, etc. Friendship Press is the only church-owned ecumenical publisher in the United States.

Arthur Frommer, Inc.

Publisher at New York City of popular travel guide books, including EUROPE ON FIVE DOLLARS A DAY, etc. The books are distributed by Simon & Schuster.

The Frontier Press Company

Started in Buffalo, New York, in 1907 by M.J. Kinsella; presently located in Columbus, Ohio. Its first publication, in 1908, was THE STANDARD DICTIONARY OF FACTS, a one-volume work divided into separate areas of knowledge. Between 1908 and 1927 the DICTIONARY went through seventeen editions. The next Frontier publication was MASTERS OF ACHIEVEMENT, a biographical reference work. In 1924 came the first publication of THE LINCOLN LIBRARY OF ESSENTIAL INFORMATION, a classified general encyclopedia conceived and developed by Kinsella. By 1972 the LINCOLN LIBRARY had gone through thirty-five editions.

The editor of the LINCOLN LIBRARY for many years was John Wilson Taylor; succeeding editors were Clyde Park, Ruth Tarbell, and William J. Redding. Since 1968 three more publications have been launched: THE LINCOLN LIBRARY OF SOCIAL STUDIES, THE LINCOLN LIBRARY OF LANGUAGE ARTS, and THE LINCOLN LIBRARY OF THE ARTS. After M.J. Kinsella, later owners of the Press were in order: B.S. Kinsella, H.C. Goff, Verne E. Seibert, and William H. Seibert.

Funk and Wagnalls, Inc.

Founded in 1876 in New York City by Reverend Isaak Kaufman Funk as a religious publishing house. In 1878 Adam W. Wagnalls joined him as a partner and the imprint became Funk and Wagnalls. Funk was at first regarded as a pirate because he never adhered to the prevailing trade courtesy and reprinted books without permission. Among his unauthorized editions were Dean Farrar's LIFE OF CHRIST and Edwin Arnold's THE LIGHT OF ASIA. At the same time he issued many original books in the religious and reference fields and achieved great success with THE SCHAFF-HERZOG ENCYCLOPAEDIA OF RELIGIOUS KNOWLEDGE, Meyer's COMMENTARY, (Theodore) PARKER'S BIBLE in twenty-five volumes, THE JEWISH ENCYCLOPAEDIA in twelve volumes, and TREASURY OF DAVID by Charles H. Spurgeon.

Funk is best remembered for his journal, *The Literary Digest,* which he began to publish in 1890. Very influential and phenomenally successful, it achieved a circulation of over two million by the 1930s. In 1936 it was sold to the *Review of Reviews* and was later absorbed by *Time.* In 1890 Funk started work on the STANDARD DICTIONARY OF THE ENGLISH LANGUAGE. When it was published in 1894 it became one of the major American dictionaries. Funk also published a number of other successful reference works among which were the INTERNATIONAL YEAR BOOK and Emily Post's ETIQUETTE—THE BLUE BOOK OF SOCIAL USAGE. Funk died in 1912, Wagnalls in 1924. Wilfred I. Funk took over as president and managed the company until 1940, when he sold his interest to Robert J. Cuddihy. Cuddihy built up a good trade list and a juvenile list to supplement the company's traditional reference books.

Funk and Wagnalls was acquired by Reader's Digest Association in 1965. In 1971 they sold the firm to Standard Reference Library, Inc., a subsidiary of Corinthian Broadcasting Corporation. Standard Reference Library, Inc. had been publishing Funk and Wagnalls encyclopedias under a royalty arrangement since 1941 and was principally a mass retail marketer. Standard Reference Library then changed its name to Funk and Wagnalls, Inc.

Later in 1971, Corinthian Broadcasting Corporation merged with Dun & Bradstreet and the ownership of Funk and Wagnalls was transferred to the Reuben H. Donnelley Corporation, a wholly-owned subsidiary of Dun & Bradstreet Companies, Inc. Trade publishing operations of Funk and Wagnalls were assigned to the Thomas Y. Crowell Company, a subsidiary of Dun-Donnelley Publishing Corporation, also owned by Dun & Bradstreet Companies, Inc.

Futura Publishing Company, Inc.

Set up in 1970 at Mount Kisco, New York, to publish medical and scientific books.

Gale Research Company

Established in 1954 in Detroit, Michigan, by Frederick G. Ruffner, Jr. Its first title was the ENCYCLOPEDIA OF ASSOCIATIONS, which entered its eighth edition in 1973. Gale publishes reference books, dictionaries, and directories, primarily for the library market. Among its major programs are CONTEMPORARY AUTHORS, a continuing series of bio-bibliographical works, which by 1973 covered over forty thousand authors; *Contemporary Literary Criticism,* a series composed of extensive excerpts from books and articles dealing with specific authors and their works; SOMETHING ABOUT THE AUTHOR, for younger readers; DIRECTORY OF SPECIAL LIBRARIES AND INFORMATION CENTERS: RESEARCH CENTERS DIRECTORY; NATIONAL FACULTY DIRECTORY; ENCYCLOPEDIA OF GOVERNMENTAL ADVISORY ORGANIZATIONS; BOOK REVIEW INDEX; and LIBRARY OF CONGRESS CLASSIFICATION SCHEDULES.

Another major project is *Management Information Guide,* a series, which includes, as of 1973, twenty-seven volumes, each a comprehensive bibliography of a particular facet of modern business and industry. A related project is *Gale Information Guides,* which will include twenty distinctly separate series of bibliographies in the humanities and social sciences. Gale has also published the LIBRARY OF CONGRESS AND NATIONAL UNION CATALOG AUTHOR LISTS, 1942-1962: A MASTER CUMULATION, in one hundred and fifty-two volumes. In addition, Gale has been a leader in the reprint field, in which its catalogue lists over a thousand titles.

Gambit, Incorporated

Organized in 1968 at Boston, Massachusetts, by Lovell Thompson, a former director of Houghton Mifflin Company. Associated with Thompson at the time of Gambit's founding, as editor-in-chief, was Helen Everitt, who was the first director of Radcliffe College's publishing procedures course. After her death in 1970, Mark Saxton, a director of the company since its beginning, succeeded Helen Everitt as editor-in-chief. Morgan K. Smith, also a former director of Houghton Mifflin, joined Gambit in 1972 as assistant managing director.

As a small, independent publisher, Gambit, Incorporated is devoted to history, literature, and books on urgent topics of the day. The firm's ALMANAC OF AMERICAN POLITICS, a biennial reference book, has gained considerable acceptance.

Garland Publishing, Inc.

Organized in 1969 at New York City as a reprint house.

Garrard Publishing Company

Established in 1912 in Champaign, Illinois, as the Twin City Printing Company, specializing in the printing of technical and scientific journals for professional societies. Printing these journals brought the company into contact with well-known authorities in various scientific fields.

Twin City entered publishing in 1932 with a reference book in microbiology. More reference books followed and in 1936 a new imprint, The Garrard Press, was adopted for the publishing division of the company. In 1939, under the new imprint, professional reference books related to the teaching of reading were published. At the same time manipulative teaching aids for the teaching of reading were developed.

In 1950 first books for children to read independently were published, followed by books for elementary classrooms and libraries. In 1957 the company decided to expand into curriculum-related books for children. To ensure that the books were educationally sound the services of several professional specialists in reading were obtained. In 1962 the publishing division was spun off as a separate corporation under the name of The Garrard Publishing Company. In the same year the editorial offices were moved from Champaign, to Scarsdale, New York.

Bernard Geis Associates, Inc.

Organized in 1959 by Bernard Geis in New York City. His partners included television personalities, among whom were Art Linkletter, Ralph Edwards, John Guedel, and Groucho Marx. The venture brought together a group of celebrities in the public eye to publish sensational books, which were then unabashedly promoted. The result was a string of bestsellers: Art Linkletter's THE SECRET WORLD OF KIDS, VALLEY OF THE DOLLS by Jacqueline Susann, Max Shulman's I WAS A TEEN-AGE DWARF, and Harry S. Truman's MR. CITIZEN.

By 1968 most of the partners had left Geis and the firm, as a protest against the increasingly erotic content of the Geis books. In 1969 the firm was incorporated.

Genealogical Publishing Company, Inc.

Established in 1959 at Baltimore, Maryland. Publishes books and reprints dealing with genealogical, heraldic and regional historical interests.

General Learning Corporation

Established in 1966 at Morristown, New Jersey, by a partnership of General Electric Company with Time, Inc. Time, Inc. invested Silver Burdett Company (q.v.) as its share in the venture.

Among General Learning Corporation's multi-media pre-K through secondary programs are *Bridge-To-Reading* (preschool curriculum), *Contemporary Social Science Curriculum, Silver Burdett Music, Pipeline* (monthly music education publication), *National Environmental Education Development, Intermediate Science Curriculum Study Program, Contemporary English Curriculum, Biology, Spell Correctly,* and the *Silver Burdett Mathematics System.* The *Concern* series and *We Celebrate the Eucharist* are two of the company's current religious education programs. All el-hi publications are published by the Silver Burdett Division.

Under the imprint General Learning Press, a broad variety of books and modules are published for college and university students in the fields of business, economics, science, music, the humanities, social and behavioral sciences, education, and mathematics.

GLC Educational Materials and Services, Ltd., in Agincourt, Ontario, Canada, publishes materials for the Canadian schools and markets GLC's educational products in that country. The firm was established in 1970 as a wholly-owned subsidiary.

GLC presents since its incorporation have been Richard L. Shetler (1966-1967), Francis Keppel (1967-1969), John D. Backe (1969-1973), and William K. Cordier (1973-present). Francis Keppel has been chairman of the board of GLC since its incorporation. The corporate name in 1974 was changed to Silver Burdett Company.

The Geological Society of America

Founded in 1888 at Rochester, New York, "for the promotion of the science of geology by the issuance of scholarly publications, the holding of meetings, the provision of assistance to research, and other appropriate means." It began activity as a publisher in 1889 in New York City with the serial, the *Geological Society of America Bulletin.* A substantial bequest from R.A.F. Penrose, Jr., in 1930 enabled the Society to begin publication in 1934 of its *Memoir* and *Special Paper* series and the annual *Bibliography and Index of Geology Exclusive of North America.* This journal was broadened to become the *Bibliography and Index of Geology* in 1969, featuring groups of descriptors or key words instead of abstracts, to provide geologists with an up-to-date monthly bibliographic coverage of world literature in geology.

With the publication in 1953 of the first part of a projected twenty-four part *Treatise on Invertebrate Paleontology,* the Society joined with the University of Kansas Press in a major publishing venture. An *Abstracts with Programs* series, special publications in the field of engineering geology, colored wall maps, and non-technical publications devoted primarily to Society matters are also published.

As a new venture in earth science reporting, publication of *Geology,* a monthly magazine, was initiated in September 1973. It was conceived to answer today's pressing need for rapid dissemination of research information. It has been designed to emphasize current awareness by quick publication—eight weeks from acceptance to delivery by mail.

Publications between the years 1891 and 1907 were issued from Rochester, New York. The imprint was issued from New York City from 1907 until 1967, when the headquarters of the Society were moved to Boulder, Colorado.

See, THE GEOLOGICAL SOCIETY OF AMERICA, 1888-1930; A CHAPTER IN EARTH SCIENCE HISTORY, Herman LeRoy Fairchild, 1933.

The C.R. Gibson Company

Founded in 1870 in New York City by John Gibson as John Gibson & Company. The company conducted a lithography business, printing business forms, marriage certificates, and related items. After John Gibson's death in 1895 his widow sold the business to his nephew, Charles, then president of the Gibson Art Company in

Cincinnati, Ohio. Charles moved to New York City and the firm, now known as the C.R. Gibson Company, expanded into such supplementary lines as church publications and remembrance books, issued as wedding and baby books.

In 1940 the company moved again, this time to Norwalk, Connecticut. In 1952 Charles R. Gibson retired and his grandson, Robert G. Bowman, succeeded him as president. The 1950s and 1960s were a period of dramatic growth for the company and saw its entry into the gift book field. The first gift book published in this series was THE GREATEST OF THESE IS LOVE by Audrey McDaniel. APPLES OF GOLD by Jo Petty was another all-time bestseller. It is now in its fourteenth printing with sales of over one million, four hundred thousand copies. The company publishes forty additional titles.

The K.S. Giniger Company, Inc.

Organized in 1965 at Chicago, Illinois, by Kenneth S. Giniger and Carol Giniger. Books are distributed under joint imprint arrangements with publishers in the United States and abroad. Publications include general trade, juveniles, reference, and religious books, often sold by mail order and subscription.

Ginn and Company

Founded in 1867 in Boston, Massachusetts, by Edwin Ginn. From 1870 until 1877 the firm operated as Ginn Brothers with Fred B. Ginn as the junior partner. Ginn's first publication was George Lillie Craik's ENGLISH OF SHAKESPEARE. In 1873 he employed Daniel C. Heath as an agent; within three years Heath was made a partner and the firm's name was changed to Ginn and Heath. In 1880 George A. Plimpton entered the partnership.

Some of Ginn's outstanding early programs included the *Classics for Children* series, Henry N. Hudson's SHAKESPEARE, in twenty-three

volumes, Joseph Henry Allen's LATIN GRAMMAR, William Watson Goodwin's GREEK GRAMMAR, and a *Music Series* by Luther Mason, which was the first graded series of music texts for elementary schools. Also, George Albert Wentworth's *Plane Geometry* and *Mathematics* series, Alexis Everett Frye's *Geographies,* and an American history series edited by David S. Muzzey.

In 1885 Heath withdrew from the partnership to found his own firm. Meanwhile, Ginn's business grew rapidly, leading *The American Bookseller* to comment that no educational publishing house in the country had attained similar success in an equal length of time. It was at this time, too, that William Dwight Whitney's ENGLISH GRAMMAR achieved wide classroom use. By 1890 Ginn was the sixth largest textbook firm in the United States; nevertheless it refused to join the newly formed American Book Company.

Ginn's continuing success was due to its ability to attract outstanding authors in all disciplines: David Eugene Smith in mathematics, James Harvey Robinson and David S. Muzzey in history, William McPherson and William E. Henderson in chemistry, Wallace A. Atwood and Preston James in geography, Robert A. Millikan and Henry Gordon Gale in physics, and Harold Rugg in the social sciences. Not only were the books written by those authors widely adopted but they influenced teaching and curricula in schools and colleges all over the country.

Edwin Ginn died in 1914 and was succeeded by George A. Plimpton as head of the firm. When Plimpton retired in 1931 Henry H. Hilton was elected president. In 1939 the company was incorporated and three years later Frederick A. Rice became its president. During the forties and fifties Ginn maintained its strength in the educational field with such series as *Faith and Freedom* for Catholic schools; *Ginn Basic Readers* prepared by D.H. Russell, Odille Ousley and others; the Tiegs and Adams *Social Study* series; Gerald S. Craig's *Science Today and Tomorrow* series; and the *Arithmetic We Need* series by W.A. Brownell and Irene Sauble.

Frederick A. Rice retired as president and chairman of the board of the company in the spring of 1958. He was succeeded by Homer C.

Lucas as president and Lee N. Griffin as chairman of the board. In 1960 the firm went public. During the tenure of Lucas, Ginn acquired Personnel Press, publisher of the Kuhlmann-Anderson Intelligence Tests, and Blaisdell Publishing Company, a former subsidiary of Random House.

In 1964 Grant M. Bennion was elected president and Henry Halvorson, chairman of the board of the company. During Bennion's tenure, a number of new programs were initiated and Blaisdell Publishing Company became Xerox College Publishing in 1968, when Ginn became a part of the Xerox Education Group. Robert F. Baker assumed the presidency three years later.

Ginn's new programs include *Reading 360; Responding: Ginn Interrelated Sequences in Literature; American Political Behavior;* and *Ginn Science Program; Ginn Elementary Mathematics; Individualized Mathematics System,* a full range of home economics textbooks; and *SWRL Kindergarten Program,* a research-based program originated by the Southwest Regional Laboratory for Educational Research and Development, designed to teach concepts and skills to beginning readers.

Globe Book Company, Inc.

Organized in 1919 in New York City by Murray J. Leventhal and Max Kessel as an examination review book publishing firm. The early review books were written by the partners themselves. Prior to incorporation in 1929 Leventhal bought out his partner. About 1940 the firm entered the secondary textbook field and gradually dropped out of Regents review books. Sara M. Leventhal was active during this period and served as president of the company.

In the 1950s, following the death of Murray Leventhal, his sons, Lester and Bernard, joined the firm, the former as president and the latter as executive vice president. Globe was acquired by *Esquire* in 1968.

The company specializes in materials for elementary and secondary schools, with special emphasis on materials for the underachiever. A subsidiary imprint, Learning Trends, was established in 1972 to issue lower reading level books and multi-media materials.

The Godine Press, Inc.

Organized in 1969 at Boston, Massachusetts, as a small general trade publisher.

Golden Press

Founded in 1958 as a joint venture by the Western Publishing Company, Inc. and Pocket Books, Inc., Golden Press took over the complete publication activities for the various Golden Book series of quality books and other products for children and adults. The Golden Book line was launched in 1942 with the publication of the first *Little Golden Book* volumes by Simon & Schuster, with production by Western Publishing Company and editorial work by Artists and Writers Press, which was then functioning as a wholly-owned subsidiary of Western. Since that time, many different types of Golden Book products have been published. Book production alone has totaled well over one billion volumes which have appeared in more than twenty-eight languages.

In 1964, Western purchased from Pocket Books, Inc. its fifty percent interest in Golden Press and reorganized Golden Press as a wholly-owned subsidiary. Subsequently, the Golden Press organization was absorbed into Western's Consumer Products Division and the trademarks and trade names Golden, Golden Book and Golden Press continue today to identify books for the juvenile and general markets, as well as a variety of related products for children such as games, jigsaw puzzles and other toys and playthings, phonograph records, tape cassettes and motion picture films, and a wide assortment of licensed merchandise sold by other companies under the Golden Book trademarks, such as children's clothes, furniture, novelties, bedding, jewelry, greeting cards, and many other products.

The Golden Quill Press

Established at Francestown, New Hampshire, as a publisher of poetry. It has a separate division, Marshall Jones Company, that issues trade, secondary and college textbooks.

Goodheart-Willcox Company, Inc.

Established in 1921 in South Holland, Illinois. In 1949 the firm was acquired by Floyd M. Mix and six years later George A. Fischer joined him as a partner. The company publishes textbooks on industrial arts and vocational subjects. It introduces from two to five books a year, the sale of which is promoted primarily by direct mail.

Gordon & Breach, Science Publishers, Inc.

Organized in 1961 at New York City. Publishes technical, scientific, business, behavioral science, research and trade books, and reference magazines and journals. Also issues high school and college textbooks and audio-visual materials. Is an associate of Media Directions (q.v.).

Gould Publications

A small publisher of secondary and college textbooks based at Jamaica, New York.

Great Books of the Western World

An ambitious program developed by Mortimer J. Adler and Robert M. Hutchins, who spent nine years and two million dollars to produce fifty-four volumes of selected works of seventy-one authors.

Published in 1952 by Encyclopaedia Britannica, the set included the two-volume SYNTOPI-CON that dealt with each of the one hundred and two main ideas and THE GREAT CONVERSA-TION, a discussion of the set as a whole. The GREAT IDEAS TODAY is issued as an annual supplement.

Great Outdoors Publishing Company

Established at St. Petersburg, Florida, in 1947. A small publisher of books on outdoor sports and hobbies, as well as regional history.

Warren H. Green, Inc.

Founded in 1966 in St. Louis, Missouri, by Warren H. Green. Under this imprint the firm publishes books in the fields of medicine, philosophy, and education. Using the imprint of Fireside Books, the firm also publishes books on American history, poetry, and religion.

The Stephen Greene Press

Established in 1957 in Brattleboro, Vermont, by Stephen and Janet Greene. The Press publishes adult nonfiction and has concentrated from the beginning on rural and New England Americana, ranging from A BOOK OF COUNTRY THINGS by Walter Needham and Barrows Mussey to THE VERSE BY THE SIDE OF THE ROAD (Burma Shave signs and jingles) by Frank Rowsome, Jr.

Other areas of attention by the Press have been sports, especially horses (such as THE MIND OF THE HORSE by R.H. Smythe), and skiing (THE NEW CROSS-COUNTRY SKI BOOK by John Caldwell); also humor (notably the cartoons of Ronald Searle and "Larry"); nature and conservation (five books by naturalist Ronald Rood); and home economics (notably PUTTING FOOD BY). The Press publishes the *Shortline Railroad Series* (of which the first title was 36 MILES OF TROUBLE by Victor Morse), and an occasional "literary" book such as several by/on Max Beerbohm and the poems of William Mundell (PLOWMAN'S EARTH).

The Press built its own quarters on eighty-five acres overlooking the Connecticut River in 1969, now brings out some thirty titles a year, and has about one hundred and sixty titles in print.

Greenwood Press, Inc.

Established in 1967 in New York City by Harold Mason and Harold Schwartz. Greenwood began by specializing in reprints for the library market. Its first major program, RADICAL PERIODICALS IN THE UNITED STATES, marked the beginning of an enormous growth period for the Press in the facsimile reprint field. An affiliated company, Negro Universities Press, specializes in reprinting works in Black studies. In 1968, with the acquisition of the Press by Williamhouse-Regency, Inc., and its relocation from New York City to Westport, Connecticut, Greenwood began to expand and to diversify.

A publishing division was set up to produce original works comprising monographs and professional books in the social sciences, the humanities, and the behavioral sciences. A journals division, also started at that time, now publishes nine journals, mainly in the social sciences and in the paramedical field. Greenwood's INDEX TO CURRENT URBAN DOCUMENTS lists and analyzes by subject the official municipal documents issued by one hundred and seventy-eight of the largest cities and counties in the United States.

In 1969 the company established its microform division. Rare source documents, archival material, manuscript holdings, and government documents make up the majority of Greenwood's microform programs. Among its major microfiche collections are *The State Constitutional Conventions* and *The Congressional Hearings*. Another library-oriented division was formed in 1969, the Printed Book Catalog Division, which issues the catalogs of major research libraries in printed book form. Greenwood has also entered the reference book field with its biographical dictionaries.

The company is now directed by Martin B. Berke, chairman, and Robert P. Hagelstein, president.

Gregg Publishing Company

Founded in 1899 in Chicago, Illinois, by John Robert Gregg, inventor of the Gregg shorthand system. The first edition of Gregg shorthand (title being "Lightline Phonography") was published in Liverpool, England, on May 28, 1888. The system was not successful in Great Britain at that time because the Pitman system was so deeply intrenched. Gregg came to the United States in the early 1890s; the first American edition of Gregg shorthand was published in Boston, Massachusetts, on October 16, 1893. A magazine for shorthand students was founded in 1898; its name then was *The Gregg Writer* (now called *Today's Secretary*). The New York office of the Gregg company was established in 1908. At the time of Gregg's death in 1948, he was the publisher of books on many phases of business education in addition to shorthand and typing texts. After Gregg's death, his company was merged with McGraw-Hill in 1948, and it is now a division of McGraw-Hill Book Company.

The Greystone Corporation

Established in 1938 at New York City by John Stevenson as Book Presentations. The firm purchased the Greystone Press in 1943 and changed its name to The Greystone Corporation in 1948, when fifty percent of the stock of the company was acquired by Milo Sutliff, former executive vice president of Doubleday Book Clubs. In 1957, when Sutliff retired, he resold his interest to John Stevenson. In 1972, Walter Rohrer, former publisher of Time-Life Books, became president of the firm.

Greystone's primary involvement has been in the field of mail order selling of both books and records. Starting with a number of how-to books such as COMPLETE BOOK OF SEWING, COMPLETE BOOK OF INTERIOR DECORATING, COMPLETE BOOK OF TABLE SETTING, DOLL MAKING, MR. FIX-IT, BOTTOMS-UP, EASY WAY TO MAKE AND REMODEL FURNITURE, and COMPLETE BOOK OF HOME REPAIR AND IMPROVEMENT, Greystone developed and operated several book and record clubs among which were The Fiction Book Club, The Catholic Digest Book Club, The Executive Book Club, Art Treasures of the World, The Children's Record Guild, The American Recording Society, Music Treasures of the World, and the Capitol Record Club.

In recent years, Greystone has launched several multi-volume encyclopedias. Among these are: NEW ILLUSTRATED ENCYCLOPEDIA OF GARDENING; PRACTICAL HANDYMAN ENCYCLOPEDIA; ENCYCLOPEDIA OF PHOTOGRAPHY; FOUNDATIONS OF SCIENCE; LIBRARY OF MYTHOLOGY; FAMILY PHYSICIAN A TO Z; DISCOVERING ANTIQUES; MAN AND WOMAN; THE NEW INTERNATIONAL ILLUSTRATED ENCYCLOPEDIA OF ART.

Grolier Club

A society for bibliophiles founded in New York City in 1884 by William Loring Andrews, Theodore De Vinne, Alexander W. Drake, Robert Hoe, Brayton Ives, Edward S. Mead, Albert Gallup, Arthur B. Turnure, and Samuel W. Marvin. Robert Hoe was the first president of the club.

Interested in all phases of book arts, the club has held more than three hundred exhibitions relating to books. Several publications on book arts have been issued under its imprint.

Grolier Incorporated

Started in 1895 in Boston, Massachusetts, by Walter M. Jackson in partnership with Francis A. Nichols as the Grolier Society, to publish books in fine bindings. Nichols became the first president of the company. Jackson had been associated with Estes and Lauriat and subsequently acquired an interest in ENCYCLOPAEDIA BRITANNICA. Jackson named his concern after Jean Grolier de Servières, the famous French Renaissance patron of fine printing and designer of fine bindings, and his lavishly produced and promoted books justified the name.

In 1899, Andrew E. Smith succeeded Francis A. Nichols as president, and in 1900 the Grolier Society offices were moved from Boston to New York City. The company's early publications included THE UNIVERSAL ANTHOLOGY, edited by Richard Garnett; THE MEMOIRS OF NAPOLEON, BEAUX AND BELLES, in fourteen volumes; and THE DAYS OF THE DANDIES, in fifteen volumes. Around the turn of the century Jackson acquired the American rights to THE CHILDREN'S ENCYCLOPEDIA, edited in London, England, by Arthur Mee. Re-edited for American children and retitled THE BOOK OF KNOWLEDGE, it was an instant success when Grolier published it in 1910. THE BOOK OF KNOWLEDGE remained one of Grolier's best-selling publications until 1966, when a completely new twenty-volume set, which continued to bring the magic of reading to millions of youngsters, was published under the title of THE NEW BOOK OF KNOWLEDGE.

With A.E. Smith as a dynamic associate, Jackson formed the W.M. Jackson Company to promote his reference book interests in Latin America. The company was formally incorporated as W.M. Jackson, Inc., in 1923.

In 1924 the Grolier Society secured American rights to THE BOOK OF POPULAR SCIENCE, followed five years later by the publication of LANDS AND PEOPLES, a colorful seven-volume encyclopedia of the countries of the world and its inhabitants. In 1936, Fred P. Murphy, who began as a salesman, acquired the company, incorporating it as the Grolier Society, Inc., and launched it on a program of accelerated expansion. He also acquired a controlling interest in the Americana Corporation, publisher of the ENCYCLOPEDIA AMERICANA.

In 1941 Grolier bought DOUBLEDAY'S ENCYCLOPEDIA and issued it three years later as the GROLIER ENCYCLOPEDIA, in ten volumes. RICHARDS TOPICAL ENCYCLOPEDIA, in fifteen volumes, was acquired in 1945. Also in 1945, Murphy merged the Americana Corporation into the Grolier Society, Inc., thus adding the ENCYCLOPEDIA AMERICANA to the company's growing list of publications.

The oldest of American encyclopedias, the ENCYCLOPEDIA AMERICANA was first published in Philadelphia, Pennsylvania, between 1829 and 1832 in thirteen volumes edited by a young German exile, Francis Lieber. He based his work on the seventh edition of the famous KONVERSATIONS-LEXIKON of Friedrich A.

Brockhaus. In 1903-1904 it was completely reset and published in a new sixteen-volume edition under the imprint of R.S. Peale & Company, with Frederick Converse Beach, editor of *Scientific American,* as its editor-in-chief. For a short period in the early 1900s it was published simply as THE AMERICANA, but it reverted to the encyclopedia title when it was again revised and reset in thirty volumes between 1918 and 1920 under the editorship of George Edward Rines.

In 1947 Fred P. Murphy became chairman of the board of the Grolier Society, Inc., and Edward J. McCabe, Jr., took his place as president. In 1950 the company published LE PETIT IN-FORMATEUR CANADIEN, a one-volume reference work for the Canadian market. In 1957-1958 the Canadian subsidiary, Grolier Limited, brought out the ENCYCLOPEDIA CANA-DIANA in ten volumes. The Australian market was covered by the AUSTRALIAN ENCYCLO-PEDIA in ten volumes. And to penetrate the British market, Grolier acquired the Victory Publishing Company (1956) and Mayflower Publishing Company (1957), both of London. Later, however, these two British acquisitions were exchanged for a twenty percent interest in Feffer & Simons. In 1957 Franklin Watts, Inc., an important American juvenile publishing house, was acquired.

In a reorganization in 1960, the company's name was changed to Grolier Incorporated. Another of Grolier's acquisitions came in 1961 when the company took over Spencer International Press, which had been owned in part by Sears, Roebuck. This purchase gave Grolier the rights to four additional major sets: AMERICAN PEO-PLE'S ENCYCLOPEDIA (20 volumes); THE CHILDREN'S HOUR (16 volumes); OUR WONDERFUL WORLD (18 volumes); and BASIC HOME LIBRARY (10 volumes).

In 1963, Grolier launched the entirely new ENCYCLOPEDIA INTERNATIONAL, in twenty volumes, edited by Lowell A. Martin and George A. Cornish. The work contained 12,000 pages, 37,000 articles, and 18,000 illustrations, and cost over four million dollars. In 1965 the GROLIER UNIVERSAL ENCYCLOPEDIA was published in ten volumes.

THE NEW BOOK OF KNOWLEDGE, produced under the editorship of Martha Glauber Shapp, former curriculum coordinator for the elementary schools of New York City, was published in 1966 after more than six years of editorial work and at a cost of seven million dollars. Whereas the original BOOK OF KNOWLEDGE had been topical in format, the new set was alphabetically arranged. It was curriculum-oriented, with subject headings, text, and illustrations all designed as a meaningful reference work appealing to children. THE NEW BOOK OF KNOWL-EDGE was the first American encyclopedia to be printed completely on a four-color press.

Grolier's English-language annuals published in the United States include ENCYCLOPEDIA SCIENCE SUPPLEMENT, AMERICANA AN-NUAL, THE NEW BOOK OF KNOWLEDGE ANNUAL, and the ENCYCLOPEDIA YEAR BOOK. Other annuals are published abroad. THE WORLD'S GREAT CLASSICS and THE BOOK OF ART are among the many other multi-volume works published by Grolier. For the Spanish and French markets Grolier publishes numerous reference works, including EL NUEVO TESORO DE LA JUVENTUD, MIS PRIMEROS CONO-CIMIENTOS, NUEVA ENCICLOPEDIA TE-MATICA, L'ENCYCLOPÉDIE DE LA JEU-NESSE, LE LIVRE DE CONAISSANCES, and others. In recent years the company has also acquired the Scarecrow Press, making Grolier one of the largest publishing houses in the United States.

In 1967, Fred P. Murphy's son, William J., became president of Grolier Incorporated, as E.J. McCabe, Jr., moved up to be chairman of the board, and Fred P. Murphy became chairman of the executive committee.

Grosset & Dunlap, Inc.

Founded in 1898 in New York City by George T. Dunlap and Alexander Grosset, the firm was originally called Dunlap and Grosset. In 1899 it was renamed Grosset & Dunlap.

Starting with booklets of Rudyard Kipling's works, the partners then rebound such popular novels as Hall Caine's THE CHRISTIAN. Their first big breakthrough came with the purchase of a large stock of paperback remainders of the H.B. Claflin Company, which was going out of the book business. Gradually Grosset & Dunlap turned their attention to reprints, beginning with THE DAMNATION OF THERON WARE by Harold Frederic. This was followed in 1903 by Paul Leicester Ford's JANICE MEREDITH. Other noteworthy publications during this period were Charles Major's DOROTHY VERNON OF HADDON HALL, Winston Churchill's RICHARD CARVEL, and Gilbert Parker's THE RIGHT OF WAY. It was also about this time that G.P. Brett of Macmillan arranged for Grosset & Dunlap to issue cheaper editions of Macmillan nonfiction under the series title of *Macmillan Standard Library.*

Grosset & Dunlap entered the juvenile field in 1907 by acquiring Chatterton and Peck, publishers of Edward Stratmeyer's ROVER BOYS and other juvenile books. This marked the beginning of the company's enduring interest in children's books, highlighted by the publication of such classic series as *The Bobbsey Twins* (1908), *Tom Swift* (1910), *The Hardy Boys* (1927) and *Nancy Drew* (1930).

The biggest general sellers in the early years of Grosset & Dunlap were Gene Stratton Porter's FRECKLES and A GIRL OF THE LIMBERLOST; Zane Grey's RIDERS OF THE PURPLE SAGE; THE LITTLE SHEPHERD OF KINGDOM COME and A TRAIL OF THE LONESOME PINE by John Fox, Jr.; REBECCA OF SUNNYBROOK FARM by Kate Douglas Wiggin; Owen Wister's THE VIRGINIAN; George Barr McCutcheon's GRAUSTARK; Booth Tarkington's PENROD; Peter Mark Roget's THESAURUS; and IN HIS STEPS by Charles M. Sheldon.

Grosset pioneered in the development of new outlets for paperback reprints and such new merchandising techniques as cooperative advertising, posters, and in-store displays. Beginning with BEN HUR in 1913, Grosset also exploited the possibilities of promoting tie-ins with motion pictures.

When Grosset died in 1934 Dunlap succeeded him as head of the firm. In 1944, with Dunlap ready to retire, the company was purchased by a group consisting of Random House; Little, Brown; Harper; Scribner's; and Book-of-the-Month Club. The following year Bantam Books, Inc. (q.v.) was created by Grosset & Dunlap and the Curtis Publishing Company.

During this period Grosset & Dunlap launched *Universal Library Paperbacks,* the *Illustrated Treasury of Children's Literature, Signature Books,* the *We Were There* series, and other projects. The company also acquired sixty percent of the stock of Wonder Books, Inc., a publisher of low-priced children's books, and fifty percent of the stock of Treasure Books, Inc., a publisher of low-priced coloring books and workbooks for children. Eventually both Treasure Books and Wonder Books became divisions of Grosset & Dunlap. In 1962 Grosset & Dunlap introduced *Tempo Books,* a line of inexpensive paperbacks for teenagers.

Bantam Books became a wholly-owned subsidiary in 1964.

In 1968 National General Corporation purchased both Grosset & Dunlap and Bantam Books. In late 1974 Grosset & Dunlap was sold to Filmways, Inc. and Bantam Books to IFI International. Since then, the company has greatly expanded, especially in the field of original publications. In 1973 Grosset published MARILYN, a novel biography by Norman Mailer, with pictures by the world's foremost photographers. Almost immediately the book appeared on the leading bestseller lists.

Grosset & Dunlap has a total of approximately three thousand five hundred titles currently in print. Approximately three hundred titles were published in 1973, and approximately sixty-eight percent of these were new or original publications.

Grossman Publishers

Established in 1962 in New York City by Richard L. Grossman. The firm took over the list of The Orion Press, Inc. Grossman was acquired as a subsidiary by The Viking Press but the imprint continues to be active in the field of general trade books.

Grove Press

Founded in New York City by Robert Phelps and John Balcomb in 1949. In 1951 Barney Rosset bought the firm and developed an *avant-garde* list that bore the impress of his own progressive literary tastes. He began by issuing new editions of books long out of print such as THE MONK by Matthew G. Lewis and books by Henry James. In 1954 *Evergreen Books,* quality paperbacks, was launched, followed three years later by the *Evergreen Review,* which Rosset personally edited.

Rosset established his reputation as a liberal publisher and gained national attention in the process by waging successful legal battles to bring out banned books, principally D.H. Lawrence's LADY CHATTERLEY'S LOVER and Henry Miller's TROPIC OF CANCER. At the same time the Grove imprint has brought the American reader such acknowledged masters as Bertolt Brecht, Samuel Beckett, Eugène Ionesco, Alain Robbe-Grillet, F. Dürrenmatt, John Osborne, and LeRoi Jones.

Grove has also been acclaimed for its distribution of several highly controversial films, such as "I Am Curious Yellow," "Titticut Follies," and such classics as "Masculine-Feminine" and "Film."

Grune & Stratton, Inc.

Founded in 1941 at New York City by Henry M. Stratton, a member of the medical publishing firm of Urban & Schwarzenberg of Vienna, Austria, who emigrated to the United States before World War II.

Grune & Stratton initially published journals and monographs in medicine and psychiatry, including Helene Deutsch's famous PSYCHOLOGY OF WOMEN. Later the company became one of the foremost publishers of psychological tests and special education books.

In 1968, Grune & Stratton was acquired by Harcourt Brace Jovanovich, Inc., and a year later Niels C. Buessem was named president of the company. Today, Grune & Stratton, with over seven hundred active titles, is one of the major medical specialty publishers in the United States.

Gulf Publishing Company

Established in 1916 at Houston, Texas, by Ray L. Dudley. The firm's first publication was a small weekly entitled *Gulf Coast Oil News.* The company's book publishing division was started in 1962. It publishes books in areas of the petroleum industry and scientific and technical management. It also publishes four magazines; *World Oil, Pipe Line Industry, Hydrocarbon Processing,* and *Ocean Industry.* An associated catalog division publishes three catalogs: COMPOSITE CATALOG, HYDROCARBON PROCESSING CATALOG, and PIPE LINE CATALOG.

H.P. Books

Organized in 1964 at Tucson, Arizona. Publishes leisure, hobby, automotive and motorcycle books.

Hacker Art Books, Inc.

Organized in 1946 at New York City. Reprinters of scarce and important books of art history.

Haessner Publishing

Established in 1966 at Newfoundland, New Jersey. Publishes a small list of books on sports and transportation.

Hafner Press

Organized in 1946 in New York City as the publishing division of Stechert-Hafner, Inc., (now Stechert Macmillan), which had been founded in 1872 by Gustav E. Stechert and F. Wolff as Stechert and Wolff "for the purpose of importing and selling all kinds of European literary works." In 1876, with Wolff's withdrawal, the firm was called Gustav E. Stechert. The name was abbreviated to G.E. Stechert by 1897 and again changed to G.E.

Stechert & Company in 1904. Stechert died in 1899 and the business passed into the hands of Alfred Hafner, who had been a partner since 1897. By 1914 Hafner had become the sole owner.

In 1919 Hafner's sons, Walter A. and Otto H., joined the firm, and in 1946 the company's name was changed to Stechert-Hafner, Inc., with Walter A. Hafner as its president. At the same time Hafner Publishing Company was spun off as a separate corporation of which Otto H. Hafner was the president. In 1969 both firms were acquired by Macmillan, Inc. Stechert-Hafner has been renamed Stechert Macmillan. Hafner Press is a division of Macmillan Publishing Co., Inc.

A major project launched in 1946 was the *Hafner Library of Classics.* New reprinting programs have since been undertaken emphasizing botany, medicine, and geology. Among these projects are: *Classica Botanica Americana, Contributions to the History of Geology,* and *The History of Medicine* series.

E.M. Hale and Company, Publishers

Established at Eau Claire, Wisconsin. Reprint publishers of library bound juvenile books, under the imprint of Cadmus Books. Now a division of Multi-Media Ventures, Inc.

Halkett and Laing

DICTIONARY OF ANONYMOUS AND PSEUDONYMOUS ENGLISH LITERATURE by Samuel Halkett and John Laing, 4 volumes (1882-1888), 9 volumes (1962). The standard work on anonymous authors, commonly referred to as HALKETT AND LAING.

Emerson Hall Publishers, Inc.

Organized in 1969 at New York City. Publishes a small list of books in the behavioral and social sciences, arts and letters.

Organized in Boston, Massachusetts, in 1942 by Garrison K. Hall as the Micro-Photography Company to do general-service microfilming. In 1946 the company began to apply microfilm technology to bibliographic research materials. The new technique was used to reproduce the extensive card index to world-wide literature on new plants owned by The Gray Herbarium at Harvard University. The next step was the reproduction of library card indexes and catalogs in book rather than card form. The Columbia University's CATALOG OF THE AVERY MEMORIAL ARCHITECTURAL LIBRARY was the first book catalog to be so published.

In 1959 the company's name was changed to G.K. Hall & Co. At the same time the company also developed a technology for the complex problem of cumulating indexes. The first two of these were announced in 1960: CUMULATED MAGAZINE SUBJECT INDEX, 1907-1949, and CUMULATED DRAMATIC INDEX, 1909-1949, in collaboration with F.W. Faxon. By the end of 1960 Hall had published thirty-six catalogs, indexes, and specialized publications in library science. At the end of 1971 this number had grown to three hundred. In addition to the foregoing, it consists of bibliographies of cumulated indexes and catalogs, bibliographic calendars, checklists and classification aids, necrologies, and dictionaries. Typical of the latter category is the five-volume BIOGRAPHICAL AND BIBLIOGRAPHICAL DICTIONARY OF THE ITALIAN HUMANISTS AND OF THE WORLD OF CLASSICAL SCHOLARSHIP IN ITALY, 1300-1800, compiled by Mario E. Cosenza.

Since 1960 bibliographies have formed an important part of the Hall publishing program. Among them are works like the STENDHAL FICHIER, compiled by Françoise Michel, and the BIBLIOGRAPHY OF RUSSIAN EMIGRÉ LITERATURE 1918-1968, compiled by Ludmila A. Foster. Cumulated indexes form another area of specialization. They range from the GENEALOGICAL INDEX OF THE NEWBERRY LIBRARY to POPULATION INDEX BIBLIOGRAPHY, PSYCHOLOGICAL ABSTRACTS (in collaboration with the American Psychological Association and Columbia University), and IN-

TERNATIONAL LABOUR DOCUMENTA-
TION: CUMULATIVE EDITION 1965-1969,
sponsored by the International Labour Office in
Geneva. The largest number of Hall publications,
however, are library catalogs of distinguished
library collections. Excluding supplements, over
one hundred and eighty have been published.
Three of these catalogs number over one hundred
volumes each, and nearly thirty percent have
originated in libraries and research institutions
outside the United States.

In 1969 the firm was purchased by ITT, joining its Educational and Publishing Services
Group, and Phillips A. Treleaven became the
president and chief executive officer. In 1971 the
company began to diversify its library publishing
programs. One step in this direction was the
establishment of its Large Print Division for the
visually handicapped. Titles are selected on the
basis of current appeal and include bestsellers;
each book is completely reset in 18 point type
and printed on special paper in 6″ x 9″ format
designed for ease in handling. Large Prints now
include an adult series, a young people's series
and an inspirational series.

Late in 1971 the company purchased Gregg
Press, a reprint publishing house that was founded
by Newton K. and Charles S. Gregg in 1963 as
the North American sales organization for Gregg
Press Limited of England (now Gregg International Publishers). Gregg Press had begun to
publish under its own imprint in 1967. Its facsimile reprints are published in series and deal with
research aspects of American studies. They include AMERICANS IN FICTION (70 volumes)
edited by Clarence F. Gohdes; THE MUCKRA-
KERS (39 volumes); AMERICAN HUMOR-
ISTS (28 volumes); and AMERICA AND THE
PACIFIC (18 volumes).

In 1973 the company added Twayne Publishers (q.v.) as one of its subsidiaries, and
Twayne moved its offices to Boston.

Later in 1973, G.K. Hall and Co. became distributor for Computext Communications, Ltd.,
publishers of *The Law Book Guide,* a monthly
bibliography generated from Library of Congress
MARC (*M*achine *R*eadable Cataloging) tapes.
Using computer typesetting, the system for producing the *Guide* was developed by Gerald
Swanson, founder of Computext. In 1974, G.K.

Hall became publisher of *The Law Book Guide*
and similar monthly and cumulated publications
in the fields of medicine, business and economics,
technology, government publications and conference publications. The purpose of the *Guides*
is to provide librarians and researchers with current access to complete Library of Congress cataloging for all English and French language monographs as well as for new or recatalogued serial
titles in all Roman alphabet languages.

Hammond Incorporated

Established in 1900 in New York City as C.S.
Hammond & Company. It was incorporated in
1901. Its first publication was an innovative rever-
sible map.

Hammond produces maps, atlases, globes and
books. In addition, its materials are used by many
other publishing houses and are to be found in
encyclopedias, dictionaries, textbooks, Bibles, almanacs, and other reference books. The firm
also publishes nonfiction books on nature, travel,
art, American history, and popular science. Another area of specialization is premium materials.

The third generation of the Hammond family
is now active in the company. Caleb D. Hammond
is chairman of the board and Stuart L. Hammond
is the president. In 1950 the headquarters were
moved from New York City to Maplewood, New
Jersey, and in 1966 the corporate name was
changed to Hammond Incorporated.

Harcourt Brace Jovanovich, Inc.

Founded in 1919 in New York City as Harcourt,
Brace & Howe by Alfred Harcourt, Donald Brace,
and Will D. Howe. Harcourt and Brace had been
up to that time members of the Holt establishment. Soon after the time that Howe withdrew
in 1921, S. Spencer Scott became the textbook
head, and the firm became Harcourt, Brace and
Company.

The company made a promising start with J.M.
Keynes' THE ECONOMIC CONSEQUENCES
OF THE PEACE, and within a few years of its

founding, the young firm had managed to put together an outstanding list that included books by Benedetto Croce, Van Wyck Brooks, Sinclair Lewis, Lytton Strachey, Louis Untermeyer, Walter Lippmann, and Lewis Mumford. The company also became the American publisher of the INTERNATIONAL LIBRARY OF PSYCHOLOGY, PHILOSOPHY, AND SCIENTIFIC METHOD, edited by C.K. Ogden, in one hundred and thirty-five volumes. Brace's connections with the Bloomsbury Group enabled him to obtain E.M. Forster's A PASSAGE TO INDIA and books by Virginia Woolf, Roger Fry, and Clive Bell. Under Spencer Scott, and later with Dudley Meek as manager and James M. Reid as editor-in-chief, the college and school textbook department became a major factor in the firm's financial success. Among its chief textbook authors were Ernest Hilgard, George Gaylord Simpson and Paul F. Brandwein. The juvenile department was another profitable division.

During its first decade, the Harcourt, Brace imprint appeared on a number of important books. Among them were: ABRAHAM LINCOLN by Carl Sandburg; MAIN CURRENTS OF AMERICAN THOUGHT by Vernon L. Parrington; ELIZABETH AND ESSEX by Lytton Strachey; A.L. Kroeber's ANTHROPOLOGY; Giovanni Papini's LIFE OF CHRIST; and Paul de Kruif's MICROBE HUNTERS. This tradition was continued in the 1930s and 1940s when the firm published THE AUTOBIOGRAPHY OF LINCOLN STEFFENS, NORTH TO THE ORIENT by Anne Morrow Lindbergh, THE JUST AND THE UNJUST by James Gould Cozzens, and books by Georges Simenon, Katherine Anne Porter and James Thurber.

In 1936 Hastings Harcourt, Alfred Harcourt's son, was appointed a director of the firm. When Alfred Harcourt sought to make him head of trade publishing, Donald C. Brace objected and in the ensuing struggle Alfred Harcourt resigned the presidency in 1942. Brace headed the company from 1942 until 1948, when he yielded the presidency to S. Spencer Scott. In 1947 the Reynal & Hitchcock list was acquired and Reynal was appointed manager of the trade department. He held this position until 1955 and subsequently established his own firm, Reynal and Company. In another organizational shakeup in 1953, Dud-

ley Meek and Lee Deighton left the company's textbook department, and in 1954 Scott was urged to leave by the Harcourt and Brace families, and William Jovanovich was elected president. Jovanovich is an editor and essayist (NOW, BARABBAS, Harper & Row, 1964). In the process, Harcourt, Brace lost one of its most able editors, Robert Giroux, and the later works of some of its best authors, including T.S. Eliot, Thomas Merton, Robert Lowell, Bernard Malamud, and Flannery O'Connor. It continued (or began) to publish the works of George Orwell, Mary McCarthy, Hannah Arendt, Rosamond Lehmann, William Saroyan, Jessamyn West, Günter Grass, William Golding, C.S. Lewis, Kingsley Amis, Charles A. Lindbergh, Konrad Lorenz, Anaïs Nin, and Erich Maria Remarque.

In 1960 Harcourt, Brace went public, with its shares traded on the New York Stock Exchange. Shortly afterward, a merger was effected with World Book Company and the name of the combined firm was changed to Harcourt, Brace & World. (The World Book Company had been founded in 1905 by Caspar W. Hodgson. It became nationally known for its elementary school textbooks and its educational tests, including the Metropolitan and Stanford Achievement Tests and Otis and Terman Mental Ability Tests.)

A number of works in linguistics, criticism, and programmed and multi-media instruction for schools and universities were also launched by Jovanovich about this time, in part as a result of his close work with B.F. Skinner, Paul Roberts, Northrop Frye, and Marshall McLuhan. The company also launched many paperback series: *Harvest Books, Harbrace Paperbound Library, Harbinger Books,* and *Voyager Books.* In addition, Jovanovich arranged with Helen and Kurt Wolff, who were co-founders of Pantheon Books, Hiram Haydn, one of the three founders of Atheneum, and Tony Godwin, the former managing editor of Penguin Books in Britain, to publish their books under co-publisher arrangements. The company completed more than twenty mergers and acquisitions in the years after it became public. In 1969 it acquired Academic Press, Inc., (q.v.) a publicly-held company. In addition, the company acquired Harvest Publishing Company (farm magazines and insurance); Guidance Associates (educational films); Grune & Stratton (medical books and journals) (q.v.); Beckley-Cardy (school supply and manufacture); History Book Club (q.v.); Longman Canada Limited; and four book publishing houses in Germany. It also founded or acquired more than fifty business periodicals.

In 1970 Jovanovich was elected chairman of the board and chief executive officer, and Paul D. Corbett was elected president of the company. At that time Jovanovich's contributions to the company's growth were acknowledged when its name was changed by the shareholders to Harcourt Brace Jovanovich, Inc.

In late 1974 HBJ bought Pyramid Communications, which publishes paperback books and magazines and which will be maintained as a separate company.

Harian Publications

Established in 1935 at Greenlawn, New York, by Fredric and Charlotte Tyarks. The firm specializes in books on travel, retirement, and finance. Its most popular book is TRAVEL ROUTES AROUND THE WORLD, published semiannually since 1935.

Harper & Row, Publishers

Founded in New York City in 1817 as J. & J. Harper, printers, by James and John Harper. The first book to bear their imprint as printers was SENECA'S MORALS. Their first publication was John Locke's ESSAY CONCERNING HUMAN UNDERSTANDING. Soon they turned to more profitable titles, competing successfully with the older Carey firm in Philadelphia to bring out popular fiction. Wesley Harper joined the company in 1823 and Fletcher Harper in 1825. James was in charge of the press, John looked after the finances, Wesley did manuscript reading and correspondence, and Fletcher was the editor. In 1833 the firm was renamed Harper & Brothers. When asked who was Harper and who were the Brothers, they gave the oft-quoted answer, "Either one of us is the Harper, the rest are the Brothers."

By 1830 Harper had become the largest book manufacturers and publishers in the country. One of the reasons for their success was the lack of an international copyright law which enabled them to "pirate" and print British works without payment of royalties. Harper was one of the first publishers to employ readers or literary advisers to ensure "that no works will be published by J. & J. Harper but as are interesting, instructive and moral." Harper was also the first American publisher to conceive the idea of publishing a series of books as "libraries." In 1830 it launched *Harper's Family Library,* followed by *Harper's Library of Select Novels, Harper's Boys' and Girls' Library,* and *Harper's Classical Library. Harper's School District Library* consisted of books adapted to the requirements of school-going children.

Among the numerous Harper titles on religion, the most successful were THE BOOK OF COMMON PRAYER and HARPER'S ILLUMINATED AND NEW PICTORIAL BIBLE, described as the finest piece of book-making that had yet appeared in the young United States. Richard H. Dana's TWO YEARS BEFORE THE MAST appeared on the list in 1840 and became one of the first bestsellers by an American writer. Other major projects during this period were HARPER'S LATIN LEXICON and

Joseph Wesley Harper (1830-1896)

Charles H. Haswell's ENGINEERS' AND ME-CHANICS' POCKET-BOOK. Harper & Brothers was then at the peak of its success. "The amount of books they have issued," wrote the *New York Times,* "is almost incalculable. For the last few years they have published on an average twenty-five volumes a minute for ten hours a day." Even the principle of "courtesy of trade" (q.v.), which the book trade had come to accept generally, worked to their advantage since by then they were in a position to outbid other publishers for any book they wanted.

In 1850 Harper issued its first magazine, *Harper's New Monthly Magazine.* In 1853 disaster struck and a fire destroyed the entire Harper establishment. But before long the firm had recovered from the disaster and resumed its business with even greater vigor. In 1857 *Harper's Weekly* was launched. In 1863 the firm proudly announced HARPER'S PICTORIAL HISTO-RY OF THE GREAT REBELLION IN THE UNITED STATES, a monumental undertaking that took five years to complete. In 1867 *Harper's Bazar* was added to the firm's growing list of magazines. To compete with the then current dime novels, Harper launched the *Franklin Square Library* of ten-cent books in 1878 and a series of nonfiction books in 1885 which sold for twenty-five cents.

With the death of Fletcher Harper in 1877 the last of the founding brothers had passed from the scene. Of the second generation of Harpers, Joseph W. Harper, Jr. soon dominated the enterprise. Known popularly as "Joe Brooklyn" to distinguish him from other Joseph Harpers in the family, he headed the firm until his retirement in 1894. Among the programs Joe initiated were the *Library of American Novels* and the *English Men of Letters* series. The company also began to accept more American authors, among whom Lew Wallace and Henry James were the most notable. BEN HUR by Lew Wallace became one of the all-time bestsellers on the Harper list. In 1879 *Harper's Young People* magazine was launched to compete with Century's *Saint Nicholas.*

With Joe Brooklyn's death in 1894 the Harper firm entered a period of decline. The third generation of Harpers, of whom John W. Harper was the senior, lacked the business acumen of their fathers and grandfathers and the firm fell into debt. J.P. Morgan, the largest creditor, decided that the company should be reorganized. George Harvey, owner of the *North American Review,* was engaged, with the approval of Morgan, to take charge and set the house in order. In the ensuing reorganization the Harpers were excluded from actual management and Harvey was appointed president of the company. An ironic footnote to the problems at Harper was the similar trouble at Appleton, then considered the second largest publishing house in the United States.

Harvey sold $125,000 worth of college texts and scholarly reference works on the Harper list to the American Book Company. He also succeeded in attracting such major writers as Booth Tarkington, Rex Beach, William Dean Howells, Joseph Conrad, Zane Grey, Robert W. Chambers, and Mark Twain was persuaded to return from his abortive attempt at self-publication. Woodrow Wilson's five-volume HISTORY OF THE AMERICAN PEOPLE, and the twenty-seven volume THE AMERICAN NATION edited by Albert Hart were two other ambitious ventures that the firm initiated under Harvey's supervision. In a move toward expansion, the publishing house of R.H. Russell was acquired in 1903. In 1915 Harvey left Harper to return to the *North American Review.* His place was taken by Clinton Brainard.

Under Brainard and his successor, Douglas Parmentier, the firm managed to reestablish fully its old eminence in the publishing world. They were aided by a number of brilliant editors, Frederick Duneka, Thomas B. Wells, Eugene Saxton, Frank S. MacGregor, and Cass Canfield. Canfield, at first stationed in England, brought in a number of British authors, including Philip Guedalla, J.B. Priestley and Richard Hughes. A religious department was established in 1925 under Eugene Exman. This department was further strengthened through the acquisition of the lists of the Sunday School Times Company of Philadelphia, Long and Smith, and Willett, Clark and Company. Parmentier resigned in 1929 and the next president of the company was Henry Hoyns. When he moved up to the chairmanship of the board two years later, Canfield was elected president.

During the Depression of the 1930s the Harper company undertook one of its greatest projects: the twenty-volume THE RISE OF MODERN EUROPE of which William L. Langer, the historian, was general editor. At this time also the firm acquired the Paul B. Hoeber list of medical books, which became the nucleus of a medical department. The trade list was well endowed with popular authors during the 1930s: Aldous Huxley, John Gunther, Betty Smith, Edna St. Vincent Millay, Zane Grey, Richard Wright and Louis Bromfield.

Frank S. MacGregor became president of the company in 1945. The following year Harper launched the *New American Nation Series,* a new forty-volume history, under the general editorship of Henry Steele Commager and Richard B. Morris. During the 1950s the trade department issued E.B. White's CHARLOTTE'S WEB; the ENCYCLOPEDIA OF AMERICAN HISTORY, edited by Richard Morris; John F. Kennedy's PROFILES IN COURAGE; THE WAPSHOT CHRONICLE by John Cheever; and the Jim Bishop books, THE DAY LINCOLN WAS SHOT and THE DAY CHRIST DIED.

In 1955 Raymond C. Harwood was chosen president of the company. In the same year establishment of *Harper Torchbooks* was announced, a series of quality religious books, and *Men of Wisdom,* a series of illustrated paperbacks. Several other paperback and clothbound series were also launched. Among them were *Regions of America, UNESCO History of Mankind, Science Today, Colophon Books, University Library, Cloister Library, Cathedral Library, Academy Library, Perennial Library,* and *Policy Books.* Still another major project was the HARPER ENCYCLOPEDIA OF SCIENCE in four volumes, edited by John Newman. A half interest in *Harper's Magazine* was sold to Minneapolis Star and Tribune Company in 1961.

Harper's growth during the sixties and early seventies has been marked by the merger with Row, Peterson & Company, which resulted in changing the company's name to Harper & Row, Publishers, Inc., and the acquisition of Basic Books, Inc., and Barnes & Noble. A book club department operated The Reader's Subscription and The Library of Human Behavior, but in early 1975 both clubs were sold. John Cowles, Jr.

is chairman of the board and of the executive committee. Winthrop Knowlton is the company's president and chief executive officer.

Harper's Magazine Press

Organized in 1968 in New York City as a joint venture between Harper & Row and *Harper's Magazine.* It produces primarily nonfiction. The list is small but prestigious and includes such titles as Bill Moyers' LISTENING TO AMERICA; INSIDE, LOOKING OUT by Harding LeMay; YAZOO by Willie Morris; and THE CITY GAME by Pete Axthelm.

The Harrison Company, Publishers

Established in 1908 in Atlanta, Georgia, by George W. Harrison, George W. Harrison, Jr., and J.T. Doonan. The firm was a successor to the James P. Harrison & Company (founded in 1873 by James P. Harrison) and its subsidiary, The Franklin Printing and Publishing Company set up in Atlanta in 1859. After the death of the original partners, the company passed into the hands of John M. Elliott, and associates.

The company was reorganized in 1970 under the leadership of Henry H. Blake as president and editor-in-chief and John M. Elliott as chairman of the board of directors. The firm specializes in the publication of lawbooks with emphasis on the southeastern states.

Hart Publishing Company, Inc.

Started in 1941 in New York City by Harold W. Hart. The firm began as a publisher of juveniles and built up a line called Hart Activity Books which was sold to Doubleday in 1962. An adult counterpart of these Activity Books, known as Grab A Pencil Books, has been successfully published during the last six years.

Hart's outstanding book is SUMMERHILL: A RADICAL APPROACH TO CHILD REARING by A.S. Neill, which has sold over a million copies to date. This was followed by a college-oriented series known as *For and Against Books* with such titles as CENSORSHIP: FOR AND AGAINST and MARRIAGE: FOR AND AGAINST.

Harvard University Press

Founded at Cambridge, Massachusetts, in 1913, though printing and publishing had been going on at Harvard from time to time for nearly three centuries. The first director of the Press was C.C. Lane, who served until 1920. Harold Murdock was the director from 1920 until his death in 1934. He was succeeded by Dumas Malone, the historian. Malone resigned in 1943, and Roger L. Scaife, a retired commercial publisher, served until 1947, when the twenty-year administration of Thomas J. Wilson began. Wilson elected early retirement at the end of 1967 and joined Atheneum. His associate director, Mark Carroll, succeeded him, serving until February, 1972. After two acting directors, the present head of the Press, Arthur J. Rosenthal, founder of Basic Books, took office in the fall of 1972.

The Press had its era of greatest growth and prosperity under Thomas Wilson, though many of its most distinguished undertakings had begun before his arrival, including F.L. Mott's HISTORY OF AMERICAN MAGAZINES; *The Loeb Classical Library;* the *American Foreign Policy Library;* the *Charles Eliot Norton Lectures;* and the HARVARD DICTIONARY OF MUSIC. Receipts reached three million dollars at the close of Wilson's directorship. The Press also launched the *Adams Papers,* the *John Harvard Library,* the *Emerson Journals,* and many other multi-volume projects. In 1954, with gifts from the Belknap family, the Belknap Press of Harvard University Press was set up as a separate imprint. The first work to be issued under this imprint was the HARVARD GUIDE TO AMERICAN HISTORY. Other Belknap titles include JOHN KEATS by W.J. Bate and A THEORY OF JUSTICE by John Rawls.

The Press publishes over seventy series of scholarly books, including the *Commonwealth Fund Books,* the *Harvard East Asian Series,* the *Godkin Lectures,* and the *Harvard Economic Studies.* A major new line, *Harvard Paperbacks,* was begun in 1971. Before that time the policy of the Press was to lease paperback rights to other publishers.

Harvard University Press has not had its own printing facilities since 1942, when the Harvard University Printing Office was established as a separate department. The Press is governed by two boards: the Board of Syndics controls the imprint, and the Board of Directors guides the financial affairs and general policy.

Harvey House, Inc.

Established in 1956 in New York City as Z.E. Harvey Inc., by Zola E. Harvey. It adopted the present name in 1961. The company purchased the books and stock of American Legal Publications, a publishing imprint also founded by Z.E. Harvey in 1929. Harvey House publishes two types of books: juveniles and general trade books, and the American Legal Publications publishes law case digest outlines and textbooks for law students. In 1961 the company went public. American Legal Publications is retained as a subsidiary imprint.

In mid-1974 the inventory and trade book list, together with the imprint of Harvey House, were acquired by Multi-Media Ventures, Inc., of which Lawrence F. Reeves is president.

Haskell House Publishers, Ltd.

Organized at New York City in 1964. Specializes in reprints in philosophy, criticism, Americana, language, music, bibliography, genealogy, sociology, and Negro history and culture.

Hastings House Publishers, Inc.

Established in New York City in 1936 by Walter Wenzel Frese. Its first book was A SMALL HOUSE IN THE SUN by Samuel Chamberlain, which set the tone and level of its publishing activity. It was the beginning of many Hastings House pictorial series such as *American Landmarks, Profiles in America, American Procession* and *American Guide*. Both of the last two series were edited by Henry G. Alsberg. Another innovation came with the pictorial diary calendar. The activities of Walter Frese as president of the American Institute of Graphic Arts from 1945 to 1947 led Hastings House into still another area of specialization: publication of the INTERNATIONAL POSTER ANNUAL and other books on the graphic arts.

In 1953 Russell F. Neale joined Hastings and he was responsible for development of *Visual Communication Books,* a series on the graphic arts, design, printing and photography, including such imports as the GRAPHIS ANNUAL, PENROSE ANNUAL, PHOTOGRAPHIS, etc. Hastings initiated the ILLUSTRATORS ANNUAL in 1959, in cooperation with the Society of Illustrators in New York.

Delving into more technical areas, Hastings in 1954 initiated *Communication Arts Books,* a series covering professional and educational techniques of radio, television, film, journalism, and other areas of mass communication.

The Hastings House imprint now also touches other areas. Among them are Western Americana, cookery and wine, arts and crafts. Also, a fine list of children's books with the little pine tree colophon had been developed by Jean Poindexter Colby, who, upon retirement in 1970, was succeeded by Judy Donnelly as editor.

Hawthorn Books, Inc.

Organized in 1953 in New York City as a division of Prentice-Hall under the direction of Kenneth S. Giniger to publish selected titles in nonfiction. Its concentration then was on art and religion. The first book, Alexis Carrel's REFLECTIONS ON LIFE, edited by Carrel's widow, established the imprint's direction and thrust. Two large early ventures were THE HEIRLOOM BIBLE and THE COMPLETE LIBRARY OF WORLD ART, the latter being in one hundred and fifty volumes. Perhaps the greatest of Hawthorn's achievements was the one hundred and fifty-volume TWENTIETH CENTURY ENCYCLOPEDIA OF CATHOLICISM, edited by Henry Daniel-Rops.

In 1965 Giniger resigned, and the division was sold to Fred Kerner who, in turn, sold it to W. Clement Stone, a millionaire insurance man. In 1967 the company was completely reorganized under the direction of Dale Timpe, and the emphasis of the Hawthorn list has been shifted to a wide range of general nonfiction trade books and paperbacks.

In 1969 Hawthorn purchased Meredith Press, which owned the imprints of Appleton-Century-Crofts, Channel Press, and Duell, Sloan and Pearce. Hawthorn now has a backlist of approximately one thousand titles. Authors on Hawthorn's list now include e.e. cummings, Karl Menninger, MacKinlay Kantor, Shepherd Mead, Martin Caidin, Alan Caillou, Arnold Shaw, Alfred Steinberg, Edgar N. Jackson, Elizabeth Goudge, Stephen Longstreet, and Leonard Spigelgass.

Hayden Book Company, Inc.

Founded in New York City in 1952 by James S. Mulholland, Jr. In 1972 Hayden was reincorporated as a Delaware corporation and moved to Rochelle Park, New Jersey. In 1961 it acquired John F. Rider, Inc., and Ahrens Publishing Company. In 1972 it obtained substantially all of the titles of Spartan Books, Inc., of Washington D.C.

Beginning as a technical and scientific publisher, the company has moved into textbooks and the humanities.

Hearst Books

Established in New York City as a division of Hearst Magazines. Publishes family service and reference, boating and automotive books.

Hearthside Press

Established in 1953 at Great Neck, New York. Publishers of a small list of home and garden and how-to books.

D.C. Heath & Company

Founded in 1885 at Boston, Massachusetts, by Daniel Collamore Heath "for the purpose of providing the tools of the new education." Heath had been a partner in Ginn and Heath and when he withdrew the separation was amicable and he took with him several titles in the sciences and languages. Heath admitted Charles H. Ames into partnership in 1888, William E. Pulsifer in 1889, and Winfield S. Smyth in 1893. In 1895 the partnership was reorganized as a corporation. Heath and Smyth died in 1908, and in 1910 Pulsifer and two associates, Winfield S. Smyth, Jr. and William H. Ives, purchased from the Heath estate its entire holdings of the company's stock.

Pulsifer retired from the presidency in 1927 and Smyth succeeded him. Two years later Smyth yielded control to Dudley R. Cowles. In 1946 Cowles became chairman of the board and Marvin B. Perry was elected president of the company. In 1957 John S. Smyth, son and grandson of earlier partners, succeeded Perry in the presidency. In 1962 W. Walker Cowles replaced Smyth.

Beginning with only twenty-four titles, the firm expanded rapidly. Heath had entered textbook publishing at an eminently psychological time which was ripe for a reorientation of the methods as well as the content of teaching. Heath himself believed that publishers had a responsibility to improve teaching methods and he encouraged his authors to incorporate new pedagogic techniques in the books they wrote for him. He was also one of the first to send out questionnaires to assess the educational needs of teachers and students. In 1903 Heath started the *English Belles Lettres*, a series which eventually grew to forty volumes. Many of Heath's texts were widely adopted and enjoyed preeminence in their fields. Among them were: the Bourne and Benton, Thompson, and Webster history series,

Edwin Campbell Woolley's HANDBOOK OF COMPOSITION, Rowland G. Hill and Jeremiah D.M. Ford's SPANISH GRAMMAR, Webster Wells and Hart's *Algebras,* the ELEMENTARY FRENCH GRAMMAR AND READER by W.H. Fraser, PRACTICAL LESSONS IN ENGLISH by Mary F. Hyde, the *Walsh Series in Arithmetic,* TRIGONOMETRY by Edward Albert Bowser, Ira Remson's ORGANIC CHEMISTRY, and ENGLISH IN ACTION.

In no field was Heath stronger than in that of modern languages. *Heath's Modern Language Series* were the first books to adapt the teaching of modern languages to the specialized needs of American schools and colleges. In 1901 *Heath's Home and School Classics* were launched. Published at monthly intervals they provided suitable reading material from primary grades through high school. The English list was greatly strengthened when F.W. Scott, former head of the department of English at the University of Illinois, joined the firm in 1925.

Under the administration of Dudley Cowles, the company rounded out its publishing program by increasing its attention to elementary books. For this purpose a new elementary department was created under Beryl Parker in 1938. In 1939 the first of a series of six *Walt Disney Readers* was issued, followed by the first book in the *World Neighbor* series. In 1941 a group of six animal books were published for use below the first grade. In the same year a new revised edition of the *Tressler Series of English Books* was published. This outstanding program was the first continuous English series for all grades from three to twelve.

In the mid-1950s the company published its first activity-based elementary science program, which covered all the major areas of science. The college department was also strengthened. In 1959 Heath was selected as the publisher for the HIGH SCHOOL PHYSICS TEXT prepared by the physical science study committee sponsored by Massachusetts Institute of Technology and the National Science Foundation, under the direction of Gerald R. Zecharias.

In 1961 the firm went public. Four years later the firm was acquired by the Raytheon Company. Francis S. Fox is the current chief executive and president of the company.

James H. Heineman, Inc.

Founded in 1961 at New York City by James H. Heineman. His first book, published in 1963, was THE ART AND HISTORY OF FRAMES. The firm's greatest success was THE BIOGRAPHICAL ENCYCLOPEDIA AND WHO'S WHO OF THE AMERICAN THEATER. Heineman also publishes the paperback series, *Open Letter*.

Herald House

Founded in 1860 in Plano, Illinois, as Herald Publishing House, Inc. The House's first title was INSPIRED VERSION OF THE HOLY SCRIPTURES. Moved in 1921 to Independence, Missouri. Publishers of religious books for the Reorganized Church of Jesus Christ of Latter Day Saints.

Herald Press

See, Mennonite Publishing House.

Herder & Herder

Established in New York City in 1957 as a branch of the celebrated German Catholic publishing house, Herder Verlag of Freiburg im Breisgau, which had been founded in 1801. A branch had been set up in St. Louis, Missouri, in 1873 but this was incorporated as a separate and autonomous firm in 1917.

The initial objective of Herder & Herder was to publish scholarly works in translation, especially such works as reflected the new currents in the Catholic Church after the Vatican Council.

An important facet of this program was the English-language publication of the ecumenical monthly, *Herder Correspondence*. The house also began to introduce a broadly international list of Catholic theologians to the American reading public. Among them were Karl Rahner, Thomas Merton, Teilhard de Chardin, Bernard Lonergan, Louis Evely, Gregory Baum, Leslie Dewart, Gabriel Moran, and Michael Novak. One of Herder's most outstanding religious titles—now a standard text and reference work—is A NEW CATECHISM (popularly known as the DUTCH CATECHISM), the first summary of faith after the Vatican Council.

Beginning in the late 1960s Herder and Herder began to diversify its publishing program substantially to include reference works (such as the three-volume ENCYCLOPEDIA OF PSYCHOLOGY and the eight-volume encyclopedia on MARXISM, COMMUNISM, AND WESTERN SOCIETY); an ecology series (including CELEBRATING THE EARTH and ONLY A LITTLE PLANET); a series of European science fiction in translation; a series of popular biographies of Hermann Hesse, Albert Camus, C.G. Jung, and others; a series of illustrated books (among them DISCOVERERS OF SPACE by Erich Lessing, and THE BIBLE: HISTORY AND CULTURE OF A PEOPLE); a colorful series of thirty *Playcraft* how-to-do-it booklets; gift books; and fiction. Among the newer authors on the Herder list are Kenneth Rexroth, Jorge Luis Borges, Mircea Eliade, Ernst Bloch, Paulo Freire, Francis Ponge, and Stanislaw Lem.

Two of Herder and Herder's more notable successes have been two titles on either ends of the spectrum: the controversial pictorial encyclopedia, THE SEX BOOK, and SACRAMENTUM MUNDI: AN ENCYCLOPEDIA OF THEOLOGY by Karl Rahner, who is considered one of the world's leading Catholic theologians.

In 1972 Herder and Herder became a Division of the McGraw-Hill Book Company, but in 1973 the Herder and Herder program of some five hundred titles in religion, education, psychology, sociology, and literature was acquired by The Seabury Press, Inc., where it is now carried on by Werner Mark Linz under a new imprint, Continuum Books.

Hill & Wang

Organized in 1956 in New York City by Lawrence Hill and Arthur W. Wang when they bought eighty-eight titles from the backlist of A.A. Wyn, Inc. Their plan was to publish general trade books and to develop a paperback series devoted to plays and the theatre. This line they called *Dramabooks*.

In 1959 Hill & Wang acquired the twenty-six-title *American Century Series,* dealing with American history and literature, from Sagamore Press, Inc. Later, a third line was started called *Hill & Wang Paperbacks,* which included fiction and world affairs.

The firm's most outstanding titles have been books by B. Traven, MODERN AMERICAN USAGE by Wilson Follett, and THE ELEGANT AUCTIONEERS by Wesley Towner. It has also published fiction by Elie Wiesel and Siegfried Lenz, plays by Arthur Kopit, and *belles lettres* by Mark Van Doren. A very successful picture book series was called *Terra Magica*.

In 1971 the firm was sold to Farrar, Straus & Giroux, of which it is now a division. Arthur Wang continued as editor-in-chief but Lawrence Hill left the company to start his own firm, Lawrence Hill & Company, Inc.

Hillary House Publishers

Based at New York City, the college textbook publishing division of Humanities Press, Inc.

The History Book Club

Organized in 1947 by Ray C. Dovell, who was its president until 1961 and then editorial director until 1964. Frank Melville succeeded him. The club specializes in nonfiction books of history and world affairs, history being defined as the whole record of man from ancient times to the twentieth century. The club's editorial board has included such names as Arthur Schlesinger, Jr., Stewart Holbrook, J. Frank Dobie, Bernard De Voto, Walter Millis, Dumas Malone, and Louis B. Wright.

In 1972 the club became a wholly-owned subsidiary of Harcourt Brace Jovanovich, Inc.

Hive Publishing Company

A small reprinter of scholarly books located at Easton, Pennsylvania.

Hobbs/Context Corporation

Established in 1964 at New York City. Publishes and distributes textbooks of a technical and business nature, as well as other instructional materials for education and industry.

Hobby House Press

Established in 1963 at Riverdale, Maryland. Publishes books on antiques, dolls, and the circus.

Holbrook Press, Inc.

Set up in 1967 at Boston, Massachusetts, the junior college and college textbook subsidiary of Allyn & Bacon, Inc.

Holden-Day, Inc.

Established in 1959 at San Francisco, California, by Frederick Murphy, a former western division manager for Addison-Wesley. The company publishes mainly college-level textbooks in the physical and natural sciences, economics, business administration, management, and psychology.

Holiday House, Inc.

Established in 1935 in New York City by Vernon Ives to publish fine juveniles. Early publications included a number of miniature "stocking" books, silk-screened cloth books, and nursery rhymes in the form of eighteenth-century broadsides. In its second year the company published Glen Rounds' OL' PAUL, THE MIGHTY LOGGER. In 1938 Ernest Shephard was commissioned to illustrate Kenneth Grahame's story, THE RELUCTANT DRAGON. Jim Kjelgaard's first book was published in 1941. Gladys Conklin's I LIKE CATERPILLARS was the first of many nature books which she wrote for the firm.

Other popular authors of Holiday House included Jane and Paul Annixter, Zachary Ball, Irma Simonton Black, Robert Davis, Margaret Embry, Russell Freedman, Phillip Harkins, Florence Parry Heide, Julian May, Edna Miller, and Vivian Thompson.

In 1965 Vernon Ives sold the business to John H. Briggs, Jr.

A. J. Holman Company

Organized in 1872 at Philadelphia, Pennsylvania, as A. J. Holman & Co. by A. J. Holman, George S. Lare and J. Parker Martin. As owners of the charter and stock of the Sauer family, the firm was the successor to Christopher Sauer, who had published the first German Bible in the American Colonies in 1743. Holman started his career in 1839 with Jesper Harding and through this association the firm can be traced to Solomon W. Conrad (1801); Kimber, Conrad & Co., (1806); Kimber & Sharpless (1815); Jesper Harding (1829); and William W. Harding & Co. (1859). During this time the company became one of the largest publishers of quarto Bibles in the world. The pronouncing feature was introduced by A. J. Holman Company in 1892 in their THE HOLMAN'S SUNDAY-SCHOOL TEACHERS' BIBLE.

The company continued under the management of the Holman family until the 1960s when it was absorbed by J. B. Lippincott Company.

Holt, Rinehart & Winston, Inc.

Founded in New York City in 1866 by Henry Holt and Frederick Leypoldt as Leypoldt and Holt. Holt was different from many other founding fathers of publishing because he was a religious and intellectual rebel and a lifelong Spencerian. Leypoldt was a bibliographic genius whose main interest was in the systematic aspects of publishing. But they both shared an interest in European authors and their first book was Charles Godfrey Leland's translation of MEMOIRS OF A GOOD-FOR-NOTHING by Joseph von Eichendorff. Holt concentrated on building up a strong foreign language list while Leypoldt devoted himself to the *Literary Bulletin,* the house organ. In 1871 R.O. Williams became a partner and the company name was changed to Leypoldt, Holt and Williams. In 1872 Leypoldt withdrew from the firm, taking with him the *Bulletin,* which was later to develop into the *Publishers Weekly.* The name of the firm then became Holt and Williams. Williams' departure in 1873 left Holt in sole ownership of the house and it became Henry Holt and Company.

Textbooks were the most profitable line of the new house but Holt's ambition was to make his imprint, with its striking owl device, well known for great literature. For this purpose he published during the 1870s and 1880s books by Ivan Turgenev, Thomas Hardy, Lewis H. Morgan, Henry Adams, and John Stuart Mill. In the 1890s he added William James to the list. Another of his early ventures was the *Leisure Hour Series,* which became one of the most popular in the higher class of inexpensive literature. It eventually grew into two hundred titles. The *American Science Series* was conceived and developed by Holt to introduce to American readers the excitement of scientific discovery in each of the major disciplines. Holt also functioned as a vigorous and forthright editor and his relations with his authors, William James, Henry Adams and Anthony Hope for instance, are part of literary history.

In 1897 Holt engaged Arthur Waugh as his representative in London, England. E.N. Bristol was in charge of the textbook division at that time. This department developed a number of distinguished series in every major discipline: *American Historical,* edited by C.H. Haskins; *American Mathematical,* edited by E.J. Townsend; *American Business,* edited by R.C. McCrea; *American Political Science,* edited by E.S. Corwin; and *American Social Science,* edited by H.W. Odum. Holt devoted his own attention to trade books. Among his authors during this period were

John Buchan, H.G. Wells, Romain Rolland, C.N. and A.M. Williamson, John Dewey, and Henri Bergson. He also sponsored and supervised such series as *American Nature* and *American Public Problems*. One of his favorite projects was the HOME BOOK OF VERSE by B.E. Stevenson.

In 1904 the firm acquired two new members, Donald Brace and Alfred Harcourt. Harcourt proved to be an able editor and he was responsible for adding a number of authors to Holt's fine list. Among them were Rose Macaulay, Dorothy Canfield Fisher, C.E. Montague, Walter Lippmann, Robert Frost, Walter de la Mare, Carl Sandburg, and Louis Untermeyer. Harcourt also persuaded Holt to begin publication of the *Home University Library* and *Makers of the Nineteenth Century,* the latter being a biographical series edited by Basil Williams. In 1919 Harcourt and Brace left Holt to found their own imprint.

Lincoln MacVeagh, who replaced Harcourt in the company, added Stephen Vincent Benét, Robert Benchley, Albert Einstein, Marcel Proust, and A.E. Housman to the Holt list. Toward the end of 1923 MacVeagh left the company to start the Dial Press.

Holt died in 1926. His GARRULITIES OF AN OCTOGENARIAN EDITOR is a testament to his rich and productive publishing career. In the reorganization following the death of Holt, E.N. Bristol and fellow executives acquired Holt's equity from his estate and Bristol became the company's president. But the Depression, combined with mediocre management, led to a decline in the fortunes of the firm. R.H. Thornton, who had succeeded Bristol in 1932, was voted out of office in 1939 and was replaced by Herbert Bristol, son of E.N. Bristol. In 1938 William Sloane was appointed trade editor and it was he who finally reversed the firm's decline.

Bold and perspicacious, Sloane was a friend of many writers and his efforts resulted in many bestsellers coming to Holt. Among these acquisitions were Mark Van Doren's COLLECTED POEMS, SEE HERE, PRIVATE HARGROVE by Marion Hargrove, Ernie Pyle's HERE IS YOUR WAR, Bill Mauldin's UP FRONT, and THE RAFT by Robert Trumbull. Herbert Bristol left the firm after World War II and, on Sloane's recommendation, Joseph A. Brandt was appointed president. Meanwhile a group of financiers, headed by Clint Murchison, had acquired the majority stock of the company from the Bristol family and toward the end of 1948 they compelled Brandt to leave. Sloane had left in 1946 to start his own firm.

Edward T. Rigg, the company's new president, set about revitalizing the firm. He placed particular emphasis on the textbook department. Through Murchison the *Field and Stream* magazine was obtained. Murchison's influence also resulted in two bestsellers: J. Edgar Hoover's MASTERS OF DECEIT and FOLK MEDICINE by D.C. Jarvis. By the late 1950s the company had turned the corner and had once again become very profitable. In 1958 Rigg acquired the Dryden Press and in the following year he arranged a merger effective March 1, 1960 with the John C. Winston and Company and Rinehart and Company. Holt, Rinehart & Winston, Inc. as the combined firm became known, went on to acquire Mentzer, Bush and Company in 1961 and Youth Associates Company in 1965.

In 1965 Rigg stepped down and since then the company has been directed by four presidents: Alfred Edwards, Ross Sackett, Kenneth Northrop, and Richard Abrams. In 1967 Holt, Rinehart & Winston was acquired by the Columbia Broadcasting System and it now operates as its wholly-owned subsidiary. Stanley D. Frank became president of the company in 1974.

Hoover Institution Press

A department of the Hoover Institution on War, Revolution, and Peace, established in 1919 by President Herbert C. Hoover for the purpose of collecting material on the causes of World War I. Its headquarters are at Stanford, California. Out of this initial collection grew the commitment to document causes of world unrest in the twentieth century, and a particularly strong collection on fascism and communism developed. Following the founder's wish that this material should be the basis of research and publishing, the Hoover Institution from the outset supported research and its first publication appeared in the 1920s. The early publications were primarily documentary studies and memoirs and were published through the Stanford University Press. Until 1960 publications were infrequent and by that date only approximately thirty books had been published.

In 1960 the publications program began to expand rapidly and the books were published through such houses as the University of Chicago Press, Pennsylvania State University Press, Johns Hopkins Press, Praeger, and Chandler. During the course of the 1960s the Hoover Press built up its own internal operations and by the end of the decade it was publishing virtually all of its own books.

Each year the Press publishes twenty academic titles and fifty microfilm reprints of serials. The publications appear in three series: *Publications, Bibliographical,* and *Studies.*

The *Publications* series is comprised of such scholarly monographs as LENIN AND THE COMINTERN; HUNGARY AND THE SUPERPOWERS: THE 1956 REVOLUTION AND REALPOLITIK; THE UNITED NATIONS IN PERSPECTIVE; and RULERS OF EMPIRE: THE FRENCH COLONIAL SERVICE IN AFRICA. Also included in this series are documentary studies such as EMERGING NATIONALISM IN PORTUGUESE AFRICA: DOCUMENTS, and FROM PROTEST TO CHALLENGE: A DOCUMENTARY HISTORY OF AFRICAN POLITICS IN SOUTH AFRICA, 1882-1964.

The *Bibliographical* series includes titles such as: A GUIDE TO RESEARCH AND REFERENCE WORKS ON SUB-SAHARAN AFRICA, and THE MODERN HISTORY OF ETHIOPIA AND THE HORN OF AFRICA: A BIBLIOGRAPHY.

The *Study* series includes topical studies, micro studies, and experimental publications such as GUERRILLAS IN HISTORY and THE TURKISH STRAITS AND NATO.

The microfilm publishing program of the Press draws its material almost entirely from the holdings of the Hoover Library, which specializes in political and social change in twentieth century history. Offerings include *The Hauptarchiv of the Nazi Party* and *Communist International (1919-1940),* the official journal of the Communist International.

Horizon Press

Organized 1951 at New York City. Specializes in books on art, architecture and photography.

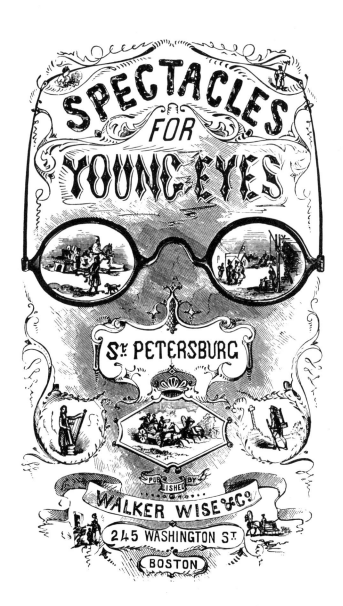

A geographic history, 1872.
Title Page.

Houghton Mifflin Company

Founded in 1880 by Henry Oscar Houghton and George Harrison Mifflin at Boston, Massachusetts. Houghton had begun his career in the trade in 1848 as a printer in the Boston shop of Freeman & Bolles, shortly buying out Freeman and changing the name of the firm to Bolles & Houghton. In 1852, having also bought out Bolles, Houghton created his own company under the name of H.O. Houghton & Company. Under this name he established in Cambridge, Massachusetts, the Riverside Press, which rapidly gained an enviable reputation for fine printing and book manufacture. In 1863, Houghton signed a contract with G. & C. Merriam Company for the printing and binding of Noah Webster's unabridged AMERICAN DICTIONARY OF THE ENGLISH LANGUAGE, a contract destined to run for over one hundred years. In 1864, in partnership with Melancthon M. Hurd, Houghton entered publishing, the firm's name being Hurd & Houghton. George Harrison Mifflin started to work for Hurd & Houghton in 1868, becoming a partner in 1872. In 1873 Hurd & Houghton acquired from James R. Osgood & Company *The Atlantic Monthly*. Three years later Hurd & Houghton bought the list of the educational publishers Crocker & Brewster (founded in 1818), thus acquiring two durable schoolbooks, Warren Colburn's INTELLECTUAL ARITHEMETIC and Andrews and Stoddard's GRAMMAR OF THE LATIN LANGUAGE.

Hurd retired in 1878 and Houghton then formed an alliance with James R. Osgood, formerly a partner in Ticknor & Fields, a Boston house dating from 1832. Osgood brought to Houghton, Osgood the great Ticknor and Fields list of New England and English writers which included Ralph Waldo Emerson, Nathaniel Hawthorne, Oliver Wendell Holmes, William Dean Howells, Henry Wadsworth Longfellow, James Russell Lowell, Henry David Thoreau, Charles Dickens, and Alfred, Lord Tennyson. In 1880 the Houghton, Osgood association was terminated and, according to the terms of the dissolution agreement, the new firm of Houghton, Mifflin & Company fell heir to the majority of the original Ticknor and Fields list.

Throughout the 1880s and 1890s Houghton, Mifflin & Company continued to develop its remarkable list of American authors, acquiring among others Edward Bellamy, Margaret Deland, Alice French, John Fiske, Lafcadio Hearn, Henry James, F. Hopkinson Smith, Kate Douglas Wiggin, and Woodrow Wilson. It also expanded its educational list by introducing a variety of series: *American Men of Letters, American Statesmen, American Commonwealths, Cambridge Poets,* and the *Riverside Literature Series* (the first educational paperbacks).

Henry Oscar Houghton died in 1895. Under Mifflin's administration the firm continued to expand in the directions Houghton had set. For editor of the *Atlantic* he secured first the services of Walter Hines Page, then of Bliss Perry; for trade editor, Ferris Greenslet. New authors continued to appear on the list of the house, notably John Buchan, Willa Cather, and Henry Adams. Large publishing and editing ventures were also undertaken, Ralph Waldo Emerson's JOURNALS and Henry David Thoreau's JOURNALS being perhaps the most outstanding. Mifflin also further enhanced the reputation of the Riverside Press by employing and giving a free hand to the book designer Bruce Rogers, whose Riverside Press Editions are today collectors' items.

In 1908, by dropping a comma and an ampersand, the firm ceased to be a partnership and became a corporation with the name Houghton Mifflin Company, the designation under which the company still operates. At this time the *Atlantic* was sold to Ellery Sedgwick.

Mifflin died in 1921 and was succeeded by Edward R. Houghton, nephew of the founder, under whose conservative administration the firm came through the depression years of the 1930s with flying colors. In 1939 E. R. Houghton yielded his position to Henry A. Laughlin. In the same year, the firm published Adolf Hitler's MEIN KAMPF.

During the 1940s Houghton's most successful authors were Lloyd C. Douglas, Anya Seton, Carson McCullers, John Dos Passos, Donald Culross Peattie, and Winston S. Churchill, whose MEMOIRS OF THE SECOND WORLD WAR was published in five volumes. The list of Houghton authors during the 1950s and 1960s is still more impressive and includes Rachel Carson, John

Kenneth Galbraith, Archibald MacLeish, Louis Auchincloss, Arthur M. Schlesinger, Jr., C. Northcote Parkinson, Agnes Sligh Turnbull, Bernard De Voto, Roger Tory Peterson, Cornelia Otis Skinner, A.B. Guthrie, Jr., and Benjamin Spock. In 1969 the firm published THE AMERICAN HERITAGE DICTIONARY OF THE ENGLISH LANGUAGE, prepared by American Heritage Publishing Company.

Throughout this century the educational division of the company has continued to develop until now it outstrips the trade division in size and profits. An early venture (1916) was the publication of Lewis M. Terman's MEASUREMENT OF INTELLIGENCE and the STANFORD REVISION OF THE BENET-SIMON INTELLIGENCE SCALE. Today Houghton Mifflin is one of the leaders in the field of educational testing. New paperback projects have continued to expand the trend set by the *Riverside Literature Series* in the *Sentry* and *Riverside Editions,* and modern mathematics texts have supplanted Colburn's INTELLECTUAL ARITHMETIC.

The importance of Houghton Mifflin's textbook division was underlined when, in 1957, the directors chose William E. Spaulding, head of the college division, to succeed Laughlin as the company's president. In 1963, Stephen W. Grant, Spaulding's successor as head of the college department, was chosen as the company's chief officer, a tradition continued in the recent appointment of Harold T. Miller, previously head of the educational division, as president.

Although Houghton Mifflin went public in 1967 and sold the Riverside Press in 1970, it still retains the independence it has enjoyed since its founding. It is one of the few historic houses which has not been absorbed by larger corporate conglomerates.

Howard University Press

Organized about 1972 at Washington, D.C. and funded by private funds. Published its first list of twelve books in spring of 1974, emphasizing academic, general trade and reference books mainly by and for Black people and other racial minorities.

Howell Book House, Inc.

Established in 1940 in New York City. The firm acquired Orange Judd Publishing Company (q.v.) and Denlinger's Dog Titles. Specializes in books about pets.

Howell-North Books

Established in 1956 at Berkeley, California, a small publisher of books dealing with Western Americana, railroads, and marine subjects.

Humanities Press, Inc.

Established in 1950 at New York City by Simon Silverman as a reprint firm. Its first reprint titles included Alfred North Whitehead's PROCESS AND REALITY and A COMMENTARY ON KANT'S CRITIQUE OF PURE REASON by Norman Kemp Smith. By 1951 the firm had become a distributor for several major British publishers, including Allen & Unwin, Routledge & Kegan Paul, Faber & Faber, and it also handled some famous series such as *The International Library of Philosophy and Scientific Method, Monographs on Social Anthropology,* and *The Muirhead Library of Philosophy.* In the mid-fifties Silverman co-founded Hillary House Publishers Ltd. with Richard Huett. He also launched Fernhill House Ltd., in 1966.

Humanities is the publisher for the American Institute of Marxist Studies (AIMS). Under an arrangement with the Van Leer Jerusalem Foundation, the company is to publish titles on the philosophy of science, political philosophy, and the behavioral sciences. Under a similar arrangement with Duquesne University Press, Humanities will handle production, marketing, and promotion of the Duquesne titles. A program has also been initiated for the publication of original works in philosophy and related disciplines.

Humanities Press has bought out Hillary House Publishers Ltd. and Fernhill House Ltd. and will no longer use either of those imprints in the future. All publishing will be done under the Humanities Press imprint.

IBC Industries, Inc.

Established in 1956 at Miami, Florida, by Lewis Leeds as International Book Distributors. The name was changed to International Book Corporation in 1966 and the firm entered educational publishing. In 1967 multi-media programs were added to the publishing line. In 1971 the firm name was changed to IBC Industries, Inc.

The Imprint Society

Established in 1970 at Barre, Massachusetts, to publish fine limited editions, Americana, and original graphic art. Purchased in spring 1974 by Crown Publishers, Inc., it will continue to operate independently as a wholly owned subsidiary.

Indiana University Press

Founded in 1950 at Bloomington, Indiana, by Bernard Perry. The first seven books were published in 1951. In the early years the Press published a number of trade titles in order to raise funds, no capital funds being available to the Press at that time.

The Press became known chiefly for its books in the fields of literary criticism, translations from classics, philosophy, and occasional trade books. In the early sixties, with John Dessauer as associate director, the Press considerably expanded its activities, publishing over sixty books a year, most of which were specialized scholarly works. This increased publication was made possible by additional subsidy from the university and assistance from Ford Foundation grants.

During the early days the Press had published a poetry series of thirty volumes but this output has now been largely reduced. The current emphasis in acquisitions is on history, public policy, political and social science, behavioral science, linguistics, the film, international affairs, music, natural history, popular culture, and books for the consumer.

The Press is also the publisher of A SELECTED EDITION OF W. D. HOWELLS for the Center for the Editions of American Authors, and two important series have been published in the field of education: *Bold New Venture Series* and the *English Curriculum Study Series*. The imprint Midland Books is used for quality paperbacks. In all, Indiana University Press has published over two hundred paperbacks, the majority under the Midland Books imprint, trade discounted to college bookstores, but included also are texts and oversized trade paperbacks. Two new series recently initiated are one on ethnic minority groups in the United States and paperback film guides.

The *Civil War Centennial Series* of the Press received a Centennial Medallion from the United States Civil War Centennial Commission in 1965. The Press also received National Book Awards in 1968 and 1971, in both instances for translations.

Industrial Press, Inc.

Founded in 1897 in New York City by Alexander Luchars. The company was among the oldest trade magazine publishers in the country and was continued when Luchars died by his son, Robert B. Luchars, and in turn by his grandson, Robert B. Luchars, Jr., who assumed the presidency of the company in 1966. A British subsidiary was established about 1900 and continues today as a separate but affiliated company.

For a number of years the company's principal publication was a monthly engineering trade magazine called *Machinery*. It entered book publishing with MACHINERY'S HANDBOOK in 1914, under the editorship of Franklin Jones. This HANDBOOK, known as the "Bible of the mechanical industries," has sold over one million eight hundred thousand copies in the course of nineteen editions.

In 1969 and 1970 the company sold its magazines and began to concentrate on book publishing. Many additional reference books and college texts were then added to its list in such fields as mechanical design and practice, industrial engineering and management, metal working and manufacturing practice, inspection and quality control, heating, ventilating, and air conditioning, plumbing, piping, and drainage, and power technology and energy.

International Arts & Sciences Press, Inc.

Established in 1958 at White Plains, New York, by Myron E. Sharpe. Its first publication was *Problems of Economics,* a monthly journal of translations from Soviet sources in the social sciences and allied fields. In the 1960s International started publishing journals of translation from other East European sources, as well as a journal entitled *Western European Education.* The *Asian Translation Series* was initiated in the late 1960s and includes six journals from Chinese sources and one from Japanese sources, all in the social sciences. In 1971 the Press launched an *International Translation* Series, five journals that publish social science materials from all parts of the world. In addition, the Press publishes *Challenge: The Magazine of Economic Affairs,* a bimonthly magazine on economic policy for economists and laymen.

The firm's book publishing program has specialized in translations from Soviet Russia and East European and Chinese sources, but its list contains an increasing number of titles by United States and Western European social scientists.

International Book Society

A subsidiary of Time-Life Books of New York City established in 1964, specializing in fine, heavily illustrated books. Most of its offerings are imports from Europe, co-produced with European publishers.

International Publishers

Established in New York City in 1924 by Alexander Trachtenberg who wrote: "International is a new publishing firm; new in fact and new in spirit and outlook. Over its imprint will appear books from the pens of writers who feel life deeply, and whose art is vivid and real." From its earliest titles, which included CHAINS by Henri Barbusse and the EIGHTEENTH BRUMAIRE OF LOUIS BONAPARTE by Karl Marx, this outlook has guided the firm. It is now the largest Marxist publishing house in the English-speaking world.

During the McCarthy period, the firm suffered economic and political harassment, including the imprisonment of Trachtenberg for violation of the Smith Act.

In 1962 International entered the quality paperback market, adopting the imprints of New World Paperbacks and Little New World Paperbacks. As a pioneer publisher of books on Black liberation, International's authors in this field include W.E.B. DuBois, Kwame Nkrumah, Henry Winston and Herbert Aptheker. The company's current list spans a wide range of subjects: current events, labor, history, political economy, fiction, and philosophy. Poetry is represented by three popular anthologies: THE NEW BLACK POETRY; POETS OF TODAY; and VOICES FROM WAH'KON-TAH.

Trachtenberg's tenure extended until 1962 when he was succeeded by James S. Allen. When Allen retired in 1973 Louis Diskin became president and editor of the company.

International Textbook Company

See, Intext, Inc.

International Universities Press. Inc.

Incorporated in 1944 in New York City by Joseph and Ester Riwkin as Medical War Books. In 1946 the company became International Universities Press, Inc. and ownership was transferred to A.S. Kagan and David Scheiner, with Scheiner serving as president until 1948. In 1948 ownership was transferred to A.S. Kagan and Paul Safro, and Kagan was the company's president until 1971. In 1971 ownership was transferred to Martin V. Azarian and Irene Azarian. Martin

Azarian then took over the presidency, which office he continues to hold.

The major publishing programs of the Press are in the field of psychiatry. Among its issues are: THE PSYCHOANALYTIC STUDY OF THE CHILD (1945-70); THE YEARBOOK OF PSYCHOANALYSIS (1945-1954); THE INDEX OF PSYCHOANALYTIC WRITINGS (14 volumes); THE ANNUAL SURVEY OF PSYCHOANALYSIS (1950-59); *Psychological Issues* (30 monographs); THE PSYCHOANALYTIC STUDY OF SOCIETY (5 volumes); THE WRITINGS OF ANNA FREUD (7 volumes); *Journal of the American Psychoanalytic Association* (1953—); *International Journal of Group Psychotherapy* (since 1951); and *Journal of Geriatric Psychiatry* (founded 1967).

The Interstate Printers & Publishers, Inc.

Founded in 1896 in Danville, Illinois, as the Commercial Printing Company. The name was changed to Interstate Printing Company in 1908 and to The Interstate Printers and Publishers, Inc., in 1939.

The firm specializes in books on agriculture, physical education, and special education.

Inter-Varsity Press

Established in 1954 and located at Downers Grove, Illinois. Specializes in religious, interdenominational books.

Intext, Inc.

Started in 1889 in Scranton, Pennsylvania, as the Colliery Engineer Company by Thomas Jefferson Foster to publish instruction texts in coal mining. The firm was incorporated in 1890 and in 1901 it became the International Textbook Company in order to publish textbooks for "the dissemination of literary, technical, educational and other information." A subsidiary corporation was also chartered, The International Correspondence Schools, which over the years has provided job-related instruction materials in one thousand courses to over eight million persons. Eventually a college textbook publishing group was developed. This was the firm's only publishing activity until 1968 when it decided to expand.

Within the course of four years the corporation acquired The John Day Company (q.v.) in 1968, Ballantine Books, Inc. (q.v.), The Steck-Vaughn Company (q.v.), and Abelard-Schuman, Ltd. (q.v.) in 1969, and the Chandler Publishing Company in 1970. These companies were then reorganized functionally. John Day and Abelard-Schuman were joined together to create Intext Press, the trade arm of Intext, Inc. The College Publishing Division (the original International Textbook Company) and Chandler were consolidated in New York in 1972 as Intext Educational Publishers, specializing in tertiary level textbooks in engineering, business administration, economics, education, mathematics, and the physical sciences. Steck-Vaughn became the el-hi text division and Ballantine Books the paperback division.

In 1974 the inventory and author contracts of Abelard-Schuman, John Day, Criterion Books, Chandler Publishing Company, and Intext Educational Publishers were sold to Thomas Y. Crowell Company. Ballantine Books was sold to Random House in 1973.

Iowa State University Press

Founded in 1924 as a student publication press on the campus of Iowa State College at Cedar Falls, Iowa. During its early years the press was guided by F.W. Beckman, head of the Department of Agricultural Journalism. The first two books under the new imprint were published during 1927-28. Further publishing had to wait until 1934 when Warren Hutton was appointed full-time editor of the Collegiate Press. The publishing program steadily progressed and Hazel Beck became editor in 1936. One title during this period that helped to focus national attention on the Press was STATISTICAL METHODS by George Snedecor. Harold E. Ingle became editor of the Press in 1938. In 1946 the name of the Press was changed to Iowa State College Press. Ingle moved on to become director of Johns Hopkins University Press in 1948 and Marshall Townsend was appointed in his place with the title of manager. When Townsend left in 1963 Merritt E. Bailey took charge as director.

Under Ingle the titles of the Press had reflected the main interests of the Iowa State College, UNIT METHOD OF SEWING, FORAGES, BETTER FARM ACCOUNTING, and YOUR FAMILY FINANCES being the more important books during this period. With Townsend came the development of regional and general scholarly publishing. A CHANGE AND A PARTING: MY STORY OF AMANA and STUDENT PILOT'S FLIGHT MANUAL were typical titles. The emphasis on the humanities was strengthened when Iowa State College became the Iowa State University and with the simultaneous change in the name of the Press to Iowa State University Press. New titles, such as INTRODUCTION TO SATIRE, THE LETTERS OF A. BRONSON ALCOTT, HOW TO LIGHT A WATER HEATER AND OTHER WAR STORIES, and CHARLES DICKENS AS SERIAL NOVELIST, are representative of the new directions at the Press.

Irish University Press, Inc.

Established at New York City in 1967 as the American branch of Irish University Press of Dublin, Ireland. The Press is a private commercial company with a board of academic advisers drawn from all universities in the Republic of Ireland and Northern Ireland. It is controlled by a group of which William Stern, a U.S. citizen, is the chief shareholder and George Lingwood and Captain Tadhg MacGlinchey are the chairman and vice-chairman respectively.

The Press gained international recognition when it published the one thousand-volume BRITISH PARLIAMENTARY PAPERS of the nineteenth century, selected and arranged in eighty-two subject areas. This has been followed by area study sets on the U.S.A., China, and Japan, facsimile series on the development of industrial society, parliamentary and congressional history, and eighty-two volumes in a limited edition of the Cuala and Dun Emer private presses of the Yeats family. Currently it is publishing a series of new books on social and clinical psychology, DOCU-

MENTS OF THE AMERICAN REVOLUTION, in twenty volumes, as well as significant reprint series on Asian studies, Black studies, Irish novels, folklore, and revolutionaries.

Many of the series and titles of the Press appear in the United States under American imprints: Barnes & Noble, Praeger, and Cornell, Duquesne, and Rutgers University Presses.

Richard D. Irwin, Inc.

Started in 1933 by Richard D. Irwin in a modest one-room Chicago, Illinois, office. Originally established under the name of Business Publications, Inc., the name of the company was changed to its present form in 1940. In 1951 the firm's physical facilities in Chicago were outgrown, necessitating a move to Homewood, Illinois.

Since its inception, Irwin has enjoyed international reputation as a leading publisher of quality books on business and economics. In order to extend the expertise of the firm to the social and behavioral sciences, a separate division, The Dorsey Press, was set up in 1959. The Dorsey Press has since become well-established as a publisher of a carefully selected, quality list of books on anthropology, sociology, history, political science, and psychology.

A new wholly-owned subsidiary and a new division were formed in 1969. The subsidiary, Business Publications, Inc., was established in Austin, Texas, and specializes in business and economics textbooks for college use. The new division, Learning Systems Company, was organized to publish, initially, a series of paperback self-review guides in programmed format for university students at all levels and for business, industrial, and governmental training programs. Its publications are identified by the name PLAIDS, an acronym for Programmed Learning Aids.

Dow Jones-Irwin, Inc., a publishing firm owned equally by Dow Jones and Company and Richard D. Irwin, was incorporated in 1964 to publish professional books for the business community. A Canadian branch, Irwin-Dorsey, Ltd. was established in 1967, and in 1972 a new international division, Irwin-Dorsey International, was set up with headquarters in London, England.

Irwin has also won recognition for its leadership in business and economics publishing by being selected as the official publisher for the American Economics Association. In addition, Irwin is the publisher for special publications sponsored by distinguished academic associations and foundations, including the S.S. Huebner Foundation for Insurance Education, the Pension Research Council, the Institute of Chartered Financial Analysts, the Leonard Davis Institute of Health Economics, and the McCahan Foundation.

As the company grew, Irwin initiated and developed a number of key series: the *Willard J. Graham Series in Accounting,* the *Irwin Series in Insurance and Economic Security,* the *Irwin Series in Management and the Behavioral Sciences,* and other series in economics, finance, and quantitative analysis for business. Many Irwin texts have become classics in their field. They include the firm's first bestseller, ECONOMICS OF TRANSPORTATION by D. Phillip Locklin and Harold Lusk's BUSINESS LAW: TEXT AND CASES. In 1961 Irwin moved up to be chairman of the board of the company. His successor as president was Harry H. Bingham, who served from 1961 to 1963. Irvin L. Grimes succeeded Bingham as president in 1963.

Jarrow Press, Inc.

Established in 1968 at Boston, Massachusetts. Publishes Episcopal, religious, and reference books.

Jenkins Publishing Company

Organized in 1965 at Austin, Texas. Specializes in secondary and college textbooks.

The Jewish Publication Society of America

Founded in 1845 by Rabbi Isaak Leeser at Philadelphia, Pennsylvania, as the American Jewish Publication Society. One of Leeser's achievements was the translation of the Hebrew Bible into English and its publication in 1853. But he was not able to muster enough support and the Society was dissolved in 1851 after publishing fourteen books. The second American Jewish Publication Society was formed in 1875. It lasted only for about three years.

The present Society was set up in 1888 under the leadership of Joseph Krauskopf and Solomon Solis-Cohen with Morris Newburger as the first president. Its first publication was OUTLINES OF JEWISH HISTORY by Lady Katie Magnus. This was followed by the monumental HISTORY OF THE JEWS in six volumes, by Heinrich Graetz. Another early title was THE PERSECUTION OF THE JEWS IN RUSSIA, issued by the Russo-Jewish Committee of London, England. One of the prime movers of the Society in the early days was Henrietta Szold, who served as secretary to the publication committee from 1893 to 1916. She is best remembered as the founder of the Hadassah.

In 1898 the Society was incorporated as a benevolent undertaking "for the publication and dissemination of literary, scientific, and religious works giving instruction in the principles of Jewish religion." In 1892 the Society began preparations for a new translation of the Bible. Out of this effort came THE HOLY SCRIPTURES ACCORDING TO THE MASORETIC TEXT published in 1917. In 1955 a new Bible project was undertaken, taking into account linguistic and archaeological advances made in recent times. The first fruit of this project was THE TORAH: THE FIVE BOOKS OF MOSES, which appeared in 1963. This was followed by THE FIVE MEGILLOTH and THE BOOK OF JONAH, THE BOOK OF PSALMS, and THE BOOK OF ISAIAH.

The hundreds of titles that have appeared under the Society's imprint would in themselves constitute a library of Jewish literature. Among them are: Salo W. Baron's SOCIAL AND RELIGIOUS HISTORY OF THE JEWS, Louis Ginzberg's THE LEGENDS OF THE JEWS, Abraham J. Heschel's THE PROPHETS, THE RISE AND FALL OF THE JUDEAN STATE by Solomon Zeitlin, A HISTORY OF THE JEWS by Solomon Grayzel, Abraham Ibn Daud's SEFER HA'QUABBALAH (Book of Tradition) edited by Gerson D. Cohen, Abraham E. Millgram's JEWISH WORSHIP, MESILLAT YESH-ARIM by Moses Hayyim Luzzatto, THE TREA-TISE TA'ANIT edited by Henry Malter, and TROTSKY AND THE JEWS by Joseph Nevada. Another popular program is a series of anthologies about Jewish holy days.

In cooperation with the American Jewish Committee the Society annually publishes THE AMERICAN JEWISH YEARBOOK, a calendar review of Jewish life the world over. Under the Covenant imprint the Society offers a series of biographies of such notables as Ben-Yehuda, Sholom Aleichem, Lillian Wald, and Albert Einstein.

The John Day Company, Inc. Publishers

Organized in 1926 by Richard J. Walsh, Trell Yocum, Cleland Austin, and Guy Holt in New York City. The company was named after John Day, the famous Elizabethan printer and bookseller. The firm was hard hit by the Depression of the 1930s and Holt left to join Whittlesey House. However, the publication of Pearl Buck's THE GOOD EARTH enabled the company to pull through without floundering. Pearl Buck was thereafter actively involved in the company's affairs, particularly after her marriage to Richard J. Walsh in 1935. Her interest in Asia led Walsh to assume the editorship of *Asia Magazine,* which had been founded many years earlier by Willard Straight.

During the late 1930s the firm's business, production, and marketing were handled first by Reynal and Hitchcock and later by Putnam's. Books on Asia dominated the John Day list, including books by such authors as Owen Lattimore, Hans Kohn, and Nathaniel Peffer. Works by Jawaharlal Nehru and Lin Yutang were also prominent on the John Day list. To promote these titles Walsh formed Asia Press in 1946. In 1944 the firm had found a bestseller in Margaret Landon's ANNA AND THE KING OF SIAM. There was also a strong interest in juveniles, and this interest has been continued to this day. The company pioneered in books for children on science and about the peoples of the world.

In 1959 Richard J. Walsh, Jr. assumed the presidency of the company. Under him the in-terest in books about Asia has been muted and greater emphasis has been placed on general trade titles. The firm also issues a number of series; among them in earlier years were the *John Day Pamphlets* and currently the *John Day Books in Special Education.*

In 1968 The John Day Company, Inc. was acquired by Intext, Inc. (q.v.) and sold to Thomas Y. Crowell in 1974.

John Knox Press

Founded in 1838 at Philadelphia, Pennsylvania, under the auspices of the General Assembly of the Presbyterian Church, as the Presbyterian Board of Publication. During the Civil War the Southern Presbyterians set up a Committee of Publication in Richmond, Virginia. This body was known as the Onward Press until 1938 when the present name was adopted. It is now the publishing arm of the Board of Christian Education of the Presbyterian Church in the United States. Its stated purpose is "to contribute to and stimulate the advancement of Biblical scholarship and Christian thought and living throughout the world by the publication and distribution of books and other printed materials." Its major publishing project in the past decade was the publication of the twenty-five-volume LAYMAN'S BIBLE COMMENTARY.

The Johns Hopkins University Press

Founded in 1878, the Johns Hopkins University Press at Baltimore, Maryland, is the oldest of the North American university presses in continuous operation. The need for a Press and the definition of its role were articulated by Daniel Coit Gilman, first president of The Johns Hopkins University when he wrote, "It is one of the noblest duties of a university to advance knowledge, and to diffuse it not merely among those who can attend the daily lectures—but far and wide." The first publication to appear under the Johns Hopkins imprint was *The American Journal of Mathematics,* edited by James J. Sylvester. The following year two other journals began publication. In 1882

Herbert B. Adams founded a monograph series entitled *The Johns Hopkins University Studies in Historical and Political Science*. This series, as well as the mathematics journal, has been published without interruption for nearly a century.

In its earliest years the Press was known as the Publications Agency of the University and its direction was the province of the University's Library Committee. In 1890 the name was changed to The Johns Hopkins Press and its executive head, Nicholas Murray, became director of the press. Murray was also the university librarian. By 1908 the Press had outgrown the plan of joint management and C.W. Dittus was given full-time responsibility for its operation, initially with the title of secretary, later as manager. The first editorial board of the Press was appointed in 1921. Representing all major divisions of the university, the board was charged with the responsibility of passing upon all manuscripts proposed for publication by the Press.

In 1948 Harold E. Ingle, formerly manager of Iowa State University Press, became the Press director. Under Ingle's guidance the Press has achieved a remarkable record of growth, from twelve books in 1948 to seventy-five new titles in 1972. In the same period the Press's annual sales volume has increased twentyfold. In 1972 the word "University" was added to its title. In 1969 a British subsidiary, The Johns Hopkins Press, Ltd., was organized and joined with similar subsidiaries of the Cornell and California university presses to form IBEG (International Book Export Group).

Perhaps the most distinguished title that the Press has published is the *variorum* edition of EDMUND SPENSER, published in eleven volumes from 1932 to 1957. Another landmark publication is the three-volume MAMMALS OF THE WORLD by Ernest P. Walker. Along with literature and life sciences, the Press publishes intensively in such areas as history, economics, the history of medicine, international politics, medical psychology, and psychiatry. Johns Hopkins also serves as publisher for the World Bank and for Resources for the Future, Inc., an independent research organization in Washington, D.C.

Many of the monograph series begun in the early years of the Press have ceased publication, and new, less formalized series have been developed in recent years. The Press now publishes actively series in architectural history, oceanography, manpower economics, geology, comparative history, and the history of ideas. The Press also publishes seven journals: *American Journal of Mathematics, Bulletin of the History of Medicine, The Johns Hopkins Medical Journal, Human Factors, ELH, MLN,* and the *American Journal of Philology.*

In March 1974 Harold E. Ingle resigned as director; he was succeeded by the former associate director, Jack G. Goellner.

See, French, John C., THE JOHNS HOPKINS PRESS: A BRIEF HISTORY, Baltimore, 1938; Hawkins, Hugh, PIONEER: A HISTORY OF THE JOHNS HOPKINS UNIVERSITY, 1874-1889, Ithaca, 1960; French, John C., A HISTORY OF THE UNIVERSITY FOUNDED BY JOHNS HOPKINS, Baltimore, 1946.

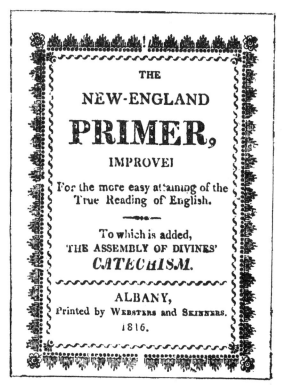

New England Primer, 1816,
Title Page

156

Johnson Publishing Company, Inc. — Book Division

Located in Chicago, Illinois. Publishes nonfiction and children's books, primarily by and about Black people.

Johnson Reprint Corporation

Established in 1946 in New York City as an offshoot of Academic Press (q.v.). The main purpose of the new firm was to reprint journals and books.

Johnson Reprint Company's major publishing programs include the fifty-volume REPORT ON THE SCIENTIFIC RESULTS OF THE VOYAGE OF H.M.S. CHALLENGER, John James Audubon's THE BIRDS OF AMERICA in full-size elephant folio, and a twelve-volume reproduction of Leonardo da Vinci's CODEX ATLANTICUS.

The firm was acquired along with Academic Press by Harcourt Brace Jovanovich, Inc., in 1969.

Jonathan David Publishers, Inc.

Founded in 1948 at Middle Village, New York, by Rabbi Alfred J. Kolatch under the name of The Jonathan David Company. It still remains in the hands of the Kolatch family. The first publication was the founder's own book, THESE ARE THE NAMES, dealing with Hebrew and English names, later revised as THE NAME DICTIONARY.

During the 1950s and 1960s the firm limited itself to adult and juvenile titles of interest to a Jewish audience, such as the ENCYCLOPEDIA OF JEWISH HUMOR by Henry D. Spalding and THE JEWISH WAY IN DEATH AND MOURNING by Maurice Lamm. In recent years it has expanded into general publishing with books such as THE FOOTBALL PLAYBOOK, ENCYCLOPEDIA OF BLACK FOLKLORE AND HUMOR, and BEN-GURION LOOKS AT THE BIBLE. In juvenile literature, it has launched two series: *Let's Talk About* and *Fun-in-Learning*.

Charles A. Jones Publishing Company

Located at Worthington, Ohio, a division of Wadsworth Publishing Company that publishes college and professional textbooks.

Marshall Jones Company

Founded in 1904 at Francestown, New Hampshire. The firm acquired the titles of Cornhill Publishing Company. Specializes in secondary and college textbooks.

Jossey-Bass, Inc., Publishers

Established in 1967 in San Francisco, California, by Allen Jossey-Bass to publish books in the social and behavioral sciences. The firm soon expanded into the field of higher education and this has become one of the main strengths of its list. Two major programs are the *Higher Education Series* and the *Behavioral Science Series*. Three journals are published in the area of higher education: *New Directions for Higher Education, New Directions for the Community College, New Directions for the School*. Future programs include an encyclopedia of international higher education and a loose-leaf subscription series of administrative aids, also considerable expansion of the social and behavioral science book series.

Jossey-Bass has a joint publication arrangement with Elsevier Publishing Company of Amsterdam. The company is now publicly owned. Jossey-Bass, Limited, London, was incorporated in early 1973.

Judson Press

Founded in 1824 in Washington, D.C. through the efforts of Samuel Cornelius and called The Baptist

General Tract Society, in order to publish and circulate tracts for American Baptists. In 1826 the headquarters were moved to Philadelphia, Pennsylvania. In 1839 the first book publications were issued: REIGN OF GRACE by Rev. Abraham Booth, CHURCH HISTORY by Isaak Backus, and MEMOIRS OF DISTINGUISHED CHRISTIANS. In 1840 the Society was reorganized as The American Baptist Publication and Sunday School Society. Four years later the title was shortened to The American Baptist Publication Society. In 1856 the New England Sabbath School Union was merged with the Society.

Until 1890 the Society was the only Baptist publishing house in existence, publishing such books "as are needed by the Baptist denomination and to provide Sunday Schools by such measures as may prove expedient." It retained the name of American Baptist Publication Society until 1964 (except for a brief period from 1870 to 1873 during which it was called The Bible and Publication Society) when it adopted the name of American Baptist Board of Education and Publication. However, in January, 1973 it became the Board of Educational Ministries of the American Baptist Churches of the U.S.A. In 1918 Judson Press was adopted as the trade imprint of the Society.

The phenomenal progress of the Society was largely due to Benjamin Griffith who was in charge from 1857 to 1893.

One of the Society's greatest bestsellers was a dog story, BEAUTIFUL JOE by Margaret Marshall Saunders. First published in 1894, it has sold over a million copies and led to a sequel, BEAUTIFUL JOE'S PARADISE.

In 1962 the headquarters of the Society were moved to Valley Forge, Pennsylvania.

Judson Press publishes a wide range of educational books for use in the churches, professional aids for ministers, and inspirational books for the laity, producing between thirty and forty books a year for those markets. Among Judson Press's bestselling authors have been Harvey Cox, Reuel Howe, and Clarence Jordan. In 1973 the Press entered international publishing with the publication of an American edition of Karl Barth's PROTESTANT THEOLOGY IN THE NINETEENTH CENTURY.

Julian Press, Inc.

Organized in 1951 in New York City. The firm took over the list of Matrix House, Ltd. Specializes in books on psychiatry and education.

Kaiman & Polon, Inc.

Organized in 1969 in New York City as publishers' representatives by Kenneth L. Kaiman and Albert L. Polon. The firm has branches in England, Israel, South Africa, Mexico, Brazil, The Philippines, Japan, and Europe. The firm participates in the book fairs at Frankfurt, Jerusalem, Cairo, and the Bienal at São Paulo, Brazil.

Augustus M. Kelley, Publishers

Established in 1947 at Clifton, New Jersey. Specializes in reprints of economics classics.

Kendall/Hunt Publishing Company

A subsidiary of William C. Brown Company, Publishers, of Dubuque, Iowa, which publishes college workbooks, manuals and supplementary textbooks.

P.J. Kenedy & Sons

Started in 1826 by John Kenedy in Baltimore, Maryland, as a small bookstore. He gravitated into publishing with a small weekly called *Kenedy's Budget of Blunders*, first issued in 1831. In 1834 he published his first Catholic work, an abridged edition of Alfonso Rodriguez's PRACTICE OF PERFECTION AND CHRISTIAN VIRTUES edited by the Reverend Edward Damphoux. THE AMERICAN SONGSTER followed the next year. Kenedy moved to New York City in 1836 and began to concentrate on serving the city's Irish Catholic population by issuing various editions of catechisms, prayer books and devotional works. When he died in 1866 the name of the business was changed to John Kenedy & Son. Patrick J., John Kenedy's son, took over the firm and through his vigorous management, and the acquisition of rival firms, by the turn of the century it became one of the forces in Catholic publishing.

Incorporated in 1904 as P.J. Kenedy & Sons, the firm remained in the ownership of the original family until 1968, when it was acquired by Crowell Collier and Macmillan (now Macmillan, Inc.). In 1895 Kenedy had been designated as Publisher to the Holy See. In this capacity the company still publishes the OFFICIAL CATHOLIC DIRECTORY.

Kennikat Press

Established in 1963 in New York City as a scholarly reprint adjunct of Ira J. Friedman, Inc., an antiquarian book firm, which had been founded in 1922 by Ira J. Friedman. On Friedman's retirement in 1960 the operation was carried on by the present management, Alice and Cornell Jaray. The two companies were subsequently sold in 1969 to Taylor Publishing Company of Dallas, Texas, a subsidiary of INSILCO Corporation of Meriden, Connecticut, but the management continued under the Jarays.

The scholarly reprint publishing of Kennikat quickly overshadowed the modest programs of its parent, the Friedman company. Kennikat's strong backlist emphasizes the humanities and the social sciences. In 1971 the firm started to publish original scholarly titles under the National University Publications imprint. The Ira J. Friedman Division is still active in regional material, publishing series of titles on New York, Pennsylvania, and the Middle Atlantic States.

Kent State University Press

Founded at Kent, Ohio, in 1965 with C. Howard Allen, Jr., as the director. In 1969 it took over the on-going publishing activities of the Antioch Press which had just suspended operations. Its best known series is *Serif,* a series of checklists and bibliographies. Other fields of strength include books of regional Ohio interest, American history, and American and English literature. In addition it publishes two journals, *Explorations in Economic History* and *Civil War History.* Paul H. Rohmann became director of the Press in 1972.

The Kirkus Service, Inc.

Organized in 1933 in New York City by Virginia Kirkus, Ruth Basham, and Alice E. Wolff as a pre-publication book review service. The service is aimed at public and academic libraries, bookshops, jobbers, publishers, magazines, book clubs, and motion picture and television producers and agents. It reviews American fiction comprehensively, nonfiction more selectively, and most juveniles from major houses. The adult book reviews appear from eight to twelve weeks in advance of publication while juvenile books are reviewed approximately four weeks prior to their publication. University presses and more specialized publishers are included on the basis of merit and general interest. There are periodic religious book supplements and each issue is indexed with cumulative indexes appearing at quarterly and semiannual intervals. A microfilm edition is in progress.

Started originally as an aid for booksellers at a time when buying in advance of publication was essential and books could not be returned to the publishers, the initial issue of the *Bulletin From Virginia Kirkus' Bookshop Service* (as it was then called) appeared in January 1933 with a subscription list of only ten bookshops. Virginia Kirkus, a former children's book editor at Harper, rapidly developed the service into an indispensable selection tool: the number of books reviewed, the size of the staff, and the subscription list all increased steadily during the thirties, forties, and fifties. In the early years the reviews emphasized popular potential; the Kirkus Service endeavored "to be informal, colloquial and readable—and not literary."

In 1962 Virginia Kirkus and Ruth Basham retired and Alice E. Wolff became the editor. Alice Wolff has consistently emphasized the qualitative as opposed to commercial potential of books under review. During her tenure as editor *Kirkus Reviews* has continued to grow; the subscription list now stands at approximately five thousand. In 1971, the *New York Review of Books* acquired the Service but it continues to operate independently.

Alfred A. Knopf, Inc.

Founded in 1915 in New York City by Alfred A. Knopf and Blanche W. Knopf. Their first announcement listed eleven titles of which seven were by Russian writers.

From the beginning Knopf was deeply concerned with the quality of his books and refused to publish anything that did not meet his standards, however salable it might be. The Borzoi imprint thus became highly respected for the appearance and quality of the books which bore its stamp. In the 1920 issue of *The Borzoi,* issued to commemorate his first five years in publishing, Knopf listed 137 authors. Among them were Kahlil Gibran, H.L. Mencken, Joseph Hergesheimer, W.H. Hudson, and E.M. Forster. In 1923 he brought out the *Borzoi Pocket Books* and two years later the *Blue Jade Library.* At the same time he arranged with Mencken and George Jean Nathan to publish a new monthly called *American Mercury.* In 1928 a juvenile department was set up and it developed into a profitable division of the company.

During the 1920s the Knopf list acquired several celebrated writers, among them: D.H. Lawrence, Thomas Mann, Oswald Spengler, and Clarence Day. In 1954 Knopf announced publication of *Vintage Books,* paperback reprints. He also experimented with paperback originals, an experiment the firm was to repeat in 1970. By 1968 Knopf could proudly count thirteen Nobel Prize winners among his authors: Knut Hamsun, Wladislaw S. Reymont, Sigrid Undset, Thomas Mann, Ivan A. Bunin, F.E. Sillanpää, Johannes V. Jensen, André Gide, Halldór Laxness, Albert Camus, Jean-Paul Sartre, Mikhail

Sholokhov, and Yasunari Kawabata. Knopf's personal interest in history was reflected in the number of historical books that he published over the years.

Celebrating fifty years as a publisher in 1965, Knopf issued an anniversary volume that contained a roster of his authors. This impressive list included some of the finest contemporary writers: Willa Cather, Max Beerbohm, John Updike, Katherine Mansfield, W.H. Hudson, Robert Graves, John Hersey, Richard Hofstadter, Eric Ambler, Jules Romains, Miguel de Unamuno, Raymond Chandler, Ezra Pound, and Elizabeth Bowen. And in recent years the firm has published John Cheever, William Humphrey, Julia Child, Chaim Potok, Doris Lessing, Ross Macdonald, Jacques Monod and T. Harry Williams.

In 1958 Alfred Knopf, Jr. resigned from the company to found Atheneum Publishers with Hiram Haydn and Simon Michael Bessie. Shortly afterwards, the senior Knopf accepted an offer to merge with Random House. Knopf continued to head the firm and retain his separate and distinct imprint. In 1966 Blanche Knopf died and was replaced as president by William A. Koshland. In 1973 Alfred Knopf retired, Koshland became chairman of the board and Robert Gottlieb was elected president of the company.

Kraus-Thomson Organization, Ltd.

Established in 1939 in New York City by Hans P. Kraus as a branch of the rare book firm he had founded in Vienna in 1932. A separate firm, Kraus Periodicals, Inc., was formed in 1946 for the purpose of importing and exporting back files of scientific and scholarly periodicals. Kraus Reprint Corporation was incorporated in 1956 in order to reprint complete files of periodicals. The two firms merged in 1968 with the Thomson International Corporation, Ltd., headed by Lord Thomson of Fleet, publisher of *The Times* of London, and became the Kraus-Thomson Organization, Ltd. Frederick Altman is president and Hans P. Kraus is the chairman.

Major publishing programs include complete series of scholarly journals in every discipline, multi-volume bibliographies, reference works, definitive editions of standard works, as well as publications of learned societies. National bibliographies have been prime programs: the ENGLISH CATALOGUE OF BOOKS (21 volumes); BIBLIOGRAPHIE DE LA FRANCE (45 volumes); BIBLIO (36 volumes); BIBLIOGRAPHIE DE BELGIQUE (75 volumes); BIBLIOGRAFIA ESPANOLA (22 volumes), and its continuations, BIBLIOGRAFIA GENERAL ESPANOLA ET HISPANO-AMERICANA (16 volumes), and BIBLIOGRAFIA HISPANICA (16 volumes); the Russian national bibliographies, KNIZHNAIA LETOPIS (218 volumes) and LETOPIS' ZHURNAL'NYKH STATEI (116 volumes); also the Italian National Bibliography, BIBLIOGRAFIA NAZIONALE ITALIANA, 1886-1957 (41 volumes).

Other monumental reference works have included INTERNATIONALE BIBLIOGRAPHIE DER ZEITSCHRIFTENLITERATUR (150 volumes); UNITED NATIONS DOCUMENTS INDEX (17 volumes); U.S. SUPERINTENDENT OF DOCUMENTS, CATALOG OF THE PUBLIC DOCUMENTS (25 volumes); PUBLIC AFFAIRS INFORMATION SERVICE BULLETIN (51 volumes); BIBLIOGRAPHY OF THE MODERN LANGUAGE ASSOCIATION OF AMERICA (21 volumes); INDEX TO THE LONDON TIMES (132 volumes); and GREAT BRITAIN, PUBLIC RECORD OFFICE, INDEX TO FOREIGN OFFICE CORRESPONDENCE, 1920-1945 (107 volumes).

Reprinted journals include Harvard University's *Quarterly Journal of Economics, Harvard Business Review, American Historical Review,* and the *Publications of the Modern Language Association of America,* as well as the journals of the American Psychological Association and the American Anthropological Association.

Kraus-Thomson is also engaged in publishing facsimiles of archival materials. Reprinted medieval source collections include the *Rolls Series* (254 volumes), and the *Monumenta Germaniae Historica* (36 volumes). Particularly hailed by librarians are the so-called Little Magazines, approximately two hundred of which have been reprinted, among them being *Hound and Horn, New Directions* and *New Freewoman.*

Since 1970 Kraus-Thomson has also been engaged in microfilm reprinting, primarily related to the reproduction of large archival files. One such program is the reproduction of a vast amount of previously unpublished source material from the Public Record Office in London. In 1972 Kraus-Thomson augmented its microfilm program with the acquisition of 3M's Micropublishing division, the International Microfilm Press. Significant microform projects obtained by Kraus-Thomson in this acquisition include a selection of titles from the Schomburg Center for Research in Black Culture of The New York Public Library, a large collection of official gazettes of foreign governments, and the transcripts of the NBC television program "Meet the Press."

Kregel Publications

Established in 1949 at Grand Rapids, Michigan. Specializes in interdenominational religious books and reprints of long out-of-print books.

R.E. Krieger Publishing Company, Inc.

Established in 1970 at Huntington, New York, to publish technical and scientific reprints.

KTAV Publishing House, Inc.

Established in 1924 by Asher Scharfstein in New York City. He published his first book in 1930. In 1946, Asher's son, Sol, joined the firm, and in 1949, another son, Bernard, also joined the firm.

The specialty of KTAV is Judaica, Hebraica, and Biblica, as well as textbooks for Jewish religious schools and college textbooks related to the field of Judaica. Its major subsidiary imprint is Friendly House and its major series programs are the *Library of Biblical Studies* and the *Library of Jewish Classics.* KTAV also publishes the ENCYCLOPEDIA FOR READERS OF THE TORAH.

Laidlaw Brothers

Formed in 1909 in New York City as The A.S. Barnes Company. In 1919 Wayne N. Laidlaw and John Laidlaw, brothers employed by D.C. Heath & Company as textbook sales representatives, bought the majority interest in the company and assumed management, Wayne in New York City and John in Chicago, Illinois. Early in 1920 the brothers purchased the remaining interest and changed the corporate name to Laidlaw Brothers, Inc. In the same year two more brothers, Richard and William, joined the firm.

The first publication of the new firm was *The Barnes Readers,* a series for elementary school use, which was already in preparation when the Laidlaws took over. From 1927 to 1932 Laidlaw also operated a trade book subsidiary known as Laird and Lee.

From 1919 to 1936 Wayne Laidlaw was the company's president; from 1936 to 1953 John Laidlaw was president of the firm. John was succeeded by his son, John Laidlaw, Jr., who served until 1968 when Robert R., another of John's sons, took over the presidency.

Laidlaw now specializes in textbooks for elementary and secondary schools with emphasis on reading, English, history, social studies, health, and mathematics. In 1964 the firm was sold to Doubleday & Company, Inc.

Lane Magazine and Book Company

Book division of *Sunset* magazine founded in 1898 at Menlo Park, California. Publishes books under the imprint Sunset Books. Specializes in how-to, building, gardening, cooking, hobby, crafts, and pictorial gift books. *See also,* Sunset Books.

Las Americas Publishing Company, Inc.

Established in 1939 in New York City. Specializes in Spanish and bilingual textbooks.

Seymour Lawrence, Inc.

Established in Boston, Massachusetts, in 1965 by Seymour Lawrence and Merloyd Ludington Lawrence. The company co-publishes books in association with Delacorte Press. Its major publishing programs are contemporary fiction and poetry, translations, children's books and books on child care and development, including the program of Publications for Parents from the Boston Children's Medical Center.

Authors whose works have appeared under the Seymour Lawrence imprint include J.P. Donleavy, Kurt Vonnegut, Jr., Katherine Anne Porter, Miguel Angel Asturias, Pablo Neruda, Jorge Luis Borges, Louis-Ferdinand Céline, Dan Wakefield, and Robert Musil.

The Lawyers Co-operative Publishing Company

The origins of this company reach back to the last century when most law books were library-owned sets that were inaccessible to and beyond the means of most attorneys. In 1882 the E.R. Andrews Co., an upstate New York printer, contracted to fulfill 2,500 private subscriptions to an inexpensive set of U.S. SUPREME COURT REPORTS solicited in advance by three law associates—J.E. Briggs, his son William, and Ernest Hitchcock. This joint enterprise, named the Lawyers Co-operative Publishing Company, was considerably oversubscribed and the fledgling company published 15,000 copies of the REPORTS for only $1.00 a volume.

This new publishing concept was so well received by the legal profession that the company soon outgrew its original location in the home of W.H. Briggs in Newark, New York, and in 1885 Lawyers Co-op moved to new quarters in Rochester, New York. Meanwhile, E.R. Andrews had purchased Hitchcock's interest in the firm and was named trustee of the company, of which he became president in 1895.

The success of the U.S. REPORTS led to the introduction of *The U.S. Digest* in 1887 and in 1888 the first series of *Lawyers Reports Annotated* was published. *Case and Comment,* the oldest legal magazine in continuous publication, was launched in 1895 under the editorship of Burdett A. Rich. A number of local books, among them NEW YORK COMMON LAW and CHANCERY REPORTS, were also issued during the early years of Lawyers Co-operative Publishing Company.

The association of Lawyers Co-op with the Bancroft-Whitney Company of San Francisco, California, began in 1896 when arrangements were made between the two companies for the publication of ROSE'S NOTES. This cooperation continued as the two houses co-produced RULING CASE LAW in 1914. Five years later Lawyers Co-op acquired Bancroft-Whitney and the two companies announced the publication of the widely used monographs on points of law called *American Law Reports* or ALR. Baker, Voorhis and Company and Bender-Moss Company were taken over in 1940.

AMERICAN JURISPRUDENCE, an encyclopedia of state and Federal law, now in its second edition, was first published in 1936, the same year in which the White Binding Company joined Lawyers Co-op. Major reference works in the same Am Jur family subsequently published were AMERICAN JURISPRUDENCE LEGAL FORMS, AMERICAN JURISPRUDENCE PLEADING & PRACTICE FORMS, AMERICAN JURISPRUDENCE PROOF OF FACTS and AMERICAN JURISPRUDENCE TRIALS.

Acquisition of the Research Institute of America (RIA) in 1964 expanded the scope of Lawyers Co-op's market to include the business sector. RIA had been founded in 1935 by Carl Hovgard to provide guidance and information to businessmen in the fields of taxation, labor, and management. RIA concentrates on the areas of profit improvement and personnel management, and publishes a weekly digest of current developments of interest to businessmen known as *Research Institute Recommendations*. Also known as an authority on tax matters, RIA provides a line of tax information services, as well as the computerized tax-return service called Autotax.

Today, the output of Lawyers Co-op includes nearly two hundred national and localized encyclopedic works. A recent example is the *United States Code Service,* an annotated Federal statute service introduced in 1972. Also, the company publishes specialized texts on specific aspects of the law, many of which have become classics in their fields, for example: WILLISTON ON CONTRACTS; COUCH ON INSURANCE; and criminal law books by F. Lee Bailey and Henry B. Rothblatt such as DEFENDING BUSINESS AND WHITE COLLAR CRIMES. Individual publications range in size from a single volume to one hundred or more. Formats range from printed books and periodicals to cassettes and machine-readable magnetic tapes.

A staff of some two hundred lawyer/editors and business specialists creates a spectrum of information services for professionals in law and business and for various branches of the government. With the aid of its highly advanced computer facilities for photocomposition, text processing, information storage, research and retrieval, LCP's Information Services Division now publishes state codes and official court reports. For example, the company used its computer technology to editorially research, update and publish all sixteen thousand sections of the *Mississippi Code of 1972*. This set of twenty-two volumes was also composed, paginated, page formatted and indexed by computer. The text material was by-producted on magnetic tape and was furnished to Mississippi as a machine-readable data bank for future legislative research and retrieval.

The president of the Lawyers Co-operative Publishing corporate complex is Thomas H. Gosnell, who succeeded G.H. Gulick in 1960.

Lea & Febiger

Traces its origin directly to Mathew Carey's publishing house founded in Philadelphia, Pennsylvania in 1785. The chronology of its evolution is as follows:

Mathew Carey 1785-1817
M. Carey & Son 1817-1821
M. Carey & Sons 1821
H.C. Carey & I. Lea 1822-1827
Carey, Lea & Carey 1827-1829
Carey & Lea 1829-1832
Carey, Lea & Blanchard 1833-1838
Lea & Blanchard 1838-1851

Blanchard & Lea 1851-1865
Lea & Blanchard 1865
Henry C. Lea 1865-1880
Henry C. Lea's Son & Company 1880-1885
Lea Brothers & Company 1885-1907
Lea and Febiger 1907 —

Though Mathew Carey's interests lay primarily in political economy and religion, medical books also figured in his list. The first of these, a pamphlet on rabies and a treatise on the care of infants, appeared in 1792. In 1820 Carey founded the second oldest medical journal in the United States—*The Philadelphia Journal,* which later became the *American Journal of the Medical Sciences.*

In 1824 Carey retired and medical books became more and more prominent on the lists of Carey's successors. In 1830 the list included eighteen medical titles out of sixty books, while in 1845 the number of medical books alone had grown to sixty-seven. By 1850 the company had become a predominantly medical book publisher as a result of New York competition in the literary field. Perhaps the most famous of the firm's titles are (Henry) GRAY'S ANATOMY and William Boyd's TEXTBOOK OF PATHOLOGY.

One of the present partners is a great-great-great-grandson of Mathew Carey while the other three are descendants of Christian C. Febiger, who joined the firm in 1865 and was made a partner in 1880.

Lerner Publications Company

Established in 1959 at Minneapolis, Minnesota, by Harry J. Lerner. Specializes in juveniles and textbooks.

Leswing Communications, Inc.

A San Rafael, California, publisher of elementary and high school textbooks in science, the social sciences, and reading.

Libra Publishers, Inc.

Established in 1960 at Roslyn Heights, New York, by William Kroll as a small private house specializing in books in the behavioral and social sciences.

Libraries Unlimited, Inc.

Founded in 1964 at Littleton, Colorado, by Bohdan S. Wynar. The firm publishes AMERICAN REFERENCE BOOKS ANNUAL and GOVERNMENT REFERENCE BOOKS: A BIENNIAL GUIDE TO U.S. GOVERNMENT PUBLICATIONS, in addition to a new series entitled *Spare Time Guides.* A wholly-owned subsidiary, Ukrainian Academic Press, publishes books of Slavic interest.

Library Journal

Established by Frederick Leypoldt, Melvil Dewey, and R.R. Bowker in New York City in 1876. Published by R.R. Bowker Company. Incorporates *School Library Journal.*

The Limited Editions Club

Organized by George Macy in New York City in 1929. Its purpose, according to its original prospectus, was "to furnish, to lovers of distinctive books, unexcelled editions of their favorite works . . . to place beautifully printed books in the hands of booklovers at commendably low prices . . . to foster in America a high regard for perfection in bookmaking . . . by publishing for its members twelve books each year, illustrated by the greatest of artists and planned by the greatest of designers." The first title so offered was THE TRAVELS OF LEMUEL GULLIVER, illustrated by Alexander King.

In 1937 Macy launched The Heritage Club and formed The George Macy Companies, Inc. Subsidiary imprints were The Readers Club and The Print Club. For several years Macy owned The Nonesuch Press of England. Macy was president of the over-all company until his death in 1956, when he was succeeded by his widow, Helen, until 1968. Their son, Jonathan, was president, 1968-70. The business was acquired in 1970 by Boise-Cascade, which, in 1972, sold the Limited Editions, Heritage, and associated clubs to Cardavon Press; Cardavon operates them in Avon, Connecticut. The president of Cardavon Press is Gordon Carroll. John M.K. Davis is chairman of the board. Distribution of club books is by subscription; subscribers receive a book every month. The Limited Editions Club is limited to two thousand members. Members receive the club's monthly journal, *The Monthly Letter of the Limited Editions Club*. Members of The Heritage Club receive *The Sandglass*.

Lion Books

Established in 1966 at New York City as a division of Sayre Publishing, Inc., by Sayre Ross. Publishes two major series: Sayre Ross Books and Bell Books. Specializes in juveniles.

Joshua Ballinger Lippincott (1814-1886)

J.B. Lippincott Company

Incorporated in 1885, but draws a direct line through a series of partnerships from Jacob Johnson's Bookstore in Philadelphia, Pennsylvania, which was originally established in 1792. Joshua Ballinger Lippincott, eventually the surviving partner, entered the book business in 1836 and later began to publish religious and trade books. By 1850 he had made enough money to acquire Grigg and Elliott, an old, well-established book jobber and medical publisher. The business then became the partnership of Lippincott, Grambo & Company, with Henry Grambo, Edward Claxton, George Remsen and Benjamin B. Willis as Lippincott's partners. Lippincott, by this coup, became the foremost publisher in Philadelphia and earned the title of Napoleon of the book trade. When Grambo retired in 1855 the name of the firm was changed to J.B. Lippincott & Company, a name which it retained until 1885 when the company was incorporated and its present name was adopted.

Lippincott's early thrust was in the field of reference books. Lippincott's PRONOUNCING GAZETTEER OF THE WORLD was issued in 1855, followed by Lippincott's DICTIONARY OF BIOGRAPHY AND MYTHOLOGY, the DICTIONARY OF BRITISH AND AMERICAN AUTHORS by S. Austin Allibone, and the CHAMBERS CYCLOPAEDIA OF ENGLISH LITERATURE. The firm also brought out seven editions of Joseph Emerson Worcester's famous DICTIONARY OF THE ENGLISH LANGUAGE. Another landmark was the publication of *Lippincott's Magazine* in 1868 under the editorship of Lloyd Smith.

Lippincott's traditional strength in medical books goes back to Grigg and Elliott, who published THE DISPENSATORY OF THE UNITED STATES OF AMERICA. By the 1870s Lippincott had become a major medical publisher of textbooks such as D.H. Agnew's PRINCIPLES AND PRACTICE OF SURGERY and G.H. Fox's PHOTOGRAPHIC ATLAS OF DISEASES OF THE SKIN, as well as the periodicals *The Medical Times* and *International Clinics*. In a related area the firm issued in 1879 the *Contemporary Science Library*. In 1897 the periodical *Annals of Surgery* also became a Lippincott publication.

Expanding into trade books, Lippincott published standard editions of Charles Dickens, Sir Walter Scott, Edward Bulwer-Lytton and William M. Thackeray, novels by Ouida, Grace Livingston Hill and Hall Caine. Also William H. Prescott's histories, Henry Schoolcraft's HISTORY OF THE INDIAN TRIBES, the VARIORUM EDITION OF SHAKESPEARE, and important biographies, one of which was THE LIFE OF JOHN QUINCY ADAMS edited by his son, Charles Francis Adams.

Lippincott died in 1886 and his oldest son, Craige, succeeded to the presidency of the firm. One important undertaking during Craige's tenure was the series *French Men of Letters,* edited by Alexander Jessup. When Craige Lippincott died in 1911 his brother J. Bertram became president of the company.

In 1914 *Lippincott's Magazine* was sold to McBride, Nast and Company. A new edition of the CHAMBERS ENCYCLOPEDIA was issued in ten volumes in 1923. In 1926 J. Bertram Lippincott became chairman of the board of the company and his son, Joseph Wharton Lippincott, was elected to be president. In 1940 Lippincott acquired the publishing house of Carrick and Evans and in 1941 it purchased Frederick A. Stokes Company, both of which firms had important authors on their lists.

After World War II Lippincott had several phenomenal bestsellers: Betty MacDonald's THE EGG AND I, Paul I. Wellman's THE WALLS OF JERICHO, James R. Ullman's THE WHITE TOWER and Gwethalyn Graham's EARTH AND HIGH HEAVEN among them. It also began publication of the *Lippincott Classics,* a series of handsomely designed and illustrated books for children. Joseph Wharton Lippincott became chairman of the board of the company in 1949, when Howard K. Bauernfeind was chosen to be president. J.W. Lippincott, Jr. was elected to replace him when Bauernfeind moved up to become chairman of the company's board at the time Joseph Wharton Lippincott retired in 1958. Also in 1958 the firm began to issue *Keystone Books,* paperback reprints.

During the sixties the Lippincott list included Harper Lee's TO KILL A MOCKINGBIRD, Muriel Spark's THE PRIME OF MISS JEAN BRODIE, and Leon Edel's monumental biography of Henry James, and a major acquisition was

the A.J. Holman Company (q.v.), the oldest publisher of Bibles in the United States.

Lippincott continues to maintain its strength in the field of medical and nursing books and is regarded as one of the largest medical publishers in the world. It also publishes over twenty medical journals. The large, distinguished juvenile list of Lippincott includes such classics as Hugh Lofting's VOYAGE OF DOCTOR DOLITTLE, Lois Lenski's STRAWBERRY GIRL and JUDY'S JOURNEY, and Jeannette Eyerly's ESCAPE FROM NOWHERE. Lippincott also has a distinctive position in the textbook field, its products ranging from the elementary and high school to the college level.

In 1972 Lippincott went public. It has recently acquired the Joseph Ballinger Company of Boston, Massachusetts, forming a new company with offices at Cambridge, Massachusetts.

The Literary Guild of America, Inc.

Established in 1922 in New York City by Samuel W. Craig, The Literary Guild was the first book club in the United States. It was incorporated in 1922. Reincorporated as The Literary Guild of America, Inc. in 1927, its first selection, under the editorship of Carl Van Doren, was ANTHONY COMSTOCK by Heywood Broun. Harold Guinzburg of Viking Press was one of the active promoters of the Guild at that time. In 1929 Nelson Doubleday acquired a minor interest in it, and the purchase was completed in 1934 when Doubleday, Inc. assumed full control of the Guild.

The Literary Guild was the first of over twenty Doubleday book clubs and programs now in operation. They include The Junior Literary Guild, Doubleday Bargain Book Club, American Garden Guild, Cook Book Guild, Fireside Theater, International Collectors Library, Junior Deluxe Editions, Military Book Club, Mystery Guild, Science Fiction Book Club, Universe Book Club, Insights Book Club, Western Writers of America, and Programs. Programs offers preselected materials, such as Know Your America Program, Science Program, and Cooking Adventures with Michael Field.

Little, Brown and Company

Founded in 1837 by Charles C. Little and James Brown although their history may be traced from Ebenezer Battelle's Bookshop founded in 1784 at Boston, Massachusetts, as follows:

1784 Ebenezer Battelle's Bookshop

1787 Acquired by Benjamin Guild

1792 Acquired by Samuel Cabot

1797 Acquired by William T. and Samuel Blake

1806 Acquired by William Andrews

1813 Acquired by Jacob A. Cummings, partner of William Hilliard.

1821 Cummings, Hilliard & Company became Carter, Hilliard and Company with Timothy Carter as the new partner. Carter engaged Charles C. Little as his clerk. James Brown began his career in 1818 in Hilliard's Cambridge, Massachusetts, store. By 1826 Brown had become Hilliard's partner in Cambridge and Little had become his partner in Boston. In 1827 Carter withdrew and Harrison Gray was admitted as a partner and the name was changed to Hilliard, Gray and Company.

When the firm of Hilliard, Gray & Company was dissolved during the Depression of 1837, Little and Brown formed a partnership to buy its assets under the name of Charles C. Little and James Brown. The present name was not assumed until 1847. Augustus Flagg became a junior partner in 1839. Brown was in charge of the general books and imports while Little devoted himself to lawbooks and Flagg looked after the bookshop. Some of their early successes were Jared Sparks' LIFE OF WASHINGTON, George Bancroft's HISTORY OF THE UNITED STATES, William H. Prescott's FERDINAND AND ISABELLA, John Bartlett's FAMILIAR QUOTATIONS, and the writings of John Adams, John Quincy Adams, Daniel Webster, and Francis Parkman. An ambitious project, begun in 1853, was a series of British poets on the model of the famous English series known as Pickering's, *Aldine Poets*. Ninety-six volumes were completed in this series under the editorship of Francis J. Child.

Brown died in 1855 and Little in 1869. After Little's death Flagg became the managing partner, a position he held until his retirement in

1884. John Bartlett, editor of FAMILIAR QUOTATIONS, was an active partner from 1868 until 1888. In 1878 Little, Brown became the American publisher of the ninth edition of ENCYCLOPAEDIA BRITANNICA.

It was under the presidency of John Murray Brown, son of James Brown, that the firm emerged as a major literary house with its own characteristic style. One major factor in this transformation was the acquisition in 1898 of Roberts Brothers with its rich list of nine hundred titles, three times as many as were on the Little, Brown list. The 1890s also witnessed the publication of THE INFLUENCE OF SEAPOWER UPON HISTORY by A.T. Mahan, Henryk Sienkiewicz's QUO VADIS, and Fannie Farmer's THE BOSTON COOKING-SCHOOL COOKBOOK.

James McIntyre was the managing partner until 1913. This was for the company a period of consolidation. In 1913 the firm was incorporated with Charles W. Allen as president. In 1925 Little, Brown entered into an agreement with *Atlantic Monthly* to produce, publish, and promote its books under a joint imprint. This arrangement is still in operation at this time. When Allen retired in 1926 Alfred R. McIntyre was named president. During McIntyre's tenure the Little, Brown commitment to fine literature was enhanced through the publication of such authors as Evelyn Waugh, C.S. Forester, A.J. Cronin, James Hilton, James Truslow Adams, Erich Maria Remarque, Mazo de la Roche, Ogden Nash, and John Marquand. It was impressive, Henry Seidel Canby remarked, how much wheat and how little chaff there was in the Little, Brown list.

Arthur H. Thornhill succeeded McIntyre as president in 1948. In addition to establishing a medical department and strengthening the legal department, Thornhill published such authors as Peter DeVries, Tom Lea, Norman Mailer, Edwin O'Connor, J.D. Salinger and Gore Vidal, who belonged to a new generation of writers. On the occasion of the firm's one hundred twenty-fifth anniversary in 1962, Arthur H. Thornhill, Jr., was elected president. In 1968 Little, Brown was acquired as a wholly-owned subsidiary by Time, Inc.

Littlefield, Adams Company

Established in 1949 at Totowa, New Jersey. Publishes college outline books. Its division, Rowman & Littlefield, issues reference books, library catalogs and bibliographies.

Litton Educational Publishing, Inc.

A Division of Litton Industries, Inc., established at New York City in 1967. *See,* American Book Company; Delmar Publishers; McCormick-Mathers Publishing Company, Inc.; D. Van Nostrand Company; Van Nostrand Reinhold Company.

Liveright

See, Horace Brisbin Liveright.

Livingston Publishing Company

Established in 1923 at Wynnewood, Pennsylvania, by Philip A. Livingston. Specializes in books on the natural sciences.

Loizeaux Brothers

Established by Paul and Timothy Loizeaux in Vinton, Iowa, in 1876. Moving east in 1879 the firm remained in New York City until 1963 when it moved to Neptune, New Jersey. During the early years they printed tracts including the *C.S. Railway Series* and the *Plain Word Series*. The founders have been continuously associated with assemblies known as Plymouth Brethren but the firm is not a denominational publishing house. Current publications are primarily Bible commentaries.

1880 marked the publication of NOTES ON THE PENTATEUCH by C.H. Mackintosh in six volumes. It was reissued in a one-volume edition in 1973. Other Loizeaux authors include H.A.

Ironside, who wrote over sixty volumes of Bible commentaries; F.W. Grant, author of the seven-volume NUMERICAL BIBLE; Arno C. Gaebelein, author of THE ANNOTATED BIBLE and other commentaries; E. Schuyler English, editor of the NEW SCOFIELD BIBLE; J. Allen Blair, radio preacher, and author of eight devotional books; and Lehman Strauss, Bible teacher, and author of a dozen volumes. The firm also publishes two periodicals, *Messenger of Peace* and *Help and Food.*

Timothy's eldest son, P. Daniel Loizeaux, joined the firm in 1890. He relinquished the ownership of the publishing company in 1945 when it was separated from the printing division. Elie T. Loizeaux, a grandson of Timothy, became the company manager in 1948.

Lothrop, Lee and Shepard Company

Organized in 1904 through the consolidation of Lee and Shepard and the Lothrop Publishing Company.

Lothrop Publishing Company, the older of the two firms, had been founded in 1868 in Boston, Massachusetts, by Daniel Lothrop and N.P. Kemp. Lothrop had "experimented with publishing" in New Hampshire as early as 1850. The following year the firm adopted the name of D. Lothrop and Company. In 1870 John C. and James E. Lothrop came into the firm and beginning in 1871 for a few years it was called Daniel Lothrop and Company. In 1875 Lothrop founded the juvenile magazine *Wide Awake*. In 1887 three more partners, W.H. Arnold, E.S. Brooks, and E.H. Pennell, entered the firm and it became the D. Lothrop Company. Daniel Lothrop died in 1892 and for a time his wife, Harriet Lothrop, managed the business. (Harriet Lothrop was one of the most prolific writers of children's books in the nineteenth century and is best remembered for her FIVE LITTLE PEPPERS AND HOW THEY GREW, published under the pseudonym Margaret Sidney.)

In 1895, with E.H. Pennell as its president, the company became Lothrop Publishing Company. Among the firm's great authors were Elbridge S. Brooks, Edna A. Brown, Sam Walter Foss, D.

Lange, Francis Rolt-Wheeler, Everett T. Tomlinson, A.T. Dudley, and Maude Lindsay.

In 1904 Lothrop's assets were taken over by the firm of Lee and Shepard, which had been founded in Boston in 1862 by William Lee and Charles Augustus Billings Shepard. Lee had formerly been a junior partner in the firm of Phillips, Sampson and Company, and Shepard had been a senior partner in Shepard, Clark and Brown, which had been in business until 1859. There was also a New York City branch of Lee, Shepard and Dillingham. In addition to popular juvenile titles by such authors as Oliver Optic and Sophie May, Lee and Shepard published Sunday School literature.

In 1943 the firm of Lothrop, Lee and Shepard was acquired by Crown Publishers, Inc., and was developed as an exclusively juvenile imprint. In 1966 Scott, Foresman and Company purchased the firm and in 1968 merged it with William Morrow & Company, Inc., a wholly-owned subsidiary. Lothrop, Lee & Shepard, now a division of William Morrow & Company, Inc., retains its own imprint.

Louisiana State University Press

Founded in 1931 at Baton Rouge, Louisiana State is the oldest and largest university press in the Deep South. The 1931 imprint was used solely to publish a series of research studies and it was not until 1935 that the Press was formally established as a separate division of Louisiana State University.

Marcus M. Wilkerson, a professor on the journalism faculty, was instrumental in founding the Press and was appointed its first director. Wilkerson developed a broad program of publishing that in time came to include four journals: the *Southern Review*, edited by Charles Pipkin, Cleanth Brooks, and Robert Penn Warren; the *Journal of Southern History*, edited by Wendell Holmes Stephenson; *Rural Sociology*, edited by T. Lynn Smith; and the *National Mathematics Magazine*, edited by Samuel T. Sanders.

In 1937 the Press embarked on a major publishing venture: A HISTORY OF THE SOUTH, a ten-volume work co-sponsored by the Littlefield

Fund for Southern History of the University of Texas. The first volume, E. Merton Coulter's THE SOUTH DURING RECONSTRUCTION, appeared in 1947 and by 1973 nine of the projected ten volumes had been published. Marcus Wilkerson served as director of the Press until his death in 1953. His successor was Donald R. Ellegood, who came to LSU in 1954. Under his direction the Press greatly expanded its list and gained national recognition for its publication of the first three volumes of Eric Voegelin's ORDER AND HISTORY.

When Ellegood left in 1963, to head the University of Washington Press, he was succeeded as director by Richard L. Wentworth. During Wentworth's tenure the Press launched a paperback series, Louisiana Paperbacks, and committed itself to a program of publication in the arts that included volumes of original poetry and short stories. It also launched the multi-volume edition of THE PAPERS OF JEFFERSON DAVIS, a project co-sponsored by the Jefferson Davis Association and Rice University. The first volume in this program was published in 1971. Wentworth left the Press in 1970 and was succeeded by Charles East.

Under East the Press has continued to stress its role as a regional publisher. In 1972 it announced plans for publication of a comprehensive one-volume ENCYCLOPEDIA OF SOUTHERN HISTORY. Other outstanding series sponsored by the Press are the *Southern Biography Series* begun in 1938, *Southern Literary Studies*, and the *Library of Southern Civilization*. Although it no longer publishes journals, the Press has one of the most active programs of publication in the creative arts of any of the scholarly publishers. Over the years the Press has won two Bancroft prizes and four Sydnor Awards, presented biannually by the Southern Historical Association.

Loyola University Press

Founded in 1912 in Chicago, Illinois, by William P. Lyons, S.J., and guided by him until 1928. From 1928 to 1960 Austin G. Schmidt, S.J., served as both director and editor of *Jesuit Studies*. In 1960 John B. Amberg, S.J., was appointed director of the Press.

One early purpose of the Press was to develop truly "Catholic textbooks comparable in teaching methods and typography with the best secular textbooks." The first of these was RELIGION: DOCTRINE AND PRACTICE by Francis B. Cassilly, S.J., which had a remarkably long life, going through twenty-five printings before it became obsolete. Other active series include Robert J. Henle's *Latin*, Mark J. Link's *High School Religion*, Michael P. Kammer's *Writing, Voyages in English*, and *Power-Tools of English*. The more recent *Communication Education Series* probes the various forms of the mass media in three different worktexts: PERSUASION, EXPLORING TELEVISION, and MASS MEDIA.

A few trade books a year bolster Loyola's backlist of scholarly works. Loyola, by modern norms, is an old, small, and independent house.

Robert B. Luce, Inc.

Established in 1961 at Washington, D.C. Publishes a small list of trade titles which are distributed by David McKay Company.

Lyons and Carnahan

Established in 1884 in Chicago, Illinois, by O.M. Powers as O.M. Powers & Company for the publication of commercial educational books. Later James A. Lyons joined Powers and the title of the firm became Lyons & Powers. During this period the company entered the elementary school market with a limited number of books. When Powers withdrew the firm's name became J.A. Lyons & Company until 1912, when James W. Carnahan was admitted to partnership. In 1918 the company was incorporated as Lyons and Carnahan. At this time the emphasis was on elementary and high school texts, particularly in the areas of language arts, mathematics, and the sciences. Lyons died in 1920 and Carnahan purchased his interest.

In 1961 the firm was acquired by the Meredith Corporation and was made a branch of its educational division. Some of the major programs of Lyons and Carnahan are: *The Young America Basic Reading Program, Word Book Spelling Series, Phonics We Use, Tomorrow's Drivers,* and *Matter, Life and Energy.*

In 1973, the firm was acquired by Rand McNally & Company and its operations have now been consolidated with those of Rand's Educational Publishing Division.

Illustration from a Webster's Speller, 1789

The MIT Press

Founded in 1932 by James R. Killian as a division of the Massachusetts Institute of Technology, at Cambridge, Massachusetts. In 1937 the responsibility for the manufacturing, marketing, and distribution of its books (under the imprint of The Technology Press) was assigned to John Wiley & Sons. This arrangement was terminated in 1962, when the Press commenced to publish under its own imprint.

Succeeding directors of the Press, including Carroll Bowen and Howard Webber, have developed the Press into one of the four largest university presses in the United States. An editorial board consisting of ten members of the faculty administers the imprint. The two all-time best-sellers of the Press are BEYOND THE MELTING POT by Nathan Glazer and Daniel Moynihan and GROOKS by Pat Hein.

Mss Information Corporation

Established in 1968 by Marc Strausberg. Prepares custom-made books of selected readings for college courses.

McCormick-Mathers Publishing Company, Inc.

Established at Wichita, Kansas, in 1912 by J.E. Mathers, County Superintendent of Schools in Butler County, Kansas, and A.G. McCormick, president of McCormick-Armstrong, a Wichita printing company. The partnership came into being in settlement of a printing bill which Mathers owed to McCormick.

For the first eighteen years the company's business consisted primarily of the production and distribution of a report card and school record form (both devised by Mathers), diplomas, and awards. It was not until 1930, after William L. Gray, another former school superintendent, became its president that the company embarked on a program of educational publishing.

In the course of his travels through southern Kansas, Gray had noticed that a number of schools were using privately produced mimeographs of a high school English text-workbook. He signed a contract with the authors, who were three teachers in East High School, Wichita, and McCormick-Mathers then published ESSENTIALS IN ENGLISH, THE LABORATORY METHOD, the first commercially produced paperbound, combined textbook-workbook designed for use in high schools. The first printing was a modest five thousand copies but over the years the total sales of the books reached fourteen million copies.

So gratifying was the immediate success of the company's initial venture into educational publishing that it discontinued its line of diplomas and forms and began to concentrate on the publication of paperbound instructional materials for elementary and high school use. In 1939 the first edition of the PLAIN ENGLISH HANDBOOK was published. Now in its sixth edition, it has sold over twelve million copies. In 1940 the first of the *Puzzle Series,* eight language arts text-workbooks, for use in kindergarten through the second grade, appeared, and the total sales of these titles is also above the twelve million mark. Another success in the language arts field is *Plain English,* a six-book junior-senior high school series, which has achieved sales of over eighteen million copies since publication of the first title in 1953.

Eventually, work-textbooks in mathematics, science, and social studies were added to the list. Then a logical step was the publication of conventional hardbound texts, which first made their appearance under the McCormick-Mathers imprint in the late 1960s and early 1970s with SKILLS IN SPELLING, and MATHEMATICS FOR DAILY LIVING. Multi-media materials followed in 1970.

William Gray was succeeded as president of the company in 1958 by C. Emil Holgerson, and under his leadership McCormick-Mathers became a subsidiary of the American Book Company in 1961. At that time the editorial office was moved to New York City, but the company's headquarters remained in Wichita until after American Book Company was acquired in 1967 by Litton Industries to form the nucleus of its educational publishing division. With the transfer of all operations out of Wichita in 1968, Holgerson retired and Charles W. Pepper, president of American Book Company, also became the president of McCormick-Mathers.

McCutchan Publishing Corporation

Established in 1963 at Berkeley, California. Specializes in college textbooks and materials for professional use.

McGrath Publishing Company

A reprint publisher in Washington, D.C. Established in 1968.

McGraw-Hill Book Company
(Division of McGraw-Hill, Inc.)

Organized in 1909 at New York City by James H. McGraw and John A. Hill through the merger of the book divisions of McGraw Publishing Company and Hill Publishing Company. McGraw Publishing had been founded in 1899 and Hill Publishing Company in 1902. Both were publishers of technical magazines. In 1907 Hill started a book publishing department with Martin M.

Foss as manager. Almost at the same time Mc-Graw established a book division under Edward Caldwell's direction. In 1909 Foss and Caldwell persuaded their principals to merge the two divisions into a new firm known as McGraw-Hill Book Company. John Hill was its first president.

Concentrating on technical titles exclusively, the new firm prospered by bringing out authoritative manuals, handbooks, and textbooks for engineers, physicists, mathematicians, and chemists. Among its early successes were Thomas E. French's MANUAL OF ENGINEERING DRAWING, Charles P. Steinmetz' ENGINEERING MATHEMATICS, Dexter Kimball's PRINCIPLES OF INDUSTRIAL ORGANIZATION, Herbert C. Hoover's PRINCIPLES OF MINING (1909), the *International Chemical Series* edited by Henry P. Talbot, ELECTRICAL ENGINEERING TEXTS edited by Harry E. Clifford, and a series of handbooks beginning with AMERICAN MACHINISTS' HANDBOOK (1908) and CHEMICAL ENGINEERS' HANDBOOK (1934). The company was also happily placed in that it could draw ideas for books and authors from the magazines of its parent companies.

Hill died in 1916 and James H. McGraw succeeded him as president of the Book Company. The magazine divisions of the two firms were then merged as McGraw-Hill Publishing Company with McGraw-Hill Book Company as a subsidiary. This merger made McGraw-Hill one of the largest technical publishing houses in the world and it proceeded to expand steadily and logically into all areas of publishing. From the physical sciences and engineering the Book Company moved into the life sciences, medicine, education, business and industry, the social sciences, and, finally, the humanities and fine arts. To serve these specialized markets McGraw-Hill Book Company established a college department in 1927, a vocational education department in 1930, a trade division, named Whittlesey House, also in 1930, a technical education department in 1941, a health education department in 1944, a Text-Film (audio-visual) department in 1945, and the Gregg Company was acquired late in 1948. A Technical Writing Service was added in 1950.

Edward Caldwell became president of the firm in 1925 when McGraw retired. Martin Foss became the president in 1926. In 1944 Foss yielded the presidency to James S. Thompson. Ill-health compelled Thompson to retire in 1946 and Curtis G. Benjamin then took over the presidency.

During the next fourteen years as president, Benjamin enlarged existing departments and added five new ones. McGraw-Hill's enormous resources also enabled it to plan and undertake large series and projects such as the *Radiation Laboratory Series* (1947) and the *National Nuclear Energy Series* in science (1948) and the *Boswell Papers* in English literature (1950). Following World War II international operations were intensified. During the 1940s the Whittlesey House imprint was gradually discontinued for adult trade titles and limited to junior books. In 1950 it was dropped entirely. In 1954 the Blakiston Company was acquired from Doubleday and reorganized as the Blakiston Division.

In addition to developing a strong high and junior high school department, McGraw-Hill entered the elementary school field with the acquisition in 1963 of the Webster Publishing Company of St. Louis, Missouri. Through the *International Student Editions,* hundreds of McGraw-Hill titles were offered at reduced prices to Asian students. And to round out its publishing program, McGraw-Hill also planned and published a number of major reference projects: THE ENCYCLOPEDIA OF WORLD ART; THE McGRAW-HILL DICTIONARY OF ART; THE McGRAW-HILL ENCYCLOPEDIA OF SCIENCE AND TECHNOLOGY; THE CATHOLIC ENCYCLOPEDIA FOR HOME AND SCHOOL; NEW CATHOLIC ENCYCLOPEDIA; ENCYCLOPEDIA OF WORLD DRAMA and the ENCYCLOPEDIA OF WORLD BIOGRAPHY. In 1965 the company announced the publication of the *World University Library,* a series of original paperbacks.

In 1960 Benjamin moved up to be chairman of the board of the company and was succeeded in the presidency by Edward E. Booher. Booher succeeded Benjamin as chairman of the board and Harold W. McGraw, Jr. became president in 1968. When Harold W. McGraw was elected president of McGraw-Hill, Inc. in 1974, he was succeeded as president of McGraw-Hill Book Company by Alexander J. Burke, Jr.

Early in the 1960s the book company's subsidiary companies established abroad began indigenous publishing programs, in London, England, and Toronto, Canada. The American Heritage Publishing Company was acquired in 1969, strengthening the company's interest in the humanities.

Other media in which the Book Company is now involved are: *testing* (CTB/McGraw-Hill; California Test Bureau acquired in 1965); *reading and numerical skills* (EDL/McGraw-Hill; Educational Development Laboratories acquired in 1966); *instructional aids* (Instructo Corporation acquired in 1970); *legal services* (*Shepard's Citations* acquired in 1966).

David McKay Company, Inc.

Founded in 1882 in Philadelphia, Pennsylvania, by David McKay, a Scot immigrant, when he purchased Rees Welsh's bookstore for $500.00 in cash and a loan of $2,500.00. A little earlier he had published his first book, Walt Whitman's LEAVES OF GRASS, which James R. Osgood had been forced to dispose of under threat of prosecution by the Attorney General of Massachusetts. The same year McKay brought out SPECIMEN DAYS, Whitman's prose writings. Both books were very successful. In 1886 McKay published a four-volume edition of Shakespeare's works. Apart from these projects, he tended to specialize in technical and reference books.

In succeeding years McKay expanded by taking over failing firms: H.C. Watts & Company in 1888; Charles De Silver & Sons in 1896; the engineering and technical books of E. Claxton & Company in 1896; the American branch of George Routledge & Sons of England in 1903; and the clothbound juveniles of Street & Smith in 1905. By this time language manuals and children's books had been added to the McKay line; *Hugo's Language Manuals* and a series of children's classics illustrated by N.C. Wyeth being among his most popular publications.

When David McKay died in 1918 his two sons, Alexander and James, took over the company. Within the next thirty years they had introduced new lines and acquired the stock of three more firms: Sun-Diet Health Library, Brentano's educational list, and the juvenile list of Reynal and Hitchcock.

In 1950 the McKay family sold the company to a small group of investors headed by Kennett Rawson and Quentin Bossi. As part of the ensuing reorganization the company's headquarters were moved from Philadelphia to New York City. In 1961, when the New York branch of Longmans, Green dissolved its partnership with the London firm, the McKay company acquired the American branch with its backlist of standard works. Over the subsequent years, McKay has also acquired Ives Washburn, Inc., Fodor's Modern Guides, Inc., Weybright & Talley, Peter H. Wyden, Inc., and Charterhouse Books, Inc.

In addition to popular books on sociology, one being Vance Packard's THE STATUS SEEKERS, the firm publishes reference books, college texts, poetry, plays, and fiction.

In late 1973 the company was bought by Morgan-Grampian Ltd. of Britain, publishers of business and consumer magazines, but will be operated as a separate company.

McKnight Publishing Company

Started in 1895 by William McKnight and his sister, Hannah, as a college bookstore near the campus of Illinois State University at Bloomington, Illinois. Their first publication was a series of desk outline maps, followed by a geography workbook series. Between 1918 and 1924 the firm enlarged its list of geography publications and added music and nature study books. The first industrial arts text was published in 1934, thus beginning a specialization in industrial vocational, and technical instructional materials. William McKnight, Jr., joined the firm in 1935, by purchasing his aunt's interest. He succeeded his father as president of the firm in 1954, and became chairman of the board when Wesley D. Stephens became president in 1968.

In its own field the firm has been innovative. In 1934 it broke publishing tradition to bring out the first paperbound series of general shop texts. The firm also publishes the yearbook publications of the American Council on Industrial Arts Teacher Education (ACIATE) and the United States Office of Education funded Industrial Arts Curriculum Project, widely accepted as an exemplary career education program.

McNally & Loftin, Publishers

Established in 1956 at Santa Barbara, California, as a small publisher of general fiction and non-fiction books, including natural history and conservation.

Macmillan Book Clubs, Inc.

Organized in 1962 at New York City as Professional and Technical Programs, Inc., when Crowell Collier and Macmillan acquired three book clubs from Basic Books, Inc.: Behavioral Science Book Service, Library of Science, and The Natural Science Book Club. Later twelve more book clubs were added: Early Learning Book Club; The Executive Program; The Grade Teacher Book Club; International Affairs Book Club; The Investors Book Club; Lawyers' Literary Club; The Library of Computer and Information Sciences; Library of Contemporary Education; Library of Political Affairs; The Library of Urban Affairs; The Nurse's Book Society; and The Woman Today Book Club.

In 1973 the subsidiary was renamed Macmillan Book Clubs, Inc., and the parent company became Macmillan, Inc.

Macmillan, Inc.

Has its origins in three publishing houses established in the nineteenth century: P.F. Collier & Son, Crowell Publishing Company and The Macmillan Company. Macmillan Publishing Co., Inc., its principal book publishing subsidiary, was established in 1869 in New York City by Alexander Macmillan as the American branch of the famous British house of Macmillan and Company. Headed by George Edward Brett, a former London, England, bookseller, the agency took over the distribution of the Macmillan titles from Scribner and Welford. In 1886 Edward Brett died and his son, George Platt Brett, was invited to head the agency as resident partner. This proved to be a wise and far-reaching choice. Within the next forty-five years the younger Brett transformed a small agency into one of the largest publishing houses in the United States.

In addition to Macmillan, Brett represented Cambridge University Press, George Bell and Sons, and the Bohn Standard Library. He also developed a strong native American list and some of his great successes came from American authors who included Owen Wister and Jack London. Following the practice of other large publishers, Brett issued a number of series: *European Statesmen, Macmillan's Novelists Library, English Men of Letters, Illustrated Standard Novels, National Studies in American Letters,* and *The Temple Shakespeare,* along with standard editions of the works of Jonathan Swift, Lord George Byron, Alfred, Lord Tennyson, and John Bartlett's CONCORDANCE TO SHAKESPEARE.

But the strength of the Macmillan list lay in its scholarly titles of permanent value. Among them were such influential books as THE MAKING OF AN AMERICAN by Jacob A. Riis, MAIN CURRENTS IN NINETEENTH CENTURY LITERATURE by George Brandes, A HISTORY OF POLITICAL THEORIES by W.A. Dunning, CUSTOM AND COMPETITION by Richard T. Ely, THE SHIFTING AND INCIDENCE OF TAXATION by Edwin R. Seligman, THE SUPREME COURT AND THE CONSTITUTION by Charles A. Beard, and THE DEVELOPMENT OF ENGLISH THOUGHT by Simon Patten. The more popular of these books were reissued in the *Macmillan Standard Library* and in the *Modern Readers Series.*

Following the death of Alexander Macmillan the agency was reorganized, in 1896, as a New York corporation owned by the parent British firm but controlled solely by Brett. An educational division was formed in 1894 and a college division, the first in the United States, followed in 1906. Further expansion led to the establishment of more divisions: a medical department in 1913, a juvenile department in 1919, and an outdoor and household arts department in 1927. Poetry also became prominent after World War I. Another major development was the publication of a line of encyclopedias and reference books, beginning with the five-volume CYCLOPEDIA OF EDUCATION, edited by Paul Monroe, in 1911. THE CYCLOPEDIA OF AMERICAN AGRICULTURE and the ENCYCLOPEDIA OF THE SOCIAL SCIENCES were two more reference book projects that were distinguished by sound scholarship.

During the 1920s Macmillan's most popular trade titles were H.G. Wells' OUTLINE OF HISTORY, THE LONDON TIMES ATLAS, and THE RISE OF AMERICAN CIVILIZATION by Charles A. and Mary Beard. When Brett died in 1936 he left behind him a house that was not only the largest in number of titles published annually but also the best organized, with over nine divisions and branch offices in different parts of the United States as well as in London, England, Canada, Australia and India.

George P. Brett, Jr., who succeeded his father as president of the firm, paid a great deal of attention to the trade department. It brought out such spectacular bestsellers as Margaret Mitchell's GONE WITH THE WIND, Rachel Field's ALL THIS AND HEAVEN TOO, Richard Llewellyn's HOW GREEN WAS MY VALLEY, and Kathleen Winsor's FOREVER AMBER. Two new series of paperbacks were introduced: *Imperial Editions* and *Crown Editions,* offering titles from the company's huge backlist.

Macmillan's growth slowed during the years of World War II but two new major books appeared shortly after it ended: B.E. Stevenson's HOME BOOK OF PROVERBS and THE LITERARY HISTORY OF THE UNITED STATES, edited by Robert Spiller, T.H. Johnson, and H.S. Canby. In 1950 Brett finally severed the firm's connections with the parent company in England when he acquired all of its controlling stock. Eight years later he yielded the presidency of the company to his son, Bruce Y. Brett.

During his very brief tenure as president, Bruce Brett launched the *Macmillan Paperback Poets,* the *Macmillan Paperbacks,* and *The Macmillan Everyman Encyclopedia.* In December 1960 Macmillan became a subsidiary of the Crowell-Collier Publishing Co., Inc. In 1965 the merged firm was renamed Crowell Collier and Macmillan, Inc., and in 1973, the parent corporation shortened its name to Macmillan, Inc. Raymond C. Hagel, president of Crowell-Collier at the time it acquired the Macmillan company, now is also chairman and chief executive officer of the corporation. Norman Pomerance is president of the publishing subsidiary, having succeeded Jeremiah

Kaplan, Macmillan, Inc. executive vice president, in that post in 1973.

During the decade from the early 1960s into the 1970s Crowell Collier and Macmillan enjoyed a period of heady growth that was marked by acquisitions and expansions not only of its book publishing activities but into related educational and cultural areas: The Free Press; P.J. Kenedy; Benziger Bruce and Glencoe; Professional and Technical Programs (to become later, Macmillan Book Clubs); Brentano's; Berlitz Schools of Languages; Stechert-Hafner, Inc. (now Stechert Macmillan); Hafner Publishing Company (now Hafner Press); Hagstrom Company; La Salle Extension University; Katharine Gibbs School; G. Schirmer; C.G. Conn; Turtox; Standard Rate & Data Service; Ferdinand Roten Galleries; Gump's; Uniforms by Ostwald; C.E. Ward; Collier-Macmillan Schools Ltd. (U.K.); and three British publishers: Cassell's; Studio Vista; and Geoffrey Chapman.

In addition to COLLIER'S ENCYCLOPEDIA and encyclopedia yearbooks, the company's reference and subscription book division published MERIT STUDENTS ENCYCLOPEDIA, the INTERNATIONAL ENCYCLOPEDIA OF SOCIAL SCIENCES, the ENCYCLOPEDIA OF PHILOSOPHY, and the ENCYCLOPEDIA OF EDUCATION. A series of school dictionaries was introduced in 1973. Another major venture was *Collier Books,* a paperback series that grew to include seven hundred books. The trade division also continued to have its share of bestsellers, notably THE GUNS OF AUGUST by Barbara W. Tuchman, INSIDE THE THIRD REICH by Albert Speer, and JONATHAN LIVINGSTON SEAGULL by Richard Bach. The company occupies a strong position in all areas of educational publishing: textbooks, supplementary materials, encyclopedias, and home study courses.

Macrae Smith Company

Founded in 1892 in Philadelphia, Pennsylvania, as the George W. Jacobs Company. In 1925 Durant L. Macrae and Allan M. Smith bought the company and renamed it Macrae Smith Company. The company remains small and independent and is currently headed by Donald P. Macrae.

Manor Books, Inc.

A paperback reprint publishing house established at New York City in 1972.

Mara Books, Inc.

Established in 1969 at Los Angeles, California, as a small privately held firm, issuing psychology and travel books.

Markham Publishing Company

Established in 1968 at Chicago, Illinois. Specializes in college textbooks.

Illustrations of the alphabet — New England Primer, 1727

Marquis Who's Who, Inc.

Established in 1898 in Chicago, Illinois, by Albert Nelson Marquis as A.N. Marquis Company. The firm's first publication was WHO'S WHO IN AMERICA, 1899-1900. Other reference works published by Marquis Who's Who, Inc. include WHO'S WHO IN FINANCE AND INDUSTRY; WHO'S WHO IN THE WORLD; WHO'S WHO IN GOVERNMENT; WHO'S WHO IN THE EAST; WHO'S WHO IN THE SOUTH AND SOUTHWEST; WHO'S WHO IN THE MID-WEST; WHO'S WHO IN THE WEST; WHO'S WHO OF AMERICAN WOMEN; WORLD WHO'S WHO IN SCIENCE; WHO WAS WHO IN AMERICA; and various alumni and organizational directories, including the DIRECTORY OF MEDICAL SPECIALISTS, published under the direction of the American Board of Medical Specialties.

The name of the firm was changed to Marquis Who's Who, Inc. in 1953, and the company was acquired by ITT as a wholly-owned subsidiary in 1969.

Media Directions, Inc.

Started in 1920 when Henry M. Snyder set out on a three-month trip to the Orient with eight trunks of sample books and returned laden with orders.

Henry M. Snyder & Company, Inc., was the first company to represent American publishers overseas. It was incorporated in 1953 at New York City with Bernard H. Ruderman as its president. An overseas sales force was created and a traffic department was set up to handle all the paperwork involved. Snyder also relieved publishers of the enormous difficulties in collecting payments by establishing a credit department with the know-how to collect moneys from abroad. It guaranteed payment on all orders under a rebilling arrangement with the publishers. To stimulate sales abroad cooperative advertising was undertaken.

The company regularly participates in major international book fairs, such as the Frankfurt Book Fair, and attends the Distripress convention each year to promote paperbacks and magazines. Book Enclosure Company was established as a subsidiary to overcome the problem of transportation costs on small orders. Another subsidiary, Book Exports, Ltd., deals exclusively with government contracts under the International Media Guaranty Program and other governmental agencies.

In 1971 Martin B. Gordon became president of the company. Under Gordon's aegis the London, England, office was expanded as a major promotion facility and a number of depositories have been set up in strategic cities around the world. To reflect its structural changes the name of the company was changed to Media Directions, Inc. Media Directions represents over one hundred fifty publishers with a range of products extending from books and magazines to audio-visual materials.

Medical Examination Publishing Co., Inc.

Founded 1960 and located at Flushing, New York, a firm that specializes in medical and paramedical books.

Memphis State University Press

Founded in 1954 at Memphis, Tennessee, through the efforts of the Herbert Herff Foundation and the Kahn Trust. It was then financed by private funds and only two of the directors were members of the university. Among its titles at that time were two reprints of classics in American history: THE ROAD TO APPOMATTOX by Bell Wiley and FROM FRONTIER TO PLANTATION IN TENNESSEE by Thomas Perkins Abernethy.

In 1967 the Press became part of the Memphis State University and it is now controlled by a committee of faculty members and administrators appointed by the university's president. While the editorial policy is aimed at the development and publication of scholarly books with broad appeal to the academic community, the Press specializes in books about Tennessee and the mid-South.

The Press also publishes the *Southern Journal of Philosophy, Acta Symbolica,* occasional research papers in anthropology, and original source materials from the Mississippi Valley Collection in the John Willard Brister Library.

Mennonite Publishing House

Founded in 1908 although the origins of Mennonite publishing go back to 1727 when Andrew Bradford published the first Mennonite book in Germantown, Pennsylvania. It was a translation of the Mennonite Confession with the title: THE CHRISTIAN CONFESSION OF FAITH OF THE HARMLESS CHRISTIANS IN THE NETHERLANDS KNOWN BY THE NAME OF MENNONISTS.

The publishing tradition was built up by the Funk family, of which Bishop Henry Funk was the founder. THE MARTYRS' MIRROR, written by a Dutch author, which he published in 1748, was a landmark in Mennonite and American publishing. Printed at the Ephrata Press it was the largest book that had been published up to that time in the American Colonies, containing 1,582 pages bound in leather and secured with heavy brass clasps. The first edition of 1,330 copies was priced at twenty shillings each. Bishop Funk's EINE RESTITUTION, published posthumously, was the largest work written by an American Mennonite author prior to the twentieth century.

The bishop died in 1763 and his work was continued by his children on a modest scale. The next prominent bookman in the Funk family was Joseph Funk, a grandson of the bishop, who set up a printing firm known as Joseph Funk & Sons in 1847. During the next fifteen years he published forty-nine books, including Paul Henkel's LUTHERAN HYMNBOOK in 1850. He died in 1862. Thereafter another member of the Funk family, one John F. Funk, in 1875 incorporated the Mennonite Publishing Company at Elkhart, Indiana, sharing the stock with Thomas Nelson & Sons, Fleming H. Revell, John C. Winston, Oxford University Press, Ginn & Company, and others. This firm went into bankruptcy in 1904.

Four years later, in 1908, the present Mennonite Publishing House was incorporated by appointed representatives of the Mennonite Church at

Scottdale, Pennsylvania. The company is still fully owned and controlled by the Mennonite Church. It publishes books under the imprint Herald Press, first adopted in 1941. Major publishing projects include the MENNONITE ENCYCLOPEDIA in four volumes; GREEK-ENGLISH CONCORDANCE TO THE NEW TESTAMENT; A PARSING GUIDE TO THE GREEK NEW TESTAMENT; and THE COMPLETE WRITINGS OF MENNO SIMONS.

Meredith Corporation

See, Better Homes & Gardens Books.

G. & C. Merriam Company

Founded in 1831, but traces its origin to 1797 and the shop of Ebenezer and Daniel Merriam in West Brookfield, Massachusetts. With a second-hand press and a few cases of battered type Ebenezer and Daniel ventured into printing and publishing. Combining frugality and daring, they printed enough books to keep themselves barely free of debt: William Perry's DICTIONARY; PSALMS by Isaac Watts; LIFE OF ANDREW JACKSON by John Henry Eaton; a few primers; and a Bible. At one time they printed Noah Webster's BLUE-BACK SPELLER without copyright clearance and were called to account by Webster himself.

After a few years Daniel Merriam gave up and went back to the farm, but his sons stayed in business. George, the eldest, and Charles opened a printing office and bookstore in Springfield, Massachusetts, in 1831, while William and Homer started as bookbinders and publishers at Greenfield, Massachusetts, later moving to Troy, New York. By the late 1830s the firm of G. & C. Merriam was already well established, with a growing business in schoolbooks, lawbooks, and Bibles. Meanwhile, the publication rights of WEBSTER'S DICTIONARY were offered to them by D. & J. Ames, its owners, but, for lack of capital, the Merriam brothers turned it down. Later, in 1844, J.S. & C. Adams of Amherst,

Massachusetts, offered to the Merriams the unbound sheets of the AMERICAN DICTIONARY, a two-volume work, the rights to which they had obtained from the heirs of Noah Webster. This time the brothers accepted the offer and thus became the owners of WEBSTER'S AMERICAN DICTIONARY OF THE ENGLISH LANGUAGE.

In their first major move after acquiring the rights to the dictionary, Merriam Company proposed a revision and enlargement of the work, in one volume, to sell at six dollars. The new revision was prepared under the chief editorship of Chauncey A. Goodrich, Webster's son-in-law and literary executor. The new work, AN AMERICAN DICTIONARY OF THE ENGLISH LANGUAGE (NEW REVISED EDITION) appeared in 1847. It contained eighty-five thousand entries together with new supplementary features, and its success was immediate. This success was all the more remarkable because it was achieved in the face of unusually vigorous competition from Joseph Worcester's UNIVERSAL AND CRITICAL DICTIONARY OF THE ENGLISH LANGUAGE which had been published in 1846. Thus began the famous "war of the dictionaries" which continued to rage until the late 1870s. This competition was a major factor in spurring the Merriams to bring out the 1864 revision of their dictionary under the chief editorship of Noah Porter. Entitled AN AMERICAN DICTIONARY OF THE ENGLISH LANGUAGE, ROYAL QUARTO EDITION, UNABRIDGED, it helped the Merriam Company to win the war with Worcester and to establish Webster's preeminence. Indeed, the name "Webster" had by then become synonymous with "dictionary" and the Merriam Company found itself the custodian of a great tradition and institution.

In 1877 Charles Merriam had sold his interest to Ivison, Blakeman, Taylor & Company, who had long been distributors of Merriam-Webster dictionaries. They put into the firm a young man of their own, Orlando M. Baker, who, on George Merriam's death in 1880, became the driving spirit of the company and eventually its president. He was responsible for initiating a program of complete revision of the dictionary. This was started in 1880 and, when Noah Porter retired in 1886 from the presidency of Yale University to accept its direction, work was pushed forward intensively. The new work appeared in 1890 under the title WEBSTER'S INTERNATIONAL DICTIONARY. It contained 175,000 listings, an addition of fifty-six thousand in twenty-six years.

The last of the Merriams retired from active participation in the company when Homer, the youngest of the brothers, relinquished the presidency in 1904. His successor was Orlando M. Baker. In 1900 a supplement to the INTERNATIONAL DICTIONARY was issued, and a major revision called the NEW INTERNATIONAL DICTIONARY was completed in 1909 under William T. Harris as the chief editor. The NEW INTERNATIONAL consisted of four hundred thousand entries. Work on a revision of the NEW INTERNATIONAL DICTIONARY, of which William Allan Neilson was editor-in-chief, was commenced in 1926. This was published in 1934. The third edition of the NEW INTERNATIONAL, the most sweeping revision in its history, appeared in 1961. Philip B. Gove was its editor-in-chief.

In 1964 the Merriam Company was acquired by Encyclopaedia Britannica. In addition to the unabridged WEBSTER'S THIRD NEW INTERNATIONAL DICTIONARY, Merriam publishes a line of other dictionaries including: WEBSTER'S NEW COLLEGIATE DICTIONARY; WEBSTER'S ELEMENTARY DICTIONARY; WEBSTER'S NEW DICTIONARY OF SYNONYMS; WEBSTER'S INTERMEDIATE DICTIONARY; WEBSTER'S BIOGRAPHICAL DICTIONARY; WEBSTER'S NEW GEOGRAPHICAL DICTIONARY; and WEBSTER'S DICTIONARY OF PROPER NAMES. The company's program for growth is marked by a greater emphasis on hard reference books.

Charles E. Merrill Publishing Company

Established by Charles E. Merrill, Sr. and Edwin C. Merrill in New York City in 1892. But the firm traces its history back to 1842 when William G. Webster, son of Noah Webster, and Lucius E. Clark founded a company known as Webster and Clark to publish educational books. They began by publishing an edition of WEBSTER'S DICTIONARY, but the firm was soon dissolved and

Clark associated himself with Jeremiah B. Austin as Clark and Austin. Later another partner, Cornelius Smith, joined the firm and it then became Clark, Austin & Smith. Most of the educational business of that firm was directed toward the Southern states and the Civil War caused its collapse.

After the war Clark resumed business as a partner of Effingham Maynard in a new firm known as Clark and Maynard. The partnership was highly successful and John Ruskin was one of their authors. When Clark retired in 1889 the firm became Effingham Maynard & Company. In 1893 Maynard merged with the Charles E. Merrill Company, which had been founded a year earlier. The new firm took the name of Maynard, Merrill & Company. Maynard died in 1899. In 1907 Charles E. Merrill, Sr., bought the Maynard interest and changed the company's name to Charles E. Merrill Company.

Merrill died in 1930 and was succeeded as president by Charles E. Merrill, Jr., who held the office until 1942. Two years later the company was acquired by a group of investors consisting of W.C. Blakey, Eleanor M. Johnson, Harold S. Brown, and The Educational Printing House, Inc. In 1946 the capital stock was transferred to American Education Press, Inc., and the company headquarters were moved to Columbus, Ohio.

Wesleyan University acquired the company, along with American Education Press, in 1949. Merrill then became the textbook division of the Wesleyan publishing operation under the name of Charles E. Merrill Book Division of Wesleyan University. Ownership was transferred to Prentice-Hall in 1958, whereupon it became known as Charles E. Merrill Books, Inc. A newly formed college division began publication at this time. In 1964 the company became independent. Three years later it was acquired by Bell & Howell, adopting its present name of Charles E. Merrill Publishing Company.

From the REED AND KELLOGG GRAMMARS of the early years through the skills workbooks of the middle years, to the modern multi-media programs of the present, Merrill has kept pace with the changes in needs and methods of education. Some of its major programs are: *The Productive Thinking Program; Merrill Linguistics Readers; Merrill Mainstream Books;*

Merrill Mathematics Skilltapes; Discovering Science; Biology: Living Systems; American Government in Action; Making Value Judgments; Arthur W. Heilman's PRINCIPLES AND PRACTICES OF TEACHING READING; Carl Rogers' FREEDOM TO LEARN; the innovative *Accounting Principles: A Multimedia Program* by Dudley Curry and Robert Frame; and all of the audio-tutorial mathematics programs authored by Robert Moon and others.

Julian Messner, A Division of Simon & Schuster, Inc.

Founded in 1933 by Julian and Kitty Messner as Julian Messner, Inc. Julian, an alumnus of Boni & Liveright and the Liveright firm, brought with him four Liveright authors, one of whom was Frances Parkinson Keyes, the popular novelist, whose books up to the present time have sold more than fifty million copies. In 1935 the trade lists of Long and Smith and Alfred H. King were purchased. With the new authors thus acquired, Messner began to publish a sizeable and varied list. A juvenile department was established in 1939 under Helen Hoke's direction. In 1943 the *Cities of America Biographies,* edited by Leo Lerman, were launched. Two years later Veritas Press, a publisher of juvenile picture books, was purchased. Julian Messner died in 1948 and Kitty Messner, who had remained in the business although by then divorced from Julian, took over the management.

Besides Frances Parkinson Keyes, the Messner list at that time included several authors of distinction: Lion Feuchtwanger, Ivy Compton-Burnett, Peter Freuchen, and Guy Endore. In 1954 Messner published THE HOLY BIBLE IN BRIEF, edited by James Reeves and designed to provide a "clear, continuous narrative that can be read as quickly and easily as a novel." In 1956 Messner achieved the greatest financial success in its history when it published PEYTON PLACE by Grace Metalious.

Kitty Messner died in 1964 and late that year the firm was purchased by Pocket Books, Inc. When Pocket Books merged with Simon & Schuster in 1966, the over-all company name was changed to Simon & Schuster, Inc., and Julian Messner became A Division of Simon & Schuster, Inc., as it now operates.

The Julian Messner Division concentrates exclusively on corollary reading books for children from grade three through high school.

The Metropolitan Museum of Art

Founded in 1870 at New York City. In 1872 it issued its first formal publication, the Museum Catalogue. The publication department was formally established in 1908. It issues handbooks and monographs, including the series *Metropolitan Seminars in Art.*

The Michigan State University Press

Founded and incorporated in 1948 as successor to the Michigan State College Press which was started on an informal basis soon after the end of World War II. The first book published under the imprint was FETTERED FREEDOM by Russel B. Nye, Pulitzer Prize winner.

The Press does not have particular specializations, series, or journals. Its director, Lyle Blair, was responsible for bringing onto the Press list the noted Indian writer, R.K. Narayan, whose works have achieved considerable critical success.

Outstanding Michigan State titles include THE AUSTRALIAN ENCYCLOPEDIA in ten volumes, edited by Alex Chisholm; THE DIARY OF JAMES GARFIELD in two volumes, edited by Frederick Williams and Harry Brown; INDIA AND WORLD CIVILIZATION in two volumes, by D.P. Singhal; THE DICTIONARY OF AGRICULTURAL AND ALLIED TERMINOLOGY, edited by John Winburne; and BROADCASTING AND GOVERNMENT: RESPONSIBILITIES AND REGULATING, by Walter Emery.

Milford House, Inc.

Established in 1967 at Boston, Massachusetts. Publishes scholarly reprints and originals in history, art, medical and dental history.

Modern Curriculum Press, Inc.

Founded 1963 at Cleveland, Ohio. Publishes text-books and guidance materials.

Modern Library

A reprint series of "the World's Best Books," including ancient and modern classics, launched by Boni and Liveright in 1917. Each volume was elegantly produced with a stained top and gold stamping, and was bound in limp craftleather. Bennett Cerf bought the series from Liveright in 1925 for $200,000.00. Subsequently it became and remains one of the imprints of Random House.

Monthly Review Press

Established in 1952 in New York City as the book publishing arm of *Monthly Review,* a leading Marxist journal. Its first publication was I.F. Stone's THE HIDDEN HISTORY OF THE KOREAN WAR. The Press published only a limited number of titles annually until 1967, when it expanded its annual output to over forty books. A paperback line, Modern Reader Paperbacks, was started in 1968.

The firm specializes in socialist books in the areas of economics, history, politics, and world affairs. The magazine, *Monthly Review,* is edited by Paul Sweezy and Harry Magdoff, and the director of the Press is Harry Braverman, a former vice president of Grove Press.

Moody Press

Founded in 1894 at Chicago, Illinois, by Dwight L. Moody under the name of The Bible Institute Colportage Association, to distribute Christian literature through inexpensive paperbacks. The first book published was C.H. Spurgeon's ALL OF GRACE and the second was THE WAY TO GOD. Those were the beginnings of the Moody Colportage Library. In 1941 the company's name was changed to Moody Press. The Press publishes mainly Bible study books, Christian educational materials, devotional books, and a full line of children's books.

Morehouse-Barlow Company, Inc.

Started in 1884 in Milwaukee, Wisconsin, as The Young Churchman Company by Linden H. Morehouse I. The history of the company, however, goes back to 1870 when Morehouse began publication of *The Young Churchman,* a religious periodical. Morehouse's first published book was Rev. Arthur Wilde Little's REASONS FOR BEING A CHURCHMAN, in 1885. Early in his career Morehouse formed alliances with the British firms of A.R. Mowbray and Company, The Faith Press, and the Dacre Press.

Upon the death of the founder, his son, Frederick C. Morehouse, succeeded to the presidency, changing the name of the firm to Morehouse Publishing Company in 1918. When Frederick C. Morehouse died in 1932, the second Linden H. Morehouse, grandson of the founder and nephew of F.C. Morehouse, became the president. In 1938 the company moved its corporate headquarters to New York City and acquired the Edwin S. Gorham Company, a bookstore, whereupon the imprint was changed to Morehouse-Gorham Company. This name prevailed until 1959 when the present name was adopted in honor of Harold C. Barlow, who had served the company for forty-three years as sales manager, treasurer, and later as vice president. Linden H. Morehouse II remained president until 1965 and Clifford P. Morehouse served from 1965 until 1969. In that year Ronald C. Barlow assumed the company's presidency.

The publications of Morehouse-Barlow reflect its primary function as a publishing service to the Episcopal Church. Among its more important books are: THE SUNDAY SCHOOL CHORISTER; GOD'S BOARD; MORNING AND EVENING PRAYER LEAFLETS; MANUAL FOR THE HOLY EUCHARIST by John H. McKenzie; WAYS AND TEACHINGS OF THE CHURCH by Lefferd M.A. Haughwout; HISTORY OF THE EPISCOPAL CHURCH by Samuel D. McConnell; and EPISCOPAL CHURCH:

ITS MESSAGE FOR MEN OF TODAY, by George Parkin Atwater. In the early 1950s the company embarked on a curriculum publishing program entitled *The Episcopal Fellowship Series* which eventually grew to fifty-nine units.

William Morrow & Company, Inc.

Organized in 1926 in New York City by William Morrow, who had been an editor-in-chief with Frederick Stokes Company. One of his associates was Thayer Hobson, who served as production manager. Success came early to the new house which had a string of notable authors that included Honoré Willsie (Morrow's wife), Margaret Mead, and Rupert Hughes. Morrow died in 1931 and a year later Hobson gained control of the company. Surviving the Depression he established Morrow as a highly visible house with the help of bestsellers such as James Hilton's LOST HORIZON, Enid Bagnold's NATIONAL VELVET, and the books of Erle Stanley Gardner, of which over one hundred and fifty million copies have been sold.

During and after World War II Morrow acquired several other publishing houses: M.S. Mill Company, Jefferson House, M. Barrows and Company, Whiteside, Inc. (formerly Women's Press), Reynal & Company, and William Sloane Associates. Of these only Reynal & Company is active as an imprint, the others having been absorbed into Morrow. In 1966 the firm joined with Temple Fielding to form a new imprint, Fielding Publications. The Morrow list has developed with such authors as Nevil Shute, Carter Dickson, Laurens van der Post, Mary Stewart, and Morris West in the adult department, and Herbert S. Zim, Carolyn Heywood, and Beverly Cleary in Morrow Junior Books, its juvenile imprint.

Hobson remained head of the company until 1959 when, on his retirement, he sold his interest to a group of younger men. The reorganized company was headed by John T. Lawrence as president. Lawrence Hughes succeeded Lawrence in that position in 1966. Hughes and his associates sold their interest to Scott, Foresman in 1968 and Morrow is now a wholly-owned subsidiary of Scott, Foresman. Hughes is still its president. The Lothrop, Lee & Shepard Company, also owned by Scott, Foresman, was merged with Morrow in 1968. Lothrop, Lee & Shepard retains its own imprint. A recent Morrow imprint is Morrow Paperback Editions, which is directed to the college market.

The C.V. Mosby Company

Founded in 1906 at St. Louis, Missouri, as a small firm of publishers' representatives, by Dr. C.V. Mosby. The first book to bear the Mosby imprint was GOLDEN RULES OF SURGERY. In 1907 the company published DIAGNOSIS AND TREATMENT OF DISEASES OF WOMEN. This became an immediate success and remained so for many years. In 1915 the company published its first two journals, *The Journal of Clinical and Laboratory Medicine* and *The International Journal of Orthodontics*.

The Mosby list has expanded steadily over the years to encompass virtually all phases of medical, dental, nursing, and allied health disciplines. This growth was stimulated when the company was acquired by The Times Mirror Company in 1967.

Mosby's most outstanding titles are: SURGICAL PATHOLOGY; OPERATIVE ORTHOPAEDICS; TEXTBOOK OF ANATOMY AND PHYSIOLOGY; PHARMACOLOGY IN NURSING; and MINOR TOOTH MOVEMENT IN GENERAL PRACTICE. Mosby also publishes thirteen medical journals.

Mountain Press Publishing Company

Established in 1948 at Missoula, Montana. Publishes a small list of medical as well as regional books.

Muhlenberg Press

Founded in 1855 as The Lutheran Publication Society of the General Synod in Philadelphia, Pennsylvania. Its first publication was THE

BLIND GIRL OF WITTENBERG. In 1919 the Society merged with the Board of Publication of the General Council and the Board of Publication of the United Synod of the South to form the Board of Publication of the United Lutheran Church in America. In 1953 the Board established the Lutheran Readers Club.

In 1962 the Muhlenberg Press imprint was superseded by a new imprint, Fortress Press (q.v.)

Music Sales Corporation

Located in New York City; publishes trade books on contemporary culture and society, folk music, jazz and blues, pop music personalities, also instruction manuals. Its books are distributed by Quick Fox, Inc.

Nash Publishing Corporation

Founded in 1969 at Los Angeles, California, by Edward L. Nash. The firm began with an initial list of eighteen titles. In 1971 Nash was acquired as a wholly-owned subsidiary by Books For Libraries, Inc., now BFL Communications, Inc. A paperback imprint is called Nash Quality Paperbacks.

As a general trade publisher, Nash's primary interest is in hardcover nonfiction capable of television promotion. Nash also published the *Principles of Freedom Series* under the auspices of the Institute for Humane Studies in Menlo Park, California. A major success was the $60.00 art book, MAXFIELD PARRISH: THE EARLY YEARS. It also publishes limited fiction, psychology books, health food books, such as the *Bircher-Benner Nutrition Guides,* a series of travel books called *Off The Beaten Track In . . . ,* and a large number of self-help and craft books.

National Bureau of Economic Research, Inc.

The Publications Division of the National Bureau of Economic Research founded in 1920 at New York City. Specializes in technical reports, abstracts, and econometric studies. Its books are distributed by Columbia University Press.

National Council of Teachers of English

Founded in Chicago, Illinois, in 1911, the National Council of Teachers of English is generally considered the largest professional subject matter organization in the world. For the past twenty years its headquarters have been in Champaign-Urbana, where it enjoys an affiliation with the University of Illinois. Its membership of approximately 100,000 is divided among elementary, high school, and college teachers of English and the language arts. To these members go one of the three Section journals: *Elementary English, English Journal,* and *College English.* The Council also publishes specialized journals: *Research in the Teaching of English, English Education, Abstracts of English Studies,* and *College Composition and Communication.*

The Council publishes approximately twenty-four books a year, typically a combination of practical advice for the classroom teacher, research reports, monographs, and book lists. A perennial bestseller has been IDEAS FOR TEACHING ENGLISH 7-8-9. In 1974 the Council inaugurated the *NCTE Guide to Teaching Materials for English 7-12,* a comprehensive overview of commercial textbooks.

Publishing decisions are made by a five-member editorial board. The current executive secretary of the Council is Robert F. Hogan and the director of publications is Paul O'Dea.

National Learning Corporation

Based at Plainview, New York, publishes learning aids for teachers' licenses, civil service, graduate and professional schools, and college entrance.

National Press Books

Established in 1947 at Palo Alto, California. Specializes in college textbooks.

National Textbook Company

Located at Skokie, Illinois. A general publisher of elementary, secondary and college textbooks, specializing in English and Western European languages.

The Naylor Company

Established in 1921 in San Antonio, Texas, by Joe O. Naylor. On Naylor's death in 1955, his wife, Rita Naylor, took over as president. The company is a regional publisher specializing in books about the Southwest.

Nazarene Publishing House

Founded in 1912 at Kansas City, Missouri, as the publishing house of the Nazarene faith.

Negro History Press

Founded in 1969 at Detroit, Michigan. Specializes in hardcover reprints. Now a division of Scholarly Press, Inc.

Nelson-Hall Company

Established in 1909 at Chicago, Illinois. Publishers of general interest nonfiction, educational, professional/reference and scholarly books.

Thomas Nelson, Inc.

Established in New York City in 1854 by Thomas Nelson II, the first British publisher to open a branch in the United States. The British parent firm had been founded in 1798 in Edinburgh, Scotland, by Thomas Nelson. The American publishing activity was transferred to Camden, New Jersey, in 1963. In 1969 the company was purchased by Royal Publishers, Inc., of Nashville, Tennessee, a group headed by Sam Moore. In 1972 the two companies merged. Nelson became the surviving company name and all major departments were transferred to Nashville.

One of the world's leading Bible publishers, Thomas Nelson sponsored the AMERICAN STANDARD VERSION and the REVISED STANDARD VERSION in 1952, and the company offers THE NEW AMERICAN BIBLE FOR CATHOLICS in several editions. In the *King James* and *Revised Standard* Bible lines Nelson offers study Bibles, gift Bibles, award Bibles, pew Bibles, reference Bibles, large-print Bibles, pulpit and lectern Bibles, and vest pocket testaments. Nelson has also published GOOD NEWS FOR MODERN MAN.

Popular Nelson juveniles include *Encyclopedia Brown Books,* the *Young Sportsman Series, Colonial Histories,* and *World Neighbor Books.* In cooperation with the Youth Research Center, Nelson publishes *Youth Forum,* a series for high school and college-age youth. In the adult range Nelson publishes the *Collectors Books,* a series for hobbyists, gift books, and inspirational books.

The company has a division called The Varsity Company which distributes Nelson books to a large number of students in over twenty states.

The New American Library, Inc.

Organized in 1948 in New York City by Kurt Enoch and Victor Weybright upon their acquisition of Penguin Books, Inc., from its British parent company, but in 1960 NAL became a subsidiary of The Times Mirror Company. In 1961 it purchased a controlling interest in Ace Books, Ltd. and Four Square Books, Ltd., both of London, England, and renamed the combined firm New English Library. NAL also owns The New American Library of Canada, Ltd.

NAL imprints include Signet (popular fiction and nonfiction), Mentor (scholarly nonfiction), Signet Classics (literary works), Plume (large-format, higher-priced titles in fiction, history, philosophy, science, and music), and Signettes (mini-books including many how-to subjects and the popular *Love Is . . .* titles). NAL is also the distributor of Award Books and co-publisher of Tiger Beat and Daw titles.

Newbury House, Publishers

Established in 1970 at Rowley, Massachusetts. Specialize in texts and reference materials in language teaching at all academic levels.

New Directions Publishing Corporation

Established by James Laughlin while he was still an undergraduate at Harvard University in 1936. During a leave of absence from Harvard, Laughlin had studied informally with Ezra Pound at Rapallo, Italy, and Pound had urged him to publish the works of a number of his friends and disciples in the United States. The first book, the annual anthology, NEW DIRECTIONS 1936, was produced by the printer of the college magazine, *The Harvard Advocate*. WHITE MULE by William Carlos Williams was probably the first important book to be published by the firm.

For the first four years Laughlin sold the books by mail or personally on the road; then, for about five years George W. Stewart took on the distribution, after which the firm did it for itself. Finally, in 1963, distribution of New Directions books was turned over to the J.B. Lippincott Company of Philadelphia, Pennsylvania, and they have remained the firm's distributors up to the present time. The business was converted from private proprietorship to a corporation in 1964 with James Laughlin and Robert M. MacGregor as the principal stockholders and with offices in New York City. A paperback program was launched in 1956 which has since become one of the chief elements of the business.

The principal publishing programs of New Directions have been *New Directions in Prose and Poetry,* anthologies of experimental and *avantgarde* writing, of which NEW DIRECTIONS 27 appeared in fall 1973; these are now published twice a year, spring and fall. Also, *The Poets of the Year,* a series of thirty-two page original poetry pamphlets which ran for forty-two numbers from 1941 to 1944; *The New Classics,* a series of pocket editions of modern classics, later replaced by paperback editions; *The Makers of Modern Literature,* a series devoted to critical studies of important modern authors; and uniform library editions of the complete works of William Carlos Williams and Tennessee Williams.

As did Alfred A. Knopf, Laughlin achieved particular distinction by importing outstanding foreign writing. He was responsible for introducing to American readers, among others, Jorge Luis Borges, Boris Pasternak, Federico García Lorca, Nicanor Parra, Gottfried Benn, Tommaso Landolfi, Giuseppe Berto, Elio Vittorini, Paul Eluard, Alfred Jarry, Pierre Reverdy, Vernon Watkins, Dylan Thomas, Henri Michaux, Raymond Queneau, and Pablo Neruda.

Laughlin performed a great service in American letters when he began to systematically publish and help to become better known Lawrence Ferlinghetti and John Hawkes, and the poetry of Thomas Merton, Denise Levertov, Henry Miller, Kenneth Patchen, Maude Hutchins, James Purdy, John Berryman, Delmore Schwartz, Carl Rakosi, Karl Shapiro, and Randall Jarrell.

With fewer than five hundred books, New Directions has been a major force in American literature in modern times.

New Hampshire Publishing Company

Organized in 1969 at Somersworth, New Hampshire. Specializes in books of regional interest. Are publishers of books for the Maine Historical Society.

New York Graphic Society, Ltd.

Established in 1925 in New York City by Anton Schutz for the distribution of etchings and other original works of art. The company later turned to the publication of reproductions and is now the world's largest publisher in that field.

In the early 1950s Schutz proposed to UNESCO a collaboration to publish a group of large-format books of color reproductions of the art treasures of United Nations member nations. The resulting UNESCO *World Art Series* brought the Society into the art book publishing field. Later publications in this area include the three-volume COMPLETE LETTERS OF VINCENT VAN GOGH, winner of the Carey-Thomas Award for Creative Publishing in 1959, and such major art books as INDIAN ART IN AMERICA; DRAWINGS OF PAUL CEZANNE; SCHOOL OF PARIS; TUTANKHAMEN; PICASSO, THE BLUE AND ROSE PERIODS.

The Society also distributes on a cooperative basis the art publications of America's major museums: the Museum of Modern Art, the Metropolitan Museum of Art, the Boston Museum of Fine Arts, and the Asia House Gallery.

In 1966 the Society was purchased by Time, Inc. Since then the publishing program has continued to expand with emphasis on original graphics and illustrated books on photography, films, architecture, crafts, and the decorative arts. Alva Museum Replicas, producer of museum quality reproductions of sculpture and jewelry, was organized as a subsidiary in 1970.

New York University Press

Founded in 1916 at New York City by Samuel A. Brown, Chancellor of the New York University. Its purpose was to publish contributions to higher learning by eminent scholars of New York University and other universities and "to give each book accepted for publication what can rarely be given by commercial publishers: the meticulous accuracy and the scholarly form appropriate to scholarly content." By 1919 the Press was proud of its list of twenty-nine titles. Arthur Huntington Nason was director of the Press from 1916 to 1933.

In the summer of 1956, under the directorship of Filmore Hyde, the Press became a separate corporation. Under Hyde's successor, William B. Harvey, the Press assumed again its noncommercial status and became responsible for financial as well as editorial duties. Malcolm C. Johnson, former vice president of R.R. Bowker Company, presently heads the Press.

Samuel Eliot Morison's THE INTELLECTUAL LIFE OF COLONIAL NEW ENGLAND, published in 1936 under the title THE PURITAN PRONAOS, is one of the proudest achievements of the Press. Gay Wilson Allen's biography of Walt Whitman, THE SOLITARY SINGER, pub-

lished in 1967, is another outstanding title and was selected for the White House library during the Kennedy administration.

Under the general editorship of Gay Wilson Allen and Sculley Bradley, the Press began the publication of THE COLLECTED WRITINGS OF WALT WHITMAN, the most comprehensive and definitive series of books on the life and works of the American poet. The biography of Walter Savage Landor by R.H. Super (1954), and Edward S. Corwin's PRESIDENT: OFFICE AND POWERS (1948) which deals with American politics, are also noteworthy titles. In 1972 Marvin Trachtenberg's study, THE CAMPANILE OF FLORENCE CATHEDRAL: GIOTTO'S TOWER received that year's Alice Davis Hitchcock Award for excellence in the field of architectural history.

New York University Press has currently over five hundred titles in print. It also publishes and distributes books for the College Art Association, The American Bar Foundation, and for various other nonprofit organizations.

Noble and Noble, Publishers, Inc.

Established in 1883 in New York City by Arthur H. Hinds, publisher, bookseller, and jobber. When Clifford Noble joined as a partner in 1886 the name became Hinds and Noble. Subsequently the publishing division changed its designation twice to reflect the various partnerships: first to Hinds, Noble and Eldredge and later to Hinds, Hayden, and Eldredge. The partnership of Hinds & Noble as booksellers and jobbers, however, continued until 1917 when the partnership was dissolved and the assets were taken over by Clifford Noble, who adopted the name of Noble & Noble. The second Noble in the title was Clifford's son, Lloyd Adams Noble, who had organized a separate publishing company about 1914.

Lloyd Adams withdrew in 1917 and four years later another son, J. Kendrick Noble, joined the firm. About this time, William R. Barnes of C.M. Barnes-Wilcox Company, publishers in Wheaton, Illinois, came to New York City and bought an interest in Noble & Noble, whereupon the company became Barnes & Noble (q.v.). In 1929 the Nobles withdrew from Barnes & Noble to resume the firm of Noble & Noble, which was incorporated in 1934. In 1925 the firm had purchased F.A. Beatty and in 1942 it acquired Simons Peckham.

Early in its career Noble & Noble expanded into school sales by preparing textbooks specifically for the New York City schools and before long the firm became the major textbook supplier to the city. One of the first publishers of adult basic education materials and remedial textbooks, the company also became well-known for its *Comparative Classics Series,* introduced in 1927. It has also been a major publisher of handwriting materials, most notable of which is its *Better Handwriting For You Series* by J. Kendrick Noble.

In 1965 Noble & Noble was acquired by Dell Publishing Co., Inc., and it now operates as a wholly-owned subsidiary. Current programs include *Spell/Write, The Yearling Individualized Reading Program, Social Studies: Man and His World, Insight, Crossroads, Falcon Books, Try: Experiences For Young Children, The Process of American Government* by Bernard Feder, and *The Noble & Noble African Studies Program.*

Northern Illinois University Press

Founded in 1965 at De Kalb, Illinois, with Jack Barker as director during the first eighteen months. Before him there was a committee headed by E. Nelson James, but the first book to appear under the imprint, HEARTLAND, was not published until 1967. The imprint is controlled by the University Press Board which consists of the dean of the Graduate School and two representatives from each of the four colleges. Richard T. Congdon has been director since 1967 and the progress the Pres has made reflects his efforts.

Northern Illinois publishes scholarly books in fields represented by the various university departments. It also publishes three major series: the *Annotated Secondary Bibliography Series of English Literature in Transition, 1880-1920;* the *Corpus Reformatorum Italicorum et Biblioteca* (in collaboration with the Newberry Library of Chicago); and *Northern Illinois University Perspectives in Geography.*

Outstanding books bearing the Northern Illinois imprint include DECOYS AND DECOY CARVERS OF ILLINOIS; DISSENT: EXPLORATIONS IN THE HISTORY OF AMERICAN RADICALISM; LIGHT FROM HEAVEN; THE SPIRITUAL CRISIS OF THE GILDED AGE; RENAISSANCE STUDIES IN HONOR OF HANS BARON; and BARTOLOME DE LAS CASAS.

Northwestern University Press

Organized in its present form at Evanston, Illinois, in 1957 as successor to an earlier Northwestern University Studies, a publishing program administered by the Graduate School of the university. Starting with a staff of three and the production of five books in its first year, the Press now produces an average of thirty titles a year. The imprint is controlled by an editorial committee. The Press began with no clear intention to specialize in any one area but over the past fifteen years, however, specializations have evolved which reflect areas of strength within the university.

One of the first books published by the Press, DAHOMEAN NARRATIVE by Melville and Frances Herskovits, initiated a series of *Northwestern University African Studies* which became a major part of the publishing program, developed in cooperation with Northwestern's pioneering African Studies Department. Recently, three new series were established: *African Urban Studies, Studies in African Religion,* and *Studies in Political Culture and National Integration.* The Press is also involved in the international publication of books on Africa through its past association with East Africa Publishing House and its cooperation with other African presses.

Another major specialization which reflects a university program is the philosophy list. *Studies in Phenomenology and Existential Philosophy,* a series which dates back to 1962, consists of important European texts in phenomenology and existentialism, in translation as well as original works in those fields. The series includes such leading twentieth century philosophers as Edmund Husserl, Martin Heidegger, Maurice Merleau-Ponty, Max Scheler, and Alfred Schutz.

A third area of concentration of the Press is in literature and literary criticism. Series have been devoted to eighteenth-century Russian literature, the Irish Revival, Renaissance drama, and both English and French medieval literature. In addition, the Press, in association with Northwestern University and Newberry Library, is publishing the definitive edition of THE WRITINGS OF HERMAN MELVILLE in fifteen volumes, under the auspices of the Center for Editions of American Authors of the Modern Language Association.

The Press also has a limited program in other fields, including communicative disorders, art, music, business, communication, geography, history, law, political science, Jungian psychology, science, and medicine.

In May of 1974 the Press announced that because of "rising deficits" it will virtually end in-house publishing operations. Existing contracts will be honored and for books in progress and in back list distribution arrangements will be made with other publishers.

W.W. Norton & Company, Inc.

Organized by William Warder Norton in 1923 at New York City as the People's Institute Publishing Company, with initial paid-in capital of $4,300.00. Its purpose was to publish *Lectures-in-Print,* a series of pamphlets to be sold to subscribers as a unit. Among the first were PSYCHOLOGY by Everett Dean Martin and BEHAVIORISM by J.B. Watson. When booksellers objected to handling packaged pamphlets, Norton began to issue them as bound books. INFLUENCING HUMAN BEHAVIOR by Harry A. Overstreet was the firm's first title to be originally published as a book. In 1925 Norton reorganized the company under his own name.

With the slogan, "Books That Live," Norton began with the determination "to publish the best books we can lay our hands on and then keep our hands on them as long as may be." An early venture in this direction was the *New Science Series,* edited by C.K. Ogden, in which he offered Bronislaw Malinowski's MYTH IN PRIMITIVE PSYCHOLOGY, SCIENCE AND POETRY by

I.A. Richards, INDUSTRIAL PSYCHOLOGY by Charles S. Meyers, and MODERN SCIENCE AND PEOPLE'S HEALTH by B.C. Gruenberg.

Norton soon expanded into music, art, philosophy, and general literature, areas in which it has consistently maintained an outstanding position with such titles as THE STORY OF MUSIC by Paul Bekker, ARTISTIC IDEALS by Daniel Mason, Bertrand Russell's PHILOSOPHY, THE MEANING OF CULTURE by John Cowper Powys, ANTHROPOLOGY AND MODERN LIFE by Franz Boas, and books by John Dewey, T.H. Morgan, and P.H. Youtz, who edited a series of studies on modernism in the arts. In 1929 Norton issued its first novel, ULTIMA THULE by Henry Handel Richardson, which became a Book-of-the-Month Club selection.

In 1930 Norton started a college department. And during the 1930s the company continued to publish books that combined popular appeal with scholarship. Among them were: Edith Hamilton's THE GREEK WAY; REVOLT OF THE MASSES by José Ortega y Gasset; THE WISDOM OF THE BODY by Walter Cannon; Victor Heiser's AN AMERICAN DOCTOR'S ODYSSEY; Lancelot Hogben's MATHEMATICS FOR THE MILLION; Karen Horney's THE NEUROTIC PERSONALITY OF OUR TIME; HISTORY OF ECONOMICS by Othmar Spann; THE BIOLOGICAL BASIS OF HUMAN NATURE by H.S. Jennings; and THE NEW VISION by Laszlo Moholy-Nagy. Norton himself was also actively involved in the war effort as chairman of the Council on Books in Wartime.

During the early 1940s the firm had a bestseller in Gordon S. Seagrave's BURMA SURGEON. It also published the sequels to this book: BURMA SURGEON RETURNS and MY HOSPITAL IN THE HILLS, and another success was Frederick Bodmer's THE LOOM OF LANGUAGE.

When Norton died in 1945 Storer B. Lunt was elected president of the firm. Under Lunt the Norton lists in music and psychiatry were expanded. Some titles were: EMOTIONAL PROBLEMS OF LIVING by O.S. English and G.H.J. Pearson; MUSIC IN OUR TIME by Adolfo Salazar; THE BIOLOGY OF SCHIZOPHRENIA by Roy G. Hoskins; Charles Berg's DEEP ANALYSIS; David Levy's NEW FIELDS OF PSYCHIATRY; COMPOSER AND CRITIC by Max

Graf; and Harry A. Overstreet's THE MATURE MIND.

In the fifties Norton's major successes were THE FALL OF A TITAN by Igor Gouzenko, Eleanor Roosevelt's IT SEEMS TO ME, and THE UGLY AMERICAN by W.J. Lederer and Eugene Burdick. In 1955 the Seagull Editions were launched; these consisted mainly of hardbound reprints. A paperback series, *Norton Library,* was introduced in 1958. In the same year George P. Brockway succeeded Lunt in the presidency.

Meanwhile, the college department was active in many fields and was particularly distinguished for its titles in English and musicology. Two of its texts in English, THE AMERICAN TRADITION IN LITERATURE and THE NORTON ANTHOLOGY OF ENGLISH LITERATURE, and two of its texts in music, THE ENJOYMENT OF MUSIC by Joseph Machlis and THE HISTORY OF WESTERN MUSIC by D.J. Grout, were widely adopted.

Norton has retained its leading position in the fields of psychoanalysis and musicology and has built up a strong list as well in literature, biography, and history. In psychiatry, Norton's major authors in the 1960s were Rollo May and Erik Erikson. In music, THE NEW COLLEGE ENCYCLOPEDIA OF MUSIC by J. A. Westrup and F.L. Harrison and A PICTORIAL HISTORY OF MUSIC by Otto L. Bettmann were outstanding titles. In the best-selling category Norton's books included W. J. Lederer's A NATION OF SHEEP, ELEANOR AND FRANKLIN by Joseph Lash, and Betty Friedan's THE FEMININE MYSTIQUE. The firm is still a closely held corporation owned entirely by its executives and other people active in its business.

Noyes Data Corporation

Established in 1959 as Noyes Development Corporation by Robert Noyes at Park Ridge, New Jersey, for the purpose of publishing technical books and market research guides, primarily for the chemical industry. In 1970 the name was changed to Noyes Data Corporation to reflect the firm's primary activity of publishing technical information and data for industry. A subsidiary imprint is the Noyes Press, which publishes books on art, archaeology, literature, and classical studies.

Oceana Publications, Inc.

Started in New York City in 1946 by Philip F. Cohen. Cohen came to America from his native England at the age of sixteen. While on his first job at the Columbia Law Library in New York City, together with a friend, Richard McKay, he put together a mimeographed booklet on marriage and divorce laws of the various states which was sold for fifty cents. After the war, Cohen set himself up as a publisher. To raise capital he began buying and selling secondhand lawbooks. On one of his trips to London in pursuit of legal rarities, he arranged with the Sinkins Brothers to print their catalog of famous rare lawbooks. He then sent this catalog to United States libraries and obtained orders totalling over $200,000.00. With this capital he began to expand. The company was incorporated in 1957 as an individual proprietorship. Four years later the headquarters were moved from New York City to Dobbs Ferry, New York.

The Oceana group consists of Oceana Publications, Glanville Publishers, Inc., publishers of bibliographical services, such as *Law Books in Print* and *Law Books Published,* and Trans-Media Publishing Company, Inc., which is responsible for microform publishing, and includes the Trial Lawyers Service Division. The group specializes in monographs, reference sets, documents collections, series, loose-leaf services, and reprints. Major series blend technical information and popular presentation such as *Legal Almanac Series* and *Business Almanac Series.* A related chronology series presents historical data in chronological form: *Presidential Chronologies, Ethnic Chronologies, Chronologies of the States,* the *American City Series,* and *Chronologies of the Nations of the World.* Loose-leaf services, such as *Digest of Commercial Laws of the World,* and *Investment Laws of the World,* are geared to international trade, while others, *U.S. Constitutions: National and State* and *Constitutions of the Countries of the World,* deal with constitutional developments. Multi-volume sets include *Consolidated Treaty Series* and *American International Law Cases.* A prime focus in all publishing efforts is the area of international law and relations and trans-national trade and investment. Through its John Marshall Division, Oceana offers rare and out-of-print books and operates the Antiquarian Legal Bookstore. In recent years Oceana publication for the school market has increased in scope and now offers such titles as THE CONSUMER AND HIS DOLLARS and ENGLISH AS A SECOND LANGUAGE.

Oceana publishes for and with many major institutions and associations, including the United Nations, Columbia University's Parker School of Foreign and Comparative Law, Columbia's Legislative Drafting Research Fund, British Institute of International and Comparative Law, New York University Vanderbilt School of Law, American Society of International Law, Carnegie Endowment, Max Planck Institute and International Legal Center. Monograph publications are extensively co-published with Sijthoff, Netherlands. Oceana distribution is world-wide, public, university and law libraries constituting a core market.

October House, Inc.

Established in 1964 at New York City. Publishes a small general nonfiction list.

Oddo Publishing, Inc.

Established in 1964 at Fayetteville, Georgia. Publishers of supplementary juvenile readers and workbooks.

O'Hara Publications, Inc.

Established in 1966 at Los Angeles, California. Publish books on the martial arts.

J. Philip O'Hara, Inc.

A small general trade publisher established at Chicago, Illinois, in 1970.

Ohio State University Press

Established at Columbus, Ohio, in 1957. Weldon A. Kefauver is its present director. Its first title was THE FISHES OF OHIO by Milton B. Trautman.

The Press operates as a division of the Ohio State University under the direction of an editorial board. Chairmanship of the editorial board devolves on the vice-provost for graduate affairs. It publishes a number of scholarly series, including the *Centenary Edition of the Works of Nathaniel Hawthorne, Calendars of American Literary Manuscripts, Law Forum Series, Modern America, The Vascular Flora of Ohio.*

The major strength of the Press is in the area of literary criticism and scholarship. THE AMERICAN NOTEBOOKS by Nathaniel Hawthorne, edited by Claude M. Simpson, THE NOVELS OF WILLIAM GOLDING by Howard S. Babb, and HOMAGE TO OCEANIA: THE PROPHETIC VISION OF GEORGE ORWELL by Ruth Ann Lief, have all been outstanding titles on the Press list. Ohio State also publishes three journals: *Journal of Higher Education, Journal of Money, Credit, and Banking,* and *Geographical Analysis.*

Ohio University Press

Established in 1964 at Athens, Ohio, with A CONSERVATIVE LOOKS AT COOPERATIVES by Raymond Miller as its first title. Cecil Hemley was director from 1964 to 1966. In 1966, Ian MacKenzie was appointed director and remained with the Press until 1973. Patricia G. Fitch became MacKenzie's successor in 1973.

The list of the Press includes nineteenth-century studies, philosophy, biography and critical studies of great English poets, including THE COMPLETE WORKS OF ROBERT BROWNING, WITH VARIANT READINGS AND ANNOTATIONS, in fourteen volumes. Due to financial stringencies the Press subsists on subsidies and co-publishes with British publishers.

Omen Press

Established in 1969 at Tucson, Arizona. Specializes in occult and metaphysical books.

101 Productions

Organized in 1969 at San Francisco, California. Publish books on domestic arts, outdoors, and travel guides, which are distributed by Charles Scribner's Sons.

The Open Court Publishing Company

Founded in 1887 by Edward C. Hegeler in La Salle, Illinois, for the purpose of "establishing ethics and religion on a scientific basis." Its first publication was *The Open Court,* a fortnightly journal edited by Paul Carus, and a scholarly quarterly journal called *The Monist* was begun in 1890. A Carus book on Buddhism, THE GOSPEL OF BUDDHA, attracted the attention of Shaku Soyen who sent his pupil, Daisetz Teitaro Suzuki, to La Salle to translate Chinese. Suzuki remained there for eleven years, translating, among other works, Lao-Tze's THE CANON OF REASON AND VIRTUE, YIN CHIH WEN, and TREATISE ON RESPONSE AND RETRIBUTION.

During this period Open Court published between ten and fifteen new books each year in the fields of philosophy, religion, psychology, mathematics, and the history of science. They published books not only by Americans (John Dewey, Charles Peirce, Edmund Montgomery, Lloyd Morgan, Lester Ward, W.T. Harris), but also by British writers (George Romanes, Augustus De Morgan, Bertrand Russell, Bernard Bosanquet,) French (Alfred Binet, Pierre Janet, Henri Poincaré, Ludwig Noire, Théodule Ribot), and German authors (Ernst Haeckel, Ernst Mach, David Hilbert, Georg Cantor, Max Müller, Gustav Fechner). They also brought out new translations of Aristotle, René Descartes, Baruch Spinoza, Gottfried Leibniz, Immanuel Kant and many other classic writers. Open Court was also one of the earliest paperback publishers in the United States.

On the death of Paul Carus in 1919, his wife, Mary, established the *Carus Mathematical Monographs* as well as *The Paul Carus Lectures* in memory of her husband. The latter are given biannually by a lecturer chosen by the American Philosophical Association and are subsequently published by Open Court. In 1962 *The Monist* was revived under the editorship of Eugene Freeman. The following year the company arranged with Paul A. Schilpp to publish his world-renowned *Library of Living Philosophers.*

Also in 1962 Blouke Carus, grandson of Paul Carus, launched an elementary textbook division and began developing the *Open Court Basic Readers.* The *Open Court Correlated Language Arts Program* utilizes intensive phonics rather than the whole-word approach to reading instruction. This program, for grades one through six, was completed in 1967. In 1970 a complete *Kindergarten Program* was published.

In 1973 *Cricket,* a magazine of fine literature for children, was launched. That year also saw Open Court expanding in the field of general, nonfiction publishing with the acquisition of Library Press. By the fall of the year the firm was bringing out twenty-two Open Court and Library Press hardcover titles plus twenty-two quality paperbacks, including such authors as Luigi Barzini, John Weightman, James Webb, Maurice Cranston, and James Koerner.

Meanwhile, Open Court maintains its reputation as a leading publisher of philosophical works by issuing books by such distinguished authors as C.I. Lewis, Brand Blanshard, Charles Hartshorne, Sidney Hook, W.V. Quine, and Sir Karl Popper.

Orbis Books

Founded in 1970 at Maryknoll, New York, as the publishing division of the Catholic Foreign Mission Society of America, popularly known as Maryknoll. The purpose of the organization, which followed earlier, less structured publishing efforts is "to alert the mind and awaken the conscience of the American community to the aspirations of the human family of the third world." In keeping with this objective Orbis publishes books on international developments, with emphasis on their religious, cultural, economic, sociological, and political implications. Orbis also offers a documentation series and a line of children's books.

Among Orbis authors are Francois Houtart, Joseph Champlin, René Laurentin, Henri de Lubac, Frederick Franck, Robert Aron, Roger Vekemans, and Arturo Paoli.

The Orbis publishing program is directed by Philip Scharper, one of the most respected Catholic editors and authors in the United States.

Oregon State University Press

Established in 1961 with offices at Corvallis, Oregon, to consolidate under one imprint various occasional books, monograph series, and journals published by the divisions of the Oregon State University since 1935.

The Press has published THE ATLAS OF THE PACIFIC NORTHWEST at five-year intervals since 1953; a quarterly journal, *Improving College and University Teaching,* since 1951; PROCEEDINGS OF THE BIOLOGY COLLOQUIUM since 1941; PROCEEDINGS OF THE PACIFIC NORTHWEST CONFERENCE ON HIGHER EDUCATION since 1946; PROCEEDINGS OF THE ASSOCIATION OF PACIFIC COAST GEOGRAPHERS since 1965; and PROCEEDINGS OF THE GENETICS INSTITUTE since 1969. The imprint is controlled by a faculty committee with J. Kenneth Munford as director.

Oriole Editions

A small scholarly reprint house established in 1970 at New York City.

Ottenheimer Publishers, Inc.

Organized in 1890 in Baltimore, Maryland, by Isaac and Moses Ottenheimer under the name of I. & M. Ottenheimer. In 1955, the firm was changed to Ottenheimer Publishers, Inc. In 1969 the control of the firm passed to a third and a fourth generation Ottenheimer, A.T. Hirsh, Jr. and A.T. Hirsh III.

Originally known for its ten-cent joke books, the company expanded into reference books, language manuals, and vest pocket dictionaries. From 1967 on the company's titles were co-produced with other publishers under their imprint. Under a recent arrangement the company has acquired the storybook rights for all the Hanna-Barbera characters, such as the Flintstones, Yogi Bear, and the Jetsons.

Outerbridge & Lazard, Inc.

Established in 1969 at New York City by David E. Outerbridge and Sidney Lazard. The firm has been acquired by E.P. Dutton Company of which it is now a division.

Oxford Book Company, Inc.

Established in 1923 at New York City. Publisher of text and workbooks, supplementary texts, review books, etc., for high school, junior college and college preparatory uses. Oxford is a division of William H. Sadlier, Inc.

Oxford University Press

Established in New York City in 1896 as the American branch of the Oxford University Press which had been founded in Oxford, England, in 1478. With John Armstrong as its first manager, the main function of the Press was that of "keeping the American public acquainted with Oxford books, both sacred and secular, and of supplying the books without avoidable delay."

Although the first important book to come directly out of the New York branch was THE SCOFIELD REFERENCE BIBLE in 1900, it was under the guidance of Geoffrey Cumberlege, director from 1928 to 1936, that Oxford became an American publishing house and a major publishing division of the Press. From 1939 to 1958 Henry Z. Walck was its president. He was succeeded by John R.B. Brett-Smith who was in turn followed by James Y. Huws-Davies. Today Oxford publishes some five or six hundred books a year, about one hundred and fifty of which originate in the New York office.

Oxford-New York's greatest strength has been in scholarly books, college and medical textbooks, Bibles, and reference books, but there have been notable trade successes, among them being: Rachel Carson's THE SEA AROUND US; Herbert J. Muller's THE USES OF THE PAST; Edmund Wilson's THE DEAD SEA SCROLLS; Richard Ellmann's JAMES JOYCE; and Arnold Toynbee's monumental A STUDY OF HISTORY. Samuel Eliot Morison has contributed many books on history, including the OXFORD HISTORY OF THE AMERICAN PEOPLE and THE EUROPEAN DISCOVERY OF AMERICA, and WHITE COLLAR by C. Wright Mills was only one of many bestselling titles in sociology. In 1962 Oxford was among the publishers of THE REVISED STANDARD VERSION of the Bible. Publishing jointly with Cambridge University Press, Oxford has sold THE NEW TESTAMENT since 1961, and most recently, THE NEW ENGLISH BIBLE.

Perhaps Oxford's most famous single publication is the thirteen-volume OXFORD ENGLISH DICTIONARY, originally appearing in 1928 and published in 1971 in a Compact Edition. The first volume (A-G) of the new Supplement was published in 1972. Henry Watson Fowler's MODERN ENGLISH USAGE, revised by Sir Ernest Gower, has also reached bestseller popularity A paperback imprint, Galaxy Paperbacks, reprints from the Oxford as well as other publishers' back lists.

Jerome S. Ozer, Publisher, Inc.

Established in 1970 at New York City. Reprints scholarly books on history and the social sciences. Also publishes texts in collaboration with Pitman Publishing Corporation.

Pacific Coast Publishers

Founded in 1950 at Menlo Park, California. A general trade publishing house that also issues teacher training, technical and professional books.

Pacific Press Publishing Assocation

Founded in 1875 in Oakland, California, as The Pacific Seventh-day Adventist Publishing Association. J.N. Loughborough was its first president. The Association was organized as a result of the efforts of James and Ellen White, early leaders in the Seventh-day Adventist Church. The first publication was a religious magazine, *Signs of the Times*. In 1888 the name was changed to Pacific Press Publishing Company, and in 1904 it was reorganized as a nonprofit association under the title Pacific Press Publishing Association.

Major divisions of the current publishing program are subscription books and trade books, distributed principally through the Seventh-day Adventist Book Centers; certain textbooks published for the Seventh-day Adventist parochial school system; and foreign language books, especially Spanish, French, German, and Ukrainian. Spanish books are produced under the imprint Publicaciones Interamericanas. Much of this growth was due to Charles H. Jones who served the Association for fifty-three years, from 1879 to 1933.

Pantheon Books

Founded in New York City in 1942 by Kurt Wolff and his wife, Helen. From 1911 until he fled Nazi Germany before World War II, Kurt Wolff had been one of Germany's most successful publishers. With the small capital of $7,500.00 the Wolffs prepared their first volumes. Their American partner, Kyrill Schabert, was in charge of administration and sales. Together they sought to keep alive in America the very books which Germany had forgotten: Hermann Broch's THE DEATH OF VIRGIL, Erich Kahler's MAN THE MEASURE, Stefan Georg's POEMS, and other works representing the German culture in exile.

In 1943 Jacques Schiffrin joined Pantheon. He had founded Bibliothèque de la Pléiade in Paris and was able to bring to Pantheon many great French writers: André Gide, Jean Vercors, Joseph Kessel, Denis de Rougemont, and Albert Camus, whose work, THE STRANGER, Pantheon published in 1946. In addition, Pantheon began to publish an increasing number of Europeans whose works were little known in America: Georges Bernanos, Paul Claudel, Bernard Berenson, Joseph Bédier, Charles Péguy, Robert Musil, Jakob Burckhardt, Jacques Maritain, Joseph Pieper, Herbert Read, and Theodor Haecker. Though most of these foreign authors created only modest sales, Pantheon had its share of bestsellers. WHEN THE MOUNTAIN FELL by C.F. Ramuz was the first of many Book-of-the-Month Club selections from Pantheon Books.

Pantheon also soon became known for its art books, a distinguished series of folios that culminated in Marc Chagall's ARABIAN NIGHTS. Pantheon's many other illustrated editions included Paul Klee's CANDIDE and Aristide Maillol's DAPHNIS AND CHLOE. Pantheon soon made its mark too in children's books, illustrated by such artists as Ben Shahn, Leo Lionni and Joseph Low.

Adding to the quality of Pantheon Books was its association with the Bollingen Foundation. Starting in 1943, Pantheon published the Bollingen Series and continued to distribute it until the late 1960s.

The fifties were marked by some extraordinary Pantheon successes: Anne Morrow Lindbergh's GIFT FROM THE SEA and the historical novels of Mary Renault, Zoé Oldenbourg, Alfred Duggan and Winifred Bryher. The great interest of

Kurt and Helen Wolff in the Orient expressed itself in a series of books on Zen, including Alan Watts' THE WAY OF ZEN. The decade for Pantheon closed with the publication of three great novels: DOCTOR ZHIVAGO by Boris Pasternak, THE LEOPARD by Giuseppe di Lampedusa, and THE TIN DRUM by Günter Grass.

In 1960 Kurt and Helen Wolff left the firm, although continuing to publish with Harcourt Brace Jovanovich. (Kurt died in 1972; Helen continues her association with Harcourt Brace Jovanovich in the area of foreign translations.) Kyrill Schabert also left the company to join the American Book Publishers Council. In 1961 Pantheon was acquired by Random House but unlike most mergers, which result in the submergence or disappearance of the smaller imprint, Pantheon has remained as a highly visible and independent division in the charge of a group of young editors led by André Schiffrin, son of Jacques. Under his direction the Pantheon list has been marked by a growing emphasis on international affairs and social history. Gunnar Myrdal exemplified the new kind of Pantheon author and his CHALLENGE TO AFFLUENCE was the first of a series of titles on contemporary social problems. Among the works that followed were Estes Kefauver's study of monopoly, IN A FEW HANDS, Richard Elman's critique of welfare programs, THE POORHOUSE STATE, and Loren Miller's THE PETITIONERS, a study of the legal system and the Negro. Jan Myrdal's REPORT FROM A CHINESE VILLAGE was the first of another series on the revolution in the life of the common people. The second book in this series, DIVISION STREET: AMERICA by Studs Terkel, was one of Pantheon's greatest successes. Pantheon's *Studies in Social History* started with Edward Thompson's masterpiece, THE HISTORY OF THE ENGLISH WORKING CLASS.

In Julio Cortázar, R.D. Laing, and Michel Foucault, Pantheon has found a new generation of creative writers. Pantheon has also initiated a major new series in the humanities, called the Anti-Textbooks, with the publication of Theodore Roszak's THE DISSENTING ACADEMY. Still another new project launched in 1973 was *The Asia Library,* to consist of books on the new Asia, with emphasis on China and Japan.

Parents' Magazine Press

A division of Parents' Magazine Enterprises, Inc., established in 1963 in New York City by Edward A. Sand. The division took over the titles of the Home Library Press. It specializes in juveniles and books for the home.

Parker & Son Publications, Inc.

Incorporated in 1898 in Los Angeles, California, as Spencer and Parker, by Tom Spencer and Robert Parker. The name of the company was changed several times, reflecting changes in partnership: Parker & Stone; Parker, Stone & Baird (1919); Parker & Baird (1935); Parker & Company (1939); and Parker & Son, Inc. (1954); at which time the Parker family acquired all outstanding stock. In 1959, the book publishing division was separately incorporated as Parker & Son Publications, Inc. The firm specializes in legal books.

Parker Publishing Company

A subsidiary of Prentice-Hall, Inc., at Englewood Cliffs, New Jersey, which publishes business, in-service educational, health and self-improvement books for the general public.

Parnassus Press

Established in 1956 at Berkeley, California. Specializes in juveniles.

Pathfinder Press

A New York City publisher specializing in labor, history, philosophy, sociology, including Afro-American, Chicano and Women's Liberation interests.

Paulist/Newman Press

Founded in 1865 at New York City by Isaac Hecker, the founder of the Paulist Community, as the Columbus Press. At the turn of the century it became the Paulist Press. It is owned by the Paulist Fathers, a Roman Catholic Missionary Society of priests. In 1963 the Paulist Press acquired Newman Press of Westminster, Maryland, a firm specializing in the publication of serious theological and religious literature. All hardbound titles of Paulist/Newman Press appear under the Newman Press imprint.

The Press publishes a wide range of religious literature, both serious and popular. Major publishing programs are: *Come To The Father* (a primary grade religious education program); *Education to Wonder* (preschool and primary grade religious education program); *Discovery* (high school religious education program); *The Old Testament Bible Series; Deus Books* (paperback line); *Ancient Christian Writers* (patristic series); and *Gift Program* (adult education program). The Press also publishes two journals, *The New Catholic World* and *The Ecumenist*. In addition Paulist Press publishes a large number of audio-visuals for the religious education market.

F.E. Peacock Publishers, Inc.

Established in 1967 at Itasca, Illinois. Specializes in college textbooks in the social and behavioral sciences.

Pelican Publishing Company

Organized in New Orleans, Louisiana, in 1926 by a group that included John McClure, who was for many years the book review editor of the *New Orleans Times-Picayune*. The first book bearing the Pelican imprint was SHERWOOD ANDERSON AND OTHER FAMOUS CREOLES by William Spratling and William Faulkner.

The firm was sold to Stuart Landry in 1926 who was publisher until his death in 1966. In that year Hodding Carter bought the company from the Landry family estate. In 1970 Milburn Calhoun acquired the firm from Carter.

Under Calhoun the publishing programs were revitalized. The *Pelican Guide Series* was initiated and the *New Orleans Architecture Series* begun. A reprint program of significant out-of-print titles is well underway. The Jackson Square Press is used as a subsidiary imprint.

Penguin Books, Inc.

Established in 1949 at Baltimore, Maryland, as a branch of the famous British paperback house founded in 1935 by Sir Allan Lane.

In 1949 Lane established a distribution center in Baltimore, Maryland, under the name of Penguin Books, Inc. Gradually the Baltimore center began to initiate books on its own and the publishing aspect of the business grew steadily. In 1962 a publishing office was opened in New York City. In addition to distribution of the British Penguin, Pelican, and Puffin lines, the American branch is now engaged in a vigorous publishing program of its own.

The Pennsylvania State University Press

Established in 1956 at University Park, Pennsylvania, "on an experimental basis" by the board of trustees of the university. Its first director was Louis H. Bell. Earlier, in 1953, the university had made a foray into the field of publishing when its Department of Public Information had published PENN STATE YANKEE: THE AUTOBIOGRAPHY OF FRED LEWIS PATTEE. After Bell's death in 1958, T. Rowland Slingluff, Jr. was named acting director of the Press. In 1959 his appointment was made permanent and a faculty committee was established to control the imprint.

Publications of the Press have included multi-volume series in art, art history, music, literary criticism, science, engineering, agriculture, and the social sciences. Two series of particular note are the multi-volume CORPUS PALLADIANUM, and the annual YEARBOOK OF COMPARATIVE CRITICISM. Its program has involved the Press in international collaborative efforts. The Press also publishes five journals:

The Chaucer Review, General Linguistics, The Shaw Review, The Journal of General Education, and *Philosophy and Rhetoric.*

In 1972 the university began a reorganization of the Press in order to broaden its scope and operation. The university vice president for research and graduate studies assumed administrative responsibility for the Press. Chris W. Kentera was appointed director of the Press in 1973.

The Pequot Press, Inc.

Organized in 1947 as a partnership among the principals of the Stonington Printing Company, Stonington, Connecticut. It was incorporated in 1962. In 1970 the control of the firm was acquired by James F. Mottershead and Robert W. Wilkerson.

The Press publishes New England and Connecticut guide books, how-to books, New England histories, biographies and genealogies. A major program is the five-volume *Connecticut History Series.* A single-volume textbook on Connecticut government has been adopted as a text in the Connecticut school systems. In conjunction with the American Revolution Bicentennial Commission of Connecticut, the Press has undertaken a history of the American Revolutionary period in thirty to forty volumes.

Pergamon Publishing Company

Set up in 1968 at Elmsford, New York, as the publishing imprint of Pergamon Press, Inc. The latter organization had been founded in 1952 primarily as an independent marketing and sales organization in the Western Hemisphere to distribute the books and journals published by Pergamon Press, Ltd., Oxford, England. In 1964 Pergamon Press, Ltd. acquired Pergamon Press, Inc. from its private owners. In 1968 Pergamon Press, Inc., became a publicly-held company with Pergamon Press Ltd., holding a seventy percent interest.

Under Robert Maxwell, founder and president of the Press, and one of the most dynamic bookmen on either side of the Atlantic, Pergamon has developed an outstanding list. Major programs include the *Pergamon Unified Engineering Series,* textbooks aimed to conform to the needs of modern, integrated engineering curricula; the *Pergamon General Psychology Series;* and WESTERN MAN AND THE MODERN WORLD (a history of Western civilization), an ambitious modular textbook aimed at the high school market. In addition, the firm distributes *The Pergamon International Library,* over one thousand volumes of textbooks, supplementary readers and books for the interested layman, and various progress and monograph series reporting on the most recent scientific research in all fields.

Peter Pauper Press

A private press devoted to fine books, founded in 1928 at Mount Vernon, New York, by Peter Beilenson and Sidney W. Wallach. The business has been continued since the death of Peter Beilenson by his wife, Edna Beilenson.

Pflaum/Standard

Begun in 1885 by George A. Pflaum in Dayton, Ohio, with a parochial school periodical entitled *The Young Catholic Messenger.* In ensuing years the original publishing operation expanded, first, with increased frequency of issues of *The Young Catholic Messenger,* and later, with additional periodicals to meet the varying reading levels of youngsters. By 1951 Pflaum was publishing five such weekly periodicals, *The Messengers,* and one monthly entertainment magazine, *Treasure Chest.*

In 1968, when the company was sold to Standard International Corporation of Andover, Massachusetts, its publishing program touched these areas: 1) periodical publishing: *The Messengers; Witness/Discover,* three religious education periodicals for students; *Catechist, Today's Catholic Teacher* and *Modern Media Teacher,* three professional magazines for educators. 2) textbook publishing: *Dimensions of Personality; The Prep Program,* language arts paperbacks. 3) adult religious books: Pflaum Press, hardbound books;

Witness Books, paperbacks for discussion groups. 4) teaching aids: film/media study textbooks, posters, photovisuals, picture dictionary, filmstrips, and a variety of teaching materials.

By 1971, having divested itself of its periodicals and closed down its hardbound book division, Pflaum was concentrating its publishing efforts on religious education and expanding its public education program. The company relinquished its divisional status with Standard International Corporation, now called Standex, and aligned itself with another Standex division, Standard Publishing of Cincinnati, Ohio. At the same time the company's name was changed to Pflaum/Standard.

Phaedra, Inc.

Established in 1965 in New York City by Oscar deLiso, noted author and translator. Publishes plays and filmscripts in English and foreign languages.

Philosophical Library

Founded in 1941 at New York City by Dagobert D. Runes, Jewish immigrant and philosopher, whose book, THE DICTIONARY OF PHILOSOPHY, was the firm's first publication. Specializes in reference and scholarly books.

The Pierian Press

Established in 1968 at Ann Arbor, Michigan, by C. Edward Wall. Publishes library-oriented reference books and indexes, including WORDS AND PHRASES INDEX and CONSUMERS INDEX.

In 1973 the Press launched the *Reference Services Review,* a quarterly guide to reference books.

Pilot Books

Established in 1959 at New York City. Specializes in financial and business books.

Pinnacle Books

A general paperback reprint house in New York City that issues fiction and nonfiction titles.

The Piper Company

Established in 1967 at Blue Earth, Minnesota. A small general trade book publishing house.

Pitman Publishing Corporation

Established in 1890 in New York City by Charles A. Pitman as Isaac Pitman & Sons, a branch of the British firm of the same name which had been founded in 1837. In 1933 the company was reorganized as Pitman Publishing Corporation.

The firm publishes primarily materials for business education, textbooks on education, Russian language, social studies, and books on arts and crafts and film. A subsidiary imprint is Initial Teaching Alphabet (i/t/a) Publications, Inc., which publishes books for beginning readers. In 1974 Fearon Publishers was acquired.

Platt & Munk

Established in New York City in 1920 as a partnership by George Platt, a British salesman, with Arnold Munk. The firm was the successor to a series of earlier partnerships: Platt & Hurst, Platt & Nourse and Platt & Peck. The Munk brothers, Arnold and Alex, took over the firm in the 1940s.

In 1959 Platt & Munk was sold to Pyramid Rubber Company, which eventually became Questor Education Products Company. David Dreiman was president of the firm until 1964, when Murray H. Rhein assumed its direction with the title of executive vice president. Platt & Munk acquired *Wee Books for Wee Folks* titles from the Henry Altemus Company and took over the lists of Excelsior Publishing House and A.L. Chatterton & Company. The firm has two affiliates: Cupples & Leon Company and Peggy Cloth Books.

Playboy Press

The book publishing division of Playboy Enterprises, Inc., of Chicago, Illinois. Publishes general interest male-oriented fiction, nonfiction, and anthologies derived from *Playboy* magazine.

Plays, Inc.

The book publishing division of *Plays-The Drama Magazine for Young People,* founded in 1941 at Boston, Massachusetts. Publishes anthologies of plays for young people as well as books on puppetry, drama, and the dance.

Plenum Publishing Corporation

Established in 1946 in New York City, now one of the world's leading publishers of scientific and technical publications. Beginning with an extensive program of cover-to-cover translations of Russian scientific books and journals, Plenum has expanded its program considerably in recent years. It now has an extensive original English language book and journal program in all the sciences and produces publications for the advanced, scientific research community. In 1973 Plenum began a new imprint, Plenum/Rosetta Editions, which provides high-level, scientific titles in a low-priced, paperback format for student adoptions and individual researchers.

Today, the cover-to-cover translation program continues, and in addition to the more than eighty Soviet journals in its translation program, Plenum has just begun the Plenum/China Program—authoritative, cover-to-cover translations of the major, scientific journals out of China since the Cultural Revolution. Plenum also publishes original, English language journals under the Plenum Press imprint.

Da Capo Press, Inc., a subsidiary of Plenum, publishes high-quality, scholarly reprints in such fields as art, architecture, music, American civilization, and travel.

The IFI/Plenum Data Company, another subsidiary, publishes and markets *The Uniterm Index to U.S. Chemical and Chemically Related Patents.*

It also operates a research bureau for chemical patents. In 1972, IFI/Plenum acquired from Du Pont the rights and data relating to Du Pont's system for machine retrieval of patent information. In addition, in 1973, the subsidiary started IFI/Document Transmission which specializes in obtaining Federal documents from government agencies.

The Plough Publishing House

Established in 1962 at Rifton, New York. A Protestant, religious publishing house affiliated with the Society of Brothers.

Pocket Books

Founded by Simon and Schuster, Inc., in 1939 under the direction of Robert de Graff. The firm launched a new trend in publishing with 25-cent paperback books.

In 1944 Marshall Field acquired controlling interest in the company. It was reacquired by Leon Shimkin in 1957 and merged with Simon and Schuster in 1966.

The greatest Pocket Books successes have been Dr. Benjamin Spock's THE POCKET BOOK OF BABY AND CHILD CARE, the MERRIAM-WEBSTER POCKET DICTIONARY, and the mysteries of Erle Stanley Gardner and Agatha Christie.

Popular Library

Founded in 1946 in New York City by Ned L. Pines. Pines began his career in 1930 as a publisher of movie and romance magazines under the name of Affiliated Magazines, Inc. In 1954 Affiliated Magazines and Popular Library were merged as Popular Library, Inc. The firm went public in 1962, and four years later Frank P. Lualdi became publisher, president, and director. In 1967 the Perfect Film and Chemical Corporation acquired substantially all the outstanding stock of the company. The firm changed hands again in 1971 when it was sold to the CBS

Publications Division of the Columbia Broadcasting System. James E. Galton now serves as publisher and chief executive.

Popular Library publishes approximately three hundred and fifty new books each year. Under an arrangement with Doubleday it has exclusive paperback rights to the Crime Club mystery books. The firm's greatest successes have been WEBSTER'S NEW WORLD DICTIONARY and Harper Lee's TO KILL A MOCKINGBIRD. A special division handles the creation and marketing of pocket-sized books for commercial and industrial companies.

Potomac Books, Inc.

Established in 1964 at Washington, D.C. Specializes in books regional to Washington, D.C.

Clarkson N. Potter, Inc.

Established in 1959 at New York City by Clarkson N. Potter. It is now a division of Crown Publishers, Inc. It publishes a small annual list with emphasis on Americana and the contemporary scene.

Praeger Publishers, Inc.

Founded in 1950 in New York City as Frederick A. Praeger, Inc., by Frederick A. Praeger, who was born into a publishing family in Vienna, Austria, where he got his grounding in book publishing. He came to the United States in 1938 and later served the U.S. Military Government in Germany in various intelligence and editorial capacities. His early list was to some extent an expression of Praeger's wide-ranging interests and concerns.

In 1966 the Praeger firm was acquired by Encyclopaedia Britannica as a wholly-owned subsidiary and the name of the company was changed to Praeger Publishers, Inc., in 1969. Frederick A. Praeger left the firm in 1968 and was succeeded as president by George Aldor, a fellow Viennese, who had joined the company in 1960. Aldor led the firm until his retirement in 1972. His successor was David R. Replogle, who continued at the same time to head Britannica's other major subsidiary, G. & C. Merriam Company. In 1974 Replogle yielded the presidency to Charles Van Doren.

The Praeger list has been known as a primary source of comprehensive works dealing with international affairs, art, economics, sociology, and contemporary culture, with special strengths in political science, area studies, urban affairs, military affairs, biography, music, and films. It is a major source of art paperbacks, background and reference books on world affairs, and classics in current history. Under this imprint also appear studies and projects of dozens of foundations, institutes, university centers, and research organizations. In recent years Praeger has developed a strong general trade list covering most areas of nonfiction and has also strengthened its college list, both in basic texts in the arts and the various social sciences as well as supplementary reading materials.

Among Praeger's outstanding series are: *Nations of the Modern World; Library of African Affairs; World of Art; Ancient People and Places; Phaidon Great Artists Collection; The Praeger Library of U.S. Government Departments and Agencies; Praeger History of Civilization; Key Concepts in Political Science; Praeger Film Library; American Art and Artists; Documentary Monographs in Modern Art; Praeger Library of Chinese Affairs; Praeger World Affairs Atlases.* A landmark was the publication of the five-volume PRAEGER ENCYCLOPAEDIA OF ART, published in 1971. The *Praeger Special Studies Series,* launched in 1964, makes available significant, policy-oriented research on U.S. and international economics, social and political developments, and urban affairs. A Young Readers Department was added in 1969. Among its programs are ongoing series such as *George School Readings on Developing Lands, How They Live and Work,* and *Voices from the Nations.* A trade paperback imprint known as Praeger Paperbacks was started by Praeger in 1959, and college paperbacks are published under the Praeger University Series and Praeger Paperbound Texts imprints.

Praeger acquired Phaidon Press Ltd. in 1969, a British publishing firm renowned for its art books, and distributes Phaidon titles in the United States.

Prayer Book Press, Inc.

Founded in 1933 at Bridgeport, Connecticut. A subsidiary of Media Judaica, Inc., the firm specializes in Jewish prayer books.

Dime Novels — Popular Reading from the 1860s to early 1900s

Prentice-Hall, Inc.

Organized in 1913 by Charles W. Gerstenberg and Richard P. Ettinger in order to publish the former's book, MATERIALS OF CORPORATION FINANCE. Since their own names were too long when combined as a title for a firm they adopted the maiden names of their mothers and thus Prentice-Hall was born. Encouraged by the success of their first book, they began to publish more titles on taxation, law, corporate finance, and economics. This publishing activity was all the more remarkable because it was a venture carried on by the partners during their spare time: Ettinger himself did not give up his job as a teacher until 1922.

A fortuitous circumstance led them into loose-leaf publishing of information on taxation, finance, estates, management and labor, and government regulations. In 1919 they had published a book on income and excess profits taxation. A revision of Federal tax regulations made this book obsolete, forcing the partners to consider remaindering the bulk of their edition. They then conceived the idea of issuing business information in loose-leaf form for sale by subscription.

In 1923 Prentice-Hall established a textbook division (one of whose early successes was H.A. Finney's PRINCIPLES OF ACCOUNTING) which has become one of the world's leading textbook publishers, particularly in the fields of business, history and art. The trade department, started in 1937 under David Dunlap, was most successful in its inspirational, self-help, and humor books among which were: Norman Vincent Peale's THE POWER OF POSITIVE THINKING and A GUIDE TO CONFIDENT LIVING; Claude Bristol's THE MAGIC OF BELIEVING; Frank Bettger's HOW I RAISED MYSELF FROM FAILURE TO SUCCESS IN SELLING; Abigail Van Buren's DEAR ABBY; John A. Schindler's HOW TO LIVE 365 DAYS A YEAR; and Art Linkletter's KIDS SAY THE DARNDEST THINGS. In 1953 a second trade division, known as Hawthorn Books (q.v.), was organized.

In 1955 Ettinger became chairman of the board and his son-in-law, John G. Powers, was appointed president of the company. The tenure of Powers was marked by a series of acquisi-

tions: Allyn and Bacon in 1951, Charles E. Merrill Books in 1957, Iroquois Publishing Company in 1960, National Foreman's Institute also in 1960, Carr-Speirs Corporation, and the New York Institute of Finance. Powers also established during this period two subsidiaries, Atherton Press and Wadsworth Publishing Company. Another venture was The Center for Applied Research in Education, which sponsored and supervised the Library of Education. A new paperback series, Spectrum Books, was begun, which publishes many course-oriented series in the humanities, including the influential *Twentieth Century Views,* edited by Maynard Mack, which consists of original critical studies of major contemporary authors. Still another ambitious venture begun about that time was THE MODERN NATIONS IN HISTORICAL PERSPECTIVE, edited by Robin W. Winks, in fifty volumes. The *American Forts Series* was also launched, with Stewart H. Holbrook as editor.

By 1964 Prentice-Hall was one of the largest publishing houses in the United States, consisting of over nineteen divisions and subsidiaries, including a profitable book club division with twenty-four units. In the same year Powers resigned.

Under the new president, Paul R. Andrews, another son-in-law of Ettinger, a series of divestitures were announced. Atherton Press was sold to Charles D. Lieber Associates, Hawthorn Books to Fred Kerner, Allyn and Bacon to Columbia Broadcasting System, Inc., and Wadsworth to its own executives. Before Ettinger died in 1971, Prentice-Hall was established as a major force in international book sales, and three new college and junior college textbook houses were formed: Winthrop Publishers, Inc., in Cambridge, Massachusetts; Goodyear Publishing Co., Inc., in Pacific Palisades, California; and Reston Publishing Company, Inc., in Reston, Virginia.

With Paul Andrews elected chairman of the board in 1971, Frank J. Dunnigan, then the executive vice president and treasurer, was named president and became the chief executive officer of the company. The acquisition of several firms that were leaders in specialized areas of audio-visual materials has opened new educational markets. In 1973, three departments of Appleton-Century-Crofts were acquired, including a prestigious line of medical and nursing textbooks.

The Press of Case Western Reserve University

Formally established in 1938 as the Press of Western Reserve University, Cleveland, Ohio, though the earliest book to bear the Press imprint was CHAUCER ESSAYS AND STUDIES: A SELECTION FROM THE WRITINGS OF OLIVER FARRAR EMERSON, published in 1929. Until 1965 the Press existed in name only to publish one or two books a year and the executive offices were located in the university library.

In October of 1965, Howard R. Webber was appointed director of the Press, and a grant of money from the Leonard Hanna, Jr. Foundation enabled the university to establish a full-fledged professional press. In 1967 when Western Reserve University and Case Institute of Technology were federated to form Case Western Reserve University the imprint of the Press was altered accordingly. In 1971 William R. Crawford succeeded Webber as director.

The Press published the first three volumes of the series, *History of Jewish Literature,* before selling it, and still publishes the major series, *Studies in Eighteenth-Century Culture.* Some of the outstanding titles of the Press include: ABORTION, SOCIETY, AND THE LAW, edited by David F. Walbert and J. Douglas Butler; DEATH AND DYING: CURRENT ISSUES IN THE TREATMENT OF THE DYING PERSON, edited by Leonard Pearson; THE CHOOSING PEOPLE: VOTING BEHAVIOR IN ISRAEL, by Alan Arian; JUSTICE IS THE CRIME: PRETRIAL DELAY IN FELONY CASES, by Lewis R. Katz, Lawrence B. Kitwin, and Richard H. Bamburger; and JAMES JOYCE'S EARLY FICTION by Homer O. Brown.

In 1973 the board of trustees of the university voted to discontinue the publishing of new books. The university has now condensed and reorganized the Press so that a smaller staff handles advertising and promotion of the book list and carries on the general business activities of the Press, including the reprinting of certain books whose print runs have sold out. Thus the Press still functions on a narrower basis and is continuing to market its inventory.

Price/Stern/Sloan Publishers, Inc.

Established in 1962 in Los Angeles, California, by L.L. Sloan, Roger Price and Leonard Stern. The firm publishes general trade books, mostly originals in softcover. It has had one bestseller in hardcover, HOW TO BE A JEWISH MOTHER by Dan Greenburg.

Princeton University Press

Founded in 1905 at Princeton, New Jersey, and incorporated in 1910 "for the promotion of scholarship," the Press received little support from the university. It owed its founding largely to Whitney Darrow, who served as its first director from 1905 to 1917, and to Charles Scribner, who donated the Gothic building in which the Press's offices still are housed. The first book of the Press, John Witherspoon's LECTURES IN MORAL PHILOSOPHY, had to wait until 1912 for publication.

A number of distinguished directors followed Darrow: Paul G. Tomlinson from 1917 to 1937; Joseph Brandt from 1937 to 1941; Datus C. Smith, Jr. from 1942 to 1952; and Herbert S. Bailey, Jr. since 1954. Tomlinson was responsible for such distinguished titles as Albert Einstein's THE MEANING OF RELATIVITY and Henri Pirenne's MEDIEVAL CITIES. Under Smith the Press made rapid strides. It published Henry D. Smyth's ATOMIC ENERGY FOR MILITARY PURPOSES, BETWEEN WAR AND PEACE by Herbert Feis, and other notable scholarly books.

For initiating the multi-volume edition of THE PAPERS OF THOMAS JEFFERSON the Press received the Carey-Thomas Award for Creative Publishing in 1951. In 1959 the Press undertook a similar project to publish in a similar edition THE PAPERS OF WOODROW WILSON. Another important undertaking was the publication of a new edition of Henry D. Thoreau's writings in twenty-four volumes. It also issued Soren Kierkegaard's writings in thirteen volumes. In 1967 the Press became the publisher of the Bollingen Series sponsored by the Bollingen Foundation. In 1971 it was announced that the

Press would publish a complete edition of THE WRITINGS OF ALBERT EINSTEIN.

Princeton books have won the Pulitzer Prize in History five times, as well as many other prizes. George F. Kennan's RUSSIA LEAVES THE WAR won a National Book Award in 1957.

Today the Press publishes about one hundred new scholarly volumes and thirty-five paperbacks each year.

Prindle, Weber & Schmidt, Inc.

Organized in 1965 at Boston, Massachusetts, by Paul E. Prindle, Arthur L. Weber and Robert Schmidt. The firm specializes in college mathematics textbooks. The Willard-Grant Press, Inc. is an affiliate company.

Prometheus Books

Established in 1970 at Buffalo, New York. Specializes in books on humanism and ethics.

Prospect House, Inc.

A Washington, D.C. publisher of a small list dealing with political and social topics.

Pruett Publishing Company

A division of Pruett Press, Inc. of Boulder, Colorado, that publishes a small list of books on Western Americana, Colorado and regional history, railroads, and the outdoors.

Public Affairs Press

Founded in 1938 in Washington, D.C. by M.B. Schnapper. It publishes six different types of publications: popular books, reference books, scholarly studies, monographs, pamphlets, and pictorial histories. Most of the scholarly monographs appear in the Annals Series: *Annals of American Economics; Annals of American Government; Annals of American Sociology;* and *Annals of American History.* Pictorial histories cover the labor movement, the Republican and Democratic Parties, symbols of the nations, American journalism, etc.

The Press has also co-published with the American Council of Learned Societies, the American Friends Service Committee, the American Political Science Association, Woodrow Wilson Foundation, the AFL-CIO, American Council on Public Affairs, the Twentieth Century Fund, and the American Civil Liberties Union.

The impressive roster of Public Affairs Press authors includes Walter Cronkite, Jack Anderson, Ralph Nader, Mohandas Gandhi, Julian Huxley, Harry S. Truman, Hans Morgenthau, Walter Reuther, Jules Romains, Lewis Mumford, Arnold Toynbee, Gamal Abdel Nasser, and Bernard Baruch.

Publishers Trade List Annual

Founded in 1873 by Frederick Leypoldt as UNIFORM TRADE LIST ANNUAL. A consolidated catalogue of all leading publishers, it is published by the R.R. Bowker Company.

Publishers Weekly

American book industry journal issued by R.R. Bowker Company of New York City. Founded in 1872 by Frederick Leypoldt as the *Publishers' and Stationers' Weekly Trade Circular.* It grew out of Leypoldt's earlier *Literary Bulletin* (founded in 1868) and the *Monthly Book Trade Circular* (founded in 1869). In 1873 Leypoldt's *Weekly Trade Circular* was merged with George W. Childs' *American Literary Gazette and Publishers' Circular* (incorporating *Norton's Literary Gazette and Publishers' Circular*) and renamed *Publishers Weekly.* Editors have been: Frederick Leypoldt; Richard R. Bowker; Frederic G. Melcher; Mildred C. Smith; Chandler B. Grannis; Arnold Ehrlich.

Since 1876 the journal has attempted to list every book published in America.

Purdue University Studies

Established in 1960 at West Lafayette, Indiana, as the book publishing arm of Purdue University. The Purdue Research Foundation, an independent corporation allied with the university, is the copyright holder and funding agency, while the university furnishes office space and equipment and meets the salaries of the staff.

THE PARADOX OF GEORGE ORWELL by Richard Voorhees, (1961) was the first publication to appear under the Purdue University Studies imprint. Since then Purdue University Studies has published over forty titles in areas of literature, American studies, history, political science, biography, and veterinary medicine.

G.P. Putnam's Sons

Established by George Palmer Putnam in 1848 in New York City. In 1833 Putnam entered the firm of Wiley & Long, a partnership of John Wiley and George Long. On the departure of Long in 1840, the firm became Wiley and Putnam. In 1848 this partnership was dissolved and Putnam set himself up as an independent publisher under his own name with a good-sized list of belletristic titles that he had received as his share at the dissolution of his partnership with Wiley. He made a promising start with A FABLE FOR CRITICS by James Russell Lowell and Washington Irving's THE SKETCH BOOK. His very first catalogue included books by Thomas Carlyle, James Fenimore Cooper, Leigh Hunt, Thomas Hood, Samuel Taylor Coleridge, and Edgar Allan Poe. One unexpected success in this early period was THE WIDE, WIDE WORLD by Susan Warner, the phenomenal sale of which became "one of the wonders of publishing history." *Putnam's Monthly Magazine* was launched in 1853 but it proved to be more of a critical than a financial success.

In 1862 financial troubles forced Putnam to hand over his business to the Boston firm of Hurd and Houghton and to accept a position as a collector of internal revenue. He resumed business in 1866 with his son, George Haven Putnam, as partner, calling the firm G.P. Putnam & Son.

George Palmer Putnam (1814-1872)

Two years later, with the entrance of John Bishop Putnam, another son, into the business, the firm became G.P. Putnam & Sons. It was changed to G.P. Putnam's Sons when a third son, Irving, joined the business in 1871. George Haven Putnam then took over the active direction of the firm from his father.

George Palmer Putnam died in 1872. So highly regarded was he in the publishing community that a committee of publishers, including Henry Holt, Andrew Armstrong, Alfred Houghton, and John Wiley, undertook the responsibility of staving off creditors until the three sons could reorganize the business.

George Haven Putnam was active in the copyright movement and was one of the founders of the American Publishers' Copyright League. He was an author in his own right and his two books, AUTHORS AND THEIR PUBLIC IN ANCIENT TIMES and BOOKS AND THEIR MAKERS DURING THE MIDDLE AGES, are models of historical scholarship. Among his contributions to publishing are the many series which he initiated: *The Story of Nations, The Heroes* of Nations, *The Writings of the Fathers of the Republic, Ariel Booklets, American Waterways, Historic Towns of America, Nature Field Books,* and a popular science series edited by J. McKeen Cattell. Theodore Roosevelt was a partner in the firm from 1884 to 1886 and an occasional author.

In the early 1900s Putnam issued many limited de luxe editions and sets. Among them were the Camden Edition of Walt Whitman's works in ten volumes, the Sunnyside Edition of the writings of Washington Irving, the Pathfinder Edition of James Fenimore Cooper's works and the Reader's Edition of the writings of Edgar Allan Poe. The *New Knickerbocker Novels* consisted of reprints of backlist titles sold at fifty cents a copy. From 1905 to 1920 Putnam's also acted as the agent of the Cambridge University Press, of England.

By the 1920s George Palmer Putnam, nephew of Major George Haven Putnam, had become an active member of the firm and his personal interest in travel and exploration was reflected in titles published, such as Roy Chapman Andrews' ON THE TRAIL OF ANCIENT MAN, Charles A. Lindbergh's WE, and LITTLE AMERICA by Admiral Richard E. Byrd. He also published books by William Beebe and Amelia Earhart, and is best remembered as being the husband of Amelia Earhart.

When George Haven Putnam died in 1930, his heirs sold their stock in the company to Melville Minton and Earle Balch. In 1936 Putnam's acquired the firm of Coward-McCann but retained that imprint as an autonomous subsidiary. In 1944 Minton assumed full control of the Putnam company.

Under Minton's direction the Putnam list was revitalized by the acquisition of such bestselling titles as Sholem Asch's EAST RIVER, MARY, and THE NAZARENE; BRITISH AGENT by Bruce Lockhart; DISCOVERY by Admiral Richard E. Byrd; THE EGYPTIAN by Mika Waltari; and A KING'S STORY by the Duke of Windsor.

In 1955 Melville Minton died and his son, Walter Minton, succeeded to the presidency. Walter Minton introduced Capricorn Books, quality paperbacks of backlist titles from the Putnam list. A new juvenile division was also organized and developed with characteristic vigor. In 1966 Putnam's acquired the Berkley Publishing Corporation (q.v.) thus becoming the first trade house to have a mass paperback subsidiary.

The Pyne Press

Established in 1970 at Princeton, New Jersey. Publishes books on American art and architecture, antiques, and social history.

Pyramid Communications, Inc.

Founded in 1949 in New York City as Almat Publishing Corp. and Pyramid Books by Alfred R. Plaine and Matthew Huttner. The company went public in 1962 under the name of Pyramid Publications, Inc., and in 1969 it merged with the Walter Reade Organization, Inc., where it operated as Pyramid Publications Division and subsequently as Pyramid Communications, Inc., a wholly-owned subsidiary. In 1971, an investing group headed by Huttner acquired all of the outstanding capital stock of Pyramid, and later that year made a public stock offering.

Pyramid books are published under a variety of imprints including: Pyramid Books (mass-market paperbacks); Pyramid House (hardcover books); Pyramid Gift Editions (high-priced quality paperbacks); Family Library (religious and inspirational paperbacks); Hi-Lo and Willow (paperbacks for younger readers); Pyramid Primary Dictionary Series; Little Paperback Classics; Worlds of Science; Living Art Editions.

The company also issues twenty-two special interest magazines in the decorating, hair styling, diet, humor, and sports fields, some of which are published by a wholly-owned subsidiary, Hewfred Publications, Inc.

In late 1974 Pyramid Communications was purchased by Harcourt Brace Jovanovich. Matthew Huttner remained as president and Pyramid is operated as a separate company.

Quadrangle/The New York Times Book Company

Established in Chicago, Illinois, in 1959 by Alexander J. Morin as Quadrangle Books, Inc. In 1970 the firm was acquired by The New York Times Company and became Quadrangle/The New York Times Book Company. It specializes in nonfiction and college texts in both hard cover and paperbound printings.

Harlin Quist Books

Established in 1966 at New York City by Harlan Quist. Publishes children's books and posters.

Ramparts Press, Inc.

A California publisher at Palo Alto of books on politics, current affairs, and economics. These are distributed by Monthly Review Press.

R and E Research Associates

Established in 1967 at San Francisco, California, by Robert D. Reed and Adam S. Eterovich. Specialize in ethnic material, history, and sociology.

Rand McNally and Company

Established in 1856 in Chicago, Illinois, as a print shop by William H. Rand, Rand McNally is the oldest publisher in Chicago. In 1864 Andrew McNally, Rand's foreman, became a partner. The corporation bearing the same name as at present was incorporated in 1873. As railroad and commercial printers they specialized at first in tickets and timetables. The first publication to include strip maps, other than in timetables, was the WESTERN RAILWAY GUIDE published in 1869.

THE INTERNATIONAL BANKERS DIRECTORY was first published in 1876, and has been in continuous publication since. In 1880 the BUSINESS ATLAS was produced, and now continues in print annually as COMMERCIAL ATLAS AND MARKETING GUIDE.

Rand McNally introduced school maps and globes in 1880, and has maintained a leading place among educational map makers. The late J. Paul Goode had a long association with the company, editing a wall map series and GOODE'S SCHOOL ATLAS, still published under the title GOODE'S WORLD ATLAS.

A Department of General Literature was formed in 1884, and hundreds of titles were published prior to World War I. Sets of classics, popular fiction, even paperback novels sold by "hawkers" on railroad trains, were printed and distributed. A textbook department was set up in 1890.

A separate juvenile division was established to publish fiction and nonfiction works which continues to produce higher-priced juveniles and inexpensive books. The Trade Publishing Division produces adult nonfiction, as well as atlases, maps and globes.

In 1948 Thor Heyerdahl's KON TIKI proved to be a bestseller. In 1950 Rand McNally published the new COSMOPOLITAN ATLAS which received the Carey-Thomas Award for Creative Publishing. Still in publication, and revised annually, COSMOPOLITAN ATLAS is one of many atlases produced by Rand McNally. Most significant of these is THE INTERNATIONAL ATLAS, first published in 1969 in the United States, and since then in Italy, Germany, England, Sweden, Denmark, Japan and Spain.

The development of the wax engraving method of map making in 1872, adopted and improved by Rand McNally, made the corporate name synonymous with maps and map making the world over. The first PHOTO-AUTO GUIDES, produced in 1909, were followed by AUTO TRAILS MAPS and ROAD ATLASES. Today, millions of road maps are produced annually by Rand McNally for oil companies, which distribute them to the motoring public.

When William Rand retired in 1894 his equity was acquired by Andrew McNally and the business has been owned by his family ever since. The current president, Andrew McNally III, is a great-grandson of the company's founder. The widespread manufacturing and production facilities of the firm are directed from office headquarters in Skokie, a Chicago suburb. There are also subsidiary operations in Mexico, Canada, and Europe.

Random House, Inc.

Started in 1925 at New York City by Bennett Cerf and Donald Klopfer. Cerf, a former partner in the Liveright company, had acquired the *Modern Library* from that troubled firm for two hundred thousand dollars and soon made it an extremely profitable imprint. With Elmer Adler, the typographical expert, as an adviser, the partners established the Random House imprint to issue de luxe classics in the tradition of Nonesuch Press and Golden Cockerel Press, of which they were the agents. When the Depression of the 1930s wiped out the market for expensive limited editions, Cerf turned to regular book publishing.

One stroke of good luck brought national recognition to the young firm. In 1933 Cerf decided to publish James Joyce's ULYSSES. The resulting censorship and the legal decision that the book was not obscene made publishing history. In the same year Cerf arranged with Eugene O'Neill to publish all of his works. In 1934 Random House published REMEMBRANCE OF THINGS PAST by Marcel Proust, which it had acquired from A. and C. Boni. Another major undertaking at that time was the *Lifetime Library*. This included classics from Plato to Havelock Ellis.

When Random House took over the firm of Smith and Haas, Robert K. Haas and Harrison Smith became members of the company and they brought with them many distinguished authors, including William Faulkner, André Malraux, Robert Graves, Isak Dinesen, and Jean de Brunhoff, author of the bestselling *Babar* books. Similarly, when Harry Maule joined Random House in 1939, he brought with him from Doubleday Sinclair Lewis, Vincent Sheean, and Mignon G. Eberhart. The firm made its first entry into the college and reference markets with the AMERICAN COLLEGE DICTIONARY, edited by Clarence L. Barnhart.

By the end of World War II Random House had become a major house, with numerous trade successes on every one of their annual lists. In the 1940s the firm published John O'Hara, Truman Capote, James Michener, Irwin Shaw, Moss Hart, and Robert Penn Warren. In the 1950s the juvenile list was strengthened with many popular series such as the *Dr. Seuss* books, *Landmark Books, Allabout Books,* and *Gateway Books. The Looking Glass Series,* which was started in 1958 by Jason Epstein as a hardback line, was later acquired by Random House. In 1959 Random House went public.

The following three years were marked by a series of imaginatively planned acquisitions that brought into the company three of the quality houses of the country. In 1960 it acquired A.A. Knopf, Inc., (q.v.) and L.W. Singer Publishing Company (q.v.), an educational publisher based in Syracuse, New York, and Beginner Books, Inc., owned by Dr. Seuss. In 1961 Pantheon Books (q.v.) was purchased. In 1965 Random House itself was acquired by RCA, Inc., in a move that reflected, in the words of Cerf, "our conviction that publishing and electronics are natural partners." Cerf moved up to become chairman of the board of the company in 1965 and Robert Bernstein then became the president. Cerf died in 1970 and his chairmanship was taken by Donald Klopfer. In January, 1973, Random House acquired Ballantine Books (q.v.), as a wholly-owned subsidiary. A new division, The Random House Documentary Reference Series publishes multi-volume sets for the library market.

Raven Press

Organized in 1964 at New York City. Specializes in professional and textbooks in medicine and related sciences.

Reardon, Baer and Company

Founded in 1957 at Cleveland, Ohio. Specializes in textbooks, reading tests, and guidance materials. The Modern Curriculum Press is a division of the firm.

Regents Publishing Co., Inc.

Started in 1910 in New York City by Samuel Goldberg, a graduate electrical engineer of the Columbia School of Engineering, and a colleague, Theodore Cohen. Neither had any credit standing and their capital was $500.00 which Cohen borrowed from his mother-in-law. Their contract was a verbal agreement and a handshake to share the business equally.

The word "Regents" in the name had a special meaning. Because they regarded the formal students' preparatory texts for the Regents examinations as too difficult, too lengthy and too obscure, they planned to publish simplified, supplementary texts and review materials. Paradoxically, their first publication was a seventh and eighth grade elementary book on geography, the printing and paper for which were purchased on credit granted to them on the merits of the manuscript submitted. Their first series of question-and-answer reviews was successful and was soon identified as the *Blue Books*.

After a few years the partnership was dissolved, Cohen established his own business and Goldberg became sole owner of Regents, continuing to publish texts and review materials for many years. In 1948, Robert J. Dixson submitted to Goldberg a small book on a hitherto disregarded field, GRADED EXERCISES IN ENGLISH FOR THE FOREIGN-BORN, which he had written and published himself. This book in time was re-written, re-edited, enlarged and re-issued many times and probably made Regents the first publisher of books written specifically for the foreign-born, and so identified.

Between 1948 and 1956, Dixson wrote and Regents published over sixty titles at different levels and on different aspects of English for the foreign-born and English as a second language. Known as the *Dixson English Series,* all these books have gone into countless editions and continue to receive world-wide distribution and reputation.

In 1958, when Goldberg died, the business was sold to and merged with the Latin American Institute Press, Inc., a company which Dixson had founded. In 1966, the two merged companies, under the one corporate title of Regents Publishing Co., Inc., were bought by Simon & Schuster.

In 1972, Simon & Schuster sold Regents to Hachette of France. Regents continues to operate in New York City as a wholly-owned subsidiary of Hachette.

Henry Regnery Company

Founded in 1948 at Chicago, Illinois, by Henry Regnery. The firm published a very small list until 1957, when it bought the Reilly and Lee Company, (q.v.). In 1971 the Cowles Book Company was acquired.

Trade books are published under the Cowles and Regnery imprints, examination test books under the Cowles imprint, juveniles under the Reilly and Lee imprint, and primary college reading material under a Gateway imprint.

In 1967 Henry Regnery moved up to become chairman of the board and Harvey Plotnick became president of the company.

Reilly and Lee Company

Established in 1900 in Chicago, Illinois, by Frank K. Reilly and Sumner C. Britton as the Madison Book Company. In 1902 the firm was incorporated as the Reilly and Britton Company. Britton was president until 1913 and Reilly from 1913 until 1932. William F. Lee was admitted as a partner in 1919, when the firm became the Reilly and Lee Company. Frank J. O'Donnell became president in 1932. In 1957 the firm was acquired by Henry Regnery Company but the imprint was retained for juvenile books.

Among Reilly and Lee's great successes have been the books of L. Frank Baum including the LAND OF OZ, the books of Edgar A. Guest, including his HEAP O' LIVIN', books of Tony Wons including TONY'S SCRAP BOOK, and Lulu Hunt Peter's DIET AND HEALTH.

Reinhold Publishing Corporation

Organized in 1915 at New York City by Ralph W. Reinhold and associates as the Chemical Catalog Company to publish the *Chemical En-*

gineering Catalog. In 1919 they published the first of their many reference works, THE CONDENSED CHEMICAL DICTIONARY. Also in 1919 Reinhold established the Pencil Point Press as a separate concern to issue *Pencil Points*, a magazine for architects, designers and draftsmen. *Pencil Points* developed into *Progressive Architecture* in 1945. The press also issued books on architecture and the arts, mostly advanced technical books such as THE CITY by Eliel Saarinen; Clinton H. Cowgill and Ben J. Small's ARCHITECTURAL PRACTICE; MATERIALS FOR ARCHITECTURE by Caleb Hornbostel; CITIES by Lawrence Halprin; WAYS WITH WATERCOLOR by Ted Kautzky; OIL PAINTING by Henry M. Gasser; and LAYOUT by Raymond A. Ballinger. In 1933 Chemical Catalog Company and Pencil Point Press were merged into Reinhold Publishing Corporation.

Reinhold retired in 1950. His equity in the business was sold to his associates, of whom Philip H. Hubbard became president. A college department was established in 1958 and a trade department in 1963. The latter department brought out titles on embroidery, crafts, and creative hobbies. A series of original paperbacks were also launched in 1964 for students in art, architecture, and design.

About this time Reinhold launched an encyclopedia program which soon developed into the firm's most productive and successful activity. Titles in this series include the ENCYCLOPEDIA OF CHEMISTRY by George L. Clark and Gessner Hawley; ENCYCLOPEDIA OF THE BIOLOGICAL SCIENCES by P. Gray; ENCYCLOPEDIA OF ENGINEERING MATERIALS AND PROCESSES by H.R. Clauser; ENCYCLOPEDIA OF MANAGEMENT by C. Heyel; and ENCYCLOPEDIA OF ELECTRONICS by C. Susskind.

By 1965, when it merged with Medical Economics, Inc., to form the Chapman-Reinhold Company, the firm had a backlist of over six hundred titles and also published four journals and two chemical annuals. Its strength in this field made it a natural acquisition in 1968 for Litton Industries. It was subsequently merged with Van Nostrand Company to form Van Nostrand-Reinhold Company, a division of Litton Educational Publishing, Inc.

From 1920 until 1972 Reinhold published the monograph series of the American Chemical Society.

Reprint Company

Established in 1959 at Spartanburg, South Carolina. Specializes in reprints of Colonial Americana and Revolutionary War histories.

Research Press Company

Established in 1969 at Champaign, Illinois. Specializes in educational and psychological books.

Fleming H. Revell Company

Founded in Chicago, Illinois, in 1870 by Fleming H. Revell, brother-in-law of the famous evangelist, Dwight L. Moody. The firm began by publishing a small religious monthly called *Everybody's Paper*. Its first book publication was W.P. McKay's GRACE AND TRUTH. The concern soon became one of the first independent and nondenominational publishing houses in America, aiming at "the promotion of Christian principles and the faith and the furtherance of world-wide evangelism." A branch office was set up in New York City in 1887 and in 1904 the headquarters were transferred to that city. In 1881 the firm purchased the stock of W.G. Holmes Company, and in 1893 it bought the Toronto Willard Tract Depository. George Doran began his publishing career with Revell in the 1890s. The firm moved to Old Tappan, New Jersey, in the 1950s. It is still in the control of the original family.

The Revell imprint has sponsored such bestselling authors as Dale Evans Rogers, George Beverly Shea, Anita Bryant, Charles L. Allen, and Helen Steiner Rice. Reference books, such as Frank Mead's ENCYCLOPEDIA OF RELIGIOUS QUOTATIONS and TARBELL'S TEACHER'S GUIDE form another facet of Revell's activity. Revell publishes under three imprints: Revell

Books, comprising Bible commentaries, sermons, inspirational poetry and prose, family guidance books, and studies of church and Christianity; Spire Books, inspirational paperbacks, including Spire Christian comics; and Manna Books, serving outreach ministries, youth groups, and other specialized markets. Revell has also a cooperative publishing arrangement with Chosen Books.

After the death of Fleming H. Revell, the presidency passed to his son, Fleming H. Revell, Jr. Succeeding him as presidents of the firm were William R. Barbour, Sr., a nephew of Fleming H. Revell, Wilbur H. Davies, and William R. Barbour, Jr.

Review & Herald Publishing Association

Founded in 1855 in Battle Creek, Michigan, by James White. The firm's first book publication was DANIEL AND THE REVELATION by Uriah Smith. Incorporated in 1861 as the Seventh-Day Adventist Publishing Association. The headquarters of the Association were transferred to Washington, D.C. in 1906. Publishes religious, medical, and educational books for members of the Seventh Day Adventist faith.

Paul R. Reynolds, Inc.

The first literary agency in the United States, founded in 1892 in New York City by Paul R. Reynolds, Sr. In 1927 Paul R. Reynolds was succeeded in the presidency of the firm by his son, Paul R. Reynolds, Jr.

The firm has represented many successful authors, including Dorothy Canfield Fisher, Willa Cather, F. Scott Fitzgerald, George Bernard Shaw, Booth Tarkington, P.G. Wodehouse, Irving Wallace, Malcolm X, Morris West, Margery Allingham, Agnes Sligh Turnbull, Howard Fast, William L. Shirer, and Tom Wicker.

The Ridge Press, Inc.

Established in 1957 at New York City. Publishes books on graphics, photography, and other general nonfiction.

The Rio Grande Press

Founded in 1962 at Glorieta, New Mexico. Specializes in books dealing with the Southwest.

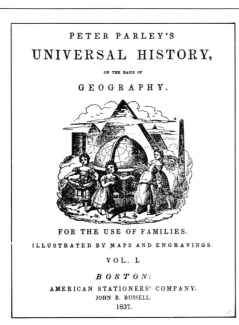 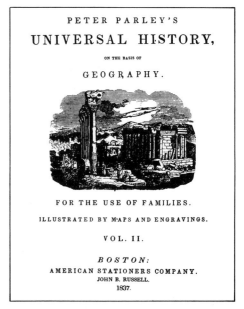

Peter Parley's Universal History Based on Geography, 1837, 2 vols., Title Pages

The Ward Ritchie Press

Founded in 1932 by Ward Ritchie, an area printer in Pasadena, California. His first publication was THE YOUTH OF HAMLET: AN INTERPRETATION, by John J. Slocum, which was printed on a handpress in an edition limited to twenty-five copies.

The majority of the books published by Ward Ritchie were elegantly designed limited editions which earned for the press the title of "De Vinne of the West." Among its titles that have found a place in the annual Fifty Books of the Year selected by the American Institute of Graphic Arts are: XV POEMS FOR THE HEATH BROOM; NEXT STEPS IN CONSUMER EDUCATION; CUBA LIBRE by Nicolás Guillén; POETRY, GONGORISM AND A THOUSAND YEARS by Robinson Jeffers; CHAFING DISH COOK BOOK by Helen Evans Brown; EL MOLINO VIEJO by Robert Glass Cleland; ELENA'S FIESTA RECIPES by Elena Zelayeta; CALIFORNIA GOLD RUSH VOYAGES, 1848-1849, edited by John E. Pomfret; A CHINESE PRINTING MANUAL; JOHN MARIN; BOOKS WEST SOUTHWEST by Lawrence Clark Powell; and THE NEWHALL RANCH by Ruth Waldo Newhall.

In 1940 the name of the parent firm was changed to Anderson and Ritchie, and in 1953 to Anderson, Ritchie and Simon, to reflect the addition of Gregg Anderson and Joseph Simon as partners.

Ward Ritchie has been traditionally a publisher of fine Americana but it now has added several new lines, including juveniles and three new series entitled *Western Travel, Leisure Time Books,* and *Cooking Classics.*

In 1974 the company was sold to Raymar Book Corporation, a trade wholesaler.

The Rockefeller University Press

Founded in New York City in 1958 as the publications arm of The Rockefeller University. The Press specializes in scientific books and journals.

Rodale Press, Inc.

Founded in 1930 at Emmaus, Pennsylvania, by J.I. Rodale as a general magazine and book publishing company. Some of its early titles included the WORD FINDER by J.I. Rodale and OUR LADY by Upton Sinclair. During the 1930s Rodale Press also published *Fact Digest,* which achieved a circulation of one hundred thousand.

In 1942 Rodale started publishing *Organic Gardening* magazine, and from that time on the majority of his titles have been in the fields of organic gardening, natural health, and ecology. *Prevention* magazine was started in 1950. In 1970 Prevention Book Club and Organic Gardening and Farming Book Club were started. In addition to the trade department the company has a health food store publishing program and a paperback series.

The Press is now headed by J.I. Rodale's son, Robert Rodale.

The Ronald Press Company

Established at New York City in 1900. Specializes in college textbooks, and professional and reference books.

Richard Rosen Press, Inc.

Established in 1960 at New York City by Richard Rosen. Specializes in books about the theater, journalism, and guidance. An associated imprint, Richard Rosen Associates, Inc., founded also in 1960, specializes in how-to and cookbooks.

Fred B. Rothman & Company

A law book publisher located at South Hackensack, New Jersey. Rothman Reprints, Inc., a reprinter, is an affiliate company.

Rowman & Littlefield

A division of Littlefield, Adams & Company of Totowa, New Jersey, which publishes reference and scholarly books, as well as library catalogues and bibliographies.

Roy Publishers

A general publisher in New York City that issues a small, distinguished list of trade books.

Russell & Russell Publishers

Established in 1953 at New York City. The firm acquired The Harbor Press and was in turn acquired by Atheneum Publishers. It specializes in scholarly reprints.

Rutgers University Press

Founded in 1936 as a division of the Department of Alumni and Public Relations of Rutgers University at New Brunswick, New Jersey, with Earl Silvers as director. By 1944 when Silvers was succeeded by Earl Schenck Miers, the Press had become a separate entity. Under Miers the Press undertook in 1953 the publication of the nine-volume COLLECTED WORKS OF ABRAHAM LINCOLN edited by Roy Basler. Earlier, the LINCOLN READER, edited by Paul Angle, had been a Book-of-the-Month Club selection and had sold over a half million copies in three months.

In 1949 the university trustees created the Rutgers Press Council, an advisory body consisting of twelve members from the academic and the business worlds, and Harold Munger came to the Press as director. Under Munger the list reflected the university's growing stature in many academic fields: microbiology, engineering, biology, history, and geology. Munger left the press in 1953 and was succeeded as director by Roger Shugg.

When Shugg resigned in 1954, to become director of the University of Chicago Press, William Sloane was appointed director. Sloane, a distinguished publisher in his own right, strengthened the list in all areas. Among the major series that bear his impress are *The Rutgers Byzantine Series* edited by Peter Charanis, the *World History of the Jewish People* in twenty-odd volumes, and nine volumes of poetry by John Ciardi. One Press book, WILLIAM TROY: SELECTED ESSAYS, won a National Book Award in 1968. Over thirty percent of the book sales of the Press come from one special area of publishing: the widely known *Jersey Books,* many of which are issued in paperback.

William H. Sadlier, Inc.

Founded in 1832 in New York City as D. & J. Sadlier by Dennis and James Sadlier. Dennis was born in Ireland, came to America at the age of twelve, and was apprenticed as a bookbinder. From the beginning he specialized in Catholic literature and Bibles and among his publications were the annual SADLIER'S CATHOLIC DIRECTORY and the *New York Tablet.* When he died in 1885, he left his business to his wife, Julia, and his oldest son, James F. A nephew, William H., had established a Catholic textbook house in 1876 called William H. Sadlier. When William died in 1887, his business was carried on by his widow, Annie M. Sadlier. In 1912 the firm of D. & J. Sadlier was absorbed by William H. Sadlier. The firm was incorporated in 1930, at which time Frank X. Sadlier became the president. Frank died in 1939 and was succeeded as president in turn by his wife. In 1969 the firm went public. It is still directed by the Sadlier family with F. Sadlier Dinger, chairman of the board, and Ralph J. Fletcher, president of the company.

Sadlier's earlier textbook programs were entitled the *Excelsior Series* and were in such areas as reading, arithmetic, and geography. In the 1930s the firm produced the very successful *Social Geography Series* by Frederick K. Branom and Helen M. Ganey. Other major programs have included the *History Series* by Philip J. Furlong; PROGRESS IN ARITHMETIC by Paulita Campbell; the *On Our Way Series* and *New Life Series* by Maria Aymes and Frank Buckley;

WORLD CULTURE GROUPS by Kempton Webb; the *Sadlier Geography Series* by Marion Lyons and George H. McVey. The firm has also since 1936 been a pioneer in paperback textbook publishing.

During the course of the last thirty years, the company has made three major acquisitions: Schwartz, Kerwin & Fauss in 1944, and the Oxford Book Company and the Keystone Education Press in 1972. Sadlier continues to expand and to diversify. It has an audio-visual department producing educational kits, records, and albums in various subject areas. It now offers new textbook programs in mathematics, social studies, science, and reading.

Sage Publications, Inc.

Organized in 1964 in New York City, Sara Miller McCune was the first president of the company. The firm moved to Beverly Hills, California, in 1966. Sage (not to be confused with the Russell Sage Foundation) defines itself as the publisher of professional social science and issues over thirty scholarly journals (including three abstract periodicals), seven series of professional and research papers, a biweekly newsletter, over twelve annual serial titles, in addition to an average of twelve to fifteen new clothbound book titles per year (some in irregular series and bibliographies) and, beginning in 1974, twenty to thirty quality paperbacks per year (mostly original editions in the *Sage Library of Social Research*).

Within the broad area of social science, Sage publishes primarily in specialized subfields. Thus in urban affairs, it publishes *Urban Affairs Quarterly, Urban Research News, Sage Urban Studies Abstracts, Urban Life and Culture* (quarterly), *Latin American Urban Research* (annual), *Urban Affairs Annual Review.*

In comparative and international studies, it publishes *Comparative Political Studies, International Studies Quarterly, Journal of Interamerican Studies and World Affairs,* SAGE INTERNATIONAL YEARBOOK OF FOREIGN POLICY STUDIES, *Sage Professional Papers in Comparative Politics, Sage Professional Papers in International Studies, Sage Cross-National Re-*search *Series* and a *Comparative Legislative Research Publishing Program*

In military studies and peace studies, the company publishes *Sage Research Progress Series on War, Revolution and Peacekeeping, Sage Series on Armed Forces and Society, The Journal of Conflict Resolution,* and *The International Journal of Group Tensions.*

In criminal justice systems, it publishes *Criminology, Criminal Justice and Behavior,* (both quarterlies), SAGE CRIMINAL JUSTICE SYSTEM ANNUALS, INTERNATIONAL YEARBOOK OF DRUG ADDICTION AND SOCIETY and *Sage Series on Politics and the Legal Order.*

Other areas in which Sage is developing a significant program include environmental studies, Black studies, educational policy, youth studies, communication research, American politics, administrative and policy sciences, simulation and gaming, and public finance.

In 1971 Sage Publications Ltd. was formed in London as a British subsidiary. It publishes under its own imprint the *Journal of Contemporary History, Sociological Analysis and Theory,* and books (primarily in series).

St. John's University Press

Founded at Jamaica, New York, in 1960. Subject areas of its publications include: Asian Culture; Asia in the Modern World; Asian Classics; Business; Literature; Medicine; Music; Philosophy; Science; Sociology; and History. A limited number of textbooks, mainly in psychology, are also issued.

St. Martin's Press

Set up in 1952 in New York City as the American branch of the Macmillan Company of London, England. The Press is completely autonomous of the parent firm in editorial policies.

St. Martin's was originally dedicated to publishing American editions of Macmillan (London) books. A major turning point, however, was the publication of ANATOMY OF A MURDER which became an international bestseller. Subsequently, under its then president, Ian McKenzie, St. Martin's embarked on an ambitious program of publishing domestic fiction. With the advent of its next president, Frank A. Upjohn, the emphasis shifted to a more conservative imports program, concentrating on reference works, musicology, and history. Under Upjohn's successor, Thomas J. McCormack, the publishing program was accelerated from forty-two trade titles in 1969 to two hundred and ten in 1973, and from sixty-one college titles to one hundred and ten in 1973. Of the two hundred and ten trade books, some forty are fiction, ten juveniles, and the rest general nonfiction and art books. The percentage of domestic books is increasing and is currently about twenty-five percent.

Reference books continue as an important component of St. Martin's list, especially with the acquisition of St. James Press, a London, England, publisher specializing in this area. In addition, the college department is also branching into basic texts, anthologies, and readers, particularly in the social sciences and literature.

Howard W. Sams & Company, Inc., Publishers

Established in Indianapolis, Indiana, in 1946 by Howard W. Sams as a small electronics research and publishing firm. A short time later he formed the Waldemar Press.

In 1958 Sams took over the older publishing house of Bobbs-Merrill and helped to revitalize it. Both Sams and Bobbs-Merrill were acquired by ITT in 1966.

Sams has a number of subsidiaries in the field of technical publishing: Editors and Engineers, and American Handbook and Textbook Company, Inc., in addition to divisions that include Theodore Audel & Company, Inc., Intertec Publishing Corporation and The Research & Review Service of America, Inc.

Sams specializes in basic text and technical books on radio, television and electronics, as well as vocational guides.

San Francisco Book Company, Inc.

Organized in 1971 at San Francisco, California, by Ernest and Anita Walker Scott to publish general interest trade books, fiction and nonfiction. Some co-publishing is done with Houghton Mifflin.

Porter Sargent Publisher

Founded by Porter Edward Sargent at Boston, Massachusetts, in 1915. His first publication was THE HANDBOOK OF PRIVATE SCHOOLS which he himself compiled. Sargent's publishing activities have expanded under the guidance of his son and successor, Francis Porter Sargent.

The *Handbook* series, of which THE HANDBOOK OF PRIVATE SCHOOLS was the first, now includes the ACADEMIC UNDERACHIEVER, GUIDE TO SUMMER CAMPS AND SUMMER SCHOOLS, and SCHOOLS ABROAD. *The Special Education Series* is comprised of texts and guidebooks in the area of special education, including a biennial volume entitled DIRECTORY OF EXCEPTIONAL CHILDREN, first published in 1954. *The Extending Horizons* series, dealing with new directions in sociology and unified knowledge, was launched with the publication in 1955 of Petr Kropotkin's MUTUAL AID. This series has gradually expanded to include contemporary affairs, social studies, and social pathology. Representative titles in this series are THE BLACK SEVENTIES, READINGS IN U.S. IMPERIALISM, DAMS AND OTHER DISASTERS, and THE POLITICS OF NONVIOLENT ACTION.

Saturday Review Press

Founded in 1968 at New York City as McCall Books. The imprint became Saturday Review Press when Saturday Review Industries took over the *Saturday Review* magazine and McCall Books. When Saturday Review Industries went bankrupt in 1973 the Press was sold to E.P. Dutton & Company, of which it is now a division. It publishes general trade books with emphasis on the contemporary scene.

W.B. Saunders Company

Established in 1888 at Philadelphia, Pennsylvania, by Walter Burns Saunders. The first book to carry the imprint was QUIZ COMPEND OF PHYSIOLOGY by Hobart Amory Hare, a question and answer book priced at $1.00. This was the initial title in a series of twenty-four. The *Blue Series,* as the books were called, played an important part in establishing the Saunders name with medical students. Another series known as *Saunders Manual Series* included such titles as SURGERY by J. Chalmers Da Costa, DISEASES OF THE EYE by George Edmund De Schweinitz, NOSE, THROAT, AND EAR by Edward Baldwin Gleason, and PRACTICE IN MEDICINE by Arthur Albert Stevens. In 1892 the first of the *American Textbook Series* was published. This was the AMERICAN TEXTBOOK OF SURGERY by W.W. Keen and J. William White. PRACTICE OF MEDICINE by William Pepper followed in 1894. In 1899 Saunders went to Germany to study medical lithography and one result was the LEHMANN HAND ATLASES. In 1900 Saunders published the AMERICAN ILLUSTRATED MEDICAL DICTIONARY by W. Newman Dorland, and in 1901 ENCYCLOPEDIA OF PRACTICAL MEDICINE by Hermann Nothnagel. At this time a British branch was opened in London.

Saunders died in 1905 and the firm was incorporated the following year as the W.B. Saunders Company. In 1907 the company entered the nursing book field with three textbooks. 1912 marked the publication of SURGICAL CLINICS OF JOHN B. MURPHY, the progenitor of the MEDICAL CLINICS OF NORTH AMERICA and SURGICAL CLINICS OF NORTH AMERICA. Saunders also specialized in multi-volume works such as PEDIATRICS by I.A. Abt, in eight volumes; OPERATIVE SURGERY by Warren Stone Bickham, in six volumes; BEDSIDE DIAGNOSIS by George Blumer, in three

volumes; and OBSTETRICS AND GYNECOLOGY by Arthur Hale Curtis, in three volumes. In 1925 the company made a vigorous entry into the college textbook field. In 1936 Lawrence Saunders was elected president of the firm.

During the World War II years Saunders became publishers to the National Research Council, supplying thousands of books to the medical corps of the armed forces. In 1946 an international department was established.

In 1948 A.C. Kinsey's SEXUAL BEHAVIOR IN THE HUMAN MALE was published, followed five years later by SEXUAL BEHAVIOR IN THE HUMAN FEMALE. These two books have been regarded as the first popular bestsellers in the medical book field. Meanwhile, Saunders standard textbooks, such as TEXTBOOK OF MEDICINE by Russell L. Cecil and Robert L. Loeb and TEXTBOOK OF PEDIATRICS by Waldo E. Nelson, continued to sell widely in revised editions.

In 1956 Harry R. Most was elected president of the company. In 1968 the firm was acquired by Columbia Broadcasting System, Inc. In 1972 Most was appointed president of CBS Education International and T. vanden Beemt became the president of Saunders. The company has maintained a regular growth pattern and is prominent in dental and veterinary, as well as medical, college, and nursing publishing. In recent years it has developed audio-visual programs in all of the educational areas which it serves.

The Scarecrow Press

Established in Washington, D.C. in 1950 by Ralph R. Shaw "to publish scholarly works in limited editions at a reasonable price." It began publishing with Alfred Hessel's HISTORY OF LIBRARIES in an edition of 500 copies. The Press was soon established on a firm basis that permitted it to bring out twenty-five to fifty reference tools and scholarly works a year in short editions of 1,000 copies. The firm was incorporated in 1954 and shortly after that the controlling interest was sold to Albert Daub. Later the firm merged with Grolier, Inc.

Scarecrow has several on-going series of major importance: *The Historical and Cultural Dictionary Series of Latin America, Africa and Asia; Author Bibliographies Series; American Imprints Series; American Theology Library Association Monograph and Bibliography Series;* and the *History of Medicine Series.*

Scarecrow Press titles have been represented on the Outstanding Reference Books list every year since 1964. The Press has three separate imprints: Scarecrow Press, Scarecrow Reprint, and Mini-Print. Eric Moon is the company's president.

Schenkman Publishing Company

Founded and incorporated in 1961 in Cambridge, Massachusetts, by Alfred S. Schenkman. From its birth the firm enjoyed unusual support from the academic community. It has over two hundred planning consultants in eight different disciplines. Schenkman at first concentrated on sociology and anthropology but later produced books on psychology, political science, history, economics, and biology. Even the first three titles reflect these additional areas of Schenkman's strength: THE GREEK AND ROMAN WORLD by W.G. Hardy; THE ECONOMIC IMPACT OF THE CIVIL WAR by Ralph Andreano; and EGO SYNTHESIS IN DREAMS by Richard Jones.

Schenkman sponsors several outstanding series, among which are: *Great Concepts of the Western World, Schenkman Series in Socio-Economic Change, States and Societies of the Third World, International Studies in Political and Social Change, Schenkman Series on Contemporary Ethics, Schenkman Advances in Psychology Series,* and the *American Forum Series.*

G. Schirmer, Inc.

Founded in New York City in 1848 as Kerksieg and Breusing. Gustav Schirmer, who became manager in 1854, acquired the business in 1861 and renamed it Beer and Schirmer. The name was changed to G. Schirmer in 1866 and the firm was incorporated in 1893.

Schirmer's publications included the *Scholastic Series* in two hundred volumes, *The Library of Musical Classics,* Waldo Selden Pratt's HISTORY OF MUSIC and BAKER'S BIOGRAPHICAL DICTIONARY OF MUSICIANS. Rudolph Ernest Schirmer, who succeeded his father as president of the company in 1907, founded the *Musical Quarterly* in 1915.

The firm was acquired by Macmillan in 1969 and now operates as one of its divisions.

Schocken Books, Inc.

Established in New York City in 1945 as a successor to Schocken Verlag, Berlin, Germany, founded in 1931 by Salman Schocken.

Schocken's original purpose was to provide German Jews with books on a wide variety of subjects at a high intellectual level. Among the first books under the Schocken imprint were the works of S.Y. Agnon, a young Hebrew writer who was to win the Nobel Prize for Literature in 1966. In 1934, Schocken acquired world rights to the writings of Franz Kafka, then practically unknown, who has since been recognized as one of the major writers of this century. With the advent of the Nazi regime in 1933, Schocken recognized that the need for good Judaica books had greatly increased and he responded by stepping up the pace of his publications. In the next five years more than two hundred titles were issued, among them the works of Martin Buber, who had an important share in the firm's editorial planning. Before the Gestapo closed his firm in Berlin in 1938, Schocken had established the Schocken Publishing House in Tel-Aviv, Israel, which is now one of the major Israeli publishing imprints. The German firm was not revived after World War II.

In 1945 Schocken brought his publishing activities to New York City, where he continued in English much of the program of the Berlin house. In the early 1960s, the Judaica and Kafka programs were greatly broadened when Schocken's son-in-law, T. Herzl Rome, took over the firm. Rome expanded into other related fields: sociology, psychology, education, art, history, religion, and literary criticism. He also introduced a major quality paperback list which has now grown to over four hundred titles. In 1964 the basis for a strong education list was provided with the publication of some of the seminal works of Maria Montessori.

Early publications in Negro sociology (E. Franklin Frazier, W.E.B. DuBois) evolved, with the expansion of Black Studies programs, into the *Sourcebooks in Negro History*. Similar evolutions led to the *Studies in the Life of Women* and *Studies in the Libertarian and Utopian Tradition*. In the continuing process of finding new expressions for old traditions, Schocken has developed publications in ecology, nonviolence, and alternate life styles.

Schocken Books is now headed by Theodore Schocken, who has been connected with the firm since its inception in 1945.

Scholarly Press, Inc.

Established in 1968 at St. Clair Shores, Michigan. The firm is a reprinter in hardcover of scholarly books.

Scholarly Resources, Inc.

Established in 1971 at Wilmington, Delaware, the company issues reprints and original books and microform publications in the humanities, the physical and social sciences.

Scholastic Magazines, Inc.

Founded in 1920 by M.R. Robinson, who started from a room in his parents' house near Pittsburgh, Pennsylvania. The firm, which went public in 1969, has had its corporate headquarters in New York City since 1931.

Scholastic creates and distributes educational materials for students and teachers from preschool through high school. It also publishes for the library and trade division through Four Winds Press, Starline Editions, and Citation Press.

Scholastic publishes thirty-one magazines with a combined circulation of more than twelve and a half million copies per issue for distribution to classrooms. The weekly and monthly magazines range across the grade-level spectrum of prekindergarten through grade twelve in language arts, reading, current affairs, social studies, science, homemaking, sports, physical education, and art and the humanities.

The firm operates five classroom book clubs: See-Saw, Lucky, Arrow, Teen Age, and Campus, covering K-12 with four hundred thousand chapters and a total membership of fifteen million. Scholastic entered the paperback book club field in 1947 as classroom distributor for Bantam Books. In 1949 it acquired Teen Age Book Club from Pocket Books. Since that time it has published its own paperback reprints as well as originals in paperback.

Scholastic pioneered in developing individualized multi-media learning programs combining printed materials with audio-visual materials—cassettes, records, slides, motion picture films, transparencies, and posters. Many of these supplementary materials and programs are being bought and used as part of the basic curriculum. Among them are: *Individualized Reading from Scholastic, Beginning Concepts, I Can,* and *Go* for preschool and elementary grades; *Art & Man, Scholastic Literature Units, Action, Contact, World Cultures Filmstrip Units, The Scholastic Black Culture Program,* and *American Adventures* for high school.

Scholastic has an International Division with subsidiary companies in Canada, the United Kingdom, Australia, New Zealand, and Japan. In addition, a New York Export Department serves the needs of educators in U.S. Armed Forces Dependents' Schools abroad and sells direct to foreign countries.

Scholastic International, a new division of the company, was formed in 1971 to organize summer study and travel programs abroad for high school students and teachers.

M.R. Robinson is currently chairman of the board of the company, and John P. Spaulding, who was elected president in 1971, died in 1974. He was succeeded by Richard Robinson.

Abner Schram

Organized in 1967 at New York City as a division of Schram Enterprises, Ltd. The firm specializes in art and art history.

Science & Behavior Books, Inc.

Publishers, at Ben Lomond, California, of professional books in psychiatry, psychology, and related fields.

Science Research Associates, Inc.

Founded in 1938 in Chicago, Illinois, by Lyle M. Spencer, then a graduate student at the University of Chicago, to publish guidance materials.

In 1942 SRA entered the educational testing field with its publication of interest, ability and achievement tests among which were the *Kuder Preference Record,* the *Iowa Tests of Educational Development* and the *SRA Achievement Series.* SRA is a leading publisher in the field of measurements tailored to the needs of the individual. Its individual skills profiles alert teachers, students and parents to specific academic strengths and weaknesses and show the development of the student's academic growth throughout his school years. More recently SRA has published DIAGNOSIS®: AN INSTRUCTIONAL AID (DIA) which enables teachers to diagnose a student's instruction that will fulfill these needs.

SRA also serves as a contract testing agency to meet the needs of businesses, government agencies, schools and colleges for the development and administration of special tests. It an-

nually provides tests to the *American College Testing Program* (ACT), which furnishes admissions data to more than eight hundred colleges.

In 1957 SRA began publication of individualized materials of instruction with the development of the *SRA Reading Laboratory®.* The laboratories contain carefully graded color-coded reading selections which individualize reading instruction in the classroom. Similar materials have been developed by SRA to provide supplemental individualized instruction in language arts, mathematics, and social studies.

SRA also provides a wide range of basal programs such as: *Our Working World,* a social science program for elementary pupils; the *SRA Basic Reading Program;* and the *Distar® Instructional System,* a program to teach reading language arts and arithmetic to educationally disadvantaged pupils with learning problems. In 1974 SRA published a new basal mathematics program for grades K-8 called the *Mathematics Learning System* (MLS).

In 1965 SRA established their first international subsidiary at Don Mills in Ontario, Canada. Subsidiaries have since been established in the United Kingdom, Australia, and most recently, in France, with distributors for products in parts of Africa and Northern Europe. In Canada, stress is being placed on the development of materials in the communications skills areas, primarily for pupils at the elementary through high school levels of training. At the college level, data-processing, business, and English publications are being developed. In the United Kingdom, SRA, Ltd., is one of the largest suppliers of reading materials for elementary age pupils. SRA PTY. Ltd., in Australia is stressing the areas of reading and language arts for elementary levels. Their plans include expansion of materials for both the high school and college levels of training. In France, SRA, SA is developing materials for elementary through high school. Materials developed in France will represent SRA's efforts to produce materials in a language other than English.

SRA's college division in Palo Alto, California, publishes materials in the fields of data processing, computer science, English and teacher education. It has recently begun to publish texts in business and economics. SRA became a wholly-owned subsidiary of IBM in 1964.

Scott, Foresman and Company

Organized in 1896 when W. Coates Foresman joined his brother, Hugh A. Foresman, and E.H. Scott, who had been in partnership since 1894. The company was preceded by an earlier partnership established in 1890 by E.H. Scott and C.J. Albert known as Albert, Scott and Company. The 1896 incorporation was with Scott as president, Hugh Foresman as vice president and sales manager, and Coates Foresman as treasurer, and it took place at Chicago, Illinois.

At the outset Scott, Foresman and Company acquired the school list of George Sherwood Book Company. This was later augmented with the educational titles of S.C. Griggs and Company. Soon the firm began to build up a strong list in both high school and elementary school areas. With the publication in 1909 of the ELSON GRAMMAR SCHOOL READERS, described as the "modern McGuffey," Scott, Foresman began its long and profitable association with basic reading instructional materials. In 1930 the ELSON-GRAY BASIC READERS were prepared under the authorship of William S. Gray and the editorial direction of Harry Johnston. Charles H. Ward's texts in English and Edwin Greenlaw's *Literature and Life* series were also widely adopted.

Everyday Problems in Science, by W.L. Beauchamp and C.J. Pieper, published in 1925, marked the company's entry into the science textbook field. Other major projects in the 1930s and 1940s were STUDY ARITHMETIC by J.W. Studebaker and F.B. Knight, OUR COUNTRY, PAST AND PRESENT by V.L. Webb and William Nida, the *Elson-Gray Life-Reading Service,* texts, and *Thorndike-Barnhart* series of graded dictionaries.

Scott died in 1928 and Hugh A. Foresman headed the firm until 1943. Robert C. McNamara took over management in that year and remained in charge until 1955. Willis H. Scott was president from 1955 to 1960. Also in 1960 the stock of the company, which until then had been privately held, was offered to the public. Following this transition, Scott, Foresman began to expand with the acquisition of other publishing houses. William Morrow & Company, Inc., was acquired in 1967. In the same year South-Western Publishing Company was merged with Scott,

Foresman. Lothrop, Lee & Shepard, which had been acquired in 1965, was made a part of William Morrow & Company. In 1971 the company purchased a majority interest in Gage Educational Publishing Limited of Toronto, Canada. These subsidiaries represent the broadening nature of Scott, Foresman's activities. Presidents since 1960 have been Theron T. Chapman (1960-64), Darrel E. Peterson (president 1964-1970, chairman of the board, chief executive officer, 1970—), and Kenneth W. Lund (1970-73).

Charles Scribner's Sons

Established in 1846 in New York City by Charles Scribner and Isaac D. Baker as Baker and Scribner. They began by buying the stock of John S. Taylor, the first partner of Moses Dodd. Their first publication was in 1846, THE PURITANS AND THEIR PRINCIPLES by Edwin Hall. In the same year they published their first bestseller, NAPOLEON AND HIS MARSHALS by Reverend J.T. Headley. Headley followed this success with two more bestsellers: WASHINGTON AND HIS GENERALS and THE SACRED MOUNTAINS. Indeed, Headley's books may be said to have established the new firm on a sound financial base. Religion was another important element in the early Scribner lists and among numerous publications in this field was a Biblical Commentary by Johann Peter Lange in twenty-six volumes.

When Baker died in 1850 Scribner carried on the business under his own name. In 1857 a separate importing subsidiary was formed known as Scribner, Welford & Company, in which Charles Welford was a partner. This subsidiary maintained its separate identity until 1891 when it was merged with the parent company. In 1864 Andrew G. Armstrong was admitted as a partner.

In 1865 Scribner launched his first magazine, *Hours At Home*. In 1870 this magazine was transformed into *Scribner's Monthly* with J.C. Holland as editor and a new subsidiary, Scribner and Company, as the publisher. *Scribner's Monthly,* it has been said, did more for the cause of American letters and a popular knowledge of good art than any other single force. Shortly afterwards *Scribner's Monthly* was joined by

St. Nicholas, an even more famous illustrated magazine for boys and girls. Both of these magazines were later sold to the Century Company which renamed *Scribner's Monthly* to become the *Century* magazine. *Scribner's Magazine* was revived in 1886 under the editorship of Edward L. Burlingame.

When Scribner died in 1871 his son, John Blair Scribner, became president of the company and in 1872 the firm was reorganized as Scribner, Armstrong & Company. In 1878 Scribner bought Armstrong's interests and the company then assumed its present name of Charles Scribner's Sons.

About that time Scribner's entered the textbook field with Arnold Henry Guyot's GEOGRAPHY; NATURAL HISTORY by Sanborn Tenney; the Edward Austin Sheldon *Readers;* and PHYSICS by Le Roy Clark Cooley. Scribner's school books were later sold to Ivison, Blakeman, Taylor & Company. One successful title that sold over two hundred thousand copies was Marion Harland's COMMON SENSE IN THE HOUSEHOLD. The *Library of Choice Fiction* was started in 1872.

Scribner's modern era may be said to have begun when the second Charles Scribner succeeded to the presidency of the company on the death of his brother, John Blair Scribner, in 1879. One of his innovations was a subscription department to sell high-priced subscription books through the mails. Among the sets and series offered by this department were the twenty-four-volume ENCYCLOPAEDIA BRITANNICA; THE POPULAR HISTORY OF THE UNITED STATES by William Bryant and Sidney Gay; BLACK ATLAS OF THE WORLD; CYCLOPEDIA OF PAINTERS AND PAINTINGS; CYCLOPEDIA OF MUSIC AND MUSICIANS; THE ARTS OF JAPAN; AMERICAN YACHTS; IN DARKEST AFRICA by Henry Stanley; THE CAMPAIGNS OF THE CIVIL WAR; and the *Library of Travel* edited by Bayard Taylor.

In the 1880s and 1890s Scribner's trade department was extremely active and published books by Leo Tolstoy, Robert Louis Stevenson, George Santayana, Frances Hodgson Burnett, Sidney Lanier, Henry Adams, Frank Stockton and James M. Barrie. To strengthen its religious list during this period Scribner bought the Christian Literature Company which published the *Post-Nicene Fathers* and the *American Church History* series.

Scribner's reputation continued to attract major writers in the early twentieth century. Henry James, Richard Harding Davis, John Galsworthy, Edith Wharton, F. Scott Fitzgerald, Ernest Hemingway and Thomas Wolfe were among the great writers whose works appeared under the Scribner imprint. Scribner's success in attracting younger writers was due in large measure to their able editors who included W.C. Brownell, Edward Burlingame, Robert Bridges, and Maxwell E. Perkins. Perkins is credited with discovering and nursing the talents of F. Scott Fitzgerald and Thomas Wolfe, with both of whom he established extraordinarily fruitful and intimate relationships.

Outside the list of Scribner's traditional authors, there were also other notable bestsellers of which they could be proud: THE LITTLE SHEPHERD OF KINGDOM COME and THE TRAIL OF THE LONESOME PINE by John Fox; THE WIND IN THE WILLOWS by Kenneth Grahame; FROM HERE TO ETERNITY by James Jones; and THIS SIDE OF INNOCENCE by Taylor Caldwell. In addition, Scribner's experimented with inexpensive series: *Literary Lives* (1904), the *Modern Student's Library* (1917), and the *Scribner Library* (1960). A new generation of reference books that began with THE DICTIONARY OF AMERICAN BIOGRAPHY sponsored by the American Council of Learned Societies was continued with the DICTIONARY OF AMERICAN HISTORY, edited by James Truslow Adams, the DICTIONARY OF SCIENTIFIC BIOGRAPHY edited by Charles C. Gillispie, under the auspices of the American Council of Learned Societies, and the DICTIONARY OF THE HISTORY OF IDEAS in four volumes. In the religious field Scribner's published such outstanding Catholic and Protestant writers as Jacques Maritain and Reinhold Niebuhr.

In 1939 the *Scribner's* magazine was discontinued, bringing to an end a literary era.

The second Charles Scribner yielded the presidency to his brother Arthur in 1928. Arthur Scribner died in 1932 and the third Charles Scribner then succeeded to the presidency of the company. He headed the firm until his death in 1952, when the fourth Charles Scribner took over control of this "house of noble proportions," as *Publishers Weekly* once called it.

The Scrimshaw Press (California)

Established in 1969 at San Francisco, California. Issues a small list of nonfiction, specializing in fine photography.

Scripta Publishing Corporation

Established in 1961 as the publishing division of Scripta Technica, Inc., at Washington, D.C. The company publishes a small number of books and journals in science and engineering.

Scroll Press, Inc.

Established at New York City in 1965. The company specializes in juveniles.

The Seabury Press, Inc.

Founded in 1951 as the official publishing house of the Episcopal Church in the United States. Though primarily intended to develop and market new curriculum materials, it soon added special editions of the Prayer Book and Hymnal to its list and developed its own list of religious books, a paperback series in 1964, and the *Seabury Books for Young People* in 1965. The Press also established a bookstore and a retail mail operation for books of all publishers.

The Press publishes not only theological and scholarly works but also titles dealing with major political and social issues. Its roster of authors includded Reuel Howe, James Cone, Jacques Ellul, Frederick Buechner, and Richard Hettlinger. In 1973, the Seabury Press acquired from McGraw-Hill the publishing program of Herder and Herder which, in addition to its ecumenical list of religious books, includes titles in the areas of social, behavioral, educational and literary concern. Werner Mark Linz, former Herder and Herder executive, became president of Seabury Press in 1973.

E.A. Seemann Publishing, Inc.

Established in 1971 at Miami, Florida, to publish popular adult nonfiction and juveniles.

Shambhala Publications, Inc.

Established in 1969 at Berkeley, California. Specializes in books on the occult and related subjects.

Sheed & Ward, Inc.

Established in New York City in 1940 as a branch of the distinguished British firm that had been founded in 1926 by Frank Sheed and Maisie Ward.

Sheed and Ward, who were also authors in their own right, built up a strong Catholic list that included works of Hilaire Belloc, G.K. Chesterton, Francois Mauriac, Jacques Maritain, León Bloy, and Nikolai Berdyaev. The New York branch continues to publish books noted for their social activism and uncompromising quality.

In 1973, the firm was sold to Universal Press Syndicate. UPS plans to continue the Sheed & Ward tradition and to move the firm simultaneously into general trade publishing. James F. Andrews is editor and president of the company.

Shengold Publishers, Inc.

Established in 1954 at New York City. Publishes books of Jewish interest.

Sherbourne Press

Started in 1963 at Los Angeles, California, by Louis W. and Ruth Linetsky. By 1968 it had become a closely held corporation owned solely by Ruth Linetsky. Most popular titles bearing the Sherbourne imprint are in the *For The Millions* series, on psychic phenomena, the occult, and Eastern religions. The *Sherbourne Handbook* titles deal with a wide variety of other subjects, such as diet, exercise, the stock market, auto repairing, and astrology.

The Shoe String Press, Inc.

Established in 1952 at Hamden, Connecticut, as a partnership by Frances and John Ottemiller to publish scholarly reprints in small editions. It was incorporated in 1958 with John Ottemiller as president. In the early years the Press published mostly reprints along with original titles of bibliography and professional library literature. Gradually more original titles have been added and the proportion of those in the fields of history and literary criticism has increased. By the late 1960s an import program of British books was expanded until about one-third of the annual publications consisted of imported books.

In 1968, following her husband's death, Frances Ottemiller became president of the company. In 1970 she married William Rutter, former director of ALA Publishing Division, and as vice president he is actively associated with the firm. In 1961 Shoe String adopted Archon Books as an imprint for scholarly titles, originals, reprints, and imported titles, and in 1970 it added the imprint Linnet Books for titles in the library sciences, educational theory, and information retrieval. The original imprint, Shoe String, is used occasionally to continue an earlier series.

Sierra Club Books

Founded in 1892 at San Francisco, California, as the publishing division of The Sierra Club. Publishes books on the environment, natural resources, ecology, and conservation. Distribution is out of New York City by Charles Scribner's Sons.

Silver Burdett Company

Founded in 1885 in Boston, Massachusetts, by Edgar O. Silver as a small music publishing company. In the following year a partnership was formed with M. Thatcher Rogers called Silver Rogers & Company. In 1888 Rogers sold his interest to Frank W. Burdett and the business was incorporated in 1892 as Silver, Burdett & Company. Later it became simply Silver Burdett Company.

The firm's first publication was the NORMAL MUSIC COURSE, which was purchased by Edgar Silver from Appleton and issued in an improved edition. Its success encouraged Silver to bring out textbooks which incorporated sound learning and teaching techniques. THE NORMAL COURSE IN READING (1888), THE NORMAL COURSE IN SPELLING, NORMAL COURSE IN NUMBERS, and NORMAL COURSE IN WRITING followed.

In 1890 Silver Burdett opened an office in Chicago, Illinois, to facilitate sales in the Midwest. Meanwhile, new series were launched: *Stepping Stones to Literature* in 1900, *Progressive Road to Reading* (1909), and *Pathway to Reading* (1925). In 1903 and 1904 the stock and lists of the Morse Company and the Potter and Putnam Company were acquired outright and the Silver Burdett headquarters were moved to New York City. Later, high school and college texts were added to the list, while the music texts continued to find the widest acceptance. Among these were *The Modern Music Series* (1901), *The Progressive Music Series* (1914), and *The Music Hour* (1927). In 1935 the firm introduced its *Unit-Activity Reading Series,* followed ten years later by the *Learning To Read Series* and in 1944 by *New Music Horizons.*

From the end of World War II through the 1960s, the company grew significantly, expanding into international markets and into the new audio-visual field. Texts continued to be the publisher's mainstay, however, and a sampling of the outstanding programs produced during those years includes several landmarks: *Making Sure of Arithmetic* (1945) and its successor, *Modern Mathematics Through Discovery* (1964), *Word Power Through Spelling* (1950), *Making Music*

Your Own (1966), and *Mankind in Time and Place* (1969).

Edgar O. Silver died in 1909; the succeeding presidents of the company were Arthur Lord (1909-1914), Haviland Stevenson (1914-1927), George L. Buck (1927-1942), Burr L. Chase (1942-1960), Earl E. Welch (1960-1964) who, in 1962, arranged the sale of the company to Time, Inc., and Craig T. Senft (1964-1967). In 1922 the headquarters of the firm were moved to Newark, New Jersey, in 1936 back to New York City, and in 1955 to Morristown, New Jersey.

In 1966 Silver Burdett became the nucleus of General Learning Corporation (q.v.). Silver Burdett distinguished all of GLC's kindergarten-through secondary educational materials. In 1974 General Learning Corporation was renamed Silver Burdett Company.

Simon & Schuster, Inc.

Established in New York City in 1924 by Richard Simon and M. Lincoln Schuster. Their capital was a modest $4,000 and an intense interest in books acquired early in their careers when Simon was a book salesman for Boni & Liveright and Schuster a teacher of journalism. The firm began, in Simon's words, "with a truckload of ideas and a mass of adolescent enthusiasms but not a single book or contract or author . . . it conditioned us in the very early days to a special sort of publishing activity that I might roughly call 'planned publishing.' " This kind of planned publishing, with its mix of made books, popular bestsellers and serious literature, was one of Simon & Schuster's major contributions to the art of publishing.

Their first title, THE CROSS-WORD PUZZLE BOOK, was published under a made-up imprint, The Plaza Publishing Company, because the two partners did not want—having greater ambitions in mind—to start off as a game-book publisher. Next year two Common Sense Books appeared: THE COMMON SENSE OF MONEY AND INVESTMENTS and the COMMON SENSE OF TENNIS. But the first breakthrough came with the publication of Will Durant's THE STORY OF PHILOSOPHY, which sold over a

half million copies and brought national recognition to the young firm.

The early Simon & Schuster lists were representative. Popular books such as Robert Ripley's BELIEVE IT OR NOT, Mortimer Adler's HOW TO READ A BOOK, and Ernest Dimnet's THE ART OF THINKING appeared cheek by jowl with more serious scholarly works such as Leon Trotsky's HISTORY OF THE RUSSIAN REVOLUTION, Edward Dahlberg's BOTTOM DOGS, and IN DEFENSE OF SENSUALITY by John Cowper Powys. Both partners had an uncanny instinct for what would sell in the marketplace and a sense of what the public wanted to read. More often than not they would create a book based on this sensed need and then proceed to create a public to read it. Later Schuster recalled "the sheer exquisite excitement of taking the editorial initiative and discovering needs yet to be met by books yet unwritten." This brand of imaginative publishing was best exemplified by such books as THE BIBLE DESIGNED TO BE READ AS LIVING LITERATURE, Thomas Craven's A TREASURY OF ART MASTERPIECES, A TREASURY OF GILBERT AND SULLIVAN, and Lincoln Schuster's A TREASURY OF THE WORLD'S GREAT LETTERS.

Many of the successes were the brain children of Leon Shimkin, who had joined the firm as a bookkeeper and had quickly risen to become a partner. Shimkin was an apt practitioner of the Simon & Schuster philosophy of publishing and two of his projects became phenomenal bestsellers: Dale Carnegie's HOW TO WIN FRIENDS AND INFLUENCE PEOPLE and the J.K. Lasser TAX GUIDES. The Inner Sanctum Books were also introduced about this time.

In 1939 Simon & Schuster made publishing history by launching the first successful paperback imprint in America—Pocket Books—under the direction of Robert de Graff. This imprint carried a step further the firm's efforts to "democratize the creation and distribution of books in America." Another landmark was the publication in 1942 of the Little Golden Books, juvenile color books at 25 cents each. In the same year the firm published Wendell Willkie's ONE WORLD.

In 1944 Marshall Field Enterprises acquired both Simon & Schuster and Pocket Books. Thirteen years later Schuster and Shimkin reacquired the firm of Simon & Schuster while at the same time Shimkin and James Jacobson bought back Pocket Books. Richard Simon had earlier relinquished his interest in both firms.

After World War II Simon & Schuster had a number of bestsellers almost every publishing season. Included were such outstanding books as Joshua Liebman's PEACE OF MIND, Herman Wouk's AURORA DAWN, Laura Z. Hobson's GENTLEMAN'S AGREEMENT, Bertrand Russell's HISTORY OF WESTERN PHILOSOPHY, Nikos Kazantzakis's ZORBA THE GREEK, A TREASURY OF WORLD'S GREAT SPEECHES edited by Houston Peterson, James R. Newman's THE WORLD OF MATHEMATICS, Max Lerner's AMERICA AS A CIVILIZATION, Clarence Darrow's ATTORNEY FOR THE DAMNED, Alexander King's MINE ENEMY GROWS OLDER, THE WAR MEMOIRS OF CHARLES DE GAULLE, THE LONGEST DAY: JUNE 6, 1944 by Cornelius Ryan, and Charles Chaplin's MY AUTOBIOGRAPHY. William Shirer's THE RISE AND FALL OF THE THIRD REICH won the Carey-Thomas Award for Creative Publishing in 1960.

In 1966 Shimkin acquired Schuster's fifty percent stock in the firm and merged Simon & Schuster into Pocket Books, Inc., a public company. The corporate name was then changed to Pocket Books. Besides Pocket Books, Simon & Schuster's subsidiary imprints now include Julian Messner (corollary reading books for children, grade three through high school), Monarch Press (review books for junior and senior high school and college), Trident Press (a hardcover imprint), and Washington Square Press, an imprint used to designate curriculum-oriented materials for the educational market. A Reference, Technical & Review Book Division has been organized to bring out Monarch Literature Notes, Monarch College Outlines, Selected Academic Readings, business directories and reference books. Young Readers Press (q.v.) was acquired in 1972.

In January 1973 Leon Shimkin became chairman of the board and chief executive of the company; Seymour Turk became the president.

In June 1975 Simon & Schuster, Inc. was merged into Gulf + Western Industries, Inc.

William Sloane Associates

Organized in 1946 at New York City by William Sloane with Helen Taylor, Keith Jennison and Norman Hood as associates. Sloane had been a brilliant editor at Holt to which firm he had brought new life and fresh blood.

Sloane's first list was prestigious and balanced. It included THUNDER OUT OF CHINA by Theodore H. White and Annalee Jacoby, and books by Mark Van Doren, Ernie Pyle, and Edith Heinrich. In 1947 two popular authors, Marion Hargrove and Bill Mauldin, joined the list. In the same year Sloane took over Holt's *The American Men of Letters Series*. This series received the Carey-Thomas Award in 1949. In 1948 Sloane engaged James Van Toor to organize a college department. Two of the partners, Helen Taylor and Keith Jennison, left the firm at this time as a result of differences with Sloane.

During the early fifties the firm fell under a cloud and, beset by financial troubles in spite of a superior list, was acquired by William Morrow. In 1955 Sloane became the director of Rutgers University Press. He died in 1974.

The Smith

Established in New York City in 1966. The company specializes in poetry and other nonfiction. Its books are distributed by Horizon Press.

The Allen Smith Company

A law book publisher, founded in 1947 at Indianapolis, Indiana.

Patterson Smith Publishing Corporation

Established in 1968 at Montclair, New Jersey. The company issues a series in criminology and law enforcement.

Peter Smith

Established in 1929 at Gloucester, Massachusetts. Specializes in reprints of out-of-print books.

Smithsonian Institution Press

Founded at Washington, D.C. in 1848 "for the diffusion of knowledge" through the efforts of Joseph Henry, the first secretary of the Smithsonian Institution, who formulated a plan for both scholarly and popular publications, with emphasis on basic research.

In 1848 the first volume of the series *Smithsonian Contributions to Knowledge* appeared: ANCIENT MONUMENTS OF THE MISSISSIPPI VALLEY by Ephraim G. Squier and E.H.D.E. Hamilton. Over the years several other important series have appeared under the Smithsonian imprint: *Smithsonian Miscellaneous Collections* (1862); *Bulletins of the United States National Museum* (1875); *Proceedings of the National Museum* (1879); *Bulletins of the Bureau of American Ethnology* (1887); *Annals of the Astrophysical Observatory* (1900); and *Annual Reports of the Board of Regents to Congress.*

Eight series are currently active: *Smithsonian Studies in Air and Space; Smithsonian Contributions to Anthropology; Smithsonian Contributions to Astrophysics; Smithsonian Contributions to Botany; Smithsonian Contributions to the Earth Sciences; Smithsonian Contributions to Paleobiology; Smithsonian Contributions to Zoology;* and *Smithsonian Studies in History and Technology.*

Secretary Henry's plan had also called for publication of separate treatises on subjects of general interest. Under this mandate the Press began in 1966 a program of trade book publishing in art, history, and science. The Press also collaborates with commercial publishers on specific projects.

Something Else Press, Inc.

Established in 1965 at West Glover, Vermont. Specializes in modern art books and curiosa.

The Southern Illinois University Press

Founded in 1956, at Carbondale, Illinois, in the second wave of new university presses established after World War II. The Press succeeded a previous organization, the Southern Illinois University Editorial Board, which had been established in 1953. In 1969, with the opening of a second campus of the university, the Press imprint became Southern Illinois University Press: Carbondale and Edwardsville. Other imprints established by the Press are Crosscurrents/Modern Critiques (1962); Crosscurrents/Modern Fiction (1966); Arcturus Books[R] (1963); and Pleiades Records[R] (1968). The first, and present, director and editor is Vernon Sternberg, who organized the Press in 1956.

The major publishing programs of the Press have been principally in the humanities. An early multi-volume work, THE LONDON STAGE, 1660-1800, was begun in 1959 and completed in eleven volumes in 1970. A successor to this work, now underway, is THE BIOGRAPHICAL DICTIONARY OF ACTORS AND ACTRESSES ON THE LONDON STAGE, 1660-1800. It will be in twelve volumes, the first two of which were published in 1973. Other multi-volume works published by the Press are THE PAPERS OF ULYSSES S. GRANT, a projected fifteen-volume work; THE EARLY WORKS OF JOHN DEWEY, 1882-1898, a five-volume work completed in 1972; and a projected forty-volume ILLUSTRATED FLORA OF ILLINOIS.

A basic and large part of the Press publishing program, and an early impetus to its growth, has been the development of a series of books in modern world literature. *Crosscurrents/Modern Critiques,* begun in 1962, under the general editorship of Harry T. Moore, is now more than one hundred titles strong and provides a core around which seasonal lists are built. Ancillary to the Modern Critiques series is the *Crosscurrents/Modern Fiction* series, also under the general editorship of Harry T. Moore, in which marked success has been achieved by such titles as SAVE ME THE WALTZ, a new edition of the novel by Zelda Fitzgerald. The acquisition of R. Buckminster Fuller's works, beginning with a paperback reprint of his NINE CHAINS TO THE MOON in 1963 through the original publishing of OPERATING MANUAL FOR SPACESHIP EARTH in 1969, added significantly to the Press's developing backlist. Other distinguished authors whose books have appeared under one of the Press imprints are Paul Weiss, Malcolm Cowley, Caresse Crosby, and Kay Boyle.

In 1968 the Press ventured into educational materials publishing with the establishment of its *Pleiades Records*ᴿ for the systematic recording of the *Davidson-Appel Historical Anthology of Music* under license from Harvard University Press. This series was designed to complement the Arcturus Booksᴿ paperback line, begun by the Press in 1963. The Press also publishes films and educational tests.

Southern Methodist University Press

Founded in Dallas, Texas, in 1937 under the directorship of John H. McGinnis as the University Press in Dallas. In its first year the new Press published only one book: NATURALISTS OF THE FRONTIER by Samuel Wood Geiser. The second, J. Frank Dobie's JOHN C. DUVAL: FIRST TEXAS MAN OF LETTERS, appeared in 1939.

During its first five years the Press had no full-time paid employees. The first regular part-time employee was Allen Maxwell, who began work on that basis in 1939 after having worked as a volunteer for the *Southwest Review*. In 1941 he became managing editor of that journal, which had been published at the university since 1924 and was taken over by the new Press in 1937. When Maxwell was called into war service in 1942 the Press appointed its first full-time director, Donald Day, who served until 1945. During his tenure the Press initiated a cooperative publishing program with the Texas Folklore Society. In 1946 Maxwell returned to the Press as director.

During the 1940s regional titles were predominant on the Press list, the most successful example of this emphasis being J .Frank Dobie's GUIDE TO LIFE AND LITERATURE IN THE SOUTHWEST. The 1950s saw a broadening of interest to include the fields of literary criticism, literary history, religion, international

law, philosophy, and international economics. In the field of literary criticism and history the Press has published Carlos Gonzalez Peña's monumental HISTORY OF MEXICAN LITERATURE, W.M. Frohock's THE NOVEL OF VIOLENCE IN AMERICA, and a number of books on Mark Twain, including MARK TWAIN: SELECTED CRITICISM. Four other great American writers were the subjects of critical studies by the Press: MOBY-DICK: CENTENNIAL ESSAYS; THOREAU: A CENTURY OF CRITICISM; HOWELLS: A CENTURY OF CRITICISM; and THE IMAGE OF EUROPE IN HENRY JAMES. Charles S. Braden's CHRISTIAN SCIENCE TODAY has been the most important religious title of the Press, while international law has been represented by COMMUNISM VERSUS INTERNATIONAL LAW by Ann Van Wynen Thomas, and TYRANNY ON TRIAL: THE EVIDENCE AT NUREMBURG by Whitney R. Harris.

In addition to the outstanding Texas Folklore Society series, the Press has issued a number of other series, such as the *Texas Folklore Society Paisano Books*, the *Range Life Series*, the *Arnold Foundation Series in Government*, the *Southern Methodist University Studies*, the *American Resort Series*, the *Fondren Science Series*, the *Scott-Hawkins Social Studies*, the *Southwest Artists Series*, *Southern Methodist University Studies in Jurisprudence*, and *Southern Methodist University Contributions in Anthropology*. Also issued as sponsored publications, but not in numbered series, have been the *Jno. E. Owens Foundation Publications and Lectures* (in international economics), the *Law Institute of the Americas Studies*, and the *SMU Law School Studies*.

Among award-winning books of the Press have been RACE: THE HISTORY OF AN IDEA IN AMERICA by Thomas F. Gossett, which won the Ralph Waldo Emerson Award of Phi Beta Kappa, and THE ARTS OF THE FRENCH BOOK, which was selected as one of the Fifty Books of the Year by the American Institute of Graphic Arts.

Journal publication was a major activity during the early years of the Press. However, at present, the *Southwest Review*, edited by Margaret L. Hartley, is the only journal it publishes.

The Press adopted its present name in 1951. Paperbacks are issued over a subsidiary imprint known as Mustang Books.

The Southwestern Company

Established in 1965 at Nashville, Tennessee. Now a subsidiary of The Times Mirror Company, Southwestern issues Bibles, dictionaries and encyclopaedic books.

South-Western Publishing Company, Inc.

Started in 1903 at Cincinnati, Ohio, as Southern Publishing Company by James W. Baker, J.C. Woodward, and Hu Woodward. Baker, a teacher in Knoxville Business College, Knoxville, Tennessee, wrote a textbook on bookkeeping which he believed to be far superior to those then available. J.C. Woodward provided the funds to print this book, 20TH CENTURY BOOKKEEPING AND OFFICE PRACTICE, and thereby founded a publishing imprint.

The company was incorporated under the name of South-Western Publishing Company in 1904 and moved to Cincinnati, Ohio, in 1910. In 1967 the company, until then a closed corporation, was merged with Scott, Foresman & Company, and reorganized as its wholly-owned subsidiary.

South-Western publishes business and economics textbooks for high schools, colleges, business schools, and vocational technical schools. It also has an active publications program in Spanish.

Robert Speller & Sons, Publishers, Inc.

Established in 1930 at New York City by Robert Speller. Among the firm's publishing programs are the *Makers of History* series and the sixteen-volume ENCYCLOPAEDIA OF AMERICAN WOODS, edited by Ellwood Scott Harrar. Since 1970 the firm has been publishing the magazine, *East Europe,* former organ of Radio Free Europe.

Robert Speller's two sons, Robert Jr. and Jon P., are associated with the firm. A subsidiary imprint, The Mohawk Press, existed from 1930 to 1932.

Springer Publishing Company, Inc.

Established in New York in 1951 by Bernhard J. Springer, scion of the famous Springer publishing family which founded the German Springer-Verlag.

The initial list included books in specialized areas of medicine such as neurology, psychiatry, and pharmacology, as well as veterinary medicine. During the mid-50s, Springer embarked on the program that today still represents the backbone of the firm's list, quality books for nurses. The company has since developed into one of the leading publishers of nursing books in the United States. Springer handled distribution of Springer-Verlag titles in the United States until 1964, when the latter firm established its own branch office in New York City. In the 1960s Springer broadened its list by adding titles in theoretical and clinical psychology.

Since the death of Bernhard Springer in 1970, his wife, Ursula Springer, carries on the business in the capacity of president. Under her direction, the firm has steadily grown in sales, staff, and scope. New areas that have been added to the publishing program include community health care and educational research (the area in which Ursula Springer holds a doctorate).

Springer-Verlag New York, Inc.

Set up in New York City in 1964 as a subsidiary of the well-known German scientific publishing company, Springer-Verlag, (formerly Julius Springer, established in 1842 with branches in Heidelberg and Berlin). This company is not to be confused with Verlag Axel Springer of Hamburg/Berlin or the Springer Publishing Company of New York.

In addition to over one hundred and forty international scientific journals, Springer-Verlag

New York publishes advanced scholarly books and series in all areas of science. Among the major publishing programs are: *Applied Mathematical Sciences; Applied Physics and Engineering;* ATLAS OF MAMMALIAN CHROMOSOMES; the BEILSTEIN ENCYCLOPEDIA OF ORGANIC CHEMISTRY; GMELIN HANDBOOK OF INORGANIC CHEMISTRY; CURRENT TOPICS IN MICROBIOLOGY AND IMMUNOLOGY; CURRENT TOPICS IN PATHOLOGY; *Ecological Studies;* ENCYCLOPEDIA OF PHYSICS; ENCYCLOPEDIA OF PLANT PHYSIOLOGY; encyclopedias of the main medical disciplines; ERGEBNISSE DER MATHEMATIK; GRUNDLEHREN DER MATHEMATISCHEN WISSENSCHAFT; HANDBOOK OF EXPERIMENTAL PHARMACOLOGY; HANDBOOK OF SENSORY PHYSIOLOGY; *Heidelberg Science Library;* Landolt Boernstein's NUMERICAL DATA AND FUNCTIONAL RELATIONSHIPS IN SCIENCE AND TECHNOLOGY; *Lecture Notes in Mathematics; Library of Exact Philosophy;* PHYSICS AND CHEMISTRY IN SPACE; RECENT RESULTS IN CANCER RESEARCH; *Residue Reviews; Springer Tracts in Modern Physics;* the *UICC Monograph Series;* and *Virology Monographs.*

Stackpole Books

Established in 1931 at Harrisburg, Pennsylvania, by Edward J. Stackpole, Jr., as The Military Service Publishing Company, the publishing arm of a commercial printing firm. Until 1934 the company published only technical and professional books for military personnel. Later a separate division, Stackpole Sons, was set up for the publication of fiction, nonfiction, and poetry. Publishing from 1939 to 1946 was again limited to military subjects because of paper quotas.

In 1947 the Stackpole Company was formed in order to publish general nonfiction in the categories of history, firearms, sports, and leisure-time activities. It was known briefly as Stackpole and Heck, Inc. A college textbook division was formed in 1950 and lasted until 1956. The Military Service Publishing Company and the Stackpole Company were then merged in 1959.

Out of the merger in 1964 a new firm was organized with the trade name of Stackpole Books.

James Rietmulder was president of the company from 1964 to 1972. Clyde P. Peters, executive vice president, succeeded him as chief executive officer. Stackpole Books became an affiliate of Commonwealth Communications Services, Inc., in 1968.

Standard Educational Corporation

Started in 1909 in Chicago, Illinois, by the Welles Brothers as the Welles Brothers Company to publish AITON'S ENCYCLOPEDIA, a five-volume work compiled by George B. Aiton of Minneapolis, a school inspector for the State of Minnesota. Shortly afterward H.M. Stanford, professor of science at the Moorhead (Minnesota) State Normal School was engaged to direct the continuing editorial work and to prepare a supplement of outlines and study guides. In 1912 this set was published in six volumes and renamed the STANDARD REFERENCE WORK. Within a few years H.M. Stanford acquired a majority share in the company.

One of the main problems of the new encyclopedia was sales, and Stanford offered one of the most successful encyclopedia salesmen of the day, Warren H. Ward, then a sales manager for World Book, the opportunity, which he accepted, to become part owner of the company if he would take charge of sales. Business grew rapidly and when Stanford retired in 1929 Ward bought his interest.

Weathering the Depression of the 1930s, Ward decided to expand. Meanwhile the name of the company had been changed to Standard Education Society and later to its present name of Standard Educational Corporation. The reference set, by then called NEW STANDARD ENCYCLOPEDIA, was enlarged into ten volumes and later, in the 1940s, into fourteen volumes, and rearranged in a unit letter system. In the early 1950s John Goodland was engaged as chairman of Standard's advisory board and to help formulate policy for a complete revision of the set. In

1955 Douglas W. Downey was engaged as editor to rewrite and expand the encyclopedia. The set is still in fourteen volumes but it has now grown to more than ninety-two hundred pages, or about double the number it had when the program was launched.

In 1947 a set of books for young children called THE CHILD'S WORLD was published in six volumes, later enlarged to eight. The firm also publishes CHILD'S HORIZONS in seven volumes, and WORLD PROGRESS, a quarterly supplement, is offered as a yearbook in four issues in a special binder.

Warren Ward's son-in-law, Louis S. Ewing, who joined the company in 1948, became its president in 1966, when Ward moved up to the chairmanship of the board.

Standard Publishing

Established in 1872 in Cincinnati, Ohio, by Isaac Errett, R.W. Carroll, and Russell Errett. It grew out of a weekly religious journal, *Christian Standard,* founded in Cleveland, Ohio, in 1866, edited by Isaac Errett and backed by a group of Christian businessmen among whom was James A. Garfield, who was later to become President of the United States. In 1869 Errett moved his paper to Cincinnati and joined forces with Carroll, a successful book publisher, to found the Standard Publishing Company. Standard was in the forefront as a publisher of lesson materials and periodicals for Sunday School classes of all ages.

Russell Errett, son of Isaac, continued as general manager of the company until 1931. Upon his death, the business was owned by his family and managed on their behalf by a son-in-law, Harry Baird, and Willard Mohorter, a long-time editor of *Christian Standard.* In 1955, with both Baird and Mohorter reaching retirement age, the company was sold to John Bolten of Andover, Massachusetts, and he operated it as The Standard Publishing Foundation until 1957. In that year, following a reorganization, the assets of the company were purchased by the newly formed Standard International Corporation. Standard continues to maintain its reputation as a leading independent evangelical publishing house.

Stanford University Press

Founded at Stanford, California, in 1925 though the imprint had been used as early as 1895 and a series of monographs, the *University Series,* was regularly published from 1908 on. The 1895 book, first to bear the imprint, was a thirty-nine page pamphlet, THE STORY OF THE INNUMERABLE COMPANY by David Starr Jordan, first president of Stanford University. Will A. Friend was appointed manager of the Press and served from 1920 to 1945. In 1945 the first director of the Press was appointed, Donald P. Bean, formerly manager of publications of the University of Chicago Press. Leon E. Seltzer has been director of the Press since 1956.

The publishing program of the Press in the social sciences and humanities is strongest in the fields of history, political science, and anthropology (with particular strength in books dealing with Latin America, China, Japan, and modern Europe), psychology, literature and linguistics, and economics. In the sciences the principal effort is in the biological and natural sciences, with a strong tradition going back to David Starr Jordan's own works, THE GENERA OF FISHES (1917-20) and A CLASSIFICATION OF FISHES (1923), reissued in 1963.

Major titles published by the Press include: BETWEEN PACIFIC TIDES, by Edward F. Ricketts and Jack Calvin (1939); THE ANCIENT MAYA, by Sylvanus G. Morley and George W. Brainerd (1956); THE COMPLETE WORKS OF MONTAIGNE: ESSAYS, TRAVEL JOURNAL, LETTERS, translated by Donald M. Frame (1957); A HISTORY OF JAPAN by Sir George Sansom (three volumes; 1958-63); FLORA OF ALASKA AND NEIGHBORING TERRITORIES by Eric Hultén (1968); THE LAST STAND OF CHINESE CONSERVATISM by Mary Clabaugh Wright (1957); and PEARL HARBOR: WARNING AND DECISION by Roberta Wohlstetter (1962).

Stanwix House

Established in 1946 in Pittsburgh, Pennsylvania. Specializes in materials for and about special education.

State University of New York Press

Organized in 1966 at Albany, New York, as the successor to the university's scholarly publications program which had been established in 1956. The Press is the publisher of the multivolume LETTERS OF LOUIS D. BRANDEIS and THE WORKS OF JAMES FENIMORE COOPER (an Associated Edition of the Center for Editions of American Authors) and the journal *Dante Studies: Journal of the Dante Society of America*.

Stechert-Hafner, Inc.

See, Hafner Press.

Steck-Vaughn Company

Founded in 1936 as a publishing division of The Steck Company, a printing firm established in 1912 in Austin, Texas, by E.L. Steck. The new division, known as The Steck Company, Publishers, was set up and directed by R.H. Porter. In 1962 the company was sold to Jack C. Vaughn and three years later a new corporation, known as Steck-Vaughn Company, acquired all of the publishing business. In 1969 the company was sold to Intext, Inc. (q.v.), which retained the imprint with H.F. Teague as president of Steck-Vaughn.

The firm specializes in adult education and el-hi texts. Major publishing programs in these areas include the series: *Family Development; General Education; Human Values;* and *Working With Numbers.* Environmental programs include ABCS OF THE TOTAL ENVIRONMENT and the series, *Wing Books* and *Wildlife.*

Stein and Day

Established in 1962 in New York City by Sol Stein and Patricia Day. Sol Stein, a successful novelist in his own right, realized that an economic transformation had taken place in American publishing whereby subsidiary rights had become the principal source of income for trade publishers. Stein therefore sought to build up a trade list with strong subsidiary rights potential. The emphasis of the company during its first decade was on fiction, medical books, and biography. THE STEIN AND DAY INTERNATIONAL MEDICAL ENCYCLOPEDIA was selected by eight book clubs. In 1969 the firm published its first paperbacks.

In 1972 the company began to buy and develop motion picture properties as a principal.

In mid-1973 the executive and editorial offices of the company were moved to suburban Briarcliff Manor, New York, making Stein and Day the first company that publishes trade bestsellers regularly to move its offices outside of New York City.

Sterling Publishing Company, Inc.

Established in 1949 at New York City by David A. Boehm. The firm specializes in general reference and informational books.

Straight Arrow Press

Established in 1970 at San Francisco, California. As a division of *Rolling Stone,* the company publishes fiction and nonfiction which is distributed by Quick Fox, Inc., a sales organization owned jointly by Straight Arrow and Music Sales Corporation.

Lyle Stuart, Inc.

Started in 1956 by Lyle Stuart in New York City with THE PULSE TEST by Arthur Coca as the first title. In 1957 he published two titles, both of them stemming from his monthly newspaper, *The Independent,* three in 1958 and four in 1959. In 1962 the firm was incorporated and ten years later it went public.

Stuart acquired University Books Inc., and its affiliated book club, The Mystic Arts Book Society, as a gift when he agreed to direct its then bankrupt affairs. The company was penniless, owed $350,000. Without putting an additional dollar into the company, Stuart repaid all creditors one hundred cents on the dollar within seven months and showed a $100,000 profit.

Stuart also bought Citadel Press, Inc., which was in financial distress. He retained Allan J. Wilson and Morris Sorkin as executives. Sorkin had co-founded the thirty-year-old Citadel company. Stuart paid overdue bills owed by Citadel of more than a half-million dollars. Within a year, the company had its first clear profit in two decades. Its volume now almost equals that of the parent company. Citadel pioneered the interest in books about films. Its *The Films of . . .* series now has more than sixty titles.

The Lyle Stuart imprint is associated with daring and with controversy. From THE SENSUOUS WOMAN to THE RICH AND THE SUPER-RICH (both number one bestsellers), it covers the range of taboo-breaking and authority-defying. Various titles have challenged and exposed the FBI, the CIA, Internal Revenue Service and the Mafia. In recent years explosive titles have included THE WASHINGTON PAYOFF; KISSINGER: THE ADVENTURES OF SUPER-KRAUT; THE ANARCHIST COOKBOOK, and George Seldes' NEVER TIRE OF PROTESTING.

H.S. Stuttman Co., Inc.

A mail order, subscription house established in New York City in 1948.

Summy-Birchard Company

Founded by Clayton F. Summy in 1888 at Chicago, Illinois. Summy, a piano and organ teacher, opened a store in 1888 and began publishing that same year. In 1931 John F. Sengstack bought the company from Summy. John Sengstack remained president until 1958 when he was succeeded by his son, David K. Sengstack, the current president, whose son, Jeff S. Sengstack, joined the company in 1972.

During the 1950s and 1960s the Sengstacks acquired several other publishing companies: Creative Music Publishers (1953); Southwestern Music Publishers (1956); Chart Music Publishing House (1960); James Allan Dash, formerly Baltimore Music Company, (1961); Traficante Music Publishing Company, including Polyphonic Publications, (1961); C.C. Birchard & Company (1957); Arthur P. Schmidt Company (1960); and McLaughlin & Reilly Company (1969). The last three of these were the most important. Arthur P. Schmidt started as a music dealer-publisher in 1876 and was notable for fostering American composers. Clarence C. Birchard had been a representative for textbook publishers before starting his own business. He also took a particular interest in American music, commissioning American composers to write for his pioneering basal music series for schools, called *A Singing School.* McLaughlin & Reilly Company was a merger of the Liturgical Music Company and the Catholic Music Company. It concentrated on publishing music for the Catholic Church, including a number of hymnals. It also issued *Music For Life,* a basal series designed for parochial schools. After the acquisition of C.C. Birchard & Company, Summy-Birchard issued another school music series, the *Birchard Music Series,* and it also ventured briefly into magazine publishing with the *Piano Teacher,* Roberta Savler, editor, (1958-66) and *The Musical Courier,* Peter Jacobi, editor (1961-63). The company also operated a concert management bureau as a subsidiary, National Concert and Artists Corporation—Civic Concert Service (1961-1973).

The company at present specializes in instructional materials, including the *Frances Clark Library for Piano Students,* and the violin method by the renowned pedagogue, Shinichi Suzuki.

Sunset Books

A separate division of Lane Magazine & Book Company of Menlo Park, California, since 1949. Has published books and booklets derived from *Sunset* magazine, which was founded in 1914. Publishes about 125 books per year. Nearly two million copies of WESTERN GARDEN BOOK, formerly "Sunset Garden Book" have been sold. Its list includes travel, home repairs, cooking, hobby and crafts books, as well as fine pictorial volumes.

The Swallow Press

Founded in 1940 at Chicago, Illinois, by Alan Swallow as Swallow and Critchlow. The imprint was changed to Alan Swallow and after Alan Swallow left the firm, it became The Swallow Press. The company specializes in literature and *bêlles lettres* and publishes both reprints and originals.

Swedenborg Foundation

Founded 1849. From offices in New York City, it issues the theological works of Emanuel Swedenborg.

Sweet Publishing Company

Established at Austin, Texas, in 1947. The firm publishes a small list of religious books and religious curriculum materials.

Syracuse University Press

Founded in 1943 at Syracuse, New York, by the then Chancellor of Syracuse University, William P. Tolley. The first full-time director was William A. Miller, who was appointed in 1945. When Miller retired in 1955 he was succeeded as director of the Press by Donald P. Bean, one of the founders of the Association of American University Presses. Upon Bean's retirement in 1960, Richard G. Underwood became director. Underwood is the author of a report, PRODUCTION AND MANUFACTURING PROBLEMS OF AMERICAN UNIVERSITY PRESSES. From 1954 to 1972, the university printing plant, known as Orange Publishing Company, was merged with the Syracuse University Press under the administrative control of the director of the Press.

The publishing program of the Press is broad and varied, especially in the humanities and the social sciences. Among its active publications are: A CRITICAL BIBLIOGRAPHY OF FRENCH LITERATURE; PROCEDURAL ASPECTS OF INTERNATIONAL LAW; SAGAMORE ARMY MATERIALS RESEARCH CONFERENCE PROCEEDINGS; and the *Special Education and Rehabilitation Monograph, Syracuse Geographical* and *Syracuse Wood Science* series.

Syracuse has devoted particular attention to the publication of books relating to New York State and the Iroquois Indians. Books in the *New York State Studies Series* are scholarly works while *York State Books* are directed to a popular readership. In 1970 the New York State Council on the Arts cited the Press for its regional publishing program. Two Press books have received the Award of Merit from the American Association for State and Local History.

The Press also publishes the periodical *Symposium, A Quarterly Journal in Modern Foreign Literatures,* and it acts as distributor for books published by Union College, Schenectady, New York, the Adirondack Museum, and the American University of Beirut, Lebanon. The Press is governed by a board of directors and the imprint is controlled by a ten-member editorial committee.

TAB Books

Organized in 1964 at Summit, Pennsylvania. The firm acquired the titles of the Gernsback Library. It specializes in technical manuals for the electronics industries and hobbyists.

T.F.H. Publications, Inc.

Established in 1952 at Neptune City, New Jersey, as the book division of the magazine, *Tropical Fish Hobbyist*. Specializes in books on pets, and gardening. All-Pets Books, Inc., is a subsidiary.

Taplinger Publishing Company, Inc.

Established in New York City by Richard J. Taplinger in 1955. Its first title was THE BRONZE CHRIST by Yoshiro Nagayo.

The firm has been long active in the areas of natural history, conservation, Asian studies, and paranormal studies. Its successful titles in these areas include *The Many Worlds of Wildlife Series* by Richard Perry; OWLS: THEIR NATURAL AND UNNATURAL HISTORY by John Sparks and Tony Soper; and LINDA GOODMAN'S SUN SIGNS by Linda Goodman.

Taplinger also distributes books published by Carnegie Endowment for International Peace, Columbia Books, Gamut Press, Garrett Publications, McKnight Publishing Company, and Topaz Books.

J.P. Tarcher, Inc.

Based in Los Angeles, California, originally a packaging operation established by Jeremy P. Tarcher. Since 1972 has been publishing nonfiction under its own imprint.

Taylor Publishing Company

Established in 1939 at Dallas, Texas, by J.W. Taylor, Jr. The company specializes in elementary and secondary textbooks. Dukane Press, Inc. is a subsidiary.

Teachers College Press

Founded in 1904 in New York City, it was then known as the Bureau of Publications, its current name being adopted in 1965. The Bureau was in part a service organization that catered to the internal needs of the college—it published syllabi and other course materials for faculty and students. In 1905 it began a much wider venture with the publication of the first volume of TEACHERS COLLEGE CONTRIBUTIONS TO EDUCATION, a series that eventually extended to nine hundred and seventy-four volumes. The CONTRIBUTIONS were derived in part from the doctoral dissertations of students and partly from the ongoing research and theoretical work of faculty members. The series ended in 1951.

Throughout his tenure as Dean of Teachers College, James Earl Russell served as directing editor of the Bureau of Publications. During his directorship Edward L. Thorndike's pioneering EDUCATIONAL PSYCHOLOGY (1913) helped to establish publication standards of high quality and importance in the field of educational studies. Later directors of the Bureau and the Press included Professor C.J. Tidwell, Professor Max R. Brunstetter, Hamden L. Forkner, Jr., Richard de Haan, John Calam, and the present director, Robert Bletter.

The Press also initiated the publication of nationally used reading tests originally developed by Arthur I. Gates and now supervised by Walter H. MacGinitie, known as the *Gates-MacGinitie Reading Tests*. These tests and other reading practice materials, such as the *Gates-Peardon Reading Exercise*s and the *McCall-Crabbs Standard Test Lessons in Reading* represent an important part of the sales volume of the Press. Current publishing activity of the Press covers the whole spectrum of scholarly and professional materials in education.

Technomic Publishing Company, Inc.

Established in 1965 at Westport, Connecticut, the company issues scientific and technical books.

Templegate Publishers

A small trade publisher, established in 1947 at Springfield, Illinois.

Temple University Press

Founded in 1969 at Philadelphia, Pennsylvania, by Maurice English under a directive from the university's president Paul R. Anderson. The first book under the Temple imprint appeared in 1970: MARXISM AND RADICAL RELIGION, edited by John C. Raines and Thomas Dean.

The programs of the Press include series in the fields of contemporary religious thought, comparative literature, and urban studies. In June, 1973 the Press published ACUPUNCTURE THERAPY, the first practical manual for doctors on acupuncture as it is currently practiced in China. This had a second impression in November, 1973.

The Press also issues *The Journal of Ecumenical Studies,* and it has a contractual arrangement to publish and distribute books for the University of Delaware Press.

Texas A. & M. University Press

Established in 1974 to publish general books with emphasis on Texas and the Southwest. Frank H. Wardlaw, former director of University of Texas Press, was appointed director.

Texian Press

Established in 1961 at Waco, Texas, the company specializes in authentic Texas history.

Theatre Arts Books

Established in 1948 at New York City by Robert M. MacGregor when he took over the book publishing department of *Theatre Arts Monthly.*

At that time it had six books in print, including AN ACTOR PREPARES by Constantin Stanislavski and ACTING: THE FIRST SIX LESSONS by Richard Boleslavsky. Theatre Arts later branched out into other fields, such as costume, stage design, and ballet. It has currently over one hundred and thirty books in print. George Zournas is a partner and assistant director of the firm.

Theosophical Publishing House

Located at Wheaton, Illinois, the company has British and Indian branches. It publishes books on theosophy, Eastern mysticism and world religions under the imprint of Quest Books.

The Third Press

Established in 1969 in New York City by Joseph O. Okpaku, the Press is the first major Black-owned publishing house in the United States. Nigerian-born Okpaku is also the editor of the *Journal of the New African Literature and the Arts,* which he had started while still a graduate student at Stanford University. The first Third Press title was VERDICT!: THE EXCLUSIVE PICTURE STORY OF THE TRIAL OF THE CHICAGO 8, with drawings by Verna Sadock and text by Okpaku.

The roster of authors of the Press includes the Senghalese poet-president, Leopold Senghor, the Nigerian novelist, Chinua Achebe, David Ben-Gurion, and film director Roman Polanski. A juvenile imprint, Odarkai Books, has issued THIRD WORLD VOICES FOR CHILDREN, edited by Robert E. McDowell and Edward Lavitt, and GLOWCHILD AND OTHER POEMS by Ruby Dee. In 1972 the Press launched two new series: one, books on literary criticism starting with JAMES BALDWIN: A CRITICAL STUDY by Stanley Macebuh; and the other, pictorial histories, of which A PICTORIAL HISTORY OF THE JEWISH PEOPLE was the first title.

Charles C. Thomas, Publisher

Publisher of textbooks on medicine, law, police science, and technical subjects. Located at Springfield, Illinois.

Thomas Law Book Company, Inc.

Founded in 1885 in St. Louis, Missouri, as the F.H. Thomas Law Book Company, Inc., by F.H. Thomas, J.G. Lodge, and A.M. Thomas. The company was the successor to an earlier partnership known as Soule, Wentworth and Thomas. In 1920 the firm name was changed to Thomas Law Book Company, Inc.

Thomas Publishing Company

Established in 1890 in Philadelphia, Pennsylvania, by H. Mark Thomas to publish directories. The firm was incorporated in 1898 and later moved to New York City. The firm publishes the THOMAS REGISTER OF AMERICAN MANUFACTURERS and other directories and industrial trade publications.

Thor Publishing Company

Located at Ventura, California, the company issues books dealing with sports, recreation, and physical education in both hard and softcover editions. It specializes in books on judo, karate, jiujitsu and related books for self-defense.

Time Incorporated Book Clubs

Organized in 1969 when Time Inc. of New York City acquired the Book Find Club and the Seven Arts Society from George Braziller. The Book Find Club had been established before World War II and the Seven Arts Society shortly after it. The Seven Arts Society has been developed to become a wide-ranging club concerned with all the arts and now offers not only books but sculpture reproductions, records, graphics, and related items. The Book Find Club's parameters have been similarly expanded to include, along with scholarly books, general trade titles, both fiction and nonfiction.

In 1971, Time Inc., established a Fortune Book Club for businessmen, and a Sports Illustrated Book Club for lovers of the active life. The Fortune Book Club assumes that its management-level audience has wide-ranging interests in economics, politics and public affairs, as well as business and finance. The Sports Illustrated Book Club is largely devoted to books on spectator sports, but it also offers some instructional books and books on participant sports.

In early 1974 management and operation of Fortune Book Club and Sports Illustrated Book Club were turned over to Book-of-the-Month Club, while Book Find Club was discontinued.

TIME-LIFE Books

Established in 1961 in New York City as a division of Time Inc. Joan D. Manley is the current publisher of the division, which originally grew out of the success of the large pictorial books Time Inc. published in the 1950s and adapted from LIFE magazine's feature articles (e.g. LIFE PICTORIAL HISTORY OF WORLD WAR II (1950); THE WORLD WE LIVE IN (1955); THE WORLD'S GREAT RELIGIONS (1957).

Starting with the thirty-four-volume *LIFE WORLD LIBRARY* in September, 1960, TIME-LIFE Books has concentrated primarily on series publishing of books with original texts, photographic and art work. Each book is written by a recognized author/authority for a specific area, as for example: Sir Maurice Bowra, Classical Greece; Roger Tory Peterson, The Birds; and Elizabeth Bishop, Brazil.

Among the TIME-LIFE Books series are *TIME-LIFE Library of Art*, 27 volumes; *LIFE Science Library*, 26 volumes; *LIFE Nature Library*, 25 volumes; *Great Ages of Man*, 21 volumes; *Foods of the World*, 27 volumes; *LIFE Library of Photography*, 17 volumes; and *American Wilderness* and *The Old West*, each scheduled to contain at least 20 volumes.

Although it publishes only twenty to thirty new titles each year, TIME-LIFE Books is among the ten largest book publishers in the United States. TIME-LIFE Books are sold by mail order and since 1968 they have also been sold through retail stores.

In September, 1973 TIME-LIFE Books had printed and sold eight hundred thousand copies of a $20.00 volume, THE BEST OF LIFE, prior to the book's official publication date. According to Eliot Fremont-Smith, book editor of *New York* magazine, this made "publishing history . . . (with) gross receipts on the order of $12 million . . . for a single hardcover venture, nothing like this has been seen before."

The Times Mirror Company

See, Harry N. Abrams, Inc.; Matthew Bender & Company, Inc.; Denoyer-Geppert Company; C.V. Mosby Company; New American Library, Inc.; The Southwestern Company; World Publishing Company; Year Book Medical Publishers, Inc.

Other subsidiaries owned by The Times Mirror Company include Fuller & Dees Marketing Group, Inc. and Popular Science Publishing Company, Inc.

The Touchstone Press

Established in 1965 at Beaverton, Oregon. Specializes in trail guide and field identification guide books.

Touchstone Publishing Company

Established in 1969 at Louisville, Kentucky. Issues a small nonfiction list.

Transaction Books

Established in 1969 at New Brunswick, New Jersey, as a division of Transaction, Inc., and issues text and reference books, mainly in the social sciences.

Transatlantic Arts, Inc.

Established in 1933 at Levittown, New York, the company is a distributor of reference, textbooks, and paperbacks.

Trend House

Established in 1958 at Tampa, Florida, as a division of Trend Publications, Inc., to publish a limited list of general nonfiction books.

Trident Press

See, Simon & Schuster, Inc.

Troubador Press, Inc.

Organized in 1956 at San Francisco, California. Publishes a small list of craft, hobbies, and how-to books.

Tudor Publishing Company

Founded in 1933 by Max Salop in New York City as an adjunct to his remainder book business, Harlem Book Company. In the early years Tudor published only reprints. In 1939 Salop purchased The Penn Publishing Company, a Philadelphia, Pennsylvania, firm that published mainly juveniles. About this time Tudor began to publish original books, some of them under the Penn imprint.

When Salop died in 1947 the business was sold to Sydney Feldman and Norman Blaustein, both of whom had worked for the firm for many years. Feldman was company president from 1947 to 1969. In 1968 the company was acquired by Computer Applications. When Computer Applications went into receivership in 1970, Tudor, along with Harlem Book Company and the Paris, France, firm of XXe Siècle, an art publisher, was sold back to Norman Blaustein and Leon Amiel. The company was then incorporated as part of Wm. Penn Publishing Corporation with Amiel as the president.

Tudor has come to specialize in art and design books, in which area it publishes a number of series: *Practical Art and Design Series, Little Art Library, Great Painters,* and *Twentieth Century Art-Homage Series.* Tudor's outstanding art titles include: THE COMPLETE AIRBRUSH BOOK by S. Ralph Maurello; PERSPECTIVE DRAWING HANDBOOK by Joseph D'Amelio; HANDBOOK OF DECORATIVE DESIGN AND ORNAMENT by Mary Jean Alexander; JOAN MIRO: LITHOGRAPHS by Michel Leiris and Fernand Mourlot; FOLKLORE AND SYMBOLISM OF FLOWERS, PLANTS, TREES by Ernst and Johanna Lehner. The firm also publishes the art journal, *XXe Siecle-XXth Century Art.* Among its international co-productions are the *World of . . .* series and *Most Beautiful Animals* series with Minerva, and art dictionaries with Hazan.

The Harlem Book Company distributes the *Cameo Series, World Mythology Series,* and *Illustrated Juvenile Classics* for Hamlyn of London, England.

Tudor Publishing Company is now also issuing important definitive works on contemporary artists, such as the *Miro Catalogue Raisonne of Graphics* and several books on the various aspects of Chagall's work, including THE MONUMENTAL WORKS OF MARC CHAGALL, edited by G. di San Lazzaro, THE BIBLICAL MESSAGE by Marc Chagall, THE STAINED-GLASS WINDOWS OF MARC CHAGALL, 1957-1970 by Robert Marteau.

Charles E. Tuttle Publishing Company

Established in 1832 at Rutland, Vermont, as the George A. Tuttle Company by George Albert Tuttle. Beginning as a printing firm, it developed into a publishing house. When George A. Tuttle retired in 1872 his business was continued by his sons and called The Tuttle Company. Incorporated in 1885, the company was headed until 1893 by Harley C. Tuttle. After Harley's death control of the company passed to Egbert C. Tuttle under whom the firm, by then known

as The Tuttle Publishing Company, began to specialize in genealogies and town histories.

In 1935 the Charles E. Tuttle Company was established by Charles E. Tuttle, a grandson of George Albert. An authority on Vermontiana, Charles Tuttle developed the firm as a major antiquarian book firm. Upon his death in 1943 his son, Charles E. Tuttle, Jr., inherited the business. As an army captain in World War II and later in the Civil Information and Education Section of United States General Headquarters, Tokyo, Japan, Charles, Jr. had worked on important research projects linked to the Japanese news media. This background was to determine the new direction of the company. Tuttle opened the Tokyo branch of his firm in 1948.

The company now specializes in books on Japan and the Orient, called appropriately Books to Span the East and West. In 1971 a paperback line called Tut Books was launched.

In addition to publishing, Tuttle operates the largest literary agency in Japan, acts as an importer and exporter of books, sponsors reprints, sells American encyclopedias, and appraises literary properties.

Twayne Publishers, Inc.

Organized in 1948 in New York City by Jacob Steinberg. As a former teacher of Chinese at Columbia University, Steinberg's initial interest was in undertaking the publication of Chinese classics in translation. The title Twayne, a play on Rudyard Kipling's 'twain,' was an expression of Steinberg's desire to promote the meeting of East and West. Twayne's first offering was the *Twayne Library of Modern Poetry,* which eventually included ten volumes, edited by John Ciardi. A significant feature of this series was the recognition given to major Black poets such as Claude McKay and Melvin B. Tolson. Another early publication that gained recognition was SEX, LITERATURE AND CENSORSHIP by D.H. Lawrence.

In 1961 Twayne launched the first of the numerous series with which the imprint has become identified: *Twayne's United States Authors Series,* edited by Sylvia E. Bowman of Indiana University. This series has grown to become one of the largest projects in American literary history, with over two hundred and twenty titles now in print. Encouraged by the success of this first series, the company launched *Twayne's English Authors Series* in 1964 and *Twayne's World Authors Series* in 1966. The former includes over one hundred and sixty titles and the latter nearly three hundred.

In a logical development, Twayne began to issue the *Introductions to World Literature Series,* edited by Jacob Steinberg, in 1966, providing anthologies of readings in modern Bulgarian, Greek, Polish, Rumanian, Spanish and Yugoslav literature. In the following year Twayne also announced the *Library of Scandinavian Literature,* jointly published with the American-Scandinavian Foundation, and, in 1972, the *Library of Netherlandic Literature,* published in cooperation with the Foundation for the Promotion of the Translation of Dutch Literary Works of Amsterdam, Holland. The series concept was further expanded with four more open-end programs in related fields: *Twayne's Rulers and Statesmen of the World,* edited by H.L. Trefousse; *The Immigrant Heritage of America Series,* edited by Cecyle S. Neidle; *The National Histories Series,* edited by Sherman D. Spector; and *The Great Educators Series,* edited by Samuel Smith. From Simon and Schuster's Washington Square Press, Twayne acquired the *Great American Thinkers Series.* This is now being continued under the title *Great Thinkers Series,* edited by Thomas S. Knight and Arthur W. Brown.

Twayne also publishes a number of individual volumes which are of interest to the general scholarly reader.

In January of 1973 Twayne merged with G.K. Hall & Co. of Boston, Massachusetts. Although a New York office and warehouse are still maintained, all editorial, production, and sales activities have been transferred to Boston.

Tyndale House Publishers

Founded in 1962 at Wheaton, Illinois, by the noted Christian missionary, Kenneth N. Taylor. The firm specializes in Bibles and inspirational books. TYNDALE'S LIVING BIBLE is one of the best-selling Bibles in the United States.

Frederick Ungar Publishing Co., Inc.

Founded in 1941 by Frederick Ungar, a native of Vienna, Austria, who had co-founded the Phaidon Verlag (now the Phaidon Press, London, England) and then established Saturn Verlag. He started in New York City with a number of his titles that had been steady sellers in Europe, among which were RIRE ET APPRENDRE and LACHEN UND LERNEN. During World War II Ungar issued books in German and English as well as a number of reprints of German technical books under license from the Alien Property Custodian. New titles were added with emphasis on translations from the German, language texts, and scholarly books, including bilingual dictionaries.

In 1945 Ungar purchased Stephen Daye Press, a firm that published regional and general books. This continues to be a second imprint, though it has been less actively used in recent years. During the 1950s much of the Ungar list consisted of reprints of scholarly titles, especially in a series called *American Classics.* By the 1960s, however, a major shift was made to original publishing in the fields of literature, including literary criticism, and reference books in literature.

Among the reference works the ENCYCLOPEDIA OF WORLD LITERATURE IN THE 20TH CENTURY and THE LITERATURES OF THE WORLD IN ENGLISH TRANSLATION: A BIBLIOGRAPHY (a multi-volume series) are important contributions. *A Library of Literary Criticism* comprises volumes on modern American, British, German, Slavic, and Romance literatures. Other successful series have been *Milestones of Thought, Modern Literature Monographs,* and *World Dramatists.* Translations in the field of the humanities have been expanded to include French, Spanish, and other languages. Paperbacks were also launched in selected titles (about two hundred), and a part of the Ungar list continues to be devoted to mathematics, engineering, geodesy, and astronomy, including several standard works.

Unicorn Press, Inc.

Established in 1966 at Santa Barbara, California. Specializes in theatre books and literature.

Union of American Hebrew Congregations

Founded in 1873 at New York City. Publishes Jewish religious books, textbooks, histories, biographies, and teaching aids.

United Church Press

The Publication Division of the United Church of Christ founded in Philadelphia, Pennsylvania, through a merger of the Pilgrim Press and the Christian Education Press.

The Pilgrim Press had been founded in 1832 in Boston, Massachusetts, as the Congregational Sunday-School and Publishing Society. In 1868 it merged with the Congregational Board of Publication (established in 1829 as the Doctrinal Tract and Book Society) under the name of The Congregational Sabbath-School and Publishing Society. In 1919 this name was shortened to Congregational Publishing Society, and Pilgrim Press was adopted as its trade imprint.

The Christian Education Press was founded in 1828 in Chambersburg, Pennsylvania, as the Board of Christian Education and Publication by the General Synod of the Evangelical and Reformed Church. From 1849 to 1864 it was under private ownership. It was resumed under the General Synod's direction in Philadelphia, Pennsylvania. From 1899 to 1940 it published books under the trade imprint of Heidelberg Press and since 1940 under the imprint of Christian Education Press.

United Educators, Inc.

Established in 1931 at Lake Bluff, Illinois. Specialize in encyclopedias and subscription books, one of which is the AMERICAN EDUCATOR ENCYCLOPEDIA.

United States Naval Institute

Founded in 1873 at Annapolis, Maryland, by a group of naval officers for discussion of professional and scientific subjects. The constitution also directed that "whenever the papers read and the record of discussions growing out of them shall accumulate in quantities sufficient . . . they shall be prepared for issue in pamphlet form." These pamphlets became the *United States Naval Institute Proceedings. The Proceedings* became a quarterly in 1879, a bimonthly in 1914, and a monthly in 1917.

The Institute entered the book publishing field in 1899 with THE LOG OF THE GLOUCESTER, the adventures of an armed yacht in the war with Spain in 1898. The first edition of THE BLUEJACKETS' MANUAL, a guide for enlisted men of the U.S. Navy, appeared in 1902. This title is now in its nineteenth edition. Over the years other guidebooks were written and published for the maritime services, among them being the NAVAL OFFICER'S GUIDE, the MARINE OFFICER'S GUIDE, the COAST-GUARDSMAN'S MANUAL, HANDBOOK FOR MARINE NCOs, and NAVAL AVIATION GUIDE.

The Institute's backlist of over two hundred titles deals with all aspects of ship handling, engineering, electronics, international law, oceanography, meteorology, and the fundamentals of naval science. Textbooks constitute a major part of the list, headed by the venerable Dutton's NAVIGATION AND PILOTING. Other books published by the Institute include reference books, such as SERVICE ETIQUETTE, and SHIPS AND AIRCRAFT OF THE U.S. FLEET, as well as naval biographies and histories.

In 1962 the Institute published the first NAVAL REVIEW, an annual volume of thoughtful essays and articles on world sea power, which is now offered as a special May issue of the *Proceedings*. The Institute also publishes reproductions of fine nautical paintings and conducts an oral history program. The imprint is controlled by a six-member board of directors, all serving officers of the U.S. Navy, Marine Corps, and Coast Guard.

Universal Publishing and Distributing Corporation

Established in New York City in 1947 by Arnold E. Abramson as a magazine publishing house. The purpose of the company was to explore the possibilities of what was then known as hobby publishing, which has since evolved as special-interest publishing. The initial name of the company was United Publishers. The first title over this imprint was a collection of cartoons from the Army newspaper service called *The Wolf* by Leonard Sansone. It was a considerable success. The first magazine issued was *Smart Knitting,* followed by *Smart Sewing* and *Smart Crochet.*

By 1950 the business was beginning to have growing pains and could not be operated on a part-time basis by Abramson, who was still holding down the job of executive vice president with Farrell Publishing Corporation. Abramson resigned from Farrell to take over the direction of United Publishers, which had been incorporated in 1947, and the name of the company was changed to Universal Publishing and Distributing Corporation.

In 1950 Universal launched its first major magazine, *Family Handyman.* Late in 1959 it started *Golf* magazine and *Ski Life* magazine. Eventually the company bought *Ski* magazine and merged its own *Ski Life* with it. In 1972 both *Golf* and *Ski* were sold to the Times Mirror Group. In recent years the company has also acquired the Science Fiction Group of magazines made up of *Galaxy* and *If.*

In mid-1950 Universal moved into the paperback book field with non-rack-sized paperbacks known as *Universal Giants.* Eventually, this led to the establishment of the Universal Award Book Corporation as a subsidiary paperback imprint. Award now publishes approximately 140-150 books a year specializing in original series and special-interest titles. Its series include *Nick Carter, Secret Mission, The Liquidator, Hawk, Donovan's Devils, Combat, McCloud, Hec Ramsey, Adam 12,* and *Apes.* In addition, Award publishes large segments of the John Creasey series and the Victor Canning books.

In 1961 the company became publicly owned and in 1969-70 it acquired Tandem Books Ltd., a small British paperback house. This subsidiary, now known as Universal-Tandem Publishing Company Ltd., publishes and distributes Award books in the United Kingdom.

Universal owned two subsidiary educational paperback imprints. One, known as Ramapo House, was sold to Random House in 1973; the other, Vocational Guidance Manuals, was sold to a subsidiary of the Louisville, Kentucky, *Courier-Journal* in 1974.

Universe Books

Established in 1956 at New York City. Specializes in social and cultural history, and international affairs.

The University of Alabama Press

Founded in 1945 at University, Alabama, by president Raymond R. Paty with James B. McMillan as acting director. Its first publication was NEW HORIZONS IN PUBLIC ADMINISTRATION, a symposium of papers. For seventeen years, from 1945 to 1962, McMillan built the Press from its beginning in one room to a respectable position among university presses, with a strong backlist including one hundred case studies of the *Inter-American Case Program* (since sold to Bobbs-Merrill), *The Alabama Review,* a quarterly journal of Alabama history, and *The Publications of The American Dialect Society.*

In 1963 Ernest A. Seemann was appointed director of the Press. Seemann continued to concentrate on political science, public administration, and regional publishing, offering such titles as ALABAMA BIRDS by Thomas A. Imhof and ALABAMA CONFEDERATE READER by Malcolm C. McMillan. Seemann also developed a strong series in philology and linguistics. When Seemann resigned in 1967, Morgan L. Walters was named as his successor.

Walters, who came to the Press after twenty years in commercial publishing, continued to strengthen the list of the Press in public administration, political science, and regional studies, but broadened the range of the Press to include philosophy and religion, American and European history, bibliography, literary criticism, biography (including a monumental biography of Moses Mendelssohn by Alexander Altmann), and a series of Judaic studies. The Press has a fairly ambitious program of translations in those fields and continues to build its titles of regional and Alabaman interest, examples being ATLAS OF ALABAMA, HISTORICAL ATLAS OF ALABAMA, and WILD FLOWERS OF ALABAMA. In addition to *The Alabama Review* and the *Publications of the American Dialect Society* the Press also publishes a Spanish language journal, *Revista de Estudios Hispánicos.*

Books of the Alabama Press have received numerous awards from the Association of State and Local History and the Southern Book Competition.

Illustrations — American Juvenile Primer, 1838

241

The University of Arizona Press

Founded at Tucson, Arizona, in 1959 under the former university president Richard A. Harvill. Robert Plant Armstrong was the first director of the Press and Jack L. Cross the second. In 1965 Marshall Townsend was brought from the University of Chicago Press (previously having directed Iowa State University Press for fifteen years) to be the director and under him the Press has become a major publisher, helping to fulfill, in his words, "the university's prime function of sharing knowledge." The publishing programs of the Press include the monographs and papers of the Association of Asian Studies, the *Anthropological Papers of the University of Arizona,* the series of the Institute of Government Research, and the historical journal, *Arizona and the West.*

In 1972 the Press became the official publisher for the Viking Fund Series in Anthropology, thus underlining its reputation in the fields of anthropology, arid lands studies, Indian and Southwestern history, and Far Eastern studies. Four area bibliographies and additional individual titles have been published in the *Far Eastern Studies Series,* in addition to the Asian Association monographs. Certain Press titles have become classics in their field: Edward H. Spicer's CYCLES OF CONQUEST; Clara Lee Tanner's SOUTHWEST INDIAN CRAFT ARTS and SOUTHWEST INDIAN PAINTING; Lyman Benson's THE CACTI OF ARIZONA; and Charles O. Hucker's THE TRADITIONAL CHINESE STATE IN MING TIMES.

University of California Press

Founded at Berkeley, California, in 1893 when the Regents of the University of California appropriated $1,000.00 for the publication of research papers, although the first Committee on Publications (afterwards known as the Editorial Committee of the Academic Senate) was appointed in 1885. The first monographs to bear the imprint, one in education and one in geology, were published in 1893. The first manager of the Press, Albert Allen, was primarily a copy editor and a sales manager. During the next forty years more than fifty-five series were established to accommodate almost every department of the university. The Editorial Committee determined policy and controlled the imprint.

In 1932, dissatisfied faculty members persuaded President R.G. Sproul to appoint a San Francisco fine printer, Samuel T. Farquhar, to replace Joseph Flinn, who had been superintendent of the university's printing office for forty-five years. In the same year Farquhar was also appointed manager of the Press. Following this reorganization the printing and publishing departments were consolidated and a sales office was established. The pattern of publication in the succeeding years was complicated by problems of funding, by the national depression, by World War II, and by a local power struggle. Only in the late 1940s did the situation begin to reverse itself; even then the number of books published could hardly be considered impressive, as few as six, rarely more than twenty in a year. But they were varied in content and were noted for fine printing.

After the death of Farquhar in 1949, August Frugé was appointed to be the new manager of the Press with the title of director. The printing and publishing departments were separated once again and the Press turned its energies toward the book program and began the development of a professional publishing organization and list. Since 1950 the University of California Press has become one of the larger publishing houses in the English-speaking world, issuing about one hundred and fifty books each year.

There are two regular paperback series: Cal Paperbacks (trade) and Campus Books (text) as well as a series of *California Natural History Guides.* The number of monograph series has been greatly reduced but each year still sees the appearance of about forty titles in several of the remaining series. There are nine scholarly journals, including two of fairly wide interest, *Asian Survey* and *Film Quarterly.* The publishing program includes many areas of special interest: Asian studies, African studies, classical literature and history, film history and criticism, botany, and others. The list also includes many items of translated poetry and some translated fiction.

The Press is organized on the sponsoring editor system with parallel editorial offices in Berkeley and Los Angeles. The imprint is still controlled by the Editorial Committee of the Academic Senate.

Books of the Press are warehoused in Richmond, California, and in New York City. Sales offices are maintained in Berkeley, California, and in New York City. A subsidiary company, University of California Press Ltd., stocks books in London, England, and sells in Great Britain, Africa, and throughout the continent of Europe.

The University of Chicago Press

Founded at Chicago, Illinois, in 1891 by President William Rainey Harper "not as an incident, an attachment, but . . . as an organic part" of his new university. Its publishing activities did not begin until D.C. Heath joined the university in organizing the Press as a private corporation in 1892. In 1894 this corporation was dissolved and the university resumed sole ownership of the Press. By this time the fledgling house had issued five books of which John Dewey's THE SCHOOL AND SOCIETY is still in print. It had also launched or taken over five journals of which three survive: the *Journal of Political Economy,* the *Journal of Near Eastern Studies,* and the *Journal of Geology.* By 1906 the number of journals published by the Press had grown to fourteen and eight new monograph series had been initiated, ranging from *Studies in Classical Philology* to *Physiological Archives.*

The appointment of Newman Miller as director of the Press in 1900 gave it the advantage of a stable administration that lasted for nineteen years. Miller's tenure was marked by the first great venture of the Press into large-scale book publishing: the series called the DECENNIAL PUBLICATIONS, in twenty-eight volumes, to celebrate the university's first ten years. The DECENNIAL PUBLICATIONS also led to the organization of an efficient proofreading and copyediting section and from this section came the first typewritten sheets of rules for typographical accuracy, consistency and style, that developed into the well-known book, A MANUAL OF STYLE, which was first published in 1906.

When Miller died in 1919 the university trustees decided on a major reorganization. The bookstore was separated from the Press and the publication and manufacturing departments were made autonomous, with Donald P. Bean as manager of the publication department. At the same time the Press was given a new governing body called the Board of University Publications. Through the 1920s and 1930s the publication department operated in the black and even accumulated a small reserve. It was also a period of big projects, proliferating series, and experimental ventures. Edgar Goodspeed's THE NEW TESTAMENT: AN AMERICAN TRANSLATION, which was later combined with J.J. Powis Smith's translation of the Old Testament, THE COMPLETE BIBLE: AN AMERICAN TRANSLATION, was one of the all-time bestsellers. A DICTIONARY OF AMERICAN ENGLISH ON HISTORICAL PRINCIPLES won for the Press the Carey-Thomas Award for Creative Publishing.

To mark Geoffrey Chaucer's six hundredth anniversary, the Press published THE CANTERBURY TALES in eight volumes, edited by John M. Manly and Edith Rickert. This set is still considered a model of textual criticism and editing.

In 1926-27, with a five-year grant of $100,000.-00 for the publication of non-commercial books from the Laura Spelman Rockefeller Memorial Foundation, old series took on new life and new ones multiplied. *The University of Chicago Science Series* was strengthened with titles by two Nobel Prize winners: Albert A. Michelson's STUDIES IN OPTICS and Werner Heisenberg's PHYSICAL PRINCIPLES OF THE QUANTUM THEORY. Typical of the new series were *Studies in Public Administration* initiated in 1934 and the *University of Chicago Sociological Series* launched in 1926, which included THE NEGRO FAMILY IN THE UNITED STATES by E. Franklin Frazier, THE PROFESSIONAL THIEF by Edwin H. Sutherland, THE GANG by Frederic M. Thrasher, and THE GHETTO by Louis Wirth. Equally productive were the four series of the Oriental Institute established by James H. Breasted in 1919: *Oriental Institute Publications, Studies in Ancient Oriental Civilizations, Oriental Institute Communications,* and *Assyriol-*

ogical Studies. But the most profitable Press books during this period proved to be the *New Plan* textbooks in the physical and biological sciences.

Donald Bean resigned in 1940 and in 1944 Joseph A. Brandt was invited to take full charge of the Press with the title of director. Although Brandt remained as director for only eighteen months, he turned the list in the direction of trade books, one of which, THE ROAD TO SERFDOM by Friedrich A. Hayek, made its own way onto the national bestseller lists. Brandt's successor in the directorship was William T. Couch and he did much to strengthen the Press list in philosophy and public policy. His tenure saw the publication of THE COMPLETE GREEK TRAGEDIES; A DICTIONARY OF AMERICANISMS by Mitford M. Mathews; the initial volume of Paul Tillich's SYSTEMATIC THEOLOGY; Ernst Cassirer's THE RENAISSANCE PHILOSOPHY OF MAN; and THE CASE OF GENERAL YAMASHITA, A. Frank Reel's controversial book; to say nothing of the UNIVERSITY OF CHICAGO SPANISH-ENGLISH DICTIONARY, compiled and edited by Carlos Castillo and Otto F. Bond (1948), one of the all-time best-selling paperbacks.

When Couch's career at Chicago was cut short in 1951 by disagreements with the university's administration, Rollin D. Hemens became acting director for a year. In 1954 Roger W. Shugg was appointed director. In 1956, only a few months after Cornell University Press led the way, Chicago launched its Phoenix paperbacks. The Press also initiated some major new series: *Chicago History of American Civilization,* edited by Daniel J. Boorstin; *Folktales of the World,* edited by Richard M. Dorson; *Chicago in Fiction,* edited by Saul Bellow; *Patterns of Literary Criticism,* published jointly with the University of Toronto Press; *Monuments of Renaissance Music,* edited by Edward E. Lowinsky; the *Papers of James Madison;* and *The Collected Papers of Enrico Fermi.*

In 1967 when Roger Shugg retired, Morris Philipson became his successor. The Press serves as publisher to the Rice University, Washington University in St. Louis, Missouri, the Newberry Library, and the American Bar Foundation.

University of Georgia Press

Founded in 1938, at Athens, Georgia, for the stated purpose of "publishing scholarly books and monographs." The Press functions as a department of the university and the imprint is controlled by a twelve-member faculty committee appointed by the university president. Ralph Stephens is the director.

The Press has several series in progress: a *Paperback Monograph* series; *Wormsloe Foundation Publications,* comprising source materials and studies in Colonial history; *Mercer University Lamar Lecture Series in Southern Literature,* and *History,* published annually; *University of Georgia Anthropology Series; Contemporary Poetry;* the *Chaucer Library,* in collaboration with the Chaucer Library Committee of the Modern Language Association; and *South Atlantic Modern Language Association Annual Award Books.*

The University of Illinois Press

Founded at Urbana, Illinois, in 1918 with H.E. Cunningham as its first director, although the imprint had appeared on a few scattered titles as early as the first decade of the century. The early years were characterized by publication of paperbound monograph series in language and literature, the biological, social and medical sciences, and one quarterly, *The Journal of English and Germanic Philology.* A facsimile edition of John Milton's writings, a series of Shakespearean studies, Scandinavian studies, classics, and literary criticism, were the more notable hardbound titles that were issued.

Expansion of the publishing program and the present organization of the Press began to take shape in 1948, when Wilbur Schramm was made director (1948-1952) and Miodrag Muntyan executive editor (director since 1952). Publishing at the rate of seventy-five titles annually, the Press now has a backlist of over six hundred titles, five series of monographs, and six quarterly journals including the *American Journal of Psychology.* Its Illini Books paperback series, begun in 1962, consists of reprints from its own backlist, led by GRIERSON'S RAID by D.A. Brown and Werner von Braun's THE MARS PROJECT.

A series begun in 1952 on *Contemporary American Painting* was published annually until 1957 and biennially since then. Current new series include a projected fifteen-volume edition of THE BOOKER T. WASHINGTON PAPERS edited by Louis R. Harlan, two volumes of which were published in 1972, and a series on *Music in American Life.*

In 1958 and 1959 the Press began experimental editions of two works which were to have major impact on teaching, testing, and remediation programs: one, THE ILLINOIS TEST OF PSYCHOLINGUISTIC ABILITIES (ITPA) by Samuel A. Kirk and James J. McCarthy, and two, UICSM HIGH SCHOOL MATHEMATICS by Max Beberman and Herbert E. Vaughn. The Press also has a strong communications list in such titles as MATHEMATICAL THEORY OF COMMUNICATION by Claude E. Shannon and Warren Weaver; MASS COMMUNICATIONS by Wilbur Schramm, and PROCESS AND EFFECTS OF MASS COMMUNICATIONS by Wilbur Schramm and Donald F. Roberts; FOUR THEORIES OF THE PRESS by Frederick Siebert, Theodore Peterson and Wilbur Schramm; and MAGAZINES IN THE TWENTIETH CENTURY by Theodore Peterson. Another major project is *Cross Cultural Universals of Affective Meaning* by Charles E. Osgood, William H. May and Murray S. Miron, a cross-cultural study and comparison of twenty-six languages, which has been in process for ten years.

The subject range of the Press list is suggested by its bestselling titles: SCIENCE IN THE BRITISH COLONIES OF NORTH AMERICA by Raymond Stearns, which won a National Book Award in 1970; ECOLOGY OF NORTH AMERICA by Victor Shelford; LIFE IN A MEXICAN VILLAGE by Oscar Lewis; GALVANIZED YANKEES by D.A. Brown; THE PEOPLE OF PUERTO RICO, THEORY OF CULTURE CHANGE and CONTEMPORARY CHANGE IN TRADITIONAL SOCIETIES by Julian Steward; SHORES OF AMERICA by Sherman Paul; SYMBOLIC USE OF POLITICS by Murray Edelman; URBAN LAND USE PLANNING by F. Stuart Chapin; and NATIONAL PARTY PLATFORMS by Kirk H. Porter and Donald Bruce Johnson, which is updated every four years.

The University of Iowa Press

Established in 1938 in Iowa City, Iowa, but only a few monograph series and an occasional book were published until 1969 when the Press launched a formal publishing program with THE MYXOMYCETES by George W. Martin and C.J. Alexopoulos.

Under the direction of John Simmons since 1969, the Press concentrates on the publication of results of original research with an emphasis on creative arts. The imprint is controlled by a twelve-member editorial board drawn from the university's faculty with two members from the student body.

The Press currently publishes three series: the *Iowa Translation Series* under the general editorship of Paul Engle; *Studies in the Psychology of Music* with Edwin Gordon as general editor; and the *Short Fiction Series.* Outstanding Iowa titles include: MODERN CHINESE POETRY, translated by Wai-lim Yip; THE BEACH UMBRELLA by Cyrus Colter, (1970 Iowa School of Letters Award for Short Fiction); OLD MORALS, SMALL CONTINENTS, DARKER TIMES by Philip F. O'Connor; and THE BURNING by Jack Cady. The latter two were recipients of Iowa's short fiction awards for 1971 and 1972.

The University of Massachusetts Press

Founded at Amherst, Massachusetts, in 1963 on the recommendations of a committee appointed by President John W. Lederle of the university under the chairmanship of Sidney Kaplan. Leone Barron Stein was chosen as the first director and a faculty committee was constituted to administer the imprint. The Press publications have been predominantly in history, political science, Black studies, philosophy and poetry. The poetry program is actively maintained by publication of the works of James Scully, Anne Halley, Don Junkins, Ishmael Reed, and Robert Francis. One of the first publications of the Press was a limited edition of A CHECKLIST OF THE PUBLICATIONS OF THOMAS BIRD MOSHER OF PORTLAND, MAINE, by Benton L. Hatch. The Press has also published FIGURES OF DEAD

MEN by Leonard Baskin and works illustrated by the artist.

Over the years the Press has in addition developed a translation program, making available in English the works of such writers as Kurt Tucholsky, Henri Desroche, Nicolás Guillén, André Chouraqui, Simone Weil, Jacques Derrida, and Aleksander Nikitenko.

Beginning in the summer of 1973, the Press initiated publication of the previously unpublished works of W.E.B. Du Bois, under the editorship of Herbert Aptheker.

In 1974 the Press issued the first volume in a series devoted to Massachusetts politics, co-sponsored by the Institute of Governmental Services.

University of Massachusetts Press titles, designed by Richard Hendel, have frequently been selected for inclusion in the AIGA Fifty Books of the Year and the AAUP Book Show.

University of Miami Press

Founded in 1947 at Coral Gables, Florida, on the recommendation of Hervey Allen, the novelist, who was on the university's board of trustees. Under the title of University Editor, the Press was first headed by Malcolm Ross, who directed it from 1947 to 1960. For the next three years Marjory Stoneman Douglas headed the Press. In 1967 Ernest A. Seemann of the distinguished German publishing family was appointed director.

The major publishing programs of the Press include a number of scholarly series: *University of Miami Linguistics, Studies in Tropical Oceanography,* and *Books of the Theatre,* the latter in cooperation with the American Theatre Association. Translation projects are also a distinctive feature of the Press activity. These include Gerhard Ritter's monumental study of German militarism, THE SWORD AND THE SCEPTER, in four volumes; classic linguistic works, such as Wilhelm von Humboldt's LINGUISTIC VARIABILITY AND INTELLECTUAL DEVELOPMENT, Antoine Meillet's GENERAL CHARACTERISTICS OF THE GERMANIC LANGUAGES, and Emile Benveniste's PROBLEMS IN GENERAL LINGUISTICS; also pioneering folklore studies by Paulo de Carvalho-Neto, and two

works by the existentialist philosopher, Karl Jaspers.

The University of Michigan Press

Founded at Ann Arbor, Michigan, in 1930 with Frank E. Robbins as the managing editor and later, from 1945 to 1954, as director. In 1954 the first full-time director was appointed, Fred D. Wieck, who broadened the publication program, set up a professional sales organization, and instituted royalty contracts for authors. He resigned in 1961 and the next year Glenn Gosling became director of the Press. In 1972 Gosling was appointed consultant to the Dean of the Graduate School and John Scott Mabon became acting director of the Press. Walter E. Sears is now director of the Press and Mabon is associate director.

In the early years the Press concentrated on series that had been previously published under the aegis of the University of Michigan. These were: *Humanistic History and Political Science; Papers of the Michigan Academy of Science, Arts, and Letters; Language and Literature; Linguistics; Contributions in Modern Philology.* Most of the series were jacketless and issued in drab, uniform bindings stamped with gold.

In the period of growth under Fred Wieck and Glenn Gosling many new broad-based series were initiated: *Ann Arbor Science Library; The Complete Prose Works of Matthew Arnold,* edited by R.H. Super; the *Thomas Spencer Jerome Lectures;* the *University of Michigan History of the Modern World; Middle English Dictionary; Michigan Mathematical Journal;* and *Ann Arbor Paperbacks.*

The Press now operates under the control of an executive committee and the imprint is controlled by an editorial committee of from six to eleven members appointed by the Executive Board of the Graduate School, with the director a member *ex officio.*

The University of Minnesota Press

Founded at Minneapolis, Minnesota, in 1925 as a department of the university. The Press began active operations two years later. The imprint is controlled by a University Press Committee, which includes the director of the Press. Margaret S. Harding, the founding director, served from 1927 until her retirement in 1953. Helen Clapesattle, the author of THE DOCTORS MAYO, was director from 1953 until 1957, when John Ervin, Jr. took over.

The Press publishes, in addition to scholarly works and books for course use at the college level, regional books concerned with Minnesota and the upper midwest, books of general interest nationally and internationally, and plays for the theater. One of the major projects of the Press is the series of *University of Minnesota Pamphlets on American Writers* initiated in 1959 and completed in 1972 with the publication of one hundred and three titles providing authoritative introductions to American writers. A continuing scholarly series published by the Press, in collaboration with the University of Minnesota Center for Philosophy of Science, is the *Minnesota Studies in the Philosophy of Science,* of which Herbert Feigl and Grover Maxwell are the general editors. The Press also publishes tests and non-book materials. In this category is the *Minnesota Multiphasic Personality Inventory* (MMPI), a psychological test originally published in 1942 and now published by the Psychological Corporation under license from the Press. In addition to the test itself the Press has published a number of books dealing with various aspects of the use or findings of the MMPI and these books are among the titles that contribute to its strong list in psychology.

Among the plays published by the Press is the first English-language edition of a play by Aleksandr Solzhenitsyn, *Candle In the Wind.* An important play series under the Press imprint is called *Playwrights for Tomorrow.* This series offers collections of plays written by playwrights who have been associated with the University of Minnesota's Office for Advanced Drama Research.

Three of the most popular books issued by the Press deal with the Minnesota outdoors: CANOE COUNTRY, SNOWSHOE COUNTRY, and THE GEESE FLY HIGH, all written by Florence Page Jaques and illustrated by her husband, Francis Lee Jaques, the noted nature ar-

tist. Of continuing popularity with a national audience, also, are COMMON EDIBLE MUSHROOMS by Clyde M. Christensen and SCULPTURE IN WOOD and SCULPTURE WITH A TORCH, both by John Rood.

Among the works that have brought international recognition to the Press are PIONEERS AND CARETAKERS: A STUDY OF NINE AMERICAN WOMEN NOVELISTS by Louis Auchincloss; JOHN GREENLEAF WHITTIER'S POETRY: AN APPRAISAL AND A SELECTION by Robert Penn Warren; PATERNALISTIC CAPITALISM by Andreas G. Papandreou; PARABLES FOR THE THEATER: TWO PLAYS BY BERTOLT BRECHT, translated by Eric Bentley; TAHITIAN JOURNAL by George Biddle; ALMS FOR OBLIVION by Edward Dahlberg; ISLAM: A WAY OF LIFE and CAPITAL CITIES OF ISLAM by Philip K. Hitti; and an important project in the field of history, the ten-volume *Europe and the World in the Age of Expansion* series edited by Boyd C. Shafer.

The University of Missouri Press

Founded at Columbia, Missouri, in 1958, under the direct supervision of the Dean of Extra-Divisional Administration of the university, the imprint being controlled by a committee of faculty members. With the expansion of the university from a single-campus to a four-campus institution in 1963 the Press became a part of the administrative body for the university system, operating under the office of the president. The faculty committee has, since that time, been appointed by the president and its membership represents all four campuses as well as the spectrum of the university's scholarly disciplines. In 1969 Thomas Lloyd, former executive director of the AAUP, was appointed director of the Press.

The Press specializes in scholarly books and monographs, regional books, poetry, short fiction, and drama. The *University of Missouri Studies,* a series, begun as a broad program under university auspices, is now a specialized imprint of the Press. *Breakthrough Books,* a series offering original creative matter, and *Literary Frontiers,* a parallel series offering criticism of contemporary trends, are new directions in the Press's publishing program. Hellmut Lehmann-Haupt's THE GÖTTINGEN MODEL BOOK and Thomas Hart Benton's DRAWINGS and THE ARTIST IN AMERICA are three of the outstanding titles of the Press.

University of Nebraska Press

Founded at Lincoln, Nebraska, in 1941, although the imprint was used as far back as 1922 by the university's printing division. The Press was created with the twofold purpose of publishing books in the scholarly disciplines and books of particular interest to the people of Nebraska and the Great Plains region. Emily Schossberger was the first editor of the Press; its first book was issued in 1942. During Schossberger's seventeen-year tenure (1941-1958) the Press published a total of eighty-one titles.

In 1959, consequent upon a decision of the Board of Regents to stimulate the publications program with increased institutional support, the Press was reorganized. Bruce H. Nicoll was appointed director with full managerial powers. Since that time the program of the Press has expanded greatly; it has published as many as eighty-three titles annually. In 1960 it began to publish quality paperbound books, originals and reprints, known as *Bison Books.* In cooperation with the Department of English, University of Nebraska-Lincoln, the Press also publishes the literary quarterly *Prairie Schooner.* The *Schooner* has had three editors: Lowry C. Wimberly (1927-56); Karl Shapiro (1956-62); and Bernice Slote, since 1962.

The publishing programs emphasized are in agricultural economics, anthropology and ethnology, drama, history, literature and criticism, philosophy, political science and law, psychology, sociology, and Western Americana. The following series have been published: *Nebraska Symposia on Motivation* (annual volumes since 1953); *Regents Renaissance Drama; Regents Restoration Drama; Regents Critics; Studies in Medieval and Renaissance History* (annual vol-

umes since 1964); *Pioneer Heritage;* and *Regents Continental Drama.* In 1962 the Press launched a multi-volume project devoted to the early and uncollected writings of Willa Cather, the fifth volume of which appeared in 1973. The Press has also published contributions by such famed American authors as Wright Morris, S.N. Behrman, A.B. Guthrie, Jr., and Jessamyn West.

University of Nebraska Press books have received their share of honors, among them the Christian Gauss Phi Beta Kappa award, the Explicator award, and the Chap-Book award of the Poetry Society of America, all for critical works, and two Golden Spur awards of the Western Writers of America for nonfiction Westerns.

In 1974 Bruce H. Nicoll retired. David H. Gilbert became the director, succeeding Frederick M. Link, who had been acting executive director.

University of New Mexico Press

Established in 1930 at Albuquerque, New Mexico, as a department of the university with Paul A.F. Walter, Jr., as editor of publications. In 1931 the *New Mexico Quarterly* was started and two years later the first book bearing the Press imprint appeared: NEW MEXICO HISTORY AND CIVICS by Lansing B. Bloom and Thomas C. Donnelly. A second book also appeared in that year: AMERICA IN THE SOUTHWEST, an anthology of Southwestern literature by T.M. Pearce and Telfair Hendon. To oversee the emerging publishing program Fred E. Harvey was named director. In 1945 Dudley Wynn became the director of the Press. The university printing plant was then made a separate department and Fred. E. Harvey became its manager. At the same time the *University of New Mexico Publications Series* was established as an independent entity with its own director, to publish scholarly monographs. It was a successor to the earlier *UNM Bulletin Series.* In 1946 Fred E. Harvey was brought back to be director of the Press. He remained in that post until 1949 when E.B. Mann took over.

In 1956 the Press underwent a major reorganization. The three related departments, The University of New Mexico Press, the *New Mexico*

Quarterly, and the *UNM Publications Series* were combined into one body under the present name, with Roland E. Dickey as director. Dickey served as director for ten years until 1966. Roger W. Shugg, former director of the University of Chicago Press, became his successor in 1967. During Shugg's term of office, the output of the Press rose to thirty titles per year and the total list passed the two hundred-title mark. When Shugg retired in July, 1973, the directorship was assumed by Hugh W. Treadwell, formerly senior editor in the Random House-A.A. Knopf College Department.

The University of North Carolina Press

Founded at Chapel Hill, North Carolina, in 1922 "to promote generally by publishing deserving books, the advancement of the arts and sciences and the development of literature." The affairs of the Press were to be directed by a board of governors. At the first meeting of this board, Louis Round Wilson, the librarian of the university, was appointed director of the Press. The first publication to bear the Press imprint appeared in 1923. It was SAPROLEGNIACEAE by W.C. Coker.

Probably the most important influence on the Press in its first decade was the founding of the Institute for Research in Social Sciences under the direction of Howard W. Odum and the securing of generous financial support for the Institute and the Press from the Laura Spelman Rockefeller Memorial Foundation. Under Odum's dynamic leadership, a series of studies on every aspect of Southern life and culture was commissioned. Eventually, these studies appeared under the imprint of the Press and gained for it immediate recognition as the principal interpreter of the South to the nation.

When Wilson resigned in 1933 he was succeeded as director by William T. Couch. Couch's intellectual gifts and deep concern for social justice resulted in a broadening of the scope of the Press. He sought to serve the interests of the general reading public by issuing juveniles, textbooks, popular regional studies and even a bestselling cookbook. At the same time he published worthwhile manuscripts in every scholarly

discipline. The Chapel Hill imprint became identified with fine scholarship, represented by such titles as SOUTHERN REGIONS OF THE UNITED STATES by Howard W. Odum, Rupert B. Vance's HUMAN GEOGRAPHY OF THE SOUTH, ATTACK ON LEVIATHAN by Donald Davidson, Cleanth Brooks' MODERN POETRY AND THE TRADITION, and AMERICA AND THE FRENCH CULTURE, 1750-1848, by Howard Mumford Jones.

Another striking contribution made by the Press at this time was the launching of a series of books on Negro life and culture. By 1950 the Press had published over one hundred books by or about Black Americans and could count among its authors such distinguished Negro scholars and writers as J. Saunders Redding, Rayford W. Logan, and John Hope Franklin.

The Press weathered the Depression of the 1930s, though with a greatly curtailed list, principally through the benefactions of the Rosenwald Fund, the Carnegie Foundation, and the General Education Board. Subsequent support from the Ford, Mellon, and Smith Reynolds foundations enabled the Press to expand both its staff and its publishing programs. In 1945 Couch resigned to accept directorship of the University of Chicago Press. His successor, Thomas J. Wilson, remained for only two years before leaving to become the director of the Harvard University Press. In 1947 Lambert Davis was chosen as the new director.

Under Davis the belletristic and history lists were strengthened. In the former field, the major titles included THE NOTEBOOKS OF THOMAS WOLFE edited by Richard S. Kennedy and Paschal Reeves; THE ACHIEVEMENT OF SHERWOOD ANDERSON by Ray Lewis White; THE POETRY OF THOMAS HARDY by J.O. Bailey; and the monumental three-volume A HISTORY OF THE SONATA IDEA by William S. Newman. Equally outstanding were some of the publications in the field of history. In 1969 WHITE OVER BLACK by Winthrop D. Jordan won both the National Book Award and the Bancroft Prize. The following year, the latter prize was accorded to another Press title: THE CREATION OF THE AMERICAN REPUBLIC, 1776-1787, by Gordon S. Wood. Both of these books were published in collaboration with the Institute of Early American History and Culture, Williamsburg, Virginia, with whom the Press has co-published more than seventy volumes during the past two decades. Davis retired as director of the Press in 1970 and was succeeded by another distinguished bookman, Matthew Hodgson.

In addition to its regular book publishing program, which by 1972 had issued over fifteen hundred titles, the Press publishes or distributes a number of monographs and journals. These include *Studies in Comparative Literature, Studies in the Germanic Languages and Literature, Social Forces, Studies in Philology, The High School Journal, The James Sprunt Studies in History and Political Science,* and the *Journal of the Elisa Mitchell Scientific Society.*

University of Notre Dame Press

Founded at Notre Dame, Indiana, in 1949. The first book to bear the new imprint was a football review. For some time occasional books were published in the sciences and theology. One early effort was the famous liturgy series of Father Matthis, and a series in medieval studies was also undertaken. Among the first of the modern Notre Dame Press books was the series *International Studies,* started in the mid-fifties under the editorship of Waldemar Gurian and currently directed by Stephen Kertesz, in which over fifty different titles have been published.

In 1960 the Press was reorganized and Emily Schossberger became its director. The next year saw the beginning of a quality paperback series. In 1972 Emily Schossberger retired. She was succeeded by James R. Langford as director. The major publishing programs of the press include *International Studies, Medieval Studies, Texts and Studies in Medieval Education, Middle English Series,* and *Mexican American Studies.*

University of Oklahoma Press

Founded at Norman, Oklahoma, in 1928 by William Bennett Bizzell, President of the University of Oklahoma. The Press formally went into operation in 1929 under Joseph A. Brandt as its director. The first publication to bear the Oklahoma imprint was a pamphlet by Duane Roller, Sr., entitled *Terminology of Physical Science.* Rather early Brandt conceived a series which serves as one of the Oklahoma Press hallmarks: *The Civilization of the American Indian.* In his ten years as director Brandt built up a solid foundation and nurtured a tradition that won national recognition.

Brandt left in 1938 to become director of the Princeton University Press but returned in 1944 as President of the University of Oklahoma. The Press continued to flourish under Brandt's successor, Savoie Lottinville. Lottinville inaugurated three new series, *American Exploration and Travel, The Western Frontier Library,* and *Centers of Civilization.* Of its total output of more than one thousand books, the Press has had a few popular bestsellers: WAH 'KON-TAH by John Joseph Mathews, DESERTS ON THE MARCH by Paul B. Sears, the FARMER'S HANDBOOK by John M. White, and PLOWMAN'S FOLLY by Edward H. Faulkner. One of Lottinville's achievements was the Oklahoma University Press fellowships in bookmaking.

Lottinville's successor and the third director of the Press is Edward A. Shaw.

University of Pennsylvania Press

Founded at Philadelphia, Pennsylvania, in 1921. The imprint, however, appears as early as 1870 as the University Press Company on *The Penn Monthly.* In 1889 a University of Pennsylvania Press was formed to publish the *University Medical Magazine,* but the modern history of the Press begins in 1921 when Phelps Soule was appointed director to establish a full-fledged publishing program. Soule remained as director until 1953. Succeeding directors were: Morse Peckham (1953-1955); Thomas Yoseloff (1955-1966); Gordon Hubel (1966-1969); and Fred Wieck (1969-1973). Robert L. Warren is the current director.

The Press publishes many series in literature, philosophy, and history: *Conduct and Communications, Folklore and Folklife, Works in Continental Philosophy,* and *Sources of Medieval*

History. Its outstanding titles include: THE PRIVATE CITY: PHILADELPHIA IN THREE PERIODS OF ITS GROWTH by Sam Bass Warner, Jr., WITCHCRAFT IN EUROPE, 1100-1700: A DOCUMENTARY HISTORY edited by Alan C. Kors and Edward Peters, KINESICS AND CONTEXT: ESSAYS ON BODY MOTION COMMUNICATION by Roy L. Birdwhistell, and LANGUAGE IN THE INNER CITY: STUDIES IN THE BLACK ENGLISH VERNACULAR by William Labor. The Press also has a paperback line called Pennsylvania Paperbacks.

University of Pittsburgh Press

Founded at Pittsburgh, Pennsylvania, in 1936 in order to publish a series of books on regional history. These books, known as the *Western Pennsylvania Series*, were written under the direction of the Western Pennsylvania Historical Survey. The Press has also published other regional titles, such as BIRDS OF WESTERN PENNSYLVANIA, WILD FLOWERS OF WESTERN PENNSYLVANIA AND THE UPPER OHIO BASIN, and EARLY ARCHITECTURE OF WESTERN PENNSYLVANIA.

In the middle 1950s the Press began to broaden the emphasis of its publication and it now publishes widely in the social sciences, the humanities, and public health. Reflecting this shift in emphasis are series such as the *Pittsburgh Series in Bibliography*, the first definitive book-length bibliographies of American and Anglo-American authors; the *Pitt Poetry Series*, which publishes among other volumes each year the winner of the United States Award of the International Poetry Forum; and the *Contemporary Community Health Series*. During the 1960s the Press published several journals, but since 1966 that program has been discontinued.

The University of South Carolina Press

Founded in 1913 at Columbia, South Carolina, and began publishing scholarly monographs in 1914 under the imprint The University Press.

Management of the Press for thirty years was a part-time activity of several professors of the university. In 1944 the Press was reorganized as a separate department of the university under its present imprint. A committee of the faculty of the university was established to control the imprint and the chairman of this committee, W.H. Callcott, was appointed acting director of the Press. In 1946 Frank Wardlaw was selected to be the first full-time director.

A volume of hunting reminiscences, MY HEALTH IS BETTER IN NOVEMBER by Havilah Babcock, published in 1947, became the first popular success of the new Press. BENEATH SO KIND A SKY, a photographic essay on South Carolina, published in 1948, with photographs by Carl Julien and words by Chapman Milling, became a classic, while Howard Quint's THE FORGING OF AMERICAN SOCIALISM, issued in 1953, became a widely adopted textbook. In 1950 Wardlaw left to become director of the newly established University of Texas Press and was succeeded in the directorship at South Carolina by Louise Jones Dubose. In 1966, Dubose having retired, Robert T. King became director.

The Press specializes in scholarly editions of historical papers and literary works, bibliographic and textual studies, the Renaissance, Shakespeare, sociology, and Oriental studies. Publications of the South Carolina Tricentennial Commission, the South Carolina Department of Archives and History, and the Institute of International Studies of the University of South Carolina are distributed by the Press under dual imprints. Publication of the SOUTH CAROLINA SHAKESPEARE in forty-two volumes began in 1974 and will continue through 1989, under the general editorship of J. Leeds Barroll.

Other major series launched by the Press include: *The Papers of John C. Calhoun*, edited by Edwin Hemphill; *The Papers of Henry Laurens*, edited by George C. Rogers; *The Centennial Edition of the Writings of William Gilmore Simms*, edited by John C. Guilds; *Proof: The Yearbook of American Bibliographical and Textual Studies*, edited by Joseph Katz; and *Shakespeare Studies: An Annual Gathering of Research, Criticism, and Reviews*, edited by J. Leeds Barroll.

The University of Tennessee Press

Established in 1940 at Knoxville, Tennessee, as a full-fledged publishing organization although the imprint may be traced back to 1898, when President Charles W. Dabney recommended the establishment of a press under which all university publications might be issued. Although the imprint appeared sporadically on a variety of publications after 1899, it had disappeared from the university scene by 1940, when another group of trustees established the Press anew, this time with a scholarly and regional publishing goal. Instead of concurrently creating a staff for the Press, the university added this new responsibility to the other publications duties of the University Editor in the Division of University Extension.

The first title under the new imprint, TENNESSEE: A POLITICAL STUDY by William H. Combs and William E. Cole, was issued that same year and it was followed by about one book a year for the next decade and a half. One of the early titles, HIWASSEE ISLAND, became an archaeological classic; others, such as CULTURE AND POLICY by René Williamson, TOWARD A NEW POLITICS IN THE SOUTH by Jasper B. Shannon, and THE FROZEN FOOD INDUSTRY by Harry Carlton, enjoyed long and successful lives; still others pioneered as studies of an agency at that time unique, the Tennessee Valley Authority.

In 1957 the Press was organized formally, elevated to departmental status and placed under its present director, Louis T. Iglehart, his mission being to develop a full-time publishing program. Subsequently the Press was further strengthened by the addition of prominent scholars to its editorial board, by the employment of editorial, production, and marketing specialists on its staff, and by the broadening of its responsibility to represent university campuses at Chattanooga, Martin, Memphis, and Nashville, as well as the original campus at Knoxville.

Growth of the Press has been steady rather than spectacular since the 1957 reorganization. Production climbed from three to four titles a year in the late 1950s to twenty new titles and reprints in the early 1970s. The Press is involved in a major Presidential papers project, having already produced the first three volumes of *The Papers of Andrew Johnson,* and within the 1970s will begin publishing the papers of Andrew Jackson in a fifty-volume series. The publishing program reflects a broad interest in history, literature, and political science, and the development of a special emphasis on natural history, anthropology, and Slavic studies. Titles range from a regional book, GREAT SMOKY MOUNTAIN WILDFLOWERS, to a pioneering study in oral history, THE SAGA OF COE RIDGE, and from a scholarly yet popular anthropological study, TRIBES THAT SLUMBER, to a standard reference book on pacifism, FOR PEACE AND JUSTICE. The Press does not generally publish paperbacks, the one exception being a series on natural history.

Cooperative publishing by the Press includes an arrangement with the Tennessee Historical Commission to co-publish selected titles in regional history. Under an agreement with the Southern Anthropological Society, the Press publishes the winning manuscripts in the annual $1,000.00 James Mooney Award Competition in anthropology.

University of Texas Press

Founded as a printing plant in 1922 at Austin, Texas, although no regular publishing was done until 1950, only occasional titles being issued in the intervening years. The modern history of the Press starts with the Couch Report prepared by W.T. Couch of the University of North Carolina Press. The report recommended the establishment of a "publishing organization clearly conceived, adequately financed, properly staffed, and instituted on a basis of permanence." The Couch Report was not implemented until 1949, when a committee, headed by Reginald Harvey Griffith, was given the task of finding a director. Frank H. Wardlaw, director of the University of South Carolina Press, accepted the job and began organization of the Press in 1950. The following year Griffith was succeeded as chairman of the faculty advisory board by the historian, Walter Prescott Webb, whose influence shaped the program of the Press for the next nine years.

The first book off the Press was significant: a translation of Garcilaso de la Vega's THE FLORIDA OF THE INCA. Among other early books of note were Philip Graham's SHOWBOATS: THE HISTORY OF AN AMERICAN INSTITUTION; the four-volume variorum edition of Lord Byron's DON JUAN; LIFE ON THE TEXAS RANGE, a collection of early range photographs by Erwin E. Smith; and FREE AND UNEQUAL by Roger Williams. The emphasis of the Press still remains in part on the Southwest, as reflected in such titles as THE INDIANS OF TEXAS, ROADSIDE FLOWERS OF TEXAS, TREES, SHRUBS, AND WOODY VINES OF THE SOUTHWEST, CACTI OF THE SOUTHWEST, SEASHELLS OF THE TEXAS COAST, and BUCK SCHIWETZ' TEXAS. Latin America is an even larger field of emphasis. Some eighty books have appeared in the *Texas Pan American Series* including translations of Augustín Yáñez' THE EDGE OF THE STORM, Juan Rulfo's THE BURNING PLAIN, Manuel Toussaint's COLONIAL ART IN MEXICO, PROFILE OF MAN AND CULTURE IN MEXICO by Samuel Ramos, Ezequiel Martínez Estrada's X-RAY OF THE PAMPA, and Garcilaso de la Vega's ROYAL COMMENTARIES OF THE INCAS.

The Texas Press also publishes the *Latin American Monograph Series* for the Institute of Latin American Studies and is the official publishing arm of the Conference on Latin American History. Other important offerings in this field are the sixteen-volume HANDBOOK OF MIDDLE AMERICAN INDIANS, published for the Middle America Research Institute at Tulane University and the six-volume PREHISTORY OF THE TEHUACAN VALLEY, published for the Peabody Foundation at Andover, Massachusetts. In addition the Press is the publishing agency of the American Folklore Society, for which it publishes *The Journal of American Folklore, Abstracts of Folklore Studies,* and two series of books.

A distinctive feature of the Texas list of over seven hundred titles is the number of series financed by private funds and gifts. These include the Texas Pan American Fund, the Elma Dill Russell Spencer Series, the Dan Danciger Publication Fund, the M.K. Brown Range Life

Series, the Blaffer Series of Southwestern Art, the Corrie Herring Hooks Fund, and the John Fielding and Lois Lassiter Maher Series.

Philip D. Jones succeeded Wardlaw as director in 1974.

University of Utah Press

Founded in Salt Lake City, Utah, in 1949 when President Ray A. Olpin of the University of Utah asked Harold W. Bentley to establish a university press that would contribute to scholarly publishing. It was joined with an existing University Printing Service, and they functioned as one department until 1963, when the Press was made a separate agency. The first title published was NEW TEETH FOR OLD, in 1949.

In 1972 a second imprint, Bonneville Books, was set up for books with local and popular appeal and for reprints of Western classics. Both imprints are controlled by the university. Press directors have been: Harold W. Bentley, 1949-1955; Philip C. Sturges, 1955-1959; A. Russell Mortensen, 1961-1964; Richard Y. Thurman, 1964-1970; and Norma B. Mikkelsen since 1971.

Two series, *Publications in the American West* and *Anthropological Papers,* indicate a focus on Western history, past and present, that evolved out of Utah's contributions to Western Americana. Outstanding titles of the Press are: FLORENTINE CODEX, ORRIN PORTER ROCKWELL, HOLE IN THE ROCK, BRIGHT ESSENCE, and OLD ONE AND THE WIND (poems).

The University of Washington Press

Established in 1909 in Seattle, Washington, when the University of Washington acquired a printing press for the campus newspaper. In 1911 the Press began to issue the *Washington Historical Quarterly,* now called the *Pacific Northwest Quarterly.* Between 1915 and 1920 several monograph series were inaugurated. The first full-length book to bear the Washington Press imprint appeared in 1920. In 1950 the Press was separated from the printing department and reorganized as the book publishing division of the university.

The backlist of the Press emphasizes art, anthropology, Asian studies, biology, ethnology, history, government, language and literature, oceanography, and regional subjects. The Press also publishes a paperback reprint series called Washington Paperbacks, and a clothbound reprint series called the *Americana Library Series*. The press in addition is the publisher of the *American Ethnological Society Monographs* which now number over fifty volumes. The imprint is controlled and supervised by the University Press Committee.

The University of Wisconsin Press

Founded at Madison, Wisconsin, in 1936 when the University of Wisconsin faculty established a committee which was "authorized . . . at its discretion to publish particularly meritorious manuscripts as books, using the imprint The University of Wisconsin Press." In the following year the first volume, REACTIONS OF HYDROGEN WITH ORGANIC COMPOUNDS OVER COPPER-CHROMIUM OXIDE AND NICKEL CATALYSTS by Homer Adkins, was published.

Headed by Livia Appel, managing editor from 1937 to 1948, and later by Thompson Webb, Jr. as director, the Press is a department of the Graduate School of the University of Wisconsin. The Wisconsin publications, although unrestricted as to origin, reflect to a large extent the scholarly interests of the university. Areas of special concentration include the history of science, African studies, and Spanish and Latin American studies. In 1967 the University of Wisconsin Press, Ltd., was incorporated and— jointly with seven other university presses, known collectively as American University Publishers Group, Ltd. (AUPG)—an office was set up in London, England.

University Park Press

Organized in 1967 at State College, Pennsylvania, by T. Rowland Slingluff, Jr., former director of the Pennsylvania State University Press. Its first publication was the INDEX OF ANTIBIOTICS FROM ACTINOMYCETES. The major thrust of the Press was toward publishing research materials in the medical and biological sciences in cooperation with overseas institutions. Long-term relationships were established for this purpose with the University of Tokyo and other academic bodies in the Far East, as well as with leading British and European publishers.

In 1971 the Press announced the North American publication of the *MTP International Review of Science,* an ambitious project that will number eventually several hundred volumes covering every major scientific discipline. In 1972 University Park was chosen to be the associate publisher of the International Research Communications System, a revolutionary publishing medium by means of which scientists in any part of the world can have immediate access to research data documented by other scientists in the same field. In the same year the Press moved its editorial offices from State College, Pennsylvania, to Baltimore, Maryland.

In 1973, the Press began expansion into fields outside its traditional medical-scientific list. PUBLIC BUDGETING SYSTEMS marked the beginning of a new list in economics, while PAPAL ROME represented the first of a planned series in art history.

In May 1974 University Park Press was purchased by CHC Corporation of Towson, Maryland, a producer of professional books and journals.

The University Presses of Florida

Founded in 1945 at Gainesville, Florida, as The University of Florida Press, "to publish, encourage, and promote original and scholarly manuscripts which will aid in developing the University as a recognized center of research and scholarship." Lewis F. Haines was its first managing editor. Its first book, FLORIDA UNDER FIVE FLAGS by Rembert W. Patrick, was published in its first year. The Press grew slowly. In 1967 it was reorganized with William B. Harvey as director. Next year the Press undertook the production of books for the Florida State University Press.

As the Press has grown, its publishing interests have gradually been channeled into two regional fields: Florida history and Latin American studies. In recent years it has published many works in eighteenth-century English literature. It has also issued works on agricultural and related subjects, mainly as they relate to Florida and the southeastern United States.

In late 1973 the Board of Regents of the State of Florida completed plans to include all of the nine universities in the state system in a statewide publishing facility. The University of Florida Press was renamed The University Presses of Florida and William B. Harvey was appointed director of the enlarged organization. Headquarters remain in Gainesville on the campus of the University of Florida.

1852 Poster Advertising Uncle Tom's Cabin

The University Press of Hawaii

Organized at Honolulu, Hawaii, in 1971 through a merger of the former University of Hawaii Press, established in 1947, and the East-West Center Press, founded in 1962. Thomas Nickerson was the founding director of the University of Hawaii Press and John Kyle of the East-West Center Press. Robert Sparks is the director of the new Press. The Press publishes books under its own as well as the East-West Center imprint and on behalf of such organizations as Friends of the Library of Hawaii and the Hawaiian Historical Society.

The University Press of Hawaii list emphasizes its interest in Asian and Pacific history, anthropology, linguistics, philosophy and literature, the natural and physical sciences, and Oceanic studies. The Press also publishes four scholarly journals: *Pacific Science, Philosophy East and West, Asian Perspectives,* and *Oceanic Linguistics,* as well as four series: *Pacific Classics; Asian Studies at Hawaii; Insects of Hawaii;* and *Pacific and Asian Languages Institute Language Series.*

The University Press of Kansas

Established in 1967 at Lawrence, Kansas, as the joint operation of The University of Kansas, Kansas State University, and Wichita State University. The University of Kansas Press, which had been in operation since 1946, was dissolved as of that date and its equipment, rights and resources were transferred to the new entity. Each university contributes to an annual subsidy applied toward the operating costs of the Press. A board of trustees composed of the academic officers of the three participating universities serves as governing board for the Press.

The earlier University of Kansas Press was directed by Clyde K. Hyder who held the title of manager and editor. Upon Hyder's retirement the Press was reorganized in 1967 with John Dessauer as director. Dessauer resigned in 1969 and John H. Langley was appointed to succeed him.

The largest publishing project undertaken under Hyder was the TREATISE ON INVER-TEBRATE PALEONTOLOGY, edited by Raymond C. Moore, and published in cooperation with the Geological Society of America. The Press now publishes the *American Presidency Series,* studies in the administration of each president of the United States.

The University Press of Kentucky

Founded at Lexington, Kentucky, in 1969 as the cooperative scholarly book publishing agency for seven state-supported universities in Kentucky: Eastern Kentucky University, Kentucky State University, Morehead State University, Murray State University, the University of Louisville, Western Kentucky University, and the University of Kentucky, including its thirteen community colleges; also two private colleges, Berea College and Centre College of Kentucky. It took over the programs, staff, and facilities of the former University of Kentucky Press, founded in 1943. The Press was enlarged with the addition of The Kentucky Historical Society as an associate member in 1971, and again in 1972 with the addition of Northern Kentucky State College, Transylvania University, and Georgetown College (the latter two, private institutions), as full members.

Through the earlier University of Kentucky Press, the present Press can trace its origins back to 1919, when the late Frank L. McVey, president of the University of Kentucky from 1917 to 1940, set up a monograph publication fund administered by a faculty committee. Lapsing during the 1930s Depression, this early book program was revived in 1939 and for the next few years was managed by McVey, who had chosen as his retirement assignment the chairmanship of the publication committee. He persuaded the university administration to set up the University of Kentucky Press in 1943. But although McVey had envisioned a central publishing agency in charge of a qualified editor, the immediate effect was only to change the name of the faculty committee.

The first title bearing the imprint of the University of Kentucky Press, A RATIONALE OF CRIMINAL NEGLIGENCE by Roy Moreland, appeared in 1944. In the next five years eight other titles were issued. One of these was A BIBLIOGRAPHY OF KENTUCKY HISTORY, the first by an off-campus author. During this period McVey was joined on the university press committee by another strong advocate of scholarly book publishing, Thomas D. Clark, head of the history department. Under a comprehensive plan developed by the two men the Press was established as a separate academic agency in 1950 with Bruce F. Denbo, a professional bookman, as its director.

An average of only five titles a year was published by the Press from 1950 to 1957. Among these, however, were THE VERBAL ICON by W.K. Wimsatt, SOUTHEAST ASIA AMONG THE WORLD POWERS by Amry Vandenbosch and THE FRONTIER MIND by Arthur K. Moore. The next five years showed a steady growth attributable only in part to the new monograph series. Three undertakings at this time were especially important. In 1958 the Mississippi Valley Historical Association (later Organization of American Historians) launched an annual competition for the best manuscript in American history and selected the University of Kentucky Press to publish the award books. The next year the first volume of THE PAPERS OF HENRY CLAY was published. This project, by the time of its completion in 1988, is expected to cost more than $600,000.00. The Press also competed successfully to become the publisher in 1962 of THE SOUTHERN APPALACHIAN REGION, a survey edited by Thomas R. Ford that established the Press as a leader in works on this area, attracting to it such titles as YESTERDAY'S PEOPLE by Jack E. Weller, and APPALACHIA'S CHILDREN by David H. Looff.

In 1967 Thomas Clark launched his campaign for a state-wide cooperative press. His plan won general approval and Victor Reynolds, then director of the pioneer cooperative University Press of Virginia, was engaged as a consultant to work out the details of the charter of the new organization. Under the charter each participating institution maintains its identity in making publishing decisions but the final approval lies with an editorial board on which each cooperating institution is represented. The editorial and sales offices are maintained on the Lexington campus of the University of Kentucky, whose president is charged with oversight of the Press. An early title of the new imprint, The University Press of Kentucky, is KENTUCKY: A PICTORIAL HISTORY, edited by J. Winston Coleman, Jr. A series on the Commonwealth's fauna and flora is underway and a number of titles on Kentucky have been prepared for the 1974 bicentennial celebration of the settlement of the state.

University Press of Virginia

Established at Charlottesville, Virginia, in 1963 with Victor Reynolds as the first director, the Press is an inter-institutional publisher serving the State of Virginia. Its first titles were four paperback reprints formerly published by Colonial Williamsburg, Inc. Two of these, THE JOURNAL OF MAJOR GEORGE WASHINGTON and SEAT OF EMPIRE by Carl Bridenbaugh, were published in 1963 and were the first books to carry the University Press of Virginia imprint.

The Press publishes and distributes for a number of organizations, including the Bibliographical Society of the University of Virginia, Colonial Williamsburg, Inc., The Virginia Historical Society, The Folger Shakespeare Library, The Winterthur Museum, the Grolier Club, the Virginia Museum of Fine Arts, Eleutherian Mills-Hagley Foundation, the Thomas Jefferson Memorial Foundation, the American Association of Architectural Bibliographers, the Columbia Historical Society, the Mariners Museum, and the Virginia Independence Bicentennial Commission. Other major projects include a standard edition of the works of Stephen Crane, edited by Fredson Bowers, for the Center for Editions of American Authors, and the PAPERS OF GEORGE WASHINGTON, edited by Donald Jackson.

The University Press of Washington, D.C.

Founded in 1949 by E.S. Larsen as The Munsey Press. The present name was adopted by President Paul Douglass of The American University to indicate the function of the press as the publishing arm of The American, George Washington, Howard, and Maryland universities. But this institutional union never materialized. The first book to appear under this imprint was INTRODUCTION TO AFRICA prepared by the Library of Congress in 1950. Early in 1951 appeared the first of the *Contributions to Learning* monographs, EGYPT AND THE ANGLO-EGYPTIAN SUDAN, also issued by the Library of Congress.

In a general reorganization in 1953 Ernest J. Vetter, then president of the Coronet Press in Virginia, was appointed director of University Press. Coronet became a UPW subsidiary. That year two important series were announced: *The Pocket Poets* and the *University Chapbooks*. Two years later S.G. Link, who had earlier served as a consultant to the Press, E.S. Larsen, A.J. Wraight of George Washington University, and Thomas Fleming, who had succeeded Vetter as director, organized the University Press Fund with the UPW as its operating agency. The fund was designed to sponsor institutional adoptions of all academic presses. Trustees of the fund were to constitute the UPW board.

In 1956 the Library of Congress made literary history by preparing for UPW THE CONGRESSIONAL ANTHOLOGY: POEMS SELECTED BY U.S. SENATORS AND REPRESENTATIVES, which became an instant bestseller. Link served briefly as director of the Press in 1956, then succeeded Larsen as chairman of the board when the latter retired. William N. Egan became the new director. Egan resigned in 1969 and was succeeded the following year by Joseph Stanley Wallace. In 1972 John Hedrick became the Press director. Meanwhile, in 1964, a new subsidiary, the Community College Press, was established with the support of four Maryland two-year colleges.

In 1969 UPW moved to the Old Riverton Post Office Building on the Dellbrook campus of the Center for Advanced Studies at Riverton, Virginia. Renamed University Press Building, this served as Virginia headquarters and depository for both UPW and the Community College Press. In 1973 the Washington office of the UPW moved to the new campus of Southeastern University in Washington, D.C. and the corporate name was expanded provisionally to The University Press of Washington, D.C.: the Publishing Division of Southeastern University.

Principal specializations of the Press have been Latin American history, European diplomatic and economic history, biography, college teaching, and *belles lettres.* Outstanding titles include: LATIN AMERICAN SOCIAL THOUGHT by Harold E. Davis; THE DIPLOMACY OF APPEASEMENT: ANGLO-FRENCH RELATIONS AND THE PRELUDE TO WORLD WAR II by Arthur H. Furnia; THE AMERICA OF CARL SANDBURG by Hazel Durnell; THE CASKET LETTERS by M.H. Armstrong Davison; COLLEGE TEACHING by J.U. Unstattd; and MANAGING COMPLEXITY: WORK, TECHNOLOGY, AND HUMAN RELATIONS by James C. Stephens. In addition to series previously noted, the Press also publishes *The American University, Administration Library, Executive Management Monographs, Excerpts from Current Literature,* and *Latin American Institute Series.*

The University Society, Inc.

Established in New York City in 1897 by George Bryan. The firm later moved to Ridgewood, New Jersey, before establishing its present headquarters in Midland Park, New Jersey.

The main types of the Society's publications are reference books, music books, and anthologies for children. Representative of the latter two categories are two widely selling sets: *The International Library of Piano Music* and *The Bookshelf for Boys and Girls.*

The control of the company is still vested in the collateral descendants of the firm's founder.

Urban Institute

Established in 1968 at Washington, D.C. Issues books and reports on urban issues.

Vanderbilt University Press

Founded in 1940 in Nashville, Tennessee, largely through the efforts of John Pomfret, Dean of the Graduate School, Vanderbilt University. An average of one title per year was issued during the first twenty years, when the imprint was controlled by a committee of faculty members and the editorial and business affairs handled as a part-time assignment by a faculty member. In 1959 the first full-time director was appointed for the Press, David Howell Jones. In that year, the Press took over publication of the Abraham Flexner Lectures in Medicine from a commercial firm, issuing THE CLONAL SELECTION THEORY OF ACQUIRING IMMUNITY by Sir McFarlane Burnet.

The Press continued to issue no more than five titles a year until Alexander Heard became chancellor of the university and the completion of a universitywide planning study in 1963-64. Since that time the Press has expanded to an average of fifteen titles a year. Outstanding among them have been SPANISH THOUGHT AND LETTERS IN THE TWENTIETH CENTURY, commemorating the centenary of the birth of Miguel de Unamuno, edited by Germán Bleiberg and Inman Fox (1966); NEW PERSPECTIVES OF BRAZIL, edited by Eric N. Baklanoff (1966); DEAFNESS IN CHILDHOOD, a symposium edited by Freeman McConnell and Paul H. Ward (1967); MIDDLE EAST OIL: A STUDY IN POLITICAL AND ECONOMIC CONTROVERSY by George W. Stocking (1970); and CORRESPONDENCE OF JAMES K. POLK, edited by Herbert Weaver and Paul H. Bergeron. The Press also publishes medical books and works of regional significance.

Vanguard Press

Founded in 1926 in New York City by the American Fund for Public Service which had been established by Charles Garland for the promotion of the labor movement in the United States. The objective of the press was to publish socially useful books for workers at low prices. After the Fund was dissolved, the firm was taken over by James Henle who headed it until 1952, when Evelyn Schrifte became president.

D. Van Nostrand Company

Founded by David Van Nostrand at New York City in 1848. Van Nostrand had been a partner with William Dwight in a bookstore in the early 1830s but the Depression of 1837 forced the business to close. For the next eleven years Van Nostrand lived in New Orleans, Louisiana, and served as a civilian aide on the staff of a friend, J.G. Barnard, who was then in the military engineering service. This association turned Van Nostrand's attention to military engineering subjects. When he returned to New York City he opened a bookstore that specialized in this field. His *Catalogue of American and Foreign Military and Naval Books* listed almost a thousand titles. His business prospered during the Civil War.

Meanwhile, in 1860, he had been appointed, through Barnard's influence, official publisher to the United States Army and Navy, and in this capacity he brought out the early texts which established his reputation: SEAMANSHIP by Captain S.B. Luce (1861) and INFANTRY TACTICS by Brigadier General Silas Casey. Luce's book was the official naval textbook of the United States Naval Academy until superseded in 1898 by Austin M. Knight's MODERN SEAMANSHIP, another Van Nostrand title, which is still available in its fifteenth edition. CASEY'S TACTICS, as that book was popularly known, had the distinction of being the standard training manual for the Union as well as the Confederate Army. Another undertaking was THE REBELLION RECORD which Van Nostrand took over from Putnam in 1863 and completed in twelve volumes.

Following the Civil War Van Nostrand's interest turned more and more to engineering and technology and, beginning in the late 1860s, his catalogues began to include a growing number of titles on mining, metallurgy, railroad engineering, and surveying, to which, in 1884, he added studies in pure and applied chemistry. From that period, too, dates Van Nostrand's *Science Series,* which eventually included one hundred twenty-seven pocket-sized volumes by the time the last title was published in 1902. In 1869 Van Nostrand started the *Electric Engineering Magazine,* which was later merged with *The American Rail-*

road Journal into *The Railroad and Engineering Journal.* The magazine was discontinued soon after Van Nostrand's death in 1888.

At Van Nostrand's death the leadership of the company was assumed by Edward Nichols Crane, a nephew by marriage, who eventually became the principal owner of the newly incorporated firm and who remained as its president until he died in 1911. Electricity and electrical engineering moved to the foreground of national interest in the 1890s and this emphasis was reflected in the Van Nostrand catalogues. The 1910 catalogue listed over one hundred fifty-seven titles in the field of electrical engineering and over one hundred titles in chemistry.

Upon Edward N. Crane's death the presidency of the company fell to his brother, Arthur McAuley Crane, who directed it for sixteen years. The company's modern era, however, may be said to have begun when Edward M. Crane, son of Edward N. Crane, became the company's president in 1927. Under his leadership came the expansion of the firm's publishing activities from the areas of science and technology almost exclusively into the broader fields of the humanities and the social sciences; from its emphasis on professional and reference books at the graduate level to the publication of college textbooks, and, after World War II, of both senior and junior high school texts; and from its role as an educational publisher to its role as a trade publisher as well. Those years also saw the organization of the company into professional and reference, college, school, trade, and international departments. Consequent on expansion, the company moved in 1955 to Princeton, New Jersey.

Among the ventures which Crane launched at this time were *Anvil Books,* quality paperbacks for college classes, consisting of original volumes in history and other social sciences, edited by Louis L. Snyder, *Insight Books,* devoted to the behavioral sciences, edited by D.G. McClelland, and *Searchlight Books,* edited by G.W. Hoffman and G.E. Pearcy, dealing with international problems. As part of its program of expansion Van Nostrand bought the high school texts of Newsom and Company, and it acquired Laurel Publishers from International Textbook Company in order to develop a list of books in the vocational arts. Crane also engaged Malcolm Johnson to organize a trade department; later a sporting books division and a juvenile division were started. In 1962 the Commission on College Physics appointed Van Nostrand to publish a series of fifty to one hundred paperbacks as supplementary texts in physics, engineering, and related sciences.

Crane died in 1964 and was succeeded in the presidency by his son, Edward M. Crane, Jr. The company was sold in 1968 to Litton Educational Publishing, Inc. Its publishing activities are now divided between two divisions of this corporation. Van Nostrand, under its president, Charles W. Pepper, continues to publish college textbooks, while Van Nostrand Reinhold, with Robert E. Ewing as its president, is responsible for the professional, reference, and trade areas.

Van Nostrand's most outstanding titles over the years include the VAN NOSTRAND'S SCIENTIFIC ENCYCLOPEDIA; the *Bell Telephone Laboratory Series* initiated in 1925; *The Library of Modern Sciences* edited by E.M. Slosson, H.E. Howe and M. Luckiesh, published in the 1920s; C.W. Swoope's LESSONS IN PRACTICAL ELECTRICITY, first published in 1898 and still on the current list in its eighteenth edition; STANDARD METHODS OF CHEMICAL ANALYSIS, first published in a single volume in 1917 and now in its sixth edition as a five-volume set; SOURCEBOOK ON ATOMIC ENERGY by Samuel Glasstone; PHYSICS by E. Hausmann and Edgar P. Slack; MODERN COLLEGE PHYSICS by Harvey White; and EARTH SCIENCE—THE WORLD WE LIVE IN by Samuel N. Namowitz.

Van Nostrand Reinhold Company

See, D. Van Nostrand Company; Reinhold Publishing Corporation.

Vedanta Press

Established in 1947 at Hollywood, California. Specializes in Indian philosophy and world religions.

Vienna House, Inc.

Established in 1970 at New York City. Specializes in books on music and issues facsimile editions.

The Viking Press

Established in New York City in 1925 by Harold K. Guinzburg and George S. Oppenheimer. They soon arranged to take over the distinguished B.W. Huebsch imprint with its pride of great authors that included Sherwood Anderson, Thorstein Veblen, James Joyce, D.H. Lawrence, and August Strindberg. Huebsch himself joined the firm as vice president and editor-in-chief, an association that lasted until his death in 1964.

Viking's first list included THE NEW AGE OF FAITH by John Langdon Davies and James Weldon Johnson's THE BOOK OF AMERICAN NEGRO SPIRITUALS. The firm published in the 1920s such notable books by hitherto unknown authors as LOLLY WILLOWES by Sylvia Townsend Warner; Elizabeth Madox Roberts' THE TIME OF MAN; POWER by Lion Feuchtwanger; and THE CASE OF SERGEANT GRISCHA by Arnold Zweig. During the 1930s Depression, it published THE LIVES OF A BENGAL LANCER by F. Yeats-Brown; Franz Werfel's FORTY DAYS OF MUSA DAGH; and WHILE ROME BURNS by Alexander Woollcott. Viking's reputation had also begun to attract newer authors, including Erskine Caldwell, Dorothy Parker and Carl Van Doren. In 1933 a juvenile department was established under May Massee. In the same year Oppenheimer withdrew from the partnership.

One landmark in the firm's history was the decision of Pascal Covici, who had previously published under his own imprint, to join Viking in 1938 and to bring with him John Steinbeck. THE GRAPES OF WRATH was published in 1939. Covici later served with Guinzburg as an editor for such authors as Saul Bellow, Arthur Miller, Lionel Trilling, Ludwig Bemelmans, and Gene Fowler. At this time Viking had three of the most brilliant editors in America: Huebsch, Covici, and Marshall Best. Later, Malcolm Cowley became consulting editor.

In 1943 the Press introduced its successful *Portable Library,* beginning the series with Alexander Woollcott's AS YOU WERE. Among its bestsellers in the 1940s and 1950s Viking published THE POWER AND THE GLORY by Graham Greene; NIGHTRUNNERS OF BENGAL by John Masters; Saul Bellow's THE ADVENTURES OF AUGIE MARCH; THE LOVE LETTERS OF PHYLLIS McGINLEY; AN EPISODE OF SPARROWS by Rumer Godden; Upton Sinclair's eleven *Lanny Budd* novels; and the detective novels of Rex Stout. THE COLUMBIA-VIKING DESK ENCYCLOPEDIA was launched in 1953 and proved to be an extremely profitable undertaking.

Harold Guinzburg died in 1961; Huebsch and Covici in 1964. Thomas H. Guinzburg, the firm's new president, strengthened the juvenile department, which had been started with such titles as THE STORY ABOUT PING and FERDINAND, and added the Viking Compass paperback series, a major new development. The Studio Books Division, inaugurated by Bryan Holme, is identified with such fine picture books as THE KENNEDY YEARS and THE WORLD IN VOGUE. The 1973 winner of the Nobel Prize in Literature was Patrick White of Australia, whose novels have all been Viking's, beginning in 1940. These enterprises have become examples of the kind of "constructive publishing" that Harold Guinzburg envisioned when he founded the company.

In 1968 Viking acquired Grossman Publishers, which continues to publish under its own imprint.

The Wadsworth Publishing Company, Inc.

Organized in 1956 at Belmont, California, by a group of associates headed by Richard P. Ettinger, Jr. and James F. Leisy as a subsidiary of Prentice-Hall. It became an independent company in 1964. Wadsworth's plan was to publish college textbooks.

Over the years Wadsworth has created and acquired several divisions and subsidiaries: Bogden & Quigley, Inc., Publishers; Brooks/Cole Publishing Company; Dickenson Publishing Company, Inc.; Duxbury Press; Charles A. Jones Publishing Company; and Prindle, Weber, and

Schmidt, Inc. Two of its successful programs have been the *Sports Skills* series and a series of issue-centered reading books for continuing education of adults.

Henry Z. Walck, Inc.

Founded in 1958 at New York City by Henry Z. Walck, Sr., who resigned as president of Oxford University Press to form his own company. Walck purchased the juvenile book department of Oxford which had been started in 1929. This list of about two hundred and seventy-five titles became the nucleus of Walck's first catalogue. Among the authors and illustrators represented on this list were Edward Ardizzone, Cathrine Barr, Ruth and Latrobe Carroll, Eleanor Farjeon, Lois Lenski, Rosemary Sutcliff and Tasha Tudor.

Assisted by Patricia Cummings Lord, Walck has developed a fine list of his own that includes such authors as Hans Baumann, Fon W. Boardman, Jr., Robert B. Jackson, Tove Jansson, Beman Lord, Osmond Molarsky, Katharine Savage, and Ian Serraillier; and such well-received series as the *Walck Fairy Tales with Historical Notes* and the *Walck Archaeologies.*

On April 1, 1973 Henry Z. Walck, Inc. became the juvenile division of the David McKay Company, Inc.

Walker and Company

Established in 1959 in New York City by Samuel S. Walker, Jr., as Publications Development Corporation. The name was later changed to Walker Publishing Company, Inc., using the imprint Walker and Company, and it remains a privately held independent corporation.

Among the fifteen titles on Walker's first list, published in 1961, were such diverse books as a biography of Casey Stengel by Clay Felker, AFFAIRS OF THE HEART, a novel by Malcolm Muggeridge, and Hesketh Pearson's A LIFE OF SHAKESPEARE. It also featured eight Connoisseur Mysteries for the more sophisticated mystery

buff. The Walker list steadily expanded during its first decade and now exceeds one hundred titles per year.

Walker authors include Isaac Asimov, Eric Sloane, John Creasey, and Harlan Ellison. The company also brings out THE WORLD TRADE ANNUAL and the UNITED NATIONS LAW REPORTS.

A major facet of Walker's publishing program is juveniles. Barbara Cooney, Millicent E. Selsam, Leonard Weisgard, and Jan Adkins are among the well-known authors and illustrators on the Walker children's books list.

In the mid-1960s Walker founded its school division, Walker Educational Book Corporation, which has launched many innovative programs for the elementary and junior high schools, known as the *Walker Geo-Board Program,* the *Walker Plays for Reading Series,* and the *Starting Tomorrow Program.*

A subsidiary imprint known as Philip Hofer Books is also active. A noteworthy publication under this imprint was LATE CAPRICHOS OF GOYA, a portfolio of six hitherto unpublished plates by Goya.

Frederick Warne & Company, Inc.

Established in 1881 in New York City as an agency of Frederick Warne & Company Ltd. of London, England, which had been founded in 1865. The firm was incorporated as a New York company in 1920. It specializes in juveniles and picture books and is the original publisher of the *Peter Rabbit* books. Still owned by the London firm, a major activity of the New York branch is distribution of the British-published books.

Warner Paperback Library

A paperback reprint house that issues both fiction and nonfiction titles including some originals, and located in New York City. Originally organized as Paperback Library, Inc., it is now a division of Warner Communications, Inc.

Warner Press, Inc.

Founded in 1881 by Daniel S. Warner as the Gospel Trumpet Company in Rome City, Indiana. In 1906 it moved to Anderson, Indiana. The Press is the publications division of the Church of God, specializing in theological and inspirational books.

Neale Watson Academic Publications, Inc.

Organized in 1971 at New York City to publish educational and library books.

Watson-Guptill Publications

Established in 1937 at New York City. The company specializes in arts and crafts, graphics and fine arts. It is now a division of Billboard Publications, Inc.

Franklin Watts, Inc.

Established at New York City in 1942 by Franklin Watts. After beginning with a few adult titles he published his first book for children, LITTLE CHOO CHOO by Helen Hoke, who later became Mrs. Franklin Watts. It was a great success and the company continued to publish juvenile books. In the years between 1946 and 1956 the company grew rapidly. It also began to publish in the United States titles originating with the Oxford University Press of London, England. Probably the best-known author-artist to arrive on the Watts list in this manner was Brian Wildsmith. In 1957 Franklin Watts became a wholly-owned subsidiary of Grolier Incorporated.

Since acquisition by Grolier, Watts has continued to expand. In 1973 two new divisions were created. The first, New Viewpoints, recently acquired from Quadrangle selected titles for the college market, primarily in the area of the social sciences, and has instituted its own publishing program. New Viewpoints is also the American distributor of Fontana academic paperbacks published by William Collins & Sons, Ltd. of London. The second division, Educational Services, serves as distributor to schools and libraries for all Watts non-books, multi-media packages and specialized book lines such as Hammond Books and Atlases, Keith Jennison Large Type Books, Howell Book House, Troll Associates audio-visual materials, Collins' *Juvenile Classics* and bilingual dictionaries, and Newsweek's *Wonders of Man.*

Franklin Watts has been especially known for many years for its nonfiction books in series for grades 1-12. The most important and extensive of these series are *Let's Find Out Books* and *First Books. The Focus Book* series, grades 7-up, concentrates on retelling outstanding events in American history, while the *World Focus Books,* also grades 7-up, cover events in world history. A new series is the *International Library* of quality nonfiction books aimed at grades 7-up. These are printed simultaneously in five countries and in four languages.

In 1973 Franklin Watts set up its first overseas venture with the creation of RSW Verlag in Esslingen, Germany, in partnership with Rizzoli Editore of Milan, Italy, and J.F. Schreiber Verlag of Esslingen.

Upon the retirement of Franklin Watts in 1970, Howard B. Graham became the president of Franklin Watts, Inc. Franklin Watts established Franklin Watts, Ltd. in London, England, which publishes books for children and which he actively operates personally.

Wayne State University Press

Founded at Detroit, Michigan, in 1941 under the editorial supervision of Alexander Brede and Joseph Norris. In 1956 Harold A. Basilius became the director and he served in that capacity until his retirement in 1970.

The primary concern of Wayne State is with literary criticism, Jewish studies, psychiatry, and education, reflected in such works as FREUD AS WE KNEW HIM edited by Hendrik M. Ruitenbeek; LET'S READ by Leonard Bloomfield and Clarence L. Barnhart; "APPROXIMATE MAN"

AND OTHER WRITINGS by Tristan Tzara, translated by Mary Ann Caws; WALT WHITMAN: A STUDY IN THE EVOLUTION OF PERSONALITY by Jan Christian Smuts, edited by Alan L. McLeod; and THE HEBREW HUMANISM OF MARTIN BUBER by Grete Schaeder, translated by Noah J. Jacobs.

In 1970 Herbert M. Schueller, former chairman of the English Department, Wayne State University, and former editor of the *Journal of Aesthetics and Art Criticism,* became director of the Press. Wayne State University Press publishes under its own imprint as well as under an alternate imprint, Savoyard, and a paperback imprint, Waynebooks. The Press also publishes six quarterly journals in the fields of literary criticism, political science, psychiatry, and human biology.

We, Inc.

Established in 1967 at Old Greenwich, Connecticut. Publishes books on military history and technique for collectors and hobbyists.

John Weatherhill, Inc.

Organized in 1962 in New York City as a trade house specializing in books on Asia and the Pacific area. The original partners were Meredith Weatherby, former editor-in-chief of Tuttle, Takeshi Yamazaki, and Thorlief Johnsen. Johnsen later sold his interest to Charles R. Temple. The firm uses a subsidiary imprint known as Wayward Press.

Weatherhill's major publishing programs are: 1) Weatherhill Books; 2) *The Heibonsha Survey of Japanese Art,* a thirty-volume history of Japanese art originally published in Japanese by Heibonsha; 3) *The Arts of Japan,* based on the Shibundo series on Japanese arts and crafts; 4) *Kapa Books,* dealing with the culture and history of the Hawaiian Islands, in collaboration with Kapa Asssociates of Hawaii.

Weatherhill also represents a number of American publishers in Japan.

Webster Publishing Company

The Webster company was founded in 1924 by Waldo P. Johnson. At that time Johnson was a salesman for another educational publishing company and during his calls on schools he became aware of the need for student workbooks. He noticed pupils laboriously copying in their notebooks exercises that the teacher had written on the blackboard. He didn't name the new company the Johnson company because there was already another publishing company using that name. He decided that the name "Webster" sounded educational — it was used for the dictionary and so was associated with an educational product.

From 1924 to 1930 Johnson published workbooks; a successful title was SHARP'S ENGLISH EXERCISES. These were followed by reading series and spellers (he introduced a new concept of teaching spelling which was part of a language arts program that emphasized meanings, uses and the functions of the words on the spelling lists). In 1962 Webster acquired the assets of Gelles-Widmer and School Aids Products Co., producers of educational games and toys. In 1963 Webster merged with McGraw-Hill, and the company is currently a division of the McGraw-Hill Book Company.

Wesleyan University Press

Founded in 1957 in Middletown, Connecticut, as part of the university's Department of School Services and Publications. The main function of the Department was the publication of weekly classroom periodicals, American Education Publications, *My Weekly Reader, Current Events,* and others. In 1965 the periodical publishing program was sold to Xerox Corporation, along with the university's printing facility in Columbus, Ohio. Wesleyan University Press, the scholarly imprint, was from its inception unrelated to *My Weekly Reader, et al.,* and now operates as a department of the university.

Particularly strong in New England studies and works in the performing arts (notably the dance), the Press is best known for the *Wesleyan Poetry Program.* Since 1959 the Press has published at least four volumes of poetry each year simultaneously in clothbound and paperback editions. Three of its poetry titles have won major awards: AT THE END OF THE OPEN ROAD by Louis Simpson (Pulitzer Prize in Poetry, 1964), BUCK-DANCER'S CHOICE by James Dickey (National Book Award for Poetry, 1966), and COLLECTED POEMS OF JAMES WRIGHT (Pulitzer Prize in Poetry, 1972).

In cooperation with Mystic Seaport, Inc., Wesleyan publishes the *American Maritime Library,* a popular series of illustrated books in American maritime history. Wesleyan is also the publisher of HISTORY AND THEORY: STUDIES IN THE PHILOSOPHY OF HISTORY. Among other outstanding Wesleyan books are: LIFE AGAINST DEATH by Norman O. Brown, AMERICA GOES TO WAR by Bruce Catton, NEW YORK LANDMARKS, edited by Alan Burnham, which won the Carey-Thomas Award for Creative Publishing in 1963, and PURITAN VILLAGE by Sumner Chilton Powell, which won the Pulitzer Prize in History in 1964.

West Publishing Company

Founded in 1876 in St. Paul, Minnesota, by John B., and Horatio D. West to "provide better service to the lawyer than he is now receiving." The firm's first publication was *The Syllabi,* a pamphlet from which its current *The National Reporter System* is derived. This supplies the American Bar with reports on the current American case-law while *The American Digest System* provides a chronological digest of American case-law.

In 1924 the Congress of the United States commissioned West Publishing Company and the Edward Thompson Company to compile THE CODE OF THE LAWS OF THE UNITED STATES, and in 1946 both firms were again commissioned to revise the FEDERAL CRIMINAL CODE and the FEDERAL JUDICIAL CODE. In addition West published THE FEDERAL CASES, UNITED STATES CIRCUIT AND DISTRICT COURT DECISIONS TO 1880, and annotated statutes for the various states, as well as large number of textbooks.

In terms of law titles West is the largest lawbook publisher in the world. West has recently entered the college textbook field.

Westernlore Press

Established at Los Angeles, California, in 1941. It is a publisher of Western Americana.

Western Publishing Company, Inc.

Established in 1907 in Racine, Wisconsin, by E.H. Wadewitz when he took over the West Side Printing Company. Roy A. Spencer, a journeyman printer, joined him as partner. Their capital was a loan of $1,500.00 and their rent was $10.00 a month. By 1910 the firm had become prosperous and the partners incorporated with a capital of $75,000.00. A lithographic press was purchased and the firm was renamed the Western Printing and Lithographing Company.

In 1916 the firm unexpectedly became a publisher when the Hamming-Whitman Publishing Company of Chicago defaulted on its bills. Western, as chief creditor, acquired the assets of Hamming-Whitman, which included popular juveniles, and thus launched itself on a second career. The Whitman Publishing Company was organized as a subsidiary and in course of time became a major producer of cheap juveniles, games, and puzzles.

Needing capital to expand, Western sold stock interest to J. Wiechers, his brother, J.C. Wiechers, and later to H.M. Benstead. When the jigsaw puzzle craze hit the country in the early 1930s the company became a major producer of those puzzles. The first *Big Little Book* titles (so called because they contained as many as three hundred and fifty pages but measured only 3½″ by 4½″) also made their appearance during that era and eventually reached peak sales of over a million copies a month. Another milestone was reached in 1933 when Western entered into its first licensing agreement with Walt Disney Productions for the exclusive book rights to all Disney features and characters. MICKEY MOUSE SAILS FOR

TREASURE ISLAND was the first of a series of books that carried the Disney name. Today many of the company's books, games, and other products make use of popular animated characters and live personalities.

The Artists and Writers Press was formed about this time as a subsidiary of Western to create packaged books for other publishers. One of its most creative ideas was that of *Little Golden Books* for Simon & Schuster. In 1957 Western acquired this series from Simon & Schuster and organized the Golden Press to produce the complete line of Golden Book products for adults and children.

In 1940 Western acquired K.K. Publications, publisher of *Mickey Mouse* comic magazine. A new series known as *Gold Key Comics* was developed under this imprint. In 1950 the Guild Press was set up to publish books and supplementary materials for parochial schools. In 1961 the Racine Press was established to publish paperbacks and hardcover books for adults. When the Odyssey Press was acquired in 1961 Racine Press became its trade imprint. Odyssey Press, organized as a college textbook house, entered the trade field with the *Odyssey Library* and coffee-table books such as LA BELLE FRANCE and TREASURY OF HUNTING. Later Odyssey Press was sold to The Bobbs-Merrill Company. Another acquisition in 1961 was the Capitol Publishing Company which produced books and educational kits.

Renamed Western Publishing Company, Inc. in 1960, the firm vigorously expanded into foreign markets, establishing Whitman Golden Limited in Canada, Americas Publishing Company in Latin America, and Les Editions des Deux Coqs d'Or in France. In 1973 it acquired a large interest in Golden Press Pty. Ltd., one of Australia's largest publishers and distributors of books to the retail trade. Most of their books are manufactured by Western and exported to Australia under an arrangement set up twenty-five years ago.

Presiding over Western's phenomenal growth over the years have been a long line of able men including the Wadewitz brothers, E.H. and W.R., Roy Spencer, E.G. Voigt, H.E. Johnson, P.H. Lyle, H.M. Benstead, and Gerald J. Slade.

The Westminster Press

Founded in Philadelphia, Pennsylvania, in 1838 by the General Assembly of the Presbyterian Church. Its first publication was PSALMS AND HYMNS in 1840. The imprint was formally adopted in 1870. In 1924 it became the Department of Publication of the then new Board of Christian Education. In 1941 it was reorganized and restaffed, and launched its present expanded book publishing program.

Westminster publishes approximately seventy new books a year, of which twenty are juvenile books, the balance being adult nonfiction. Long noted for its substantial publications in the fields of theology, biblical studies, and church education, in recent years it has also issued important works in the fields of secular education, political and social science, and ethics. It currently numbers in excess of eight hundred titles on its active backlist.

The Press also publishes educational resource materials for church schools, and hymnals and anthem books.

Westover Publishing Company

Established in 1970 at Richmond, Virginia. An affiliate of Media General, Inc., the company publishes mostly trade nonfiction. In July 1974 it was purchased by Crown Publishers but is being maintained as an independent publisher.

Weybright & Talley, Inc.

Established in 1966 in New York City by Victor Weybright and Truman M. Talley. Publishes general nonfiction and juveniles. The firm was acquired by David McKay Company, of which it is now a division.

The Bond Wheelwright Company

Established in 1949 at Freeport, Maine, by Bond Wheelwright. The company specializes in regional books and general nonfiction of a premium and promotional nature.

David White Company

Established in 1963 at New York City by David White. The firm publishes nonfiction and juveniles. It also operates the Independent Publishers' Group of which the following are members: Behavioral Publications; Donald Brown, Inc.; Emerson Hall, Inc.; Paul S. Eriksson, Inc.; Lawrence Hill and Company; Whitney Library of Design.

James T. White and Company

Founded in 1873 in San Francisco, California, by James Terry White. In 1887 he moved his headquarters to New York City where the company was incorporated in 1902. In 1888 White launched the first volume of the NATIONAL CYCLOPEDIA OF AMERICAN BIOGRAPHY, an ongoing project. The firm relocated in Clifton, New Jersey, in 1969, and it continues in the control of the original family. In recent years it has formed two new divisions, one devoted to micrographics and the other to issuing trade and reference books in the area of the performing arts.

Whitehall Company

Established in 1959 at Northbrook, Illinois. The firm publishes books in the social sciences and education, languages, and history.

Albert Whitman & Company

Started in 1919 by Albert Whitman. Whitman began his career in the 1890s when he published a street guide for New York City. It was a logical move from this to association with Hammond Publishing Company and later Rand McNally. Whitman then joined the new company of Whitman-Hamming which, in 1915, was absorbed by the Western Printing and Lithographing Company.

Whitman focused his list on children's books at the time he resumed publishing in 1919 at Chicago, Illinois, under the name of Albert Whitman & Company. The imprint of Laird and Lee and the trade division of Laidlaw Brothers were acquired in 1931, adding a series of pocket dictionaries and adult titles in a field as unusual as occult science. By 1945, however, juvenile trade books became the company's single area of concentration.

Whitman remained with the company until his death in 1962 but the ownership by 1949 had passed to five employees. William McGovern became president of the company and upon his retirement in 1961 Edward J. Wambach succeeded him.

Among popular authors and artists who have appeared under the Whitman imprint are: John Hawkinson, Laura Bannon, Janice May Udry, Jean Merrill, Kurt Wiese, Katherine Evans, Joe Lasker, Miriam Schlein, Norma Simon, and Florence Perry Heide.

Over the years, Maj. Lindman's *Snipp, Snapp, Snurr* books and Gertrude Warner's *Boxcar Children* mysteries have proved perennial Whitman favorites.

Whitston Publishing Company

Established in 1968 at Troy, New York. Specializes in bibliographies and creative anthologies of the twentieth-century *avant-garde*.

Wilderness Press

Established in 1967 at Berkeley, California. Specializes in books on the outdoors.

John Wiley & Sons, Inc.

Established in 1807 by Charles Wiley at New York City as a bookstore. This bookshop became a celebrated literary rendezvous known as The Den. The Wiley imprint first appeared in

1819 as C. Wiley & Company on a small edition of FANNY, a long, narrative poem by Fitz-Greene Halleck, a member of The Den. James Fenimore Cooper was also a member of this circle and his book, THE SPY, was another early Wiley publication.

When Charles Wiley died in 1826, his son, John Wiley, took over the business. In 1832 George Long became a partner, and the business name was changed to Wiley & Long. Next year Wiley acquired still another associate, George Palmer Putnam. When Long withdrew in 1840 the firm became Wiley & Putnam and emerged as a vigorous literary house.

The Wiley & Putnam *Library of Choice Reading,* edited by Evart A. Duyckinck, included works by Charles Dickens, William M. Thackeray, William Hazlitt, Charles Lamb, Thomas Carlyle, Johann Wolfgang Goethe, Johann Schiller, and John Ruskin. A companion series, *The Library of American Books,* included works by Nathaniel Hawthorne, Edgar Allan Poe, and Herman Melville.

At the urging of Putnam a branch was opened in London, England. This proved to be unprofitable and was closed in 1848. In the same year the partners arranged an amicable separation; Putnam took with him most of the literary titles except those of Ruskin, and Wiley retained most of the scientific and technical works. This was the field in which the firm, now known simply as John Wiley, began to concentrate. Its earliest title in science was AN INTRODUCTION OF ALGEBRA by Jeremiah Day, published in 1815. In 1839 its first text in physics appeared, and in 1855 the first text in chemistry. By the end of the Civil War the firm had become one of the largest publishers in the fields of mathematics, technology, engineering, chemistry, and mineralogy.

The stimulating force behind this growth was John Wiley's son, William H., who had joined his brother Charles as a member of the firm in 1876. An engineer by profession and a charter member of the American Society of Mechanical Engineers, William conceived the idea of issuing condensed engineering pocket books. One of these, F.E. Kidder's ARCHITECT'S AND BUILDER'S POCKET-BOOK, became a basic tool for architects. William H. Wiley's entry

into the firm also led to a change in its name to John Wiley & Sons. The firm was incorporated in 1904 with William H. Wiley as president. In 1925 he was succeeded by his nephew, William O. Wiley.

The Wiley list steadily broadened into the biological sciences, geology, statistics, metallurgy, electronics, agriculture, home economics, the social sciences, psychology, and nuclear science. Among its influential and seminal books are: INTRODUCTION TO CHEMISTRY by W.F. Ostwald; MINING ENGINEER'S HANDBOOK by R. Peele; TEXTBOOK OF GEOLOGY by L.V. Pirsson and C. Schuchert; ANIMAL PARASITES AND HUMAN DISEASES by A.C. Chandler; METHOD FOR THE IDENTIFICATION OF PURE ORGANIC COMPOUNDS by S.P. Milliken; STATISTICAL METHODS by C.B. Davenport; ELEMENTS OF ELECTRICITY by W.H. Timbie; APPLIED MECHANICS by C.E. Fuller and W.A. Johnston; ARCHITECTURAL GRAPHIC STANDARDS by C.G. Ramsey and H.R. Sleeper; PRINCIPLES OF RADIO by K. Henney; FIRST PRINCIPLES OF TELEVISION by A. Dinsdale; CYBERNETICS by N. Wiener; and EVOLUTIONARY GENETICS AND MAN by T. Dobzhansky. From 1937 until 1963 Wiley produced and marketed the Massachusetts Institute of Technology Press books.

Edward P. Hamilton, a grandson of John Wiley, assumed the presidency of the firm in 1940. Under him the firm launched a number of new series: *Biological Research; Biochemical Preparations; The Structure of Matter; Alloys of Iron Monograph Series; Organic Synthesis; Organic Reaction; Applied Mathematics;* and *Mathematical Statistics.* In 1956 W. Bradford Wiley was chosen to be president of the company when Hamilton became chairman of the company's board.

Following World War II, Wiley broadened its activities in a variety of ways. International marketing, distribution and publishing have been systematically developed, commencing with the formation in 1960 of John Wiley & Sons, Ltd. in London, initially as a distribution and marketing center and more recently as a publishing unit in its present location in Chichester. Editorial Limusa, S.A. was started in Mexico City in 1962 as a joint venture between Wiley and a syndicate of Mexican publishers to publish translations and original works in the Spanish language. Livros Tecnicos E Cientificos Editora S.A., another joint venture, for Portuguese language publication, was organized in Brazil in 1967 and enlarged substantially in 1972. Wiley Australasia Pty., Ltd., was established in 1963, and Wiley Canada Ltd. in 1968, both following the model of the British company in evolving from marketing and distribution operations into complete publishing centers.

Wiley acquired Interscience Publishers in 1961, thereby adding not only a substantial list and editorial capability in scientific and technical book publishing, but also a program of encyclopedias, such as the ENCYCLOPEDIA OF CHEMICAL TECHNOLOGY, and scientific journals such as the *Journal of Polymer Science*. Wiley became a public company after the Interscience merger and held its first annual stockholders' meeting in 1963.

Concurrently the company began the expansion of its college textbook publishing program to encompass a broad spectrum of undergraduate subjects in the social sciences, in addition to strengthening its established programs in the biological and physical sciences. Titles such as FUNDAMENTAL CONCEPTS IN BIOLOGY by Gideon E. Nelson, Gerald G. Robinson and R.A. Boolootian, THEORIES OF PERSONALITY by Calvin S. Hall and Gardner Lindzey, INTRODUCTION TO PHYSICAL GEOGRAPHY by Arthur N. Strahler, and THE LITTLE ENGLISH HANDBOOK by Edward P. Corbett, are representative of Wiley College Division titles that have become major undergraduate teaching vehicles.

Similarly, the professional and reference programs in books, encyclopedias, and journals, have undergone considerable expansion and subject broadening under the auspices of the Wiley-Interscience Division. ARCHITECTURAL GRAPHIC STANDARDS, now in its sixth edition, is a standard reference work for architects and builders. The list includes many titles in the social sciences, business, and computer applications in addition to the established lists in the sciences; the various books in computer languages by Daniel D. McCracken have reflected, and aided,

the rapidly expanding employment of data-processing in all areas of science, business, and education.

Wiley's activities have diversified further in the late 1960s with the acquisition of Becker & Hayes, Inc., specializing in professional services to libraries and library systems, and of Wiley Systems, developers of seminars and packaged programs for business and industrial training. In addition, the company has established decentralized publishing units in Los Angeles and Santa Barbara, California, Melville Publishing Company and Hamilton Publishing Company, respectively.

In 1971, Andrew H. Neilly, Jr. became the president and the chief operating officer of the company and W. Bradford Wiley continued as chairman of the board and its chief executive officer.

The Williams & Wilkins Company

Founded by John H. Williams as a printing shop in Baltimore, Maryland, in 1890. The firm was incorporated in 1892 as John H. Williams Company, Inc. In need of additional financing for his growing business, Williams took a friend, Harry B. Wilkins, as a partner and the firm became Williams & Wilkins. In 1897 the partners hired a full-time salesman, Edward B. Passano, an engineer by profession. About the turn of the century Williams sold his equity in the firm to Wilkins. In 1904 came the Great Baltimore Fire which wiped out the press. Passano, who by then was managing the business, decided to keep it going and he bought Wilkins' interest. The company has been owned by the Passano family ever since. In 1946 William Passano became president of the firm when his father, Edward Passano, died.

In 1909, largely through the influence of John J. Abel, professor of pharmacology at The Johns Hopkins University School of Medicine, Williams & Wilkins published their first journal, *The Journal of Pharmacology and Experimental Therapeutics*. This was followed by scores of journals, and the publication of journals inevitably led to the publication of books. In 1920 THE DETER-

MINATION OF HYDROGEN IONS became the first book with The Williams & Wilkins imprint. The first trade catalog was issued in 1922. The next important landmark was the acquisition in 1932 of William Wood & Company of New York, one of the oldest medical publishers in the United States, established in 1805. This acquisition added three hundred and eighty-six titles to The Williams & Wilkins list. Many of these are still widely used. Some of them are: DISEASES OF THE EYE by C. May; PHYSICAL DIAGNOSIS by F. Dennette Adams; Frederick Randolph Bailey's TEXTBOOK OF HISTOLOGY; Thomas Lathrop Stedman's MEDICAL DICTIONARY; Hamilton Bailey's PHYSICAL SIGNS IN CLINICAL SURGERY; and PRINCIPLES OF BACTERIOLOGY AND IMMUNOLOGY by W.C. Topley and Graham S. Wilson. In 1943 the medical books of Little, Brown and in 1952 the medical books of Thomas Nelson & Sons were acquired.

The 1973 catalog of Williams & Wilkins lists 340 domestic book titles and 780 which have been imported from abroad. It also lists nineteen periodicals published by the company for scientific societies, nine of which the company owns outright, eighteen foreign journals, for which the company is the distributor in the United States, and seven journals owned and published by others, to whom the company supplies all needed publishing services, are also included. The company also provides publishing services which do not include subscription fulfillment to sixty other journals. The ability to offer complete publishing services to others is one of the company's most unique features.

Wilshire Book Company

Established in 1947 in Los Angeles, California, by Melvin Powers. Wilshire specializes in nonfiction of a psychological and inspirational nature. One of its most popular titles in this area is PSYCHO-CYBERNETICS by Maxwell Maltz. Wilshire also publishes a wide range of books on horsemanship, health, astrology, bridge, hypnosis, gardening, bicycling, chess, Judaica, metaphysics, and the occult. The company has four imprint lines: Melvin Powers Self-Improvement Library, Wilshire Horse Lovers Library, Chess Lovers Library, and Wilshire Health Series.

The H.W. Wilson Company

Founded in 1898 in Minneapolis, Minnesota, by Halsey William Wilson. A bookseller located on the campus of the University of Minnesota, Wilson decided to issue his own monthly bibliography of current American trade books. This bibliography known as CUMULATIVE BOOK INDEX (CBI) first appeared in 1898 as a pamphlet of sixteen pages. There were twenty-six subscribers to it. In 1899 Wilson published the first of the four editions of the UNITED STATES CATALOG, a national trade list of books in print.

But it was with CBI that Wilson began developing his methods of gathering periodic bibliographic listings into large cumulated lists covering longer periods of time and easy to search by subject, author, and title. These methods were also applied to one of his earliest and most successful ventures, the READER'S GUIDE TO PERIODICAL LITERATURE, whose 1900-1904 cumulation featured a dictionary arrangement, with uniform subject headings, never before achieved in an American periodical index. With the READER'S GUIDE Wilson also inaugurated a service-basis system of pricing, based on potential use, which allowed his enterprise to gain a foothold in the extremely precarious business of bibliographic publishing. In 1972 Wilson could claim subscribers in more than one hundred thousand libraries in some one hundred and twenty-five countries.

The company was incorporated in 1903 and soon after moved into its own building opposite the main campus of the University of Minnesota. Publications and services proliferated and, reluctantly, Wilson left Minneapolis to be nearer to New York City. After a brief period in White Plains, N.Y., the firm settled in the Bronx in New York City. Wilson headed the firm until 1952. He was succeeded as president by Howard Haycraft. In 1967 Leo M. Weins assumed the presidency. The company is owned mainly by past and present employees and is directed by a board consisting of company officers and of prominent librarians.

Currently Wilson publishes a variety of general and specialized indexes, such as *Reader's Guide* and *Education Index;* tools for book selection and cataloging, such as *Book Review Digest* and *Children's Catalog;* biographical reference works, that include *Current Biography* and the *Authors* series; ready reference, of which *Famous First Facts* is one; for background reference, the *Reference Shelf;* for professional library materials, *Sears List of Subject Headings* and *Library Literature;* and the journal, *Wilson Library Bulletin.*

Winchester Press

Established in 1969 in New York City, it is a division of Olin Corporation. The firm's first publication was THE HISTORY OF WINCHESTER FIREARMS. It specializes in books on hunting, shooting, and outdoor sports.

Windmill Books, Inc.

Established in 1967 at New York City as a publisher exclusively of juvenile picture and storybooks, usually co-published and distributed by other publishing houses.

V.H. Winston & Sons, Inc.

Set up in 1971 at Washington, D.C. as an affiliate of Scripta Publishing Corporation. Issues books and journals in the behavioral sciences, which are distributed by Halsted Press.

Wm. H. Wise & Company, Inc.

Founded in 1888 by Wm. H. Wise, Elbert Hubbard, and Fred Dolan, Sr. The company was originally incorporated in Illinois, later in Delaware, and finally in New York. The firm was one of the earliest direct mail merchandisers of sub-

scription books. Wm. H. Wise was president of the company from 1888 to 1933; his successors were Fred Dolan Sr. (1933-34), John Crawley, Sr. (1934-63), and John Crawley Jr. (1963—). John J. Crawley & Company, Inc., Catholic publishers, was acquired in 1951.

Wise publishes many popular encyclopedias and sets, such as: CARAVAN: THE WORLD SHOPPING ENCYCLOPEDIA; TREASURE BOX: THE CHILDREN'S ENCYCLOPEDIA; CRUSADE: BIBLE STORIES FOR CHILDREN; WISE GARDEN ENCYCLOPEDIA; WISE COOKING ENCYCLOPEDIA; WISE FISHING ENCYCLOPEDIA; and ENCYCLOPEDIA OF U.S. GOVERNMENT BENEFITS.

George Wittenborn, Inc.

A spin-off in 1947 from the parent firm of Wittenborn & Company founded in 1937 by George Wittenborn, born in Germany and a trained bookseller who left that country in 1932. For the next four years he ran his own bookstore in Paris, then, feeling that war was inevitable in Europe, he, with his English wife, Joyce Phillips, and baby son, Andrew, emigrated to the United States in 1936. The next year he opened a bookstore, first working out of his family apartment near Columbia University in New York City, but soon he moved to larger premises on East 57th Street, specializing in art books.

At the suggestion of Robert Motherwell and Laszlo Moholy-Nagy, the Wittenborns, together with their partner, Heinz Schultz, started to publish a series of books on the modern art movements in Europe, with Joyce Wittenborn as supervisor of translations from French, German and Spanish. Two series were begun, *The Documents of Modern Art* (which is still active) and *The Problems of Contemporary Art.* These series were unusual in that they were the first book-sized paperbacks in the art field. In 1947 a subsidiary, first called Wittenborn, Schultz, Inc., took over the publishing side of Wittenborn & Company, becoming George Wittenborn Inc., under the guidance of George and Joyce Wittenborn after Heinz Schultz withdrew from the business in 1952.

The firm was one of the first to publish books by Jean Arp, Morris Ernst, Laszlo Moholy-Nagy, *et al.* in paperback, as well as hardcover books on the Dada painters and poets Paul Rand, André Masson, and others, and a periodical, *Possibilities,* concerned with the New York School, edited by Robert Motherwell, Harold Rosenberg and John Cage. Also another periodical, *Transformation,* edited by Harry Holtzman. More recently the firm has published, among others, books on and by Josef Albers, and the first two volumes of Paul Klee's teaching notebooks, entitled respectively THE THINKING EYE and THE NATURE OF NATURE.

Word Books

Founded at Waco, Texas, in 1965 as the publishing division of Word, Inc., a religious recording firm. Under Floyd Thatcher, vice president and executive editor, the house has built up a successful list that includes books by Keith Miller, Malcolm Boyd, Charlie Shedd, Elizabeth O'Connor, Charles Merrill Smith, Robert Raines, William Stringfellow, and Art Linkletter.

Workman Publishing Company, Inc.

Established in 1967 at New York City by Peter Workman. Issues general nonfiction and crafts books. Also co-publishes with other firms under their imprints.

World Publishing Company

Established in 1905 at Cleveland, Ohio, by Alfred Cahen as a small book bindery called Commercial Bookbinding Company. Cahen bought the World Syndicate Publishing Company in 1929. He adopted that name but shortened it to World Publishing Company in 1940. He did not enter publishing until Ben D. Zevin, his son-in-law, who had joined his firm in 1934, launched the *Tower Books* in 1939. These were hardbound reprints of standard books in public domain, priced at forty-

nine cents a copy. Encouraged by the success of these editions, Zevin issued *World Illustrated Editions,* illustrated reprints of classics, at fifty-nine cents a copy, and *Forum Books,* consisting of nonfiction and anthologies. World's Bible and dictionary lines were also established at this time.

In time World was to become one of the largest publishers of Bibles and dictionaries in the United States. Its range of dictionaries, edited by David B. Guralnik since 1948, includes eight different editions of WEBSTER'S NEW WORLD DICTIONARY OF THE AMERICAN LANGUAGE. In 1945 Zevin commissioned Bruce Rogers to design a folio Bible, now known as the BRUCE ROGERS BIBLE, issued in 1949 in a limited edition. In 1941 Zevin engaged William Targ to develop a trade department and to expand the firm's reprint activities. Targ arranged with Carl Van Doren to edit *The Living Library,* contemporary American classics at $1.00 a copy. This series appeared in 1946. In the same year a juvenile series was introduced: *Rainbow Classics,* edited by May Lamberton Becker.

World began trade publishing in earnest in 1948. One major impetus in this direction was Donald Friede, of the by then defunct firm of Covici-Friede, who joined World in 1953, bringing with him several authors. Theodore Dreiser was a World author: so were Simone de Beauvoir, Herbert Gold, Lillian Smith, Clifton Fadiman, and MacKinlay Kantor. In the late 1950s the World catalogue included such outstanding books as Richard Mason's THE WORLD OF SUZIE WONG; C.A. Bowra's THE GREEK EXPERIENCE; Ashley Montagu's THE CULTURED MAN; James Ramsey Ullman's THE DAY ON FIRE; Harry Golden's ONLY IN AMERICA; François Mauriac's THE SON OF MAN; and THE MEMOIRS OF FIELD MARSHAL BERNARD MONTGOMERY. In 1960 World purchased Meridian Books, a paperback firm.

In 1963, through an exchange of stock, The Times Mirror Company acquired World Publishing Company. At the present time, Martin P. Levin, a vice president of Times Mirror, is chairman and chief executive officer of World.

In January, 1974, World sold to William Collins Sons & Co., Ltd. of Great Britain its Bible and dictionary interests.

Worth Publishers, Inc.

Established in 1966 at New York City. Publishes undergraduate college textbooks and supplements.

The Writer, Inc.

Founded in 1887 at Boston, Massachusetts, as a journal for writers and has continued publication up to the present time. Issues books of special interest to and for writers.

Peter H. Wyden, Inc.

A small general nonfiction trade house in New York City, whose books are distributed by David McKay Company.

Xerox Education Publications

Established in 1902 by Charles Palmer Davis in the small western Massachusetts town of Agawam. The initial publication by Davis was *Current Events,* a classroom newspaper written expressly for the young and designed to provide them with important news of America and the world. From the start, the paper was a phenomenal success. Davis wrote the first issues of *Current Events* at home and had them printed in nearby Springfield, Massachusetts. He soon shifted the entire operation to Springfield.

In 1917 the Davis firm, now called American Education Press, Inc., moved to New York City where it established its own wholly-owned printing and distribution plant. Three years later the company moved again, this time to Columbus, Ohio, where it occupied from 1936 to 1954 one of the most modern buildings in the nation, built extensively of hollow glass. Meanwhile, in 1928 the company had begun its greatest period of growth with the publication of *My Weekly Reader,* directed at children in the elementary school grades. *My Weekly Reader* is the largest newspaper for children in the world, with an estimated readership of more than ten million. Its special vacation version, *Summer Weekly Reader* reaches three million homes. Another newspaper, *Current Science,* was created in 1932 to provide grammar school classrooms with the latest news in science.

In 1952 AEP was purchased by Wesleyan University and its editorial and management operations were moved to Middletown, Connecticut. In the mid-1960s the Xerox Corporation purchased AEP from Wesleyan University and made it a part of its Xerox Education Group.

In 1953 the company entered the children's book club field with Weekly Reader Children's Book Club, and in 1968 the I Can Read Book Club. The Paperback Book Club division provided low-cost paperbacks for all grade levels. The company also produced some seventy-five various publications for the classroom, including a wide range of *Unit Books* for secondary schools. In 1972 Xerox decided to separate the two divisions by creating Xerox Education Publications to produce periodicals and paperback books for schools, and Xerox Family Education Services for hardcover books and records sold to children at home.

The company meanwhile continued its innovative production of supplementary materials for the classroom. Based on the success of the *Read Magazine,* launched in 1951, the firm introduced two newspapers created especially to help poor readers to improve their reading skills, *Know Your World* and *You and Your World.* Three more periodicals were also introduced: *Discovering Science,* a news-oriented science periodical; *Urban World,* a news magazine focusing on city life; and *Issues Today,* a social studies periodical dealing with important civic issues. The company has also broadened its range of *Unit Books* for secondary school classrooms. Among them are the famed *Harvard Public Issues Series, The Black Experience in America Series, Values and Decisions,* and *Science Unit Books,* that range in subject matter from space exploration to pollution and drug addiction. Another series, *Practice Books,* helps students at all grade levels to improve knowledge and skills in reading, science, and arithmetic.

The company produces and markets 16-millimeter films and sound filmstrips through its

Xerox Films division and also markets the Xedia program comprised of children's literature on microfiche.

Yale University Press

Founded in 1908 at New Haven, Connecticut, by G.P. Day who later became treasurer of Yale University. One of the early Yale titles was B.F. Bacon's THE BEGINNINGS OF THE GOSPEL STORY. Various endowments, from alumni and friends enabled the Press to begin a substantial publishing program after World War I.

Day directed the Press for thirty-six years, one of the longest tenures in university press history. His successor was E.S. Furniss, a university officer who carried the title until 1950. N.V. Donaldson was director from 1950 until 1959, when he yielded to Chester Kerr, a widely respected scholar whose A REPORT ON AMERICAN UNIVERSITY PRESSES is a standard work on the subject.

The Yale imprint has been identified with outstanding multi-volume works: the YALE SHAKESPEARE in forty volumes; the *Yale Oriental Series* in thirty volumes; *Yale Romantic Series* in fourteen volumes; the CORRESPONDENCE OF HORACE WALPOLE in forty volumes; the PAPERS OF BENJAMIN FRANKLIN in forty volumes; the WORKS OF SAMUEL JOHNSON in fifteen volumes; and the WRITINGS OF THOMAS MORE. In addition, the Press has brought out a number of popular books of distinction, among them THE HIGHER LEARNING IN AMERICA by R.M. Hutchins, David Reisman's THE LONELY CROWD, Carl L. Becker's MODERN DEMOCRACY, Gisela M. Richter's SCULPTURE OF THE GREEKS, Thurman W. Arnold's FOLKLORE OF CAPITALISM, Henry Steele Commager's THE AMERICAN MIND, and Eugene O'Neill's LONG DAY'S JOURNEY INTO NIGHT. The publication of THE VINLAND MAP in 1965 was a landmark in the scholarship of discovery. A paperback program instituted in 1959 includes a number of titles from the rich Yale backlist.

Year Book Medical Publishers

Founded in 1900 at Chicago, Illinois, by Gustavus P. Head who, with his colleague Albert H. Andrews, published in that year a volume entitled YEAR BOOK OF NOSE, THROAT AND EAR. Its success prompted Head to make this an annual volume and to develop similar volumes in other fields of medicine. A series of *Practical Medical Year Books* was thus launched. The first volume in this new series appeared in 1901 under the imprint of The Year Book Publishers. From then on the series grew to its current size of twenty Year Books in the medical specialties and one in dentistry. In 1938 the first volume of a new series, *General Practice Manuals,* was ENDOCRINE THERAPY by Elmer Sevringhaus. After issuance of this title, the company's non-Year Book publications grew steadily.

In 1965 the company was acquired by The Times Mirror Company. At the time of the purchase the company was under the direction of Alexander M. Greene who had been its president since 1948. William F. Keller became president on Greene's retirement in 1968.

Young Readers Press

Acquired in 1972 by Simon & Schuster, Inc., this company publishes and distributes paperback books for grades kindergarten through twelve. Generally these books are reprints of original hardcover publications.

Books are sold directly to the student through book clubs. Sales material is sent to school teachers who distribute the material to the students and transmit the class order to the company.

Zondervan Publishing House

Established in 1931 by two brothers, Pat and Bernie Zondervan, in the back bedroom of their family farmhouse in Grand Rapids, Michigan. Beginning as a book distribution operation, it soon expanded into a retail bookstore, and in

1933 into a publishing house with the publication of two titles: WOMEN OF THE OLD TESTAMENT and WOMEN OF THE NEW TESTAMENT, both by Abraham Kuyper. From these small beginnings the firm has expanded. Today the Zondervan Corporation has seven divisions "united by the single goal of communicating the Word of God." Of these seven divisions the Zondervan Publishing House, the Zondervan Bible Publishers and the Zondervan Book of Life are concerned with book publishing. Zondervan's expansion has been directed by the Zondervan brothers and by Peter Kladder, Jr., who is currently the company's president.

Major publishing programs of the firm include: THE NEW INTERNATIONAL VERSION OF THE BIBLE; THE AMPLIFIED BIBLE; THE NEW TESTAMENT FROM TWENTY-SIX TRANSLATIONS; THE LAYMAN'S PARALLEL NEW TESTAMENT; THE NEW INTERNATIONAL DICTIONARY OF THE CHRISTIAN CHURCH; THE NEW EXPOSITORS BIBLE COMMENTARY; THE ZONDERVAN PICTORIAL BIBLE ENCYCLOPEDIA; the *Zondervan Bible Students Library; The Compact Bible Reference Library;* and the *Zondervan Book of Life,* a ten-volume, home Bible study set.

III

Conglomerates

BELL AND HOWELL COMPANY
Charles E. Merrill Publishing Company

CHARTER COMMUNICATIONS, INC.
Ace Books, Inc.
Dauntless Books, Inc.
G & D Publications, Inc.
Harle Publications, Inc.
U.S. Electronic Publications

CHC CORPORATION
University Park Press

**COLUMBIA BROADCASTING
SYSTEM, INC.**
CBS Consumer Publishing Division
Popular Library
CBS Educational Publishing Division
BFA Educational Media
Holt, Rinehart & Winston, Inc.
CBS Publishing Division
W.B. Saunders Company

COX BROADCASTING CORPORATION
American Photographic Book Publishing
Co., Inc. (Amphoto)

DUN & BRADSTREET, INC.
Dun-Donnelley Publishing Corporation
Thomas Y. Crowell Company
Abelard-Schuman, Ltd.
Criterion Books
The John Day Company
Funk & Wagnalls Publishing
Company
Intext Educational Publishers

ESQUIRE, INC.
Globe Book Company

FILMWAYS, INC.
Grosset & Dunlap, Inc.

GULF + WESTERN INDUSTRIES, INC.
Simon & Schuster, Inc.

IBM
Science Research Associates, Inc.

IFI INTERNATIONAL
Bantam Books, Inc.
Plenum Publishing Corporation

ITT
G.K. Hall & Company
Gregg Press
Twayne Publishers
Marquis Who's Who, Inc.
Howard W. Sams Company, Inc.
American Handbook & Textbook
Company, Inc.
Theodore Audel & Company
The Bobbs-Merrill Company, Inc.
Intertec Publishing Corporation
The Research & Review Service of
America, Inc.

INTEXT, INC.
Intext Publishers Group
Intext Press, Inc.
Steck-Vaughn Company

LITTON INDUSTRIES, INC.
Litton Educational Publishing, Inc.
American Book Company
Collectors Editions Limited
Delmar Publishers
McCormick-Mathers Publishing
Company
D. Van Nostrand Company
Van Nostrand Reinhold Company

THE NEW YORK TIMES COMPANY
Arno Press, Inc.
Cambridge Book Company
Quadrangle/The New York Times
Book Company

RADIO CORPORATION OF AMERICA
Random House, Inc.
Ballantine Books, Inc.
Beginner Books
A.A. Knopf, Inc.
Pantheon Books, Inc.

RAYTHEON COMPANY
D.C. Heath & Company

TIME, INC.
Little, Brown & Company
New York Graphic Society, Ltd.
Silver Burdett Company
Time Incorporated Book Clubs, Inc.
Time-Life Books

THE TIMES MIRROR COMPANY
Harry N. Abrams, Inc.
Matthew Bender & Company, Inc.
Denoyer-Geppert Company
Fuller & Dees Marketing Group, Inc.
C.V. Mosby Company
New American Library Inc.
Popular Science Publishing Company, Inc.
The Southwestern Company
World Publishing Company
Year Book Medical Publishers

UNIVERSAL PRESS SYNDICATE
Sheed & Ward, Inc.

WARNER COMMUNICATIONS, INC.
Warner Modular Publications, Inc.
Warner Books, Inc.
Warner Paperback Library

XEROX CORPORATION
R.R. Bowker Company
Ginn and Company
Unipub, Inc.
Xerox Education Publications
Xerox University Microfilms

IV

Multiple
Publishing Houses

ADDISON-WESLEY PUBLISHING COMPANY, INC.
    W.A. Benjamin, Inc.
    Cummings Publishing Co., Inc.
    Field Educational Publications

ALLYN AND BACON, INC.
    Holbrook Press, Inc.

AMERICAN ART ENTERPRISES, INC.
    Barclay House Books
    Books For Better Living
    Brandon Books

BARTELL MEDIA CORPORATION
    Bartholomew House Ltd.
    Macfadden-Bartell Corporation

BFL COMMUNICATIONS, INC.
    Books for Libraries Press, Inc.
    Nash Publishing Corporation

CHILDRENS PRESS
    Elk Grove Press
    Golden Gate Press
    Melmont Publishers

CONSOLIDATED BOOK PUBLISHERS
    Advance Publishers Inc.
    Catholic Press
    Culinary Arts Institute
    John A. Dickson Publishing Company
    The English-Language Institute of
        America, Inc.
    Menorah Press
    Processing & Books, Inc.

CROWN PUBLISHERS, INC.
    Barre Publishers
    The Imprint Society
    Lenox Hill Press
    Clarkson N. Potter, Inc.
    Westover Publishing Company

DELL PUBLISHING COMPANY, INC.
    The Delacorte Press
    The Dial Press
    Noble & Noble, Publishers, Inc.

DOUBLEDAY & COMPANY, INC.
    Feffer & Simons, Inc.
    J.G. Ferguson Publishing Company
    Laidlaw Brothers
    Literary Guild of America

E.P. DUTTON & COMPANY, INC.
    Outerbridge & Lazard, Inc.
    Saturday Review Press

ENCYCLOPAEDIA BRITANNICA, INC.
    F.E. Compton Company
    Library Resources, Inc.
    G. & C. Merriam Company
    Praeger Publishers, Inc.

FARRAR, STRAUS & GIROUX, INC.
    Hill & Wang
    Octagon Books

FIELD ENTERPRISES EDUCATIONAL CORPORATION
    World Book Encyclopedia, Inc.

GROLIER, INCORPORATED
    Americana Corporation
    Lexicon Publications, Inc.
    Scarecrow Press, Inc.
    Spencer International Press, Inc.
    Franklin Watts, Inc.

HARCOURT BRACE JOVANOVICH, INC.
    Academic Press, Inc.
    Grune & Stratton, Inc.
    Guidance Associates, Inc.
    HBJ Publications Division
    History Book Club
    Johnson Reprint Corporation

Media Systems Corporation
The Psychological Corporation
Pyramid Communications, Inc.
Seminar Press, Inc.

HARPER & ROW, PUBLISHERS, INC.
Barnes & Noble Books
Basic Books, Inc.

HAWTHORN BOOKS, INC.
Appleton-Century-Crofts
Channel Press
Duell, Sloan and Pearce
Meredith Press

HAYDEN BOOK COMPANY, INC.
Ahrens Book Company, Inc.
John F. Rider, Inc.
Spartan Books, Inc.

RICHARD D. IRWIN, INC.
Business Publications, Inc.
Dorsey Press
Dow Jones-Irwin, Inc.
Learning Systems Company

J.B. LIPPINCOTT COMPANY
Ballinger Publishing Company
A.J. Holman Company
Frederick A. Stokes Company

McGRAW-HILL, INC.
American Heritage Publishing
Company, Inc.
McGraw-Hill Book Company
Gregg Publishing Company
Webster Publishing Company
Shepard's Citations

DAVID McKAY COMPANY, INC.
Charterhouse Books, Inc.
Fodor's Modern Guides, Inc.
Ives Washburn, Inc.
Henry Z. Walck, Inc.
Weybright & Talley, Inc.
Peter H. Wyden, Inc.

MACMILLAN, INC.
(formerly, Crowell Collier & Macmillan, Inc.)
Benziger, Bruce & Glencoe, Inc.
Berlitz Publications, Inc.
Brentano's
Hagstrom Company, Inc.

Macmillan Book Clubs, Inc.
Macmillan Publishing Company, Inc.
The Free Press
Hafner Press (formerly Hafner
Publishing Company)
P.J. Kenedy & Sons
Macmillan Information
G. Schirmer, Inc.
Stechert Macmillan (formerly Stechert-
Hafner, Inc.)

NATIONAL LEARNING CORPORATION
Delaney Books, Inc.
Frank Merriwell, Inc.

W.W. NORTON & COMPANY, INC.
Liveright Publishing Corporation

PRENTICE-HALL, INC.
Bureau of Business Practices, Inc.
Goodyear Publishing Company, Inc.
Institute for Business Planning, Inc.
New York Institute for Finance
Parker Publishing Company
Reston Publishing Company
Winthrop Publishers, Inc.

G.P. PUTNAM'S SONS
Berkley Publishing Corporation
Coward, McCann & Geoghegan, Inc.

RAND McNALLY & COMPANY
Lyons and Carnahan

WILLIAM H. SADLIER, INC.
Keystone Education Press
Oxford Book Company, Inc.

SCOTT, FORESMAN & COMPANY
William Morrow & Company, Inc.
Lothrop, Lee & Shepard Company
South-Western Publishing Company, Inc.

THE SEABURY PRESS, INC.
Herder and Herder

SIMON & SCHUSTER, INC.
Julian Messner
Monarch Press
Pocket Books
Trident Press
Washington Square Press
Young Readers Press

LYLE STUART, INC.
Citadel Press, Inc.
Fieldcrest Books
Mystic Arts Book Society
University Books, Inc.

THE VIKING PRESS, INC.
Grossman Publishers

WADSWORTH PUBLISHING COMPANY, INC.
Bogden & Quigley, Inc., Publishers

Brooks/Cole Publishing Company
Dickenson Publishing Company, Inc.
Duxbury Press
Charles A. Jones Publishing Company
Prindle, Weber & Schmidt, Inc.

JOHN WILEY & SONS, INC.
Halsted Press
Hamilton Publishing Company
Melville Publishing Company

WILLIAMHOUSE-REGENCY, INC.
Greenwood Press
Negro Universities Press

V

Book Trade Associations

American Book Publishers Council

Established at New York City in 1946. The first president was Melville Minton. *See,* Association of American Publishers.

The American Booksellers Association (ABA)

Founded in 1900. Henry T. Coates was the first president. During its first quarter century the ABA's chief objective was the establishment and maintenance of the net-price system. Later the Association enlarged its sphere of operations and initiated several programs designed to facilitate book distribution, to knit the membership more firmly together for the purpose of mutual benefit, and to promote the cause of the book throughout America.

Among such programs has been the Clearing House, which accepted orders of individual booksellers throughout the country, had them filled, and consolidated outgoing shipments. ABA was also instrumental in the passage of the fair trade acts in most of the States of the Union. It sponsors a number of booksellers' aids: *ABA Newswire* (which lists authors' promotional appearances and forthcoming reviews in the media), The Booksellers School, *Sidelines Directory, ABA Bulletin, The ABA Book Buyer's Handbook,* the *Basic Book Lists,* and *A Manual on Bookselling.* ABA set .up the Single Copy Order Plan which makes it feasible for bookstores to order single copies of books. Since 1937 it has sponsored a series of Book and Author luncheons in New York City which are broadcast on public radio. In 1949 it joined with American Book Publishers Council and Book Manufacturers Institute in sponsoring the National Book Awards.

The Association has a current membership of over four thousand members. Its annual convention and trade exhibit is a major event in the book industry calendar.

American Book Trade Association

Founded in 1874 at Cincinnati, Ohio.

American Book Trade Union

Organized in 1873. The first president was I.C. Aston.

American Company of Booksellers

Founded in 1801 at Philadelphia, Pennsylvania, by Mathew Carey, who was also its first president.

American Copyright League

Organized in 1888 at New York City by Brander Matthews and others. *See,* its successor, Authors League of America.

American Council on Education

Founded in 1918 in Washington, D.C., as an organization of national and regional education associations and institutions of higher education. In addition to its other services, the Council publishes books and reference works on higher education. Two standard directories published by the Council are: AMERICAN UNIVERSITIES AND COLLEGES, first published in 1928, and AMERICAN JUNIOR COLLEGES, first published in 1940.

American Educational Publishers Institute

See, Association of American Publishers.

American Institute of Graphic Arts

Founded in 1914 at New York City to organize American participation in the Leipzig (Germany) Graphic Arts Exhibition. In 1923 it began its selection of *The Fifty Books of the Year,* which is now an annual exhibition held in New York City.

American Publishers Association

Organized at New York City in 1900.

American Publishers' Copyright League

Founded at New York City in 1886 by George Haven Putnam. The first president was W.H. Appleton. The League was largely responsible for enactment of the Copyright Acts of 1891 and 1909.

American Textbook Publishers Institute

Founded in 1942 in Jefferson City, Missouri. Its objective was to study all problems relating to the use of textbooks as tools of learning. Lloyd King, former State School Superintendent, Missouri, was appointed the first director. In 1944 the Institute moved to New York City. It enlarged its scope of membership in 1943 by admitting publishers of encyclopedias and reference books. In 1947 membership was expanded further to include publishers of college textbooks, in 1955 text publishers, and map publishers in 1964. An associate membership category was also established to encompass textbook associations in other countries. In 1958 Austin McCaffrey assumed the position of executive secretary.

In 1970 the Institute merged with American Book Publishers Council to form the Association of American Publishers (q.v.).

American University Press Services, Inc.

A wholly-owned subsidiary of the Association of American University Presses, Inc., established in 1964. It is concerned with the operation of the *Educational Directory,* the Exhibits Program, the Statistical Survey, and the publication of specialized bibliographies.

Association of American Publishers, Inc.

Established in 1970 by the consolidation of the American Book Publishers Council and the American Educational Publishers Institute. Its goals are:

To foster and develop a public understanding of the essential role of books in our culture and of independently created books and instructional materials in our educational institutions.

To provide effective representation of book publishing and educational publishing to governmental units and the general public.

To provide members with appropriate information concerning trade conditions, markets, copyright, manufacturing processes, taxes, duties, postage, freight, censorship movements, government programs, and other matters of importance.

To provide a framework within which the various groups and particular interests that make up the general and educational publishing industry can work to advance their collective and individual areas of concern.

To cooperate in research in the design, content, and distribution of books and educational materials.

To unify the industry into a single group so that it is able to speak with one voice on matters of common interest, as well as to articulate positions of particular groups of publishers within the Association.

A Board of Directors elected by the membership determines governing policies, plans, courses of action, and publicly announced views of the Association. The AAP is organized horizontally into divisions to provide for publishers' interests in specific markets and products: College; School; Scientific; Technical; Medical; General Trade and Mail Order/Book Club. AAP is also organized vertically across divisional lines to deal with matters of concern to all publishers, such as reading development, copyright, educational technology, freedom to read, international trade, school and library marketing and promotion, management and administration, marketing, postal fees, and Federal funding.

The Association holds regular industry-wide meetings, seminars, and workshops. Its Washington, D.C. office keeps members continually informed of problems and opportunities presented by Federal government actions through the monthly *Washington Newsletter*.

The Association of American University Presses, Inc.

Founded in 1937. The Association developed out of the informal meetings of the directors of American university presses attending the annual conference of the National Association of Book Publishers, held since the 1920s. Donald P. Bean was the prime mover behind those sessions and until 1937 the permanent acting secretary *pro tem* of the group.

In 1937 it was decided to set up a more formal organization with Bean as chairman and Charles G. Proffitt of Columbia University Press as secretary. By the 1940s the Association began to assume the form of its present size and shape with dues, elections, annual meetings, and a number of cooperative enterprises. In 1959 a central office was established in New York City.

In 1964 the Association was reorganized into two bodies: The Association of American University Presses, Inc. and American University Press Services, Inc. The Association's main activities are: rendering assistance to university presses, conducting educational and training programs, research and development projects, the AAUP Book Show, and maintaining liaison with scholarly, educational and publishing organizations within the United States and with scholarly publishers in other countries.

Authors League of America

Founded in 1911 in New York City by Arthur Train, Gelett Burgess, Joseph Vance, and Lloyd

Osbourne in order to safeguard the rights of authors. *See,* Arthur Train's MY DAY IN COURT.

Book Publishers' Bureau

Organized in 1937 at New York City, with Curtis W. McGraw as the first president.

Children's Book Council

Founded in 1945 and incorporated in 1957 as a nonprofit organization to encourage the reading and enjoyment of children's books. Its members are composed of some sixty-eight publishers of trade books for children. The Council's headquarters are in New York City.

The Council evolved from what has been, and still is, its major promotional activity, the National Children's Book Week (q.v.). In addition, the Council administers the Summer Reading Program. The Council also publishes *The Calendar,* an informative newsletter issued three times yearly, and CHILDREN'S BOOKS: AWARDS AND PRIZES, a biennial paperbound publication.

The Council supports and works with other national organizations such as the American Library Association, National Council of Teachers of English, Association for Childhood Education International, and the International Reading Association. The Council has been a donor organization for the National Book Awards Program since the introduction of a children's book category in 1969.

Copyright Society of the U.S.A.

A professional association of copyright experts founded in 1953 with headquarters in New York City.

Council on Books in Wartime

Set up at New York City in 1942. The first chairman was W.W. Norton. Disbanded shortly after the close of the war.

International Book Institute

An organization formed in 1966 in Washington D.C., under the auspices of the National Academy of Sciences to plan and coordinate U.S. international book programs and to facilitate the flow of books to and from the United States. John H. Kyle was the Institute's first director. The Institute failed to receive adequate support and was suspended in 1968.

International Book Year

A year-round and intensive celebration sponsored and coordinated by the UNESCO in 1972 to stimulate book consciousness on a world-wide scale and to study the state of the book arts, especially in relation to publication, production, and use. The program was administered in the United States by the National Book Committee.

International Copyright Association

Founded in 1868.

International Copyrights Information Center

Founded in 1969 by Franklin Book Programs as a clearing house for foreign publishers seeking information on American copyrights.

International Publishers Association

Established in 1896 in Zurich, Switzerland, to promote better relations among national publishing communities and to study the world-wide problems of the book industry. Currently the Association has thirty-three member organizations. An educational group was established in 1965.

National Association of Book Publishers

Organized in New York City in 1920 with John W. Hiltman as its first president. Reorganized in 1937 as the Book Publishers Bureau.

National Book Committee

A nonprofit association devoted to the wider and wiser use of books, founded in 1954 through the efforts of the American Library Association and the American Book Publishers Council. The three major areas of the Committee's activity were reading and library development, recognition and encouragement of the literary arts, and the preparation of field surveys and status studies. In pursuit of its objectives it co-sponsored the National Library Week, awarded the National Medal for Literature, and administered the National Book Awards. The organization consisted of an executive committee of twenty-four members and a national board of two hundred members. Late in 1974 the Committee was disbanded.

School Book Publishers' Board of Trade

Set up in 1870.

Women's National Book Association

Established in 1917 as a professional organization covering a national cross-section of women in all phases of the book industry. The Association now has over ten active chapters and there are affiliated groups in Japan and in India. Since 1940 the Association has annually granted the Constance Lindsay Skinner Award for women for distinguished contribution to the book world. In 1961 the Amy Loveman National Award was established to be given annually to a college student who collected the best personal library.

The Association publishes a semiannual, *The Book Woman,* as its official journal. Various chapters also sponsor book fairs, arrange courses on various phases of the book industry, and hold an annual reception for women attending the ALA convention. *See,* WOMEN IN THE WORLD OF WORDS.

VI

Major Prizes,
Awards, Events

Bancroft Prize

Established under the will of Frederic Bancroft and offered by Columbia University for distinguished works in American history, American diplomacy, and international relations of the United States. Three annual prizes valued at $4,000.00 each are awarded. The first was granted in 1948.

John Barnes Publisher of the Year Award

Offered by the American Booksellers Association in memory of the late John Barnes, former president of Barnes & Noble. Since 1965 two awards have been given, one to a publisher of one hundred or more titles a year, and another to a publisher of less than one hundred titles a year. The criteria are: 1) good sales representation, 2) advertising and promotion with distinction, 3) shipping and billing with maximum speed and efficiency, 4) handling correspondence with minimum red tape, and 5) evincing genuine interest in the welfare of the trade and reading public.

Bollingen Prize

An annual prize, awarded by the Library of Congress in 1949 and by Yale University Library since 1950, for achievement in American poetry.

Bowker Lectures on Book Publishing

Lecture series established in 1935 in honor of Richard Rogers Bowker and held at the New York Public Library. Each lecture deals with some aspect of book publishing.

1935 — Stokes, Frederick A., *A Publisher's Random Notes.*

1937 — Harcourt, Alfred, *Publishing Since 1900.*

1938 — Crofts, Frederick S., *Textbooks Are Not Absolutely Dead Things.*

1939 — Compton, F.E., *Subscription Books.*

1940 — Davis, Elmer, *Some Aspects of the Economics of Authorship.*

1941 — Watkins, Ann, *Literature For Sale.*

1942 — Thompson, James S., *The Technical Book Publisher in Wartime.*

1943 — Bay, Helmuth, *The History and Technique of Mapmaking.*

1944 — Brandt, Joseph A., *The University of Every Man.*

1946 — Bechtel, Louise, *Books in Search of Children.*

1947 — Fisher, Dorothy Canfield, *Book Clubs.*

1948 — McCormick, Ken, *Editors Today.*

1949 — Evans, Luther H., *Copyright and the Public Interest.*

1950 — Weeks, Edward, *The Schooling of an Editor.*

1950 — Edman, Irwin, *Unrequired Reading.*

1953 — Lewis, Freeman, *Paper-bound Books in America.*

1956 — Lacy, Dan, *Books and the Future: A Speculation.*

1959 — Huebsch, B.W., *Busman's Holiday: "What Exactly Do Publishers Do?"*

1960 — Spaulding, William E., *Look to the School.*

1964 — Knopf, Alfred A., *Publishing Then and Now, 1912-1964.*

1967 — McCabe, Edward J., Jr., *Subscription Books and the Knowledge Explosion.*

1973 — Pilpel, Harriet F., *The Recent Supreme Court Decision on Pornography.*

1974 — Ringer, Barbara, *The Demonology of Copyright.*

Caldecott Medal

Annual prize, first awarded in 1938, given to the best illustrated book for children, named in honor of Randolph Caldecott, noted British illustrator of children's books. The medal bears a relief of John Gilpin done from Caldecott's representation.

Carey-Thomas Award for Creative Publishing

Annual award established in 1942 by Frederic G. Melcher of R.R. Bowker Company to honor the most distinguished publishing achievement of the year in creative book publishing taking into account initiative, imagination, cooperation with author, appropriate manufacture, and successful promotion and marketing. The Award is named after the two great American publishers of the eighteenth century: Mathew Carey and Isaiah Thomas.

Carey-Thomas Awards

1942　Farrar & Rinehart
　　　The Rivers of America
　　　Series

1943　University of Chicago Press
　　　A DICTIONARY OF AMERICAN ENGLISH ON HISTORICAL PRINCIPLES

1944　E.P. Dutton
　　　THE WORLD OF WASHINGTON IRVING
　　　by Van Wyck Brooks

1945　Alfred A. Knopf
　　　THE AMERICAN LANGUAGE
　　　by H.L. Mencken

1946　Duell, Sloan & Pearce
　　　THE NEW WORLD
　　　by Stefan Lorant

1947　Oxford University Press
　　　A STUDY OF HISTORY
　　　by Arnold Toynbee

1948　William Sloane Associates
　　　The American Men of Letters
　　　Series

1949　Rand McNally & Company
　　　COSMOPOLITAN WORLD ATLAS

1950　Princeton University Press
　　　THE PAPERS OF THOMAS JEFFERSON
　　　edited by J.P. Boyd, *et al.*

1951　Houghton Mifflin Company
　　　LIFE IN AMERICA
　　　by Marshall B. Davidson

1952　The Macmillan Company
　　　THE DIARY OF GEORGE TEMPLETON STRONG, 1835-1875,
　　　edited by Allan Nevins and Milton H. Thomas

1953　Houghton Mifflin Company
　　　THE SECOND WORLD WAR
　　　by Winston Churchill

1954　Doubleday & Company
　　　Anchor Books

1955　Belknap Press (Harvard)
　　　THE POEMS OF EMILY DICKINSON
　　　edited by T.H. Johnson

1956　Doubleday & Company
　　　Mainstream of America
　　　Series

1957　Frederick A. Praeger
　　　THE NEW CLASS
　　　by Milovan Djilas

1958　New York Graphic Society
　　　COMPLETE LETTERS OF VINCENT VAN GOGH

1959　Oxford University Press
　　　JAMES JOYCE
　　　by Richard Ellmann

1960　Simon & Schuster
　　　THE RISE AND FALL OF THE THIRD REICH
　　　by William L. Shirer

1961　Belknap Press (Harvard)
　　　THE ADAMS PAPERS: DIARY AND AUTOBIOGRAPHY OF JOHN ADAMS

1962　Shorewood Publishers
　　　GREAT DRAWINGS OF ALL TIME

1963　Wesleyan University Press
　　　NEW YORK LANDMARKS
　　　edited by Alan Burnham

1964   Sierra Club
TIME AND THE RIVER FLOWING
and THE LAST REDWOODS in
Exhibit Format Series

1965   Doubleday and Company
THE ANCHOR BIBLE
edited by W.F. Albright and
D.N. Freedman

1966   George Braziller
THE HOURS OF CATHERINE
OF CLEVES
Introduction and Commentaries
by John Plummer

1967   Holt, Rinehart & Winston
WILDERNESS KINGDOM: THE
JOURNALS AND PAINTINGS OF
FATHER NICOLAS POINT,
translated and introduced by Joseph P.
Donnelly, S.J.

1968   W.W. Norton
THE NORTON FACSIMILE: THE
FIRST FOLIO OF SHAKESPEARE,
prepared by Charlton Hinman

1969   Alfred A. Knopf
HUEY LONG
by T. Harry Williams

1970   Random House
Maecenan Press
Chanticleer Press
PICASSO 347: COLLECTED
DRAWINGS OF PABLO PICASSO

1971   Oxford University Press
THE COMPACT EDITION OF THE
OXFORD ENGLISH DICTIONARY

1972   Yale University Press
THE CHILDREN OF PRIDE: A TRUE
STORY OF GEORGIA AND THE
CIVIL WAR
edited by Robert Manson Myers

1973   Princeton University Press
The Bollingen Series

Children's Book Week

A book week organized by the Children's Book Council and held annually in the third week of November. The beginnings of the Book Week can be traced to the 1912 American Booksellers Association Convention where E.W. Mumford delivered a paper entitled "Juvenile Readers as an Asset." This paper caught the attention of James West, Director of the Boy Scouts of America, who sought the aid of his librarian, Franklin K. Mathiews, in the organization of a program to give new direction to boys' reading. The result was the Good Book Week held by the Boy Scouts of America in 1916, in cooperation with the American Booksellers Association and the American Library Association.

Frederic G. Melcher organized the first Book Week Committee which selected the famous Book Week slogan, "More Books in the Home." The scope of the Book Week grew to such an extent that it stimulated the formation of the Children's Book Council in 1945.

Fifty Books of the Year

An exhibition organized every year by the American Institute of Graphic Arts. The selection is based on the quality of design and physical production of the books. First held in 1923.

Frankfurt Book Fair

World's largest and most prestigious international book fair held annually at Frankfurt, Germany, in September-October. The history of the fair goes back to the sixteenth century but it was revived in its present form in 1949 by the West German Publishers and Booksellers Association. The annual Peace Prize of the German book trade is awarded during the fair.

Roger Klein Award

A biennial award established in 1971 and administered by *Publishers Weekly*. It is awarded to a book editor under forty years of age, with over four years of professional experience. Juvenile book editors are excluded. The criteria are: the addition of important books and authors to the list of a publishing house; recognition of writing talent; nurturing of talented writers to reach their potential; and development of ideas for books.

National Book Awards

Literary awards honoring the year's best work in eight fields: fiction, poetry, history and biography, arts and letters, children's literature, science, philosophy and religion, and translation. Founded in 1950, the awards are sponsored by the Association of American Publishers, Association of American University Presses, American Booksellers Association, Book Manufacturers' Institute, Children's Book Council, and National Association of College Stores. They have been administered by the National Book Committee until 1974.

Newbery Medal

The John Newbery Medal awarded annually since 1922 for the most distinguished contribution to literature for American children. Named after John Newbery, London bookseller, who first conceived the idea of publishing books especially for children. The bronze medal is a gift of Frederic G. Melcher and is administered by the American Library Association.

Pulitzer Prize

Any of the annual awards for notable achievements in American journalism, letters, drama, and music administered by the trustees of Columbia University from the income of a fund set up in 1903 by Joseph Pulitzer. Under the category of letters there are separate prizes for biography, history, fiction, and poetry.

Appendices

APPENDIX 1
Commonly Used Publishing Abbreviations

a.a.	author's alterations
AAP	Association of American Publishers
AAUP	Association of American University Presses
AB	*Antiquarian Bookman*
ABA	American Booksellers Association
ABPC	*American Book Prices Current*
ABPR	*American Book Publishing Record*
abr.	abridgment; abridged
ACLS	American Council of Learned Societies
AIGA	American Institute of Graphic Arts
ALA	American Library Association
all pub.	all published
ann.	annals
annot.	annotated; annotator; annotation
anon.	anonymous; anonym
appx.	appendix
AUPS	American University Press Services
auth.	author
bd.	bound
bib., bibl., bibliog.	bibliography
bio-bibl.	bio-bibliography
biog.	biography
BIP	*Books in Print*
bk	book
BMI	Book Manufacturers Institute
BOM	Book-of-the-Month Club
BSA	Bibliographical Society of America
bull.	bulletin
cat.	catalogue
CBC	Children's Book Council
CBI	*Cumulative Book Index*
ch.	chapter
CICP	Committee to Investigate Copyright Problems
CIP	Cataloging in Publication
col.	column
comp.	1. compiler; compiled 2. complete
cont.	continued
corr.	corrected
cyc.	cyclopedia
DC	1. Dewey Classification 2. Decimal Classification
DDC	Dewey Decimal Classification
diagr.	diagram
diss.	dissertation
d.j.	dust jacket
doc.	document
dup., dupl.	duplicate

ed., edit.	editor; edition; edited
e.d.l.	edition de luxe
encyc.	encyclopedia
endp.	endpapers
enl. ed.	enlarged edition
fac., facsim.	facsimile
fasc.	fascile, fascicule
ff	folios; following
fict.	fiction
fig.	figure
f.n.	footnote
fp., front.	frontispiece
GPO	Government Printing Office
IBBY	International Board of Books for Young People
IBEG	International Book Export Group
ill., illus.	illustrated; illustration; illustrator
illum.	illuminated
inc., incompl.	incomplete
in prep.	in preparation
inscr.	inscribed; inscription
introd.	introduction
IPA	International Publishers Association
ISBN	International Standard Book Number
juv.	juvenile
l., ll.	leaf; leaves
L.C.	Library of Congress
l.c.	lower case
LJ	*Library Journal*
LMP	*Literary Market Place*
l.p.	large-paper edition
ms. mss; MS, MSS	manuscript; manuscripts
NBC	National Book Committee
n.d.	no date of publication (given)
n.e.p.	new edition pending
new ed. rev. enl.	new edition revised and enlarged
no., nos.	number; numbers
n.p.	1. no place of publication (given)
	2. no publisher (given)
n.s.; new ser.	new series
n.y.	no year (given)
o.p., O.P.	out of print
or.; orig.	original
o.s., O.S.	out of stock
p., pp.	page; pages
pam; pm; pph.	pamphlet
phot.	photograph
p.l.	preliminary leaf
pl.	plate
p.p.	privately printed
pref.	preface

prelims	preliminary pages
proc.	proceedings
pseud.	pseudonym
pt., pts.	part; parts
ptd.	printed
PTLA	*Publishers Trade List Annual*
pub.	publisher
pubd.	published
publ.	publication
PW	*Publishers Weekly*
ref.	reference
rept.	report
rev.	1. reviewed 2. revised
rev. ed., Rev. Ed.	revised edition
R & P	Rights and Permissions
RSV	Revised Standard Version
S.C.O.P.	Single Copy Order Plan
ser.	series
SG	*Subject Guide to Books in Print*
sig.	signature
subj.	subject
sup., suppl.	supplement
t.	title; tome
tab.	table
t.p.	title page
tr., trans.	translated; translator; translation
tr.	transpose
trans.	transactions
ts.	typescript
UCC	Universal Copyright Convention
UDC	Universal Decimal Classification
USOE	United States Office of Education
v., vol.	volume
v.	verso
v.p.	various publishers
WNBA	Women's National Book Association
yr.	year

advance copy   copy of a new book, final proofs, or unbound signatures, sent out in advance of publication to reviewers, booksellers, or book clubs, often without book jackets.

advance jacket   dust jacket of a forthcoming book sent to booksellers as promotional material.

advance sheets   a copy of a forthcoming book in sheets as a basis for preliminary notices, or for simultaneous publication elsewhere. The general practice is to send advance sheets for review purposes as folded, but unbound, signatures.

afterword   material at the conclusion of a book, as an epilogue. Distinguished from a foreword.

all published   statement that a publication planned to appear in several volumes will not be continued. Used as a descriptive term for an incomplete or uncompleted set.

all rights reserved   a printed notice that the right of reproducing a book or any part of it in any form will not be granted without the written consent of the owner of the copyright. This notice is required for copyright protection in Latin American countries under the Buenos Aires Convention.

almanac   1. an annual publication containing a calendar, astronomical data, and related information. 2. a yearbook designed to provide a wide range of useful information on a particular subject or for general reference.

The first almanac printed in America was AN ALMANACK CALCULATED FOR NEW ENGLAND by William Pierce, printed by Stephen Day at Cambridge, Massachusetts, in 1639. JOHN TULLEY'S ALMANAC FOR 1687, printed by Benjamin Harris in Boston, Mass., incorporated many radical improvements. Tulley began the year from January instead of March. He also added weather forecasts, advertisements, and short, pithy sayings, witticisms, and advice. The next important almanac was that of Nathanael Ames whose ASTRONOMICAL DIARY AND ALMANAC was published from 1726 until 1775.

Other almanac makers in the eighteenth century included Nathan Daboll, Dudley Leavitt, and Benjamin West. But the best known of all the early almanacs is Benjamin Franklin's POOR RICHARD'S ALMANACK which was in publication from 1733 until 1757. Benjamin Franklin's brother, James, was an almanac maker and his THE RHODE ISLAND ALMANACH FOR THE YEAR 1728, BY POOR ROBIN, may have been Benjamin's immediate model. Robert Bailey Thomas's THE FARMER'S ALMANAC, renamed OLD FARMER'S ALMANAC in 1832, is the oldest of the existing almanacs. The forerunners of the present-day general almanacs are to be found in Peter Force's NATIONAL CALENDAR issued between 1820 and 1836 and the AMERICAN ALMANAC issued between 1830 and 1861 and between 1878 and 1889. Both of those publications contained information on governments, railroads, colleges, denominations, and a chronology of the past year's events.

The first newspaper almanac was the TRIBUNE ALMANAC (of the *New York Tribune*) which had been first issued in 1856. Specialized almanacs also flourished in the nineteenth century. Among them were THE PHYSICIANS' ALMANAC; THE CHRISTIAN ALMANAC; THE MECHANICS' ALMANAC; and the WHIG ALMANAC. Among current general almanacs are WORLD ALMANAC (1868-76 and yearly since 1886), INFORMATION PLEASE ALMANAC (started 1947) and NEW YORK TIMES ENCYCLOPEDIC ALMANAC (begun 1970), renamed ASSOCIATED PRESS ALMANAC in 1973.

Americana   material relating to or printed in America or written by Americans. The term is frequently restricted to the period of history before 1820. *See also,* USiana.

American Book Publishing Record   an annual cumulative index to American books, published by R.R. Bowker Company.

American Book Prices Current issued by Luther S. Livingstone in 1895 and published annually since then as a guide to sale prices compiled from auctioneer's catalogues. Divided into four sections: (1) books (2) autographs and manuscripts (3) broadsides and (4) maps and charts. Currently it is published by Columbia University Press.

anthology a collection of poems or prose selections from the writings of one or various authors. The term was first used by Greek author Agathias in A.D. 550.

author appearance an author's presence at various public functions, television and radio programs, and autographing parties, in order to generate publicity for his books.

author-publisher a writer who publishes his own works.

author's rights under the U.S. Copyright Act the author of a copyrighted work has the right to print, publish, reproduce, and sell, as well as the right to translate, adapt and dramatize. Any or all of these rights may be assigned under contract.

back list all the in-print titles on a publisher's list that were published before the current publishing season.

back matter material that follows the text in a book including appendices, addenda, author's notes, glossary, bibliography, and index.

banned in Boston (of a book) prohibited from public sale on extremely puritanical grounds. Many books, including Walt Whitman's LEAVES OF GRASS, were so banned in Boston because they offended the "proper Bostonians."

battledore an early form of primer, common in the late 18th century, made of folded paper or cardboard which, when opened out, resembled a hornbook without handle.

Berne Convention The International Copyright Union for the Protection of Literary and Artistic Works, 1888, an agreement adhered to by forty-two signatory countries. This agreement has been subject to revisions every twenty years. Under the Convention a signatory country extends full copyright protection to all works properly copyrighted in every other signatory country. Any work published in a non-signatory country will enjoy such protection only if it is published simultaneously in a signatory country. The United States is not a signatory to this Convention. *See also,* Universal Copyright Convention.

bestseller a current popular book sold in large numbers. Frank Luther Mott defines a bestseller as a book which achieves a total sale equal to one percent of the population for the decade in which it is published. This would mean a sale of over two million copies in the 1970s. Bestseller lists are compiled weekly by *The New York Times Book Review* and *Publishers Weekly*.

better seller a title having a steady, but not a spectacular, sale.

bibliography 1. the systematic description and classification of books according to subject, class, period, author, country, provenance, or a particular press or publisher. Usually divided into enumerative, analytical, and descriptive. 2. a list of the sources of information on a given subject or the works of a given author or publisher. 3. a list of the books and articles referred to by an author in the course of his book or used by him as source material. 4. the comparative study of books as physical objects, especially as a means of determining their history and the transmission of texts.

book according to a UNESCO definition in 1950, a non-periodical literary publication containing forty-nine or more pages, not counting the covers. According to the U.S. Post Office a book must have twenty-four or more pages, of which at least twenty-two are printed, permanently bound, and consisting wholly of reading matter.

book club an organization that selects books, generally of recent publication, for distribution to subscribers at reduced rates. A member of a book club usually receives an expensive book premium on joining and agrees to purchase a minimum number of books during a year. Some book clubs offer book dividends after a certain number of books have been purchased within a year while others offer an unlimited selection at a discount. Most book clubs have an outside board of judges and publish monthly bulletins for their members.

book fair an exhibition, usually held periodically, featuring books sponsored by a group of booksellers, publishers, or similar agencies. Some book fairs include talks by authors and book promotional activities. The first book fair to be held in the United States was the Marshall Field Book Fair in 1919. *The New York Times* held a book fair in 1936 and in 1937.

book industry the production, publishing and selling of books considered together as a broad segment of the economy.

The Booklist journal, formerly *The Booklist and Subscription Books Bulletin,* founded by the American Library Association to evaluate subscription books.

book packaging the production of a well-designed and usually heavily illustrated volume by a firm that does not publish it but sells it to a publisher. Book packaging involves conceiving the idea of a book, deciding on and hiring the writers and illustrators, creating a dummy, selecting the type, and arranging for printing and binding. Ridge Press owned by Jerry Mason, Gemini Smith owned by Bradley Smith, and Chanticleer Press owned by Paul Steiner are well-known firms engaged in book packaging.

book publishing consultant a firm or individual that provides technical and professional services to publishers, especially in the fields of management, design, market research, foreign and subsidiary rights, special editorial projects, international operations, production, book clubs, and multi-media programs.

Books in Print an index to the *Publishers' Trade List Annual* published annually since 1948 by R.R. Bowker Company.

book trade retail bookselling considered as a distinct branch of the book industry.

book week a week set aside for cooperative promotion of books and reading and usually sponsored by a group or organization. It may be devoted to the promotion of books in general as is the National Library Week or to a special type of book, *e.g.* the Catholic Book Week or Children's Book Week.

Bowdlerize to omit from an author's edited works words or passages considered to be offensive or indelicate after the manner of Thomas Bowdler (1754-1825).

Buenos Aires Convention copyright convention signed by seventeen Latin American countries in 1910. It supplemented an earlier agreement governing copyright known as the Montevideo Convention of 1886. The Buenos Aires Convention was itself revised by the Washington Convention of 1946.

Cataloging in Publication (CIP) a service program sponsored by the Library of Congress to provide professional cataloging data to publishers prior to publication so that the data can be printed in the books, usually on the copyright page. Full galleys are submitted to the Library of Congress in advance of publication; the data is sent to the publishers without charge.

CIP is intended to speed the delivery of books to library readers and to reduce cataloging time and the cost of cataloging for the nation's libraries.

censorship the term applied to any of the following acts: (a) prohibiting the sending of a book through the mail; (b) preventing the passage of a book through the Customs; (c) enjoining the sale of a book in a bookstore; (d) removing a book from a library; or (e) restricting in any way its availability to readers.

Among literary classics banned in America have been JURGEN by James Branch Cabell, LEAVES OF GRASS by Walt Whitman, OIL by Upton Sinclair, ELMER GANTRY by Sinclair Lewis, AN AMERICAN TRAGEDY by Theodore Dreiser, THREE WEEKS by Elinor Glyn, ULYSSES by James Joyce, BAD GIRL by Viña Delmar, MARRIED LOVE by Marie Stopes, THE SEX SIDE OF LIFE by Mary Ware Dennett, CASANOVA'S HOMECOMING by Arthur Schnitzler, LADY CHATTERLEY'S LOVER by D.H. Lawrence, TROPIC OF CANCER and TROPIC OF CAPRICORN by Henry Miller, MEMOIRS OF HECATE COUNTY by Edmund Wilson, LOLITA by Vladimir Nabokov, and THE NAKED LUNCH by William Burroughs.

The Watch and Ward Society of Boston, Massachusetts, and The Society for the Suppression of Vice in New York City, the latter under the direction of Anthony Comstock and John S. Sumner, were very active censorship organizations. Books prohibited by the Catholic Church are listed in the *Index Librorum Prohibitorum*.

chapbook   a popular form of literature that flourished in America from 1725 to 1825. The chapbooks were generally 5½ by 3½ inches in size, usually of anonymous authorship, printed on cheap paper, and four to twenty-four pages in length. In content they ranged from crime to romance, adventure, biography, jokes, astrology, the occult, songs, Indian captivity tales, and religion. Some achieved wide popularity, one being A WONDERFUL DISCOVERY OF A HERMIT WHO LIVES UPWARDS OF TWO HUNDRED YEARS. Benjamin Franklin's WAY TO WEALTH, Samuel Richardson's PAMELA, and Henry Fielding's TOM JONES also appeared as chapbooks.

By far the most popular categories of chapbooks were romances and tales of sexual misbehavior, such as THE HISTORY OF JANE SHORE (mistress of Henry IV), and THE HISTORY OF FAIR ROSAMOND (mistress of Henry II). Some chapbooks were adapted from classics and had some literary merit, *e.g.,* TRISTRAM SHANDY and MOLL FLANDERS.

Chapbooks were sold by peddlers known as chapmen and they were also sold in stationery shops.

Children's Books in Print   an annual publication of R.R. Bowker Company. Contains an author-title index, grade levels, and an index to illustrators.

Classification Décimale Universelle   a classification system based on the Dewey Decimal classification but expanded and modified.

coffee-table book   a large book valued more for its lavish illustrations and fine format than its contents. Often placed on a coffee table to enhance the décor of a room; hence its name.

collected works   a complete edition containing all of an author's published and unpublished works under one imprint.

colophon   1. literally, finishing touch. A note at the end of the text proper giving the title of the work, the name of the author, the name of the printer or the publisher or both, and the place and date of printing. Now largely superseded by the title page. 2. a publisher's identifying symbol.

coloring book   a book of drawings that may be colored with crayons or watercolors. Generally for use by a child.

composite book   a book on a single subject written by several authors in collaboration or a book of works by several authors collected by an editor.

comstockery   the suppression or censorship of works of genuine literature and art for supposed obscenity. A word coined by George Bernard Shaw.

Congressional Edition   a special edition of United States Senate and House journals, reports, and documents, grouped in series, and numbered consecutively.

continuous revision   a policy of periodical updating of reference books, such as encyclopedias, by insertion of alterations and supplementary material into standing matter. Additional pages are usually numbered A,B,C, and so on.

cookbook   a book of recipes. The first cookbook published in the United States was THE COMPLEAT HOUSEWIFE; OR, ACCOMPLISHED GENTLEWOMAN'S COMPANION issued in 1742 by William Parks, in his Williamsburg, Virginia, press. The first cookbook to be compiled by an American was AMERICAN COOKERY by Amelia Summers, published in 1796 at Hartford, Connecticut, by Hudson & Goodwin. Other popular cookbooks followed in its wake: Eliza Leslie's 75 RECEIPTS, Lydia Maria Child's THE FRUGAL HOUSEWIFE, and THE YOUNG HOUSEKEEPER'S FRIEND by Mary Cornelius. But it was only after the Civil War that the modern bestsellers made their appearance: Marion Harland's NATIONAL COOK BOOK and Fannie M. Farmer's BOSTON

COOKING-SCHOOL COOK BOOK, which was first published in 1896.

cooperative advertising   arrangement for promoting a publisher's books over a dealer's name. The bookseller and publisher agree to share advertising costs.

cooperative publishing   *See, vanity publishing.*

copy edit   to make a manuscript consistent with the house style and to check it for typographical errors and errors in grammatical construction.

copyright   the exclusive right to publish, produce, and sell a work granted by law to its author for a specified number of years. Under the United States code of 1909 book copyright depends upon publication with notice of copyright on title page or verso. The copyright notice consists of three elements: the word "copyright" followed by the name of the copyright owner and the date of publication. For the protection of the Universal Copyright Convention the symbol © should follow the word "copyright" on books published after 1957, and the statement "All Rights Reserved" should follow the name of the publisher for protection in Latin American countries under the Buenos Aires Convention.

United States copyright is registered in the Copyright Office in Washington, D.C. through the deposit of two copies of the work manufactured in America (in the case of works in foreign languages only one copy need be deposited) along with an application on Form A or other appropriate form, duly notarized, and the fee for registration ($6.00). The application may be made by the author or his representative. Statutory United States copyright currently extends for twenty-eight years and may be renewed for another twenty-eight years if applied for by the author, his heirs, or other lawful designate, during the twenty-seventh year of the original copyright.

copyright, ad interim   under the 1949 amendment ad interim U.S. copyright is granted to books in the English language first published abroad. To secure this copyright a foreign copy bearing a notice of American copyright must be deposited in the Copyright Office in Washington, D.C. within six months of original publication. The book must be accompanied by a request for registration and a statement of the name and nationality of the author and of the copyright owner and the date of publication. Ad interim copyright is valid for five years in the United States during which time a total of 1,500 copies of the original edition may be imported by an authorized agent. To continue the American copyright an edition must be manufactured and published in the United States.

copyright, British   British copyright law requires the deposit of a copy of every book published in the United Kingdom in the British Museum, the National Libraries of Scotland and Wales and the University Libraries of Oxford, Cambridge, and Trinity College, Dublin. Penalty for failure to do so does not involve forfeiture of copyright but a fine. Copyright extends for life and fifty years for all works published within the United Kingdom and its dominions. Publication has been defined in British law as the offering for sale of sufficient copies of a work to meet reasonable public demand. British manufacture is not a required condition for copyright.

copyright, Canadian   Canada is not a signatory to the Universal Copyright Convention but the amended Canadian Copyright Act of 1931 incorporates most of the British provisions. Canadian manufacture is required for works originally published in countries that are not signatories to the Universal Copyright Convention.

copyright, common law   unlimited protection extended under common law to the unpublished works of authors, whether foreign or domestic, if not voluntarily registered in the Copyright Office.

copyright, inter-American   copyright governed by the Montevideo Convention of 1886, the Buenos Aires Convention of 1910, and the Washington Convention of 1946. Under the Buenos Aires Convention, signed by seventeen Latin American countries, the statement "All Rights Reserved" following the name of the publisher is deemed effective copyright notice. Brazil and Canada are the only countries in the Western

Hemisphere that belong to the Berne Convention. Argentina, Brazil, Chile, Costa Rica, Cuba, Ecuador, Haiti, Mexico, and the United States are signatories to the Universal Copyright Convention.

copyright, international   *See,* Berne Convention, *also,* Universal Copyright Convention.

copyright date   the date of copyright as given in the copyright notice.

copyright deposit   free copy or copies required to be sent to a copyright office or designated libraries within a certain period of publication in accordance with copyright law.

copyright fees   the fee for registration of any published work under copyright laws in the U.S. is now $6.00. This must be accompanied by two copies of the book (one in the case of books of foreign origin). For registration of renewal of copyright the fee currently is $4.00.

Copyright Act of 1790   the first Federal copyright law enacted as "An Act for the encouragement of learning by securing copies of maps, charts, and books, to the authors and proprietors of such copies, during the times therein mentioned." This act was based on Article 1, Section 8 of the Constitution, which granted Congress the power "to promote the progress of science and useful arts, by securing for limited times to authors and inventors the exclusive right to their respective writings and discoveries." The term of copyright was limited to fourteen years. In 1831 this term was extended to twenty-eight years with an option of renewal for another fourteen years. Copyright was held inapplicable to imported books, books by non-residents, and books printed and published outside the United States.

copyright notice   legal notice of copyright protection on the title page or verso consisting of the word copyright, followed by the symbol © (in the case of books published after 1957), the name of the copyright owner, the statement All Rights Reserved, and the date of publication, in that order.

courtesy of the trade   before the copyright law came into force, an announcement by a publisher of his intention to publish any English book caused other publishers to withdraw from bidding for it. Later extended to give each publisher first claim on the authors on his list.

cum licentia   literally, with permission. A notice indicating that the book has been published with ecclesiastical or secular sanction. Also, *cum privilegio.*

Cumulative Book Index, The   a complete listing of books published in the United States in the English language, compiled by H.W. Wilson Company and first issued in 1898. It contains an author, title, and subject index.

departmental edition   an edition of the publications of the executive departments of the U.S. government.

deposit copy   copy of a book deposited on publication in specified libraries under the copyright laws.

depository library   1. a library designated under copyright laws to receive without charge one or more copies of every book published in a country. 2. a library designated to receive without charge copies of all United States government publications.

Dewey decimal classification   a system of book classification, based on the decimal points, devised by Melvil Dewey in 1876 and revised periodically. The main divisions are:

000	General Works	500	Pure Science
100	Philosophy	600	Technology
200	Religion	700	The Arts
300	Social Sciences	800	Literature
400	Language	900	History

dime novel   popular fiction of a romantic or sensational nature published in paper covers, which had a vogue in America between 1860 and 1900. Prominent publishers of dime novels were Beadle and Adams, George Munro, Street and Smith, Robert M. DeWitt, J.S. Ogilvie Company, Frank Tousey, Frank Starr Company, Norman L. Munro, Nickel Library Company, George Sibley Company, and Thomas & Talbot. Dime novel series are listed in *Collector's Journal,* v. 4. *Also known as* yellowback.

discount   a deduction from list price offered by a publisher to the trade as well as schools and libraries according to a fixed schedule, usually a sliding scale based on the quantity ordered. A long discount is a full trade discount, normally forty per cent or more. A short discount is less than forty per cent, and given, as a rule, on textbooks, technical books and university press publications.

easy book   children's illustrated book for the youngest readers.

edition   1. as defined by Ronald Brunlees McKerrow, the British scholar, the whole number of copies of a book printed at any time or times from one setting-up of type (including copies printed from stereotype or electrotype plates made from that setting-up of type) without substantial changes. *Distinguished from* impression. 2. one of the forms in which a book is published with respect to the text or the format.

>   **abridged edition**   one that retains the sense of a work but uses fewer words.

>   **authorized edition**   published with the consent of the author or his representative, or the subject, or family of the subject, of a biography.

>   **author's edition**   the complete or collected works of an author with a uniform binding and collective title.

>   **collected edition**   uniform edition of an author's previously published works. A collected edition is not necessarily a complete edition.

>   **compact edition**   a concentrated version, usually in smaller format, from which extraneous matter has been deleted.

>   **corrected edition**   reprinting of an original edition in order to remove basic errors of fact or to add factual data.

>   **critical edition**   issue of a well-known work or classic distinguished by scholarly textual criticism.

>   **definitive edition**   an authoritative or final version of an author's work or works.

edition de luxe   limited edition printed on quality paper with fine illustrations, often specially bound and signed by the author.

editio minore   the first separate printing of a work previously included in a larger volume.

editio princeps   the first printed edition.

enlarged edition   a new edition expanded in size or volume through the addition of fresh material or illustrations.

export edition   edition of a book intended for the overseas market to which a lower rate of royalty applies. It is usually supplied at less than the normal wholesale rates.

expurgated edition   edition from which objectionable parts in the original text have been Bowdlerized.

facsimile edition   exact copies of a book made by offset or photomechanical process.

false first edition   an edition claimed as first edition by the publisher when there has been a previous edition issued by a different publisher.

first edition   all copies of a book as first printed and published. Repeated printings from the same type plates or stereos without major textual alterations are still part of the first edition.

first American edition   used to distinguish the first edition manufactured in the United States of a work previously published abroad.

first separate edition   the first edition printed within its own covers of a publication previously published as part of another work.

folio edition   an edition published in folio form.

hardbound edition   binding of stiff cardboard and cloth. *Also,* paper over boards.

illlustrated edition   one containing photographs, drawings, prints, etc., or any other form of illustrative matter in addition to the text.

inclusive edition   a complete edition of all of an author's works.

large paper edition   an edition printed on paper sized larger than the regular one, with wider margins.

large-print edition   an edition printed for the visually handicapped in larger type than usual. *Also,* large-type.

library edition   1. a higher priced edition of a book with stronger binding, intended for the library market. 2. a uniformly bound set or series for private libraries. *Also,* library binding.

limited edition   a special, de luxe edition of a volume or set consisting of a specified number of copies, consecutively numbered. Limited editions are usually sold only to collectors by subscription.

new edition   an edition substantially revised by the author or editor and incorporating additional material. *See also,* revised edition.

original edition   the first published version of a work.

paperbound edition   bound in heavy paper stock, usually varnished. *Also,* paperback.

parallel edition   one in which different texts of the same work are printed side by side, *e.g.,* the original and its translation, or two versions.

period edition   an edition issued in the style associated with the historical period of its subject, or a reprint issued in the style of the original.

pirated edition   an unauthorized and often illegal edition published and distributed without the permission of or payment to the owner of the copyright. *See also,* transatlantic piracy.

revised edition   a new printing of an original version which includes new matter that brings data up to date, corrects errors, supplies additional information and/or illustrations.

small paper edition   an edition printed on paper of smaller size than that of the regular edition.

special edition   an edition of a standard work or by a standard author with some distinctive feature, such as a new format or binding, more illustrations, or a new introduction.

text edition   an edition of a standard work prepared for use in schools and colleges, frequently including questions and answers and test material. A text edition carries a lower discount and a lower price than the trade edition.

title edition   an edition distinguished from another edition of the same book by a different title page.

trade edition   an edition sold to the general public, as distinguished from the text or library editions of the same book.

unauthorized edition   an edition issued without the consent of the author, original publisher, or subject of a biography. No actual infringement of copyright is customarily involved in such an edition.

unexpurgated edition   an uncensored complete edition of a book, including passages or portions deleted in expurgated or censored editions.

variorum edition   1. an edition of a classic containing the notes of various editors and commentators. 2. an issue of a book containing variant versions of the text.

editor   person who prepares an edition and directs its publication. As distinguished from an author, an editor prepares for publication writings not his own. An editor performs any or all of the following functions: collection and arrangement of material, revision and correction of the manuscript, review and elucidation of the text, addition of notes and other critical matter, preparation of copy for the printer, and supervision of design of the book and its printing.

acquisition editor   editor in charge of acquiring manuscripts and maintaining contacts with authors and agents.

area editor   an editor charged with books and programs on a specific subject such as religion, art, American history, etc.

associate editor   an editor ranking below a full editor and above an assistant editor.

copy editor   an editor who checks a manuscript against the house style manual and corrects and standardizes spelling, punctuation, etc. His other functions may include checking accuracy of facts and marking copy for the printer.

editor-in-chief   1. editor having managerial and policy-making responsibility for a project. 2. the principal editor of a publishing house or a publication.

executive editor   the principal editor of a project concerned with the coordination of the work of various editors, time schedules, and liaison with art and production departments.

managing editor   an editor ranking below an editor-in-chief and above an executive editor, concerned chiefly with editorial supervision and business management.

search editor   an editor charged with planning and developing new ideas for books, scouting out leads, evaluating manuscripts, and encouraging and advising authors and potential authors. More often called a consulting editor.

el-hi   elementary school and high school markets considered together.

El-Hi Textbooks in Print   an annual publication of R.R. Bowker Company listing elementary and secondary school textbooks classified by subject, with author and title index. Also lists professional reference books, teaching aids, and programmed materials in book form.

ephemera   published materials of passing interest, *e.g.* pamphlets.

erotica   literature that emphasizes sexual love or serves to arouse sexual feelings. As distinguished from pornography, erotica may have some literary value.

export representative   an organization handling the promotion and sale of books outside the country of their origin. Feffer and Simons, Inc., Media Directions, Inc., and Kaiman and Polon, Inc., are the major American export representatives.

extra illustrated   having extra illustrations that were not part of the original edition. The additional material—pictures, documents, or engravings—are trimmed to fit the size of the book and then mounted. Also called "Grangerized" after James Granger, British publisher, who, in 1769, published his BIOGRAPHICAL HISTORY OF ENGLAND with blank leaves interleaved for the addition of portraits.

facsimile reprint   reset of an out of print work in which identical face and size of type are used.

faction   blend of fact and fiction. Used as a collective term for fictionalized narratives of real events.

factual book   an information book as distinguished from one fictionalized or designed for recreational reading.

Fair Trade Agreement   litigation between American Publishers Association and R.H. Macy Company led to fair trade legislation in New York State. In 1935 the Feld-Crawford Fair Trade Act was passed. Several New York publishers signed an agreement to maintain a fixed price on their books for a definite period. The New York Supreme Court declared the Feld-Crawford Act unconstitutional and this decision was upheld by the New York State Court of Appeals in 1936. On appeal the United States Supreme Court upheld the fair trade legislation and since then practically every state has passed fair trade laws covering the price maintenance of books.

fair use   principle embodied in copyright law that permits use of portions of copyrighted materials without the sanction of the copyright owner provided the use (a) is fair and reasonable and does not exceed 250-300 words in length, (b) does not substantially impair the value of the material so used, (c) does not curtail the reasonable profits of the owner, and (d) is for the purpose of advancing scholarship and is accompanied by fair comment.

fascicle   one of the sections of a book issued in parts prior to its being published in complete form. Each installment usually consists of quires covered with a paper wrapper. *Also,* fascicule, *fasciculus.*

Festschrift   literally, festival writing. A collection of original essays or addresses by students or colleagues of a scholar and published in his honor, generally on the occasion of an anniversary celebration.

fictitious imprint   an imaginary imprint used to evade legal restrictions, to mask piracy, or to protect the author's anonymity.

first impression   the total number of copies printed at one time without removing the type or plates from the press and issued together.

Florence Agreement   an international agreement sponsored by the UNESCO and signed by over thirty countries, including the United States. The agreement provides for the elimination or reduction of tariffs on books and other scientific, educational, and cultural materials.

folio   1. a sheet of paper folded once to give two leaves or four pages. 2. a book of the largest size printed on sheets folded only once. A folio is usually more than eleven inches in height. 3. a sheet or leaf numbered on the front side only. 4. the page number.

front matter   matter preceding the text in a book, in this order: (1) bastard title or fly title, (2) a list of books by the same author or other books in the same series, (3) frontispiece, (4) title page, (5) copyright page (with country of origin and number of printings, if more than one), (6) dedication, (7) preface or foreword, (8) table of contents, (9) list of illustrations, (10) introduction, and (11) half title. Frontispiece, copyright page, and list of books appear on the verso and the others on the recto.

fugitive material   material of passing interest printed for limited distribution as, for instance, programs.

get-out   the number of copies of a book that must be sold to enable a publisher to cover initial costs of publishing the book.

giant book   a three-dimensional blow-up of a book for display purposes.

giftbook   an illustrated annual publication of prose and poetry, popular in the early part of the nineteenth century.

Grolier List   list issued by the Grolier Club of New York City entitled "One Hundred Books Famous in English Literature," often cited by collectors.

Harvard Classics   library of literary classics of all nations, known as the *Five-Foot Shelf.* Edited by Charles W. Eliot in fifty volumes, it was published by P. F. Collier, 1909 to 1910. Now owned by Macmillan, Inc.

hidden bestsellers   books which have tremendous sales but which do not appear on bestseller lists. Some examples are THE BIBLE, schoolbooks, cookbooks, and THE BOY SCOUT MANUAL.

hornbook   a leaf of paper containing the alphabet, the ten digits, and the Lord's Prayer, protected by a translucent plate of horn and mounted on a tablet of wood with a handle. Used from the sixteenth to early eighteenth centuries as a primer.

house style   approved style incorporating standardized rules with regard to grammar, spelling, capitalization, punctuation, abbreviation, etc., followed by a publishing house in preparing copy.

how-to book   a book of detailed instructions in a household or practical art, a hobby or recreational activity.

illustrated book   a book containing pictorial illustrations. The first book illustration in the United States was a woodcut map of New England that appeared in William Hubbard's NARRATIVE OF THE INDIAN WARS, published by John Foster in Boston in 1677.

imprimatur   literally, let it be printed. Originally, official license authorizing the publication of a book printed on the verso of the title page. The term survives only in the Catholic Church and is used to indicate that the book contains nothing contrary to the doctrines of the Church. *Also, nihil obstat, cum licentia.*

imprint   1. the publisher's name. 2. the publisher's name and device and the place and date of publication at the foot of the title page. 3. the printer's name on the verso of the title page or at the foot of the last printed page of the final signature.

Index Expurgatorius   a list of books that the Roman Catholic Church forbids its members to read until objectionable parts have been deleted or changed.

Index Librorum Prohibitorum   a list of books that the Roman Catholic Church totally forbids its members to read.

Index Translationum   international bibliography of translations published by UNESCO beginning in 1949. A similar annual was published by the League of Nations from 1932 to 1940.

International Standard Book Number   an identification number for books consisting of ten digits made up of the following parts: (1) group identifier (language, national, geographical, or other), (2) publisher identifier, (3) title identifier, (4) check digit. When written or printed it is preceded by the letters ISBN and each element is separated by a hyphen or space, as for example: ISBN 91-8523-201-7. The group identifier is allocated by an international standard book number agency. This number will be based on the title output of the group concerned. The publisher identifier is allocated within the group by the internal agency appointed for this purpose. This number will be based on the title output of the publisher concerned. The title identifier is determined by the length of the preceding numbers. The check digit is calculated on a modulus of 11 with weights 10-2, using X in lieu of 10 where 10 would occur as a check digit. The International Standard Book Number should be printed on the back of the title page or at the foot of the title page. It should also appear at the foot of the outside back cover or at the foot of the back of the jacket.

introduction   the preliminary section of a book in which the author or a friend explains the organization and limits of the work.

irregular serial   a publication in book form issued at intervals of more than a year.

Library of Congress Card   a classified catalogue card printed by the Library of Congress Card Division for distribution to libraries. The card number, secured in advance from the Division when a book is ready for manufacture, is usually printed on the verso of the title page.

Library of Congress classification   a system of book classification developed by and used in the Library of Congress. It consists of an expandable notation of figures and letters.

Library of the World's Best Literature   a collection edited by Charles Dudley Warner and others in thirty-one volumes and published in 1897. Better known as the *Warner Library*.

literary agent   an author's representative who finds a publisher for his manuscript and handles his rights. The agent is usually paid a commission of ten per cent by the author. A literary agent may also help a publisher to secure the kind of books he requires.

Literary Market Place   a business directory of American publishing issued annually by R.R. Bowker Company since 1940. It also contains a register of personnel in publishing and allied fields and a buyer's guide for materials and services in the book industry.

logo   a trade name designed in a particular form or style; logotype.

made book   a book conceived inside a publishing house which then finds an author to write it and picture researchers to illustrate it.

mass market paperbacks   low-priced paperbacks distributed through magazine distribution channels to supermarkets, drug stores, newsstands, and other outlets. *Distinguished from quality paperbacks.*

monograph series   a series of related monographs issued by a learned society in uniform style with a collective title.

National Bibliography   a complete list of books published in a country, continuously updated through supplements.

National Biography   collection of biographies of notable persons living in or associated with a particular country.

National Library Week   a week set aside for the intensive promotion of books and reading. It is organized annually by the National Book Committee in the United States and held in April. The program was inaugurated in 1958 and is now one of the major events of the American book trade.

nihil obstat literally, nothing hinders. A Catholic censor's sanction of publication, usually printed on the verso of the title page.

non-book   a book without any literary merit, often consisting more of pictures than text and designed to exploit a passing fad or vogue.

noncommercial book   a publication by associations, foundations, corporations, or special agencies for limited distribution, usually on a courtesy basis, that is not sold through normal trade channels.

nonfiction novel   a factual account written in the form of a novel. *See also,* faction.

numbered copy   a copy of a book in a limited edition which has a notice in the colophon stating the total number of copies printed and the individual copy number. Originated by Gian Battista Bodoni.

offset   a printing process in which a metal lithographic plate prints on a rubber-covered cylinder which in turn transfers the image to the paper. Offset printing is commonly used for reprints and picture books. *Also,* photo offset lithography.

omnibus   a one-volume reprint edition of the collected works of an author, or a collection of related articles or stories by various authors.

one-shot   the reprinting of the full text or an abridgment of a book in one issue of a periodical as distinguished from a serialized reprinting.

onomasticon   a dictionary of proper names, giving their origin, form, and meaning.

option   a right to buy or sell a literary property within a given length of time.

pamphlet   1. a small, independent publication with fewer pages than a book, stitched but not bound and usually enclosed in paper covers. The maximum number of pages in a pamphlet varies from 32 to 100 pages. 2. earlier, a controversial treatise on a topic of current interest.

pamphlet volume   a bound volume containing a number of separate pamphlets with a general title page and a table of contents.

part issue   one of the installments in which a work that is published in parts appears. When the issue is complete it is bound in binding cases supplied by the publisher.

picture researcher   person familiar with photo and picture sources who selects illustrations to accompany the text in a book.

popular copyright   a term used in the nineteenth century to denote a low-priced reprint of a popular book issued through arrangement with the copyright owners, often manufactured by using the original plates.

postface   explanatory matter following the body of the text as distinguished from preface.

preliminary matter   those pages that precede the text in a book, with independent pagination in Roman numerals, often printed after the text has been set. *Also,* front matter.

printed as manuscript   1. printed from an unedited manuscript. 2. printed for private circulation only.

printed but not published   (of a printed book) not offered for sale for legal or other reasons.

private book club   an association of bibliophiles often publishing fine editions for its members or engaged in activities of interest to book collectors. The Grolier Club and the Limited Editions Club are two important private book clubs in the United States.

privately printed (of a book) 1. printed by a private press. 2. printed by an author-publisher for private circulation. 3. printed clandestinely to evade the law.

privately published published by author-publisher for private circulation.

private press 1. a press that prints fine books for limited circulation. As defined by Eric Gill, "a private press prints solely what it chooses to print whereas a public press prints what its customers demand of it." 2. a press where books are hand-set and hand-printed.

Proctor Order a chronological system of arranging incunabula developed by Robert Proctor. The main subgroupings of the system are: by country, by place, and by printer.

prospectus 1. plan of a work to be published, with specimen pages and a table of contents. 2. a descriptive circular containing specimen pages, representative illustrations, and style of binding, used in soliciting orders.

public domain the legal status of a book whose copyright has expired. In the United States this is twenty-eight years after publication if the copyright has not been renewed. If renewed, the copyright extends to fifty-six years. To be "in public domain" means to be available for free and unrestricted use.

publisher a person or firm in the business of issuing printed materials to the public. Though publishing has developed as a business apart from bookselling and printing (especially since the middle of the nineteenth century), production and distribution are still two of the most important functions of a publisher. His other functions include manuscript acquisition, editing and picture researching, art work, promotion, and the handling of copyright, subsidiary rights, and some other author's rights. Ultimately, he is an entrepreneur dealing in books.

publisher's agreement arrangement between a publisher and an author under which a book is published and sold. Payment of royalties, calculated on a sliding scale and based on actual sales, is the most common arrangement. Profit-sharing agreements are less common but some-times more advantageous to the author. Under a commission agreement, an author pays the publisher a fixed commission for handling his book. The last type of arrangement involves the outright sale of copyright by the author to the publisher for a mutually agreed consideration.

publisher's mark an emblem, device, or logo used by a publisher as his trade mark. *Also,* colophon.

publisher's series an open-ended collection of reprints of standard books, not necessarily related by subject, which a publisher issues in uniform format with a collective series title. *Everyman's Library, Modern Library,* and *World Classics* are notable examples of such series.

publishing as defined by Chandler B. Grannis, the whole intellectual and business procedure of selecting and arranging to make a book and of promoting its ultimate use.

"publish or perish" an expression used for the publication by college or university teachers of books or scholarly articles; regarded as an imperative for advancement in the academic community.

quality paperbacks higher-priced paperbound books sold through regular book outlets.

reader one who reads manuscripts critically for a publisher or literary agent to determine their publishability.

recto the right hand page of an open book, usually bearing an odd number.

red book a book containing a list, as of employees in an organization, hotels and motels.

reference matter section of a book that contains notes, bibliography, appendices, and indexes.

regional publishing publishing of books exclusively or primarily oriented to local history and interests.

religious press denominational book publishers collectively. Includes Judson Press and Broadman Press (Baptist), Westminster Press (Presbyterian), Pilgrim Press (Congregationalist), Beacon Press (Unitarian), Abingdon Press

(Methodist), Concordia Publishing House (Lutheran), Morehouse-Barlow (Episcopalian), Bloch Publishing Company (Jewish), and Sheed and Ward and P.J. Kenedy (Catholic).

remainders a publisher's overstock of unsold, slow-selling titles disposed of as a lot at considerably reduced prices.

reprint publishing a branch of publishing specializing in the reprints of scholarly works in the public domain. Such reprints, usually made by offset, are sold directly to libraries by direct mail.

reprint series a collection of selected books in a particular subject reprinted and issued as a series with a general title.

Revised Standard Version an American Protestant revision of the New Testament published in 1946 and of the whole Bible in 1952.

Revised Version a revision of the Authorized Version, or the King James Version, of the Bible, published 1881-1885.

rights and permissions rights to a literary property and permission to use and exploit them. The rights include: (1) publication; (2) syndication and serialization; (3) book club; (4) paperback reprint; (5) dramatization; (6) motion picture; (7) radio and television; (8) reprint and reproduction; (9) foreign publication; (10) condensation; (11) anthology; (12) translation; (13) quotation; (14) recording; (15) electronic reproduction, storage and retrieval.

royalty a mutually agreed percentage of the published price of a book paid to its author in respect of copies sold, the payment being governed by a contract. The percentage may vary from house to house, from author to author, and from edition to edition.

scout a peripatetic editor looking for new and promising writers and exploring ideas for new books.

serial a publication issued at regular intervals or in successive parts and generally intended to be continued indefinitely. Serials include periodicals, annuals, and proceedings of societies.

serial rights the right to reprint in a magazine or newspaper. First serial rights pertain to prepublication use (usually of extracts from a book) and second serial rights to usage after publication of a story, book, or other matter. Serialization need not be in parts but can also be a one-time excerpt.

series 1. a number of separate works issued in uniform style with a collective general title. 2. each of two or more volumes of collected writings on the same subject issued in sequence, *e.g.,* American Poets, second series.

series title the collective title of a series as distinguished from the titles of the individual books comprising the series.

service a publisher who supplies current information in a specialized area at regular intervals. The information is organized for ready reference and is generally in loose-leaf form.

set a series of works by the same author or on the same subject issued in uniform style and designed to be sold as a unit.

sheets the unbound pages of a book, either folded or flat. *Also, in sheets.*

signature 1. a section of a book consisting of a folded printed sheet. *Also,* gathering, section, quire. 2. the letter, mark, or figure at the foot of the first page of this section for the guidance of the binder. *Also,* signature mark.

Single Copy Order Plan a plan devised and administered by the American Booksellers Association that ensures full trade discount to dealers on single copies by reducing their handling charges at the publishers' end.

sleeper an initially unpromising book that achieves wide sale and unexpected success with little promotion.

society publication an official publication of a society or association.

Spanish Americana material about American countries or regions south of the United States, books printed in that region, or written by or about Spanish Americans.

318

state publication   any printed material published by the authority of a government.

Stockholm Protocol   international agreement known as the Protocol Regarding Developing Countries signed at Stockholm on July 14, 1967. It permits a developing country to restrict international copyright protection by reducing the basic term of copyright to life-plus-twenty-five years and by providing for compulsory licensing of translations for educational and cultural purposes.

styling   checking a manuscript against the house style manual and standardizing spelling, punctuation, capitalization, etc. Styling is commonly done by copy editors.

Subject Guide to Books in Print   an annual bibliography published by R.R. Bowker Company listing American books in print arranged according to subject matter under Library of Congress subject headings.

subject series   a number of books often written by different authors, uniform in format, scope, and method, often under a general editor.

subscription book   a book or set of books sold by subscription agents or by direct mail. The practice arose in the eighteenth and nineteenth centuries when expensive works had to be underwritten in advance by a sufficient number of subscriptions. Subscribers who responded to the preliminary announcement were asked to pay part of the price in advance.

subsidiary rights   incidental rights to a literary property other than initial volume publication rights. *See also,* rights and permissions.

suppressed   (of a book)   withdrawn from circulation or publication by the author or publisher or by legal or ecclesiastical order.

tie-in   1. promotion of a book by emphasizing its relation to a motion picture, play, or television program, especially through an advertisement featuring the two together. 2. a book thus promoted.

trade book   a book sold to the general public through regular outlets, such as bookstores, as distinguished from subscription books and textbooks.

trade publisher   a publisher who issues a wide spectrum of books for the general public, as distinguished from one who publishes special books appealing to a limited audience, as for example textbooks, scientific books, etc.

trade terms   the schedule of discounts extended to the book trade by a publisher, including conditions of sale governing return of unsold copies, shipping, cooperative advertising, etc.

transatlantic piracy   unauthorized publication of books of British origin in the United States and of American origin in Britain before passage of the U.S. Copyright Law of 1909.

Universal Copyright Convention   an agreement sponsored by UNESCO in 1952 under which signatory countries, including the United States, extend to literary works published in member countries full, equal, and reciprocatory copyright protection.

universal decimal classification   an adapted form of Dewey Decimal Classification suitable for specialized information and documentation.

USiana   Americana relating to the United States only. Term coined by Wright Howes.

vanity publisher   a publisher who publishes books at the author's risk and expense. *Also,* subsidy publisher.

verso   the left hand page of an open book, usually bearing an even number.

warehouse publishing   publication of titles more for prestige than for profit.

yellowback   a cheap, popular novel bound in yellow covers, popular in nineteenth century America.

Baehr, William, *Denominational Publishing in the United States.* Urbana, Ill.: University of Illinois Press, 1929.

Bailey, Herbert S., *The Art and Science of Book Publishing.* New York, N.Y.: Harper & Row, 1970.

Ballou, Robert O., *A History of The Council on Books in Wartime.* New York, N.Y.: Council on Books in Wartime, 1946.

Bean, Donald P., *Report on American Scholarly Publishing.* Chicago, Ill.: mimeographed, 1929.

Beswick, Jay W., *The Work of Frederick Leypoldt, Bibliographer and Publisher.* New York, N.Y.: Bowker, 1942.

Bigelow, John, (ed.), *The Autobiography of Benjamin Franklin.* Philadelphia, Pa.: J.B. Lippincott, 1868.

Bingley, Clive, *Book Publishing Practice.* Hamden, Conn.: The Shoe String Press, 1966.

Bliss, Arthur Ames, *Theodore Bliss, Publisher and Bookseller. A Study of Character and Life in the Middle Period of the XIX Century.* Norwalk, O.: American Publishers Company, 1911.

Bowker Company, annual issue, New York, N.Y. *Bowker Annual of Library and Book Trade Information.*

Bradley, Edward, *Henry Charles Lea: A Biography.* Philadelphia, Pa.: University of Pennsylvania Press, 1931.

Bradsher, E.L., *Book Publishers and Publishing.* From *Cambridge History of American Literature,* vol. 4, pp. 533-553. New York, N.Y.: Putnam's, 1917-21.

——, *Mathew Carey, Editor, Author, and Publisher: A Study in American Literary Development.* New York, N.Y.: Columbia University Press, 1912.

Buckingham, J.T., *Personal Memoirs and Recollections of Editorial Life.* Boston, Mass.: Ticknor, Reed and Fields, 1852.

Burke, W.J. and Howe, Will D. (revised by Weiss, Irving R.), *American Authors and Books.* New York, N.Y.: Crown Publishers, 1972.

Burlingame, Roger, *Of Making Many Books: A Hundred Years of Reading, Writing and Publishing.* New York N.Y.: Scribner, 1946.

Campbell, William J., *The Collection of Franklin Imprints in the Museum of the Curtis Publishing Company, with a Short-Title Checklist of All the Books, Pamphlets, Broadsides, &c., Known to Have Been Printed by Benjamin Franklin.* Philadelphia, Pa.: Curtis Publishing Company, 1918.

Canfield, Cass, *The Publishing Experience.* Philadelphia, Pa.: University of Pennsylvania Press, 1968.

——, *Up & Down & Around: A Publisher Recollects the Time of His Life.* New York, N.Y.: Harper's Magazine Press, 1971.

Carey, Mathew, *Autobiographical Sketches, in a Series of Letters Addressed to a Friend.* Philadelphia, Pa.: John Clarke, 1829.

Carpenter, Charles, *History of American Schoolbooks.* Philadelphia, Pa.: University of Pennsylvania Press, 1963.

(Robert Carter & Brothers), *Robert Carter: His Life and Work, 1807-1889.* New York, N.Y.: Anson D.F. Randolph, 1891.

Charvat, William, *Literary Publishing in America, 1790-1850.* Philadelphia, Pa.: University of Pennsylvania Press, 1959; Rosenbach Publications Series.

Cheney, O.H., *Economic Survey of the Book Industry, 1930-31. (The Cheney Report).* New York, N.Y.: Bowker, 1960.

Childs, George W., *Recollections.* Philadelphia, Pa.: J.B. Lippincott, 1890.

Clark, Aubert J., *The Movement for International Copyright in Nineteenth Century America.* Washington, D.C.: Catholic University of America Press, 1960.

Clark, Harry, *A Venture in History: the Production, Publication, and Sale of the Works of Hubert Howe Bancroft*. Berkeley, Calif.: University of California Press, 1973.

Crain, G.D., Jr. (ed.), *Teacher of Business: The Publishing Philosophy of James H. McGraw*. Chicago, Ill.: Advertising Publications, 1944.

Crowell, Thomas Irving, *Thomas Young Crowell, 1836-1915: A Biographical Sketch*. New York, N.Y.: Thomas Y. Crowell, 1926.

Day, G.P., *The Function and Organization of University Presses*. New Haven, Conn.: Yale University Press, 1915.

Derby, J.C., *Fifty Years Among Authors, Books and Publishers*. New York, N.Y.: Carleton, 1884.

Doran, George H., *Chronicles of Barabbas, 1884-1934*. New York, N.Y.: Harcourt, Brace, 1935.

——, *Further Chronicles and Comment, 1952*. New York, N.Y.: Rinehart, 1952.

Doubleday, Frank Nelson, *A Few Indiscreet Recollections*. Garden City, N.Y.: Privately printed, 1928.

——, *More Indiscreet Recollections: A Postscript*. Garden City, N.Y.: Privately printed, 1929.

——, *He's Done It Again: More Indiscreet Recollections*. Garden City, N.Y.: Privately printed, 1933.

Dunlap, George T., *The Fleeting Years: A Memoir*. New York, N.Y.: Privately printed, 1937.

Elder, William, *A Memoir of Henry C. Carey*. Philadelphia, Pa.: H.C. Baird & Company, 1880.

Ellsworth, W.W., *A Golden Age of Authors: A Publisher's Recollection*. Boston, Mass.: Houghton Mifflin, 1919.

Fields, James T., *Biographical Notes and Personal Sketches, with Unpublished Fragments and Tributes from Men and Women of Letters*. Boston, Mass.: Houghton Mifflin, 1881.

——, *Yesterdays With Authors*. Boston, Mass.: Houghton Mifflin, 1900.

Fisher, Vardis, *The Caxton Printers in Idaho: A Short History*. Cincinnati, O.: Society of Bibliosophers, 1944.

Fisher, William A., *One Hundred and Fifty Years of Music Publishing in the United States. An Historical Sketch with Special Reference to the Pioneer Publisher, Oliver Ditson Company, Inc., 1783-1933*. Boston, Mass.: Ditson, 1933.

Fleming, E. McClung, *R.R. Bowker, Militant Liberal*. Norman, Okla.: University of Oklahoma Press, 1952.

Friede, Donald, *The Mechanical Angel: His Adventures and Enterprises in the Glittering 1920's*. New York, N.Y.: A.A. Knopf, 1948.

Gardiner, C. Harvey, *Prescott and his Publishers*. Carbondale, Ill.: Southern Illinois University Press, 1959.

Gilmer, Walker, *Horace Liveright, Publisher of the Twenties*. New York, N.Y.: David Lewis, 1970.

Goodrich, Samuel G., *Recollections of a Lifetime*. (2 vols.) New York, N.Y.: Auburn, Miller, Orton & Mulligan, 1856.

——, *Peter Parley's Own Story: From the Personal Narrative of the Late Samuel G. Goodrich*. New York, N.Y.: Sheldon & Company, 1864.

Grannis, Chandler B., *What Happens in Book Publishing*. New York, N.Y.: Columbia University Press, 1967.

Greenslet, Ferris, *Under the Bridge: An Autobiography*. Boston, Mass.: Houghton Mifflin, 1943.

Gross, Gerald, *Editors on Editing*. New York, N.Y.: Grosset & Dunlap, 1962.

——, *Publishers on Publishing*. New York, N.Y.: Grosset & Dunlap, 1961.

Growoll, Adolf, *American Book Clubs: Their Beginnings and History, and a Bibliography of their Publications*. New York, N.Y.: Dodd, Mead, 1897.

——, *Frederick Leypoldt: Biographical and Bibliographical Sketch*. New York, N.Y.: Dibdin Club, 1899.

Gunn, John W., *E. Haldeman-Julius—The Man and His Work*. Girard, Kansas: Haldeman-Julius, 1924.

Hackett, Alice Payne, *Seventy Years of Bestsellers: 1895-1965*. New York, N.Y.: Bowker, 1967.

Haldeman-Julius, Emanuel, *My First 25 Years*. Girard, Kansas: Haldeman-Julius, 1949.

——, *My Second 52 Years*. Girard, Kansas: Haldeman-Julius, 1949.

——, *The First Hundred Million*. New York, N.Y.: Simon & Schuster, 1928.

Harcourt, Alfred, *Some Experiences*. Riverside, Conn.: 1951.

Harmon, Eleanor, *The University as Publisher*. Toronto, Ont.: University of Toronto Press, 1961.

Hart, James D., *The Popular Book: A History of America's Literary Taste*. New York, N.Y.: Oxford University Press, 1950.

Hawes, Gene R., *To Advance Knowledge: A Handbook on American University Press Publishing*. New York, N.Y.: American University Press Services, 1967.

Henderson, Kathryn, *Trends in American Publishing*. Urbana, Ill.: University of Illinois School of Library Science, 1968. (Allerton Park Institute Publications No. 14.)

Hilton, Henry Hoyt, *Observations and Memories*. Boston, Mass.: Ginn, 1947.

Holt, Henry, *Garrulities of an Octogenarian Editor*. Boston, Mass.: Houghton Mifflin, 1923.

Hubbard, Elbert, *Impressions: Being Short Sketches and Intimacies Concerning Elbert Hubbard, The Roycroft and Things Roycroftie, Together With Some Autobiography*. East Aurora, Ill.: Roycrofters, 1921.

——, *The Roycroft Shop: A History*. East Aurora, Ill.: The Roycroft Press, 1908.

Hungerford, Herbert, *How Publishers Win: A Case Record Commentary on Personal Experiences and Interviews with Prominent Publishers Showing How Books and Periodicals are Made and Marketed*. Washington, D.C.: Ransdell, 1931.

International Bibliography of the Book Trade and Librarianship. New York, N.Y.: Bowker, 1970.

Jamieson, John Alden, *Editions for the Armed Services, Inc. A History, Together with the Complete List of 1324 Books Published for American Armed Forces Overseas*. New York, N.Y.: Editions For the Armed Services, Inc., 1948.

Johnson, Robert Underwood, *Remembered Yesterdays*. Boston, Mass.: Little, Brown, 1923.

Jovanovich, William, *Now, Barabbas*. New York, N.Y.: Harcourt, Brace, 1960.

——, *Now, Barabbas*. New York, N.Y.: Harper, 1964.

Kaser, David, *The Cost Book of Carey & Lea, 1825-1838*. Philadelphia, Pa.: University of Pennsylvania Press, 1963.

——, *Messrs. Carey & Lea of Philadelphia: A Study In the History of the Book Trade*. Philadelphia, Pa.: University of Pennsylvania Press, 1957.

Kerr, Chester, *American University as Publisher. A Digest of a Report on American University Presses*. Norman, Okla.: University of Oklahoma Press, 1949.

Kilgour, Raymond L., *Lee and Shepard: Publishers for the People*. Hamden, Conn.: Shoe String Press, 1965.

——, *Messrs. Roberts Brothers, Publishers*. Ann Arbor, Mich.: University of Michigan Press, 1952.

Kimber, Sidney A., *The Story of An Old Press: An Account of the Hand Press Known as the Stephen Daye Press, Upon Which Was Begun in 1638 the First Printing in British North America*. Cambridge, Mass.: Harvard University Press, 1939.

Kramer, Sidney, *A History of Stone & Kimball and Herbert S. Stone & Co., With a Bibliography of their Publications, 1893-1905*. Chicago, Ill.: N.W. Forgue, 1940.

Kujoth, Jean S., *Book Publishing: Inside Views*. Metuchen, N.J.: Scarecrow Press, 1971.

Lane, Robert Frederick, *The Place of American University Presses in Publishing*. Chicago, Ill.: University of Chicago Press, 1942.

Latham, Harold S., *My Life in Publishing*. New York, N.Y.: Dutton, 1965.

Laylander, O.J., *The Chronicles of a Contented Man*. Chicago, Ill.: A. Kroch, 1928.

Lea, Arthur H., *Henry Charles Lea, 1825-1909*. Philadelphia, Pa.: Privately printed, 1910.

Lehmann-Haupt, Hellmut; Wroth, Lawrence C., and Silver, Rollo, *The Book in America: History of the Making and Selling of Books in the United States*. New York, N.Y.: Bowker, 1951.

Leslie, Frank, *A Brief History of Frank Leslie's Publishing House*. New York, N.Y.: Leslie, 1887.

Littlefield, G.E., *Early Boston Booksellers, 1642-1711.* Boston, Mass.: Club of Odd Volumes, 1900.

Lottinville, Savoie, et al., *Some Notes on University Press Publishing.* Norman, Okla.: University of Oklahoma Press, 1947.

Lynch, Kathleen M., *Jacob Tonson, Kit-Cat Publisher.* Knoxville, Tenn.: University of Tennessee Press, 1971.

Lyon, Peter, *Success Story: The Life and Times of S.S. McClure.* New York, N.Y.: Scribner, 1963.

Madison, Charles A., *Book Publishing in America.* New York, N.Y.: McGraw-Hill, 1966.

——, *The Owl Among the Colophons: Henry Holt as Publisher and Editor.* New York, N.Y.: Henry Holt & Co., 1966.

Mangione, Jerre, *The Dream and the Deal. The Federal Writers Project.* Boston, Mass.: Little, Brown, 1973.

Mann, Dorothea Lawrance, *A Century of Bookselling: The Story of the Old Corner Book Store on the Occasion of Its One Hundredth Birthday.* Boston, Mass.: Old Corner Book Store, 1928.

Marble, Annie Russell, *From 'Prentice to Patron: The Life Story of Isaiah Thomas.* New York, N.Y.: Appleton-Century, 1935.

Marshall, John, *Publication of Books and Monographs by Learned Societies.* Washington, D.C.: American Council of Learned Societies, 1931.

Matthews, Annie Harmon, *Thomas Bird Mosher of Portland, Maine.* Portland, Me.: Southworth-Anthoensen Press, 1941.

McClure, S.S., and Cather, Willa, *My Autobiography.* New York, N.Y.: Frederick Stokes, 1914.

Melcher, Frederic G., *Friendly Reminiscences of A Half Century Among Books and Bookmen.* New York, N.Y.: Book Publishers Bureau, 1945.

Merritt, LeRoy C., *The United States Government as Publisher.* Chicago, Ill.: University of Chicago Press, 1943. (University of Chicago Studies in Library Sciences.)

Miller, William, *The Book Industry.* New York, N.Y.: Columbia University Press, 1949.

Moore, John W., *Historical, Biographical & Miscellaneous Gatherings in the Form of Disconnected Notes Relative to Printers, Printing, Publishing & Editing Books, Newspapers, Magazines & Other Literary Productions.* Concord, N.H.: Republican Press Association, 1886.

Mora, Imre, *The Publisher's Practical Dictionary in 20 Languages.* New York, N.Y.: Bowker, 1974.

Mordell, Albert, *The World of Haldeman-Julius.* New York, N.Y.: Twayne Publishers, 1960.

Morley, Christopher, *"Effendi" (Frank Nelson Doubleday, 1862-1934.)* Garden City, N.Y.: Privately printed, 1934.

Mott, Frank Luther, *Golden Multitudes: The Story of Bestsellers in the United States.* New York, N.Y.: Macmillan, 1947.

Munsey, Frank A., *The Founding of the Munsey Publishing-House: Quarter Century Old.* New York, N.Y.: De Vinne Press, 1907.

Murray, William, *Adventures in the People Business. The Story of World Book.* Chicago, Ill.: Field Enterprises Educational Corp., 1966.

Nemeyer, Carol A., *Scholarly Reprint Publishing in the United States.* New York, N.Y.: Bowker, 1972.

Nickerson, Thomas, *Trans-Pacific Scholarly Publishing.* Honolulu, Haw.: University Press of Hawaii, 1963.

Optimus Magister, Bonus Liber. Chicago, Ill.: Loyola University Press, 1953.

Page, Walter Hines, *A Publisher's Confession.* Garden City, N.Y.: Doubleday, Page, 1905.

Parton, James, *George W. Childs: A Biographical Sketch.* Philadelphia, Pa.: Collins, 1870.

Pearson, Edmund, *Dime Novels; or, Following an Old Trail in Popular Literature.* Boston, Mass.: Little, Brown, 1929.

Perry, Bliss, *Park-Street Papers.* Boston, Mass.: Houghton Mifflin, 1908.

Pratt, John Barnes, *A Century of Book Publishing, 1838-1938: Historical and Personal.* New York, N.Y.: A.S. Barnes, 1938.

——, *Personal Recollections: Sixty Years of Book Publishing*. New York, N.Y.: A.S. Barnes, 1942.

——, *Seventy-Five Years of Book Publishing, 1838-1913*. New York, N.Y.: A.S. Barnes, 1913.

Profiles in Book Publishing. New York, N.Y.: *Book Production Magazine,* Freund Publishing Co., 1963.

Pulsifer, W.E., *A Brief Account of the Educational Publishing Business in the United States*. Atlantic City, N.J.: 1921.

Reid, James M., *An Adventure in Textbooks*. New York, N.Y.: Bowker, 1969.

Renetzky, Alvin, and Greene, Jon S., *Directory of Scholarly and Research Publishing Opportunities*. Los Angeles, Calif.: Academic Media, 1971.

Rogers, Denis R., *Munro's Ten Cent Novels, 1863-77*. Fall River, Mass.: Edward T. LeBlanc, 1958.

Roselle, Daniel, *Samuel Griswold Goodrich, Creator of Peter Parley: A Study of His Life and Work*. Albany, N.Y.: State University of New York Press, 1968.

Schick, Frank L., *The Paperbound Book in America: The History of Paperbacks and their European Antecedents*. New York, N.Y.: Bowker, 1958.

Scudder, Horace E., *Henry Oscar Houghton: A Biographical Outline*. Cambridge, Mass.: Riverside Press, 1897.

Sears, Helen L., *American University Presses Come of Age*. Syracuse, N.Y.: Syracuse University Press, 1959.

Sheehan, Donald H., *This Was Publishing: A Chronicle of the Book Trade in the Gilded Age*. Bloomington, Ind.: Indiana University Press, 1952.

Shove, Raymond Howard, *Cheap Book Production in the United States, 1870-1891*. Urbana, Ill.: University of Illinois Press, 1937.

Shugg, Roger, *The Two Worlds of University Publishing*. Lawrence, Kan.: University of Kansas Libraries, 1967.

Silver, Rollo G., *The Boston Book Trade, 1800-1825*. New York, N.Y.: New York Public Library, 1949.

Skeel, Emily Ellsworth Ford, (ed.), *Mason Locke Weems: His Works and Ways*. (3 vols.) Norwood, Mass.: Plimpton Press, 1929.

Smith, Datus C., *A Guide to Book Publishing*. New York, N.Y.: Bowker, 1966.

Spieseke, Alice Winifred, *The First Textbooks in American History and Their Compiler, John M'Culloch*. New York, N.Y.: Columbia University, Teachers College, 1938.

Steiger, Ernst, *Dreiundfünfzig Jahre Buchhändler in Deutschland und Amerika*. New York, N.Y.: E. Steiger, 1901.

Stern, Madeleine B., *Imprints on History: Book Publishers and American Frontiers*. Bloomington, Ind.: Indiana University Press, 1952.

Stevens, Abel, *Life and Times of Nathan Bangs, D.D.* New York, N.Y.: Carlton and Porter, 1863.

Stone, John Paul, *Inexpensive Reprint Series*. Urbana, Ill.: University of Illinois Press, 1930.

Strouse, Norman H., *Thomas Bird Mosher—The Passionate Pirate*. Cleveland, O.: Rowfant Club, 1960.

Sutton, Walter, *Western Book Trade: Cincinnati as a 19th Century Publishing and Book Trade Center*. Columbus, O.: Ohio State University Press, 1961.

Sweet, Arthur P., *The Trade Book and the Book Trade: A Study in the Terminology and Structure of American Publishing*. Rochester, N.Y.: University of Rochester Press, 1954.

Tanselle, Thomas, *Guide to the Study of United States Imprints*. (2 vols.) Cambridge, Mass.: Belknap Press, Harvard University Press, 1972.

Taraporevala, Russi Jal, *The American Book Industry*. Bombay, India: Taraporevala, 1966.

Tebbel, John, *A History of Book Publishing in the United States*. Vol. I, *The Creation of an Industry, 1630-1865*. New York, N.Y.: Bowker, 1972.

——, *Paperback Books A Pocket History*. New York, N.Y.: Pocket Books, 1964.

Thayer, John Adams, *Astir: A Publisher's Life Story*. Boston, Mass.: Small, Maynard, 1910.

——, *Out of the Rut: A Business Life Story*. New York, N.Y.: Dillingham, 1912.

Thomas, Benjamin Franklin, *Memoir of Isaiah Thomas by His Grandson.* Boston, Mass.: 1874.

Ticknor, Caroline, *Hawthorne and His Publisher.* Boston, Mass.: Houghton Mifflin, 1913.

Tryon, Warren S., *Parnassus Corner: A Life of James T. Fields, Publisher to the Victorians.* Boston, Mass.: Houghton Mifflin, 1963.

——, and Charvat, William, (eds.), *The Cost Books of Ticknor and Fields and their Predecessors, 1832-1858.* New York, N.Y.: Bibliographical Society of America, 1949.

Turner, Mary, *Bookman's Glossary.* New York, N.Y.: Bowker, 1961.

Uhlan, Edward, *The Rogue of Publishers' Row: Confessions of a Publisher.* New York, N.Y.: Exposition Press, 1956.

Underwood, Richard G., *Production and Manufacturing Problems of American University Presses.* New York, N.Y.: Association of American University Presses, 1960.

United Brethen Publishing House, *Historical Sketch of the United Brethren Publishing House, 1834-1894.* Dayton, Ohio: United Brethren Publishing House, 1894.

Ward Ritchie Press, *The Ward Ritchie Press and Anderson, Ritchie & Simon.* Los Angeles, Calif.: Ward Ritchie Press, 1961.

Weber, Carl J., *The Rise and Fall of James Ripley Osgood.* Waterville, Me.: Colby College Press, 1959.

Weber, Olga S., *Literary and Library Prizes.* New York, N.Y.: Bowker, 1973.

Weiss, Harry B., *A Book About Chapbooks: The People's Literature of Bygone Times.* Trenton, N.J.: Privately printed, 1942.

——, *Printers and Publishers of Children's Books in New York City, 1698-1830.* New York, N.Y.: New York Public Library, 1948.

——, *Samuel Wood & Sons: Early New York Publishers of Children's Books.* New York, N.Y.: New York Public Library, 1942.

——, *Solomon King, Early New York Bookseller and Publisher of Children's Books and Chapbooks.* New York, N.Y.: New York Public Library, 1947.

Weybright, Victor, *The Making of a Publisher: A Life in the 20th Century Book Revolution.* New York, N.Y.: Reynal-Morrow, 1967.

Winterich, John T., *The Grolier Club, 1884-1967: An Informal History.* New York, N.Y.: The Grolier Club, 1967.

Wood, W.C., *One Hundred Years of Publishing, 1804-1904: A Brief Historical Account of the House of William Wood and Company.* New York, N.Y.: William Wood & Co., 1904.

Wroth, Lawrence C., *Parson Weems: A Biographical and Critical Study.* Baltimore, Md.: Eichelberger Book Company, 1911.

——, *William Parks, Printer and Journalist of England and Colonial America; with a List of the Issues of His Several Presses and a Facsimile of the Earliest Virginia Imprint Known to Be in Existence.* Richmond, Va.: William Parks Club, 1926.

Yard, Robert Sterling, *The Publisher.* Boston, Mass.: Houghton Mifflin, 1913.

Bibliography II – Company Histories

American Baptist Publication Society

> *After Eight Decades: The Story of the American Baptist Publication Society.* Philadelphia, Pa.: American Baptist Publication Society, 1908.

> Barnes, Lemuel Call; Barnes, Mary Clark, and Stephenson, Edward M., *Pioneers of Light: The First Century of the American Baptist Publication Society, 1824-1924.* Philadelphia, Pa.: American Baptist Publication Society, 1924.

> Blackall, C.R., *A Story of Six Decades.* Philadelphia, Pa.: American Baptist Publication Society, 1885.

> Brown, J. Newton, *History of the American Baptist Publication Society, from Its Origin in 1824, to Its Thirty-Second Anniversary in 1856.* Philadelphia. Pa.: American Baptist Publication Society, 1856.

> Stevens, Daniel Gurden, *The First Hundred Years of the American Baptist Publication Society.* Philadelphia, Pa.: American Baptist Publication Society, 1924.

American Book Company

> Livengood, W.W., *Our Heritage: Being a Brief History of the American Book Company and an Account of Sundry Textbooks and their Authors.* New York, N.Y.: American Book Company, 1947.

American Education Publications

> Martz, Charles E., *History of American Education Publications, Inc., 1902-1965.* Columbus, O.: American Education Publications, 1965.

American Tract Society

> Bliss, Seth, *A Brief History of the American Tract Society, Instituted at Boston, 1824, and its Relations to the American Tract Society at New York, Instituted 1825.* Boston, Mass.: T.R. Marvin, 1857.

> *Proceedings of the First Ten Years; to which is Added A Brief View of the Principal Religious Tract Societies of the World.* Boston, Mass.: Flagg and Gould, 1824.

W.H. Anderson Company

> *Fifty Years of Good Law Books, 1887-1937: Commemorating the Fiftieth Anniversary of the Founding of W.H. Anderson Company, Cincinnati,* Cincinnati, O.: W.H. Anderson, 1937.

Appleton-Century-Crofts

> Chew, S.C., *Fruit Among the Leaves: An Anniversary Anthology.* New York, N.Y.: Appleton-Century-Crofts, 1950.

> *The House of Appleton-Century.* New York, N.Y.: Appleton-Century, 1936.

> Overton, Grant, *Portrait of a Publisher and the First Hundred Years of the House of Appleton, 1825-1925.* New York, N.Y.: Appleton, 1925.

Association Press

> James, Selwyn, *Association Press, the First Fifty Years: 1907-1957.* New York, N.Y.: Association Press, 1957.

Augustana Book Concern

> Holmgrain, O.V., *Augustana Book Concern, 1889-1914.* Rock Island, Ill.: Augustana, 1914.

> Nystrom, Daniel, *A Ministry of Printing: History of the Publication House of Augustana Lutheran Church, 1889-1962.* Rock Island, Ill.: Augustana, 1962.

> Olson, Ernest W., *Fiftieth Anniversary, 1884-1934, Augustana Book Concern: Publishers to the Augustana Synod Since 1889.* Rock Island, Ill.: Augustana, 1934.

Baker, Voorhis & Company

One Hundred Years in Business, 1820-1920. New York, N.Y.: Baker, Voorhis, 1920.

Banks & Company

A Business Centenary: The Oldest Law Publishing House in the United States. Albany, N.Y.: Banks & Co., 1904.

Beadle and Adams

Johannsen, Albert, *The House of Beadle and Adams and Its Dime and Nickel Novels: The Story of a Vanished Literature,* (3 vols.) Norman, Okla.: University of Oklahoma Press, 1950.

Blakiston Company, The

One Hundred Years, 1843-1943. Philadelphia, Pa.: Blakiston, 1943.

Bobbs-Merrill Company, Inc., The

Casey, Robert J., *The Bobbs-Merrill Company.* Indianapolis, Ind.: Bobbs-Merrill, 1945.

The Hoosier House. Indianapolis, Ind.: Bobbs-Merrill, 1923.

Book-of-the-Month Club, Inc.

Lee, Charles, *The Hidden Public: The Story of the Book-of-the-Month Club.* New York, N.Y.: Doubleday, 1958.

Century Company, The

Cable, G.W., *A Memory of Roswell Smith.* New York, N.Y.: De Vinne Press, 1892.

The Story of Century Company, 1870-1923. New York, N.Y.: Century, 1923.

Cokesbury Press

Fifteen Years and an Idea: A Report, 1923-1938. Nashville, Tenn.: Cokesbury, 1938.

Columbia University Press

Reflections on Seventy-Five Years of Publishing. New York, N.Y.: Columbia University Press, 1968.

Coward, McCann, Inc.

A Brief History of Coward-McCann, Inc., Publishers, 1928-1953. New York, N.Y.: Coward, McCann, 1953.

Dodd, Mead & Company

Dodd, Edward H., Jr., *The First Hundred Years: A History of the House of Dodd, Mead, 1839-1939.* New York, N.Y.: Dodd, Mead, 1939.

Doubleday & Company

See, Doubleday, Frank Nelson, (Bibliography I).

E.P. Dutton & Company, Inc.

Seventy-Five Years; or, The Joys and Sorrows of Publishing and Selling Books at Dutton's from 1852 to 1927. New York, N.Y.: Dutton, 1927.

Encyclopaedia Britannica

Kogan, Herman, *The Great EB: The Story of the Encyclopaedia Britannica.* Chicago, Ill.: University of Chicago Press, 1958.

Estes & Lauriat

Kilgour, R.L., *Estes & Lauriat, a History, 1872-1898, With a Brief Account of Dana Estes and Company 1898-1914.* Ann Arbor, Mich.: University of Michigan Press, 1957.

Sargent, George H., *Lauriat's 1872-1922: Being a Sketch of Early Boston Booksellers, With Some Account of Charles E. Lauriat Company and its Founder, Charles E. Lauriat.* Boston, Mass.: Privately printed, 1922.

Ginn & Company

Lawler, Thomas B., *Seventy Years of Textbook Publishing: A History of Ginn and Company, 1867-1937.* Boston, Mass.: Ginn, 1938.

Laylander, O.J., *The Ginn Sketchbook.* Boston, Mass.: Athenaeum Press, 1933.

Outline of the Life of Edwin Ginn, Including his Preparation for the Publishing Business and the Establishment of Ginn and Company. Boston, Mass.: Athenaeum Press, 1908.

Who is Edwin Ginn? New York, N.Y.: American Book Company, 1895.

Harper & Row

Abbott, Jacob, *The Harper Establishment; or, How the Story Books Are Made.* New York, N.Y.: Harper, 1855.

Exman, Eugene, *The Brothers Harper: A Unique Publishing Partnership And its Impact on the Cultural Life of America from 1817 to 1853.* New York, N.Y.: Harper, 1965.

——, *The House of Harper: One Hundred and Fifty Years of Publishing.* New York, N.Y.: Harper, 1967.

Harper, J. Henry, *The House of Harper: A Century of Publishing in Franklin Square.* New York, N.Y.: Harper, 1912.

——, *I Remember.* New York, N.Y.: Harper, 1934.

Harvard University Press

The Story of Harvard University Press Told by a Friend, Being an Informal History on the Occasion of the Fiftieth Anniversary of its Founding. Cambridge, Mass.: Harvard University Press, 1963.

D.C. Heath & Company

Forty Years of Service: Published in Commemoration of the Fortieth Anniversary of D.C. Heath & Company. Boston, Mass.: D.C. Heath, 1925.

Houghton Mifflin Company

Ballou, Ellen B., *The Building of the House: Houghton Mifflin's Formative Years.* Boston, Mass.: Houghton Mifflin, 1970.

Laughlin, Henry A., *An Informal Sketch of the History of Houghton Mifflin Company.* Cambridge, Mass.: Riverside Press, 1957.

Fifty Years of Publishing: A History of the Educational Department of Houghton Mifflin Company. Boston, Mass.: Houghton Mifflin, 1930.

A Portrait Catalogue of the Books Published by Houghton, Mifflin & Company, with a Sketch of the Firm, Brief Descriptions of the Various Departments, and Some Account of the Origin and Character of the Literary Enterprises Undertaken. Boston, Mass.: Riverside Press, 1905-6.

A Sketch of the Firm of Houghton Mifflin & Company, Publishers. Cambridge, Mass.: Riverside Press, 1890.

Johns Hopkins Press

French, John C., *The Johns Hopkins Press: A Brief History, 1878-1938.* Baltimore, Md.: The Johns Hopkins Press, 1938.

P.J. Kenedy & Sons

Healey, Robert C., *A Catholic Book Chronicle: The Story of P.J. Kenedy & Sons, 1826-1951.* New York, N.Y.: Kenedy, 1951.

Alfred A. Knopf, Inc.

The Borzoi 1920: Being a Sort of Record of Five Years' Publishing. New York, N.Y.: Knopf, 1920.

The Borzoi 1925: Being a Sort of Record of Ten Years of Publishing. New York, N.Y.: Knopf, 1925.

Alfred A. Knopf, Quarter Century. Norwood, Mass.: Plimpton Press, 1940.

Portrait of a Publisher, 1915-1965. (2 vols.) New York, N.Y.: Typophiles, 1965.

Lea & Febiger

One Hundred Years of Publishing, 1785-1885. Philadelphia, Pa.: Lea Brothers, 1885.

One Hundred and Fifty Years of Publishing, 1785-1935. Philadelphia, Pa.: Lea & Febiger, 1935.

Limited Editions Club

Quarto-Millenary: The First 250 Publications and the First 25 Years, 1929-1954, of the Limited Editions Club. New York, N.Y.: Limited Editions Club, 1959.

Ten Years and William Shakespeare: A Survey of the Publishing Activities of The Limited Editions Club from October 1929 to October 1940. New York, N.Y.: Limited Editions Club, 1940.

J.B. Lippincott Company

The Author and His Audience, With a Chronology of Major Events in the Publishing History of J.B. Lippincott Company. Philadelphia, Pa.: Lippincott, 1967.

A Brief History of a Great Book House. Philadelphia, Pa.: Lippincott, 1893.

Little, Brown and Company

Hillard, George Stillman, *A Memoir of James Brown.* Boston, Mass.: Privately printed, 1856.

Books From Beacon Hill: The Story of the Boston Publishing House of Little, Brown and Company, 1837-1926. Boston, Mass.: Little, Brown, 1926.

One Hundred Years of Publishing, 1837-1937. Boston, Mass.: Little, Brown, 1937.

One Hundred and Twenty-Five Years of Publishing, 1837-1962. Boston, Mass.: Little, Brown, 1962.

Lutheran Publication Society

Sixtieth Anniversary of the Organization of the Lutheran Publication Society, 1855-1915. Philadelphia, Pa.: Lutheran Publication Society, 1915.

Macmillan Company

The Macmillan Company. New York, N.Y.: Macmillan, 1954.

Marquis Who's Who, Inc.

Larson, Cedric A., *Who: Sixty Years of American Eminence, the Story of "Who's Who in America."* New York, N.Y.: McDowell, Obolensky, 1958.

McGraw-Hill Book Company

Burlingame, Roger, *Endless Frontiers: The Story of McGraw-Hill.* New York, N.Y.: McGraw-Hill, 1959.

Imprint On An Era. New York, N.Y.: McGraw-Hill, 1966.

The Story of Forty Years of Growth. New York, N.Y.: McGraw-Hill, 1949.

Ten Years. New York, N.Y.: McGraw-Hill, 1919.

Twenty-Fifth Anniversary, 1909-1934. New York, N.Y.: McGraw-Hill, 1934.

Mennonite Publishing House

Hostetler, John A., *God Uses Ink: The Heritage and Mission of the Mennonite Publishing House After Fifty Years.* Scottdale, Pa.: Herald Press, 1958.

Mennonite Publishing House . . . 1908-1933. Scottdale, Pa.: Mennonite Publishing House, 1933.

G. & C. Merriam Company

The House That Merriam-Webster Built. Springfield, Mass.: G. & C. Merriam, 1940.

Leavitt, Robert K., *Noah's Ark, New England Yankees, and the Endless Quest: A Short History of the Original Webster Dictionaries, with Particular Reference to their First Hundred Years as Publications of G. & C. Merriam Company.* Springfield, Mass.: G. & C. Merriam, 1947.

One Hundredth Anniversary of the Establishment of G. & C. Merriam Company, Springfield, Massachusetts, 1831-1931; Publishers of the Merriam-Webster Dictionaries Since 1843. Springfield, Mass.: G. & C. Merriam, 1931.

Methodist Publishing House (Methodist Book Concern)

Jennings, H.C., *The Methodist Book Concern.* New York, N.Y.: Methodist Book Concern, 1924.

Lanahan, John, *The Era of Frauds in the Methodist Book Concern at New York.* Baltimore, Md.: Methodist Book Depository, 1896.

Pilkington, James Penn, *The Methodist Publishing House: A. History.* Nashville, Tenn.: Abingdon Press, 1968.

Since 1789: The Story of the Methodist Publishing House. Nashville, Tenn.: Abingdon Press, 1964.

Whitlock, William F., *The Story of the Book Concerns.* Cincinnati, O.: Jennings & Pye, 1903.

Oxford University Press

Redman, Ben Ray, *The Oxford University Press, New York, 1896-1946.* New York, N.Y.: Oxford University Press, 1946.

Peter Pauper Press

Recalling Peter: The Life and Times of Peter Beilenson and his Peter Pauper Press. New York, N.Y.: Typophiles, 1964.

Pocket Books

Lewis, Freeman, *A Brief History of Pocket Books, 1939-1967.* New York, N.Y.: Pocket Books, 1967.

Presbyterian Board of Publication

Rice, Willard M., *History of the Presbyterian Board of Publication and Sabbath-School Work.* Philadelphia, Pa.: Presbyterian Board of Publication, 1882.

Princeton University Press

Bailey, Herbert S., Jr., *Princeton University Press: Publlishers for the World of Learning.* New York, N.Y.: Newcomen Society, 1958.

Darrow, Whitney, *Princeton University Press: An Informal Account of Its Growing Pains . . .* Princeton, N.J.: Princeton University Press, 1951.

Tomlinson, Paul G., *Princeton University Press, 1905-1935.* Princeton, N.J.: Princeton University Press, 1935.

G.P. Putnam's Sons

Putnam, George Haven, *A Memoir of George Palmer Putnam, Together with a Record of the Publishing House Founded by Him.* New York, N.Y.: Putnam, 1903.

——, *Memories of a Publisher, 1865-1915.* New York, N.Y.: Putnam, 1915.

——, *Memories of My Youth, 1844-65.* New York, N.Y.: Putnam, 1914.

Putnam, George Palmer, *Wide Margins: A Publisher's Autobiography.* New York, N.Y.: Harcourt, Brace, 1942.

Rand McNally & Company

McNally, Andrew, III, *The World of Rand McNally.* New York, N.Y.: Newcomen Society, 1956.

Scott, Foresman and Company

    A Half Century of Scott-Foresman Progress. Chicago, Ill.: Scott, Foresman, 1933.

    Foresman, Hugh A., *These Things I Remember.* Chicago, Ill.: Scott, Foresman, 1949.

Seabury Press

    A History of the Seabury Press. Greenwich, Conn.: Seabury Press, 1956.

Silver Burdett Company

    Silver Burdett Company: A History from 1885 to 1941. Boston, Mass.: Silver Burdett, 1941.

Frederick A. Stokes Company

    The House of Stokes, 1881-1926: A Record, Together with Some Letters from Authors, on the Forty- Fifth Anniversary of the Establishment of the Publishing House of Frederick A. Stokes Company. New York, N.Y.: Stokes, 1926.

Street & Smith

    The Greatest Publishing House in the World. New York, N.Y.: F. Presbrey Co., 1905.

    Reynolds, Quentin, *The Fiction Factory; or, From Pulp Row to Quality Street: The Story of 100 Years of Publishing at Street & Smith.* New York, N.Y.: Random House, 1955.

University of California Press

    Farquhar, Samuel T., *The University of California Press: A Western Center of Scholarly Publishing.* Berkeley, Calif.: University of California Press, 1940.

University of Chicago Press

    Shugg, Roger, *The University of Chicago Press.* Chicago, Ill.: University of Chicago Press, 1966.

D. Van Nostrand Company

    Crane, Edward, *A Century of Book Publishing, 1848-1948.* New York, N.Y.: Van Nostrand, 1948.

West Publishing Company

    Law Books By the Million: An Account of the Largest Law-Book House in the World. St. Paul, Minn.: West Publishing Company, 1901.

Western Publishing Company

    The Story of Western: Fifty Years of Progress. Racine, Wisc.: Western, 1957.

John Wiley & Sons, Inc.

    The House of Wiley. New York, N.Y.: John Wiley, 1940, 1948.

    Matheson, Martin, *The First One Hundred and Fifty Years: A History of John Wiley and Sons, Incorporated, 1807-1957.* New York, N.Y.: John Wiley, 1957.

Williams and Wilkins Company

    After Seventy-Five Years, 1890-1965. Baltimore, Md.: Williams & Wilkins, 1965.

    A Quarter Century in the Service of Science, 1925-1950. Baltimore, Md.: Williams & Wilkins, 1950.

H.W. Wilson Company, The

    Lawler, John L., *The H.W. Wilson Company: Half a Century of Bibliographic Publishing.* Minneapolis, Minn.: University of Minnesota Press, 1950.

Yale University Press

    Day, Clarence, *The Story of the Yale University Press Told By A Friend.* New Haven, Conn.: Yale University Press, 1920.

APPENDIX 5
Company Addresses

ABC-CLIO, INC.
Box 4397, Riviera Campus
Santa Barbara, California 93103

AMS PRESS, INC.
56 East 13th Street
New York, N.Y. 10003

ABBEY PRESS
St. Meinrad, Indiana 47577

ABELARD-SCHUMAN LIMITED
257 Park Avenue South
New York, N.Y. 10010

ABINGDON PRESS
201 Eighth Avenue South
Nashville, Tennessee 37202

HARRY N. ABRAMS, INC.
110 East 59th Street
New York, N.Y. 10022

ACADEMIC PRESS, INC.
111 Fifth Avenue
New York, N.Y. 10003

ACE BOOKS
1120 Avenue of the Americas
New York, N.Y. 10036

ACROPOLIS BOOKS LTD.
2400 – 17th Street, N.W.
Washington, D.C. 20009

ADDISON-WESLEY PUBLISHING CO., INC.
Reading, Massachusetts 01867

AERO PUBLISHERS, INC.
329 Aviation Road
Fallbrook, California 92028

ALBA HOUSE
2187 Victory Boulevard
Staten Island, New York 10314

ALDINE PUBLISHING COMPANY
529 South Wabash Avenue
Chicago, Illinois 60605

ALEC R. ALLENSON, INC.
635 East Ogden Avenue
Naperville, Illinois 60540

ALLYN & BACON, INC.
470 Atlantic Avenue
Boston, Massachusetts 02210

AMERICAN BIBLE SOCIETY
1865 Broadway
New York, N.Y. 10023

AMERICAN BOOK COMPANY
450 West 33rd Street
New York, N.Y. 10001

AMERICAN CHEMICAL SOCIETY
1155 – 16th Street N.W.
Washington, D.C. 20036

AMERICAN ELSEVIER PUBLISHING CO., INC.
52 Vanderbilt Avenue
New York, N.Y. 10017

AMERICAN HERITAGE PUBLISHING CO., INC.
1221 Avenue of the Americas
New York, N.Y. 10020

AMERICAN LIBRARY ASSOCIATION
50 East Huron Street
Chicago, Illinois 60611

AMERICAN MANAGEMENT ASSOCIA-TIONS, INC.
135 West 50th Street
New York, N.Y. 10020

AMERICAN MATHEMATICAL SOCIETY
Box 6248
Providence, Rhode Island 02904

AMERICAN PERSONNEL & GUIDANCE
ASSOCIATION
1607 New Hampshire Avenue, N.W.
Washington, D.C. 20009

AMERICAN PHILOSOPHICAL SOCIETY
104 South Fifth Street
Philadelphia, Pennsylvania 19106

AMERICAN PHOTOGRAPHIC BOOK
PUBLISHING COMPANY, INC.
(AMPHOTO)
East Gate & Zeckendorf Boulevards
Garden City, N.Y. 11530

AMERICAN SOCIETY FOR TESTING
AND MATERIALS
1916 Race Street
Philadelphia, Pennsylvania 19103

AMERICAN TECHNICAL SOCIETY
848 East 58th Street
Chicago, Illinois 60637

AMURU PRESS, INC.
161 Madison Avenue
New York, N.Y. 10016

ANCHOR BOOKS
Doubleday & Company, Inc.
277 Park Avenue
New York, N.Y. 10017

THE W.H. ANDERSON COMPANY
646 Main Street
Cincinnati, Ohio 45201

ANN ARBOR SCIENCE PUBLISHERS,
INC.
Drawer 1425
Ann Arbor, Michigan 48106

ANTHROPOSOPHIC PRESS, INC.
258 Hungry Hollow Road
Spring Valley, N.Y. 10977

ARBOR HOUSE PUBLISHING
COMPANY, INC.
757 Third Avenue
New York, N.Y. 10017

ARCHITECTURAL BOOK PUBLISHING
COMPANY, INC.
10 East 40th Street
New York, N.Y. 10018

ARCO PUBLISHING COMPANY, INC.
219 Park Avenue South
New York, N.Y. 10003

ARLINGTON HOUSE, INC.
165 Huguenot Street
New Rochelle, N.Y. 10801

ARNO PRESS, INC.
330 Madison Avenue
New York, N.Y. 10017

JASON ARONSON, INC.
59 Fourth Avenue
New York, N.Y. 10003

ASHLEY BOOKS, INC.
Box 768
Port Washington, N.Y. 11050

ASIA PUBLISHING HOUSE, INC.
420 Lexington Avenue
New York, N.Y. 10017

ASSOCIATION PRESS
291 Broadway
New York, N.Y. 10007

ASTOR-HONOR, INC.
67 Southfield Avenue
Stamford, Connecticut 06904

ATHENEUM PUBLISHERS
122 East 42nd Street
New York, N.Y. 10017

THE ATLANTIC MONTHLY PRESS
8 Arlington Street
Boston, Massachusetts 02116

AUERBACH PUBLISHERS INC.
121 North Broad Street
Philadelphia, Pennsylvania 19107

AUGSBURG PUBLISHING HOUSE
426 South Fifth Street
Minneapolis, Minnesota 55415

J.J. AUGUSTIN, INC. –PUBLISHER
Locust Valley, New York 11560

AURORA PUBLISHERS INC.
118 16th Avenue South
Nashville, Tennessee 37219

AVE MARIA PRESS
Notre Dame, Indiana 46556

AVI PUBLISHING COMPANY
Box 831
Westport, Connecticut 06880

AVON BOOKS
959 Eighth Avenue
New York, N.Y. 10019

BFL COMMUNICATIONS, INC.
1 Dupont Street
Plainview, New York 11803

BNA BOOKS
1231 – 25th Street N.W.
Washington, D.C. 20037

THE BAKER & TAYLOR COMPANY
6 Kirby Avenue
Somerville, New Jersey 08876

BAKER BOOK HOUSE
1019 Wealthy Street, S.E.
Grand Rapids, Michigan 49506

BAKER'S PLAYS
Walter H. Baker Company
100 Chauncy Street
Boston, Massachusetts 02111

BALLANTINE BOOKS, INC.
201 East 50th Street
New York, N.Y. 10022

BALLINGER PUBLISHING COMPANY
17 Dunster Street
Cambridge, Massachusetts 02138

BANCROFT-WHITNEY COMPANY
301 Brannan Street
San Francisco, California 94107

BANKS-BALDWIN LAW PUBLISHING COMPANY
1904 Ansel Road
Cleveland, Ohio 44106

BANTAM BOOKS, INC.
666 Fifth Avenue
New York, N.Y. 10019

BARCLAY HOUSE BOOKS
21322 Lassen Street
Chatsworth, California 91311

A.S. BARNES & COMPANY, INC.
Forsgate Drive
Cranbury, New Jersey 08512

BARNES & NOBLE BOOKS
10 East 53rd Street
New York, N.Y. 10022

CLARENCE L. BARNHART INC.
1 Stone Place
Bronxville, N.Y. 10708

RICHARD W. BARON PUBLISHING CO., INC.
201 Park Avenue South
New York, N.Y. 10003

BARRE PUBLISHERS
South Street
Barre, Massachusetts 01005

BARRON'S EDUCATIONAL SERIES INC.
113 Crossways Park Drive
Woodbury, N.Y. 11797

BASIC BOOKS, INC., PUBLISHERS
10 East 53rd Street
New York, N.Y. 10022

WILLIAM L. BAUHAN, INC.
Dublin, New Hampshire 03444

BEACON PRESS
25 Beacon Street
Boston, Massachusetts 02108

BEHAVIORAL PUBLICATIONS, INC.
72 Fifth Avenue
New York, N.Y. 10011

BEHRMAN HOUSE, INC.
1261 Broadway
New York, N.Y. 10001

BELLMAN PUBLISHING COMPANY
Box 164
Arlington, Massachusetts 02174

BELMONT TOWER BOOKS, INC.
185 Madison Avenue
New York, N.Y. 10016

MATTHEW BENDER & COMPANY, INC.
235 East 45th Street
New York, N.Y. 10017

BENEFIC PRESS
10300 W. Roosevelt Road
Westchester, Illinois 60153

THE BENJAMIN COMPANY, INC.
485 Madison Avenue
New York, N.Y. 10022

W.A. BENJAMIN, INC.
2725 Sand Hill Road
Menlo Park, California 94025

CHAS. A. BENNETT COMPANY, INC.
809 W. Detweiller Drive
Peoria, Illinois 61614

W.S. BENSON & COMPANY
109 East Fifth Street
Austin, Texas 78767

ROBERT BENTLEY, INC.
872 Massachusetts Avenue
Cambridge, Massachusetts 02139

BENZIGER BRUCE & GLENCOE, INC.
8701 Wilshire Boulevard
Beverly Hills, California 90211

NORMAN S. BERG, PUBLISHER
Sellanraa, Box 88384
Dunwoody, Georgia 30338

BERKLEY PUBLISHING CORPORATION
200 Madison Avenue
New York, N.Y. 10016

BERLITZ PUBLICATIONS, INC.
866 Third Avenue
New York, N.Y. 10022

BETHANY FELLOWSHIP, INC.
6820 Auto Club Road
Minneapolis, Minnesota 55438

THE BETHANY PRESS
Box 179, 2640 Pine Street
St. Louis, Missouri 63166

BETTER HOMES & GARDENS BOOKS
1716 Locust Street
Des Moines, Iowa 50336

**BIBLIOGRAPHICAL SOCIETY OF
AMERICA**
Box 397, Grand Central Station
New York, N.Y. 10017

**BIBLO & TANNEN BOOKSELLERS &
PUBLISHERS, INC.**
63 Fourth Avenue
New York, N.Y. 10003

BINFORDS & MORT
2505 S.E. 11th Avenue
Portland, Oregon 97242

WALTER J. BLACK, INC.
Flower Hill
Roslyn, N.Y. 11576

BLACK SPARROW PRESS
Box 25603
Los Angeles, California 90025

JOHN F. BLAIR, PUBLISHER
1406 Plaza Drive
Winston-Salem, North Carolina 27103

BLOCh PUBLISHING COMPANY, INC.
915 Broadway
New York, N.Y. 10010

BENJAMIN BLOM, INC.
2521 Broadway
New York, N.Y. 10025

CLARK BOARDMAN COMPANY, LTD.
435 Hudson Street
New York, N.Y. 10014

THE BOBBS-MERRILL CO., INC.
4300 West 62nd Street
Indianapolis, Indiana 46268

BOBLEY PUBLISHING CORPORATION
311 Crossways Park Drive
Woodbury, N.Y. 11797

BOOK-OF-THE-MONTH CLUB, INC.
280 Park Avenue
New York, N.Y. 10017

BOOKS FOR LIBRARIES PRESS, INC.
1 Dupont Street
Plainview, N.Y. 11803

BOSTON TECHNICAL PUBLISHERS
728 Dedham Street
Newton, Massachusetts 02159

THOMAS BOUREGY & COMPANY, INC.
22 East 60th Street
New York, N.Y. 10022

R.R. BOWKER COMPANY
1180 Avenue of the Americas
New York, N.Y. 10036

BOWMAR
Box 3623
Glendale, California 91201

BOYD & FRASER PUBLISHING COMPANY
3627 Sacramento Street
San Francisco, California 94118

BRADBURY PRESS, INC.
2 Overhill Road
Scarsdale, New York 10583

BRANDEN PRESS, INC.
221 Columbus Avenue
Boston, Massachusetts 02116

BRANDON BOOKS
21322 Lassen Street
Chatsworth, California 91311

CHARLES T. BRANFORD COMPANY
28 Union Street
Newton Centre, Massachusetts 02159

GEORGE BRAZILLER, INC.
1 Park Avenue
New York, N.Y. 10016

BRIGHAM YOUNG UNIVERSITY PRESS
209 University Press Building
Provo, Utah 84601

BROADMAN PRESS
127 Ninth Avenue North
Nashville, Tennessee 37234

BROADSIDE PRESS
12651 Old Mill Place
Detroit, Michigan 48238

BRO-DART PUBLISHING COMPANY
1609 Memorial Avenue
Williamsport, Pennsylvania 17701

THE BROOKINGS INSTITUTION
1775 Massachusetts Avenue, N.W.
Washington, D.C. 20036

BROOKS/COLE PUBLISHING COMPANY
540 Abrego Street
Monterey, California 93940

WILLIAM C. BROWN COMPANY,
PUBLISHERS
2460 Kerper Boulevard
Dubuque, Iowa 52001

BROWN UNIVERSITY PRESS
129 Waterman Street
Providence, Rhode Island 02912

BRUNNER/MAZEL, INC.
64 University Place
New York, N.Y. 10003

BUCKNELL UNIVERSITY PRESS
Lewisburg, Pennsylvania 17837

BUREAU OF NATIONAL AFFAIRS, INC.
1231 – 25th Street N.W.
Washington, D.C. 20037

BURGESS PUBLISHING COMPANY
7108 Olms Lane
Minneapolis, Minnesota 55435

CADILLAC PUBLISHING COMPANY, INC.
220 Fifth Avenue
New York, N.Y. 10001

CAHNERS BOOKS
89 Franklin Street
Boston, Massachusetts 02110

CALLAGHAN & COMPANY
6141 North Cicero Avenue
Chicago, Illinois 60646

CAMBRIDGE BOOK COMPANY
488 Madison Avenue
New York, N.Y. 10022

CAMBRIDGE UNIVERSITY PRESS
32 East 57th Street
New York, N.Y. 10022

THE CARDAVON PRESS, INC.
Avon, Connecticut 06001

CAROLRHODA BOOKS, INC.
241 First Avenue North
Minneapolis, Minnesota 55401

CATHOLIC PRESS
1727 South Indiana Avenue
Chicago, Illinois 60616

THE CATHOLIC UNIVERSITY OF AMERICA PRESS
620 Michigan Avenue, N.E.
Washington, D.C. 20017

THE CAXTON PRINTERS, LTD.
Caldwell, Idaho 83605

CENTURY HOUSE, INC.
Watkins Glen, New York 14891

CHANTICLEER PRESS, INC.
424 Madison Avenue
New York, N.Y. 10017

CHARTER COMMUNICATIONS, INC.
1120 Avenue of the Americas
New York, N.Y. 10036

THE CHATHAM PRESS, INC.
15 Wilmot Lane
Riverside, Connecticut 06878

CHELSEA HOUSE PUBLISHERS
70 West 40th Street
New York, N.Y. 10018

CHELSEA PUBLISHING COMPANY, INC.
159 East Tremont Avenue
Bronx, New York 10453

CHEMICAL PUBLISHING COMPANY, INC.
200 Park Avenue South
New York, N.Y. 10003

CHILDRENS PRESS
1224 West Van Buren Street
Chicago, Illinois 60607

THE CHILD STUDY PRESS
50 Madison Avenue
New York, N.Y. 10010

CHILTON BOOK COMPANY
Chilton Way
Radnor, Pennsylvania 19089

CHRISTIAN PUBLICATIONS INC.
25 South Tenth Street
Harrisburg, Pennsylvania 17101

THE CHRISTIAN SCIENCE PUBLISHING SOCIETY
1 Norway Street
Boston, Massachusetts 02115

CHRONICLE BOOKS
54 Mint Street
San Francisco, California 94103

CITADEL PRESS, INC.
120 Enterprise Avenue
Secaucus, New Jersey 07094

ARTHUR H. CLARK COMPANY
1264 South Central Avenue
Glendale, California 91204

CLIFF'S NOTES, INC.
Box 80728
Lincoln, Nebraska 68501

COLLECTORS EDITIONS LIMITED
185 Madison Avenue
New York, N.Y. 10016

COLLEGE & UNIVERSITY PRESS
263 Chapel Street
New Haven, Connecticut 06513

**WILLIAM COLLINS SONS &
COMPANY, LTD.**
215 Park Avenue South
New York, N.Y. 10003

**COLORADO ASSOCIATED UNIVERSITY
PRESS**
1424 – 15th Street
Boulder, Colorado 80302

COLUMBIA UNIVERSITY PRESS
562 West 113th Street
New York, N.Y. 10025

F.E. COMPTON COMPANY
425 North Michigan Avenue
Chicago, Illinois 60611

CONCORDIA PUBLISHING HOUSE
3558 South Jefferson Avenue
St. Louis, Missouri 63118

THE CONFERENCE BOARD, INC.
845 Third Avenue
New York, N.Y. 10022

CONSOLIDATED BOOK PUBLISHERS
1727 South Indiana Avenue
Chicago, Illinois 60616

COOPER SQUARE PUBLISHERS, INC.
59 Fourth Avenue
New York, N.Y. 10003

CORINTH BOOKS
29 Perry Street
New York, N.Y. 10014

CORNELL MARITIME PRESS, INC.
Cambridge, Maryland 21613

CORNELL UNIVERSITY PRESS
124 Roberts Place
Ithaca, New York 14850

CORNERSTONE LIBRARY, INC.
630 Fifth Avenue
New York, N.Y. 10020

R.D. CORTINA COMPANY, INC.
136 West 52nd Street
New York, N.Y. 10019

COWARD, McCANN & GEOGHEGAN, INC.
200 Madison Avenue
New York, N.Y. 10016

CRANE, RUSSAK & COMPANY
347 Madison Avenue
New York, N.Y. 10017

**CREATIVE EDUCATIONAL
SOCIETY, INC.**
123 South Broad Street
Mankato, Minnesota 56001

CRESCENDO PUBLISHING COMPANY
48–50 Melrose Street
Boston, Massachusetts 02116

THOMAS Y. CROWELL COMPANY
666 Fifth Avenue
New York, N.Y. 10019

**CROWELL COLLIER AND
MACMILLAN, INC.**
866 Third Avenue
New York, N.Y. 10022

CROWN PUBLISHERS, INC.
419 Park Avenue South
New York, N.Y. 10016

CURTIS BOOKS, INC.
Chestnut East Building
Philadelphia, Pennsylvania 19107

DA CAPO PRESS, INC.
227 West 17th Street
New York, N.Y. 10011

THE STUART L. DANIELS CO., INC.
431 Fifth Avenue
New York, N.Y. 10016

THE DARTNELL CORPORATION
4660 Ravenswood Avenue
Chicago, Illinois 60640

DAUGHTERS OF ST. PAUL
50 St. Paul's Avenue
Jamaica Plain
Boston, Massachusetts 02130

DANIEL DAVEY & COMPANY, INC.
410 Asylum Street
Hartford, Connecticut 06103

F.A. DAVIS COMPANY
1915 Arch Street
Philadelphia, Pennsylvania 19103

DAW BOOKS, INC.
1301 Avenue of the Americas
New York, N.Y. 10019

JOHN de GRAFF, INC.
34 Oak Avenue
Tuckahoe, New York 10707

MARCEL DEKKER, INC.
305 East 45th Street
New York, N.Y. 10017

DELL PUBLISHING COMPANY, INC.
1 Dag Hammarskjold Plaza
New York, N.Y. 10017

DELMAR PUBLISHERS
50 Wolf Road
Albany, New York 12205

T.S. DENISON & COMPANY, INC.
5100 West 82nd Street
Minneapolis, Minnesota 55437

DENLINGER'S PUBLISHERS
Box 189
Fairfax, Virginia 22030

DENOYER-GEPPERT COMPANY
5235 Ravenswood Avenue
Chicago, Illinois 60640

DESERET BOOK COMPANY
44 E. South Temple Street
Salt Lake City, Utah 84110

DETERMINED PRODUCTIONS, INC.
Box 2150
San Francisco, California 94126

THE DEVIN-ADAIR COMPANY
1 Park Avenue
Old Greenwich, Connecticut 06870

THE DIAL PRESS
1 Dag Hammarskjold Plaza
New York, N.Y. 10017

JOHN A. DICKSON PUBLISHING COMPANY
1727 South Indiana Avenue
Chicago, Illinois 60616

DIGEST BOOKS, INC.
540 Frontage Road
Northfield, Illinois 60093

DIMENSION BOOKS, INC.
Box 811
Denville, New Jersey 07834

DODD, MEAD & COMPANY
79 Madison Avenue
New York, N.Y. 10016

DOUBLEDAY & COMPANY, INC.
277 Park Avenue
New York, N.Y. 10017

DOVER PUBLICATIONS, INC.
180 Varick Street
New York, N.Y. 10014

DRAKE PUBLISHERS, INC.
381 Park Avenue South
New York, N.Y. 10016

DRAMA BOOK SPECIALISTS/ PUBLISHERS
150 West 52nd Street
New York, N.Y. 10019

THE DRAMATIC PUBLISHING COMPANY
86 East Randolph Street
Chicago, Illinois 60601

DRAMATISTS PLAY SERVICE, INC.
440 Park Avenue South
New York, N.Y. 10016

DROKE HOUSE/HALLUX, INC.
Box 2027, 116 West Orr Street
Anderson, South Carolina 29621

DUFOUR EDITIONS, INC.
Chester Springs, Pennsylvania 19425

DUKE UNIVERSITY PRESS
Box 6697, College Station
Durham, North Carolina 27708

DUNELLEN PUBLISHING COMPANY, INC.
386 Park Avenue South
New York, N.Y. 10016

DUQUESNE UNIVERSITY PRESS
Pittsburgh, Pennsylvania 15219

E.P. DUTTON & COMPANY, INC.
201 Park Avenue South
New York, N.Y. 10003

THE ECONOMY COMPANY
1901 North Walnut Avenue
Oklahoma City, Oklahoma 73105

EDGEMOOR PUBLISHING COMPANY
805 Durham Drive
Houston, Texas 77007

EDUCATORS PUBLISHING SERVICE, INC.
75 Moulton Street
Cambridge, Massachusetts 02138

WILLIAM B. EERDMANS PUBLISHING COMPANY
255 Jefferson Avenue, S.E.
Grand Rapids, Michigan 49502

ENCYCLOPAEDIA BRITANNICA, INC.
425 North Michigan Avenue
Chicago, Illinois 60611

PAUL S. ERIKSSON, INC.
119 West 57th Street
New York, N.Y. 10019

M. EVANS & COMPANY, INC.
216 East 49th Street
New York, N.Y. 10017

FAIRCHILD PUBLICATIONS, INC.
7 East 12th Street
New York, N.Y. 10003

FAIRLEIGH DICKINSON UNIVERSITY PRESS
Rutherford, New Jersey 07070

FARNSWORTH PUBLISHING COMPANY, INC.
78 Randall Avenue
Rockville Centre, N.Y. 11570

FARRAR, STRAUS & GIROUX, INC.
19 Union Square West
New York, N.Y. 10003

FAWCETT PUBLICATIONS, INC.
1515 Broadway
New York, N.Y. 10036

F.W. FAXON COMPANY, INC.
15 Southwest Park
Westwood, Massachusetts 02090

FEARON PUBLISHERS
6 Davis Drive
Belmont, California 94002

FEFFER & SIMONS, INC.
31 Union Square West
New York, N.Y. 10003

FREDERICK FELL PUBLISHERS, INC.
386 Park Avenue South
New York, N.Y. 10016

J.G. FERGUSON PUBLISHING COMPANY
6 North Michigan Avenue
Chicago, Illinois 60602

HOWARD FERTIG, INC., PUBLISHER
80 East 11th Street
New York, N.Y. 10003

THE FIDELER COMPANY
31 Ottawa Avenue, N.W.
Grand Rapids, Michigan 49502

FIDES PUBLISHERS, INC.
Box F
Notre Dame, Indiana 46556

FIELD ENTERPRISES EDUCATIONAL
CORPORATION
510 Merchandise Mart Plaza
Chicago, Illinois 60654

FLEET PRESS CORPORATION
160 Fifth Avenue
New York, N.Y. 10010

FODOR'S MODERN GUIDES, INC.
750 Third Avenue
New York, N.Y. 10017

FOLLETT PUBLISHING COMPANY
1010 West Washington Boulevard
Chicago, Illinois 60607

FORDHAM UNIVERSITY PRESS
2546 Belmont Avenue
Bronx, New York 10458

FORTRESS PRESS
2900 Queen Lane
Philadelphia, Pennsylvania 19129

THE FOUNDATION PRESS, INC.
170 Old Country Road
Mineola, N.Y. 11501

FOUNTAINHEAD PUBLISHERS, INC.
475 Fifth Avenue
New York, N.Y. 10017

FRANCISCAN HERALD PRESS
1434 West 51st Street
Chicago, Illinois 60609

BURT FRANKLIN
235 East 44th Street
New York, N.Y. 10017

FRANKLIN BOOK PROGRAMS, INC.
801 Second Avenue
New York, N.Y. 10017

THE FREE PRESS
866 Third Avenue
New York, N.Y. 10022

JAMES E. FREEL & ASSOCIATES
535 Ramona
Palo Alto, California 94301

MILLER FREEMAN PUBLICATIONS, INC.
500 Howard Street
San Francisco, California 94105

W.H. FREEMAN AND COMPANY
PUBLISHERS
660 Market Street
San Francisco, California 94104

FREEMAN, COOPER & COMPANY
1736 Stockton Street
San Francisco, California 94133

SAMUEL FRENCH, INC.
25 West 45th Street
New York, N.Y. 10036

FRESHET PRESS INC.
90 Hamilton Road
Rockville Centre, N.Y. 11570

FRIENDSHIP PRESS
475 Riverside Drive
New York, N.Y. 10027

ARTHUR FROMMER, INC.
70 Fifth Avenue
New York, N.Y. 10011

THE FRONTIER PRESS COMPANY
250 East Town Street
Columbus, Ohio 43215

FUNK & WAGNALLS, INC.
55 East 77th Street
New York, N.Y. 10021

FUNK & WAGNALLS PUBLISHING
COMPANY
666 Fifth Avenue
New York, N.Y. 10019

FUTURA PUBLISHING COMPANY, INC.
295 Main Street
Mount Kisco, N.Y. 10549

GALE RESEARCH COMPANY
Book Tower
Detroit, Michigan 48226

GAMBIT, INC.
306 Dartmouth Street
Boston, Massachusetts 02116

GARLAND PUBLISHING, INC.
10 East 44th Street
New York, N.Y. 10017

GARRARD PUBLISHING COMPANY
1607 North Market Street
Champaign, Illinois 61820

BERNARD GEIS ASSOCIATES, INC.
128 East 56th Street
New York, N.Y. 10022

GENEALOGICAL PUBLISHING CO., INC.
521-23 St. Paul Place
Baltimore, Maryland 21202

GENERAL LEARNING CORPORATION
(See, Silver Burdett Company)

GEOLOGICAL SOCIETY OF AMERICA
3300 Penrose Place
Boulder, Colorado 80301

THE C.R. GIBSON COMPANY
Knight Street
Norwalk, Connecticut 06856

THE K.S. GINIGER COMPANY, INC.
1727 South Indiana Avenue
Chicago, Illinois 60616

GINN AND COMPANY
191 Spring Street
Lexington, Massachusetts 02173

GLOBE BOOK COMPANY, INC.
175 Fifth Avenue
New York, N.Y. 10010

THE GODINE PRESS, INC.
306 Dartmouth Street
Boston, Massachusetts 02116

GOLDEN PRESS
c/o Western Publishing Company
1220 Mound Avenue
Racine, Wisconsin 53404

THE GOLDEN QUILL PRESS
Francestown, New Hampshire 03043

GOODHEART-WILLCOX COMPANY
123 West Taft Drive
South Holland, Illinois 60473

GORDON AND BREACH, SCIENCE PUBLISHERS, INC.
1 Park Avenue
New York, N.Y. 10016

GOULD PUBLICATIONS
208-01 Jamaica Avenue
Jamaica, N.Y. 11428

GREAT OUTDOORS PUBLISHING COMPANY
4747 – 28th Street North
St. Petersburg, Florida 33714

WARREN H. GREEN, INC.
10 South Brentwood Boulevard
St. Louis, Missouri 63105

STEPHEN GREENE PRESS
Box 1000
Brattleboro, Vermont 05301

GREENWOOD PRESS, INC.
51 Riverside Avenue
Westport, Connecticut 06880

GREGG PUBLISHING COMPANY
1221 Avenue of the Americas
New York, N.Y. 10020

GREYSTONE CORPORATION
225 Park Avenue South
New York, N.Y. 10003

GROLIER CLUB
47 East 60th Street
New York, N.Y. 10022

GROLIER INCORPORATED
575 Lexington Avenue
New York, N.Y. 10022

GROSSET & DUNLAP, INC.
51 Madison Avenue
New York, N.Y. 10010

GROSSMAN PUBLISHERS
625 Madison Avenue
New York, N.Y. 10022

GROVE PRESS, INC.
53 East 11th Street
New York, N.Y. 10003

GRUNE & STRATTON, INC.
111 Fifth Avenue
New York, N.Y. 10003

**GULF PUBLISHING COMPANY,
BOOK DIVISION**
Box 2608
Houston, Texas 77001

H.P. BOOKS
Box 50640, Kino Station
Tucson, Arizona 85703

HACKER ART BOOKS INC.
54 West 57th Street
New York, N.Y. 10019

HAESSNER PUBLISHING, INC.
Box 89
Newfoundland, New Jersey 07435

HAFNER PRESS
866 Third Avenue
New York, N.Y. 10022

E.M. HALE AND COMPANY, PUBLISHERS
20 Waterside Plaza
New York, N.Y. 10010

EMERSON HALL PUBLISHERS, INC.
62 West 85th Street
New York, N.Y. 10024

G.K. HALL & COMPANY
70 Lincoln Street
Boston, Massachusetts 02111

HAMMOND INCORPORATED
Maplewood, New Jersey 07040

HARCOURT BRACE JOVANOVICH, INC.
757 Third Avenue
New York, N.Y. 10017

HARIAN PUBLICATIONS
1000 Prince Street
Greenlawn, N.Y. 11740

HARPER & ROW, PUBLISHERS, INC.
10 East 53rd Street
New York, N.Y. 10022

HARPER'S MAGAZINE PRESS
2 Park Avenue
New York, N.Y. 10016

THE HARRISON COMPANY
178 Pryor Street, S.W.
Atlanta, Georgia 30303

HART PUBLISHING COMPANY, INC.
15 West Fourth Street
New York, N.Y. 10012

HARVARD UNIVERSITY PRESS
79 Garden Street
Cambridge, Massachusetts 02138

HARVEY HOUSE, INC., PUBLISHERS
20 Waterside Plaza
New York, N.Y. 10010

HASKELL HOUSE PUBLISHERS, LTD.
280 Lafayette Street
New York, N.Y. 10012

HASTINGS HOUSE, PUBLISHERS, INC.
10 East 40th Street
New York, N.Y. 10016

HAWTHORN BOOKS, INC.
260 Madison Avenue
New York, N.Y. 10016

HAYDEN BOOK COMPANY, INC.
50 Essex Street
Rochelle Park, New Jersey 07662

HEARST BOOKS
250 West 55th Street
New York, N.Y. 10019

HEARTHSIDE PRESS
445 Northern Boulevard
Great Neck, N.Y. 11021

D.C. HEATH & COMPANY
125 Spring Street
Lexington, Massachusetts 02173

JAMES H. HEINEMAN, INC.
475 Park Avenue
New York, N.Y. 10022

HERALD HOUSE
Drawer HH
Independence, Missouri 64055

HERALD PRESS
616 Walnut Avenue
Scottdale, Pennsylvania 15683

HERDER & HERDER
c/o The Seabury Press, Inc.
815 Second Avenue
New York, N.Y. 10017

HILL & WANG
19 Union Square West
New York, N.Y. 10003

HILLARY HOUSE PUBLISHERS
450 Park Avenue South
New York, N.Y. 10016

HISTORY BOOK CLUB
40 Guernsey Street
Stamford, Connecticut 06904

HIVE PUBLISHING COMPANY
Box 1004
Easton, Pennsylvania 18042

HOBBS/CONTEXT CORPORATION
441 Lexington Avenue
New York, N.Y. 10017

HOBBY HOUSE PRESS
4701 Queensbury Road
Riverdale, Maryland 20840

HOLBROOK PRESS, INC.
470 Atlantic Avenue
Boston, Massachusetts 02210

HOLDEN-DAY, INC.
500 Sansome Street
San Francisco, California 94111

HOLIDAY HOUSE, INC.
18 East 56th Street
New York, N.Y. 10022

A.J. HOLMAN COMPANY
Box 956, East Washington Square
Philadelphia, Pennsylvania 19105

HOLT, RINEHART AND WINSTON, INC.
383 Madison Avenue
New York, N.Y. 10017

HOOVER INSTITUTION PRESS
Stanford University
Stanford, California 94305

HORIZON PRESS
156 Fifth Avenue
New York, N.Y. 10010

HOUGHTON MIFFLIN COMPANY
2 Park Street
Boston, Massachusetts 02107

HOWARD UNIVERSITY PRESS
Howard Hall
Washington, D.C. 20001

HOWELL BOOK HOUSE, INC.
730 Fifth Avenue
New York, N.Y. 10019

HOWELL-NORTH BOOKS
1050 Parker Street
Berkeley, California 94710

HUMANITIES PRESS, INC.
450 Park Avenue South
New York, N.Y. 10016

IBC INDUSTRIES, INC.
7200 Biscayne Boulevard
Miami, Florida 33138

THE IMPRINT SOCIETY
Barre, Massachusetts 01005

INDIANA UNIVERSITY PRESS
Tenth & Morton Streets
Bloomington, Indiana 47401

INDUSTRIAL PRESS, INC.
200 Madison Avenue
New York, N.Y. 10016

INTERNATIONAL ARTS & SCIENCES
PRESS, INC.
901 North Broadway
White Plains, N.Y. 10603

INTERNATIONAL PUBLISHERS
COMPANY, INC.
381 Park Avenue South
New York, N.Y. 10016

INTERNATIONAL UNIVERSITIES
PRESS, INC.
239 Park Avenue South
New York, N.Y. 10003

THE INTERSTATE PRINTERS &
PUBLISHERS, INC.
19 North Jackson Street
Danville, Illinois 61832

INTER-VARSITY PRESS
Box F
Downers Grove, Illinois 60515

INTEXT PUBLISHERS GROUP
257 Park Avenue South
New York, N.Y. 10010

IOWA STATE UNIVERSITY PRESS
Ames, Iowa 50010

IRISH UNIVERSITY PRESS, INC.
485 Madison Avenue
New York, N.Y. 10022

RICHARD D. IRWIN, INC.
1818 Ridge Road
Homewood, Illinois 60430

JARROW PRESS, INC.
29 Commonwealth Avenue
Boston, Massachusetts 02116

JENKINS PUBLISHING COMPANY
Box 2085
Austin, Texas 78767

JEWISH PUBLICATION SOCIETY
OF AMERICA
1528 Walnut Street
Philadelphia, Pennsylvania 19102

THE JOHN DAY COMPANY, INC.
257 Park Avenue South
New York, N.Y. 10010

JOHN KNOX PRESS
341 Ponce de Leon Avenue, N.E.
Atlanta, Georgia 30308

THE JOHNS HOPKINS UNIVERSITY
PRESS
Baltimore, Maryland 21218

JOHNSON PUBLISHING CO., INC. –
BOOK DIVISION
820 South Michigan Avenue
Chicago, Illinois 60605

JOHNSON REPRINT CORPORATION
111 Fifth Avenue
New York, N.Y. 10003

JONATHAN DAVID PUBLISHERS, INC.
68-22 Eliot Avenue
Middle Village, N.Y. 11379

CHARLES A. JONES PUBLISHING
COMPANY
4 Village Green, S.E.
Worthington, Ohio 43085

MARSHALL JONES COMPANY
Francestown, New Hampshire 03043

JOSSEY-BASS, INC., PUBLISHERS
615 Montgomery Street
San Francisco, California 94111

JUDSON PRESS
Valley Forge, Pennsylvania 19481

JULIAN PRESS, INC.
150 Fifth Avenue
New York, N.Y. 10011

KAIMAN & POLON, INC.
456 Sylvan Avenue
Englewood Cliffs, New Jersey 07632

AUGUSTUS M. KELLEY, PUBLISHERS
305 Allwood Road
Clifton, New Jersey 07012

KENDALL/HUNT PUBLISHING COMPANY
2460 Kerper Boulevard
Dubuque, Iowa 52001

P.J. KENEDY & SONS
c/o Macmillan, Inc.
866 Third Avenue
New York, N.Y. 10022

KENNIKAT PRESS INCORPORATED
90 South Bayles Avenue
Port Washington, N.Y. 11050

KENT STATE UNIVERSITY PRESS
Kent, Ohio 44242

THE KIRKUS SERVICE INC.
60 West 13th Street
New York, N.Y. 10011

ALFRED A. KNOPF, INC.
201 East 50th Street
New York, N.Y. 10022

KRAUS-THOMSON ORGANIZATION LTD.
Route 100
Millwood, New York 10546

KREGEL PUBLICATIONS
525 Eastern Avenue S.E.
Grand Rapids, Michigan 49501

R.E. KRIEGER PUBLISHING COMPANY, INC.
Box 542
Huntington, N.Y. 11743

KTAV PUBLISHING HOUSE, INC.
120 East Broadway
New York, N.Y. 10002

LAIDLAW BROTHERS
Thatcher & Madison Streets
River Forest, Illinois 60305

LANE MAGAZINE & BOOK COMPANY
Menlo Park, California 94025

LAS AMERICAS PUBLISHING COMPANY, INC.
40-22 23rd Street
Long Island City, N.Y. 11101

SEYMOUR LAWRENCE, INC.
90 Beacon Street
Boston, Massachusetts 02108

THE LAWYERS CO-OPERATIVE PUBLISHING COMPANY
Aqueduct Building
Rochester, N.Y. 14603

LEA & FEBIGER
600 South Washington Square
Philadelphia, Pennsylvania 19106

LERNER PUBLICATIONS COMPANY
241 First Avenue North
Minneapolis, Minnesota 55401

LESWING COMMUNICATIONS INC.
750 Adrian Way
San Rafael, California 94903

LIBRA PUBLISHERS, INC.
391 Willets Road
Roslyn Heights, N.Y. 11577

LIBRARIES UNLIMITED, INC.
Box 263
Littleton, Colorado 80120

LIBRARY JOURNAL
R.R. Bowker Company
1180 Avenue of the Americas
New York, N.Y. 10036

THE LIMITED EDITIONS CLUB
Avon, Connecticut 06001

LION BOOKS
111 East 39th Street
New York, N.Y. 10018

J.B. LIPPINCOTT COMPANY
East Washington Square
Philadelphia, Pennsylvania 19105

LITERARY GUILD OF AMERICA
277 Park Avenue
New York, N.Y. 10017

LITTLE, BROWN AND COMPANY
34 Beacon Street
Boston, Massachusetts 02106

LITTLEFIELD, ADAMS & COMPANY
81 Adams Drive
Totowa, New Jersey 07512

LITTON EDUCATIONAL
PUBLISHING, INC.
450 West 33rd Street
New York, N.Y. 10001

LIVERIGHT
386 Park Avenue South
New York, N.Y. 10016

LIVINGSTON PUBLISHING COMPANY
18 Hampstead Circle
Wynnewood, Pennsylvania 19096

LOIZEAUX BROTHERS
1238 Corlies Avenue
Neptune, New Jersey 07753

LOTHROP, LEE & SHEPARD COMPANY
105 Madison Avenue
New York, N.Y. 10016

LOUISIANA STATE UNIVERSITY PRESS
Baton Rouge, Louisiana 70803

LOYOLA UNIVERSITY PRESS
3441 North Ashland Avenue
Chicago, Illinois 60657

ROBERT B. LUCE, INC.
2000 N Street, N.W.
Washington, D.C. 20036

LYONS & CARNAHAN
Box 7600
Chicago, Illinois 60680

THE M.I.T. PRESS
28 Carleton Street
Cambridge, Massachusetts 02142

Mss. INFORMATION CORPORATION
655 Madison Avenue
New York, N.Y. 10021

McCORMICK-MATHERS PUBLISHING
COMPANY
450 West 33rd Street
New York, N.Y. 10001

McCUTCHAN PUBLISHING CORPORATION
2526 Grove Street
Berkeley, California 94704

McGRATH PUBLISHING COMPANY
821 15th Street N.W.
Washington, D.C. 20005

McGRAW-HILL BOOK COMPANY
1221 Avenue of the Americas
New York, N.Y. 10020

DAVID McKAY COMPANY, INC.
750 Third Avenue
New York, N.Y. 10017

McKNIGHT PUBLISHING COMPANY
Bloomington, Illinois 61701

McNALLY & LOFTIN, PUBLISHERS
Box 1316
Santa Barbara, California 93102

MACMILLAN BOOK CLUBS, INC.
866 Third Avenue
New York, N.Y. 10022

MACMILLAN, INC.
866 Third Avenue
New York, N.Y. 10022

MACRAE SMITH COMPANY
225 South 15th Street
Philadelphia, Pennsylvania 19102

MANOR BOOKS INC.
432 Park Avenue South
New York, N.Y. 10016

MARA BOOKS, INC.
2840 West Rowena Avenue
Los Angeles, California 90039

MARKHAM PUBLISHING COMPANY
Box 7600
Chicago, Illinois 60680

MARQUIS WHO'S WHO, INCORPORATED
200 East Ohio Street
Chicago, Illinois 60611

MEDIA DIRECTIONS, INC.
One Park Avenue
New York, N.Y. 10016

MEDICAL EXAMINATION PUBLISHING
CO., INC.
65-36 Fresh Meadow Lane
Flushing, N.Y. 11365

MEMPHIS STATE UNIVERSITY PRESS
Memphis, Tennessee 38152

MENNONITE PUBLISHING HOUSE
(See, Herald Press)

MEREDITH CORPORATION
1716 Locust Street
Des Moines, Iowa 50336

G. & C. MERRIAM COMPANY
47 Federal Street
Springfield, Massachusetts 01101

CHARLES E. MERRILL PUBLISHING
COMPANY
1300 Alum Creek Drive
Columbus, Ohio 43216

JULIAN MESSNER
1 West 39th Street
New York, N.Y. 10018

METROPOLITAN MUSEUM OF ART
Fifth Avenue & 82nd Street
New York, N.Y. 10028

MICHIGAN STATE UNIVERSITY PRESS
1405 South Harrison Road
East Lansing, Michigan 48824

MILFORD HOUSE, INC.
85 Newbury Street
Boston, Massachusetts 02116

MODERN CURRICULUM PRESS, INC.
13900 Prospect Road
Cleveland, Ohio 44136

MODERN LIBRARY
Random House, Inc.
201 East 50th Street
New York, N.Y. 10022

MONTHLY REVIEW PRESS
62 West 14th Street
New York, N.Y. 10011

MOODY PRESS
820 North LaSalle Street
Chicago, Illinois 60610

MOREHOUSE-BARLOW COMPANY, INC.
14 East 41st Street
New York, N.Y. 10017

WILLIAM MORROW & COMPANY, INC.
105 Madison Avenue
New York, N.Y. 10016

THE C.V. MOSBY COMPANY
11830 Westline Industrial Drive
St. Louis, Missouri 63141

MOUNTAIN PRESS PUBLISHING
COMPANY
279 West Front Street
Missoula, Montana 59801

MUSIC SALES CORPORATION
33 West 60th Street
New York, N.Y. 10023

NASH PUBLISHING CORPORATION
9255 Sunset Boulevard
Los Angeles, California 90069

NATIONAL BUREAU OF ECONOMIC
RESEARCH, INC.
261 Madison Avenue
New York, N.Y. 10016

NATIONAL COUNCIL OF TEACHERS
OF ENGLISH
1111 Kenyon Road
Urbana, Illinois 61801

NATIONAL LEARNING CORPORATION
20 DuPont Street
Plainview, New York 11803

NATIONAL PRESS BOOKS
285 Hamilton Avenue
Palo Alto, California 94301

NATIONAL TEXTBOOK COMPANY
8259 Niles Center Road
Skokie, Illinois 60076

NAVAL INSTITUTE PRESS
(See, U.S. Naval Institute Press)

NAYLOR COMPANY
1015 Culebra Avenue
San Antonio, Texas 78201

NAZARENE PUBLISHING HOUSE
Box 527
Kansas City, Missouri 64141

NEGRO HISTORY PRESS
Box 5129
Detroit, Michigan 48236

NELSON-HALL COMPANY
325 West Jackson Boulevard
Chicago, Illinois 60606

THOMAS NELSON INCORPORATED
407 Seventh Avenue South
Nashville, Tennessee 37203

THE NEW AMERICAN LIBRARY INC.
1301 Avenue of the Americas
New York, N.Y. 10019

NEWBURY HOUSE, PUBLISHERS
68 Middle Road
Rowley, Massachusetts 01969

**NEW DIRECTIONS PUBLISHING
CORPORATION**
333 Avenue of the Americas
New York, N.Y. 10014

NEW HAMPSHIRE PUBLISHING COMPANY
15 Interstate Drive
Somersworth, New Hampshire 03878

NEW YORK GRAPHIC SOCIETY LTD.
140 Greenwich Avenue
Greenwich, Connecticut 06830

NEW YORK UNIVERSITY PRESS
Washington Square
New York, N.Y. 10003

NOBLE & NOBLE, PUBLISHERS, INC.
1 Dag Hammarskjold Plaza
New York, N.Y. 10017

**NORTHERN ILLINOIS UNIVERSITY
PRESS**
De Kalb, Illinois 60115

NORTHWESTERN UNIVERSITY PRESS
1735 Benson Avenue
Evanston, Illinois 60201

W.W. NORTON & COMPANY, INC.
500 Fifth Avenue
New York, N.Y. 10036

NOYES DATA CORPORATION
Mill Road & Grand Avenue
Park Ridge, New Jersey 07656

OCEANA PUBLICATIONS, INC.
Dobbs Ferry, New York 10522

OCTOBER HOUSE, INC.
160 Avenue of the Americas
New York, N.Y. 10013

ODDO PUBLISHING, INC.
Storybook Acres, Beauregard Boulevard
Fayetteville, Georgia 30214

OHARA PUBLICATIONS INC.
5455 Wilshire Boulevard
Los Angeles, California 90036

J. PHILIP O'HARA, INC.
20 East Huron Avenue
Chicago, Illinois 60611

OHIO STATE UNIVERSITY PRESS
Hitchcock Hall, 2070 Neil Avenue
Columbus, Ohio 43210

OHIO UNIVERSITY PRESS
Administrative Annex
Athens, Ohio 45701

OMEN PRESS
3705 North Old Sabino Canyon Road
Tucson, Arizona 85715

101 PRODUCTIONS
834 Mission Street
San Francisco, California 94103

OPEN COURT PUBLISHING COMPANY
1039 Eighth Street
LaSalle, Illinois 61301

ORBIS BOOKS
Maryknoll, New York 10545

OREGON STATE UNIVERSITY PRESS
101 Waldo Hall
Corvallis, Oregon 97331

ORIOLE EDITIONS
19 West 44th Street
New York, N.Y. 10036

OTTENHEIMER PUBLISHERS, INC.
1632 Reisterstown Road
Baltimore, Maryland 21208

OUTERBRIDGE & LAZARD, INC.
201 Park Avenue South
New York, N.Y. 10003

OXFORD BOOK COMPANY, INC.
11 Park Place
New York, N.Y. 10007

OXFORD UNIVERSITY PRESS, INC.
200 Madison Avenue
New York, N.Y. 10016

JEROME S. OZER, PUBLISHER, INC.
475 Fifth Avenue
New York, N.Y. 10017

PACIFIC COAST PUBLISHERS
Campbell Avenue at Scott Drive
Menlo Park, California 94025

PACIFIC PRESS PUBLISHING ASSOCIATION
Mountain View, California 94042

PANTHEON BOOKS, INC.
201 East 50th Street
New York, N.Y. 10022

PARENTS' MAGAZINE PRESS
52 Vanderbilt Avenue
New York, N.Y. 10017

PARKER & SON PUBLICATIONS, INC.
6500 Flotilla Street
Los Angeles, California 90022

PARKER PUBLISHING COMPANY
Englewood Cliffs, New Jersey 07632

PARNASSUS PRESS
4080 Halleck Street
Emeryville, California 94704

PATHFINDER PRESS
410 West Street
New York, N.Y. 10014

PAULIST/NEWMAN PRESS
1865 Broadway
New York, N.Y. 10023

F.E. PEACOCK PUBLISHERS, INC.
401 West Irving Park Road
Itasca, Illinois 60143

PELICAN PUBLISHING CO., INC.
630 Burmaster Street
Gretna, Louisiana 70053

PENGUIN BOOKS INC.
7110 Ambassador Road
Baltimore, Maryland 21207

THE PENNSYLVANIA STATE
UNIVERSITY PRESS
215 Wagner Building
University Park, Pennsylvania 16802

PEQUOT PRESS, INC.
Old Chester Road
Chester, Connecticut 06412

PERGAMON PUBLISHING COMPANY
Fairview Park
Elmsford, New York 10523

PETER PAUPER PRESS
629 North MacQuesten Parkway
Mount Vernon, New York 10552

PFLAUM/STANDARD
2285 Arbor Boulevard
Dayton, Ohio 45439

PHAEDRA, INC.
49 Park Avenue
New York, N.Y. 10016

PHILOSOPHICAL LIBRARY, INC.
15 East 40th Street
New York, N.Y. 10016

THE PIERIAN PRESS
Box 1808
Ann Arbor, Michigan 48106

PILOT BOOKS
347 Fifth Avenue
New York, N.Y. 10016

PINNACLE BOOKS
275 Madison Avenue
New York, N.Y. 10016

THE PIPER COMPANY
120 North Main Street
Blue Earth, Minnesota 56013

PITMAN PUBLISHING CORPORATION
6 East 43rd Street
New York, N.Y. 10017

PLATT & MUNK
1055 Bronx River Avenue
Bronx, New York 10472

PLAYBOY PRESS
919 North Michigan Avenue
Chicago, Illinois 60611

PLAYS, INC.
8 Arlington Street
Boston, Massachusetts 02116

PLENUM PUBLISHING CORPORATION
227 West 17th Street
New York, N.Y. 10011

THE PLOUGH PUBLISHING HOUSE
Rifton, New York 12471

POCKET BOOKS
630 Fifth Avenue
New York, N.Y. 10020

POPULAR LIBRARY
600 Third Avenue
New York, N.Y. 10016

POTOMAC BOOKS, INC.
Box 40604
Washington, D.C. 20016

CLARKSON N. POTTER, INC.
419 Park Avenue South
New York, N.Y. 10016

PRAEGER PUBLISHERS, INC.
111 Fourth Avenue
New York, N.Y. 10003

PRAYER BOOK PRESS, INC.
1363 Fairfield Avenue
Bridgeport, Connecticut 06605

PRENTICE-HALL, INC.
Englewood Cliffs, New Jersey 07632

THE PRESS OF CASE WESTERN
RESERVE UNIVERSITY
Quail Building
Cleveland, Ohio 44106

PRICE/STERN/SLOAN PUBLISHERS, INC.
410 North La Cienega Boulevard
Los Angeles, California 90048

PRINCETON UNIVERSITY PRESS
Princeton, New Jersey 08540

PRINDLE, WEBER & SCHMIDT, INC.
20 Newbury Street
Boston, Massachusetts 02116

PROMETHEUS BOOKS
923 Kensington Avenue
Buffalo, New York 14215

PROSPECT HOUSE, INC.
7777 Leesburg Pike
Falls Church, Virginia 22043

PRUETT PUBLISHING COMPANY
Box 1560
Boulder, Colorado 80302

PUBLIC AFFAIRS PRESS
419 New Jersey Avenue, S.E.
Washington, D.C. 20003

PURDUE UNIVERSITY STUDIES
South Campus Courts-D
West Lafayette, Indiana 47907

G.P. PUTNAM'S SONS
200 Madison Avenue
New York, N.Y. 10016

THE PYNE PRESS
291 Witherspoon Street
Princeton, New Jersey 08540

PYRAMID COMMUNICATIONS, INC.
919 Third Avenue
New York, N.Y. 10022

QUADRANGLE/THE NEW YORK TIMES
BOOK COMPANY
10 East 53rd Street
New York, N.Y. 10022

HARLIN QUIST BOOKS
192 East 75th Street
New York, N.Y. 10021

RAMPARTS PRESS INC.
Box 10128
Palo Alto, California 94303

R AND E RESEARCH ASSOCIATES
4843 Mission Street
San Francisco, California 94112

RAND McNALLY & COMPANY
Box 7600
Chicago, Illinois 60680

RANDOM HOUSE, INC.
201 East 50th Street
New York, N.Y. 10022

RAVEN PRESS
1140 Avenue of the Americas
New York, N.Y. 10036

REARDON, BAER & COMPANY
13900 Prospect Road
Cleveland, Ohio 44136

REGENTS PUBLISHING COMPANY, INC.
2 Park Avenue
New York, N.Y. 10016

HENRY REGNERY COMPANY
180 North American Avenue
Chicago, Illinois 60601

REPRINT COMPANY
116 Hillcrest Offices, Box 5401
Spartanburg, South Carolina 29301

RESEARCH PRESS COMPANY
2612 North Mattis Avenue
Champaign, Illinois 61820

FLEMING H. REVELL COMPANY
Old Tappan, New Jersey 07675

REVIEW & HERALD PUBLISHING
ASSOCIATION
Takoma Park
Washington, D.C. 20012

PAUL R. REYNOLDS, INC.
599 Fifth Avenue
New York, N.Y. 10017

THE RIDGE PRESS, INC.
25 West 43rd Street
New York, N.Y. 10036

THE RIO GRANDE PRESS, INC.
La Casa Escuela
Glorieta, New Mexico 87535

THE WARD RITCHIE PRESS
3044 Riverside Drive
Los Angeles, California 90039

THE ROCKEFELLER UNIVERSITY
PRESS
York Avenue & East 66th Street
New York, N.Y. 10021

RODALE PRESS
33 East Minor Street
Emmaus, Pennsylvania 18049

THE RONALD PRESS COMPANY
79 Madison Avenue
New York, N.Y. 10016

RICHARDS ROSEN PRESS, INC.
29 East 21st Street
New York, N.Y. 10010

FRED B. ROTHMAN & COMPANY
57 Leuning Street
South Hackensack, New Jersey 07606

ROWMAN & LITTLEFIELD
81 Adams Drive
Totowa, New Jersey 07512

ROY PUBLISHERS, INC.
30 East 74th Street
New York, N.Y. 10021

RUSSELL & RUSSELL PUBLISHERS
122 East 42nd Street
New York, N.Y. 10017

RUTGERS UNIVERSITY PRESS
30 College Avenue
New Brunswick, New Jersey 08901

WILLIAM H. SADLIER, INC.
11 Park Place
New York, N.Y. 10007

SAGE PUBLICATIONS, INC.
275 South Beverly Drive
Beverly Hills, California 90212

ST. JOHN'S UNIVERSITY PRESS
Grand Central & Utopia Parkways
Jamaica, New York 11439

ST. MARTIN'S PRESS, INC.
175 Fifth Avenue
New York, N.Y. 10010

HOWARD W. SAMS & COMPANY, INC.,
PUBLISHERS
4300 West 62nd Street
Indianapolis, Indiana 46268

SAN FRANCISCO BOOK COMPANY, INC.
321 Pacific Avenue
San Francisco, California 94111

PORTER SARGENT, PUBLISHER
11 Beacon Street
Boston, Massachusetts 02108

SATURDAY REVIEW PRESS
201 Park Avenue South
New York, N.Y. 10003

W.B. SAUNDERS COMPANY
West Washington Square
Philadelphia, Pennsylvania 19105

SCARECROW PRESS, INC.
52 Liberty Street
Metuchen, New Jersey 08840

SCHENKMAN PUBLISHING CO., INC.
3 Mt. Auburn Place
Cambridge, Massachusetts 02138

G. SCHIRMER, INC.
866 Third Avenue
New York, N.Y. 10022

SCHOCKEN BOOKS INCORPORATED
200 Madison Avenue
New York, N.Y. 10016

SCHOLARLY PRESS, INC.
22929 Industrial Drive East
St. Clair Shores, Michigan 48080

SCHOLARLY RESOURCES, INC.
1508 Pennsylvania Avenue
Wilmington, Delaware 19806

SCHOLASTIC BOOK SERVICES
50 West 44th Street
New York, N.Y. 10036

ABNER SCHRAM
1860 Broadway
New York, N.Y. 10023

SCIENCE & BEHAVIOR BOOKS, INC.
Box 11457
Palo Alto, California 94306

SCIENCE RESEARCH ASSOCIATES, INC.
259 East Erie Street
Chicago, Illinois 60611

SCOTT, FORESMAN AND COMPANY
1900 East Lake Avenue
Glenview, Illinois 60025

CHARLES SCRIBNER'S SONS
597 Fifth Avenue
New York, N.Y. 10017

THE SCRIMSHAW PRESS (CALIFORNIA)
149 Ninth Street
San Francisco, California 94103

SCRIPTA PUBLISHING CORPORATION
1511 K Street, N.W.
Washington, D.C. 20005

SCROLL PRESS, INC.
22 East 84th Street
New York, N.Y. 10028

THE SEABURY PRESS, INC.
815 Second Avenue
New York, N.Y. 10017

E.A. SEEMANN PUBLISHING, INC.
Box K
Miami, Florida 33156

SHAMBHALA PUBLICATIONS INC.
2045 San Francisco Street
Berkeley, California 94709

SHEED & WARD, INC.
475 Fifth Avenue
New York, N.Y. 10017

SHENGOLD PUBLISHERS, INC.
45 West 45th Street
New York, N.Y. 10036

SHERBOURNE PRESS
1640 South La Cienega Boulevard
Los Angeles, California 90035

THE SHOE STRING PRESS, INC.
995 Sherman Avenue
Hamden, Connecticut 06514

SIERRA CLUB BOOKS
597 Fifth Avenue
New York, N.Y. 10017

SILVER BURDETT COMPANY
250 James Street
Morristown, New Jersey 07960

SIMON & SCHUSTER, INC.
630 Fifth Avenue
New York, N.Y. 10020

THE SMITH
5 Beekman Street
New York, N.Y. 10038

THE ALLEN SMITH COMPANY
1435 North Meridian Street
Indianapolis, Indiana 46202

PATTERSON SMITH PUBLISHING
CORPORATION
23 Prospect Terrace
Montclair, New Jersey 07042

PETER SMITH
6 Lexington Avenue
Gloucester, Massachusetts 01930

SMITHSONIAN INSTITUTION PRESS
Washington, D.C. 20560

SOMETHING ELSE PRESS, INC.
Box H
Barton, Vermont 05822

SOUTHERN ILLINOIS UNIVERSITY
PRESS
Box 3697
Carbondale, Illinois 62901

SOUTHERN METHODIST UNIVERSITY
PRESS
Dallas, Texas 75275

THE SOUTHWESTERN COMPANY
Box 820
Nashville, Tennessee 37202

SOUTH-WESTERN PUBLISHING
COMPANY
5101 Madison Road
Cincinnati, Ohio 45227

ROBERT SPELLER & SONS,
PUBLISHERS, INC.
10 East 23rd Street
New York, N.Y. 10010

SPRINGER PUBLISHING CO., INC.
200 Park Avenue South
New York, N.Y. 10003

SPRINGER-VERLAG NEW YORK INC.
175 Fifth Avenue
New York, N.Y. 10010

STACKPOLE BOOKS
Cameron & Kelker Streets
Harrisburg, Pennsylvania 17105

STANDARD EDUCATIONAL
CORPORATION
130 North Wells Street
Chicago, Illinois 60606

STANDARD PUBLISHING
8121 Hamilton Avenue
Cincinnati, Ohio 45231

STANFORD UNIVERSITY PRESS
Stanford, California 94305

STANWIX HOUSE, INC.
3020 Chartiers Avenue
Pittsburgh, Pennsylvania 15204

STATE UNIVERSITY OF NEW YORK
PRESS
99 Washington Avenue
Albany, New York 12210

STECK-VAUGHN COMPANY
Box 2028
Austin, Texas 78767

STEIN & DAY PUBLISHERS
Scarborough House
Briarcliff Manor, N.Y. 10510

STERLING PUBLISHING COMPANY, INC.
419 Park Avenue South
New York, N.Y. 10016

STRAIGHT ARROW BOOKS
625 Third Street
San Francisco, California 94107

LYLE STUART, INC.
120 Enterprise Avenue
Secaucus, New Jersey 07094

H.S. STUTTMAN COMPANY, INC.
404 Park Avenue South
New York, N.Y. 10016

SUMMY-BIRCHARD COMPANY
1834 Ridge Avenue
Evanston, Illinois 60204

SUNSET BOOKS
Lane Magazine & Book Company
Menlo Park, California 94025

THE SWALLOW PRESS, INC.
1139 South Wabash Avenue
Chicago, Illinois 60605

SWEDENBORG FOUNDATION
139 East 23rd Street
New York, N.Y. 10010

SWEET PUBLISHING COMPANY
Box 4055
Austin, Texas 78765

SYRACUSE UNIVERSITY PRESS
Box 8, University Station
Syracuse, New York 13210

TAB BOOKS
Blue Ridge Summit, Pennsylvania 17214

T.F.H. PUBLICATIONS, INC.
211 West Sylvania Avenue
Neptune City, N.J. 07753

TAPLINGER PUBLISHING COMPANY, INC.
200 Park Avenue South
New York, N.Y. 10003

J.P. TARCHER, INC.
9110 Sunset Boulevard
Los Angeles, California 90069

TAYLOR PUBLISHING COMPANY
1550 West Mockingbird Lane
Dallas, Texas 75221

TEACHERS COLLEGE PRESS
1234 Amsterdam Avenue
New York, N.Y. 10027

TECHNOMIC PUBLISHING CO., INC.
265 West State Street
Westport, Connecticut 06880

TEMPLEGATE PUBLISHERS
Box 963
Springfield, Illinois 62705

TEMPLE UNIVERSITY PRESS
Philadelphia, Pennsylvania 19122

TEXAS A. & M. UNIVERSITY PRESS
College Station, Texas 77843

TEXIAN PRESS
1301 Jefferson Street
Waco, Texas 76702

THEATRE ARTS BOOKS
333 Avenue of the Americas
New York, N.Y. 10014

THEOSOPHICAL PUBLISHING HOUSE
Box 270
Wheaton, Illinois 60187

THE THIRD PRESS
444 Central Park West
New York, N.Y. 10025

CHARLES C. THOMAS, PUBLISHER
301-27 East Lawrence Avenue
Springfield, Illinois 62717

THOMAS LAW BOOK COMPANY
1909 Washington Avenue
St. Louis, Missouri 63103

THOMAS PUBLISHING COMPANY
461 Eighth Avenue
New York, N.Y. 10001

THOR PUBLISHING COMPANY
Box 1782
Ventura, California 93001

TIME INCORPORATED BOOK CLUBS, INC.
95 East Putnam Avenue
Greenwich, Connecticut 06830

TIME-LIFE BOOKS
Time & Life Building
Rockefeller Center
New York, N.Y. 10020

THE TIMES MIRROR COMPANY
280 Park Avenue
New York, N.Y. 10017

THE TOUCHSTONE PRESS
Box 81
Beaverton, Oregon 97005

TOUCHSTONE PUBLISHING COMPANY
Box 21318
Louisville, Kentucky 40221

TRANSACTION BOOKS
Rutgers – The State University
Rutgers, New Jersey 08903

TRANSATLANTIC ARTS, INC.
North Village Green
Levittown, New York 11756

TREND HOUSE
Box 2350
1306 West Kennedy Boulevard
Tampa, Florida 33601

TRIDENT PRESS
630 Fifth Avenue
New York, N.Y. 10020

TROUBADOR PRESS, INC.
126 Folsom Street
San Francisco, California 94105

TUDOR PUBLISHING COMPANY
221 Park Avenue South
New York, N.Y. 10003

CHARLES E. TUTTLE COMPANY, INC.
28 East Main Street
Rutland, Vermont 05701

TWAYNE PUBLISHERS, INC.
c/o G.K. Hall & Company
70 Lincoln Street
Boston, Massachusetts 02111

TYNDALE HOUSE PUBLISHERS
336 Gundersen Drive
Wheaton, Illinois 60187

FREDERICK UNGAR PUBLISHING
CO., INC.
250 Park Avenue South
New York, N.Y. 10003

UNICORN PRESS, INC.
Box 3307
Greensboro, North Carolina 27402

UNION OF AMERICAN HEBREW
CONGREGATIONS
838 Fifth Avenue
New York, N.Y. 10021

UNITED CHURCH PRESS
1505 Race Street
Philadelphia, Pennsylvania 19102

UNITED EDUCATORS, INC.
Tangley Oaks Educational Center
Lake Bluff, Illinois 60044

U.S. NAVAL INSTITUTE PRESS
(Naval Institute Press)
Annapolis, Maryland 21402

UNIVERSAL PUBLISHING & DISTRIB-
UTING CORPORATION
235 East 45th Street
New York, N.Y. 10017

UNIVERSE BOOKS
381 Park Avenue South
New York, N.Y. 10016

UNIVERSITY OF ALABAMA PRESS
Drawer 2877
University, Alabama 35486

THE UNIVERSITY OF ARIZONA PRESS
Box 3398
Tucson, Arizona 85722

UNIVERSITY OF CALIFORNIA PRESS
2223 Fulton Street
Berkeley, California 94720

UNIVERSITY OF CHICAGO PRESS
5801 Ellis Avenue
Chicago, Illinois 60637

UNIVERSITY OF GEORGIA PRESS
Athens, Georgia 30602

UNIVERSITY OF ILLINOIS PRESS
Urbana, Illinois 61801

UNIVERSITY OF IOWA PRESS
Iowa City, Iowa 52242

UNIVERSITY OF MASSACHUSETTS PRESS
Amherst, Massachusetts 01002

UNIVERSITY OF MIAMI PRESS
Drawer 9088
Coral Gables, Florida 33124

THE UNIVERSITY OF MICHIGAN PRESS
Ann Arbor, Michigan 48106

UNIVERSITY OF MINNESOTA PRESS
2037 University Avenue S.E.
Minneapolis, Minnesota 55455

UNIVERSITY OF MISSOURI PRESS
107 Swallow Hall
Columbia, Missouri 65201

UNIVERSITY OF NEBRASKA PRESS
901 North 17th Street
Lincoln, Nebraska 68508

UNIVERSITY OF NEW MEXICO PRESS
Albuquerque, New Mexico 87106

UNIVERSITY OF NORTH CAROLINA PRESS
Box 2288
Chapel Hill, North Carolina 27514

UNIVERSITY OF NOTRE DAME PRESS
Notre Dame, Indiana 46556

UNIVERSITY OF OKLAHOMA PRESS
1005 Asp Avenue
Norman, Oklahoma 73069

UNIVERSITY OF PENNSYLVANIA PRESS
3933 Walnut Street
Philadelphia, Pennsylvania 19104

UNIVERSITY OF PITTSBURGH PRESS
127 North Bellefield Avenue
Pittsburgh, Pennsylvania 15260

UNIVERSITY OF SOUTH CAROLINA PRESS
Columbia, South Carolina 29208

UNIVERSITY OF TENNESSEE PRESS
Communications Building
Knoxville, Tennessee 37916

UNIVERSITY OF TEXAS PRESS
Box 7819, University Station
Austin, Texas 78712

UNIVERSITY OF UTAH PRESS
Building 513
Salt Lake City, Utah 84112

UNIVERSITY OF WASHINGTON PRESS
Seattle, Washington 98105

UNIVERSITY OF WISCONSIN PRESS
Box 1379
Madison, Wisconsin 53701

UNIVERSITY PARK PRESS
Chamber of Commerce Building
Baltimore, Maryland 21202

THE UNIVERSITY PRESS OF HAWAII
535 Ward Avenue
Honolulu, Hawaii 96814

THE UNIVERSITY PRESS OF KANSAS
366 Watson Library
Lawrence, Kansas 66045

THE UNIVERSITY PRESS OF KENTUCKY
Lexington, Kentucky 40506

THE UNIVERSITY PRESS OF VIRGINIA
Box 3608, University Station
Charlottesville, Virginia 22903

UNIVERSITY PRESS OF WASHINGTON, D.C.
Southeastern University
University Press Building
Riverton, Virginia 22651

UNIVERSITY PRESSES OF FLORIDA
15 N.W. 15th Street
Gainesville, Florida 32601

UNIVERSITY SOCIETY, INC.
25 Cottage Street
Midland Park, N.J. 07432

URBAN INSTITUTE
2100 M Street, N.W.
Washington, D.C. 20037

VANDERBILT UNIVERSITY PRESS
Nashville, Tennessee 37235

VANGUARD PRESS, INC.
424 Madison Avenue
New York, N.Y. 10017

D. VAN NOSTRAND COMPANY
450 West 33rd Street
New York, N.Y. 10001

VAN NOSTRAND REINHOLD COMPANY
450 West 33rd Street
New York, N.Y. 10001

VEDANTA PRESS
1946 Vedanta Place
Hollywood, California 90068

VIENNA HOUSE, INC.
342 Madison Avenue
New York, N.Y. 10017

THE VIKING PRESS, INC.
625 Madison Avenue
New York, N.Y. 10022

WADSWORTH PUBLISHING COMPANY, INC.
Belmont, California 94002

HENRY Z. WALCK, INC.
750 Third Avenue
New York, N.Y. 10017

WALKER & COMPANY
720 Fifth Avenue
New York, N.Y. 10019

FREDERICK WARNE & COMPANY, INC.
101 Fifth Avenue
New York, N.Y. 10003

WARNER PAPERBACK LIBRARY
75 Rockefeller Plaza
New York, N.Y. 10019

WARNER PRESS, INC.
1200 East Fifth Street
Anderson, Indiana 46012

NEALE WATSON ACADEMIC PUBLICA-
TIONS, INC.
156 Fifth Avenue
New York, N.Y. 10010

WATSON-GUPTILL PUBLICATIONS
1 Astor Plaza
New York, N.Y. 10036

FRANKLIN WATTS, INC.
730 Fifth Avenue
New York, N.Y. 10019

WAYNE STATE UNIVERSITY PRESS
5980 Cass Avenue
Detroit, Michigan 48202

WE, INC.
Box 131
Old Greenwich, Connecticut 06870

JOHN WEATHERHILL, INC.
149 Madison Avenue
New York, N.Y. 10016

WESLEYAN UNIVERSITY PRESS
356 Washington Street
Middletown, Connecticut 06457

WEST PUBLISHING COMPANY
50 West Kellogg Boulevard
St. Paul, Minnesota 55102

WESTERNLORE PRESS
5117 Eagle Rock Boulevard
Los Angeles, California 90041

WESTERN PUBLISHING COMPANY, INC.
1220 Mound Avenue
Racine, Wisconsin 53404

THE WESTMINSTER PRESS
Witherspoon Building
Philadelphia, Pennsylvania 19107

WESTOVER PUBLISHING COMPANY
333 East Grace Street
Richmond, Virginia 23219

WEYBRIGHT AND TALLEY, INC.
750 Third Avenue
New York, N.Y. 10017

THE BOND WHEELWRIGHT COMPANY
Porter's Landing
Freeport, Maine 04032

DAVID WHITE COMPANY
60 East 55th Street
New York, N.Y. 10022

JAMES T. WHITE & COMPANY
1700 State Highway 3
Clifton, New Jersey 07013

WHITEHALL COMPANY
601 Skokie Boulevard
Northbrook, Illinois 60062

ALBERT WHITMAN & COMPANY
560 West Lake Street
Chicago, Illinois 60606

WHITSTON PUBLISHING COMPANY
Box 322
Troy, New York 12181

WILDERNESS PRESS
2440 Bancroft Way
Berkeley, California 94704

JOHN WILEY & SONS, INC.
605 Third Avenue
New York, N.Y. 10016

THE WILLIAMS & WILKINS COMPANY
428 East Preston Street
Baltimore, Maryland 21202

WILSHIRE BOOK COMPANY
12015 Sherman Road
North Hollywood, California 91605

THE H.W. WILSON COMPANY
950 University Avenue
Bronx, New York 10452

WINCHESTER PRESS
205 East 42nd Street
New York, N.Y. 10017

WINDMILL BOOKS, INC.
201 Park Avenue South
New York, N.Y. 10010

V.H. WINSTON & SONS, INC.
1511 K Street, N.W.
Washington, D.C. 20005

WM. H. WISE & COMPANY, INC.
336 Mountain Road
Union City, New Jersey 07087

GEORGE WITTENBORN, INC.
1018 Madison Avenue
New York, N.Y. 10021

WORD, INC.
4800 West Waco Drive
Waco, Texas 76703

WORKMAN PUBLISHING CO., INC.
231 East 51st Street
New York, N.Y. 10022

WORLD PUBLISHING COMPANY
110 East 59th Street
New York, N.Y. 10022

WORTH PUBLISHERS, INC.
70 Fifth Avenue
New York, N.Y. 10011

THE WRITER, INC.
8 Arlington Street
Boston, Massachusetts 02116

PETER H. WYDEN, INC.
750 Third Avenue
New York, N.Y. 10017

XEROX EDUCATION PUBLICATIONS
245 Long Hill Road
Middletown, Connecticut 06457

YALE UNIVERSITY PRESS
302 Temple Street
New Haven, Connecticut 06511

**YEAR BOOK MEDICAL PUB-
LISHERS, INC.**
35 East Wacker Drive
Chicago, Illinois 60601

YOUNG READERS PRESS, INC.
1 West 39th Street
New York, N.Y. 10018

ZONDERVAN PUBLISHING HOUSE
1415 Lake Drive S.E.
Grand Rapids, Michigan 49506

INDEX

Guide to Index - As alphabetized, names of individuals precede names of companies.

Barron's Educational Series,
Inc., 71-72
Barron's Textbook Exchange.
See Barron's Educational
M. Barrows and Company.
See William Morrow & Co.
Bartell Media Corporation, 283-285
Barthel, Martin C.
See Concordia Publish. House
Bartlett, John. *See* Little, Brown
Basham, Ruth. *See* Kirkus Service
Basic Books, Inc., Publishers, 72.
See also Crowell Collier &
Macmillan; Harper & Row
Basilius, Harold A.
See Wayne State Univ. Press
Bauernfeind, Howard K.
See J. B. Lippincott Co.
William L. Bauhan, Inc., 72
Bay Psalm Book, 4.
See also Cambridge Press
Beach, Frederick Converse.
See Grolier Incorporated
C. B. Beach & Company.
See F. E. Compton Co.
Beacon Press, 72-73
Beadle, Erastus F.
See Irwin P. Beadle & Co.
Beadle, Irwin P., 4.
See also George P. Munro
Beadle & Adams.
See Irwin P. Beadle & Co.
Irwin P. Beadle & Company, 4
Bean, Donald P. *See* Assoc. of
American Univ. Presses;
Stanford Univ. Press;
Syracuse Univ. Press;
Univ. of Chicago Press
Beatty, F. A. *See* Noble and Noble
Beck, Hazel.
See Iowa State Univ. Press
Beckley-Cardy Company, The.
See Benefic Press;
Harcourt Brace Jovanovich
Beckman, F. W.
See Iowa State Univ. Press
Beemt, T. vanden.
See W. B. Saunders Co.
Behavioral Publications, Inc., 73
Behrens, Rudolph.
See Dick & Fitzgerald
Behrens Publishing Company.
See Dick & Fitzgerald
Behrman House, Inc., 74
Beilenson, Edna.
See Peter Pauper
Beilenson, Peter. *See* Peter Pauper
Belknap Press.
See Harvard Univ. Press
Bell, Louis H. *See*
Pennsylvania State Univ. Press
Bell, Robert, 4-5
Bell & Howell Company, 279-280
Bellman Publishing Company, 74
Belmont Tower Books, Inc., 74
Bemis, James D., 5
Bender, John T.
See Matthew Bender & Co.
Bender, John T., Jr.
See Matthew Bender & Co.
Bender, Matthew, 74
Bender, Matthew, Jr., 74
Bender, Matthew, III, 74
Matthew Bender & Company,
Inc., 74. *See also*
Times Mirror Co.
Bender-Moss Company.
See Lawyers Co-op.
Benefic Press, 74

Benjamin, Curtis G.
See McGraw-Hill Book Co.
Benjamin, Roy.
See Benjamin Co. Inc.
Benjamin, Ted.
See Benjamin Co. Inc.
Benjamin, William A.
See W. A. Benjamin, Inc.
Benjamin Company, Inc.,
The, 74-75
W. A. Benjamin, Inc., 75.
See also Addison-Wesley
Bennett, Charles A., 76
Bennett, Harry.
See Chemical Publishing
Chas. A. Bennett Co., Inc., 76
Bennion, Grant M.
See Ginn and Co.
Bennion, Samuel O.
See Deseret Book
W. C. Benson & Company, 76
Benstead, H. M.
See Western Publish. Co.
Bentley, Harold W.
See Univ. of Utah Press
Robert Bentley, Inc., 76
Benton, William.
See Encyclopaedia Britannica
Benziger Inc.
See Benziger Bruce & Glencoe
Benziger Bruce and Glencoe,
Inc., 76. *See also* Macmillan, Inc.
Norman S. Berg, Publisher, 77
Berke, Martin B.
See Greenwood Press
Berkley Publishing Corporation,
77. *See also*, G. P. Putnam's Sons
Berlitz, Maximilian D.
See Berlitz Publications
Berlitz Publications, Inc., 77.
See also Macmillan Inc.
Berne Convention, 306
Bernstein, Robert.
See Random House
Bessie, Simon Michael.
See Atheneum
Best, Marshall. *See* Viking
Bethany Fellowship, Inc., 77
Bethany Press, The, 77
Better Homes & Gardens Books, 77.
See also Meredith Corp.
Bibliographical Society of
America, The, 77-78
Bibliography — #1-General
Reference, Biographies &
Memoirs, 321-326.
#2-Company Histories, 327-332
Biblo, Jack. *See* Biblo & Tannen
Biblo & Tannen Booksellers
& Publishers, Inc., 78
Binford, Maurice.
See Binfords & Mort
Binford, Maurice, Jr.
See Binfords & Mort
Binford, Ormond.
See Binfords & Mort
Binford, Peter.
See Binfords & Mort
Binford, Thomas.
See Binfords & Mort
Binfords & Mort, Publishers, 78
Bingham, Harry H.
See Richard D. Irwin, Inc.
C. C. Birchard & Company.
See Summy-Birchard
Birmingham, Matthew T., Jr.
See Matthew Bender & Co.
Bizzell, Wiliam Bennett.
See Univ. of Oklahoma Press

Black, Douglas M.
See Doubleday & Co.
Black, Theodore M.
See Walter J. Black, Inc.
Black, Walter J., 78
Walter J. Black, Inc., 78-79
Black Sparrow Press, 79
Blair, Lyle.
See Michigan State Univ. Press
John F. Blair, Publisher, 79
Blaisdell Publishing Company.
See Ginn and Co.
Blake, Frederick H.
See American Book Co.
Blake, Henry H.
See The Harrison Co.
Blakeman, Birdseye.
See American Book Co.;
Ivison, Blakeman, Taylor
Blakeman, Louis H.
See Ivison, Blakeman, Taylor
Blakiston, Kenneth M., 5
Blakiston, Presley, 5
Blakiston Company, The, 5.
See also McGraw-Hill Book Co.
P. Blakiston's Son & Company, 5
Blanchard & Lea.
See Henry Charles Lea;
Sheldon & Co.
Blaustein, Norman.
See Tudor Publishing
Bledsoe, Thomas. *See* Beacon Press
Bletter, Robert.
See Teachers College Press
Bloch, Charles E.
See Bloch Publishing
Bloch, Edward.
See Bloch Publishing
Bloch and Company.
See Bloch Publishing
Bloch Publishing Company, 79
Benjamin Blom, Inc., 79
Blue and Gold Series, 5
Blue Ribbon Books, 5-6.
See also A. L. Burt Co.;
Dodd, Mead
Board of Educational Ministries
of the American Baptist
Churches of the U.S.A.
See Judson Press
Boardman, P. Clark.
See Clark Boardman Co.
Clark Boardman Company,
Ltd., 79-80
Bobbs, W. C.
See Bobbs-Merrill
Bobbs-Merrill Company, Inc.,
The, 80. *See also*
Howard W. Sams & Co.; ITT
Bobley, Edward, 81
Bobley, Harry W., 81
Bobley Publishing, 81
Boehm, David A.
See Sterling Publishing
Boehm, Eric H.
See ABC-Clio
Bogden & Quigley, Inc.,
Publishers. *See*
Wadsworth Publishing
Boise-Cascade.
See Limited Editions Club.
Bollingen Prize, 295
Bollingen Series, 81
Bolten, John.
See Standard Publishing
Bond, Raymond T.
See Dodd, Mead

Cowles, Dudley R.
  See D. C. Heath & Co.
Cowles, John, Jr.
  See Harper & Row
Cowles, W. Walker.
  See D. C. Heath & Co.
Cowles Book Company.
  See Henry Regnery Co.
Cowley, Malcolm. See Viking
Cowperthwait and Company.
  See American Book Co.
Cox, W. J.
  See Encyclopaedia Britannica
Cox Broadcasting Corporation,
  279-280
Coykendall, Frederick.
  See Columbia Univ. Press
Cozzens, William L.
  See Row, Peterson & Co.
Craig, Samuel W.
  See Literary Guild
Crane, Arthur McAuley.
  See D. Van Nostrand Co.
Crane, Edward M.
  See D. Van Nostrand Co.
Crane, Edward M., Jr.
  See Crane, Russak;
  D. Van Nostrand Co.
Crane, Edward Nichols.
  See D. Van Nostrand Co.
Crane, William N.
  See Ivison, Blakeman, Taylor
Crane and Company.
  See American Book Co.
Crane, Russak & Company, Inc., 97
Craven, Robert H.
  See F. A. Davis Co.
Crawford, William R. See
  Press of Case Western Reserve
Crawley, John.
  See Wm. H. Wise & Co.
Crawley, John, Jr.
  See Wm. H. Wise & Co.
John J. Crawley & Company, Inc.
  See Wm. H. Wise & Co.
Creative Age Press.
  See Farrar, Straus & Giroux
Creative Educational Society,
  Inc., 97-98
Crescendo Publishing Company, 98
Criterion Books.
  See Abelard-Schuman
Crocker, Uriel, 13
Crocker & Brewster.
  See Uriel Crocker;
  Houghton Mifflin
Crofts, Frederick S.
  See Appleton-Century-Crofts
F. S. Crofts & Company.
  See Appleton-Century-Crofts
Cross, Jack L.
  See Univ. of Arizona Press
Crowell, Robert L.
  See Thomas Y. Crowell Co.
Crowell, Thomas Young, 98-99
Crowell, T. Irving.
  See Thomas Y. Crowell Co.
Crowell Publishing Company.
  See Macmillan, Inc.
Crowell-Collier Publishing
  Company, 99.
  See also Macmillan, Inc.
Crowell, Collier and Macmillan,
  Inc.
  See Macmillan, Inc.
Thomas Y. Crowell Company,
  98-99. See also
  Abelard-Schuman; John Day Co.
  Intext Educational

Crown Publishers, Inc., 99-100;
  283. See also Barre Publishing;
  Imprint Society;
  Clarkson N. Potter, Inc.;
  Westover Publishing
Cudahy, E. I. See Callaghan & Co.
Cudahy, Michael.
  See Callaghan & Co.
Cudahy, Sheila.
  See Farrar, Straus & Giroux
Cuddihy, Robert J.
  See Funk and Wagnalls
Cumberlege, Geoffrey.
  See Oxford Univ. Press
Cummings, Jacob Abbott.
  See William Hilliard
Cummings, Lew Addison.
  See Addison-Wesley
Cummings, Melbourne Wesley.
  See Addison-Wesley
Cummings, Hilliard & Company.
  See William Hilliard
Lew A. Cummings Company.
  See Addison-Wesley
Cummings Publishing Company,
  Inc. See Addison-Wesley
Cuneo, John F.
  See Consolidated Book
Cunningham, H. E.
  See Univ. of Illinois Press
Cupples & Leon Company.
  See Platt & Munk
Curtis, J. J.
  See Bobbs-Merrill
Curtis Books, Inc., 100

D

Da Capo Press, Inc.
  See Plenum Publish. Corp.
Dale, J. W.
  See Robert Clarke & Co.
Stuart L. Daniels Company,
  Inc., The, 100
Darling, Edward See Beacon Press
Darrow, Whitney.
  See Princeton Univ. Press
Dartnell Corporation, The, 100
Daub, Albert. See Scarecrow Press
Daughters of St. Paul, Inc., 100
Daniel Davey & Company, Inc., 100
Davies, Charles.
  See A. S. Barnes & Co.
Davies, Wilbur H.
  See Fleming H. Revell Co.
Davis, Albert H.
  See F. W. Faxon Co.
Davis, Albert H., Jr.
  See F. W. Faxon Co.
Davis, Charles Palmer.
  See Xerox Education
Davis, Elizabeth Irene Craven.
  See F. A. Davis Co.
Davis, Frank Allston.
  See F. A. Davis Co.
Davis, John M. K.
  See Cardavon Press;
  Limited Editions Club
Davis, Lambert.
  See Univ. of No. Carolina Press
Davis, Thomas.
  See Johnson and Warner
F. A. Davis Company, 101
Davison, Peter.
  See Atlantic Monthly Press
Daw Books, Inc., 101
Day, Donald. See
  Southern Methodist Univ. Press
Day, Frederick Holland.
  See Copeland and Day

Day, G. P.
  See Yale Univ. Press
Day, Matthew.
  See Bay Psalm Book;
  Cambridge Press
Day, Patricia. See Stein and Day
Day, Stephen. See
  Bay Psalm Book;
  Cambridge Press
Stephen Daye Press.
  See Frederick Ungar Publishing
de Graff, Robert.
  See Pocket Books;
  Simon & Schuster
John de Graff, Inc., 101
de Haan, Richard.
  See Teachers College Press
de Kay, George C.
  See M. Evans & Co.
de Liso, Oscar. See Phaedra
Charles De Silver & Sons.
  See David McKay Co.
Deighton, Lee. See
  Harcourt Brace Jovanovich
Dekker, Marcel, 101
Dekker, Maurits.
  See American Elsevier;
  Marcel Dekker, Inc.;
  Interscience Publishers
Marcel Dekker, Inc., 101
Delacorte, George T., Jr.
  See Dell Publishing
Delacorte Press.
  See Dell Publishing
De La Mare Publishing Company.
  See Dodd, Mead
Delaney Books, Inc.
  See National Learning
Dell Publishing Co., Inc.,
  101; 283-285
Delmar Publishers, 101-102.
  See also Litton Educational
Dembo, Bruce F.
  See Univ. Press of Kentucky
Denison, T. S., 102
T. S. Denison and Company,
  Inc., 102
Denlinger's Publishers, 102
Denoyer, L. Philip.
  See Denoyer-Geppert
Denoyer-Geppert, 102.
  See also Times-Mirror Co.
Derby, Henry.
  See Robert Clarke & Co.
Derby, J. C., 13-14
Derby and Jackson.
  See J. C. Derby & Co.
Derby and Miller.
  See J. C. Derby & Co.
J. C. Derby & Company, 13-14
Deseret Book Company, 102-103
Dessauer, John.
  See Indiana Univ. Press;
  Univ. Press of Kansas
Determined Productions, Inc., 103
Devin-Adair Company, The, 103
Dewey decimal classification, 310.
  See also Melvil Dewey
Dewey, Melvil, 14
Dial Press, The, 103.
  See also Dell Publishing
Dibble, William.
  See Drake Publishers
Dibble, William (Mrs.).
  See Drake Publishers-
Dick, Harris Brisbane.
  See Dick & Fitzgerald
Dick, William Brisbane.
  See Dick & Fitzgerald

Hodgson, Caspar W. *See*
Harcourt Brace Jovanovich
Hodgson, Matthew. *See*
Univ. of No. Carolina Press
Hoe, Robert. *See* Grolier Club
Paul B. Hoeber. *See*
Harper & Row
Philip Hofer Books.
See Walker & Co.
Hoffman, B. D. *See* Dial Press
Hogan, Robert F. *See* National
Council of Teachers of English
Holbrook Press, Inc., 144.
See also Allyn & Bacon
Holden-Day, Inc., 144
Holgerson, C. Emil. *See*
McCormick-Mathers
Holiday House, Inc., 144-145
Holland, Robert E., S. J.
See Fordham Univ. Press
Holman, A. J., 145
A. J. Holman Company, 145.
See also J. B. Lippincott Co.
Holme, Bryan. *See* Viking
Holt, Guy. *See* John Day Co.
Holt, Henry, 25. *See also*
Holt and Rinehart;
Holt, Rinehart & Winston
Henry Holt and Company. *See*
Holt, Rinehart & Winston
Holt and Rinehart, 35. *See also*
John C. Winston Co.
Holt, Rinehart & Winston, Inc.,
145-146. *See also* Columbia
Broadcasting; Holt & Rinehart;
Mentzer, Bush; Rinehart & Co.;
John C. Winston Co.
Home Library Press.
See Parents' Magazine
Hood E. H. *See* Bobbs-Merrill
Hood, Norman. *See*
William Sloane Associates
Hooper, Horace. *See*
Encyclopaedia Britannica
Hooper, Horace (Mrs.). *See*
Encyclopaedia Britannica
Hooper, T. Albert
See Deseret Book
Hoover Institution Press, 146-147
Horizon Press, 147
Hornstein, Gabriel.
See AMS Press
Houghton, Edward R. *See*
Houghton Mifflin
Houghton, Henry Oscar. *See*
Houghton Mifflin;
James Ripley Osgood
Houghton Mifflin Company, 13, 30,
34, 57, 148-149. *See also*
Ballantine
Hovgard, Carl *See* Lawyers Co-op.
Howard, Bailey K. *See*
Field Enterprises
Howard University Press, 149
Howe, Will D. *See*
Harcourt Brace Jovanovich
Howe, W. T. H. *See*
American Book Co.
Howell Book House, Inc., 149. *See
also* Orange Judd Publish. Co.;
Franklin Watts
Howell-North Books, 149
Howell, Soskin & Co. *See* Crown
Howley, Roger. *See*
Cornell Univ. Press
Hoyns, Henry. *See* Harper & Row
Hubbard, Elbert II. *See*
Roycroft Publish. Shop

Hubbard, Elbert Green. *See*
Roycroft; Wm. H. Wise & Co.
Hubbard, Philip H. *See*
Reinhold Publish. Corp.
Hubbard Press. *See*
M. A. Donohue & Co.
Hubel, Gordon. *See*
Univ. of Pennsylvania Press
Huebsch, Benjamin W., 21.
See also Viking
Huett, Richard. *See* Humanities
Hughes, Lawrence. *See*
Wm. Morrow & Co.
Humanities Press, Inc., 149.
See also Duquesne Univ. Press;
Hillary House
Human Sciences, Inc. *See*
Behavioral
Hunter, William A. *See*
Baker & Taylor
Hurd, Melancthon M. *See*
Houghton Mifflin; Sheldon & Co.
Hurd and Houghton. *See*
Houghton Mifflin;
G. P. Putnam's
Hutchins, Robert M. *See*
Great Books
Huttner, Matthew. *See* Pyramid
Hutton, Warren. *See*
Iowa State Univ. Press
Huws-Davies, James Y.
See Oxford Univ. Press
Hyde, Filmore. *See*
New York Univ. Press
Hyder, Clyde K. *See*
Univ. Press of Kansas

I

IBC Industries, Inc., 150
IBM, 279-280
IFI International. *See*
Bantam; Plenum Publish. Corp.
ITT, 279-280
Ide, Lemuel. *See*
E. P. Dutton & Co.
Ide and Dutton. *See*
E. P. Dutton & Co.
Iglehart, Louis T. *See*
Univ. of Tennessee Press
Imprint Society, Inc., 150. *See
also,* Barre Publishing; Crown
Indian Bible, 21
Indiana University Press, 150
Industrial Press, Inc., 150-151
Ingle, Harold E. *See*
Iowa State Univ. Press;
Johns Hopkins Univ. Press
Inman, John, 21
International Arts & Sciences
Press, Inc., 151
International Book Corporation.
See IBC Industries
International Book Distributors.
See IBC Industries
International Book Institute, 292
International Book Society, 151.
See also TIME-LIFE Books
International Book Year, 292
International Copyright
Association, 292
International Copyrights
Information Center, 292
International Publishers, 151
International Publishers
Association, 292
International Standard Book
Number, 315

International Textbook Company.
See Intext, Inc.
International Universities Press,
Inc., 151-152
Interscience Publishers. *See*
Marcel Dekker, Inc;
John Wiley & Sons
Interstate Printers & Publishers,
Inc., The, 152
Inter-Varsity Press, 152
Intext Educational Publishers.
See Intext, Inc.
Intext, Inc., 152; 279-280
Iowa State University
Press, 152-153
Irish University Press, Inc., 153
Iroquois Publishing Company.
See Prentice-Hall, Inc.
Irwin, Richard D., 153
Richard D. Irwin, Inc., 153-154;
283-285
Ives, Vernon. *See* Holiday House
Ives, William H. *See*
D. C. Heath & Co.
M. J. Ives & Company.
See Irwin P. Beadle & Co.
Ives Washburn, Inc.
See David McKay Co.
Ivison, David, 22
Ivison, David B., 22. *See also*
American Book Co.
Ivison, H. C. *See* J. C. Derby & Co.;
Ivison, Blakeman, Taylor
Ivison, Blakeman & Company, 22
Ivison, Blakeman, Taylor &
Company, 22. *See also*
American Book Co.;
G. & C. Merriam Co.
Ivison & Phinney, 22
Ivison, Phinney, Blakeman &
Company, 22

J

Jackson, Edwin. *See*
J. C. Derby & Co.
Jackson, Walter M. *See*
Encyclopaedia Britannica;
Grolier Inc.
Jackson Square Press.
See Pelican Publishing
George W. Jacobs Company.
See Macrae Smith
Jacobson James.
See Simon & Schuster
Jacoby, Kurt. *See* Academic Press
James, Joseph A., 22
James, Uriah P., 22
J. A. James & Company, 22
Jaray, Alice. *See* Kennikat
Jaray, Cornell. *See* Kennikat
Jarrow Press, Inc., 154
Jefferson House.
See Wm. Morrow & Co.
Jefferson Law Book Company.
See W. H. Anderson Co.
Jenkins Publishing Company, 154
Jennison, Keith. *See*
Wm. Sloane Associates
Jensen, Oliver. *See*
American Heritage
Jewett, John P., 22
Jewish Publication Society of
America, The, 154-155
Joel, George. *See* Dial Press
John Day Company, Inc.,
Publishers, The, 155
See also Intext Inc.
John Knox Press, 155

374

McCarty, William. *See*
  Johnson & Warner
McClure, John. *See* Pelican
McClure, S. S. *See* Doubleday
  & Co.; McClure, Phillips
McCormack, Thomas J.
  See St. Martin's
McCormick, A. G. *See*
  McCormick-Mathers
McCune, Sara Miller. *See* Sage
McDowell, David. *See* Crown
McGinnis, John H. *See*
  Southern Methodist Univ. Press
MacGlinchey, Captain Tadhg.
  See Irish Univ. Press
McGovern, William. *See*
  Albert Whitman & Co.
McGraw, Curtis W. *See*
  Book Publishers' Bureau
McGraw, Harold W., Jr.
  See McGraw-Hill Book
McGraw, James H. *See*
  McGraw-Hill Book
MacGregor, Frank S.
  See Harper & Row
MacGregor, Robert M. *See*
  New Directions; Theatre Arts
McGuffey, William Holmes.
  See McGuffey Readers
McIntyre, Alfred R. *See*
  Little, Brown
McIntyre, James. *See* Little, Brown
McKay, Alexander. *See*
  David McKay Co.
McKay, David, 173
McKay, James. *See*
  David McKay Co.
MacKenzie, Ian. *See*
  Ohio Univ. Press; St. Martin's
McKnight, Hannah. *See*
  McKnight Publishing
McKnight, William. *See*
  McKnight Publishing
McKnight, William, Jr. *See*
  McKnight Publishing
McLoughlin, Charles, 27-28
McLoughlin, Edmund, 27-28
McLoughlin, James G., 27-28
McLoughlin, John, 27-28
McLoughlin, John, Jr., 27-28
McLoughlin, Patrick. *See*
  Behavioral
McMillan, James B. *See*
  Univ. of Alabama Press
McMurtrie, Douglas C. *See*
  American Imprints Inventory
McNally, Andrew. *See*
  Rand McNally
McNally, Andrew III. *See*
  Rand McNally
McNamara, Robert C. *See*
  Scott, Foresman
MacVeagh, Lincoln. *See* Dial
  Press; Holt, Rinehart & Winston
McVey, Frank L. *See*
  Univ. Press of Kentucky
McCall Books. *See*
  Saturday Review
McCarty and Davis. *See*
  Johnson & Warner
McClure, Phillips & Company, 27
McCormick-Mathers Publishing
  Company, Inc., 171. *See also*
  American Book Co.
McCutchan Publishing
  Corporation, 171
McDowell, Obolensky, Inc.
  See Astor-Honor

McGrath Publishing Company, 171.
  See also Catholic Univ. of
  America Press
McGraw-Hill, Inc., 283-285.
  See also McGraw-Hill Book
McGraw-Hill Book Company,
  171-173. *See also* American
  Heritage; Blakiston Co.; Gregg
  Publishing; Webster Publishing
McGraw-Hill Publishing Company.
  See McGraw-Hill Book
McGuffey Readers, 27. *See also*
  American Book Co.;
  Truman & Smith
David McKay Company, Inc., 173;
  283-285. *See also* Fodor's;
  Longmans, Green; Henry Z.
  Walck, Inc.; Ives Washburn;
  Weybright & Talley;
  Peter H. Wyden, Inc.
McKnight Publishing
  Company, 173
McLoughlin Brothers, 27-28
McMullen Books, Inc. *See*
  Farrar, Straus & Giroux
McNally & Loftin, Publishers, 174

M

MIT Press, The, 170
Mss Information Corporation, 170
Mabie, Hamilton Wright.
  See Dodd, Mead
Mabon, John Scott. *See*
  Univ. of Michigan Press
Mackin, J. C. *See*
  Creative Educational
Macmillan, Alexander.
  See Macmillan, Inc.
Macmillan Company, The.
  See Macmillan Inc.
Macmillan, Inc., 174-175; 283-285.
  See also Benziger, Bruce &
  Glencoe; Berlitz; Brentano's;
  Peter Fenelon Collier;
  Crowell-Collier; Crowell-Collier-
  Macmillan; Free Press;
  Hafner Publish.; P. J. Kenedy;
  Stechert Hafner; G. Schirmer
Macmillan Book Clubs, Inc., 174.
  See also Macmillan, Inc.
Macmillan Publishing Company,
  Inc. *See* Crowell-Collier Publish.
  Co.; Macmillan, Inc.
Macrae, Donald P. *See*
  Macrae Smith
Macrae, Durant L. *See*
  Macrae Smith
Macrae, Elliott Beach.
  See E. P. Dutton & Co.
Macrae, John. *See*
  E. P. Dutton & Co.
Macrae, John, Jr. *See*
  E. P. Dutton & Co.
Macrae, John III. *See*
  E. P. Dutton & Co.
Macrae Smith Company, 175-176
Macy, George. *See*
  Limited Editions Club
Macy, Helen. *See*
  Limited Editions Club
Macy, Jonathan. *See*
  Limited Editions Club
Madison Book Company.
  See Reilly and Lee
Magnet Books, Inc. *See*
  Frederick Fell Publishing
Malone, Dumas. *See*
  Harvard Univ. Press

Manley, Joan D. *See*
  TIME-LIFE BOOKS
Mann, E. B. *See*
  Univ. of New Mexico Press
Manning, Robert. *See*
  Atlantic Monthly
Manning & Loring. *See*
  Benj H. Sanborn & Co.
Manor Books, Inc., 176
Mansbridge, F. Ronald. *See*
  Cambridge Univ. Press
Mara Books, Inc., 176
Markham Publishing Company, 176
Marquis, Albert Nelson.
  See Marquis Who's Who
Marquis Who's Who, Inc., 176.
  See also ITT
Marriner, Robie D. *See*
  American Book Co.
Martin, J. Parker. *See*
  A. J. Holman Co.
Mason, Harold. *See* Greenwood
Mason, Lowell, Jr. *See*
  Truman & Smith
Mason, Baker & Pratt. *See*
  Baker & Taylor
Mason Brothers. *See*
  Sheldon & Co.
Massee, May. *See*
  Doubleday & Co.; Viking
Mathers, J. E. *See*
  McCormick-Mathers
Matrix House, Ltd. *See*
  Julian Press
Matthews, Brander. *See*
  American Copyright League
Maule, Harry. *See* Random House
Maxwell, Allen. *See*
  Southern Methodist Univ. Press
Maxwell, Robert. *See* Pergamon
Maxwell, William, 28
Maynard, D. D. *See*
  American Book Co.
Maynard, Effingham, 28
Effingham Maynard &
  Company, 28
Maynard, Merrill & Company.
  See Effingham Maynard
Mead, Edward S. *See* Dodd, Mead
Media Directions, Inc., 177.
  See also Gordon & Breach
Media Judaica, Inc.
  See Prayer Book
Medical Economics, Inc. *See*
  Reinhold Publish. Corp.
Medical Examination Publishing
  Co., Inc., 177
Meek, Dudley. *See*
  Harcourt Brace Jovanovich
Melcher, Frederic Gershom, 28.
  See also R. R. Bowker Co.;
  Publishers Weekly
Melmont Publishers. *See*
  Childrens Press
Melville, Frank. *See*
  History Book Club
Melville Publishing Company.
  See John Wiley & Sons
Memphis State University
  Press, 177
Mennonite Publishing House,
  177-178
Mentzer, John P. *See*
  Mentzer, Bush
Mentzer, Bush & Company, 28.
  See also Holt, Rinehart &
  Winston
Meredith, Hugh. *See*
  Benjamin Franklin

National Learning Corporation,
183; 283-285
National Library Week, 316
National Press Books, 183
National Textbook Company, 184
Naval Institute Press. See
United States Naval Institute
Naylor, Joe O. See Naylor Co.
Naylor, Rita. See Naylor Co.
Naylor Company, The, 184
Nazarene Publishing House, 184
Neale, Russell F. See
Hastings House
Negro History Press, 184.
See also Scholarly Press
Negro Universities Press.
See Greenwood
Neilly, Andrew H., Jr. See
John Wiley & Sons
Nelson-Hall Company, 184
Thomas Nelson, Inc., 184
New American Library, Inc., The,
184. See also Times-Mirror Co.
Newbery Medal, 298. See also
Frederic G. Melcher;
Isaiah Thomas
Newburger, Morris. See
Jewish Publication Society
Newbury House, Publishers, 185
New Directions Publishing
Corporation, 185
New England Primer, The, 29-30.
See also Benjamin Harris
New Hampshire Publishing
Company, 185
Newman, Mark H. See
Ivison, Blakeman, Taylor
Mark H. Newman & Company.
See Ivison, Blakeman, Taylor
Newman Press. See
Paulist/Newman
Newsom and Company. See
D. Van Nostrand Co.
New York Graphic Society, Ltd.,
185-186. See also Time, Inc.
New York Society For the
Suppression of Vice.
See Anthony Comstock
New York Times Company,
279-280
New York Times Media
Corporation. See
New York Times Co.
New York University Press, 186
Nichols, Francis A. See
Grolier, Inc.
Nickerson, Thomas. See
Univ. Press of Hawaii
Nicoll, Bruce H. See
Univ. of Nebraska Press
Niles, Thomas. See No Name
Series; Roberts Bros.
Noble, G. Clifford. See Barnes &
Noble Books; Noble and Noble
Noble, J. Kendrick. See
Noble and Noble
Noble, Lloyd Adams. See
Noble and Noble
Noble and Noble, Publishers, Inc.,
186-187. See also Barnes &
Noble Books; Dell
No Name Series, 30.
See also Roberts Bros.
Noonday Press, Inc. See
Farrar, Straus & Giroux
Norris, Eben. See
T. S. Denison & Co.

Norris, Joseph. See
Wayne State Univ. Press
Northern Illinois University
Press, 187
Northrop, Kenneth. See
Holt, Rinehart & Winston
Northwestern University
Press, 187-188
Norton, Charles B., 30. See also
Charles B. Richardson
Norton, William Warder, 188-189.
See also Council on Books
in Wartime
W. W. Norton & Company, Inc.,
188-189; 283-285. See also
Liveright
Noyes, Robert. See Noyes Data
Noyes Data Corporation, 189

O

Oakley Mason & Co. See
Baker & Taylor
Ivan Obolensky, Inc. See
Astor-Honor
Oceana Publications, Inc., 189-190
Octagon Books, Inc. See
Farrar, Straus & Giroux
October House, Inc., 190
Oddo Publishing, Inc., 190
O'Dea, Paul. See
National Council of Teachers
O'Donnell, Frank J. See
Reilly & Lee
Odum, Howard W. See Univ. of
No. Carolina Press
Odyssey Press. See Bobbs-Merrill;
Western Publish. Co.
Ogilvie, John Stuart, 30
J. S. Ogilvie Company, 30. See also
United States Book
O'Hara Publications, Inc., 190
J. Philip O'Hara, Inc., 190
Ohio State University Press, 190
Ohio University Press, 190-191
Okpaku, Joseph O. See Third Press
Olson, Ernest L. See
Brigham Young Univ. Press
Oman, William M. See Dodd, Mead
Omen Press, 191
101 Productions, 191
O'Neil, John J. See Avi
Onward Press. See
John Knox Press
Open Court Publishing Company,
The, 191
Oppenheimer, George S.
See Viking
Orbis Books, 192
Oregon State University Press, 192
Oriole Editions, 192
Orion Press, Inc., The. See
Grossman Publishers
Osgood, James Ripley, 30-31.
See also Houghton Mifflin
James R. Osgood and Company,
30-31. See also E. P. Dutton &
Co.; Houghton Mifflin;
Ticknor & Fields
Ottemiller, Frances. See
Shoe String
Ottemiller, John. See Shoe String
Ottenheimer, Isaac, 192
Ottenheimer, Moses, 192
Ottenheimer Publishers, Inc., 192
Otterbein Press, The, 31
Outerbridge, David E. See
Outerbridge & Lazard

Outerbridge & Lazard, Inc.
See also E. P. Dutton & Co.
Outlet Book Company, Inc.
See Crown
Owen, John, 31
Oxford Book Company, Inc., 192.
See also Wm. H. Sadlier, Inc.
Oxford University Press, 192-193
Jerome S. Ozer, Publisher,
Inc., 193

P

Pablos, Juan, 31
Pacific Coast Publishers, 193
Pacific Press Publishing
Association, 193
Page, Lewis C. See Estes &
Lauriat; L. C. Page & Co.
Page, Walter Hines. See
Doubleday & Co.;
Houghton Mifflin
L. C. Page and Company, 31.
See also Estes & Lauriat;
Farrar and Straus
Pantheon Books, 193-194. See also
Bollingen Series; Random House
Paperback Library, Inc. See
Warner Paperback
Parents' Magazine Press, 195
Park, Clyde. See Frontier Press
Parker, Beryl. See
D. C. Heath & Co.
Parker, Robert. See Parker & Son
Parker & Son Publications,
Inc., 195
Parker Publishing Company, 195
See also Prentice-Hall, Inc.
Parks, William, 31-32
Parmentier, Douglas. See
Harper & Row
Parnassus Press, 195
Parry, Alva H. See Deseret Book
Parton, James. See
American Heritage
Passano, Edward B. See
Williams & Wilkins
Passano, William. See
Williams & Wilkins
Pathfinder Press, 195
Patterson & Clarke. See
Robert Clarke & Co.
Patterson, Woodford. See
Cornell Univ. Press
Paty, Raymond R. See
Univ. of Alabama Press
Paulist/Newman Press, 195
Payne, Michael. See
Bucknell Univ. Press
F. E. Peacock Publishers, Inc., 195
Pearce, Charles A. See
Duell, Sloan & Pearce
Peckham, Morse. See Univ. of
Pennsylvania Press
Pegasus Division. See
Bobbs-Merrill
Peggy Cloth Books. See
Platt & Munk
Pelican Publishing Company,
195-196
Pell, Arthur. See
Horace Brisbin Liveright
Pellegrini & Cudahy. See
Farrar, Straus & Giroux
Pencil Point Press. See
Reinhold Publishing
Penguin Books, Inc., 196
The Penn Publishing Company.
See Tudor